Da

ANDALUCÍA

'almond trees, cacti, olive groves and mountains that drop steeply away to the silver ribbon of a stream below'

CADOGANguides

Contents

Introducing

The Guide

Reference

Maps

About the authors

Dana Facaros and **Michael Pauls** have written over 30 books for Cadogan Guides, including the entire Spain series. They have lived all over Europe, but have recently hung up their castanets in an old *presbytère* near the Lot.

About the updater

Mary-Ann Gallagher has lived everywhere from New York to Tokyo, but still thinks nothing compares to Spain. She has updated a dozen guides for Cadogan, as well as writing regularly for other travel publications.

Updater's acknowledgements

Besos and huge thanks to my dream team – Susannah, Adolfo, José Ángel (Machote) and Candido. *Muchas gracias* to Nacho from *mu* magazine, Fernando at Sevilla Apartamentos, and Miguel in Granada. Extra-special thanks to Dana and Michael who make every step in Andalucía such a treat, to Andrew, my willing chauffeur and beach expert, and to Christine and Linz at Cadogan – you are stars!

Cadogan Guides
Highlands House, 165 The Broadway,
London SW19 1NE
info.cadogan@virgin.net
www.cadoganguides.com

The Globe Pequot Press
246 Goose Lane, PO Box 480, Guilford,
Connecticut 06437–0480

Cover and photo essay design by Kicca Tommasi
Book design by Andrew Barker
Cover photographs by John Miller
Maps © Cadogan Guides,
drawn by Map Creation Ltd
Managing Editor: Christine Stroyan
Editor: Lindsay Porter
Art Direction: Sarah Rianhard-Gardner
Proofreading: Héloïse McGuinness
Indexing: Isobel McLean
Production: Navigator Guides Ltd

Printed in Italy by Legoprint
A catalogue record for this book is available from the British Library
ISBN 1-86011-103-3

Please help us to keep this guide up to date. We have done our best to ensure that the information in this guide is correct at the time of going to press, but places and facilities are constantly changing, and standards and prices in hotels and restaurants fluctuate. We would be delighted to receive any comments concerning existing entries or omissions. Authors of the best letters will receive a copy of the Cadogan Guide of their choice.

Andalucía a photo essay

by John Ferro Sims

RUPO ESCOLAR DE NIÑOS
IGUEL DE CERVANTES

PUESTO DE SOCORRO
EN EL SINDICATO
ADMINISTRACION DE
LOTERIAS

STO
47
CUENTAS
DE
AHORRO
benetton

The Alhambra, Granada

Arcos de la Frontera, bull run

Almeria

Tarifa

Granada

Cádiz

The Alhambra, Granada

Alcazár, Sevilla

Granada

Jerez de la Frontera, train station

Huelva, Aztec calendar

El Burgo

Coast near Nerja

Almodovar

Sevilla

San Roque, semana santa

About the photographer

John Ferro Sims was born of Anglo-Italian parents in Udine, Italy. He worked successfully for five years as an investment analyst before quitting the world of money for a career as a professional photographer, which has taken him around the world. He has published 9 books.

Introduction

There is a story about haughty Queen Isabel, so proud of her conquest of the godless Moors of Andalucía, that sums up this region's sad history. The Moors, lovers of art and poetry, were also the great architects of water, making the dry hills of the south into lush fields and gardens; Spanish folk tales often speak of them almost as sorcerers. During the campaigns against Granada, Isabel found herself lodging at the Alcázar of Córdoba, where an old Moorish water wheel in the Guadalquivir churned up water for the pools and fountains of the Alcázar gardens. After a few nights Isabel ordered it be dismantled – it disturbed her sleep.

The ghost of Islamic al-Andalus still haunts the south; a more graceful and delicate spirit could not be desired. In the gardens and palaces, and in the white villages, this great, lost civilization is a separate reality that shines through centuries of Spanish veneer. And what of the new Andalucía, after its centuries of trouble, of oppression and inquisitions, expulsions, poverty and emigration? It's looking pretty well, thank you, with its exuberant life and culture, and a delightful, fun-loving population of generally sane and friendly people, as much of an attraction as the land itself. Andalucía is a minefield of unexploded stereotypes: sequined matadors and strumming guitars, torrid flamenco and hot-blooded Gypsies, orange blossom and jasmine. They may be hard to avoid, but then again, why try? Few regions of Europe have been blessed with such stereotypes. Visitors never weary of them, and the Andalucians certainly don't either; they cultivate and polish them with the greatest of care.

Today, with its green and white flag flying proudly on every public building, autonomous, democratic Andalucía may have the chance to rediscover itself. With a fifth of Spain's population, its biggest tourist industry, and potentially its richest agriculture, it has great promise for the future. And as the part of Spain with the longest and most brilliant artistic heritage – not only from the Moors, but from the troubled, creative, post-Reconquista Andalucía that has given Spain Velázquez, García Lorca, de Falla and Picasso – the region may find it still has the resources once more to become the leader in Spain's cultural life.

For its size, Andalucía contains a remarkable diversity of landscapes – from Spain's highest mountains to endless rolling hills covered with olive trees, Europe's biggest marshland preserve and even some patches of desert. And no other part of Spain can offer so many interesting large cities. Andalucía is a world unto itself; it has as many delights to offer as you have time to spend.

A Guide to the Guide

The five introductory chapters, which provide an incisive glimpse of the history and culture of this hybrid corner of Europe, are followed by up-to-date travel and practical information – all you'll need to set you on your way. Throughout the guide the narrative is interspersed with detailed listings, providing considered recommendations and points of reference. For Spanish vocabulary, flick to the language section at the back of the book.

Chapter Divisions
PORTUGAL
BADAJOZ
CIUDAD REAL
ALBACETE
MURCIA
HUELVA
SEVILLA
CÓRDOBA
JAÉN
GRANADA
ALMERÍA
MÁLAGA
CÁDIZ
09
SEVILLA
10
CÓRDOBA AND JAÉN
11
HUELVA, CÁDIZ
AND GIBRALTAR
12
MÁLAGA
13
GRANADA AND ALMERÍA
Huelva
Sevilla
Córdoba
Jaén
Granada
Almería
Málaga
Cádiz
Gibraltar
Ceuta
(Spain)
Tangier
MOROCCO
Sierra Nevada
Costa del Sol
STRAITS OF GIBRALTAR
ATLANTIC
OCEAN
MEDITERRANEAN SEA
N
40 km
20 miles

Sevilla

The whimsical charms of Andalucía's capital city, with its colourful *barrios* and great monuments, are the primary subject of the first gazetteer chapter, with side-steps into nearby Roman Itálica, Moorish Carmona and Estepa with its Baroque showpieces.

Córdoba and Jaén

From Sevilla we head up the long valley of the Río Guadalquivir into the heart of Andalucía and the provinces of Córdoba and Jaén. Flanked by the broad spine of the Sierra Morena to the north (famous for good hunting and cured hams), and a sea of sunflowers and olive groves to the south, the river is dotted with fine *andaluz* towns, from the citadel of Córdoba itself (and the remarkable Mezquita) to neatly clipped Baeza and Úbeda, with their unrivalled ensembles of Renaissance architecture.

Huelva, Cádiz and Gibraltar

For this chapter we move to the Costa de la Luz, western flank of Andalucía's famous coastline (and less-developed sister of the Costa del Sol). Inland, through forests of holm oak and cork, lie hidden the little-visited villages of the Sierra de Aracena – an easy day out from Huelva by car. Heading on down the coast past Las Marismas (Europe's greatest marshland wildlife reserve) we come to the hundred shades of Cádiz, Europe's oldest city (or so it claims). The province is packed with diversions, from the *bodegas* of Jerez – synonymous with sherry – to the moist micro-climate of the Sierra de Grazalema, home to golden eagles and species of pre-Ice Age flora. We also offer a taste of North Africa proper, with an excursion across the Straits from Algeciras. Finally, from the smoky souks of Tangier we hop back across 8 miles of water for the ultimate culture shock: pie and mash and red phone booths in Gibraltar, that peculiar British enclave at the southern tip of Europe.

Málaga: The Costa del Sol

The Mediterranean's biggest playground, this is the one region of Andalucía that needs little introduction. As well as conveying the true excitement (or horror, depending on your temperament) of this adrenaline-charged and multinational coastline, we seek to dig up the hidden delights of Málaga province, including the towns and villages of the Serranía de Ronda.

Granada and Almería

Anyone with more than a few days to spare in Andalucía comes to Granada, drawn by the Moorish excess of the Alhambra, survivor of the lost world of al-Andalus. After a tour of this great fortified palace, our final gazetteer chapter guides you through the gardens and whitewashed neighbourhoods of the city, with the backdrop of Spain's tallest mountain, Mulhacén, to the north, and the delightful villages of Las Alpujarras to the south. Beyond the mountains of the Sierra Nevada lie the arid and lonely eastern reaches of Granada province and Almería, a landscape immortalized in countless spaghetti westerns. Finally, we hit Almería itself, the crystal waters of the Costa de Almería and trendy Mojácar, set on a hill 'like a pile of sugar cubes'.

History

03

Prehistory

Southern Spain has been inhabited since remotest antiquity. The area around Huelva is only one of the places in Spain where remains from the early Pleistocene have been found, and some finds on the peninsula suggest somebody was poking about as far back as one million years ago. Only 250,000 years ago, they were making tools out of elephant tusks, when they were lucky enough to catch one. A site near – of all places – the centre of Marbella is currently being excavated for its Middle-Palaeolithic remains. Neanderthal man wandered all over Spain some 50,000 years ago, and Gibraltar seems to have been one of his favourite locations. Later people, the devious and quarrelsome *homo sapiens*, contributed the simple cave paintings in the Cueva de la Pileta and some other sites near Ronda *c.* 25,000 BC – nothing as elaborate as the famous paintings at Altamira and other sites in northern Spain, though they date from about the same time.

The great revolution in human affairs known as the **Neolithic Revolution**, including the beginnings of agriculture and husbandry, began to appear around the Iberian coasts *c.* 6000 BC. By the 4th millennium BC, the Neolithic people had developed an advanced culture, building dolmens, stone circles and burial mounds all along the fringes of western Europe – Newgrange, Avebury, Stonehenge, Carnac. In southern Spain, they left the huge tumuli at Antequera called the Cueva de Romeral and the Cueva de Menga. By *c.* 3200 BC, they had learned to make use of copper, and a metal-working nation created the great complex at Los Millares near Almería, a veritable Neolithic city with fortifications, outer citadels and a huge tumulus surrounded by circles of standing stones. Los Millares and sites associated with it began to decline about 2500 BC, and most of them were abandoned by 2000 BC, replaced by different, bronze-working peoples who often founded their settlements on the same old sites.

1100–201 BC

The native Iberians learn that if you've got a silver mine in your backyard, you'll never be lonely

In the 2nd millennium BC, while early civilizations rose and fell in the Middle East and eastern Mediterranean, the west remained a backwater – southern Spain in particular found nothing to disturb its dreams until the arrival of the **Phoenicians**, who 'discovered' Spain perhaps as early as 1100 BC (that is the traditional date; many archaeologists suspect they didn't appear until 900 or 800 BC). As a base for trading, they founded Gades (Cádiz), claimed to be the oldest city in western Europe, and from there they slowly expanded into a string of colonies along the coast. The Phoenicians were after Spain's mineral resources – copper, tin, gold, silver and mercury, all in short supply in the Middle East at this time – and their trade with the native Iberians made the Phoenicians the economic masters of the Mediterranean (the flood of Andalucían silver from the Río Tinto mines into the Middle East caused one of history's first recorded spells of inflation, in the Assyrian Empire). Such wealth eventually attracted the Phoenicians' bitter rivals, the **Greeks**, who arrived in 636 BC and founded a trading post at Mainake near Málaga, though they were never to be a real force in the region.

The great mystery of this era is the fabled kingdom of **Tartessos**, which covered all or part of Andalucía; the name seems to come from Tertis, an ancient name of the Guadalquivir River. Phoenician records mention it, as does Herodotus, and it may be the legendary 'Tarshish' mentioned in the Book of Kings, its great navy bringing wares of Spain and Africa to trade with King Solomon. With great wealth from the mines of the Río Tinto and the Sierra Morena, Tartessos may have appeared about 800–700 BC. Very little is known of the real story behind the legends of Tartessos, but they reflect the fact that Iberian communities throughout the peninsula were rapidly gaining in wealth and sophistication. Archaeologists refer to the 7th and 6th centuries as the 'orientalizing period' of Iberian culture, when the people of Spain were adopting wholesale elements of life and art from the Phoenicians and Greeks. Iberians imported Greek and Phoenician art, and learned to copy its themes and techniques for themselves. They developed an adaptation of the Phoenician alphabet, and began an agricultural revolution that has shaped the land up to this day with two new crops brought to them by their eastern visitors – the grape and the olive.

By the 6th century, the Phoenicians of the Levant were under Babylonian rule, and **Carthage**, their western branch office, was building an empire out of their occupied coasts in Spain, Sicily and North Africa. About 500 BC, the Carthaginians gobbled up the last remains of Tartessos and other coastal areas and stopped the Greek infiltration. The Carthaginians maintained the status quo until 264–241 BC, when Rome drubbed them in the **First Punic War**.

Before that, Carthage had been largely a sea power. After Rome built itself a navy and beat them, the Carthaginians changed tack and rebuilt their empire as a land power, based on the resources and manpower of Spain. Beginning in 237, they established military control throughout most of the peninsula under **Hamilcar Barca**. This, along with other factors, alarmed Rome enough to reopen hostilities. In the rematch, the **Second Punic War** (218–201 BC), Hamilcar's son **Hannibal** marched off to Italy with his elephants and a largely Spanish army. Meanwhile the Romans under **Scipio Africanus** entered Spain by sea. At first, Scipio's intention was merely to cut off Hannibal's supply routes to Italy. But it was a brilliant stroke, and under Scipio's able command the Romans were able to eventually gain control of all Iberia, winning important battles at Bailén in 208, and Alcalá del Río, near Sevilla, the following year. After that, Scipio was able to use Spain as a base to attack Carthage itself, forcing Hannibal to evacuate Italy and leading to total victory for Rome.

201 BC–AD 409

The Romans muscle in, and do the Spaniards the way the Spaniards would one day do the Mexicans

Unlike their predecessors, the Romans were never content to hold just a part of Spain. Relentlessly, they slogged over the peninsula, subjugating one Celtic or Iberian tribe after another, a job that was not entirely completed in northern Spain until AD 220. Even then, rebellions against Rome were frequent and bloody, including a major one in Andalucía in 195. Rome had to send its best – Cato, Pompey, Julius Caesar and Octavian (Augustus) were all commanders in the Spanish conquest. Caesar, in fact, was briefly governor in Andalucía, the most prosperous part of the peninsula, and the one that adapted most easily to Roman rule and culture.

Not that Roman rule was much of a blessing. Iberia, caught in the middle of a huge geopolitical struggle between two powerful neighbours, had simply exchanged one colonial overlord for another. Both were efficiently rapacious in the exploitation of the all-important mines, keeping the profits for themselves alone. As in every land conquered by the legions, most of the best land was collected together into huge estates owned by the Roman élite, on which the former inhabitants were enslaved or reduced to the status of tenant farmers. The Iberians had reasons to resist as strongly as they did.

At first the Romans called Andalucía simply 'Further Spain', but eventually it settled in as **Baetica**, from the Bætis, another ancient name for the Guadalquivir river. During the first three centuries AD, when the empire was at its height, Baetica became a prosperous, contented place – by grace of its great mineral and agricultural wealth the richest part of the empire west of Italy and Tunisia. Baetica poured out oceans of plonk for the empire; the Romans sniffed at its quality but they were never shy about ordering more. In Rome today you can see a 48m (160ft) hill called Monte Testaccio, made entirely of broken amphorae – most of them from Spain. Besides wine, oil and metals, another export was dancing girls; Baetica's girls were reputed to be the hottest in the empire. And for the choicer Roman banquets, there was *garum*, a highly prized condiment made of fish guts. Modern gourmets have been trying to guess the recipe for centuries.

New cities grew up to join Cádiz, Itálica and Málaga. Of these, the most important were **Hispalis** (Sevilla) and **Corduba** (Córdoba), which became Baetica's capital. Other towns owe their beginnings to the common Roman policy of establishing colonies populated by army veterans, such as Colonia Genetiva Iulia Ursa – modern Osuna. Among the cosmopolitan population were Iberians, Celts, Phoenicians, Italians, and a sizeable minority of **Jews**. During the Diaspora, Rome settled them here in great numbers, as far from home as they could possibly put them; they would play an important and constructive role in Spanish life for the next 1,500 years. The province also had a talent for keeping in the mainstream of imperial politics and culture. Vespasian had been governor here, and Baetica gave birth to three of Rome's best emperors: Trajan, Hadrian and Theodosius. It also contributed almost all the great figures of the 'silver age' of Latin literature – Lucan, both Senecas, Martial and Quintilian. None of these, of course, were really 'Andalucíans' except by birth; all were part of the thin veneer of élite Roman families that owned nearly everything, and monopolized colonial Spain's political and cultural life. Concerning the other 99 per cent of the population, we know very little.

409–711

Finally rid of its Roman bosses, Spain hasn't a minute before some malodorous blue-eyed Teutons come to take their place

By the 4th century, the crushing burden of maintaining the defence budget and the government bureaucracy sent Spain's economy, along with the rest of the empire's, into a permanent depression. Cities declined, and in the countryside the landowners gradually squeezed the majority of the population into serfdom or outright slavery. Thus when the bloody, anarchic **Vandals** arrived in Spain in 409, they found bands of rural guerrillas, or *bagaudae*, to help them in smashing up the remnants of the Roman system. The Vandals moved on to Africa in 428, leaving nothing behind but, maybe, the name Andalucía – some believe it was originally Vandalusia.

The next uninvited guests were the **Visigoths**, a ne'er-do-well Germanic folk who had caused little trouble for anyone until they were pushed westwards by the Huns. After making a name for themselves by sacking Rome under their chief Alaric in 410, they found their way into Spain four years later, looking for food. By 478 they had conquered most of it, including Andalucía, and they established an independent kingdom stretching from the Atlantic to the Rhône. The Visigoths were illiterate, selfish and bloody-minded, but persistent enough to endure, despite endless dynastic and religious quarrels; like most Germans, they were Arian heretics. There weren't many of them; estimates of the original invading horde range up to some 200,000, and for the next three centuries they would remain a warrior élite that never formed more than a small fraction of the population. For support they depended on the landowners, who were making the slow but logical transition from Roman *senatores* to feudal lords. An interruption to their rule, at least in the south, came in 553; Justinian's reviving eastern empire, having already reclaimed Italy and Africa, tried for Spain too. Byzantine resources proved just enough to wrest Andalucía from the Visigoths, but the overextended empire was hardly able to hold all its far-flung conquests for very long. Over the following decades the Visigoths gradually pushed them back, though some coastal bases remained in Byzantine hands as late as the Arab invasion.

Despite all the troubles, Andalucía at least seems to have been doing well – probably better than anywhere else in western Europe – and there was even a modest revival of learning in the 7th century, the age of St Isidore (*c.* 560–636), famous scholar of Sevilla. King Leovigild (573–86) was an able leader; his son Reccared converted to orthodox Catholicism in 589; both helped bring their state to the height of its power as much by internal reform as military victories. Allowing the grasping Church a share of power, however, proved fatal to the Visigoths. The Church's depredations against the populace and its persecutions of Jews and heretics made the Visigothic state as many enemies within as it ever had beyond its borders. By the time of King Roderick, a duke of Baetica who had usurped the throne in one of the kingdom's periods of political turbulence, Visigothic Spain was in serious disarray.

711–756

The Spaniards are conquered by a people they had never before heard of

The great wave of Muslim Arab expansion that began in Mohammed's lifetime was bound to wash up on Spain's shores sooner or later. A small Arab force arrived in Spain in 710, led by **Tarif**, who gave his name to today's Tarifa on the Straits. The following year brought a larger army – still only about 7,000 men – under **Tariq ibn-Ziyad**, with the assistance of dissident Visigoths opposed to Roderick, and a certain Count Julian, Byzantine ruler of Ceuta, who supplied the ships to ferry over the Arab-Berber army; Tariq quickly defeated the Visigoths near Barbate, a battle in which Roderick was killed. Toledo, the Visigothic capital, fell soon after, and a collection of Visigothic nobles were on their way to Baghdad in chains as presents to the caliph. Within five years, the Arabs had conquered most of the peninsula, and they were crossing the Pyrenees into France.

The ease of the conquest is not difficult to explain. The majority of the population was delighted to welcome the Arabs and their Berber allies. The overtaxed peasants and persecuted Jews supported them from the first. Religious tolerance was guaranteed under the new rule; since the largest share of taxes fell on non-believers, the Arabs were happy to refrain from forced conversions. The conquest, however, was never completed. A small Christian enclave in the northwest, the kingdom of Asturias, survived following an obscure but symbolic victory over the Moors at Covadonga in 718. At the time, the Arabs would barely have noticed; Muslim control of most of Spain was solid, but hampered almost from the start by dissension between the Arabs, the neglected Berbers, the large numbers of Syrians who arrived later, in another army sent from the east, and among the various tribes of the Arabs themselves. The Berbers had the biggest grudge. Not only did the Arabs look down on them, but in the distribution of confiscated lands they were not given their promised fair share. The result was a massive **Berber revolt** in 740. This was put down with some difficulty, but it was only one of a number of troubles, as fighting between the various Arab princes kept Spain in an almost continuous state of civil war. Between the feuding invaders, Spain suffered through one of the darkest centuries in its history.

756–929

Spain becomes al-Andalus, and things are looking up

Far away in Damascus, the political struggles of the caliphate were being resolved by a general massacre of the princes of the Umayyad dynasty, successors of Mohammed; a new dynasty, the Abbasids, replaced them. One young Umayyad escaped – **Abd ar-Rahman**; he fled to Córdoba, and took power with the support of Umayyad loyalists there. After a victory in May 756, he proclaimed himself emir, the first leader of an independent emirate of al-Andalus. At first, Abd ar-Rahman was only one of the contending petty princes fighting over a ruined, exhausted country.

Eventually he prevailed over them all, though the chronicles of the time are too thin to tell us whether he owed his ascendence to military talent, good fortune or just simple tenacity. It took him over thirty years of fighting to do the job and, besides rival Arabs, he had to contend with invading Christian armies sent by Charlemagne in the 770s – a campaign that, though unsuccessful, left us the legend of Roland at Roncesvalles, source of the medieval epic *Chanson de Roland*.

Under this new government, Muslim Spain gradually recovered its strength and prosperity. Political unity was maintained only with great difficulty, but trade, urban life and culture flourished. Though their domains stretched as far as the Pyrenees, the Umayyad emirs referred to it all as **al-Andalus**. Andalucía was its heartland and Córdoba, Sevilla, and Málaga its greatest cities, unmatched by any others in western Europe. Abd ar-Rahman kept his capital at Córdoba and began the Great Mosque there, a brilliant and unexpected start to the culture of the new state.

After Abd ar-Rahman, the succession passed without difficulty through Hisham I (788–96), Al-Hakim I (796–822), and Abd ar-Rahman II (822–52), all of them sound military men, defenders of the faith and patrons of musicians and poets. Abd ar-Rahman I's innovations, the creation of a professional army and palace secretariat, helped considerably in maintaining stability. The latter, called the *Saqaliba*, a civil service of imported slaves, was made up largely of Slavs and black Africans. The new dynasty seems also to have worked sincerely to establish justice and balance among the various contentious ethnic groups. In the days of Abd ar-Rahman I, only a fifth of al-Andalus's population was Muslim. This figure would rise steadily throughout the existence of al-Andalus, finally reaching 90 per cent in the 1100s, but emirs would always have to deal with the concerns of a very cosmopolitan population that included haughty Arab aristocrats prone to factionalism, leftover Roman and Visigothic barons, who might be Christians or *muwallads* (converts to Islam), Iraqis, Syrians, Yemenites, and various other peoples from the eastern Muslim world, Berbers (who made up the bulk of the army), Jews, slaves from the furthest corners of three continents and all the old native Iberian population.

One weakness, shared with most early Islamic states, was the personal, non-institutional nature of rule. Individuals and groups could address their grievances only to the emir, while governors in distant towns had so much authority that they often began to think of themselves as independent potentates – a cause of frequent rebellions in the reigns of Mohammed I (852–86) and Abd Allah (888–912). Closer to home, discontented *muwallads* in the heart of Andalucía coalesced around the rather mysterious figure of **Umar ibn-Hafsun**. After his rebel army was defeated in 891, he and his followers took refuge in the impregnable fortress of Bobastro, in the mountains near Antequera, carrying on a kind of guerrilla war against the emirs. Later Christian propagandists claimed ibn-Hafsun as a Christian. Though this is unlikely, a church can still be seen among the ruins of Bobastro. After ibn-Hafsun's death, his sons held out until Bobastro was finally taken in 928.

A less serious problem, though a bothersome one, was the **Vikings**, who raided Spain's coasts just as they did all others within the reach of their longboats. Even though their raids took them as far as Sevilla, al-Andalus was better able to fight off the Northmen than any of the Christian states of Europe; under the reign of **Abd ar-Rahman II**, al-Andalus made itself into a sea power, with bases on both the Mediterranean and the Atlantic. In those days, interestingly enough, al-Andalus held on to two key port towns in North Africa, Ceuta and Melilla, to guard its southern flank – just as Spain does today. The pirates of Fraxinetum, La Garde-Freinet in southern France, made life miserable for the Provenceaux and helped keep the western Mediterranean a Muslim lake; they too acknowledged the sovereignty of Abd ar-Rahman.

929–1008

A caliph rises in the west, and a great civilization reaches its noonday

In the tenth century, al-Andalus enjoyed its golden age. **Abd ar-Rahman III** (912–61) and **al-Hakim II** (961–76) collected tribute from the Christian kingdoms of the north, and from North African states as far as Algiers. In 929, Abd ar-Rahman III assumed the title of caliph, declaring al-Andalus entirely independent of any higher political or religious authority. Umayyad Al-Andalus was in fact cooperating closely with the Abbasid caliphate in Baghdad, but Shiite heretics in North Africa had declared their own caliph at Tunis, and Abd ar-Rahman, who like all the emirs was orthodox in religion, was not about to let himself be outranked by an upstart neighbour. After the peaceful reign of al-Hakim II, a boy caliph, Hisham II, came to the throne in 976. In a fateful turn of events, effective power was seized by his minister Abu Amir al-Ma'afiri, better known by the title he assumed, **al-Mansur** ('the Victorious', known to the Christians as Almanzor). Though an iron-willed dictator with a penchant for bloody slaughter of anyone suspected of opposing him, al-Mansur was also a brilliant military leader, one who resumed the offensive against the growing Christian kingdoms of the north. He recaptured León, Pamplona and Barcelona, sacked almost every Christian city at least once, and even raided the great pilgrimage shrine at Santiago de Compostela in Galicia, stealing its bells to hang up as trophies in the Great Mosque of Córdoba.

A more resounding al-Andalus accomplishment was keeping in balance its diverse and increasingly sophisticated population, all the while accommodating three religions and ensuring mutual tolerance. At the same time, they made it pay. Al-Andalus' cities thrived, far more than any of their neighbours, Muslim or Christian, and the countryside was more prosperous than it has been before or since. The Arabs introduced cotton, rice, dates, sugar, oranges, artichokes and much else. Irrigation, begun under the Romans, was perfected; contemporary observers counted over 200 *nurias*, or water wheels, along the length of the Guadalquivir, and even parched Almería became a garden. It was this 'agricultural revolution', the application of eastern crops and techniques to a land perfectly adapted for them, that made all the rest possible. It meant greater wealth and an increased population, and permitted the growth of manufacturers and commerce far in advance of anything else in western Europe.

At the height of its fortunes, al-Andalus was one of the world's great civilizations. Its wealth and stability sustained an impressive artistic flowering – obvious today, even from the relatively few monuments that survived the Reconquista. Córdoba, with al-Hakim's great library, became a centre of learning; Málaga was renowned for its singers, and Sevilla for the making of musical instruments. Art and life were also growing closer. About 822, the famous **Ziryab** had arrived in Córdoba from Baghdad. A great musician and poet, mentioned often in the tales of the *Thousand and One Nights*, Ziryab also revolutionized the manners of the Arabs, introducing eastern fashions, poetic courtesies, and the proper way to arrange the courses of a meal. It wasn't long before the élite of al-Andalus became more interested in the latest graft of Shiraz roses than in riding across La Mancha to cross swords with the barbaric Asturians.

When Christian Europe was just beginning to blossom, al-Andalus and Byzantium were its exemplars and schoolmasters. Religious partisanship and western pride have always obscured the relationship; how much we really owe al-Andalus in scholarship – especially the transmission of Greek and Arab science – in art and architecture, in technology, and in poetry and the other delights of civilization, has never been completely explored. Contacts were more common than is generally assumed. Christian students often found their way to Toledo or Córdoba – like the French monk, one of the most learned Christians of his day, who became Pope Sylvester II in 997.

Throughout the 10th century, the military superiority of al-Andalus was great enough to have finally erased the Christian kingdoms, had the caliphs cared to do so; it may have been a simple lack of aggressiveness and determination that held them back, or perhaps simply a constitutional inability of the Arab leaders to deal with the green, chilly, rainy world of the northern mountains. The Muslim–Christian wars of this period cannot be understood as a prelude to the Crusades, or to the bigotry of Fernando and Isabel. Pious fanaticism, in fact, was conspicuously lacking on both sides, and if the chronicles detail endless wars and raids, they were always about booty, not religion. Al-Andalus had its ambassadors among the Franks, the Italians, the Byzantines and the Ottonian Holy Roman Empire, and it usually found no problem reaching understandings with any of them. In Spain itself, dynastic marriages between Muslims and Christians were common, and frontier chiefs could switch sides more than once without switching religions. The famous **El Cid** would spend more time working for Muslim rulers than Christians, and all the kings of León had some Moorish blood. Abd ar-Rahman III himself had blue eyes and red hair (which he dyed black to keep in fashion); his mother was a Basque princess from Navarre.

1008–1085

Disaster, disarray; al-Andalus breaks into pieces

It is said that the great astronomer Maslama of Madrid, who was also court astrologer at Córdoba, foretold the end of the caliphate just before his death in 1007. A little political sense, more than knowledge of the stars, would have sufficed to demonstrate that al-Andalus was approaching a crisis. After the death of al-Mansur in 1002, the political situation began to change dramatically. His son, Abd al-Malik al-Muzaffar, inherited his position as vizier and *de facto* ruler and held the state together until his death in 1008, despite increasing tensions. All the while, Hisham II remained a pampered prisoner in the sumptuous palace-city of **Medinat al-Zahra**, outside Córdoba. The lack of political legitimacy in this ministerial dictatorship, and the increasing distance between government and people symbolized by Medinat al-Zahra, contributed to the troubles that began in 1008. Historians suggest that the great wealth of al-Andalus had made the nation a bit jaded and selfish, that the rich and powerful were scarcely inclined to compromise or sacrifice for the good of the whole. The old Arab aristocracy, in fact, was the most disaffected group of all. Al-Mansur's conquests had been delivered by a kind of new model army, manned by Berber mercenaries. With their military function gone, the nobles saw their status and privilege steadily eroding.

Whatever the reason, the caliphate disintegrated with startling suddenness after 1008. Nine caliphs ruled between that year and 1031, most of them puppets of the Berbers, the Saqaliba or other factions. Civil wars and city riots became endemic. Al-Mansur's own Berber troops, who felt no loyalty to any caliph, caused the worst of the troubles. They destroyed Medinat al-Zahra, and sacked Córdoba itself in 1013. By 1031, when the caliphate was formally abolished, an exhausted al-Andalus had split into at least 30 squabbling states, run by Arab princes, Berber officers or even former slaves. Almost overnight, the balance of power between Muslim and Christian had reversed itself. In 999, al-Mansur had been sacking the towns of the north as far as Pamplona. Only a decade later, the counts of Castile and Barcelona were sending armies deep into the heart of al-Andalus, intervening by request of one party or the other.

The years after 1031 are known as the **age of the *taifas***, or of the 'Party Kings' (*muluk al tawa'if*), so-called because most of them owed their position to one of the political factions. Few of these self-made rulers slept easily in an era of constant intrigues and revolts, shifting alliances and pointless wars. The only relatively strong state was that of Sevilla, founded by former governor **Mohammed ibn-Abbad**, who was also the richest landowner in the area. For political legitimacy he claimed to rule in the name of the last caliph, who had disappeared in the sack of Medinat al-Zahra, and miraculously reappeared (ibn-Abbad's enemies claimed the 'caliph' was really a lookalike mat weaver from Calatrava). Ibn-Abbad was unscrupulous, but effective; his successes were continued by his sons, who managed to annexe Córdoba and several other towns. Under their rule Sevilla replaced stricken Córdoba as the largest and most important city of al-Andalus.

1085–1212

Moroccan zealots come to Spain's defence, if only for a while

The total inability of the 'Party Kings' to work together made the 11th century a party for the Christians. Nearly all the little states were forced to pay heavy tribute to Christian kings; that, and the expenses of their lavish courts and wars against each other, led to sharply higher taxes and helped put an end to a 200-year run of economic expansion. **Alfonso VI**, King of Castile and León, collected tribute from most of the *taifas*, including even Sevilla. In 1085, with the help of the legendary warrior El Cid, he captured Toledo. The loss of this key fortress-city alarmed the *taifas* enough for them to request assistance from the **Almoravids** (*al-Murabitun*, the 'warrior monks') of North Africa, a fanatical fundamendalist movement of the Berbers that had recently established an empire stretching from Morocco to Senegal, with its capital at the newly-founded city of Marrakech.

The Almoravid leader, **Yusuf ibn-Tashufin**, crossed the Straits and defeated Alfonso in 1086. Yusuf liked al-Andalus so much that he decided to keep it; by 1110 the Almoravids had gobbled up the last of the surviving *taifas* and had reimposed Muslim rule as far as Saragossa. Under their rule, al-Andalus became more of a consciously Islamic state than it had ever been before, uncomfortable for the Christians and even for the cultured Arab aristocrats, with their gardens and their poetry (and their long-established custom of dropping in on Christian monasteries for a forbidden glass of wine). The chronicles give some evidence of Almoravid oppression directed against Christian communities, and even deportations; religious prejudices were hardening on both sides, especially since the Christians evolved their crusading ethos in the 1100s, but the Almoravids did their best to help bigotry along.

Popular rebellions against the Almoravids in the Andalucían cities were a problem from the start, and a series of big ones put an end to their rule in 1145; al-Andalus rapidly dissolved into confusion and a second era of 'Party Kings'. Two years later Almoravid power in Africa was defeated and replaced by that of the **Almohads**, a nearly identical military-religious state. The Almohads (*al-Muwahhidun*, 'upholders of divine unity') began with a Sufi preacher named ibn-Tumart, proselytizing and proclaiming *jihad* among the tribes of the Atlas mountains of Morocco. By 1172 the Almohads had control of most of southern Spain. Somewhat more tolerant and civilized than the Almoravids, their rule coincided with a cultural reawakening in al-Andalus, a period that saw the building of La Giralda in Sevilla. Literature and art flourished, and in Córdoba lived two of the greatest philosophers of the Middle Ages: the Arab, Ibn Rushd (Averroës), and the Jew, Moses Maimónides. The Almohads nevertheless shared many of the Almoravids' limitations. Essentially a military regime, with no deep support from any part of the population, they could win victories over the Christians (as at Alarcos in 1195) but were never able to take advantage of them.

1212–1492

Al-Andalus falls to the eaters of pork; one small corner remains to the faithful

At the same time, the Christian Spaniards were growing stronger and gaining a new sense of unity and national consciousness. The end for the Almohads, and for al-Andalus, came with the **Battle of Las Navas de Tolosa** in 1212, fought near the traditional site for climactic battles in Spain – the Despeñaperros pass, gateway to

Andalucía. Here, an army from all the states of Christian Spain under Alfonso VII (1126–57) destroyed Almohad power for ever. Alfonso's son, **Fernando III** (1217–52), captured Córdoba (1236) and Sevilla (1248), and was made a saint for his trouble. The people of Sevilla would have found it ironic; breaking with the more humane practices of the past, Fernando determined to make al-Andalus's capital a Christian city once and for all, and after starving the population into submission by siege he expelled every one of them, allowing them to take only the goods they could carry. **Alfonso X** (the Wise, 1252–84), noted for his poetry and the brilliance of his court, completed the conquest of western Andalucía in the 1270s and 1280s.

In the conquest of Sevilla, important assistance had been rendered by one of Fernando's new vassals, **Mohammed ibn-Yusuf ibn-Nasr**, an Arab adventurer who had conquered Granada in 1235. The **Nasrid Kingdom of Qarnatah** (Granada) survived partly from its cooperation with Castile, and partly from its mountainous, easily defensible terrain. For the next 250 years it would be the only remaining Muslim territory on the peninsula. Two other factors helped keep Granada afloat. One was a small but very competent army, which made good use of a chain of strong border fortresses in the mountains to make Castile think twice about any serious invasion. Granada was also able to count on help from the Marenid emirs of Morocco, who succeeded to power in North Africa after the collapse of the Almohad state. The Marenids half-heartedly invaded Spain twice, in 1264 in support of a Muslim revolt, and again in 1275; for a long time afterwards they were able to hold on to such coastal bases as Algeciras, Tarifa and Gibraltar.

As a refuge for Muslims from the rest of Spain, Granada became al-Andalus in miniature, a sophisticated and generally peaceful state, stretching from Gibraltar to Almería. It produced the last brilliant age of Moorish culture in the 14th century, expressed in its poetry and in the art of the Alhambra. It was not, however, always a happy land. When they were not raiding Granada's borders, the Castilians enforced heavy tributes on it, as they had with the Party Kings of the 11th century. It wasn't easy to prosper under such conditions, and things were made worse by the monopoly over trade and shipping forced on the Granadans by the predatory Genoese, who in those days were an affliction to Christian and Muslim Spaniards alike. Affected by a permanent siege mentality, and filled with refugees from the lands that had been lost, Granada seems to have acquired the air of melancholy that still clings to the city today.

In the rest of Andalucía, the Reconquista meant a profound cultural dislocation, as the majority of the Muslim population chose to flee the rough northerners and their priests. The Muslims who stayed behind (the ***mudéjares***, meaning those 'permitted to remain') did not fare badly at first. Their economy remained intact, and many Spaniards remained fascinated by the extravagant culture they had inherited. In the 1360s, King Pedro of Castile (1350–69) was signing his correspondence 'Pedro ben Xancho' in a flowing Arabic script, and spending most of his time in Sevilla's Alcázar, built by artists from Granada. There was even a considerable return of Muslim populations, to Sevilla and a few other towns from which they had been forced out; this took place with the approval of the Castilian kings, who needed their labour and skills to rebuild the devastated land. Throughout the period, though, the culture and the society that built al-Andalus were becoming increasingly diluted, as Muslims either left or converted, while the Castilians imported large numbers of Christian settlers from the north. Religious intolerance, fostered as always by the Church, was a growing problem.

1492–1516

A rotten queen and a rotten king send the Andalucians down a road of misery

The final disaster, for Andalucía and for Spain, came with the marriage in 1469 of **King Fernando II of Aragón** and **Queen Isabel I of Castile**, opening the way, ten years later, for the union of the two most powerful states on the peninsula. The glory of the occasion has tended to obscure the historical realities, and writers too often give a free ride to two of the most vicious and bigoted figures in Spanish history. If Fernando and Isabel did not invent genocide, they did their hypocritical best to sanctify it, forcing a maximalist solution to a cultural diversity they found intolerable. As state-sponsored harassment of the *mudéjares* increased across Spain, the 'Catholic Kings' also found the time was right for the extinction of Granada. Fernando, a tireless campaigner, nibbled away at the Nasrid borders for a decade, until little more than the capital itself remained. It had not been easy, but Fernando was fortunate enough to have one of the greatest soldiers of his day running the show – Gonzalo de Córdoba, El Gran Capitán, who would later use the tactics developed on the Granada campaign to conquer southern Italy for Spain.

Granada fell in 1492, completing the Reconquista; Fernando and Isabel expelled all the Jews from Spain the same year; their **Inquisition** – founded by Fernando and Isabel, not by the Church, and entirely devoted to their purposes – was in full swing, terrorizing 'heretical' Christians and converted Jews and Muslims and effectively putting an end to all differences of opinion, religious or political. In the same year, **Columbus** (who had been present at the fall of Granada) sailed from Andalucía to the New World, initiating the Age of Discovery.

Under the conditions of Granada's surrender in 1492, the *mudéjares* were to be allowed to continue their religion and customs unmolested. Under the influence of the Church, in the person of the famous Archbishop of Toledo, Cardinal Cisneros, Spain soon reneged on its promises and attempted forced conversion, a policy cleverly designed to justify itself by causing a revolt. The **First Revolt of the Alpujarras**, the string of villages near Granada in the Sierra Nevada, in 1500, resulted in the expulsion of all Muslims who failed to convert – the majority of the population had already fled – as well as decrees prohibiting Moorish dress and un-Christian institutions such as public bathhouses.

Beyond that, the Spanish purposely impoverished the Granada territories, ruining their agriculture and bankrupting the important silk industry with punitive taxes and a ban on exports. The Inquisition enriched the Church's coffers, confiscating the entire property of any converted Muslims who could be found guilty of backsliding in the faith. A second revolt in the Alpujarras occurred in 1568, after which Philip II ordered the prohibition of the Arabic language and the dispersal of the remaining Muslim population throughout the towns and cities of Castile. By this time, paranoia had a partial justification. Spain was locked in a bitter struggle against the Ottoman Empire, and the Turks had established bases as close as the Maghreb coast; the threat of a Muslim revival was looking very real. But paranoia was not directed at Muslims alone. In the same year, the Inquisition began incinerating suspected Protestants in Sevilla, and the systematic persecution of the *conversos* – Jews who had converted to Christianity, in some cases generations before – was well under way. Intolerance had become a way of life.

1516–1700

The new Spain chokes on its riches and power, and Andalucía suffers the most

In the 16th century, the new nation's boundless wealth, energy and talent were squandered by two rulers even more vile than Los Reyes Católicos. Carlos I, a Habsburg who gained the throne by marriage when Fernando and Isabel's first two heirs died, emptied the treasury to purchase his election as Holy Roman Emperor. Outside Spain he is better known by his imperial title, **Charles V** (1516–56), a sanctimonious tyrant who had half of Europe in his pocket and dearly wanted the other half. His megalomaniac ambitions bled Spain dry, a policy continued by his son **Philip II** (1556–98), under whom Spain went bankrupt three times.

Throughout the century, Andalucía's ports were the base for the exploration and exploitation of the New World. Trade and settlement were planned from Sevilla, and gold and silver poured in each year from the Indies' treasure fleet; in the 16th century the city's population increased fivefold, to over 100,000. Unfortunately, what money did not immediately go to finance the wars of Charles and Philip was gobbled up by the nobility, the Genoese and German bankers, or by inflation – the 16th-century 'price revolution' caused by the riches from America. The colonies needed vast amounts of manufactured goods, and had solid bullion to pay for them, but despite Sevilla's monopoly on the colonial trade, Andalucía found itself too badly misgoverned and economically primitive to supply any of them.

The historical ironies are profound. Awash in money, and presented with the kind of opportunity that few regions ever see through their entire history, Andalucía instead declined rapidly from one of the richest and most cultured provinces of Europe to one of the poorest and most backward. Fernando and Isabel had begun the process, distributing the vast confiscated lands of the Moors to their friends, or to the Church and military orders; from its birth the new Andalucía was a land of huge estates, exploited by absentee landlords and worked by sharecroppers – the remnants of the original population as well as the hopeful colonists from the north, most of whom were reduced in a generation or two to virtual serfdom. It was the story of Roman

Spain all over again, and in the end Andalucía found that it had become just as much a colony as Mexico or Peru.

By the 17th century, the destruction of Andalucía was complete. The Inquisition's terror had done its work, eliminating any possibility of intellectual freedom and reducing the population to the lowest depths of superstition and subservience. Their trade and manufactures ruined, the cities stagnated; agriculture suffered as well, as the complex irrigation systems of the Moors fell into disrepair and were gradually abandoned. The only opportunity for the average man lay with emigration, and Andalucía contributed more than its share to the American colonies. The shipments of American bullion peaked about 1610–20, and after that the decline was precipitous. As for the last surviving Muslims, the *moriscos*, they were expelled from Spain in 1609. The greatest concentration of them, surprisingly, was not in Andalucía, but in the fertile plains around Valencia. The king's minister, the Duke of Lerma, was a Valencian, and apparently he came up with the plan in hope of snatching some of their confiscated land. The leaders of the Inquisition opposed the expulsions, since they made most of their profits shaking down *moriscos*, but the land-grabbers won out, and by 1614 some 275,000 Spanish Muslims had been forced from their homes.

1700–1931

Bourbon reformers, Napoleonic hoodlums, and a long parade of despots cross the stage; the Andalucians start to fight back

For almost the next two centuries, Andalucía has no history at all. The perversity of Spain's rulers had exhausted the nation. Scorned for its backwardness, Spain was no longer even taken seriously as a military power. The **War of the Spanish Succession**, during which the English seized Gibraltar (1704), replaced the Habsburgs with the Bourbons, though their rule brought little improvement. Bourbon policies, beginning with **Philip V** (1700–46) followed the lead of their cousins in France, and a more centralized, rationalized state did attempt to bring improvements in roads and other public works, as well as state-sponsored industries in the French style, such as the great royal tobacco factory in Sevilla. The high point of reform in the 18th century was the reign of **Carlos III** (1759–88), who expelled the Jesuits, attempted to revive trade and resettled the most desolate parts of Andalucía. New towns were founded – the Nuevas Poblaciones – such as La Carolina and Olavide, though in such a depressed setting that the foreign settlers Carlos brought in could not adapt, and the new towns never really thrived. One bright spot was an ancient city, long in the shadows, that found a new prominence. Cádiz, which succeeded Sevilla as the major port for the colonial trade, became in these years one of the most prosperous and progressive cities in Spain.

Despite three centuries of decay, Andalucíans responded with surprising energy to the French occupation during the **Napoleonic Wars**. The French gave them good reason to, stealing as much gold and art as they could carry, and blowing up castles and historical buildings just for sport. As elsewhere in Spain, irregulars and loyal army detachments assisted the British under Wellington. In 1808, a force made up mostly of Andalucíans defeated the French at the **Battle of Bailén**. In 1812, a group of Spanish liberals met in Cádiz to declare a constitution, and under this the Spanish fitfully conducted what they call their **War of Independence**.

With victory, however, came not reforms and a constitution, but reaction and the return of the Bourbons. For most Andalucíans, times may have been worse than ever, but Romantic-era Europe was about to discover the region in a big way. The trend had already started with Mozart's operas set in Sevilla, and now the habit resumed with Washington Irving's *Tales of the Alhambra* in 1832, and Richard Ford's equally popular *Handbook for Travellers in Spain* in 1845. Between the lost civilization of the Moors, which Europeans were coming to value for the first time, and the natural colour of its daily life, backward, exotic Andalucía proved to be just what a jaded continent was looking for. The region provided some of the world's favourite stereotypes, from gypsies and flamenco to *toreadores* and Don Juans. Bizet's *Carmen* had its debut in 1873.

The real Andalucíans, meanwhile, were staggering through a confusing century that would see the loss of Spain's American colonies, coups, counter-coups, civil wars on behalf of pretenders to the throne (the two Carlist Wars of the 1830s and 1870s), a short-lived First Republic in 1874 and several *de facto* dictatorships. Andalucía, disappointed and impoverished as ever, contributed many liberal leaders. It also knew a mining boom, especially at the famous Río Tinto mines in Huelva province, the same that had been worked in Phoenician times. Typically, in what had become a thoroughly colonial economy, all the mines were in the hands of foreign, mostly British owners, and none of the profits stayed in Andalucía. The desperate peasantry, living at rock bottom of an archaic feudal structure, became one of the most radicalized rural populations in Europe.

At first, this manifested itself as simple outlawry, especially in the Sierra Morena (and in northern Spain, Corsica, Sardinia, southern Italy, north Africa – the 19th century was a great age for bandits all over the Mediterranean). In 1870, an Italian agitator and associate of Bakunin named Giuseppe Fanelli brought **Anarchism** to Andalucía. In a land where government had never been anything more than institutionalized oppression, the idea was a hit; Anarchist ideas and institutions found a firmer foothold in Spain than anywhere else in Europe, oddly concentrated in two very different milieus: the backward Andalucían peasantry and the modern industrial workers of Barcelona. Anarchist-inspired guerrilla warfare and terrorism increased steadily in Andalucía, reaching its climax in the years 1882–6, directed by a secret society called the **Mano Negra**. Violence continued for decades, met with fierce repression by the hated but effective national police, the Guardia Civil. In 1910 the national Anarchist trade union, the CNT, was founded at a congress in Sevilla.

Despite their poverty and troubles, Andalucíans could occasionally make a game attempt to show they were at least trying to keep up with the modern world – most spectacularly at the 1929 *Exposición Iberoamericana*, Sevilla's first World Fair, which left the city a lovely park and some impressive monuments. The Fair project had been pushed along by Spain's dictator of the 1920s, General **Miguel Primo de Rivera**. Though a native Andalucían, from Jerez, Primo de Rivera did little else for the region. Rising discontent forced his resignation in 1929, and two years later municipal elections turned out huge majorities all over Spain for republican parties. King Alfonso XIII abdicated, and Spain was about to become a very interesting place.

1931–9

Civil War – the second Reconquista

The coming of the democratic **Second Republic** in 1931 brought little improvement to the lives of Andalucía, but it opened the gates to a flood of political agitation from extremists of every faction. Andalucía often found itself in the middle, as in 1932 when General Sanjurjo attempted unsuccessfully to mount a coup from Sevilla. Peasant rebellions intensified, especially under the radical right-wing government of 1934–6, when attempted land seizures led to such incidents as the massacre at Casas Viejas in 1934. Spain's alarmed Left formed a Popular Front to regain power in 1936, but street fighting and assassinations were becoming daily occurrences, and the new government seemed powerless to halt the country's slide into anarchy. In July 1936 the army uprising, orchestrated by Generals **Francisco Franco** and **Emilio Mola**, led to the **Civil War**. The Army of Africa, under Franco's command, quickly captured eastern Andalucia, and most of the key cities in the province soon fell under Nationalist control. The Army of Africa, battle-hardened from campaigns against the Rif in the mountains of Spanish Morocco in the 1920s, was the most effective force in the Spanish Army. Many of its battalions were made up of native Moroccans, who brought with them another bitter Spanish irony: generals fighting in the name of old Christian, monarchist Spain, bringing mercenary Muslim troops into the country for the first time in 500 years.

In Sevilla, a flamboyant officer named Gonzalo Queipo de Llano (later famous as the Nationalists' radio propaganda voice) singlehandedly bluffed and bullied the city into submission, and then led an armoured column to destroy the working-class district of Triana. In arch-reactionary Granada, the authorities and local fascists massacred thousands of workers and Republican loyalists, including the poet Federico García Lorca. Málaga, the last big town under Republican control, fell to Mussolini's Italian 'volunteers' in February 1937. Four thousand more loyalists were slaughtered there, and Franco's men bombed and strafed civilian refugees fleeing the city. Thereafter Andalucía saw little fighting though its people shared fully in Nationalist reprisals and oppression; Franco, who had spent most of his career in the colonial service, had no problem using the same terror tactics on fellow Spaniards that the army had habitually practised on Africans. A Nationalist officer estimated that some 150,000 people were murdered in Andalucía by 1938, and in Sevilla alone at that time the Nationalists were still shooting up to 80 people a day.

1939–the Present

Forty years of Francisco Franco, and finally, a happy ending

After the war, in the dark days of the 1940s, Andalucía knew widespread destitution and, at times, conditions close to famine. Emigration, which had been significant ever since the discovery of America, now became a mass exodus, creating the huge Andalucían colonies in Madrid and Barcelona, and smaller ones in nearly every city of northern Europe.

Economic conditions improved marginally in the 1950s, with American loans to help get the economy back on its feet, and the birth of the Costa del Sol on the empty coast west of Málaga. A third factor, often overlooked, was the quietly brilliant planning of Franco's economists, setting the stage for Spain's industrial take-off of the 1960s and '70s. In Andalucía, their major contributions were industrial programmes around Sevilla and Cádiz and a score of dams, providing cheap electricity and ending the endemic, terrible floods.

When **King Juan Carlos** ushered in the return of democracy, Andalucíans were more than ready. **Felipe González**, the socialist charmer from Sevilla, ran Spain from 1982 to 1996, and other Andalucíans are well represented in every sector of government and society. They took full advantage of the revolutionary regional autonomy laws of the late 1970s, building one of the most active regional governments, and giving Andalucía some control over its destiny for the first time since the Reconquista. And in other ways, history seems to be repeating itself over the last 20 years: the Arabs have returned in force, building a mosque in the Albaicín in Granada, making a home from home along the western Costa del Sol, and bringing economic if not exactly cultural wealth to the area; Jews once more are free to worship, and do so in small communities in Málaga, Marbella and Sevilla. In 1978 the first synagogue to be built since the Inquisition was consecrated at El Real in Málaga province.

Five centuries of misery and misrule, however, cannot be redeemed in a day. The average income in Andalucía is less than half of that in Catalunya or the Basque country; the unemployment rate, despite the relief which tourism brings along the coast, often stands at a brutal 40 per cent. None of this will be readily apparent unless you visit the more dismal suburbs of Sevilla or Málaga or the mountain villages of Almería province, where the new prosperity is still a rumour. In the flashy, vibrant cities and the tidy whitewashed villages, Andalucíans hold fast to their ebullient, extrovert culture, living as if they were at the top of the world.

Art and Architecture

Until the coming of the Moors, southern Spain produced little of note, or at least little that has survived. To begin at the beginning, there are the 25,000-year-old cave drawings at the Cueva de la Pileta, near Ronda, and Neolithic dolmens near Antequera and Almería. No significant buildings have been found from the Tartessians or the Phoenicians, though remains of a 7th-century BC temple have been dug up at Cádiz. Not surprisingly, with their great treasury of metals, the Iberians were skilled at making jewellery and figurines in silver and bronze (also ivory, traded up from North Africa where elephants were still common). They built walled towns on defensible sites, and their most significant religious buildings (besides the eastern-style temples built by the Phoenicians and Carthaginians) were great storehouses where archaeologists have discovered caches containing thousands of simple ex-voto statuettes.

Real art begins with the arrival of the Greeks in the 7th century BC. The famous Lady of Elche in the Madrid museum, though found in the region of Murcia, may have been typical of the Greek-influenced art of all the southern Iberians; their pottery, originally decorated in geometrical patterns, began to imitate the figurative Greek work in the 5th century BC. The best collections of early work are in the Archaeological Museum at Sevilla and the museum at Málaga – though everything really exceptional ends up in Madrid.

During the long period of Roman rule, Spanish art continued to follow trends from the more civilized east (ruins and amphitheatres at Itálica, Carmona, Ronda; a reconstructed temple at Córdoba; museums in Sevilla, Córdoba and Cádiz). Justinian's invasion in the middle of the 6th century BC brought new influences from the Greek world, though the exhausted region by that time had little money or leisure for art. Neither was Visigothic rule ever conducive to new advances. The Visigoths were mostly interested in gaudy jewellery and gold trinkets (best seen not in Andalucía, but in the museums of Madrid and Toledo). Almost no building work survives; the Moors purchased and demolished all of the important churches, but made good use of one architectural innovation of the Visigothic era, the more-than-semicircular 'horseshoe' arch.

Moorish

The greatest age for art in Andalucía began not immediately with the Arab conquest, but a century and a half later, with the arrival of Abd ar-Rahman and the establishment of the Umayyad emirate. The new emir and his followers had come from Damascus, the old capital of Islam, and they brought with them the best traditions of emerging Islamic art from Syria. 'Moorish' art, like 'Gothic', is a term of convenience that can be misleading. Along with the enlightened patronage of the Umayyads, this new art catalysed the dormant culture of Roman Spain, creating a brilliant synthesis; of this, the first and finest example is **La Mezquita**, the Great Mosque of Córdoba.

La Mezquita was recognized in its own time as one of the wonders of the world. We are fortunate it survived, and it is chilling to think of the (literally) thousands of mosques, palaces, public buildings, gates, cemeteries and towers destroyed by the Christians; the methodical effacement of a great culture. We can discuss Moorish architecture from its finest production, and from little else. As architecture, La Mezquita is full of subtleties and surprises (*see* p.141). Some Westerners have tended to dismiss the Moorish approach as 'decorative art', without considering the philosophical background, or the expression of ideas inherent in the decoration. Figurative art was prohibited in Islam, and though lions, fantastical animals and human faces peek out frequently from painted ceramics and carvings, for more serious matters artists had to find other forms. One of them was Arabic calligraphy, which soon became an Andalucian speciality. In architecture and the decorative arts, the emphasis was on repetitive geometric patterns, mirroring a Pythagorean strain that had always been present in Islam; these made the pattern for an aesthetic based on a meticulously clever arrangement of forms, shapes and spaces, meant to elicit surprise and delight. The infinite elements of this decorative universe, and the mathematics that underlie them (*see* **Topics**, pp.59–62) come together in the most unexpected of conclusions – a reminder that unity is the basic principle of Islam.

The 'decorative' sources are wonderfully eclectic, and easy enough to discern. From Umayyad Syria came the general plan of the rectangular, many-columned mosques, along with the striped arches; from Visigothic Spain, the distinctive horseshoe arch. The floral arabesques and intricate, flowing detail, whether on a mosque window, a majolica dish or a delicately carved ivory, are the heritage of late-Roman art, as can be clearly seen on the recycled Roman capitals of La Mezquita itself. The Umayyads in Syria had been greatly impressed by Byzantine mosaics, and had copied them in their early mosques. This continued in Spain, often with artists borrowed from Constantinople. Besides architectural decoration, the same patterns and motifs appear in the minor arts of al-Andalus, in painted ceramics, textiles and in metalwork, a Spanish speciality since prehistoric times – an English baron of the time might have traded an entire village for a fine Andalucían dagger or brooch.

Such an art does not seek progress and development in our sense; it shifts slowly, like a kaleidoscope, carefully and occasionally finding new and subtler patterns to captivate the eye and declare the unity of creation. It carried on, without decadence or revolutions, until the end of al-Andalus and beyond. The end of the caliphate and the rise of the Party Kings, ironically enough, was an impetus for art. Now, instead of one great patron there were thirty, with thirty courts to embellish. Under the Almoravids and Almohads, a reforming religious fundamentalism did not mean an end to art, though it did cut down some of its decorative excesses. The Almohads, who made their capital at Sevilla, created the **Torre del Oro** and the tower called **La Giralda**, model for the great minarets of Morocco.

The Christian conquest of Córdoba, Sevilla, and most of the rest of al-Andalus (1212–80), did not finish Moorish art. The tradition continued intact, with its Islamic foundations, for another two centuries in the kingdom of Granada. In the rest of

Spain, Muslim artists and artisans found ready employment for nearly as long; their *mudéjar* art briefly contended with imported styles from northern Europe to become the national art of Spain. Most of its finest productions are not in Andalucía at all; you can see them in the churches and synagogues of Toledo, the towers of Teruel and many other towns of Aragón. The trademarks of *mudéjar* building are geometrical decoration in *azulejo* tiles and brickwork, and elaborately carved wooden *artesonado* ceilings. *Mudéjar* styles and techniques would also provide a strong influence in Spain, for centuries to come, in all the minor arts, from the *taracea* inlaid woodcraft of Granada to fabrics, ceramics and metalwork. And the Moorish love of intricate decoration would resurface again and again in architecture, most notably in the Isabelline Gothic and the Churrigueresque.

Granada, isolated from the rest of the Muslim world and constantly on the defensive, produced no great advances, but this golden autumn of Moorish culture brought the decorative arts to a state of serene perfection. In the **Alhambra** (built in stages throughout the 14th century, during the height of the Nasrid kingdom), where the architecture incorporates gardens and flowing water, the emphasis is on panels of ornate plaster work, combining floral and geometric patterns with calligraphy – not only Koranic inscriptions, but the deeds of Granada's kings and contemporary lyrical poetry. Another feature is the stucco *muqarnas* ceilings (sometimes called 'stalactite ceilings'), translating the Moorish passion for geometry into three dimensions.

Granada's art and that of the *mudéjares* cross paths at Sevilla's **Alcázar**, expanded by Pedro the Cruel in the 1360s; artists from Granada did much of the work. Post-1492 *mudéjar* work can also be seen in some Sevilla palaces, such as the **Palacio de las Dueñas** or the **Casa de Pilatos**. The smaller delights of late Moorish decorative arts include painted majolica ware, inlaid wooden chests and tables (the *taracea* work, still a speciality of Granada), and exquisite silver and bronze work in everything from armour to astronomical instruments; the best collection is in the Alhambra's **Museo Nacional de Arte Hispano-Musulmán**.

Gothic and Renaissance

For art, the Reconquista and the emergence of a united Spain was a mixed blessing. The importation of foreign styles gave a new impetus to painting and architecture, but it also gradually swept away the nation's Moorish and *mudéjar* tradition, especially in the south, where it put an end to 800 years of artistic continuity. In the 13th and 14th centuries, churches in the reconquered areas were usually built in straightforward, unambitious Gothic, as with **Santa Ana** in Sevilla, built under Pedro the Cruel, and the simple and elegant parish churches of Córdoba. In the 1400s, Gothic lingered on without noticeable inspiration; Sevilla's squat and ponderous cathedral, the largest Gothic building anywhere, was probably the work of a German or Frenchman.

The Renaissance was a latecomer to Andalucía, as to the rest of Spain. In 1506, when the High Renaissance had already hit Rome, the Spaniards were building a Gothic chapel in Granada for the tombs of Fernando and Isabel. This time, though, they had an architect of distinction: **Enrique de Egas** (*c.* 1445–1534), who had already created important works in Toledo and Santiago de Compostela, made the Capilla Real Spain's finest late-Gothic building, in the lively style called 'Isabelline Gothic', which roughly corresponds to the contemporary French Flamboyant or English Perpendicular. Isabelline Gothic is only one part of the general tendency of Spanish art in these times, which has come to be called the **Plateresque**. A *platero* is a silversmith or a jeweller, and the style takes its name from the elaborate decoration applied to any building, whether Gothic or Renaissance.

The Plateresque in the decorative arts had already been established in Sevilla (the huge cathedral retablo, begun in 1482), and would continue into the next century (the cathedral's Capilla Real and sacristy, and the 1527 Ayuntamiento, by Diego de Riaño). Other noteworthy figures of this period are the Siloés: **Gil de Siloé**, a talented sculptor, and his son **Diego**, who came to Andalucía after creating the famous Golden Staircase in Burgos cathedral, and began the cathedrals at Granada (1526) and Úbeda. The Granada cathedral provided a precursor for High Renaissance architecture in Spain; Diego de Siloé was responsible for most of the interior, taking over the original Gothic plan and making it into a lofty, classical space in a distinctive, personal style. He is also responsible for the cathedral of Guadix, and contributed to the Capilla del Salvador at Úbeda.

Charles V took a personal interest in Granada, and de Siloé had a hard time convincing the king that his new architecture was really an advance over the more obvious charms of Isabelline Gothic. Charles eventually came around, while at the same time mainstream Renaissance architecture arrived with **Pedro Machuca** (1485–1550), who had studied in Italy. Strongly influenced by the monumental classicism of Bramante, his imposing Palacio de Carlos V (1527–8), built for the king in the Alhambra at Granada, was the most famous and influential work of the Spanish Renaissance; it actually predates the celebrated High Renaissance Roman palaces it so closely resembles. Andalucía's Renaissance city is Úbeda, with an ensemble of exceptional churches and palaces. Its Sacra Capilla del Salvador contains some of the finest Renaissance reliefs and sculpture in Spain.

In the stern climate of the Counter-Reformation, architecture turned towards a disciplined austerity, the *estilo desornamentado* introduced by **Juan de Herrera** at Philip II's palace-monastery of El Escorial, near Madrid. Herrera gave Sevilla a textbook example in his Lonja, a business exchange for the city's merchants (1582). His most accomplished follower, **Andrés de Vandelvira**, brought the 'unornamented style' to a striking conclusion with his Hospital de Santiago in Úbeda, and other works in Úbeda and Baeza; he also began the ambitious cathedral at Jaén.

Baroque and Beyond

This style, like the Renaissance, was slow in reaching southern Spain. One of the most important projects of the 17th century, the façade for the unfinished Granada cathedral, wound up entrusted to a painter from Granada, **Alonso Cano** (1601–67), called in his time the 'Spanish Michelangelo' for his talents at painting, sculpture and architecture. The idiosyncratic and memorable result (1664), with its three gigantic arches, shows some appreciation for the new Roman style, though it is firmly planted in the Renaissance. Real Baroque arrived three years later, with Eufrasio López de Rojas's façade for Jaén Cathedral (1667).

The most accomplished southern architect in the decades that followed was **Leonardo de Figueroa** (1650–1730), who combined Italian styles with a native Spanish delight in colour and patterns in brickwork; he worked almost entirely in Sevilla (El Salvador and San Luís, both begun 1699, Colegio San Telmo, 1724, and the Convento de la Merced, now the Museo de Bellas Artes). His son Ambrosio Figueroa continued in the same style. Spanish sculpture was largely a matter of gory realism done in wood, as in the work of **Juan Martínez Montañés** (Sevilla cathedral). **Pedro de Mena** (1628–88), an artist from Granada known for wood sculpture, started out as Alonso Cano's assistant, and later did the relief panels in the choir of Málaga cathedral.

The 17th century has often been described as a golden age of painting in Andalucía. It begins with **Francisco Pacheco** of Sanlúcar de Barrameda (1564–1664). Not much of a painter himself, Pacheco is still a key figure in the beginning of this Andalucían school: founder of an academy, teacher and father-in-law of Velázquez, author of an influential treatise, the *Arte de la Pintura* – and official censor to the Sevilla Inquisition. Giving ample room for exaggeration, this 'golden age' does include **Velázquez** (1599–1660), a native *sevillano* who left the region for ever in 1623 when he became painter to the king. Almost none of his work can be seen in the south. Of those who stayed behind, the most important was Alonso Cano. Cano studied sculpture under Montañés, and painting under Pacheco alongside Velázquez. His work often has a careful architectonic composition that betrays his side career as an architect, but seldom ranges above the pedestrian and devotional. Cano's sculpture, often in polychromed wood, can be seen in Granada cathedral, including the *Immaculate Conception* (1655) that many consider his masterpiece.

Francisco Herrera of Sevilla (1576–1656) shows more backbone, in keeping with the dark and stormy trends of contemporary Italian painting, under the influence of Caravaggio. His son, Francisco Herrera the younger (1627–85) was a follower of Murillo who spent little time in Sevilla. One of the most intriguing painters of the time is **Juan Sánchez Cotán** (1561–1627), the 'father of Baroque realism' in Spain, noted for his strange, intense still lifes. Sánchez Cotán, whose work had a great influence on Zurbarán, spent the last years of his life as a monk in Granada.

Best of all is an emigrant from Extremadura, **Francisco de Zurbarán** (1598–1664), who arrived in Sevilla in 1628. He is often called the 'Spanish Caravaggio', and though his contrasts of light and shadow are equally distinctive, this is as much a disservice as a compliment. Set in stark, bright colours, Zurbarán's world is an unearthly vision of monks and saints, with portraits of heavenly celebrities that seem painted from life, and uncanny, almost abstract scenes of monastic life like the *Miracle of Saint Hugo* in Sevilla's Museo de Bellas Artes. Later in life, Zurbarán went a bit soft, coming increasingly under the influence of his younger contemporary Murillo. Seeing the rest of his work would require a long trip across two continents; Napoleon's armies under

Maréchal Soult stole hundreds of his paintings, and there are more than 80 in the Louvre alone.

In the next generation of southern artists, the worst qualities of a decaying Spain are often painfully evident. Sculpture declined precipitously, with artists adding glass eyes and real human hair in an attempt to heighten even more the gruesome realism of their religious subjects. Among the painters, **Bartolomé Estebán Murillo** (1617–82), another *sevillano*, is the best of the lot; two centuries ago he was widely considered among the greatest painters of all time. Modern eyes are often distracted by the maudlin, missal-illustration religiosity of his saints and Madonnas, neglecting to notice the exceptional talent and total sincerity that created them. Spaniards call his manner the *estilo vaporoso*. Zurbarán's and Murillo's reputations suffered a lot in the 19th century from the large number of lesser works by other painters who copied their subjects and styles, and whose works were later attributed to the two masters. Murillo founded the Academy of Painting at Sevilla and was its first leader; he died after a fall from the scaffolding in 1682.

Somewhat harder to digest is **Juan de Valdés Leal** (1622–90), who helped Murillo organize the Sevilla Academy. His work is considerably more intense and dramatic than Murillo's, and he is best known for the ghoulish, death-obsessed allegories he painted for the reformed Don Juan, Miguel de Mañara, at the Hospital de la Caridad in Sevilla (these two artists can be compared in Sevilla's museum and at the Caridad). After 1664, the head of sculpture at the Academy was **Pedro Roldán** (1624–99). Born in Antequera, Roldán was a fellow student of Pedro de Mena at Granada. Roldán was perhaps the most notable exponent of the Spanish desire to combine painting, sculpture and architecture in unified works of art. He is best known for his altarpiece at Sevilla's Caridad, which Valdés Leal polychromed, and he also contributed works for the facade of Jaén Cathedral. Roldán's daughter Luisa became a sculptor too – the only Spanish woman ever to become a king's court sculptor (for Charles II).

If any style could find a natural home in Spain, it would be the **rococo**. Eventually it did, though a lack of energy and funds often delayed it. Spain's most important architecture in this time, the elaborately decorated work of the Churriguera family and their followers, is mostly in the north, in Salamanca and Madrid. In Andalucía, **Vicente Acero** introduced the tendency early on, with a striking façade for the cathedral at Guadix. He had a chance to repeat it on a really important building project, the new Cádiz cathedral, but the money ran out, and the result was a stripped-down Baroque shell – ambition without the decoration. The great Fábrica de Tabacos in Sevilla (1725–65), the largest project of the century in Andalucía, met a similar end, leaving an austere work, an unintentional precursor of the neoclassical. Whenever the resources were there, Andalucían architects responded with a tidal wave of eccentric embellishment worthy of the Moors – or the Aztecs. Pre-Columbian architecture may have been a bigger influence on Spain than is generally credited; judge for yourself at the chapel and sacristy of the Cartuja in Granada (1747–62), the most blatant interior in Spain.

Elsewhere, the decorative freedom of the rococo led to some unique and delightful buildings, essentially Spanish and often incorporating eclectic references to the styles of centuries past. José de Bada's church of San Juan de Dios (1737–59) in Granada is a fine example. In Córdoba, there is the elegant Convento de la Merced (1745), and the *Coro* of the cathedral, inside La Mezquita, a 16th-century Gothic work redecorated (1748–57) with elaborate stucco decoration by **Juan de Oliva** and stalls and overall design by **Pedro Duque Cornejo**. Sevilla, in its decline, was still building palaces, blending the new style with the traditional requirements of a patio and grand staircase; the best of the century's palaces, however, is in Écija, the Palacio de Peñaflor (1728). Many smaller towns, responding to the improved economic conditions under Philip V and Charles III, built impressive churches, notably in Priego de Córdoba, Lucena, Utrera, Estepa and Écija.

In view of all Andalucía's troubles, it should not be surprising that little has been produced in the last two centuries. **Pablo Picasso**, born in Málaga, was the outstanding example of the artist who had to find his inspiration and his livelihood elsewhere. Despite the lack of significant recent architecture, Andalucíans hold on to the glories of their past with tenacity; splashes of *azulejo* tiles and Moorish decoration turn up in everything from bus stations and market houses to simple suburban cottages. For some 500 years now, Andalucíans have most often been constrained by their sorry history to follow styles and inspirations from outside. Few regions of Europe, however, can show such a remarkable heritage of locally nurtured arts and crafts, styles and motifs, the heritage of both Moor and Christian. Now that prosperity and confidence are slowly coming back, we might hope that Andalucía can find something in its old glories that fits a modern age, and amaze and delight the world once again.

Topics

Bullfights

In Spanish newspapers, you will not find accounts of the bullfights (*corridas*) on the sports pages; look in the 'arts and culture' section, for that is how Spain has always thought of this singular spectacle. Bullfighting combines elements of ballet with the primal finality of Greek tragedy. To Spaniards it is a ritual sacrifice without a religion, and it divides the nation irreconcilably between those who find it brutal and demeaning, an echo of the old Spain best forgotten, and those who couldn't live without it. Its origins are obscure. Some claim it derives from Roman circus games, others that it started with the Moors, or in the Middle Ages, when the bull faced a mounted knight with a lance.

There are bullrings all over Spain, and as far afield as Arles in France and Guadalajara, Mexico, but modern bullfighting is quintessentially Andalucían. The present form had its beginnings around the year 1800 in Ronda, when Francisco Romero developed the basic pattern of the modern *corrida*; some of his moves and passes, and those of his celebrated successor, Pedro Romero, are still in use today.

The first royal *aficionado* was Fernando VII, the reactionary post-Napoleonic monarch who also brought back the Inquisition. He founded the Royal School of Bullfighting in Sevilla, and promoted the spectacle across the land as a circus for the discontented populace. Since the Civil War, bullfighting has gone through a period of troubles similar to those of boxing in the USA. Scandals of weak bulls, doped-up bulls, and bulls with the points of their horns shaved have been frequent. Attempts at reform have been made, and all the problems seem to have decreased bullfighting's popularity only slightly.

In keeping with its ritualistic aura, the *corrida* is one of the few things in Andalucía that begins strictly on time. The show commences with the colourful entry of the *cuadrillas* (teams of bullfighters or *toreros*) and the *alguaciles*, officials dressed in 17th-century costume, who salute the 'president' of the fight. Usually three teams fight two bulls each, the whole taking only about two hours. Each of the six fights, however, is a self-contained drama performed in four acts. First, upon the entry of the bull, the members of the *cuadrilla* tease him a bit, and the *matador*, the team leader, plays him with the cape to test his qualities. Next comes the turn of the *picadores*, on padded horses, whose task is to slightly wound the bull in the neck with a short lance or pica, and the *banderilleros*, who agilely plant sharp darts in the bull's back while avoiding the sweep of its horns. The effect of these wounds is to weaken the bull physically without diminishing any of its fighting spirit, and to force it to keep its head lower for the third and most artistic stage of the fight, when the lone *matador* conducts his *pas de deux* with the deadly, if doomed, animal. Ideally, this is the transcendent moment, the matador leading the bull in deft passes and finally crushing its spirit with a tiny cape called a *muleta*. Now the defeated bull is ready for 'the moment of truth'. The kill must be clean and quick, a sword thrust to the heart. The corpse is dragged out to the waiting butchers.

More often than not the job is botched. Most bullfights, in fact, are a disappointment, especially if the *matadores* are *novilleros* or beginners, but to the *aficionado* the chance to see one or all of the stages performed to perfection makes it all worthwhile. When a *matador* is good, the band plays and the hats and handkerchiefs fly; a truly excellent performance earns as a reward from the president one, or both, of the bull's ears; or rarely, for an exceptionally brilliant performance, both ears and the tail.

You'll be lucky to see a bullfight at all; there are only about 500 each year in Spain, mostly coinciding with holidays or a town's fiesta. During Sevilla's *feria* there is a bullfight every afternoon at the famous Maestranza ring, while the rings in Málaga and Puerto de Santa María near Cádiz are other major venues. Tickets can be astronomically expensive and hard to come by, especially for a well-known *matador*; sometimes touts buy out the lot. Get them in advance, if you can, and directly from the office in the *plaza de toros* to avoid the hefty commission charges. Prices vary according to the sun – the most expensive seats are entirely in the shade.

City Slickers

You're on the train for Córdoba, passing the hours through some of the loneliest landscapes in Europe. For a long time, there's been nothing to see but olive trees – gnarled veterans, some of them planted in the time of Fernando and Isabel. You may see a donkey pulling a cart. At twilight, you pull in at the central station, and walk four blocks down to the Avenida del Gran Capitán, an utterly Parisian boulevard of chic boutiques and pompous banks, booming with traffic. The loudspeakers from the *Galerías Preciados* department store broadcast the latest chart singles.

You don't often see Andalucians going off on picnics in the country. The ground is dry, vegetation usually sparse, and the sun can seem like a death-ray even in winter. Climate has always forced people here to seek their pleasure elsewhere; it is the impetus behind their exquisite gardens, and it has made them the most resolutely urban people in Europe. In city centres the air is electric, a cocktail of motion, colour, and fragrances that goes to your head like the best *manzanilla*. It has probably had much the same ambience for over 2,000 years; the atmosphere may be hard to recapture, but we can learn a lot by looking at decoration and design.

We know little about city life in Roman times – only that for relatively small populations, towns such as Itálica had amphitheatres and other amenities comparable to any in the empire. The cities of Moorish Spain were a revelation, with libraries, public gardens and street lighting at a time when feudal Europe was scratching its carrot rows with a short stick. Their design, similar to that of North African and Middle Eastern cities, can be discerned (with some difficulty) in parts of Granada, Córdoba and Sevilla today. It is difficult to say what aspects of the design of Andalucía's Moorish cities are legacies from Roman Baetica, and what was introduced by the Moors themselves. Enclosure was the key word in Moorish architecture: a great mosque and its walled courtyard occupied the centre, near the fortified palace (*alcázar or alcazaba*) and its walled gardens. Along with the markets and baths, these were located in the *medina*, and locked up behind its walls each night. The residential quarters that surrounded the *medina* were islands in themselves, a maze of narrow streets where the houses, rich or poor, looked inwards to open patios while turning blank walls to the street. Some of these survive, with their original decoration, as private homes in Granada's Albaicín.

In Roman times, the patio was called a *peristyle*. The gracious habit of building a house around a colonnaded central court was perfected by the Greeks, and became common across the Roman Mediterranean. Today, while most of us enjoy the charms of our cramped flats and dull, squarish houses, the Andalucíans have never given up their love of the old-fashioned way. In Córdoba especially, the patios of the old quarters spill over with roses, wisteria and jasmine; each year there is a competition for the prettiest. Besides the houses, some of the cellular quality of Moorish cities survived the Reconquista. In 16th-century Sevilla, thick with artful bandits, the silversmiths had their own walled quarter (and their own cops to guard it). The Moorish urban aesthetic evolved gracefully into the modern Andalucían: the simple, unforgettable panorama of almost any town – an oasis of brilliant white rectangularity, punctuated sharply by upright cypresses and by the warm sandstone of churches, palaces and towers.

One Spanish invention, combining Italian Renaissance planning with native tradition, was the arcaded, rectangular square usually called the *Plaza Mayor*. The best are in Madrid and Salamanca, but many Andalucían towns have one, and there is a huge dilapidated specimen in Córdoba. Architecturally unified – the four walls often seem like a building turned inside-out – the *Plaza Mayor* translated the essence of the patio into public space. Such a square made a perfect stage for the colourful life of a Spanish city. Spanish theatres in the great age of Lope de Vega and Calderón took the same form, with three sides of balconies, the fourth for the stage, on the narrow end, and a Shakespearean 'pit' at ground level. In the last two centuries, while the rest of Spain continued to create innovations in urban design and everyday pageantry, impoverished Andalucía contributed little – some elegant bullrings, certain exquisite redesigns of the old Moorish gardens, a few grand boulevards like the Alameda of Málaga and the *paseos* of Granada, and some eccentric decorations, such as the gigantic, sinister stone birds of prey that loom over most city centres – symbols of an insurance company.

Since the 1970s and the end of Francoism, one can sense a slickness gathering momentum: a touch of anonymous good design in a shop sign, new pavements and lighting, ambitious new architecture with a splash of colour and surprise. The *El Corte Inglés* department store in Málaga has been known to be entirely covered in computer-controlled electric lights at Christmas, nearly a vertical acre of permanent fireworks, flashing peacock tails and other patterns in constantly changing, brilliant colours – as spectacular and futuristic a decoration as any city has ever had. Watch out for these sharp Andalucíans – and for Spaniards in general. While we fog-bound northerners are nodding off with Auntie at twelve o'clock, they may well be plotting the delights of the future.

Dust in the Wind

The poets of al-Andalus devoted most of their attention to sensuous songs of love, nature, wine, women and boys, but amidst all the lavish beauty there would linger, like a *basso continuo*, a note of refined detachment, of melancholy and futility. Instead of forgetting death in their man-made paradises, the poets made a point of reminding their listeners of how useless it was to become attached to these worldly delights. After all, only God is forever, and why express love to something that would one day turn to dust? Why even attempt to build something perfect and eternal – the main ingredients of the lovely, delicate Alhambra are plaster and wood. The Nasrid kings, were they to return, might be appalled to find it still standing.

The Christians who led the Reconquista had no time for futility. In their architecture and art they built for eternity, plonking a soaring church right in the middle of the Great Mosque and an imperial palace on the Alhambra – literal, lapidarian, emanating the power and total control of the temporal Church and State. Their oppression reduced the sophisticated songs of the Moorish courts to a baser fatalism. The harsh realities of everyday life encouraged people to live for the moment, to grab what happiness they could in an uncertain world. This uncertainty was best expressed by the 17th-century Spanish playwright Pedro Calderón de la Barca, especially in his great *La Vida es Sueño* (Life is a Dream), known as the Catholic answer to *Hamlet*.

There wasn't much poetry in Granada between 1492 and the advent of Federico García Lorca, born in 1898 in the Vega just outside of town. Lorca, a fine musician as well as a poet and playwright, found much of his inspiration in what would be called nowadays Granada's 'alternative' traditions, especially those of the Gypsies. In 1922, Lorca was a chief organizer of Granada's first *cante jondo* festival, designed to bring flamenco singing to international attention and prevent it from sliding into a hack-neyed Andalucían joke. In 1927, he published the book of poems that made him the most popular poet in Spain, the *Romancero Gituno* (Gypsy Ballads); his plays, like *Bodas de Sangre* (Blood Wedding) and *Yerma* (The Barren One), have the lyrical, disturbing force of the deepest *cante jondo*.

But of post-Reconquista Granada he was sharply critical, accusing Fernando and Isabel of destroying a much more sophisticated civilization than their own – and as for the modern inhabitants of Granada, they were an imported reactionary bourgeois contingent from the north, not 'real' Andalucíans. Lorca criticized, but he kept coming back, and had dreams of bringing the city's once great culture back to life.

In Granada, a commemorative park at Víznar marks the spot where, on 18 August 1936, local police or rebel soldiers took Lorca and shot him dead. No one knows who gave the orders, or the reason why; the poet had supported the Republic but was not actively political. When news of his secret execution leaked out, it was an embarrass-ment to Franco, who managed to hush up the affair until his own death. But most historians agree that the killing was a local vendetta for Lorca's outspoken views of his home town, a blood sacrifice to the stone god of Fernando and Isabel and Charles V who fears all change, closing (one can only hope) once and for all the circle of bittersweet futility, frustration, and death.

Flamenco

For many people, flamenco is the soul of Spain – like bullfighting – and an essential part of the culture that sets it apart from the rest of the world. Good flamenco, with that ineffable quality of *duende*, has a primitive, ecstatic allure that draws in its listeners until they feel as if their very hearts were pounding in time with its relentless rhythms, their guts seared by its ululating Moorish wails and the sheer drama of the dance. Few modern experiences are more cathartic.

As folklore goes, however, flamenco is newborn. It began in the 18th century in Andalucía, where its originators, the Gypsies, called one another '*flamencos*' – a derogatory term believed to date back to the days when Charles V's Flemish (*flamenco*) courtiers bled Spain dry. These Gypsies, especially in the Guadalquivir delta cities of Sevilla, Cádiz and Jerez, sang songs of oppression, lament and bitter romance, a kind of blues that by the 19th century began to catch on among all the other downtrodden inhabitants of Andalucía.

Yet despite flamenco's recent origins, the Andalucían intelligentsia, especially Lorca and Manuel de Falla, found (or invented) much to root it deeply in the south's soil and soul. Its rhythms and Doric mode are as old as Andalucía's ancient Greek settlers; its spirit of improvisation and spontaneity date from the famous Córdoba school of music and poetry, founded in 820 by Abu al-Hassan Ali ibn Nafi, better known as Ziryab, the 'Blackbird'; the half-tonal notes and lyrics of futility of the *cante jondo*, or deep song, the purest flamenco, seem to go straight back to the Arab troubadours of al-Andalus. But just how faithfully the music of al-Andalus was preserved among the Gypsies and others to be reincarnated as flamenco will never be known; the Arabs knew of musical notation, but disdained it in their preference for improvisation.

By the late 19th century, flamenco had gone semi-public, performed in the back rooms of cafés in Sevilla and Málaga. Its very popularity in Spain, and the enthusiasm set off by Bizet's *Carmen* abroad, began seriously to undermine its harsh, true quality. At the same time, flamenco's influence spread into the popular and folk repertories to create a happier, less intense genre called the *sevillana* (often songs in praise of you know where). When schoolchildren at a bus stop in Cádiz burst into an impromptu dance and hand-clapping session, or when some old cronies in Málaga's train-station bar start singing and reeling, you can bet they're doing a *sevillana*.

In the 1920s attempts were made to establish some kind of standards for the real thing, especially *cante jondo*, though without lasting results; the 'real, original flamenco' was never meant to be performed as such, and will only be as good as its 'audience'. This should ideally be made up of other musicians and flamenco *aficionados*, whose participation is essential in the spontaneous, invariably late-night combustion of raw emotion, alcohol, drugs and music, to create *duende*.

Flamenco not only remains popular in Spain, but is undergoing something of a renaissance. It all started in the 1970s and 1980s when Paco de Lucía, a native of Algeciras, took his art to the international stage, fusing it with jazz. Paco's music is a must for any lover of flamenco guitar and he continues to produce traditional records as well as recording crossover with other musicians like John McLaughlin and Al Di Meola. Within Spain, Ketama, a popular Gypsy band from Granada, have fused flamenco with rock, and singers like Niña Pastori are following in their wake. On a pop level, flamenco has achieved an international audience thanks to the Gypsy Kings (who are French) and the Michael Flatley-style dance spectaculars of Joaquín Cortés.

The Founding Father

Andalucía for itself, for Spain and for Humanity.

So reads the proud device on the regional escutcheon, hurriedly cooked up by the Andalucíans after the regional autonomy laws of the 1970s made them masters in their own house once again. Above the motto we see a strong fellow, mythologically underdressed and accompanied by two lions. Though perhaps more familiar to us for his career among the Hellenes, he is also the first Andalucían – HERCULES DOMINATOR FUNDATOR.

The Greeks themselves admit that Hercules found time for two extended journeys to the distant and little-known West. In the eleventh of his Twelve Labours, the Apples of the Hesperides caper, he made it as far as the environs of Tangier, where he dispatched the giant Antaeus. The tenth Labour brought Hercules into Spain, sailing in the golden goblet of Helios and using his lion skin for a sail. In the fabled land of Tartessos, on the 'red island' of Erytheia, he slew the three-headed titan Geryon and stole his cattle. Before heading back to Greece, he founded the city of Gades, or Cádiz, on the island (Cádiz, surrounded by marshes, is almost an island). He also erected his well-known Pillars, Gibraltar and Mount Abyle, across the way in Africa. His return was one of the all-time bad trips; whenever you're crazed and dying on some five-hour 'semi-direct' Andalucían bus ride (say, Granada to Córdoba via Rute), think of Hercules, marching Geryon's cows through Spain and over the Pyrenees, then making a wrong turn that took him halfway down the Italian peninsula before he noticed the mistake. After mortal combats with several other giants and monsters, he finally made it to Greece – but then his nemesis, Hera, sent a stinging blue-tail fly to stampede the cattle. They didn't stop until they reached the Scythian Desert. To most people, Hercules is little more than mythology's most redoubtable Dog Warden, rounding up not only Cerberus, the Hound of Hell, but most of the other stray monsters that dug up the roses and soiled the footpaths of the Heroic Age. But there is infinitely more than this to the character of the most-travelled, hardest-working hero of them all. In antiquity, wherever Hercules had set foot the people credited him with founding nations and cities, building roads and canals, excavating lakes and draining swamps. And there is the intellectual Hercules, the master of astronomy and lord of the zodiac, the god of prophecy and eloquence who taught both the Latins and the Spaniards their letters. One version has it that the original Pillars of Hercules were not mountains at all, but columns, like those of the Temple of Jerusalem, and connected with some alphabetical mysticism.

Ancient mythographers had their hands full, sorting out the endless number of deities and heroes known to the peoples of Europe, Africa and the Middle East, trying to decide whether the same figure was hiding behind different names and rites. Varro recorded no fewer than 44 Hercules, and modern scholars have found the essential Herculean form in myths from Celtic Ireland to Mesopotamia. Melkarth, the Phoenician Hercules, would have had his temples in southern Spain long before the first Greek ever saw Gibraltar. Not a bad fellow to have for a founding father – and a reminder that in Andalucía the roots of culture are as strong and as deep as in any corner of Europe.

Getting Them Back

In the 1970s Robert Graves recalled overhearing two Londoners talking about their vacations: 'I went to Majorca this year,' says one. Her friend asks, 'Where's that?' and receives the answer, 'I don't know, I flew.' But the boom years of the Spanish package tour are definitely over. The drop in visitors is ringing alarm bells in Spain, and Europe's most intelligent and capable tourism bureaucracy is making a determined effort to put the country back in its former position by means of a far-sighted and extensive change of image.

The downmarket profile of resorts like Torremolinos will take a long time to change in the minds of the foreign public, who understandably but somewhat mistakenly connect it with tattooed lager louts, late-night punch-ups and raucous discos belting out music until dawn. There's a fair degree of snobbery involved in these attitudes; who in Britain, for example, boasts of having just spent a holiday on the Costa del Sol, with destinations such as Turkey, Florida and the Caribbean beckoning at affordable prices? The principal obstacle to attracting and sustaining mass tourism is the quality of holiday and destination on offer. Whilst the independent traveller is happy to pack guidebook, camera and sensible shoes, and head off on a cultural pilgrimage to Granada's Alhambra, Córdoba's Mezquita, Sevilla's Giralda or the Cádiz Carnival, and along the way experience and indulge in the *real* Andalucía, the majority of visitors are interested in less ethereal pursuits, and the ingredients for their fun are beaches, hotels, food and entertainment at a reasonable price.

Spain can meet these criteria; too well, some malcontent Hispanophiles would say – those who think that the country has sacrificed its integrity to provide monstrous concrete resort playgrounds, paint them white and pass them off as Andalucían *pueblos*. So what can be done? It's too late to tear down what already exists, but it's time the government pushed the stop button on the coastal developments, on the Costa del Sol particularly, but no less so on the Costa de la Luz, where full-scale construction would mean, and in some places has already meant, the ruination of an untamed stretch of coast. Control future development, improve the existing infrastructure and abolish Spain's reputation as solely a paradise for sun-seeking tipplers, and maybe more visitors will come for the most genuine of motives – to get a balanced view of a country rich in history, culture and fun.

Hot-blooded Andalucían Women

Andalucía holds roughly a fifth of Spain's people, which means more than one-tenth of the population consists of the most sultry, sensuous women in Europe. Ah, *señores*, how they arch their supple torsos in an improvised *sevillana*, clicking their magic castanets! *Dios*, how provocative they are behind the iron grilles of their windows with their come-hither burning black eyes over flickering fans, each serenaded by her handsome guitar-strumming *caballero*, tossing him a red rose of promise and desire!

Ever since the first boatload of dancing girls from Cádiz docked at the slave-markets of ancient Rome, the women of Andalucía have had to put up with this – an extraordinary reputation for grace, beauty, and amorous dispositions. Travellers' accounts and novels elaborate on their exotic charms, spiced by the languor of the Moorish harem odalisque and the supposed promiscuity of the passionate Gypsy. After all, when Leporello counts off his master's conquests in Mozart's *Don Giovanni*, which country comes out on top? Spain, of course, with 1,003 victims to the arch libertine's art of persuasion.

Nothing kept this fond male fancy afloat as much as the fact that nubile Andalucían women were tantalizingly inaccessible, thanks to a rigid Latin code of honour second to none. It took the Industrial Revolution, the Sevilla tobacco factory, and a French visitor, Prosper Mérimée, to bring this creature of the imagination out into the open, in the form of the beautiful Gypsy Carmen in 1845, rendered immortally saucy in Bizet's opera of 1873. Step aside, Don Juan, or be stepped on! This new stereotype was as quick to light up a cheroot as to kick aside her sweetheart for a strutting matador in tight trousers. Not surprisingly, it wasn't long before the tobacco factory and its steamy, scantily-clad examples of feminine pulchritude (labouring for a handful of pesetas each day) attracted as many tourists as the Giralda tower.

Alas, where is the kitsch of yesteryear? Modern young Andalucían women are, like modern Andalucían men, among the most normal, mentally well-balanced people in the world. Ask them about the cloistered *señoritas* of the past and they'll laugh. Ask them about the unbridled Carmen, and they'll laugh. Ask them about the bizarre wind called the *solano* that troubles Cádiz in the springtime, a wind that in the old days drove the entire female population en masse to the beach, where they would fling off their clothes and dive into the sea to seek relief while the local cavalry regiment stood guard. Ask them about it, and they'll just laugh.

Roses of the Secret Garden

Western art and Islamic art are two worlds that will never agree. Even today, the sort of folk who believe in the divinity of Michelangelo or the essential greatness of the Baroque can be found in print, sniffing at the art of the Alhambra as merely 'decorative'. On the other side, you will discover a state of mind that can dismiss our familiar painting and sculpture as frivolous, an impious obsession with the appearances of the moment that ignores the transcendent realities beneath the surface. A powerful idea was in the air in the 7–8th centuries, perhaps a reaction against the worldliness and incoherence that drowned classical civilization. It was not limited to Islam alone; the 'iconoclastic' controversy in Byzantium, following the attempt of Emperor Leo III to end the idolatrous veneration of icons, was about the same issue.

However this argument started, Islam grew up with an aversion to figurative art. At the same time, Islam was gaining access to the scientific and mathematical heritage of Greece and Rome, and finding it entirely to its liking. A new approach to art gradually took form, based on the sacred geometry of Byzantine architecture, and on a trend of mathematical mysticism that goes back to Pythagoras. Number, proportion and symmetry were the tools God used to create the world. The same rule could be found in every aspect of creation, and could be reproduced in art by the simple methods of Euclidean geometry. This geometry now found its place not only in the structure of a building, but also in its decoration.

Once the habit of thinking this way was established, it profoundly affected life and art in all the Islamic world, including Spain. The land itself became a careful mosaic, with neat rows of olive trees draped over the hills and the very beans and carrots in the gardens laid out in intricate patterns (Andalucían farmers still do it: you can see a remarkable example of such a landscape from the *mirador* in Úbeda). While nature was being made to imitate art, Muslim artists, consciously or not, often imitated the hidden processes of nature – the Córdoba mosque grew like a crystal with the columns and aisles of each new addition. Often, they created novelties by changing scales, reducing and replicating old forms to make new, more complex ones. One example of this is the Visigothic horseshoe arch. You can see it in its simplest form at Córdoba or Medinat al-Zahra; later, as in Sevilla's Alcázar, the same arch is made of smaller versions of itself. And in the Alhambra, you'll see arches made of arches made of arches, seeming to grow organically down from the patterns on the walls. A tree or a snowflake finds its form in much the same way. Fans of chaos theory, take note – the Moors had anticipated fractals and Koch curves 600 years ago.

Three dimensions is the domain of the mundane shell, the worldly illusion. The archetypes, the underlying reality, can be more fittingly expressed in two. With their straight-edge and compass, Islamic artists developed a tradition of elaborate geometrical decoration, in painted tiles, stucco, or wooden grilles and ceilings. The highest levels of subtlety reached by this art were in Isfahan, Persia, in Egypt, and in Granada. The foundation, as in all constructive geometry, is the circle – *man's heart is the centre, heaven the circumference*, as a medieval Christian mystic put it. From this, they wove the exquisite patterns that embellish the Alhambra, exotic blooms interlaced in rhythms of 3, 5, 6, 8 or 12. This is not the shabby, second-hand symbolism of our times. A 12-pointed flower does not *symbolize* the firmament and the 12 signs of the zodiac, for example; it *recalls* this, and many other things as well. For philosophers, these patterns could provide a meditation on the numerical harmony of creation; for the rest of us, they stand by themselves, lovely, measured creations, whispering a sweet invitation to look a bit more closely at the wonders around us. The patterns of the Alhambra haunt Andalucía to this day. In Granada especially, these geometric flowers

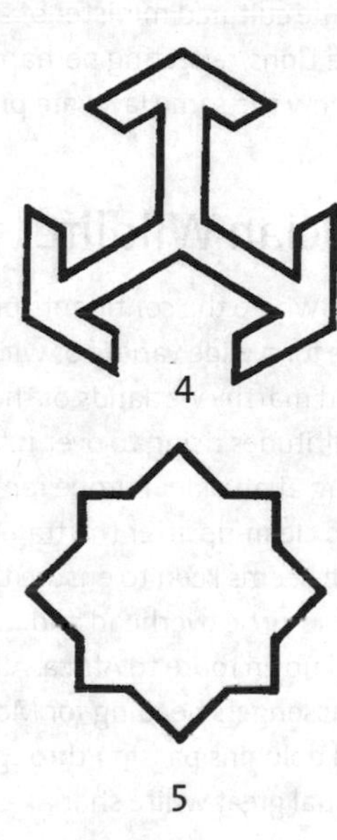

are endlessly reproduced on *azulejo* tiles in bars and restaurants, and in the *taracea* (marquetry) work boxes and tables sold in the Alcaicería.

One of the favourite games of the Islamic artists was filling up space elegantly, in the sense that a mathematician understands that word. In geometry, only three regular polygons, when repeated, can entirely fill a flat plane: the hexagon (as in a honeycomb); the square (as on a chessboard); and the equilateral triangle. Some not-so-regular polygons (any triangle or parallelogram, for example) can do it too. Try and find some more complex forms; it isn't easy. One modern artist fascinated by these problems was M. C. Escher, whose tricks of two-dimensional space are beloved of computer programmers and other Pythagoreans of our own age. Figures 1, 2 and 4 on this page can fill a plane. The second, with a little imagination and geometrical know-how, could be made into one of Escher's space-filling birds or fish. Figure 3 doesn't quite do the job, but properly arranged it creates a secondary pattern of eight-pointed stars (fig.5) in between. For a puzzle, try and multiply each of the first four on paper to fill a plane. Answers can be found on the walls of the Alhambra.

By now, you may suspect that these shapes were not employed without reason. In fact, according to the leading authority on such matters, Keith Critchlow (in his book *Islamic Patterns*), the patterns formed by figs.1 and 3 mirror the symmetrical arrangement of numbers in a magic square. Triangular figs.2 and 4 are based on the *tetractys*, a favourite study of the Pythagoreans. But a Spanish Muslim did not need to be a mathematician to appreciate the lesson of this kind of geometry. Everyone understood the basic tenet of Islam – that creation is One: harmonious and complete. Imagine some cultured minister of a Granadan king, musing under the arcades of the Court of the Lions, reflecting perhaps on the nature that shaped the roses in the court, and how the same laws are proclaimed by the ceramic blossoms within.

Andalucían Wildlife

Andalucía, where the continents once met, is one of western Europe's last important havens for a wide variety of wildlife. The land ranges from the long sandy beaches and marshy wetlands of the western coast through the craggy shores of the east, with altitudes rising to over 11,500ft (3,500m) in the Sierra Nevada. A few pristine areas hinting at an older Europe remain hidden in the land's pockets and, aside from the botched clean-up after the tragic pollution of the Doñana wetlands in 1998, the government seems keen to ensure that they remain untouched. Wolves and lynx still prowl, raptors circle overhead and in spring and autumn millions of migrating birds flock to fuel up en route to Africa. Although the seas are now too polluted to teem with life, passengers heading for Morocco on the ferry will be unlucky not to see whales and dolphins passing through the straits, and there have even been reports of the occasional great white shark.

Mammals

Although wolves, lynx and wild boar roam in Andalucía there is little reason to shudder if you walk alone in the hills – you'll be very lucky to see one, and even if you do, it's likely to be a rear view. There are fewer than 1,200 pardel lynx and only 75 wolves hunting in the Doñana and the Sierra Morena. Smaller mammals are more numerous – rabbits and hares abound, garden dormice hang around in trees, often close to houses. These are prey to martens, mongooses, wildcats, badgers and weasels. Otters are still plentiful, although rarely seen, while the pale Algerian hedgehog has evolved longer legs and larger ears than its European counterpart, presumably to help it escape from under the wheels of the increasing number of cars that speed along Andalucía's roads.

Little pipistrelle bats flutter by day and larger noctules flap by night. A fine country for bats, is Spain. Almost everywhere in the country (but especially around Granada) you'll see clouds of them cavorting in the twilight, zooming noiselessly past your ears and doing their best to ensure you get a good night's sleep by gobbling up all the mosquitoes they can. Spaniards don't mind them a bit, and the medieval kings of Aragón even went so far as to make them a dynastic emblem, derived from a Muslim Sufi symbol. Lots of bats, of course, presumes lots of caves, and Spain has more than its share. The famous grottoes of Nerja and Aracena are only a couple of the places where you can see colossal displays of tinted, aesthetically draped stalactites. Hundreds were decorated in one way or another by Palaeolithic man; even though the most famous, at Altamira, are closed to the public, you can still see some cave art by asking around for a guide in Vélez Rubio west of Murcia. This last area, from Vélez as far west as Granada, actually has a huge population still living in caves – quite cosily fitted out these days – and in Granada itself you can visit the 'Gypsy caves' for a little histrionic flamenco and diluted sherry.

Finally, there are Spanish ibex, red and fallow deer (as well as emigré Corsican mouflon) in the hills of the Sierra Nevada, Cazorla and the Serranía de Ronda.

Reptiles and Amphibians

The most unusual of Andalucía's reptiles is the *Amphibisbaenia* which looks, at first glance, like a giant pork sausage. Closer inspection reveals it to be a caecilian – a subterranean reptile that slips in somewhere between snake and lizard on the reptile family tree. Caecilians spend much of their time underground chasing worms, surfacing for a breather only during the night or after heavy rain. You're more likely to see a snake or a lizard. Chameleons stick to the coast, wall lizards are everywhere and little chirrupping geckoes hunt for small insects near outside lights or in hotel rooms. Of the eight species of snake, only the latastes viper, ugly, with a horn on the end of its nose, is venomous. Other reptiles with protuberances include the very rare spur-thighed tortoises whose habitats in northeastern Almería and Doñana are under threat from development and pollution.

Marsh frogs are the most vocal of the amphibians and green tree frogs the most beautiful. These share Andalucía with fifteen other species including the sharp-ribbed salamander and a variety of toads and newts.

Birds

Andalucía's most numerous wildlife enthusiasts are ornithologists who descend on the region in spring and autumn to follow the flocks of migrating birds on their way to or from Africa. Hundreds of binoculars trace the movements of storks and huge raptors as they soar ever higher over the rock of Gibraltar catching thermals to prepare for the crossing.

Winter and summer visitors like little bitterns, purple herons, bee-eaters and golden orioles find safe haven in Andalucía's growing number of protected areas. This is the only place in Europe where you will find the Spanish imperial eagle, black-shouldered kite, red-necked nightjar, azure-winged magpie, marbled duck and numerous others. And it's the only place in the world (aside from the Maghreb) where you'll find white-headed duck, rescued from the brink of extinction by a conservation effort that began just under twenty years ago. Other rarities include the shy purple gallinule, betrayed by its bright red legs and the collared pratincole that breeds in the Guadalquivir marshes. Europe's largest colony of greater flamingoes crowd the salt lake of Fuente de Piedra near Málaga and hordes of shrieking swifts swoop around church towers and blocks of flats everywhere.

Insects

Ornithologists rub shoulders with lepidopterists in Andalucía – there are thirty different species of blues alone here, along with clouded yellows, swallowtails,

Spanish fritillaries and marbled whites and the spectacular two-tailed pasha, which is as large as a small bird. There are even sporadic visitors from across the Atlantic including the milkweed and the American painted lady. Moths include the humming-bird hawk moth and the great peacock moth, both of which fly during the day.

Among the other insects are bright green praying mantis, who compete with geckoes in the hunt for southern Spain's ubiquitous flies, industrious dung beetles and a variety of invisible but omnipresent cicadas and crickets.

Plant Life

Among the 5,000 species of flowering plant in Andalucía are 150 which are unique to the region. In spring the meadows of the Cádiz coast fill the air with scent and the countryside with colour. Wild lupins, convolvulus and orchids vie with irises, mallows and a hundred dancing butterflies in an area that has never known pesticides.

Aromatic herbs and alpine flowers bloom a few months later on the higher ground, when the snow is at its thinnest, and on the lower slopes of the Serranía de Ronda there is still a small isolated forest of the rare pinsapo fir.

Food and Drink

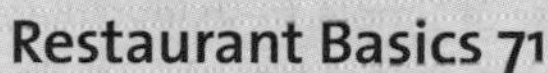

Read an old guidebook to Spain and, when the author gets around to the local cooking, expressions like 'eggs in a sea of rancid oil' and 'mysterious pork parts' or 'suffered palpitations through garlic excess' pop up with alarming frequency. One traveller in the 18th century fell ill from a local concoction and was given a purge 'known on the comic stage as angelic water. On top of that followed four hundred catholic pills, and a few days later...they gave me *escordero* water, whose efficacy or devilry is of such double effect that the doctors call it ambidexter. From this I suffered agony'.

You'll fare better; in fact, the chances are you'll eat some of the tastiest food you've ever had at half the price you would have paid for it at home. The massive influx of tourists has had its effect on Spanish kitchens, but so has the Spaniards' own increased prosperity and, perhaps most significantly, the new federalism. Each region, each town even, has come to feel a new interest and pride in the things that set it apart, and food is definitely one of those; the best restaurants are almost always those that specialize in regional cooking.

Regional Specialities

Food

The greatest attraction of *andaluz* cuisine is the use of simple, fresh ingredients. Seafood plays a big role, and marinated or fried fish (*pescaditos fritos*, known in Sevilla as *pescaíto frito*) is a speciality. (The traditional marinade, or *adobo*, is a mixture of water, vinegar, salt, garlic, paprika, cumin and marjoram.) Other specialities include the wholesome broth made with fish, tomato, pepper and paprika, and the famous cured hams of Jabugo and Trevélez. Almost everybody has heard of gazpacho; there are literally dozens of varieties, ranging from the *porra* of Antequera made with red peppers, to the thick, tasty Córdoban version, *salmorejo*, sometimes topped with finely chopped ham and boiled egg. Olives, preserved in cumin, wild marjoram, rosemary, thyme, bay leaves, garlic, savoury fennel and vinegar, are a particular treat, especially the plump, green manzanilla olives from Sevilla.

In Granada, an unappetizing mixture of brains, bulls' testicles, potatoes, peas and red peppers results in a very palatable *tortilla de Sacromonte*, and many restaurants in the city work wonders with slices of beef *filete* or loin larded with pork fat and roasted with the juice from the meat and sherry. However, watch out for odd little dishes like *revoltillos,* whose name gives you a fair warning of what flavours to expect in this subtle dish of tripe, rolled and secured with the animal's intestines, mercifully lined with ham and mint.

The province of Cádiz takes the place of honour in *andaluz* cuisine; its specialities to look out for are *cañaillas* (sea snails), *pastel de pichón* (pigeon pâté), *calamares con habas* (squid with broad beans), *archoba* (a highly seasoned fish dish) or *bocas* (small crabs). Córdoba, too, has a fine culinary tradition, including dishes with a strong Arab and Jewish influence, like *calderetas* (lamb stew with almonds). But Córdoba is also the home of one of the most famous *andaluz* dishes, *rabo de toro*, a spicy concoction of oxtail, onions and tomatoes. Also try the *buchón* (rolled fish filled with ham, dipped in breadcrumbs, then fried). As one might expect, the Sierras offer dishes based on the game and wild herbs found in the mountains. Here, freshwater lakes teem with trout, and wild asparagus grows on the slopes. The town of Jaén is particularly well known for its high-quality oil and vinegar, and delectable salads are a feature of most menus (try the *pipirrana*).

Fish and seafood, fresh from the coast, dominate cuisine in Málaga but there are plenty of gazpachos, particularly *ajo blanco con uvas* – a creamy white almond and garlic soup with grapes. Prawns and mussels are plump and, served simply with lemon, are divine. The Costa del Sol's traditional beachside delicacy is sardines, speared on a stick and cooked over a wood fire – best when eaten with a good salad and washed down with chilled white wine. *Boquerones* (often mistaken for the peculiarly English whitebait but in fact a variety of anchovy) feature widely in restaurants and tapas bars, along with *pijolas*, small hake that suffer the indignity of being sizzled with tail in mouth. Forget British fried fish; in Málaga *fritura mixta* is one of Spain's culinary art forms.

Nearly every village in the province has its own dessert, usually influenced by the Moors. Try the almond tarts in Ardales, the honey-coated pancakes in Archidona and the mixture of syrup of white roses, oil and eggs called *tocino de cielo* in Vélez. There again you can always substitute a sweet Málaga dessert wine for pudding – delicious sipped with dry biscuits.

All over Andalucía you will find *pinchitos*, a spicier version of its Greek cousin the *souvlaki*, a mini-kebab of lamb or pork marinated in spices. To finish off your meal there are any number of desserts (*postres*) based on almonds and custards, and the Arab influence once again shows through in, for example, the excellent sweetmeats from Granada and the *alfajores* (puff pastry) from Huércal, Almería.

The presence of 1.5 million foreign residents, mainly clustered along the southern coast, has had an effect on the culinary scene of the Costa del Sol, although Spanish restaurants still manage to hold their own. A bewildering choice of Indonesian, Belgian, Swedish, Chinese, French, Italian and numerous other nationalities' cuisines confront the tourist. The standard is in fact quite high in most 'ethnic' restaurants, and prices are reasonable because of the fierce competition. A host of British establishments (mostly pubs) offer the whole shebang: roast beef, Yorkshire pudding and three veg, and apple pie and custard, and all for bargain prices.

Drink

No matter how much other costs have risen in Spain, **wine** (*vino*) has remained awesomely inexpensive by northern European or American standards; what's more, it's mostly very good and there's enough variety from the regions for you to try something different every day. If you take an empty bottle into a *bodega*, you can usually bring it out filled with the wine that suits your palate that day. A *bodega* can be a bar, wine cellar or warehouse, and is worth a visit whatever its guise.

Menu Reader

Hors d'œuvres (*Entremeses*)

aceitunas olives
alcachofas con mahonesa artichokes with mayonnaise
ancas de rana frogs' legs
caldo broth
entremeses variados assorted hors d'œuvres
huevos de flamenco baked eggs in tomato sauce
gambas pil pil shrimp in hot garlic sauce
gazpacho cold soup
huevos al plato fried eggs
huevos revueltos scrambled eggs
sopa de ajo garlic soup
sopa de arroz rice soup
sopa de espárragos asparagus soup
sopa de fideos noodle soup
sopa de garbanzos chickpea soup
sopa de lentejas lentil soup
sopa de verduras vegetable soup
tortilla Spanish omelette, with potatoes
tortilla a la francesa French omelette

Fish (*Pescados*)

acedías small plaice
adobo fish marinated in white wine
almejas clams
anchoas anchovies
anguilas eels
angulas baby eels (elvers)
ástaco crayfish
atún tuna fish
bacalao codfish (usually dried)
besugo sea bream
bogavante lobster
bonito tunny
boquerones anchovies
caballa mackerel
calamares squid
cangrejo crab
centollo spider crab
chanquetes whitebait
chipirones cuttlefish
... en su tinta ...in its own ink
chirlas baby clams
lubina sea bass
escabeche pickled or marinated fish
gambas prawns
langosta lobster
langostinos giant prawns
lenguado sole
mariscos shellfish

If you want to learn how to discern a *fino* from an *amontillado*, go to one of the warehouse *bodegas* of Jerez where you can taste the sherry as you tour the site. When dining out, a restaurant's *vino del lugar* or *vino de la casa* is always your least expensive option; it usually comes out of a barrel or glass jug and may be a surprise either way. Some 20 Spanish wine regions bottle their products under strict controls imposed by the Instituto Nacional de Denominaciones de Origen (there is almost always a little maps of the region pasted on the back of the bottle). In many parts of Andalucía you may have difficulty ordering a simple bottle of white wine, as, on requesting *una botella de vino blanco de la casa*, you will often be served something resembling diluted sherry. To make things clear, specify a wine by name or by region – for example *una botella de Rioja blanco* – or ask for *un vino seco*, and the problem should be solved. Spain also produces its own champagne – *cava* – which seldom has the depth of the French, nor the lightness of an Italian *prosecco*, but is refined enough to drink alone. The principal house, Cordoniú, is always a safe bet. Some *andaluz* wines have achieved an international reputation for high quality. Best known is the *jerez*, or what we in English call **sherry**. When a Spaniard invites you to have a *copita* (glass) it will nearly always be filled with this Andalucían sunshine. It comes in a wide range of varieties: *manzanillas* are very dry; *fino* is dry, light and young (the famous Tío Pepe); *amontillados*, from the slopes around Montilla in Córdoba province, are a bit sweeter and rich; *olorosos* are very sweet dessert sherries, and can be either brown, cream, or *amoroso*.

mejillones mussels
merluza hake
mero grouper
navajas razor-shell clams
ostras oysters
pejesapo monkfish
percebes barnacles
pescadilla whiting
pez espada swordfish
platija plaice
pulpo octopus
rape monkfish
raya skate
rodaballo turbot
salmón salmon
salmonete red mullet
sardinas sardines
trucha trout
veneras scallops
zarzuela fish stew

Meat and Fowl (*Carnes y Aves*)

albóndigas meatballs
asado roast
bistec beefsteak
buey ox
callos tripe
cerdo pork
chorizo spiced sausage
chuletas chops
cochinillo sucking pig
conejo rabbit
corazón heart
cordero lamb
faisán pheasant
fiambres cold meats
filete fillet
hígado liver
jabalí wild boar
jamón de York raw cured ham
jamón serrano baked ham
lengua tongue
lomo pork loin
morcilla blood sausage
paloma pigeon
pato duck
pavo turkey
perdiz partridge
pinchitos spicy mini kebabs
pollo chicken
rabo de toro bull's tail with onions and tomatoes
riñones kidneys
salchicha sausage

The white wines of Córdoba grown in the Villaviciosa region are again making a name for themselves, after being all but wiped out by phylloxera in the last century. In Sevilla, wine is produced in three regions: Lebrija, Los Palacios (white table wines); and Aljarafe, where full-bodied wines are particular favourites. Jaén also has three wine-producing regions. Torreperogíl, east of Úbeda, produces wine little known outside the area, but extremely classy. Take your bottle along to the local *bodega* when you are here, as many wines are on tap only. In Bailén, the white, rosé and red table wines resemble those of the more famous La Mancha vineyards. In the west of the province, Lopera white wines are also sold from the barrel. Málaga and Almería do not produce much wine, although the sweet, aromatic wines of Málaga are famous (and famously undrinkable to most English palates, but persevere). Two grapes, muscatel and Pedro Ximénez, define Málaga province wines and sherries. All are sweet, enjoyed with gusto in bars and the best known are the Málaga Virgen.

Many Spaniards prefer **beer** (*cerveza*), which is also good, though not quite the bargain wine is. The most popular brands are Cruzcampo and San Miguel – most bars sell it cold in bottles or on tap; try Mahou Five Star if you see it. Imported whisky and other spirits are pretty inexpensive, though even cheaper are the versions Spain bottles itself, which may come close to your home favourites. Gin, believe it or not, is often drunk with Coke. Bacardi and Coke is a popular thirst-quencher but beware, a Cuba Libre is not necessarily a rum and Coke, but Coke with anything, such as gin or

salchichón salami
sesos brains
solomillo sirloin steak
ternera veal

Note: *potajes, cocidos, guisados, estofados, fabadas* and *cazuelas* are all different kinds of stew.

Vegetables (*Verduras y Legumbres*)

ajo garlic
alcachofa artichoke
apio celery
arroz rice
arroza a la marinera rice, saffron and seafood
berenjena aubergine (eggplant)
cebolla onion
champiñones mushrooms
col, repollo cabbage
coliflor cauliflower
endibia endive
ensalada salad
espárragos asparagus
espinacas spinach
garbanzos chickpeas
judías (verdes) French beans
lechuga lettuce
lentejas lentils
patatas potatoes
...fritas/salteadas ...fried/sautéed
...al horno ...baked
pepino cucumber
pimiento pepper
puerro leek
remolacha beetroot (beet)
setas Spanish mushrooms
zanahoria carrot

Fruits (*Frutas*)

albaricoque apricot
almendras almonds
cerezas cherries
ciruela plum
ciruela pasa prune
frambuesas raspberries
fresas strawberries
...con nata ...with cream
higos figs
limón lemon
manzana apple
melocotón peach
melón melon
naranja orange
pera pear
piña pineapple

vodka – you have to specify; then, with a flourish worthy of a matador, the barman will zap an ice-filled tumbler in front of you, and heave in a quadruple measure. No wonder the Costa del Sol has a staggering six chapters of Alcoholics Anonymous.

Coffee, tea, all the international soft-drink brands and *Kas*, the locally made orange drink, round out the average café fare. If you want tea with milk, say so when you order, otherwise it may arrive with a piece of lemon. Coffee comes with milk (*café con leche*) or without (*café solo*). Spanish coffee is good and strong, and if you want a lot of it order a *doble* or a *solo grande*; one of those will keep you awake through the guided tour of any museum.

Food and Drink in Gibraltar

In the past, to say that eating out in Gibraltar could be a depressing experience was a compliment. Sausage, beans and chips have long been the zenith of Gibraltar's culinary achievement, with only a handful of exceptions. However, food here is no longer solely restricted to authentic pub grub and fish 'n' chips (although both are still widely available). For the best restaurants on the Rock, get out of the environs of Main Street and head for the recently developed Queensway Quay, or the more established Marina Quay, where you will find a reasonable selection of seafood, Italian dishes and even tapas treats. Away from the quays, olive oil, the sun-dried tomato, or anything

plátano banana
pomelo grapefruit
sandía watermelon
uvas grapes

Desserts (*Postres*)

arroz con leche rice pudding
bizcocho/pastel/torta cake
blanco y negro ice cream and coffee float
flan crème caramel
galletas biscuits (cookies)
helado ice cream
pajama flan with ice cream
pasteles pastries
queso cheese
requesón cottage cheese
tarta de frutas fruit pie
turrón nougat

Drinks (*Bebidas*)

agua con hielo water with ice
agua mineral mineral water
...sin/con gas ...without/with fizz
batido de leche milkshake
café (*con leche*) coffee (with milk)
cava Spanish champagne
cerveza beer
chocolate hot chocolate
jerez sherry
granizado slush, iced squash
leche milk
té (*con limón*) tea (with lemon)
vino (*tinto, rosado, blanco*) wine (red, rosé, white)
zumo de manzana apple juice
zumo de naranja orange juice

Restaurant Vocabulary

menu *carta/menú*
bill/check *cuenta*
change *cambio*
set meal *menú del día*
waiter/waitress *camarero/a*
Do you have a table? *¿Tiene una mesa?*
for one/two? *¿... para uno/dos?*
What is there to eat? *¿Qué hay para comer?*
Can I see the menu, please? *Déme el menú, por favor*
Do you have a wine list? *¿Hay una lista de vinos?*
Can I have the bill (check), please? *La cuenta, por favor*
Can I pay by credit card? *¿Puedo pagar con tarjeta de crédito?*

grilled (as opposed to fried) is almost unheard of. The least dangerous dining in the centre of town is probably Indian cuisine, where standards do rise a little. Chinese is largely inedible.

You can drink to your heart's content in Gibraltar (wend your way to one of the 360 or so pubs on the Rock), but your liver may be happy to know that costs are about double the Spanish equivalent. Pub opening times follow Britain's – open all day till 11pm. Wines and spirits are cheap in the supermarkets and off-licences, but no bargain in restaurants or pubs.

Restaurant Basics

Sticklers for absurd bureaucracy, the Spanish government rates **restaurants** by forks (this has become a bit of a joke – a car repair shop in Granada has rated itself two wrenches). The forks have nothing to do with the quality of the food, though they hint somewhat at the prices. Unless it's explicitly written on the bill (*la cuenta*), service is not included in the total, so tip accordingly. Be careful, though: eating out in southern Spain – especially away from the Costa and big towns – is still a hit-and-miss affair. You will need luck as well as judgement. Spain has plenty of bad restaurants; the worst offenders are often those with the little flags and 10-language menus in the most touristy areas. But common sense will warn you off these. On the other hand, kitsch 'Little Chef' type cut-outs are rampant along country roads, beckoning you inside – and, unlike in the UK, they're not necessarily indicative of a second-class establishment.

If you dine where the locals do, you'll be assured of a good deal, if not necessarily a good meal. Almost every restaurant offers a *menú del día*, or a *menú turístico*, featuring an appetizer, a main course, dessert, bread and drink at a set price, always cheaper than if you had ordered the items *à la carte*. These are always posted outside the restaurant, in the window or on the plywood chef at the door; decide what you want before going in if it's a set-price menu, because these bargains are hardly ever listed on the menu the waiter gives you at the table.

One step down from a restaurant are ***comedores*** (literally, dining-rooms), often tacked on to the backs of bars, where the food and décor are usually drab but cheap, and ***cafeterías***, usually those places that feature photographs of their offerings of *platos combinados* (combination plates) to eliminate any language problem. ***Asadores*** specialize in roast meat or fish; ***marisquerías*** serve only fish and shellfish – you'll usually see the sign for '*pescados y mariscos*' on the awning. Keep an eye out for ***ventas***, usually modest family-run establishments offering excellent *menús del día* for working people. They specialize in typical *andaluz* dishes of roast kid or lamb, rabbit, paella, game (partridge crops up often) and many pork dishes, chorizo sausage and varieties of ham. Visit one on a Sunday lunchtime when all the Spanish families go out – with a bit of luck things may get out of hand, and guitars and castanets could appear from nowhere, in which case abandon all plans for the rest of the day.

If you're travelling on a budget, you may want to eat one of your meals a day at a **tapas bar** or *tasca*. Tapas means 'lids', since they started out as little saucers of goodies served on top of a drink. They have evolved over the years to become the basis of the world's greatest snack culture. Bars that specialize in them have platter after platter of delectable tidbits – shellfish, mushrooms baked in garlic, chicken croquettes, *albóndigas*, the ubiquitous Spanish meatball, quails' eggs and stews. (*Tortilla* is seldom as good as it looks, unless you like eating re-heated shoe-leather.) All you have to do is pick out what looks best and point to it. At about €1 a go, it doesn't really matter if you pick a couple of duds. Order a *tapa* (hors-d'œuvre), or a *ración* (big helping) if it looks really good. It's hard to generalize about prices, but on average €5 of tapas and wine or beer really fill you up. Sitting down at a table rather than eating at the bar may attract a token surcharge. Another advantage of tapas is that they're available at what most Americans or Britons would consider normal dining hours. Spaniards are notoriously late diners; 2pm is the earliest they would consider sitting down to their huge 'midday' meal – at Jerez's premier restaurant, no self-respecting local would be seen dead in the place before 4pm. Then after work at 8pm a few tapas at the bar hold them over until supper at 10 or 11pm. After living in Spain for a few months this makes perfect sense, but it's exasperating to the average visitor. On the coasts, restaurants tend to open earlier to accommodate foreigners (some as early as 5pm) but you may as well do as the Spaniards do.

See 'Eating Out', p.85, in **Practical A–Z** for restaurant price categories.

Travel

07

Getting There

By Air from the UK

British Airways flies up to six times a day to Andalucía, with 22 flights a week from London (Gatwick and Heathrow) to Málaga, five flights a week from Gatwick to Sevilla and two flights daily (from both Gatwick and Heathrow) to Gibraltar; flights are operated by GB Airways. The Spanish airline, **Iberia**, operates on many of the same routes, and also offers direct services from the UK to Alicante, Jerez de la Frontera, and Sevilla. **Air Europa** has daily flights to Madrid, with connections to Málaga and Sevilla. **Monarch Airlines** operates scheduled and chartered services from Luton to Alicante and Málaga, with increased frequency in summer. Málaga is a popular destination for low-cost carriers. **British Midland's** budget airline, **bmibaby,** has daily services in summer from East Midlands Airport and Cardiff (flights three times a week in winter). **MyTravelLite** has services from Birmingham to Málaga and **easyJet** operates services from London Luton, Gatwick, Stanstead and Liverpool to Málaga.

APEX and other discounted fares carry various restrictions, such as minimum and maximum stays, and no change of reservation is allowed. They do, however, represent substantial savings on standard published fares. Most companies offer promotional fares from time to time outside the peak seasons of mid-summer, Christmas and Easter, although a degree of flexibility over travel dates may be necessary to secure them.

Airline Carriers

UK

Air Europa, t 0870 240 1501, *www.air-europa.co.uk.*
Air France, t (020) 8759 2311, *www.airfrance.com.*
Alitalia, t 0870 544 8259, *www.alitalia.it.*
British Airways, t 0845 773 3377, *www.britishairways.com.*
British Midland/bmibaby, t 0870 607 0555, *www.flybmi.com.*
easyJet, t 0870 600 000, *www.easyjet.com.*
Iberia, t 08705 341 341, *www.iberia.com.*
KLM, t 08705 074 074, *www.klmuk.com.*
Lufthansa, t 0845 773 7747, *www.lufthansa.com.*
Monarch Airlines, t 08700 40 50 40, *www.monarch-airlines.com.*
MyTravelLite, t 08701 564564, *www.mytravelite.com.*

USA

Air Canada, toll free **t** 1 888 247 2262, *www.aircanada.ca.*
American Airlines, toll free **t** 800 433 7300, *www.americanairlines.com.*
Continental Airlines, toll free **t** 800 231 0856, *www.continentalairlines.com.*
Iberia, toll-free **t** 800 772 4642, *www.iberia.com.*
United Airlines, toll free **t** 800 538 2929, *www.united.com.*

Other Airlines with Routes via Europe

British Airways, toll free **t** 800 247 9297, *www.britishairways.com*
KLM, toll free **t** 800 777 5553, *www.klm.com.*
Lufthansa, toll free **t** 800 645 3880, *www.lufthansa.com.*
Virgin Atlantic, toll free **t** 800 862 8621, *www.virginatlantic.com.*

Charters and Special Deals

UK and Ireland

Flightline.com, t 0870 040 1757, *www.flightlineinternational.com.*
STA Travel, 117 Euston Road NW1 and 86 Old Brompton Road SW7, **t** 0870 160 6070, *ww.statravel.co.uk.*
USIT Now, 19–21 Aston Quay, O'Connell Bridge, Dublin 2, **t** (01) 602 1600; 16 Mary Street, Galway, **t** (091) 565 177; *www. usitnow.ie.* Foutain Centre, College Street, Belfast BT1 6ET; **t** (028) 90 327 111, *www.usitnow.com.*

USA

Council Travel, t 1 8888 COUNCIL, *www.counciltravel.com.*
STA Travel, 48 E 42nd St, New York, NY 10017, **t** 800 777 0112, *www.sta-travel.com.*

Charter Flights

These can be incredibly cheap, and offer the added advantage of departing from local airports. Companies such as **Thomson**, **Airtours** and **Unijet** offer return flights from as little as £60. This can sometimes include basic accommodation, but nobody expects you to make use of this facility. Some of the best deals have return dates limited strictly to one week or two and sometimes four, the maximum allowed under the regulations. In many cases a return charter ticket is a big saving over a one-way regular fare, even if your itinerary means you have to let the return half lapse. Check your local economy travel agent, or in your local paper, or the Sunday papers. In London, look in the *Evening Standard* and *Time Out*. TV Teletext and the Internet are also good sources of information on cheap charter flights to Spain, with some remarkable last-minute deals.

Get your ticket as early as possible, but try to be sure of your plans, as there are no refunds for missed flights – most travel agencies sell insurance, and indeed, most charter companies now insist upon it so that you don't lose all your money if you become ill and have to cancel. Students and those under 26 have the additional option of special discount charters, departing from the UK, but make sure you have proof of student status. An official STA Youth Go-25 card costs £7.

By Air from the USA

There are numerous carriers that serve Spain. Most regular flights from the USA or Canada are to Madrid or Barcelona. **Iberia**, the national airline, offers fly-drive deals and discounts. From anywhere in the USA, you can use Iberia's toll-free number, **t** 800 772 4642, or log on at *www.iberia.com*. Remember that some of the best transatlantic deals are to London, from where you should be able to get a low-cost flight to Spain departing within a day or two of your arrival. This is an especially cheap way to go in the off season. The Sunday *New York Times* has the most listings.

Charter Flights

These require a bit more perseverance to find, though you can save considerably on the cost of a regular or even APEX flight – currently a charter from New York to Madrid varies between $400–700 depending on the season, with winter charters from New York to Málaga at around $350. You may want to weigh this against the current transatlantic fares to London, where in most cases you will be able to get a low-cost flight to Spain departing within a day or two of your arrival. This is an especially cheap way to go in the off season. The Sunday *New York Times* has the most listings.

Useful Travel Websites

Flights

www.cheapflights.co.uk
www.opodo.com

Holidays

www.ebookers.com
www.eurobookers.com
www.expedia.co.uk
www.justcities.com
www.lastminute.com
www.online-travellers.co.uk
www.packyourbags.com

By Sea

Sea links between the UK and Spain are operated by Brittany Ferries and P&O Ferries. This is a good way to go if you mean to bring your car, motorbike, caravan or bicycle, but book well in advance – prices rise dramatically as the ferries fill up.

Brittany Ferries operates between Plymouth and Santander twice weekly, and prices for foot passengers are roughly equivalent to a charter flight; children of 4–15 go for slightly over half-price, under-4s free. Prices for vehicles vary according to size and season: high season is from late June until early September, when the return fare for a driver plus car is £550, and about £45 per person for additional passengers. Fares drop to about £280 return in low season. An adult foot passenger pays from £130 return in high season, dropping to £75 out of season. These fares do not include on-board accommodation, which you have to take; in the high season, this costs from £4–6 for a reclining seat, and from £21 per person based upon four people sharing a four-berth cabin, to £135 or more for a deluxe twin-berth cabin. There are also cheaper 5- and 10-day returns. The 24–27hr crossing can be rough.

P&O European Ferries operates the Portsmouth–Bilbao route with crossings twice weekly throughout the year except for a three-week break in January. Peak season runs from mid-July to mid-August when the return fare for an average-length car and four adults is £1156, including accommodation in a four-berth cabin. This drops to £694 in the winter months. Return fare for an adult foot passenger in peak season is £359, £170 out of season, including accommodation in a two-berth cabin. P&O fares include accommodation on all crossings, and prices vary dramatically according to the date and time of sailing. Children ages 4–15 travel just over half-price and under-4s go free. Good value 5- and 8-day mini-breaks are also available.

Brittany Ferries: Millbay Docks, Plymouth PL1 3EW, **t** 08705 360 360, *www.brittanyferries.com*. In Santander the address is the Estación Marítima, **t** 94 221 4500.

P&O Ferries Ltd: Peninsular House, Wharf Road, Portsmouth, PO2 8TA, **t** 0870 2424 999. In Bilbao, Cosmé Echevarrieta 1, 48009 Bilbao, **t** 9) 423 4477.

By Rail

From London to Andalucía takes at least a day and a half and requires a change of trains in Paris and Madrid or Barcelona. A two-month return, London–Madrid costs from £270; for London–Sevilla you will need to change in Madrid anyway. Students, those under 26 and holders of a Senior Citizen's Railcard can get reductions. Time can be saved by taking the Eurostar rail service, **t** 08705 186 186, which runs very frequently and takes three hours from London (Waterloo) to Paris (Gare du Nord). Fares are lower if booked at least 14 days in advance.

If you've been a resident in Europe for the past six months you can take advantage of the **InterRail pass or the Eurodomino rail pass**, available at main rail stations or any travel agent. The InterRail passes are available for unlimited travel within one to four zones throughout Europe and are valid for 12 days, 22 days or one month. Prices range from £119 for 12 days' travel in one zone, to £249 for one month's travel in four zones. The Eurodomino pass allows you 3–8 days unlimited travel in first or second class within a one-month period on Spanish railways and costs between £73 (for 3 days' travel in second class) to £207 (for 8 days' travel in first class). There are discounts on both rail passes for under-26s.

Bookings: rail tickets to Spain from England, or vice versa, and couchette and sleeper reservations in France, can be obtained from **Rail Europe**, 179 Piccadilly, London, W1 (take your passport), or booked and paid for over the telephone, **t** 08705 848 848, or online, *www.raileurope.co.uk* (which is also a good source of information on the different passes available).

Tickets for local Spanish services can be obtained from certain UK travel agents, but bookings must be made weeks in advance.

The American **EurRail pass**, which must be purchased before you leave the States, is a good deal only if you plan to use the trains every day in Spain and elsewhere – and it's not valid in the UK, Morocco or countries outside the European Union. For those under 26, a month of travel is $644, 21 days is $518, and two weeks is $410; those over 26 can get a one-month pass for $918, a 21-day pass for $740 or a 15-day pass for $572. In Spain you'll have to pay supplements for any kind of express train. Contact: **CIT Tours**, 15 West 44th Street, New York 10173 **t** 800 248 7245, or buy tickets online at *www.raileurope.com*.

By Bus or Coach

One major company, **Eurolines**, offers departures several times a week in the summer (twice a week out of season, but you may have to change) from London to Spain, along the east coast as far as Alicante, or to Algeciras via San Sebastián, Burgos, Madrid, Córdoba, Granada and Málaga. Journey time is 37 hours from London to Málaga, and 40 hours to Algeciras. Fares from London to Málaga start from £136 return for under-25s, £149 for over-26s. The European Apex ticket (non-refundable and booked at least 7 days in advance) costs just £79. Peak season fares

Special Interest Holidays and Tour Operators

Golf

The south coast of Spain is teeming with golf courses – there are more than 50 of them on the Costa del Sol. Most hotels nearby cater specifically for the golfer and there are numerous specialist golf operators, some of which are listed below. There is a list of courses and fees at *www.andalucian-golf-booking.com*.

Language

Language courses generally last 2–12 weeks. Course fees average €300 for 2 weeks; private tuition costs around €12–20 per hour. Accommodation can be arranged, whether boarding with families or in an apartment. Contact the **Instituto Cervantes**, 102 Eaton Square, London, **t** (020) 7235 0353, *www.cervantes.co.uk* for information and listings of approved language schools in Andalucía or for details of language courses in the UK.

Some Specialist Language Centres

Granada: Escuela de Español de las Alpujarras, C/Natalio Rivas 1, 18001 Granada, **t** 95 829 22 19. Offers language courses integrated with activities in the Alpujarras area, including cycling, hiking, horseriding, cooking and flamenco dancing.

Málaga: Instituto de Español Picasso, Pza de la Merced 20, 29080 Málaga, **t** 95 221 39 32, *www.instituto-picasso.com*.

Marbella: Instituto Internacional de Idiomas, C/Los Almendros s/n, Edif. Las Palmeras, 29600 Marbella, **t** 95 282 21 91.

Nerja: Escuela de Idiomas, Almirante Ferrandiz 73, 29780 Nerja, Málaga, **t** 95 252 20 96, *www.idnerja.es*.

Spas

In Andalucía there's a spa to cater for every complaint, from allergies to rheumatism.

Cádiz: Balneario Fuente Amarga, Avda de Fuente Amarga s/n, 11130 Chiclana de la Frontera, **t** 95 640 05 20, *www.terra.es/personal/vitini*.

Granada: Balnearios Alhama de Granada, 18120 Alhama de Granada, **t** 95 835 00 11, *www.grupoalessa.com/nextel/balnearios andalucia/alhama.html*.

Jaén: Balneario de Marmolejo, Ctra Balneario s/n, 23770 Marmolejo, **t** 95 354 04 04.

Málaga: Balneario de Carratraca, Baños 1, 29551 Carratraca, **t** 95 245 80 71.

Specialist Tour Operators

Abercrombie & Kent International, 1520 Kensington Road, Oak Brook, IL 60521, toll free **t** 800 323 7308, and in the UK, Sloane Square House, Holbein Place, London SW1W 8NS, **t** 0845 0700610, *www.abercrombiekent.co.uk*. Up-market holidays and villas.

ACE Study Tours, Sawston Road, Babraham, Cambridge CB2 4AP, **t** (01223) 835 055, **f** (01223) 837394, *www.study-tours.org*. Organizes art, architecture, archaeology and natural history tours.

Al-Andalus Expreso, booked through Cox & King's (*see* below). Offers luxury train tours across Andalucía.

Andalucian Adventures, Washpool, Horsley, Glos, GL6 0PP, **t** (01453) 834137, *info@andalucian-adventures.co.uk, www.andalucian-adventures.co.uk*. Walking and painting tours in southern Spain.

Alternative Travel Group, 69–71 Banbury Road, Oxford OX2 6PE, **t** (01865) 310 399. Arranges walking tours around Andalucía.

Andante Travel, The Old Barn, Old Road, Alderbury, Salisbury, SP5 3AR, Wilts, **t** (01722) 713 800, *www.andantetravels.co.uk*. Arranges archaeological and historical study tours of Roman Spain.

Andrew Brock Travel, 29a Main St, Lyddington, Oakholm, Rutland, LE15 9LR, **t** (01572) 821 330. Walking holidays in southern Andalucía.

Aviación del Sol, Apartado 344, 29400 Ronda (Málaga), **t/f** 95 287 72 49. Specializes in hot-air ballooning in the Serranía de Ronda.

Bird Holidays, 10 Ivegate, Yeadon, Leeds, LS19 7RE, **t/f** (0113) 391 0510. *www.britishbirdguides.org.uk*. Arranges bird-watching holidays in the Coto Doñana National Park (Huelva), and around Tarifa.

Cabalgar-Rutas Alternativas, 18412 Bubión (Granada), **t/f** 95 876 3135. Offers horse riding and 4x4 trips in the sierras of Granada and to the coast of Almería.

Cadogan Travel, 9–10 Portland Street, Southampton SO14 7EB, **t** (01703) 828 300, *www.cadoganholidays.com*. Upmarket holidays (including golfing holidays) in Gibraltar, southern Spain and Morocco.

Cortijo Romero, Little Grove, Grove Lane, Chesham, HP5 3QQ, **t** (01494) 782720, **f** (01494) 776066, *www.cortijo-romero.co.uk*. Alternative holidays (personal developement, yoga Tai Chi etc) in a rural farmhouse.

Cox & King's Travel Ltd, Gordon House, 10 Green Coat Place, London SW1P 1PH, **t** (020) 7873 5000. Agents for the al-Andalus luxury train tour of Andalucía.

CV Travel, 43 Cadogan Street, London SW3 2PR, **t** 0870 606 0802 (24-hour brochure service: **t** 0870 603 9018). Small luxury hotels and up-market villas on the coast and inland

Dolphin Safari, Marina Bay, Gibraltar, PO80, **t** 95 677 19 14, *www.dolphinsafari.gi*. Arranges dolphin-spotting trips from May to October.

Equitour, **t** (01993) 849489, *www.equitour.co.uk*. Riding holidays throughout Spain.

Exodus, 9 Weir Road, London SW12 0LT, **t** (020) 8675 5550, *www.exodus.co.uk*. Offers walking tours throughout Spain.

Learning for Pleasure, Apartado 25, Las Limas, 11330 Jimena de la Frontera (Cádiz), **t** 95 664 01 02, **f** 95 664 12 89. Offers courses in painting, creative writing, cooking, herbal medicine and gardening, and organizes riding and walking tours.

Longshot Golf Holidays, Meon House, College Street, Petersfield, Hants GU32 3JN, **t** (01730) 268 621, *www.longshotgolf.co.uk*.

Loymer Tours, Avda. Constitución, 21, Cómpeta **t** 95 251 62 04, **f** 95 251 63 24, *info@loymertours.com, www.loymertours.com*. Rents rural cottages in Andalucía and apartments on the Costa del Sol. Also does car hire.

Marketing Ahead Inc., 433 Fifth Avenue, New York, NY 10016, **t** (212) 686 9213, **f** (212) 686 02 71, *www.marketingahead.com*. Leading *parador* agents in the USA.

Mundicolor Holidays, 276 Vauxhall Bridge Road, London SW1V 1BE, **t** (020) 7828 6021, *www.mundicolor.co.uk*. Specializes in tailor-made resort, national park, and *parador* holidays throughout Spain; it also offers a luxury train tour of Andalucía and gastronomy and wine tours.

Naturetrek, Cheriton Mill, Cheriton, Alresford, Hampshire SO24 ONG, **t** (01962) 733 051, *www.naturetrek.co.uk*. Runs bird-watching and botanical tours in Andalucía and the Coto Doñana.

Nevadensis, C/Verónica s/n, 18411 Pampaneira (Granada), **t** 95 876 31 27, **f** 95 876 30 01, www.nevadensis.com. Organizes walking tours, mountaineering, cross-country skiing.

Page & Moy Ltd, 136–140 London Road, Leicester LE2 1EN, **t** (0116) 250 7000, *www.page-moy.com*. Offers cultural guided tours throughout Spain.

Peregrine Holidays, 15 Grange Place, Bridge St, Witney, Oxfordshire, OX28 4 BS, **t** (01993) 849489. Offers bird-watching tours. Linked to Equitour (*see* above).

Plantagenet Tours, 85 The Grove, Moordown, Bournemouth BH9 2TY, **t** (01202) 521 895, *www.plantagenettours.com*. A changing programme of cultural tours in Andalucía and Catalunya run by a passionate, learned and entertaining ex-college professor.

Prospect Music & Art Tours, 36 Manchester Street, London W1 U7LH, **t** (020) 7486 5704, **f** (020) 7486 5868, *sales@prospecttours.com*. Arranges tours led by art historians.

Ramblers Holidays, Box 43, Welwyn Garden City, Herts AL8 6PQ, **t** (01707) 331 133, *www.ramblersholidays.co.uk*. Offers walking tours in the Sierra Nevada.

Rancho Los Lobos, 11339 Estación de Jimena (Cádiz), **t** 95 664 04 29, **f** 95 664 11 80, *www.rancholoslobos.com*. Riding holidays.

Safari Andalucía, Apartado 20, 29480 Gaucín, (Málaga), **t** 95 215 11 48, **f** 95 215 13 76. Walking holidays in the Serranía de Ronda with tented camp and hunting lodge accommodation and mules to carry baggage.

Sierra Cycling Tours, Urb. Pueblo Castillo 7, Fuengirola (Málaga) 29640, **t** 95 247 17 20 mobile 616 295 251. Cycling in the sierras.

The Spirit of Andalucía, c/o Sally von Meister, Apartado 20, El Nobo, 29480 Gaucín, (Málaga), **t** 95 215 13 03, **f** 952 11 72 07, *spirit@mercuryin.eswww.elnobu.co.uk*. Offers courses in cooking and painting.

Tall Stories, Brassey House, New Zealand Avenue, Walton on Thames, Surrey, KT12 1QD, **t** (01932) 252 002, **f** (01932) 252 970, *www.tallstories.co.uk. Adventure holidays.*

Unicorn Holidays, 2–10 Crossroad, Tadworth, KT20 5UJ, **t** (01737) 812 255. Specializes in tailor-made holidays, with high-quality character hotels and *parador* accommodation.

between 1 July and 31 August are slightly higher. There are discounts for anyone under 26, senior citizens and children under 12. The national coach companies operate services that connect with the continental bus system. In the summer, the coach is the best bargain for anyone over 26; off-season you'll probably find a cheaper charter flight.

The Spanish Tourist Office in London can also provide details of UK–Spain bus services.

Eurolines, 52 Grosvenor Gardens, London SW1, **t** (020) 7730 8235, *www.eurolines.com or www.gobycoach.com*.

By Car

From the UK via France, ferries from Portsmouth cross to Cherbourg, Caen, Le Havre and St-Malo. From any of these ports the most direct route takes you to Bordeaux, down the western coast to the border at Irún, and on to San Sebastián, Burgos and Madrid, from where you can head south and choose your entry point into Andalucía.

An alternative route is from Paris to Perpignan, crossing the border at the Mediterranean side of the Pyrenees, then along the coast to Barcelona, where the E15 will take you south. Both routes take an average of two days' steady driving.

You may find it more convenient and less tiring to try the ferry from Portsmouth to Bilbao or Plymouth to Santander, which cuts out driving through France and saves expensive autoroute tolls. For the scenery, opt for one of the routes over the Pyrenees, through Puigcerdá, Somport-Canfranc or Andorra, but expect heavy traffic; if you're not in a hurry, take the classic route through Roncesvalles, Vall d'Arán, or through Tarbes and Aragnouet through the tunnel to Parzán.

Entry Formalities

Passports and Visas

There are no formal entry requirements for EU passport holders, regardless of the purpose or duration of the visit.Nationals of the EU countries that are signatories to the *Schengen* agreement no longer require even a passport. However, the UK is *not* a signatory and passengers arriving at Spanish airports from the UK must still present a valid passport.

Holders of US, Canadian, Australian and New Zealand passports can enter Spain for up to 90 days without a visa; visitors from other countries will need a visa, available from any Spanish consulate. For Gibraltar there are no extra visa requirements for USA citizens, and EU nationals have the same rights and status as in the UK. For the most up-to-date information, check with the Spanish embassy or consulate in your home country.

Spanish Consulates

Australia: Level 24, St Martin's Tower, 31 Market St, Sydney NSW 2000, **t** (02) 61 74 33.

Canada: 1 West Mount Square, Montreal H3Z 2P9, **t** (514) 935 5235; 200 Cross Street West, Toronto, Ontario **t** (416) 977 1661.

France: 165 Blvd Malesherbes, 75840 Paris, **t** 01 44 29 40 00.

Germany: Steinplatz 1, Berlin **t** (30) 315 09 251/315 09 251.

Ireland: 17a Merlyn Park, Ballsbridge, Dublin 4, **t** (1) 269 1640.

Italy: Palacio Borghese, Largo Fontanella di Borghese, 00186 Roma, **t** 06 687 82 64.

Netherlands: Frederiksplein 34, 1017 XN Amsterdam, **t** (20) 620 3811.

New Zealand: New Zealanders should contact the Spanish Embassy in Canberra: 15 Arkana St, Yarralumla ACT2600, P.O.B. 9076, Deakin ACT 2600, **t** 62 73 35 55.

UK: 20 Draycott Place, London SW3 2RZ, **t** (020) 7589 8989; 1a Brook House, 70 Spring Gardens, Manchester M2 2BQ, **t** (0161) 236 1233, **f** (0161) 228 7467; 63 North Castle Street, Edinburgh EH2 3LJ, **t** (0131) 220 1843.

USA: 545 Boylston Street, Boston, MA 02116, **t** (617) 536 2506; 180 North Michigan Avenue, Chicago, IL 60601, **t** (312) 782 4588; 2655 Le Jeune Road, 203 Coral Gables, Florida, **t** (305) 446 5511; 5055 Wilshire Blvd, Suite 960 Los Angeles, CA 90036, **t** (323) 938 0158; 150 East 58th Street, New York, NY 10155, **t** (212) 355 4080; 2375 Pennyslvania Avenue NW, Washington, DC 20009, **t** (202) 728 2330.

Customs

Customs are usually easy to get through – unless you come in via Morocco, when they'll search everything. EU limits for goods from a tax-free shop are: 1 litre of spirits or 2 litres of liquors plus 2 litres of wine and 200 cigarettes. Larger quantities (10 litres of spirits, 90 litres of wine, 110 litres of beer, 800 cigarettes) can be taken through Customs if they have been bought locally in a non-tax-free shop, you are travelling between EU countries, and you can prove they are for private consumption.

If you are travelling from the UK or the USA, don't bother to pick up any alcohol in transit – it's cheaper to buy drink off the supermarket shelves in Spain.

Getting Around

By Air

Internal flights in Spain are primarily on Iberia and Air Europa. However, there are several other carriers on national routes, such as the Alitalia service between Málaga and Barcelona. In Andalucía you'll find airports in Almería, Córdoba, Granada, Jerez (Cádiz), Málaga, Sevilla, and Melilla in North Africa. Prices are less of a bargain than they used to be, although if you shop around and are willing to travel at night you can pick up some cheap deals, especially if you're going on a round trip. Also, check out the national charters in Spanish travel agencies.

Iberia Offices

Almería: Almería Airport, **t** 95 021 37 95/7.
Granada: Pza Isabel la Católica 2, **t** 95 822 75 92.
Jerez: Airport, **t** 95 615 00 10.
Málaga: Molina Larios 13, **t** 95 213 61 47.
Sevilla: Avda de la Buhaira, 8, **t** 95 422 89 01.
Gibraltar: Padre Santaella, Primera Izq 04004, **t** 95 023 86 84.

You can also call Iberia throughout Spain on their 24hr number in Madrid, **t** 902 400 500. Otherwise log on to *www.iberia.com*.

By Sea

The *Transmediterránea* line operates services from the Spanish mainland to the Balearic Islands, North Africa and the Canary Islands. In **Málaga**, Estación Marítima, 29016, **t** 902 45 46 45, *www.trasmediterranea.com*.

UK Agents: Southern Ferries, 179 Piccadilly, London W1V 9DB, **t** (020) 7491 4968, **f** (020) 7491 3502.

By Rail

Mister Traveller, take the Spanish Train!
RENFE brochure

Democracy in Spain has made the trains run on time, but Western Europe's most eccentric railway company, **RENFE**, still has a way to go. The problem isn't the trains themselves; they're almost always clean and comfortable, and do their best to keep to the schedules, but the new efficient RENFE remains so complex it will foul up your plans at least once. There are no fewer than 13 varieties of train, from the luxury **TEE** (Trans-Europe Express) to the excruciating *semidirecto* and *ferrobús*, which stop at every hamlet to deliver mail.

The best are the **Talgo** trains, speedy and stylish beasts in gleaming stainless steel; the Spaniards are very proud of them. **TER** trains are almost as good. Note that a majority of lines are still, incredibly, single-track, so whatever train you take, you'll still have to endure delays for trains coming the other way. This said, there has been one great leap forward in Spanish rail transport in the last few years, and that is the introduction of **AVE** services – high-speed rail links – originally developed for the Sevilla Expo in 1992.

Every variety of train has different services and a different price. RENFE ticket people and conductors can't always get them straight, and confusion is rampant, except again on Talgo and AVE routes where the published prices are straightforward. There are discounts for children (under-4s free; 4–12 half-price), large families, senior citizens (half-price) and regular travellers, and 25 per cent discounts on *Días Azules* ('blue days') for round-trip tickets only. 'Blue days' are posted in the RENFE calendars in every station. Interpretations of the rules for these discounts differ from one ticket-window to the next, and you may care to undertake protracted negotiations over them like the Spanish do. There is a pass for people under 26, the *tarjeta joven*, and BIGE or BIJ youth fares are available from TIVE offices in large cities.

For information and tickets, call the RENFE information line, **t** 902 24 02 02, or book online at *www.renfe.es* (the website is available in English). Always buy tickets in advance if you can; one of RENFE's little tricks is to close station ticket-windows 10 minutes before your train arrives. Other stations don't open the ticket-windows until the train is a couple of minutes away, causing panic and confusion. Don't rely on the list of trains posted; always ask at the station or travel office. **Fares** are generally considerably lower than in the UK, but there are supplements on the faster trains that can put another 80 per cent on top of the basic price. If you plan to do a lot of riding on the rails, buy the *Guía RENFE*, an indispensable government publication with all the schedules and tariffs, available from any station newsagent.

Rail Excursions

Andalucia's answer to the *Transcantábrica*, which operates in northwest Spain, is the *Al-Andalus Expreso*, a luxury tour taking passengers from Sevilla to Córdoba, Granada, Málaga and Jerez. Although expensive, the carriages are done out in period décor and the cuisine is superb. The trip takes 4–5 days, but a common complaint is that the train spends an excessive amount of time in a railway siding while passengers are bussed to the sights.

Contacts for Al-Andalus Expreso

UK: Cox & King's Travel Ltd, Gordon House, 10 Green Coat Place, London SW1P 1PH, **t** (020) 7873 5000.

USA: Marketing Ahead Inc., 433 Fifth Avenue, New York, NY 10016, **t** 800 223 1356, **f** (212) 686 0271, *Mahrep@aol.com*, *www.marketingahead.com*

By Car

This is certainly the most convenient way of getting about, and often the most pleasurable. However, bear in mind that only a few hotels – the more expensive ones – have garages or any sort of parking, and in cities parking is always difficult. A useful tip to remember is that space which appears to be private – e.g. underground car parks of apartment blocks and offices – is often public, and rates are usually modest. Spain's highway network is adequate, usually in good repair, and sometimes impressive. The system of *autopistas* (motorways) is constantly expanding. Spanish road building is remarkable for its speed if not always its durability.

Once you venture off the beaten track, be prepared for a few surprises; some roads in Andalucía wind tortuously up mountainsides, with steep drops into gorges below. The old N340 along the coast is much safer with the addition of frequent lane-changing slip roads, bridges and underpasses, while the new bypasses around Fuengirola and Marbella have been built to genuine motorway standards. Travelling between Málaga and Gibraltar, which used to be known as 'mortuary mile', is undoubtedly much safer than it was thanks to a new motorway, which bypasses the towns between Estepona and Algeciras.

To drive in Spain you'll need registration and insurance documents, and a driving licence. If you're coming from Ireland or the UK, adjust the dip of your headlights to the right. Drivers with a valid licence from an EU country, the USA, Canada or Australia no longer need an international licence. Americans should not be intimidated by driving in Europe. Learn the international road-sign system (charts available to members from most auto clubs), brush up on your gear-changing technique, and get used to the idea of few signals and traffic constantly converging from all directions. Seat belts are mandatory. The speed limit is 100kph (62 mph) on national highways, unless marked, and 120kph (75 mph) on motorways. Drive with the utmost care at all times – having an accident will bring you untold headaches, and to make matters worse, many Spaniards drive without insurance.

Hitchhiking is likely to involve a long, hot wait. Drivers in Andalucía rarely give lifts.

Car Hire

This is slightly cheaper than elsewhere in Europe. The big international companies are the most expensive, and seldom the most service-orientated. Smaller companies will, for example, deliver a car to your hotel when you want it, and collect it again when you no longer require it. On the costas, prices for the smallest cars begin at about €220 per week, which includes unlimited mileage and full insurance (CDW), according to season. An all-in weekly rate for a two-door Opel Corsa in mid-season picked up from and returned to Málaga Airport should be about €280. If your rental begins at Málaga Airport, try booking it locally in advance. You will do no better than with **Mustang Rent-a-Car**, Aeropuerto de Málaga, **t** 95 223 51 59, **f** 95 288 33 13. Apart from offering good rates and friendly service, Mustang is also a car-repair garage – worth remembering if your own car breaks down or needs attention; you can hire another while it's being repaired. Two other firms with a good reputation are **Marinsa**, **t** 95 223 23 04, **f** 95 223 99 25, and **Helle Hollis**, **t** 95 224 55 44, **f** 95 224 51 86. Local firms, such as **Turarche**, C/Roger de Flor 1 (by the bus station), **t** 95 231 80 69, **f** 95 231 63 42, *www.turarche.es*, also rent mopeds and bicycles, especially in tourist areas. If you would like to pre-book from the UK, try **Holiday Autos**, **t** 08705 300 400, **Auto Europe**, **t** 0800 169 6414, or **Hertz**, **t** 08705 996 699. Check if your airline offers any car deals when you book your ticket. However, pre-booked car rentals offer no refunds should your plans change.

Taxis

The average fare within a city will be €5–10. Taxis are not always metered, but the drivers are usually honest; they are entitled to certain surcharges (for luggage, night or holiday trips, to the train or airport, etc), and if you cross the city limits they can usually charge double the fare shown. It's easy to hail a cab from the street, and there will always be a few around the stations.

By Bus

With literally dozens of companies providing services over Andalucía, expect choice at the price of confusion. Not all cities have bus stations; in some there may be a dozen little offices spread around town for each firm. Buses, like the trains, are cheap by northern European standards, but still no bargain; if you're travelling on the cheap, you'll find that transportation is your biggest expense. Usually, whether you go by train or bus will depend on simple convenience; in some places the train station is far from the centre, in others the bus station is. As is the custom at RENFE stations, tickets on the inter-city bus routes are sometimes sold at the last minute.

Small towns and villages can normally be reached by bus only through their provincial capitals. Buses are usually clean, dependable and comfortable, and there's plenty of room for baggage in the compartment underneath. On the more luxurious buses that link the main cities of Andalucía, as well as the services along the coast, you get air-conditioning and even a movie (*Rambo, Kung Fu*, sappy Spanish flicks from the Franco era or locally produced rock videos). **Tourist information offices** are the best sources for information.

City Buses

Every Spanish city has a perfectly adequate system of public transportation. You won't need to make much use of it, though, for in almost every city all attractions are within walking distance of each other. City buses usually cost around €0.90, and if you intend to use them often there are books of tickets called *abonamientos* or *bono-bus*, or *tarjeta* cards to punch on entry, available at reduced rates from tobacco shops. Bus drivers will give change but often don't accept notes of more than €10. In many cities, the bus's entire route will be displayed on the signs at each stop (*parada*). And don't take it for granted that the bus will stop just because you are waiting – nearly every stop apart from the terminus seems to be a *request* stop. Flamboyant signals and throwing yourself across its path are the only ways of ensuring the bus will stop for you.

Practical A–Z

Children

Spaniards adore children, and they'll welcome yours almost everywhere. Baby foods, and other supplies are widely available, but don't expect to find babysitters except at the really smart hotels; Spaniards always take their children with them, even if they're up until 4am. Nor are there many special amusements for children, though these are beginning to spring up with Spain's new prosperity, for better or worse; traditionally Spaniards never thought of their children as separate little creatures who ought to be amused. Ask at a local tourist office for a list of attractions in its area geared towards children.

Climate and When to Go

Andalucía is hot and sunny in the summer, generally mild and sunny by day in the winter – in fact, with an average 320 days of sunshine in the region, you can count on more sun here than anywhere else in Europe. Autumn weather is normally warm and comfortable, but can pack a few surprises, from torrential rains to droughts. The mild winters in coastal regions give way to warm springs with minimal rainfall. Temperatures inland can be considerably lower, especially in the mountainous regions, and the *Levante* wind can make life uncomfortable, even in summer, when it will not only blow your beach umbrella away, but might even make you a bit kooky. For comfort, spring and autumn are the best times to visit; winter is generally pleasant on the Mediterranean coast, but can be damp and chilly inland. Spanish homes (and hotel rooms) are not made for winter; you'll probably be more comfortable outside.

Climate in Gibraltar

Gibraltar's climate is, of course, Mediterranean, but it also manifests the characteristic cloud and rain of British weather. The moisture-laden *Levante* batters Gibraltar's shores and is forced up the sheer face of the rock, to condense in the lower temperatures at the top, forming a dense cloud that can be seen for miles; during the winter months the cloud deposits a sometimes relentless shower.

Disabled Travellers

Facilities for disabled travellers are limited within Spain and public transport is not particularly wheelchair-friendly, though RENFE usually provides wheelchairs at main city stations. You are advised to contact the Spanish Tourist Office, which has compiled a fact sheet and can give general information on accessible accommodation, or any of the organizations that specifically provide services for people with disabilities.

Organizations in Spain

ALPE Turismo para Todos, C/Casarrubuelos 5, Madrid, **t** 91 448 08 64. Publishes a useful hotel guide that lists facilities for disabled travellers.

ONCE (Organización Nacional de Ciegos de España), Consejo General de la ONCE, C/ José Ortega y Gasset 18, 28006 Madrid, **t** 91 577 37 56, *www.once.es*. The Spanish association for the visually impaired.

Organizations in the UK

Holiday Care Information Unit, 2nd Floor Imperial Buildings, Victoria Road, Horley, Surrey RH6 7PZ, **t** (01293) 774535, **f** (01293) 784647, Minicom 01293 776943,

Average Temperatures in °C (°F)

	Jan		April		July		Oct	
	max	min	max	min	max	min	max	min
Sevilla	15 (59)	6 (43)	23 (74)	11 (52)	35 (95)	21 (70)	26 (79)	14 (58)
Málaga	17 (63)	9 (49)	21 (70)	13 (56)	29 (84)	21 (70)	23 (74)	16 (61)
Cádiz	15 (59)	8 (47)	21 (70)	12 (54)	29 (84)	20 (68)	23 (74)	15 (59)

Average Monthly Rainfall in mm (inches)

	Jan	April	July	Oct
Sevilla	99 (4)	80 (3)	0 (0)	37 (1.5)

www.holidaycare. org.uk. Information packs for people with special needs, covering accessible hotels, attractions and activity holidays.

RADAR (Royal Association for Disability and Rehabilitation), 12 City Forum, 250 City Road, London EC1V 8AF, **t** (020) 7259 3222, *www.radar.org.uk*. Has a wide range of travel information.

Royal National Institute for the Blind,105 Judd St, WC1H 9NE, **t** (020) 7388 1266, *www.rnib.org.uk*. Its mobility unit offers a 'Plane Easy' audio-cassette which advises blind people on travelling by plane. It will also advise on accommodation.

Tripscope, The Vassall Centre, Gill Avenue, Bristol BS16 2QQ, **t** (08457) 585 641 (for calls from within the UK charged at cheap rate), **t** + 44 117 939 7782 (from outside the UK), *www.tripscope.org.uk*. Offers advice on the practicalities of travel for elderly and disabled travellers.

Organizations in the USA

American Foundation for the Blind, 11 Penn Plaza, Suite 300, New York, NY 10001, **t** (212) 502 7600; toll free **t** 800 232 5463, *www.afb.org*. The best source of information in the USA for visually impaired travellers.

Mobility International USA, PO Box 10767, Eugene, OR 97403, **t** (503) 343 1284, *www.miusa.org*. Offers a service similar to that of its sister organization in the UK.

SATH (Society for Accessible Travel and Hospitality), Suite 610, 347 5th Avenue, New York, NY 10016, **t** (212) 447 7284, *www.sath.org*. Offers advice on travel for a small charge (free to members).

Eating Out

See also **Food and Drink** chapter, pp.71–2, for typical restaurant hours.

Price categories quoted in the 'Eating Out' sections throughout this book are prices for the set menu or for a three-course meal with drinks, per person.

Unless it's explicitly written on the bill (*la cuenta*), service in most restaurants is not included in the total, so tip accordingly. If you dine where the locals do, you'll be assured of a good deal, if not necessarily a good meal.

Restaurant Price Categories

expensive over €30
moderate €18–30
inexpensive under €18

Almost every restaurant offers a *menú del día*, or a *menú turístico*, featuring an appetizer, a main course, dessert, bread and drink at a set price, always cheaper than if you had ordered the items *à la carte*.

Electricity

The current is 225 AC or 220 V, the same as most of Europe. Americans will need converters, and the British will need two-pin adapters for the different plugs. If you plan to stay in the less expensive *hostales*, it may be better to leave your gadgets at home. Some corners of Spain have pockets of exotic voltage – 150V for example – guaranteeing a brief display of fireworks. Virtually all hotels now have the standard current.

Embassies and Consulates

Australia: Pso de la Castellana, 143 Edificio Cuzco, Madrid, **t** 91 579 04 28; Seville **t** 95 422 09 71

Canada: C/Núñez de Balboa 35, Madrid **t** 91 431 43 00; Málaga, **t** 95 222 33 46.

France: C/Salustiano Olózaga 9, Madrid, **t** 91 435 89 00; Málaga, **t** 95 222 48 88.

Germany: C/Fortuny 8, Madrid, **t** 91 557 90 00; Málaga, **t** 95 221 24 42.

Ireland: C/Claudio Coello 73, 28001 Madrid, **t** 91 576 35 00; Fuengirola, **t** 95 247 51 08.

Italy: C/Joaquín Costa 29, Madrid, **t** 91 262 55 46; Málaga, **t** 95 230 61 50.

Netherlands: Pso de la Castellana 178, Madrid, **t** 91 359 0914; Málaga, **t** 95 260 02 60.

New Zealand: Plaza de la Lealtad 2, Madrid, **t** 91 523 02 26.

UK: C/de Fernando el Santo 16, Madrid, **t** 91 319 0200; Pza Nueva 8, Sevilla, **t** 95 422 88 75; Edificio Duquesa, C/Duquesa de Parcent 8, Málaga, **t** 95 221 75 71; Gibraltar: (Vice Consulate) 65 Irish Town, **t** 78 305.

USA: C/Serrano 75, Madrid, **t** 91 577 40 00; consular office for passports, around the corner at Pso de la Castellana, 52 Pso de las Delicias 7, Sevilla, **t** 95 423 18 85; C/Martínez

Catena, Portal 6, Apartado 5B, Complejo Sol Playa, Fuengirola, **t** 95 247 48 91.

Festivals

One of the most spiritually deadening aspects of Francoism was the banning of many local and regional fiestas. These are now celebrated with gusto, and if you can arrange your itinerary to include one or two you'll be guaranteed an unforgettable holiday. Besides those listed below, there are literally thousands of others, and new ones spring up all the time. Many village patronal fiestas feature *romerías* (pilgrimages) up to a venerated shrine. Getting there is half the fun, with everyone in local costume, riding on horseback

Calendar of Events

January

First week Granada: commemoration of the city's capture by the Catholic Kings.
Málaga: Epiphany parade of Los Reyes Magos (Three Wise Men).

February

Third week Isla Cristina: winter *carnival* in coastal town. Festivities include *Entierro de las Sardina* – the burial of the sardine.

Last week Cádiz: perhaps the best carnival in Spain and certainly the oldest, with parades, masquerades, music and fireworks in abundance.

March

Easter week Sevilla: sees the most important *Semana Santa*: celebrations, with over 100 processions, broken by the singing of *saetas* (sacred laments).
Córdoba: the city's 26 processions are perhaps the most emotionally charged of all, making their way around the streets of the Great Mosque.
Málaga, Granada, Úbeda: also put on major celebrations.

April

Last week Sevilla: the capital's *Feria*, originally a horse-fair, has now grown into the greatest festival of Andalucía. Costumed parades of the gentry in fine carriages, lots of flamenco, bullfights, and drinking.

Last week Andújar (Jaén): hosts the *Romería de la Virgen de la Cabeza*, a pilgrimage from all over Andalucía that culminates in the procession to the sanctuary in the nearby Sierra Morena.

End of month Jerez: Horse Fair with equestrian events and sherry-tasting.

May

First week Almería: Peña de Taranto Cultural Week. The foremost flamenco singers meet here every year for this prestigious contest.
Navas de San Juan (north of Úbeda): in honour of *Nuestra Señora de la Estrella*, one of the most important pilgrimages in Jaén. During the night, the popular *mayos* are sung in front of the church.

First Friday Jaca: re-enacts the victory over the Moors by local women.

First week Jerez de la Frontera: much like the *Feria* in Sevilla.
Granada: *El Día de la Cruz*, where large crosses made of flowers are set up throughout the city.

Second week Córdoba: every third year the *Concurso Nacional de Arte Flamenco* takes place, with over 100 singers, guitar players and dancers.

Mid-May Marbella: if you thought this town was just for tourists, come and take part in the Marbella *Feria de San Bernabé*, a five-day extravaganza with the local population out in force.

Pentecost El Rocío (Huelva): the biggest *romería* in all Spain. Pilgrims converge on this tiny spot in Las Marismas, south of Sevilla, in gaily decorated wagons for a week of wild carrying-on. The religious aspect is strictly a secondary part of the celebrations.

Last week Sanlúcar de Barrameda: the *Manzanilla* wine fair, where vast quantities of fried fish and shellfish are consumed, helped down by equally copious amounts of *Manzanilla*; dancing, singing and sporting events are also held.

End of month Zahara de la Sierra (Cádiz): sees four days of spectacular festivities begin on the Thursday after Trinity Sunday, celebrating *Corpus Christi*.

or driving covered wagons full of picnic supplies. Music, dancing, food, wine and fireworks are all necessary ingredients of a proper fiesta, while the bigger ones often include bullfights, funfairs, circuses and competitions. *Semana Santa* (Holy Week) is a major tourist event, especially in Sevilla. The processions of *pasos* (ornate floats depicting scenes from the Passion) carried in a slow march to lugubrious tuba music, and accompanied by children and men decked out in costumes later copied by the Ku Klux Klan, are worth fighting the crowds to see. And while a certain amount of merry-making goes on after dark, the real revelry takes place after Easter, in the unmissable April *feria*. Fiestas or *ferias* are incredibly important to Andalucíans, no matter what the cost in money and lost

June

Second week Mojácar: Moorish and Christian troops re-enact the surrender of the town to the Christian army at Mojácar's annual two-day fiesta.

Mid-month Granada: start of the month-long *Festival Internacional de Música y Danza*, which attracts big names from around the world and includes classical music, jazz and ballet; flamenco competitions are also held in odd-numbered years.

Third week Alhaurín de la Torre (Málaga): fair and festival in honour of the patron San Juan; entertainment includes a parade of giant figures and the *torre del cante*, one of the best flamenco gatherings in the region.

July

First Sunday Córdoba: International Guitar Festival – classical, flamenco and Latino.

16 Málaga: *Virgen del Carmen* – decorated boats with firework displays.

Last two weeks Lebrija: flamenco festival. La Línea: summer fair.

End of month Almería: festival, including numerous jazz concerts.

August

3 Huelva: *Colombinas* – bullfights and other sporting events.

5 Trevélez (Granada): has a midnight pilgrimage up Mulhacén, Spain's highest mountain, so that pilgrims arrive exhausted but in time for prayers at midday.

First two weeks Ronda: Pedro Romero festival – bullfights, equestrian parades, folk groups.

15 Competa: wine festival.

15–16 Vejer (Cádiz): Assumption of the Virgin and San Roque festivities, with flamenco.

Mid-month Málaga: its *feria* is gaining a reputation as one of the best, with a week of concerts, bullfights, dancing and singing.

Last week Sanlúcar de Barrameda (Cádiz): exaltation of the Río Guadalquivir and major flamenco events.
Toro: *Fiesta de San Agustín*, with bulls and a 'fountain of wine'.

September

First week Jerez: has a *Vendimia* wine festival.

Second week Alájar (Huelva): As well as many other places in the region, Alájar celebrates the *Nativity of the Virgin*. Far livelier and more popular than most pilgrimages; includes carriages and riders dressed in typical Andalucían costumes.
Ronda: puts on an 18th-century-style bullfight in its historic ring.
Chipiona: flamenco, bull-running, bullfights.

Turn of month Úbeda: fair with stalls and bullfights.

October

Second week Fuengirola: *Feria del Rosario*.

Third week Jaén: festival of San Lucás, bullfights, cultural and sporting events.

December

First week Martos (Jaén): Fiesta de la Aceituna. Annual four-day olive festival celebrating the olive in all its glory.

Gibraltar Calendar

January 5 Three Kings Cavalcade.
April–June Gibraltar Festival.
October 21 Trafalgar Day.
Nov–Dec Drama Festival.

For a comprehensive guide to Andalucía's *ferias*, festivals, pageants, carnivals and cultural events, get hold of a copy of the excellent and free booklet, *52 and a half weeks*, available from most local tourist offices.

sleep; they are a celebration of being alive in a society constantly aware of the inevitability of death. Dates for most festivals tend to be fluid, flowing towards the nearest weekend; if the actual date falls on a Thursday or a Tuesday, Spaniards 'bridge' the fiesta with the weekend to create a four-day whoopee. Check dates at the tourist office in advance.

Geography

Andalucía covers the southern fifth of the **Iberian peninsula,** occupying an expanse equivalent to slightly more than half the area of Portugal. Its natural border to the north is the rugged Sierra Morena range; the wild Atlantic batters its western shores and the timid Mediterranean laps its southern coast. The **Sierra Morena** range, although reaching barely 1,200m (4,000ft), was for a long time a deterrent to northern invaders. The only natural interruption is the Pass of Despeñaperros, or the 'gateway to Andalucía'. Numerous early travellers spoke with awe of the first time they traversed this pine-clad gorge; the frontier that separated 'the land of men from the land of gods'. Arriving in Andalucía at this point provides a strong contrast indeed from the barren plains of La Mancha to the north. These peaks, rich in minerals, sweep down to the fertile **Guadalquivir plain**, widening towards the western coast to form broad salt marshes and mud flats – including the Coto Doñana National Park, one of the largest bird sanctuaries in Europe. From here, the coast as far as the Portuguese border is virtually one long sandy beach, with a hinterland of undulating farming terrain and the gentle mountains of Huelva province.

South of the Guadalquivir valley the land rises again to form the craggy **Serranía de Ronda** mountain range, home to bandits and smugglers for centuries; the terrain then descends sharply to meet the balmy palm-lined shores of the Mediterranean, with Tarifa, the furthest south you can go on mainland Europe, and a mere 12km (7½miles) from the African coast, and Gibraltar, that geological oddity of a rock, whose outline resembles one of the sentinel lions on guard at the foot of Nelson's column in London. From the Serranía de Ronda the land dips and rises eastwards till it joins the snow-capped **Sierra Nevada**, the highest peaks on mainland Spain, below which lie long beaches, tiny coves and crystal-clear water.

Dry as it is, Andalucía when properly tended has been the garden of Spain. The soil in most areas, *argiles de montmorillonite*, holds water like a sponge. The Romans first discovered how to irrigate it; the Moors perfected the system, and also introduced the palm and such crops as cotton, rice, oranges and sugar. Today most of the inhabitants of the region live in cities – it's traditionally one of the most urbanized regions in Europe – but its farmers have discovered the modern delights of tractors and of owning their own land. Unless the Habsburgs or the Francoists come back, the region will have no excuse for not making a good living. Between the towns, spaces seem vast and empty, with endless hillsides of olives, vineyards, wheat and sunflowers. Come in the spring, when the almond trees are in blossom, the oranges turn orange and wild flowers surge up along the roadsides – providing the unforgettable splash of colour that characterizes Andalucía and its warm, vibrant people.

Health and Insurance

There is a standard agreement for citizens of EU countries, entitling them to a certain amount of free medical care, but it's not straightforward. You must complete all the necessary paperwork before you go to Spain, and allow a couple of months to make sure it comes through in time. Ask for a leaflet entitled *Before You Go* from the Department of Health and fill out form E111 (available from post offices). On arrival in Spain you must take it to the local office of the *Instituto Nacional de Seguridad Social* (INSS), where you'll be issued with a Spanish medical card and some vouchers enabling you to claim free treatment from an INSS doctor. If you have a particular diet or need special treatment then obtain a letter from your doctor and get it translated into Spanish before you go. In an emergency, ask to be taken to the nearest *hospital de la seguridad social*. Before resorting to a *médico* (doctor) and his €30 fee (ask at the tourist office for a list of English-speaking doctors), go to a pharmacy and tell them your woes. Spanish *farmacéuticos* are highly skilled, and if there's a prescription medicine that you know will cure you, they'll often supply it without a doctor's note. (The newspaper *Sur* lists *farmacias* in large cities that stay open all night and every pharmacy displays a duty roster outside so you can locate one nearby which is open.)

No **inoculations** are required to enter Spain, though it never hurts to check that your tetanus jab is up to date, as well as some of the more exotic inoculations (typhoid, cholera and gamma globulin) if you want to venture on into Morocco.

The **tap water** is safe to drink in Spain, but of horrendously poor quality after periods of drought. At the slightest twinge of queasiness, switch to the bottled stuff.

Insurance

You may want to consider travel insurance, available through most travel agents. For a small monthly charge, not only is your health insured, but your bags and money as well. Some will even refund a missed charter flight if you're too ill to catch it.

Many English and English-speaking doctors now have arrangements with European insurance companies and send their account directly to the company without you, the patient, having to fork out. But whether you pay on the spot or not, be sure to save all doctors' bills, pharmacy receipts and police documents (if you're reporting a theft).

Left Luggage

Since terrorists stopped leaving bombs in rail stations, RENFE has started to reintroduce *consignas*, or left-luggage facilities; you'll have about an even chance of finding one in a bus station or small bus company office, and sometimes bars near train or bus stations are willing to let you leave your bags. But don't rely on it.

Maps

Cartography has been an art in Spain since the 12th-century Catalans charted their Mediterranean empire in Europe's first great school of map-making. The tourist offices hand out beautifully detailed maps of every town; ask for their *Mapa de Comunicaciones*, an excellent general map of the country. The best large-scale maps are produced by *Almax Editores*. Topographical maps for hikers and mountaineers can be obtained directly from Instituto Geográfico Nacional (IGN), C/General Ibáñez de Ibero 3, Madrid, **t** 91 533 31 21, *www.oan.es*; Servicio Geográfico Ejército (SGE), C/Dario Gazapo, Madrid, **t** 91 711 50 43, *www.ejercito.mde.es/publicaciones/sge*, or from bookshops, including the Librería Quera, C/Petritxol 2, Barcelona, **t** 93 318 07 43, *www.llibreriaquera.com*. If you can't wait until you get to Spain, specialist shops include Stanfords, 12 Long Acre, London WC2, **t** (020) 7836 1321, or 39 Spring Gardens, Manchester **t** (0161) 831 0250 (or *www.stanfords.co.uk*). In the USA try The Traveler's Choice Bookstore, 111 Greene St, New York, NY, **t** (212) 941 1535.

Media

The left-leaning *El País* is Spain's biggest and best national **newspaper**, closely followed in the circulation stakes by *El Mundo*, a centre-right broadsheet. Circulation for both is painfully low; Spaniards just don't read newspapers and television listing magazines and newspapers devoted exclusively to football are consistently the best-sellers.

Both papers have weekly arts and entertainment supplements. *El País* has the best regional **film** listings, indicating where you can see some great films subtitled instead of dubbed (look out for *versión original* or its abbreviation 'vo'). English films are occasionally shown on the Costa del Sol and dozens of shops rent English-language video releases. Films are cheap and Spaniards are great cinema-goers; there are lots of inexpensive outdoor movie theatres in the summer. Hollywood hearthrob Antonio Banderas is a native *malagueño*; his occasional visits to the Costa del Sol are greeted with a media frenzy.

Major British papers are available in all tourist areas and big cities and the *New York Herald Tribune* (which has a small English-language supplement from *El País*), the *Wall Street Journal*, and *USA Today* are readily available wherever Americans go. Most hit the newsstands a day late; issues of *Time* and *Newsweek* often hang about for a while.

There are also publications in English on the Costa del Sol, notably *Sur in English*, a surprisingly high-quality English-language round-up of the Málaga paper with news, good features, and a riveting classified ads section; *Costa del Sol News*, with more of the same; *Absolute Marbella* and *Essential Marbella*, two free glossy monthly magazines; and *The Reporter*, another free monthly magazine with sometimes controversial features. All British papers are flown daily to **Gibraltar**.

Money

Spain's official currency is the euro. Exchange rates vary, but until any drastic changes occur £1 is roughly €1.60 and $1 equivalent to about €0.95. Spain's city centres seem to have a bank on every street corner, and most of them will exchange money; look for the *cambio* or *exchange* signs and the little flags. There is a slight difference in the rates, though usually not enough to make shopping around worthwhile. Beware exchange offices, as they can charge a hefty commission on all transactions. You can often change money at travel agencies, hotels, restaurants or the big department stores. Most big supermarkets tend to have *telebancos* or automatic tellers.

Traveller's cheques, if they are from one of the major companies, will pass at most bank exchanges. Wiring money from overseas entails no special difficulties; just give yourself two weeks to be on the safe side, and work through one of the larger institutions (Banco Central, Banco de Bilbao, Banco Español de Crédito, Banco Hispano Americano, Banco de Santander, Banco de Vizcaya). All transactions have to go through Madrid. **Credit cards** will always be helpful in towns, rarely in the country. Few museums or monuments accept credit cards. Direct debit cards are also useful ways of obtaining money, though you should check with your bank before leaving to ensure your card can be used in Spain. But do not rely on a hole-in-the-wall machine as your only source of cash; if, for whatever reason, the machine swallows your card, it usually takes 10 days to retrieve it.

Money in Gibraltar

In Gibraltar you can use local currency, UK sterling or euros, though you'll lose a bit on the exchange rate with euros. Spanish banks in Gibraltar tend to give a better rate of exchange from sterling to euros.

National Parks

Among the parks and reserves in the Andalucían area are:

Parque Nacional Coto Doñana
Reserva Nacional de Sierra de Tejeda
Reserva Nacional de Cortes de la Frontera
Coto Nacional de la Pata del Caballo
Parque de Cabo de Gata-Níjar
Parque de la Bahía de Cádiz
Parque Natural de los Alcornocales
Parque Natural de Acantilado y Pinar de Barbate
Parque Natural de las Sierras Subbéticas de Córdoba
Parque Natural de Sierra Nevada
Laguna de la Fuente de Piedra

See also 'Wildlife Reserves', pp.99–100, and in **Topics**, 'Andalucían Wildlife', pp.62–4.

Opening Hours

Banks

Most banks are open Mon–Thurs 8.30–2.30, Fri 8.30–2 and Sat in winter 8.30–1.

Churches

The less important churches are often closed. Some cities probably have more churches than faithful communicants, and many are unused. If you're determined to see one, it will never be hard to find the *sacristán* or caretaker. Usually they live close by, and would be glad to show you around for a tip. Don't be surprised when cathedrals and famous churches charge for admission – just consider the costs of upkeep.

Shops and museums

Shops usually open from 10am. Spaniards take their main meal at 2pm and, except in the larger cities, most shops shut down for 2–3 hours in the afternoon, usually from 1pm or 2pm. In the south, where it's hotter, the siesta can last from 1pm to 5pm. In the evening most establishments stay open until 7pm or 8pm, or later still in tourist resorts.

Although their opening times have become more chaotic lately, major **museums** and historical sites tend to follow shop hours, but are shorter in the winter months, nearly all close on Mondays. We have tried to list the hours for the important sights. Seldom-visited ones have a raffish disregard for their official hours, or open only when the mood strikes them. Don't be discouraged; bang on doors and ask around.

We haven't bothered to list admission prices for all museums and sites. Usually the sum is trivial and often fluctuating – hardly anything will cost more than €3, usually much less; EU nationals are admitted free to many monuments. The Alhambra in Granada, La Mezquita in Córdoba and La Giralda in Sevilla are the most notable exceptions.

Opening Hours in Gibraltar

Shops in Gibraltar are generally open 9–6 on weekdays, and 9–1 on Saturdays; banks are open 9–3.30 weekdays only. Most sights remain open on Saturday afternoons, which can be a quiet time to visit.

Photography

Film is quite expensive everywhere; so is developing it, but in any city there will be plenty of places – many in opticians' shops (*ópticas*) or big department stores – where you can get processing done in a hurry.

Serious photographers must give some consideration to the strong sunlight and high reflectivity of surfaces (pavements and buildings) in towns. If you're there during the summer use ASA100 film.

Police Business

Crime is not really a big problem in Spain and Spaniards talk about it perhaps more than is warranted. Pickpocketing and robbing parked cars are the specialities; in Sevilla they like to take the whole car. The big cities are the places where you should be careful, especially Málaga and Sevilla. Crime is also spreading to the tourist areas, particularly the Costa del Sol. Even on the Costa, though, you're probably safer in Spain than you would be at home; the crime rate is roughly a quarter of that in Britain. Note that in Spain less than 8 grams of cannabis is legal; buying and selling it, however, is not. And anything else may easily earn you the traditional 'six years and a day'.

There are several species of **police**, and their authority varies with the area. Franco's old goon squads, the *Policía Armada*, have been reformed and relatively demilitarized into the *Policía Nacional*, whom the Spaniards call 'chocolate drops' for their brown uniforms; their duties largely consist of driving around in cars and drinking coffee. They are, however, more highly thought of than the *Policía Armada*, and their popularity increased when their commander, Lt General José Antonio Sáenz de Santa María, ordered his men to surround the Cortes to foil Tejero's attempted coup in 1981, thereby proving that he and his *Policía Nacional* were strongly on the side of the newly born democracy. The *Policía Municipal* in some towns do crime control, while in others they simply direct traffic.

Mostly in rural areas, there's the *Guardia Civil*, with green uniforms, but no longer do they don the black patent-leather tricorn hats. The 'poison dwarfs of Spain', as Laurie Lee called them, may well be one of the most efficient police forces in the world, but after a century and a half of upholding a sick social order in the volatile countryside, they have few friends. They too have been reformed; now they're most conspicuous as a highway patrol, assisting motorists and handing out tickets (ignoring 'no passing' zones is the best way to get one). Most traffic violations are payable on the spot; the traffic cops have a reputation for upright honesty.

Police Business in Gibraltar

Gibraltar has no serious crime to speak of, and given its, albeit diminishing, military status, security is tight.

Post Offices

Every city, regardless of size, seems to have one post office (*correos*) and no more. It will always be crowded, but unless you have packages to mail, you may not ever need to visit one. Most tobacconists sell stamps (*sellos*) and they'll usually know the correct postage for whatever you're sending. The standard charge for sending a letter is €0.50 (European Union) and €0.76 (North America, up to 20 grammes). Send everything air mail (*por avión*) and don't send postcards unless you don't care when they arrive. Mailboxes are bright yellow and scarce. The post offices also handle telegrams, which normally take 4hrs to arrive within Europe but are very expensive. There is also, of course, the *poste restante* (general delivery). In Spain this is called *lista de correos*, and it is as chancy as anywhere else. Don't confuse post offices with the *Caja Postal*, the postal savings banks, which look just like them. More information from *www.correos.es* (in Spanish only).

Post Offices in Gibraltar

Post offices in Gibraltar are open 9.30–6; mail sent from here in theory arrives much faster than from Spain, but don't rely on it.

Public Holidays

The Spaniards, like the Italians, try to have as many public holidays as possible. And everything closes. The big holidays, celebrated throughout Spain, are *Corpus Christi* in late May, *Semana Santa* during the week before Easter, *Asunción* on 15 August and *Día de Santiago* on 25 July, celebrating Spain's patron, Saint James.

No matter where you are, there are bound to be fireworks or processions on these dates, especially for *Semana Santa* and *Corpus Christi*. But be aware that every region, town, and village has at least one of its own holidays as well (*see* 'Festivals' above).

Public Holidays in Spain

1 Jan Año Nuevo (New Year's Day)
6 Jan Epifanía (Epiphany)
March/April Viernes Santo (Good Friday), Domingo de la Resurreccíon (Easter Sunday)
1 May Día del Trabajo (Labour Day)
May/June Corpus Christi
25 July Día de Santiago (St James's Day)
15 Aug Asunción (Assumption)
12 Oct Día de la Hispanidad (National Day)
1 Nov Todos los Santos (All Saints' Day)
6 Dec Día de la Constitución (Constitution Day)
8 Dec Inmaculada Concepción (The Immaculate Conception)
25 Dec Navidad (Christmas Day)

Public Holidays in Gibraltar

1 Jan New Year's Day
Mid-March Commonwealth Day
March/April Good Friday and Easter Monday
1 May May Day
May Spring Bank Holiday (last Monday of month)
Mid-June The Queen's Birthday
Aug August Bank Holiday (last Monday of month)
12 Sept Gibraltar Day
25 Dec Christmas Day
26 Dec Boxing Day

Shopping

There are some delightful tacky tourist wares – Toledo 'daggers', plastic bulls and flamenco dolls *ad nauseam*. There are also some good buys to be had, for instance the high-quality **leather goods** from Córdoba and the town of Ubrique, which has been producing leatherwork since Roman times. Moorish craftsmen later had a major influence on the method of treating the cured skin for export. But, though the quality is good, the design seldom compares with its Italian counterpart. While Córdoba is better known for its ornate embossed leather for furniture decoration and **filigree jewellery**, Ubrique specializes in handmade items such as diaries, suitcases, bags and wallets. If you want an everlasting memory of Andalucía, have your boots made to measure in Valverde del Camino, Huelva province – guaranteed to last a lifetime. **Ceramic** plates, pottery and colourful *azulejo* tiles are made all over Andalucía; the quality varies enormously, from the shoddy factory-made products adorning tourist shop shelves, to the sophisticated **ceramic ware** you will find in the Triana district of Sevilla. Granada is well known for its **inlaid wood** *taracea* work (chests, chessboards and music boxes), although these can be rather crudely produced. Spanish **woven goods** are reasonably priced; Sevilla produces exquisite *mantillas* and embroidered shawls, and is the centre for the extraordinary designs that adorn the bullfighter's costume. In the Alpujarras a concentrated effort is being made to revive old skills, using the wooden loom particularly, to produce the typical **woollen blankets** and **rugs** for which this area has long been known – a fascinating mixture of ancient Christian and Arab designs. Brightly coloured handwoven blankets are the claim to fame of Grazalema, a village less than 20km (12 miles) to the west of Ronda. In the province of Almería, the village of Níjar produces colourful *jarapas* – woven blankets and mats. To encourage the nation's craftsmen, the government has organized a kind of co-operative, *Artespaña*, with various outlets selling their work. In Andalucía there is one at C/Ramón Areces, s/n, Marbella, **t** 95 290 6771. More information from *www.artespana.com*.

The major **department store** chain in Spain, El Corte Inglés, often has a good selection of crafts and will ship items home for you. You can also get excellent bargains at the roving **weekly markets**, where Spaniards do much of their shopping. Local tourist offices will have details. Good-quality **antiques** can occasionally be picked up at a ***rastro*** (flea market), but they aren't the great finds they once were – Spaniards have learned what they're worth and charge accordingly. Guitars, mandolins and bagpipes, fine wooden furniture and Goya tapestries are some of the bulky, more expensive items you may want to ship home. EU citizens are not entitled to tax refunds.

Sports and Activities

Bars and **cafés** collect much of the Spaniards' leisure time. They are wonderful institutions, where you can eat breakfast or linger over a glass of beer until four in the morning; in any of them you could see an old sailor delicately sipping his camomile tea next to a young mother, baby under her arm, stopping by for a beer break during her shopping. Some have music – jazz, rock or flamenco; some have great snacks, or tapas, some have games or pinball machines. Every Spaniard is a gambler; there seem to be an infinite number of lotteries run by the State (the *Lotería Deportiva*), for the blind (ONCE), the Red Cross or the Church; there's at least one bingo-hall in every town and there are **casinos** in all major resorts. Every bar has a slot machine, doling out electronic versions of **La Cucaracha** whenever it gets lonely.

Discos and **night clubs** are easily found in the big cities and tourist spots; most are expensive. Ask around for the favourites. Watch out for posters for **concerts, ballets**, and especially for **circuses**. The little travelling Spanish troupes with their family acts, tents, tinsel and names like 'The National Circus of Japan' will charm you; they often gravitate to the major fiestas throughout the summer.

Football has pride of place in the Spanish heart, while **bullfighting** (*see* **Topics**, pp.52–3) and cycling vie for second place; all are shown regularly on television, which, despite a heavy fare of dubbed American shows, everyone is inordinately fond of watching. Both channels are state-run, but with satellite dishes outnumbering *bodegas*, who watches them anyway? Certainly not the expat coastal residents, who tune in to Sky, satellite TV in nine languages, and even the fascinatingly awful Gibraltar TV network.

Gibraltar has a number of sports clubs and associations, many of them private. For further information ask at the tourist office.

Cycling

Cycling is taken extremely seriously in Spain and you don't often see people using a bike as a form of transport. Instead, Lycra-clad enthusiasts pedal furiously up the steepest of hills, no doubt trying to reach the standards set by Miguel Indurain, who was the Spanish winner of the *Tour de France* for three years running. If you do want to bring your own **bicycle** to Spain, you can make arrangements by ferry or train; by air, you'll almost always have to dismantle it to some extent and pack it in some kind of crate. Each airline seems to have its own policy. The south of Spain would be suicide to bike through in summer, though all right in winter. **Information**: call the Cycling Federation of Andalucía, Ferraz 16, 28008 Madrid, **t** 91 542 04 21, **f** 91 542 03 41.

Fishing and Hunting

Fishing and hunting are long-standing Spanish obsessions, and you'll need to get a licence for both. Freshwater fishing permits (*permisos de pesca*) are issued from the Delegación Agencia Medio Ambiente (AMA), which has an office in each of the the provincial capital cities. A maritime recreational fishing licence (1st and 3rd Class) is required for fishing from the shore or from a boat near the coast; get it from the Delegación Provincial de la Conserjeria de Agricultura y Pesca, which also has an office in each provincial capital city. **Information:** write to the Spanish Fishing Federation, Navas de Tolosa 3, 28013 Madrid, **t/f** 91 532 83 52; or to the Instituto Andaluz de Reforma Agraria de la Junta de Andalucía, Avenida República Argentina 25, Sevilla, **t** 95 427 00 73. You can also get information from the Spanish Agricultural Office in London **t** (020) 7235 50 05. The Spanish tourist office provides a useful map of fishing in Spain, and various information leaflets.

You may bring sporting guns to Spain, but you must declare them on arrival and present a valid firearms certificate with a Spanish translation bearing a consulate stamp. Hunters (boar and deer are the big game, with quail, hare, partridges and pigeons, and ducks and geese along the coasts in the winter) are obliged to get a licence as well (*permiso de caza*) from the local autonomous community, presenting their passports and record of insurance coverage. **Information**: the Spanish tourist office, or the Spanish Hunting Federation, C/Francos Rodríguez 70, 28039 Madrid, **t** 91 311 14 11, **f** 91 450 66 08.

Football

Soccer is Spain's most popular sport, and the Spanish Primera is possibly the best football league in the world. Barcelona, Real Madrid and Valencia are the best teams to watch; fans of Málaga, Sevilla and Real Betis will argue over whose team is the best in Andalucía. The season lasts from September to June, and matches are usually trouble-free. **Information**: Spanish Football Federation, Alberto Bosch 13, 28014 Madrid, **t** 91 420 13 62, **f** 91 420 20 94, *www.rfef.es*.

Golf

English settlers built Spain's first golf course at the Río Tinto mines in the 19th century, and since the advent of Severiano Ballesteros Spaniards, too, have gone nuts for the game. The warm, sunny winters, combined with greens of international tournament standard, attract golfing enthusiasts from all over the world throughout the year. Any real-estate agent on the coast hoping to sell villas to foreigners, especially Scandinavians and the latest newcomers, the Russians, stands little chance of closing a deal unless his property is within 5mins of a golf course – or preferably *on* a golf course. It's all the rage in the Costa del Sol; the Marbella area alone boasts over two dozen fine courses, some so 'exclusive' that if you manage to get in you could find yourself teeing off next to Sean Connery. On the other hand, there is an abundance of humbler clubs where a few euros will get you a round. Most places hire out clubs. Inland you'll find courses around the big cities and, at the last count, there were 60 courses along the Costa del Sol, over a third of all golf courses in Spain. Many hotels cater specifically for the golfer and there are numerous specialist tour operators (*see* **Travel**, pp.77–8). **Information**: the Spanish tourist office, or the Royal Spanish Golf Federation, Capitán Haya 9–5, 28020 Madrid, **t** 91 555 26 82.

Hiking and Mountaineering

Thousands of hikers and mountaineers are attracted to the paths in the Sierra Nevada above Granada and the Serranía de Ronda. The tourist office or the Spanish Mountaineering Federation provide a list of *refugios*, which offer mountain shelter in many places. Some are well equipped and can supply food. Most, however, do not, so take your own sleeping bags, cooking equipment and food with you. Hiking boots are essential, as is a detailed map of the area, issued by the Instituto Geográfico Nacional, or the Servicio Geográfico Ejército (*see* 'Maps', p.89). **Information**: Spanish Mountaineering Federation, Alberto Aguilera 3, 28015 Madrid, **t** 91 445 13 82, **f** 91 445 14 38, or from the Federación Andaluza de Montanismo, C/Ant. Raíz 10, Málaga, **t** 952 39 90 04.

Horse Racing

Horse racing is centred in Madrid, but there is a winter season at the Pineda racecourse in Sevilla. **Information**: Spanish Horse Racing Federation, Plaza Marqués de Salamanca 2, 28006 Madrid, **t** 91 577 78 92, **f** 91 575 07 70, *www.rfhe.com*.

Horse Riding

Andalucía has some perfect terrain for riding, whether exploring the Serranía de Ronda, the smugglers' trails around Cádiz, or following in the hoofprints of Sir John Betjeman's wife, Penelope Chetwode, who experienced one bosom-heaving emotion after another as she boldly trekked through the Sierra Nevada on horseback in the 1960s, a journey so delightfully recorded in her journal *Two Middle Aged Ladies in Andalucía*. There are a number of stables offering organized treks.

Pelota

Pelota, although a Basque game by origin, has a following in Andalucía. This is a fast, thrilling game, where contestants wearing long basket-like gloves propel a hard ball with great force at high walls; rather like squash. The fast action on the *jai-alai* court is matched by the wagering frenzy of the spectators. **Information**: Spanish Pelota Foundation, Los Madrazos 11, 28014 Madrid, **t** 91 521 42 99, **f** 91 532 38 79.

Skiing

Many of the mountains popular with hikers at other times of the year attract ski crowds in the winter. An hour from Granada you can be among the Iberian Peninsula's highest peaks and Europe's southernmost ski resorts, whose après-ski life is steadily improving. In Spain, it's easy to arrange all-inclusive ski packages through a travel agent. A typical deal would include six nights' accommodation in a three- or four-star hotel with half board and unlimited use of ski lift for the week, at a cost of around €600. With instruction fees, count on €60–80 extra per week. **Information**: write to the tourist office or the Spanish Winter Sports Federation, C/Infanta María Teresa 14, 28016 Madrid, **t** 91 344 09 44.

Tennis

There is just as much fervour for tennis as for golf, inspired by international champion Arantxa Sánchez Vicario, and more recently by Conchita Martínez, both of whom are revered in their native Spain. Again, the best clubs are to be found on the coast, and every resort hotel has its own courts; municipal ones are rare or hard to get to. The most famous tennis school in Andalucía lies just behind Fuengirola on the Mijas road, and was owned by Australian Lew Hoad, the Wimbledon favourite of the 1950s and 1960s, until his death in 1994. If you're looking for a game in Marbella, call Los Monteros Tennis Club, **t** 95 277 17 00. **Information**: Royal Spanish Tennis Federation, Avda Diagonal 618, 08021 Barcelona, **t** 93 201 08 44.

Water Sports

Water sports are the most popular activities in the summer. You can rent a windsurf and learn how to use it at almost any resort; *aficionados* head for Tarifa, Europe's windsurfing centre and the continent's southernmost tip. If you bring your own boat, get the tourist office's literature on marinas before setting out. You have a choice of 30 along the coasts of Andalucía. There's a full calendar of sailing events and races, as well as sailing schools and rentals. A number of reservoirs have also become quite popular for water sports. **Information**: write to the Royal Spanish Sailing Federation, Luis de Salazar 12, 28002 Madrid, **t** 91 519 50 08, **f** 91 416 45 04, *www.rfev.es*.

Underwater activists flock to the Almería coast in particular for its sparkling water and abundant marine life. **Information**: Spanish Sub-Aqua Federation, Santaló 15, 08021 Barcelona, **t** 93 200 67 69, **f** 93 241 16 80, *www.fedas.es*; or contact the Federación Española de Esquí Náutico, Sabino de Arana 30, 08028 Barcelona, **t** 93 330 89 03, **f** 93 330 99 57.

Telephones

There is now one **general emergency number** in Spain and Gibraltar: **t** 112.

Save for a few annoying quirks, Spain has one of the best and cheapest telephone **systems in Europe**, although it can be rather confusing to use. All local telephone numbers in Spain contain seven digits plus a code, which now must be dialled even from within a province. In Andalucía, this code is 95. Some phone boxes accept cards and coins, although coin-operated booths are getting harder to find and it's much more usual to use pre-paid Telefónica phone cards (available from tobacconists in denominations of 5, 10, 15 and 20 euros). Instructions for use are given in English.

Overseas calls from Spain are among the most expensive in Europe; calls to the UK can cost €1.50 a minute and to the USA substantially more. The cheapest way to call abroad is to find a *locutario*, a phone centre (there are usually several around bus and train stations). Otherwise, you can buy cheap pre-paid international calling cards with a scratch-off pin number, which are cheaper than Telefónica's rates. Expect to pay a big surcharge if you telephone from your hotel or any public place that does not have a coin slot. Cheap rate is from 10pm–8am Monday–Saturday and all day Sunday and public holidays.

For calls to Spain from the UK, dial 00 followed by the country code (34), the area code and the number. For international calls from Spain, dial 00, wait for the higher tone and then dial the country code (44 for the UK; 1 for the US and Canada). To telephone Gibraltar from Spain, dial 9567 (due to change to 8563) followed by the local five-digit number. (The country code for Gibraltar if you are calling from elsewhere is 350.) To telephone abroad from Gibraltar, dial 00 followed bythe country and area codes.

Toilets

Outside bus and train stations, public facilities are rare in Spain. On the other hand, every bar on every corner has a toilet. Don't feel uncomfortable using it without purchasing something – the Spaniards do it all the time. Just ask for *los servicios* (on signs they are sometimes referred to as *aseos*).

It has to be said that public lavatories and ones in private commercial establishments have improved tremendously over the last decade. Going to the loo in a marble cubicle at an airport or petrol station can be a delightful experience!

Tourist Information

After receiving millions of tourists each year for the last three decades, no country has more information offices, or more helpful ones, or more intelligent brochures and detailed maps. Every city will have an office, and about two-thirds of the time you'll find someone who speaks English. Sometimes they'll be less helpful in the big cities in the summer. More often, though, you'll be surprised at how well they know the details of accommodation and transportation. Many large cities also maintain **municipal tourist offices**, though they're not as well equipped as those run by the Ministry of Tourism, better known as **Turismo**. Hours for most offices are Monday to Friday, 9.30–1.30 and 4–7, open on Saturday mornings, closed on Sundays.

Spanish National Tourist Offices

Australia: 203 Castlereagh Street, PO Box A-685, Sydney, **t** (02) 264 7966, **f** (02) 267 5111.

Brazil: Escritorio Espanhol de Turismo, Rua Zequinha de Abreu 78, CEP 01250 São Paulo, **t** (11) 38 65 59 99.

Belgium: Rue Royale 97, 1000 Brussels, **t** (2) 280 19 26, **f** (2) 230 21 47.

Canada: 2 Bloor Street West, Toronto, Ontario, M4W 3E2, **t** (416) 961 31 31, **f** (416) 961 19 92.

France: 43 Rue Decamps, 75784 Paris Cedex 16 **t** 01 45 03 82 50, **f** 01 45 03 82 51.

Germany: Kurfürstendamm 180, 10707 Berlin, **t** (30) 882 6036, **f** (30) 882 6661.
Myliusstraße 14, 60323 Frankfurt, **t** (69) 72 50 33, **f** (69) 72 53 13.
Schuberterstraße 10, München, **t** (89) 530 74 60, **f** (89) 532 86 80.

Italy: Via del Mortaro 19, Interno 5, Roma 00187, **t** 06 678 3106, **f** 06 679 82 72.
Via Broletto 30, Milano 20121, **t** 02 72 00 46 17, **f** 02 72 00 43 18.

Netherlands: Laan Van Meerdervoor 8, AJ Den Haag, **t** (70) 346 59 00, **f** (70) 364 98 59.

UK: 22–23 Manchester Square, London W1M 5AP, **t** (020) 7486 8070, **f** (020) 7486 8034.

USA: Water Tower Place, Suite 915, East 845 North Michigan Avenue, Chicago, IL 60611, **t** (312) 642 1992, **f** (312) 642 9817. 8383 Wilshire Boulevard, Suite 960, Beverly Hills, CA 90211, **t** (213) 658 7188, **f** (213) 658 1061. 665 Fifth Avenue, New York, NY 10022, **t** (212) 759 8822, **f** (212) 980 8864.

Gibraltar Information Bureau

UK: 179 The Strand, London WC2R 1EH, **t** (020) 7836 0777.

Where to Stay

Hotels in Spain are still bargains – though, as with prices for other facilities, Spain is gradually catching up with the rest of western Europe. One thing you can still count on is a consistent level of quality and service; the Spanish government regulates hotels intelligently and closely. Room prices must be posted in the hotel lobbies and in the rooms, and if there's any problem you can ask for the complaints book, or *Libro de Reclamaciones*. No one ever writes anything in these; any written complaint must be passed on to the authorities immediately. Hotel keepers would usually rather correct the problem for you.

The prices given in this guide are for double rooms with bath (unless stated otherwise) but do not include VAT (IVA) charged at 7% on all hotel rooms. Prices for single rooms will average about 60 per cent of a double, while triples or an extra bed are around 35 per cent more. Within the price ranges shown (*see* box), the most expensive are likely to be in the big cities, while the cheapest places are always in provincial towns. On the whole, prices throughout Andalucía are surprisingly consistent. No government could resist the chance to insert a little bureaucratic confusion, and accommodation in Spain is classified in a complex system. Look out for the **blue plaques** next to the doors of all *hoteles, hostales*, etc., which identify the classification.

If you're travelling around a lot, a good investment would be the government publication *Guía de Hoteles*, a great fat book with every classified hotel and *hostal* in Spain (except the very cheap one-star *pensiones*), available in many bookshops, €9 The government also publishes similar guides to holiday flats (*apartamentos turísticos*), campsites and *casas rurales* (rural accommodation). Another useful guide is the big, fat *Guía de Hoteles y Restaurantes de España*, one of a series of guides published annually by *El País and Aguilar*, available from almost all bookshops. Local tourist information offices will have a complete accommodation list for their province, and some can be very helpful with finding a room when things are tight.

Accommodation Price Ranges

Prices listed here and elsewhere in the book are for a double room with bathroom.

luxury over €132
expensive €78–132
moderate €48–78
inexpensive €30–48
cheap under €30

Paradores

The government, in its plan to develop tourism in the 1950s, started this nationwide chain of classy hotels to draw some attention to little-visited areas. They restored old palaces, castles and monasteries for the purpose, furnished them with antiques and installed fine restaurants featuring local specialities. *Paradores* for many people are one of the best reasons for visiting Spain. Not all *paradores* are historical landmarks; in resort areas, they are as likely to be cleanly designed modern buildings, usually in a great location with a pool and some sports facilities. As their popularity has increased, so have their prices; in most cases both the rooms and the restaurant will be the most expensive in town. *Paradores* are classed as three- or four-star hotels, and their prices range from €60 in remote provincial towns to €150 and upwards for the most luxurious. Many offer out-of-season or weekend promotional rates (including fantastic 'youth rates' which can make a *parador* cheaper than a one-star hotel). If you can afford a *parador*, there is no better place to stay. We've mentioned most of them throughout this book.

Advance Booking

Spain: Head office, C/Requena 3, 28013, Madrid **t** 91 516 66 66, **f** 91 516 66 57.

UK: Keytel International, 402 Edgware Road, London W2 1ED, **t** (020) 7616 0300, **f** (020) 7616 0317.

USA: Marketing Ahead, 433 Fifth Avenue, New York, NY 10016, **t** 800 223 1356, **f** (212) 686 0271, *www.marketingahead.com*.

More information at *www.parador.es*. Look out for their special offers.

Hoteles

Hoteles (H) are rated with from one to five stars, according to the services they offer. These are the most expensive places, and even a one-star hotel will be a comfortable, middle-range establishment. *Hotel residencias* (HR) are the same, only without a restaurant. Many of the more expensive hotels have some rooms available at prices lower than those listed. They won't tell you, though; you'll have to ask. You can often get discounts in the off season but will be charged higher rates during festivals. These are supposedly regulated, but in practice hotel-keepers charge whatever they can get. If you want to attend these events, book as far in advance as possible.

Hostales and *Pensiones*

Hostales (Hs) and *pensiones* (P) are rated with from one to three stars. These are more modest places, often a floor in an apartment block; a three-star *hostal* is roughly equivalent to a one-star hotel. *Pensiones* may require full- or half-board; there aren't many of these establishments, only a few in resort areas. *Hostal residencias* (HsR), like hotel *residencias*, do not offer meals except breakfast, and not always that. Of course, *hostales* and *pensiones* with one or two stars will often have rooms without private baths at considerable savings. Be warned: cheap *hostales* in ports (such as Málaga, Cádiz and Algeciras) can be crummy and noisy beyond belief – as you lie unable to sleep, you can only marvel at the human body's ability to produce such a wealth of unidentifiable sounds, coming through the paper-thin walls of the next room.

Fondas, Casas de Huéspedes and *Camas*

The bottom of the scale is occupied by the *fonda* (F) and *casa de huéspedes* (CH), little different from a one-star *hostal*, though generally cheaper. Off the scale completely are hundreds of unclassified cheap places, usually rooms in an apartment or over a bar and identified only by a little sign reading *camas* (beds) or *habitaciones* (rooms). You can also ask in bars or at the tourist office for unidentified *casas particulares*, private houses with a room or two; in many villages these will be the best you can do, but they're usually clean – Spanish women are manic housekeepers. The best will be in small towns and villages, and around universities.

Occasionally you'll find a room over a bar, run by somebody's grandmother, that is nicer than a four-star hotel – complete with frilly pillows, lovely old furnishings, and a shrine to the Virgin Mary. The worst are inevitably found in industrial cities or dull modern ones. It always helps to see the room first. In cities, the best places to look are right in the centre, not around the bus and train stations. Most inexpensive establishments will ask you to pay a day in advance.

Alternative Accommodation

Youth hostels exist in Spain, but they're usually not worth the trouble. Most are open only in the summer; there are the usual inconveniences and silly rules, and often hostels are in out-of-the-way locations. You'll be better off with the inexpensive *hostales* and *fondas* – sometimes these are even cheaper than youth hostels – or ask at the local tourist office for rooms that might be available in **university dormitories**. If you fancy some peace and tranquillity, the national tourist office has a list of **monasteries** and **convents** that welcome guests. Accommodation starts at about €16 a night, meals are simple and guests may usually take part in the religious ceremonies.

Camping

Campsites are rated with from one to three stars, depending on their facilities, and in addition to the ones listed in the official government handbook there are always others, rather primitive, that are unlisted. On the whole camping is a good deal, and facilities in most first-class sites include shops, restaurants, bars, laundries, hot showers, first aid, swimming pools, telephones and, occasionally, tennis courts. Caravans and camper vans converge on the more developed sites, but if you just want to pitch your little tent or sleep out in some quiet field, ask around in the bars or at likely farms. Camping is forbidden in many forest areas because of fears of fire, as well as on the beaches (though you can often get close to some quieter shores if you're discreet). If you're doing some hiking, bring a sleeping bag and stay in the free ***refugios*** along the major trails.

Information: the government handbook *Guía de Campings* can be found in most bookstores and at the Spanish tourist office; further details can be obtained from the Camping and Caravan Club, Greenfields

House, Westwood Way, Coventry CV4 8JH, t 024 7669 4995, *www.campingandcaravanningclub.co.uk* (membership necessary £27.50 plus £5 joining fee). **Reservations** for sites can be made through Federación Española de Empresarios de Camping, C/San Bernardo, 97 99 Edidificio Colomina, 28015 Madrid, t 91 448 12 34, *www.fedcamping.com*.

Resort Accommodation

Almost everything along the coasts of Andalucía has been built in the last 25 years, and anonymous high-rise buildings abound. Lately the trend has turned towards low-rise 'villages' or *urbanizaciones* built around a pool, usually on or near the beach. We've tried to include places that stand out in some way, or which are good bargains for their rating. Resorts offer a choice of hotels in every price range, though the best bargains tend to be in the places where foreigners fear to tread, or at any rate tread less – the Costa de la Luz west of Cádiz, or the small resorts close to Almería.

If you intend to spend a couple of weeks on the Costa del Sol, your best bet is to book an all-inclusive package deal from the UK or USA. Most hotels in the big resorts cater for package tours, and may not even answer a request for an individual reservation during the peak season. The coast has some stylish hotels, particularly around Marbella and the up-market areas of the western Costa del Sol. However, all sorts of bargains are to be had, especially if you plan a long-term stay in winter, a practice often followed by cold pensioners from the north. Incidentally, all beaches in Spain are public, which sounds extremely politically correct but in fact is a mixed blessing.

Where to Stay in Gibraltar

Gibraltar doesn't have the same range of accommodation, and there are no official categories; the only guide to quality is price – unfortunately not an accurate guarantee of standards anywhere. Based on Spanish categories, most hotels would fall into the two- or three-star bracket, with one or two exceptions, but don't expect any bargains – £60 is about average for a double room with bath, and there's little cheaper than that unless you go on a package deal. There are no camping facilities in Gibraltar, but plenty on the Spanish side of the border, from where you can make a day-trip. Note that if you are travelling in a caravan (camper), you will not be allowed to take it in, as the streets are narrow and congested at the best of times. You can, of course, leave it on the Spanish side, but mind where you park – you could return to find it displaying a ticket, or clamped, or simply towed away.

Wildlife Reserves

There are over 20 important wildlife reserves in Andalucía – the coast, the wetlands behind it, the scrub deserts of Almería and the mountain slopes of the Sierra Nevada. They are given different names, depending on their importance. **Reservas Naturales** are usually small sites of specific scientific interest such as lagoons or copses. **Parques Naturales** are larger and permit traditional land use within their borders. **Parques Nacionales** are of international importance with restricted access and close control of human activities.

The Coast

Most famous and most spectacular of all is the **Coto Doñana**, on the Cadiz coast, southern Spain's only Parque Nacional. Though the terrain may appear flat and monotonous at first, it consists of a range of different and distinct habitats including cork oak forest, scrubland, swamp, raised flooded areas and reedy channels filled by the Guadalquivir as it reaches the coast. These are a haven for hundreds of species of native and migratory birds including the largest population of Spanish imperial eagles in the world. These share the wetlands with pardel lynx, wild boar and 50 other species of mammals, reptiles and amphibians.

Andalucía's other important wetland areas are both close to cities. The **Marismas de Odiel** near Huelva is home to 30 per cent of the European spoonbill population and in the winter, flocks of up to 2,000 flamingos. The **Bahía de Cadiz** also has abundant birdlife, important for breeding little terns, avocets and kentish plovers.

Other significant wildlife sites along the coast include the clifftop forests of the **Acantilado y Pinar de Barbate**, the beaches and flower-filled marshlands of **Los Lances** near Tarifa and the semi-desert of the **Cabo de Gata** peninsula east of Almería.

Inland

Inland from Tarifa lies **Los Alcornocales**, one of the largest cork oak forests in the world. Some of the Lusitanian and cork oaks here are over a thousand years old, and they form a tangle with wild olives and laurels. Golden eagles nest here, as do griffon vultures and eagle owls. Los Alcornocales borders on the **Parque Natural de la Sierra de Grazalema**, part of the Serranía de Ronda, the wettest place on the Iberian peninsula, proving that the rain in Spain definitely does not fall mainly on the plain. The plants and animals seem to love it. More than 1,300 species of vascular plant thrive here, including the pinsapo, a fir found only here, the endangered *Narcissus baeticus* daffodil, irises and 27 species of wild orchid.

The **Desierto de Las Tabernas**, made famous by Sergio Mendes, Clint Eastwood and Lee Van Cleef, is a little less lush but equally full of endemic rare plant life including the toadflax, the sea lavender, the crucifer and a variety of aromatic thymes. Reptiles love it here and if you are lucky you may see an ocellated lizard, Europe's largest, at up to a metre long.

The Sierras

Wolves still live in the eastern **Sierra Morena**, which is punctuated by a series of wildlife sites and *parques naturales*, from its beginnings on the Portuguese border right through to the **Sierra de Cazorla** in the east. The **Despeñaperros**, a kilometre-deep gorge that bisects it in northern Jaén, was once the only crossing point between Andalucía and the Spanish *meseta*.

The higher **Sierra Nevada Parque Natural** which peaks at 3,482m (11,420ft) is famous for its alpine flowers, which include 70 endemic species and its butterflies. Spanish ibex, rescued from the brink of extinction in the 1940s, also live here. They are seen most easily in the evening on the lower peaks. The lower slopes, known locally as '*zona erizo*' (hedgehog zone) are shrouded in prickly scrub, and below them the valleys of the Alpujarras are filled with birdsong, butterflies and semi-tropical fruits – even custard apples grow here.

Women Travellers

On the whole, the horror stories of sexual harassment in Spain are a thing of the past – unless you dress provocatively and hang out by the bus station after dark. All Spaniards seem to melt when they see blondes, so if you're fair you're in for a tougher go. Even Spanish women sunbathe topless these days at the international *costa* resorts, but do be discreet elsewhere, especially near small villages. Apart from the coast, it often tends to be the older men who comment on your appearance as a matter of course. Whether you can understand what is being said or not, best to ignore them.

Sevilla

09

Sevilla
Antiguo Hospital Provincial
Jardines del Guadalquivir
Puente de la Barqueta
Calle de Resolana
San Juan de Ribera
Monasterio de San Clemente
Calle Calatrava
Calle de la Feria
Basilica de la Macarena
Moorish Walls
Calle Muñoz León
Convento de Capuchinos
Avenida de la Cruz Roja
Avenida de Miraflores
Río Guadalquivir
Calle de Santa Clara
Monasterio Santa Clara
Calle de Relator
Calle de San Luis
Ronda Capuchinos
Monasterio de Santa María de las Cuevas
Calle del Torneo
Calle de San Vicente
C. Eslava
Calle de Jesus del Gran Poder
Alameda Hercules
San Lorenzo
San Luis
Juan Rabadán
Puente de la Cartuja
Calle del Amor de Dios
Castellar
Bustos Tavera
San Marcos
Calle de la Enladrillada
Calle del Sol
Calle de Baños
Palacio de las Dueñas
El Fontanal
Centro
Calle Regina
Calle Gerona
San Vicente
Convento de Santa Catalina
Plaza Duque Victoria
Plaza de la Encarnación
Plaza Ponce de León
Calle José Laguillo
Calle de Alfonso XII
Plaza San Pedro
Santa Justa Train Station
Calle Marqués de Paradas
Museo de Bellas Artes
Calle de Recaredo
Puente del Cachorro
Calle Las Sierpes
Plaza Cristo de Burgos
Calle de Alhóndiga
Calle Tetuan
La Magdalena
El Salvador
Casa de Pilatos
Calle Juan Antonio Cavestany
Calle de Arjona
San Pablo
San Ildefonso
Correo de Rey
San Esteban
Reyes Católicos
Ayuntamiento
Calle Zaragoza
Plaza Nueva
Bus Station
Argote de Molina
Calle de Luis Montoto
Santa María Blanca
Avenida de la Constitución
Santa María la Blanca
El Arenal
Santa Cruz
Aqueduct (ruin)
Calle de Adriano
Catedral La Giralda
Calle de Menéndez Pelayo
Triana
Puente de Isabel II
Plaza del Altozano
C. Demetrio de los Ríos
Paseo de Cristóbal Colon
Plaza de Toros de la Maestranza
Hospital de la Caridad
Alcázar
Jacinto
Archivo de Indias
Calle Betis
Santander
San Bernardo
Santa Ana
Puerta de Jerez
Jardines de Alcázar
Pages del Corro
Torre del Oro Museo Marítimo
Calle San Fernando
Bus Station
Av. Sanjurjo
Puente de San Telmo
Avenida de Roma
Universidad
Plaza de Cuba
Avenida de Carlos V
Av. del Cid
Palacio de San Telmo
Prado de San Sebastián
Calle de Enramadilla
Avenida de la República Argentina
Avenida de Portugal
Avenida de María Luisa
Capitanía General
Los Remedios
Plaza de España
Plaza República Dominicana
Calle de la Asunción
Puente del Generalísimo
Avenida de Borbolla
Virgen de Luján
Paseo de las Delicias
Avenida Santiago Montoto
Parque de María Luisa
Parque de los Remedios
Museum of Popular Art and Customs
Calle Felipe II
N
Archaeological Museum
Puente de Alfonso XIII
1 km
1/2 mile

Getting There

By Air

Sevilla has regular flights from Madrid and Barcelona. San Pablo airport is 12km east of the city, and the airport bus is run by Amarillos Tour and leaves from the Puerta de Jerez, with a stop at the Santa Justa station. Departures every 30mins between 6.45am and 23.30pm, less frequently at weekends. For airport **information** call **t** 95 444 90 00.

By Train

Estación de Santa Justa, in the surreally named Avenida Kansas City in the northeast of town, is the modern Expo showpiece. There are several trains daily to Madrid by AVE in 2hrs 15mins, and a daily *Talgo* to Barcelona. The central RENFE office is at C/Zaragoza 29, information and reservations **t** 902 24 02 02.

By Bus

There are two bus stations in Sevilla, one at Plaza de Armas, **information t** 95 490 80 40, and one at Prado de San Sebastián, **information t** 95 441 71 11. Buses for the western side of the peninsula, including Madrid, leave from Plaza de Armas. All buses for the eastern side of the country, including Barcelona, leave from Prado de San Sebastián. Information is available from the tourist office, or from the information office inside the bus stations.

Getting Around

The narrow, twisting streets of old Sevilla are a delight to stroll around, and most of the main sights are bunched within walking distance of each other.

By Bus

There is a good city bus service; among the most useful lines are buses C4 and C3, which circle the perimeter of the old city, and lines C1 and C2, which make a larger circle and encompass Triana, La Cartuja, the main train station (Estación de Santa Justa) and the bus station on Plaza de Armas. Night bus routes are prefaced with the letter A. The tourist information office has free bus maps with explanations in English, including a table called 'How to Get There', which makes working out the routes simpler. For information, call **t** 90 071 01 71; for lost property call **t** 95 455 72 22. Buy single tickets (85 cents) on the bus; 3- or 7-day tourist passes which offer unlimited travel for a set period are available at the Prado de San Sebastián, Plaza Nueva and Plaza Encarnación.

By Taxi

Taxis are everywhere and fairly inexpensive; if you do need to call one, try Radio Taxis **t** 95 458 00 00 or Tele Taxi **t** 95 462 22 22/ 95 462 14 61.

By Bicycle/Moped

Bicycles can be rented at BiciBike, C/Miguel de Mañara 11B, **t/f** 95 456 38 38, just behind the main tourist office, near the Reales Alcazares. Rent mopeds from Rentamoto, C/Padre Mendez Casariego 17, **t** 95 441 75 00, *www.rentamoto.com*.

By Tour

Sightseeing buses and river cruises depart from the Tower of Gold (Torre del Oro). Bus tours are offered by Sevilla Tour, **t** 902 10 10 81, *www.citysightseeing-spain.com* (includes a ride in an old-fashioned tram car), and Sevirama, **t** 95 456 06 93. River cruises are offered by Cruceros Turisticos Torre del Oro, **t** 95 421 13 96; Cruceros del Sur, **t** 95 456 16 72; and Buque El Patio, Paseo de Colón 11, **t** 95 421 38 36.

Tourist Information

The permanent tourist office is very helpful; it's near the cathedral at Avenida de la Constitución 21, **t** 95 422 14 04, **f** 95 422 97 53 (*open Mon–Sat 9–7, Sun and hols 10–2*). The municipal information centre is near the María Luisa Park, on Paseo de las Delicias 9, **t** 95 450 56 00, *www.turismo.sevilla.org*. There's also an information centre at the airport, **t** 95 444 91 28, and at Santa Julia station, **t** 95 453 76 26.

Internet and Telephones

Capitán Mouse, C/O'Donnell 3, 3rd floor, **t** 95 450 14 84.

Ciber Planet, C/Juan Ramón Jiménez 12, **t** 95 408 29 12.

El Cibercafé de Sevilla/Estación Café-Metro, C/Betis 29, **t** 95 434 14 01.
Cyber Seville, C/Pérez Galdós 1, **t** 95 422 75 75.

Post Office

The main post office is on Avenida de la Constitución 32, **t** 902 19 71 97.

Shopping

All the paraphernalia associated with Spanish fantasy, such as *mantillas*, castanets, wrought iron, *azulejo* tiles and embroidery, is available in Sevilla. **C/Cuna** is the best place to find flamenco paraphernalia, and several of the convents sell jams and confectionery. **Triana**, of course, is the place to find *azulejo* tiles and perfumed soaps. If you want to pick up a First Communion outfit or any kind of religious kitsch,there is an astonishing number of shops devoted to it around the **Plaza del San Salvador**.

If you want to look the part at Feria, deck yourself out at one of several equestrian shops, including **Jara y Sedal**, C/Adriano 16.

For fashion, there is a branch of the luxurious leather store **Loewe** on the Plaza Nueva, as well as other upmarket designer shops. The most famous *sevillano* designers are **Victorio and Lucchino**, who have an outlet in the Peyré Centro, a small shopping centre on C/Álvarez Quintano. The **C/O'Donnell** has a number of more affordable boutiques.

There are two branches of **El Corte Inglés**, where the well-heeled *sevillanos* shop and, on Plaza Duque de la Victoria, a branch of Zara (also to be found at C/Velázquez) and Mango, the perennial fashion favourites.

Vértice is an international bookshop, C/San Fernando 33, **t** 95 421 16 54, near the cathedral, with a small selection of English-language literature and local guides. For a pleasant wander head for the pedestrianized **C/Sierpes**.

Where to Stay

Sevilla ✉ 41000

Hotels are more expensive in Sevilla than in most of Spain and it is advisable to book in advance. High season is March and April; during Semana Santa and the April Feria you should book even for inexpensive *hostales*, preferably a year ahead. Low season is July and August, when the inhabitants flee from the heat, and January to early March.

Luxury

*******Alfonso XIII**, C/San Fernando 2, **t** 95 491 70 00, **f** 95 491 70 99. Built by King Alfonso for the Exposición Iberoamericana in 1929, this is the grandest hotel in Andalucía, attracting heads of state, opera stars, and tourists who want a unique experience, albeit at a price. Sevilla society still meets around its lobby fountain and somewhat dreary bar. Its restaurant, **San Fernando,** is good if pricey.

*******Hotel Colón**, C/Canalejas 1, **t** 95 422 29 00, **f** 95 422 09 38, *www.solmelia.com, melia.colon@solmelia.com*. Grand and extremely comfortable. It used to be a haunt of bullfighters and their hangers-on.

******Hotel Doña María**, C/Don Remondo 19, **t** 95 422 49 90, **f** 95 421 95 46, *www.hdmaria.com, reservas@hdmaria.com*. Charming and superbly located by the cathedral. Among the mostly antique furniture are some beautifully painted headboards and four-poster beds, and there is a rooftop pool with stunning views.

******Fernando III**, C/San José 21, **t** 95 421 73 07, **f** 95 422 02 46, *www.altor.com, fernandoiii@altur.com*. Superbly located in Santa Cruz, with a pool and garden.

******Las Casas del Rey de Baeza**, Plaza Jesús de la Redención 2, **t** 95 456 14 96, **f** 95 456 14 41, *www.hospeshoteles.com, baeza@zoom.com*. Also in Santa Cruz, with an elegant white and ochre façade and pretty rooms, some overlooking the square.

******Inglaterra**, Plaza Nueva 7, **t** 95 422 49 70, **f** 95 456 13 36, *www.hotelinglaterra.es*. A gracious and typically *sevillano* hotel, with a chic clientele and well-equipped rooms.

******Tryp Macarena**, C/San Juan de Rivera 2, **t** 95 437 57 00, **f** 95 438 18 03. Situated by the Macarena walls, this is another classy establishment with a beautiful *azulejo*-tiled fountain, a swimming pool, and views over the city from the rooftop terrace.

*****Las Casas de las Mercaderes**, C/Álvarez Quintero 9/13, **t** 95 422 58 58, **f** 95 422 21 70, *www.lascasas.es*. In the Arenal district, the stylish rooms have been sympathetically restored and are arranged around an 18th-century courtyard.

Casa Numero 7, C/Virgenes 7, **t** 95 422 15 81, **f** 95 421 45 27, *www.casanumero7.com*. An utterly delightful place in the heart of Santa Cruz, like staying in an elegant private home. There are just a handful of rooms, individually decorated with antiques and paintings from the charming owner's private collection. The style is relaxed but aristocratic and the staff couldn't be nicer. A special treat.

Expensive

****__Hotel Taberna de Alabardero__, C/Zaragoza 20, **t** 95 456 06 37, **f** 95 456 36 66, *hotel.alabardero@esh.es*. The former home of a Romantic poet, the building now houses an outstanding restaurant and culinary school. Ten charming and intimate rooms, all with Jacuzzi and plush fittings, are set around the light-filled courtyard. The service is discreet and excellent, and the cuisine, sublime. Prices include breakfast in the award-winning restaurant (*see* below).

***__Hotel San Gil__, C/Parras 28, **t** 95 490 68 11, **f** 95 490 69 39, *hsangil@arrakis.es*. Near the Andalucian parliament is this beautiful ochre building from the turn of the last century, with fabulous mosaics and tiles. The modern annexe is less charming, but the rooms are large and well-equipped and there's a small rooftop pool.

***__Las Casas de la Judería__, Plaza Santa María la Blanca, Callejón de Dos Hermanos 7, **t** 95 441 51 50, **f** 95 422 21 70, *www.casasypalacios.com*. A row of charming and perfectly restored townhouses in the Santa Cruz quarter, with airy rooms set around a beautiful patio. The owners also run the slightly cheaper **Casas de las Mercaderes**, below.

__Hotel Baco__, overlooking Plaza Ponce de León 15, **t 95 456 50 50, **t** 95 456 36 54. A stalwartly old-fashioned place with a wrought-iron entrance and charming, simple rooms. Expensive in high season but very reasonable (*moderate*) out of season.

Moderate

*__Hotel Plaza Sevilla__, C/Canalejas 2, **t** 95 421 71 49, **f** 95 421 07 73. Has a beautiful neo-classical façade, the work of Aníbal González, architect of the 1929 Exposición, and is ideally placed near the restaurants and bars of San Eloy.

__Montecarlo__, C/Gravina 51, **t 95 421 75 03, **f** 95 421 68 25, *hmontecarlo@arrakis.es*. Has a bright peachy façade and quiet, recently refurbished rooms. Staff are friendly and a good source of local information.

__Hostería de Doña Lina__, C/Gloria 7, **t 95 421 09 56, **f** 95 421 86 61, *lina@arrakis.es*. In the Santa Cruz area, a charmingly kitsch place with whitewashed rooms and a terrace.

__Hotel Alcántara__, C/Xímenez de Enciso 28, **t 95 450 05 95, *www.hotelalcantara.net*. A new hotel in a converted old mansion in the centre of the Barrio Santa Cruz, with quiet, spacious, simply decorated rooms. There are rooms for three and four – a good choice for families. Friendly and family-run.

__Hotel Maestranza__, C/Gamazo 12, **t 95 422 67 66, *www.andalunet.com/maestranza*. A traditional little hotel with a tiled lobby, slightly fussy rooms and very helpful staff.

__Hostería del Laurel__, Plaza de los Venerables 5, **t 95 422 02 95, **f** 95 421 04 50, *www.sol.com/host_laurel*. Overlooking a slightly touristy square, this engagingly quirky hotel, with layered turrets and terraces, once attracted Romantic poets.

__Hotel Murillo__, C/Lope de Rueda 9, **t 95 421 60 95, **f** 95 421 96 16, *www.sol.com/hotel/murillo/*. Old-fashioned, family-run and comfortable; the prices are very reasonable for its central location in Santa Cruz. It also offers apartments.

__Hotel Rábida__, C/Castelar 24, **t 95 422 09 60, **f** 95 422 43 75, *hotel-rabida@sol.com*. In the quiet heart of El Arenal, not far from the bullring, with simple, well-equipped rooms set around two courtyards, one of which doubles as a salon with a pretty stained-glass ceiling. Excellent value for money.

__Hostal Goya__, C/Mateos Gago 31, **t 95 421 11 70, **f** 95 456 29 88. Makes up for its slight gloominess by being located on the most animated street in the *barrio*.

*__Hotel Simón__, C/García de Vinuesa 19, **t** 95 422 66 60, **f** 95 456 22 41, *hotel-simon@jet.es*. A restored 18th-century mansion in a fine position just off the Avenida de la Constitución by the cathedral. This good-value option gets booked up quickly. Pick your room carefully – they vary considerably in size and furnishings.

★**Hostal Nuevo Picasso**, C/San Gregorio 1, **t/f** 95 421 08 64, *hpicasso@arrakis.es*. One of the nicest pensions in this district, with a plant-filled entrance hall and interior courtyard hung with bric-a-brac. Rooms are attractively furnished, but over priced.

Inexpensive

★★**Córdoba**, C/Farnesio 12, **t** 95 422 74 98. Offers eight clean, bright rooms, all with a/c and en suite bathrooms. Booking essential.

★★**Hostal Atenas**, C/Caballerizas 1, **t** 95 421 80 47, **f** 95 422 76 90, *atenas@jet.es*. Quiet and very nice, in a good location between the Plaza Pilatos and the cathedral. Take a cab – it's hard to find.

★★**Hostal Naranjo**, C/San Roque 11, **t** 95 422 58 40, **f** 95 421 69 43. Located on a tranquil residential street in a tiled old building. Rooms with or without bathrooms.

★**Hostal Monreal**, C/Rodrigo Caro 8, **t** 95 421 41 66. A lively place close to the cathedral with almost too much character and a good cheap restaurant when it's open.

Cheap

For inexpensive *hostales*, the Santa Cruz quarter is, surprisingly, the best place to look, particularly on the quiet side streets off C/Mateos Gago.

★★**Hostal Londres**, C/San Pedro Mártir 1, **t/f** 95 421 28 96. Near the Fine Arts Museum, a quiet place with pretty balconies overlooking the street.

★**Argüelles**, C/Alhóndiga 58, **t** 95 421 44 55. Small with a garden and terrace.

★**Fabiola**, C/Fabiola 16, **t** 95 421 83 46. Quiet and cooler than most in summer, with a little courtyard full of plants.

★**Hostal Bailén**, C/Bailén 75, **t** 95 422 16 35. A delightful old building with a garden and courtyard in the Santa Cruz quarter. There's also a tiny two-room apartment for rent during the summer.

Apartments

If you are travelling on a budget, or with a family, renting an apartment can be a good option.

Sevilla Apartamentos, **t** 667 511 348, *www.sevillapartamentos.com*, *info@sevillapartamentos.com*. A friendly, family-run business offering immaculate studios and one- and two-bedroom apartments in the heart of the city. Highly recommended (*inexpensive*).

Apartamentos Murillo, **t** 95 421 09 59, **f** 95 421 96 16. One- and two-bedroom apartments in the heart of the Barrio Santa Cruz (*moderate*).

Eating Out

Restaurants in Sevilla are more expensive than in most of Spain, but even around the cathedral and the Santa Cruz quarter there are a few places that can simply be dismissed as tourist traps. Remember that in the evening the *sevillanos*, even more than most Andalucíans, enjoy bar-hopping for tapas, rather than sitting down to one meal.

Expensive

Taberna del Alabardero, C/Zaragoza 20, **t** 95 456 06 37. One of Sevilla's most celebrated restaurants, also home to an illustrious school for chefs. Specialities include wild-boar ragout, fresh artichokes and Jabugo ham in olive oil, and *urta* (a firm-fleshed, white fish caught locally around Rota) cooked in red wine. The staff are friendly and very knowledgeable. Head up the grand marble staircase overhung with an ornate chandelier to a series of wood-panelled dining rooms set around the central courtyard, each with a different ambience. There is also a handful of elegant guest rooms available (*see* 'Where to Stay', above). The café in the central glassed-over courtyard serves an excellent set lunch at €12, and wonderful cakes in the afternoons. There is also a sumptuous, tile-lined bar with an adventurous range of tapas.

La Albahaca, Plaza Santa Cruz 12, **t** 95 422 07 14. Situated on one of Sevilla's most delightful small squares. There is a Basque twist to many of the beautifully prepared classic dishes and the menu changes with the season. *Closed Sun*.

El Corral del Agua, Callejón del Agua 6, **t** 95 422 48 41. Well-seasoned travellers usually steer clear of cutesy wishing-wells, but the garden in which this one stands is a haven of peace, perfect for a lazy lunch or romantic dinner. Next to Washington Irving's garden.

Egaña-Oriza, C/San Fernando 41, **t** 95 422 72 11. Splendidly situated on the corner of the Jardines Alcázar, opposite the university, this is one of Sevilla's best-loved restaurants. Among its tempting delights are clams on the half-shell and a kind of *sevillano* jugged hare. *Closed Sat lunch, Sun and Aug.*

Bar España, C/San Fernando 41. Attached to the Egaña-Oriza, this tapas bar is chic, bright, cosmopolitan – and the Basque tapas are sensational.

Jaylu, C/Lopéz de Gomara, 19, **t** 95 433 94 76. You can dine here on some of the city's best and freshest seafood. *Closed Sun.*

Casa Robles, C/Álvarez Quintero 58, **t** 95 456 32 72. In a wonderful setting, with dishes combining traditional cooking and the best of new cuisine. It specializes in pastries.

Moderate

La Judería, C/Cano y Cueto, **t** 95 442 64 56. Tucked away in the old Jewish quarter, with brick arches and terracotta tiles. There is an almost bewildering range of richly flavoured regional dishes, like *rabo de toro* (oxtail stew, the house speciality), game in season, dozens of fish dishes and, to finish up, delicious homemade desserts. Great tapas in the bar, too. *Closed Tues and Aug.*

Marea Grande, C/Diego Angulo Íñiguez 16, **t** 95 453 80 00. Fish-lovers should head slightly out of the centre for this plush establishment, justly considered one of the city's finest seafood restaurants. *Closed end of Aug and Sun.*

La Dorada, Avenida Ramón y Cajal, **t** 95 492 10 66. Serves delicately prepared fish and shellfish. *Closed Sun.*

Rincón de Casana, C/Santo Domingo de la Calzada 13, **t** 95 453 17 10. Fine traditional cuisine served in rustic surroundings. *Closed Sun June–Aug.*

Becerrita, C/Recaredo 9, **t** 95 441 20 57. Run by the affable Jésus Becerra, who serves traditional *andaluz* dishes in small, intimate surroundings. *Closed Sun eve.*

Enrique Becerra, C/Gamazo 2, **t** 95 421 30 49. Enrique followed in his father's footsteps (he is the 5th generation of this family of celebrated *sevillano* restaurateurs), with this prettily tiled restaurant. The menu is based on flavoursome regional dishes accompanied by a variety of delicious breads. For dessert, try the house speciality, *pudding de naranjas Santa Paula*, made with *sevillano* marmalade from the Convent of St Paula. There is also a lively tapas bar. *Closed Sun and the last two weeks of July.*

Salvador Rojo, C/San Fernando 23, **t** 95 422 97 25. Near Hotel Alfonso XIII and yet virtually hidden. The décor is almost spartan, which is all the more reason to concentrate on the food, a selection of creative *andaluz* dishes deftly prepared by Salvador Rojo himself.

El Bacalao, Plaza Ponce de León 15, **t** 95 421 66 70. For infinite varieties of *bacalao* (dried salted cod), this delightful restaurant and tapas bar is the only place to go; some meat and game is also served. *Closed Sun eve.*

Mesón Don Raimundo, C/Argote de Molina 26, **t** 95 422 33 55. By the cathedral and set in a 17th-century convent with an eclectic décor of religious artefacts and suits of armour. No enforced abstinence here, though. You can pig out on the large selection of traditional *andaluz* dishes based on fish, shellfish and game, to the accompaniment of fine wines from an extensive list. *Closed Sun eves.*

Las Meninas, C/Santo Tomás 3, **t** 95 422 62 26. Also owned by Don Raimundo; draws big crowds for its hearty but well-priced portions.

Ox's, C/Betis 61, **t** 95 427 62 75. A delightful *asador* (grill room) with novelties from Navarra – cod-stuffed peppers, fish and steaks grilled over charcoal for a smoky piquancy. *Closed Sun eves, Mon and Aug.*

Restaurante San Marco, C/Cuna 6, **t** 95 421 24 40. Back in the winding pedestrian and shopping district, and set in an 18th-century palace with an enormous Moorish carved wooden door. The cuisine is Franco-Italian and the desserts are particularly good. There are five other branches around Sevilla. *Closed Mon lunch and Sun.*

Café del Pintor, C/Murillo 8, **t** 95 422 1502. Right in the heart of the Barrio Santa Cruz, this is a laid-back little restaurant where the chef (actually from Barcelona) cooks up all kinds of interesting goodies: delicious sautéed wild mushrooms and scrambled eggs with *bacalao*.

Inexpensive (*see* also 'Tapas Bars' below)

Río Grande, C/Betis 70, **t** 95 427 39 56. Along the Triana side of the Guadalquivir, you can dine here with a tremendous view of the Tower of Gold and La Giralda, and even join in with the whoops from the bullring opposite if a *corrida* is in progress. The kitchen here specializes in regional cuisine.

Pizzeria San Marco, Meson del Moro 6–10, **t** 95 421 43 90. Run by the same family as the Restaurante San Marco (*see* above), with excellent pizzas and a wide range of pasta dishes in an old Arabic bath-house. The prices and the relaxed, stylish décor attract a young, chatty crowd.

Bodegón Torre del Oro, C/Santander 15, **t** 95 422 08 80. The rafters here are hung with dozens of different hams and the dining room shares the space with the bar. There's a three-course set meal with wine and the *raciones* are excellent.

Casa Salva, C/Pedro del Toro 12, **t** 95 421 41 15. A tiny, unassuming and very welcoming restaurant near the Fine Arts Museum. The fresh, simple menu changes daily. *Open Mon–Fri lunch only*.

La Illustre Víctima, C/Doctor Letamandi 35 (not far from the Plaza de Alameda de Hércules). A friendly, laid-back and pleasingly chaotic café, bar and restaurant with painted murals. It serves a variety of snacks, including some pasta, couscous, *enchiladas* and *fajitas*, some suitable for vegetarians.

Vegetarian

La Mandrágora, C/Albuera 11, **t** 95 422 01 84. In a country where meat and fish reign supreme, it's a nice surprise to find this friendly vegetarian restaurant with an excellent menu; everything is home-cooked – even the piquant salsas. *Closed Sun.*

Jalea Real, C/Sor Ángela de la Cruz (at the corner of C/Jerónimo Hernández), **t** 95 421 61 03. Not far from Plaza de la Encarnación – a delightful place with a healthy and cheap three-course lunch menu.

Habanita, C/Golfo 3, **t** 6060 716 456. Tiny, friendly veggie restaurant with delicious cakes and changing art exhibitions.

Ice Cream and *Pastelerías*

La Campana, C/Sierpes 1. Delicious cakes, coffee or ice cream.

Ochoa, on C/Sierpes. Another of the city's prettiest old *pastelerías*.

Horno Santa Cruz, C/Guzmán el Bueno 12. Pretty blue and white tiles and a lovely plant-filled courtyard – the perfect place to buy your bread and pastries.

Sopa de Ganso, C/Pérez Galdós 8. Laid-back café by day; cool bar with DJs at night.

Alfalfa 10, at No.10. One of the nicest café-bars on trendy Plaza de Alfalfa, with very untypical but delicious cappuccino and strudel.

Tapas Bars

Tapas bars are an intrinsic part of daily life in Sevilla, and even the smartest restaurants, such as the Taberna del Alabardero, Egaña-Oriza, El Bacalao and many others, often have excellent tapas bars attached (*see* above).

El Rinconcillo, C/Gerona 40, **t** 95 422 31 83 (north of the cathedral, between the Church of St Pedro and the Convent of Espíritu Santo). The oldest bar in Sevilla, this is reputedly where the custom of topping a glass with a slice of sausage or a piece of bread and ham – the first tapas – began. Decorated in moody brown *azulejos*, the place dates back to 1670 and is frequented by lively *sevillano cognoscenti*, who gather to enjoy the tasty nibbles. The staff, oblivious, chalk up the bill on the bar.

Bar Manolo, on buzzing Plaza de Alfalfa. The best of several tapas bars on the square. It's lively at breakfast as well as the evening.

Bar El Refugio, C/Huelva 5. Just round the corner, with delicious fried vegetables served with a creamy *béchamel* sauce.

Bar Alicantina, Plaza del Salvador s/n. Has great *ensalada rusa* and is a favoured hangout of the young and fashionable.

La Eslava, C/Eslava 3, **t** 95 490 65 68. Many of Sevilla's best tapas bars also have dining rooms at the back; this is one of the nicest, serving a wide range of excellent tapas. The popular restaurant has a more extensive menu and can get very crowded. Highly recommended. *Closed Sun, Mon eve and Aug.*

Casa Morales, C/García de Vinuesa 11, **t** 95 422 12 42. In the Santa Cruz quarter, just a skip away from the cathedral, this is purportedly

Sevilla's second-oldest bar, with old pottery wine casks, sawdust scattered across the tiled floor and a range of simple tapas.

Bar Modesto, C/Cano y Cueto 5, **t** 95 441 68 11. Another well-established favourite with wonderful seafood tapas, and a dining room for full meals.

La Bodeguita de Santa Julia, C/Hernando Colón 1 (near the cathedral). Serves some of Sevilla's most traditional and tastiest tapas.

Bar Giralda, C/Mateo Gago 1, **t** 95 422 74 35. In an old Moorish bath-house, with a great range to choose from; popular with tourists and locals.

Hostería del Laurel, Plaza de los Venerables 5, **t** 95 422 02 95. Serves superb tapas in a room filled with hanging *jamón* and beautiful Triana tiles. The restaurant is also excellent.

Las Infantas, C/Arfe 36, **t** 95 422 96 89. Heading down towards the river, this is a very stylish bar popular with yuppies, who come for the excellent tapas. The range of dishes is limited but the quality is outstanding. Try the *chorizo* sausage or the *bacalao*.

Sol y Sombra, C/Castilla 149–51, **t** 95 433 39 35. Over in Triana, this is a very atmospheric place with sawdust on the floor, and *taurino* memorabilia. The superb tapas change daily, and there's a restaurant next door.

Kiosko de las Flores. A pretty and informal café-bar partly overlooking the river, justly celebrated for its *pescaítos fritos*.

Bodega La Albariza, C/Betis 6A, **t** 95 433 20 16. Serves its astonishing range of tapas on empty sherry casks in the bar. There is a little dining area at the back with a very reasonably priced menu.

Las Golondrinas, C/Antillano Campos 26, **t** 95 433 16 26. Come here for great *alcachofas* (artichokes) and *tortilla* in a charming tiled two-floor bar.

Bodega Santa Cruz, C/Mateo Gago (on the corner of C/Rodrigo Caro). Attracts a young university crowd and serves an excellent selection of tapas , which will be chalked up at your place at the bar.

Las Teresas, C/Sta Teresa. A traditional café-bar deep in the heart of the *Barrio Santa Cruz*, with walls lined with old photos.

Entre Calles, C/Ximenez de Encisco. An old, dark and atmospheric tapas bar.

Casa Placido, C/Meson del Moro. Serves excellent and reasonably priced tapas in an old-style tiled bar.

Entertainment and Nightlife

Bars and Clubs

Red and white signs emblazoned *Cruzcampo* hang from many of the bars; this is Sevilla's most popular **beer**, a pale brew served ice cold either on draft or in bottles. San Miguel is another favourite, and you should try Mahou Five Star if you see it.

The Plaza del Salvador fills up quickly in the evenings, so start your night with a chilled sherry at the tiny **Antigua Bodeguita** or one of its neighbours, opposite the church. Sip the sherry with the locals out in the square or lounging on the church steps, and ponder your next move. One particular pleasure, in a city which pursues so many, is to set out on a bar crawl, trying different sherries and tapas.

Many of the liveliest bars are around the Plaza de Alfalfa; head down C/Boteros for some of the buzziest. C/Pérez Galdós is another good street for popular bars, with hordes of youthful *sevillanos* and *sevillanas* spilling out on to the pavement. The Santa Cruz quarter is equally vibrant, although you'll find more young foreigners here.

Bar Berlin, C/Boteros 4. Loud, crammed and great fun.

El Garlochi, C/Boteros 26. Eccentric local bar which changes decoration with the seasons – before Semana Santa, for example, it is scented with incense and filled with flowers.

La Subasta, C/Argote de Molina 36. Whitewashed walls and an old wooden bar, on a road packed with popular bars.

Antigüedes, C/Argote de Molina 40. Has books suspended, pages flapping, from the ceiling. Close to the cathedral, it gets packed out with a mix of *guiris* (young foreigners) and locals.

Metropol, C/La Florida. Trendy bar – café by day and a *bar de copas* with DJ by night.

El Mundo o Otro Bar, C/Siete Revueltos 5, **t** 95 422 96 95. Trendy gay bar with tongue-in-cheek retro décor.

Bilindo, Pso de las Delicias s/n, **t** 95 462 61 51; **Alfonso**, Pza América s/n, **t** 95 423 37 35; **El Chile**, Pso de las Delicias s/n, **t** 95 423 56 59. These three *terrazas* are enormously popular in summer: drink and dance outdoors until dawn.

Habanilla Café, Alameda de Herculés 63. Tiled, laid-back bar and café full of arty, boho-chic *sevillanos*. The crowds spill out onto the square on summer evenings.

Café de la Prensa, C/Betis 8, **t** 95 433 34 20. A great place for a coffee or a cocktail, with a terrace overlooking the river. This is Triana's busiest street, with lots of bars and cafés to choose from.

Flamenco

If you've been longing to experience flamenco, Sevilla is a good place to do it. The most touristy flamenco factories will hit you for €10 and upwards per drink. Bars in Triana and other areas do it better for less; C/Salado and environs in Triana, for example, have some good bars. There are more venues across the river in the Santa Cruz quarter. The tourist office on Avenida de la Constitución has a notice board with details of shows.

Flamenco *Tablaos* (Shows)

These cost around €22–30 for the show plus a drink. Dinner is more expensive.

Los Gallos, Plaza de Santa Cruz s/n, **t/f** 95 421 69 81. *Sevillanas* and flamenco dancing lit by the flashes of tourist cameras. *Shows at 9 and 11.30pm.*

El Palacio Andaluz, Avenida María Auxiliadora 18B, **t** 95 453 47 20. More formal, with a 1½hr show staged for tourists in an expensive restaurant. *Shows at 7.30 and 10pm.*

El Arenal, C/Rodo 7, **t** 95 421 64 92, *www.tablaoareanal.com*. Dinner and a flamenco show daily at 9pm. Touristy but the dancers and musicians are very accomplished. *Shows at 9 and 11pm.*

Las Brujas, C/Gonzalo de Bilbao, **t** 95 441 36 51. Closed Sun. Another touristy *tablao*; dinner and a show. Accessible for those new to flamenco. *Shows at 9 and 11.30pm.*

Flamenco Bars with Live Performances

La Carbonería, C/Levíes 18. The king of modern flamenco, the late El Camarón de la Isla, used to play at this cavernous bar, which is still one of the best venues in the city for extemporaneous performances of all styles. The bar attracts a largely young, foreign crowd and there's a pretty terrace lit with fairy lights out at the back. Live performances Thursdays and occasionally Sundays.

El Tamboril, Plaza Santa Cruz s/n. Come here for *sevillanas* dancing (very similar to flamenco but slightly less tortured and frenetic).

El Simpecao, Paseo Nuestra Señora de la O. Youthful and occasionally impromptu, this place in Triana is not too far from the real thing.

Casa Anselma, C/Pagés del Corro. Another atmospheric flamenco taverna in Triana, this is as popular with *sevillanos* as it is with the foreign tourists who have just begun to discover it.

Lola de los Reyes, Avda Blas de Infante 6, **t** 95 427 75 76. Well off the beaten track, Lola's bar is set under an apartment block on the edge of Seville. Packed with locals who know all the words to the songs, Lola herself dances and belts out some spine-tingling flamenco and popular *sevillanas* accompanied by local musicians.

Music, Theatre and Opera

They do play other kinds of music in Sevilla, and two publications, *El Giraldillo* and *Ocio*, available free in bars, cafés and hotels, have listings. Again, the tourist information office is very helpful, and publishes the free *Welcome Olé* magazine with listings information.

For mainstream drama, the best-known theatre is the **Lope de Vega Theatre**, Avenida María Luisa, **t** 95 459 08 53, built for the 1929 exhibition.

The **Maestranza Theatre**, Paseo de Cristóbal Colón, **t** 95 422 33 44, *www.maestranza.com* has quickly established itself as one of the top opera houses in Europe.

Bullfighting

See a bullfight in the famous **Maestranza** if you can, but don't just turn up! Get tickets as far ahead as possible; prices at the box office, C/Adriano 37, **t** 95 422 35 06, will be cheaper than at the little stands on C/Sierpes.

Apart from in the Alhambra of Granada, the place where the lushness and sensuality of al-Andalus survives best is Andalucía's capital. Sevilla may be Spain's fourth-largest city, but it is a place where you can pick oranges from the trees, and see open countryside from the centre of town. Come in spring if you can, when the gardens are filled with birdsong and the air is heavy with the scent of jasmine and a hundred other blooms. If you come in summer, you may melt: the lower valley of the Guadalquivir is one of the hottest places in Europe. The pageant of Sevilla unfolds in the shadow of La Giralda, still the loftiest tower in Spain. Its size and the ostentatious play of its arches and arabesques make it the perfect symbol for this city, full of delightful excess and the romance of the south.

At times Sevilla has been a capital, and it remains Spain's eternal city; neither past reverses nor modern industry have been able to shake it from its dreams. That its past glories should return and place it alongside Venice and Florence as one of the jewels in the crown of Europe, a true metropolis with full international recognition, is the first dream of every *sevillano*. Sevilla is still a city very much in love with itself. Even the big celebrations of Semana Santa and Feria – although enjoyable for the foreigner (anyone from outside the city), with revelry in every café and on every street corner – are essentially private; the *sevillanos* celebrate in their own *casitas* with friends, all the time aware that they are being observed by the general public, who can peek but may not enter, at least not without an *enchufe* ('the right connection'). Sevilla is much like a beautiful, flirtatious woman: she'll tempt you to her doorstep and allow you a peck on the cheek – whether you get over the threshold depends entirely on your charm.

History: from Hispalis to Isbiliya to Sevilla

One of Sevilla's distinctions is its long historical continuity. Few cities in western Europe can claim never to have suffered a dark age, but Sevilla flourished after the fall of Rome – and even after the coming of the Castilians. Roman **Hispalis** was founded on an Iberian settlement, perhaps one of the cities of Tartessos, and it soon became one of the leading cities of the province of Baetica, as well as its capital. **Itálica**, the now ruined city, lies just to the northwest; it is difficult to say which was the more important. During the Roman twilight, Sevilla seems to have been a thriving town. Its first famous citizen, San Isidore, was one of the Doctors of the Church and the most learned man of the age, famous for his great *Encyclopedia* and his *Seven Books Against the Pagans*, an attempt to prove that the coming of Christianity was not the cause of Rome's fall. Sevilla was an important town under the Visigoths, and after the Moorish conquest it was second only to Córdoba as a political power and a centre of learning. For a while after the demise of the western caliphate in 1023, it became an independent kingdom, paying tribute to the kings of Castile. Sevilla suffered under the Almoravids after 1091, but enjoyed a revival under their successors, the Almohads, who made it their capital and built the **Giralda** as the minaret for their new mosque.

The disaster came for Muslim **Isbiliya** in 1248, 18 years after the union of Castile and León. Fernando III's conquest of the city is not a well-documented event, but it seems that more than half the population found exile in Granada or Africa preferable to

Castilian rule; their property was divided among settlers from the north. Despite the dislocation, the city survived, and found a new prosperity as Castile's window on the Mediterranean and South Atlantic trade routes (the River Guadalquivir is navigable as far as Sevilla). Everywhere in the city you will see its emblem, the word NODO (knot) with a double knot between the O and D. The word recalls the civil wars of the 1270s, when Sevilla was one of the few cities in Spain to remain loyal to Alfonso the Wise. '*No m'a dejado*' ('She has not forsaken me'), Alfonso is recorded as saying; *madeja* is another word for knot, and placed between the syllables NO and DO it makes a clever rebus, besides being a tribute to Sevilla's loyalty to medieval Castile's greatest king.

From 1503 to 1680, Sevilla enjoyed a legal monopoly of trade with the Americas, and it soon became the biggest city in Spain, with a population of over 150,000. The giddy prosperity this brought, in the years when the silver fleet ran full, contributed much to the festive, incautious atmosphere that is often revealed in Sevilla's character. Sevilla never found a way to hold on to much of the American wealth, and what little it managed to grab was soon dissipated in showy excess. There was enough to attract great artists such as Velázquez, Zurbarán and Murillo. and the city participated fully in the culture of Spain's golden age – even Don Quixote was born here, conceived by **Cervantes** while he was doing time in a Sevilla prison for debt.

It was in this period, of course, that Sevilla was perfecting its charm. Poets and composers have always favoured it as a setting. The prototypes of Bizet's Carmen rolled their cigars in the Royal Tobacco Factory, and for her male counterpart Sevilla contributed Don Juan Tenorio, who evolved through Spanish theatre in plays by Tirso de Molina and Zorrilla to become Mozart's *Don Giovanni*; the same composer also used the city as a setting for *The Marriage of Figaro*. The historical ironies are profound: amidst all this opulence, Andalucía was rapidly declining from one of the richest and most cultured provinces of Europe to one of the poorest and most backward. Over the 17th and 18th centuries the city stagnated.

In 1936, the Army of Africa, under **Franco**'s command, quickly took control of Andalucía. In Sevilla, a flamboyant officer named Gonzalo Queipo de Llano single-handedly bluffed and bullied the city into submission, and as soon as the Moroccan troops arrived he turned them loose to butcher and terrorize the working-class district of Triana. Queipo de Llano was soon to be famous as the Nationalists' radio propaganda voice, with shrill, grotesque nightly broadcasts full of sexual innuendoes about the Republic's politicians, and explicit threats of what his soldiers would do to the Loyalists' women once they were conquered.

Various industrial programmes, including a new shipbuilding industry, were started up by Franco's economists in the 1950s, stemming the flow of mass emigration and doing something to reduce the poverty of the region. But when **King Juan Carlos** ushered in the return of democracy, the city was more than ready. In the late 1970s, Andalucíans took advantage of revolutionary regional autonomy laws, building one of the most active regional governments in the country. **Felipe González**, a socialist from Sevilla, ran Spain from 1982 up to 1996, when the many political scandals of 1995 and economic discontent finally discouraged the electorate from returning him to office.

In 1992, crimped and prinked, Sevilla opened her doors to the world for **Expo '92**. Fresh romance and excess mingled with the old. New roads, new bridges and a new opera house combined with Moorish palaces and monuments in a vainglorious display that attracted 16 million visitors. But despite the massive investment, the hoped-for regeneration of the region remains a dream: more than a decade later, Seville is still paying off its bills and the pavilions that line the Expo '92 site have been semi-abandoned. Unemployment remains among the highest in Spain at more than 40 per cent, and accusations of corruption still dog local government.

The Cathedral and Around

La Giralda

Open Mon–Sat 11–5, Sun and hols 2.30–6; adm; information t 95 421 49 71.

A good place to start your tour of Sevilla is at one of Andalucía's most famous monuments. You can catch the 100m (319ft) tower of **La Giralda** peeking over the rooftops from almost anywhere in Sevilla; it will be your best friend when you get lost in the city's labyrinthine streets. This great minaret, with its *ajimeces* and brickwork arabesques, was built under the **Almohads**, from 1172 to 1195, just 50 years before the Christian conquest. Two similar minarets, built in the same period, still survive in Marrakech and Rabat in Morocco, and the trio are known as the **Three Sisters**. The surprisingly harmonious spire stuck on top is a Christian addition. Whatever sort of turret originally existed was surmounted by four golden balls stacked up at the very top, designed to catch the sun and be visible to a traveller one day's ride from the city; all came down in a 13th-century earthquake. On the top of their spire, the Christians added a huge, revolving statue of Faith as a weathervane (many writers have noted the curious fancy of having a supposedly constant Faith turning with the four winds). **La Giraldillo** – the weathervane – has given its name to the tower as a whole. The climb to the top is fairly easy: instead of stairs, there are shallow ramps – wide enough for Fernando III to have ridden his horse up for the view after the conquest in 1248. He was probably not the first to ride up – it is likely that the *muezzin* used a donkey to help him to the top to call the faithful to prayer. For those without equine support, there are plenty of viewing ledges on the way up for a breather, and a handful of glassy chambers exhibiting fragments of La Giralda's past, such as the robust 14th-century door which combines Gothic motifs and verses from the Koran, and the memorial stone of Petrus de la Cera, one of the knights who seized the city in November 1248 and couldn't bear to leave. There are also the remains of the monstrous hooks and pulleys which hoisted the stones into place.

The Biggest Gothic Cathedral in the Whole World

The same opening hours as La Giralda; both are visited with one ticket.

For a while after the Reconquista, the Castilians who repopulated Sevilla were content to use the great Almohad mosque, built at the same time as La Giralda. But

Semana Santa and Feria

The penitential rituals of the medieval *cofradías*, or fraternities, form the basis of the solemn processions at the heart of Sevilla's Semana Santa (Holy Week), although they owe their current theatrical pizzazz to the Baroque era. Every year between Palm Sunday and Easter Saturday, 57 *cofradías* hoist up their *pasos* (floats) and process through the crowds along the sinuous streets from their church to the great cathedral and back, taking, as decreed by a humane cardinal in the 17th century, the shortest possible route. Even this can take between four and twelve hours, with the occasional pit stop at a bar or local convenience. The musical accompaniment is a solemn and sonorous *marcha*, and, occasionally, a single voice will break in with a *saeta*, a soaring mournful song sung *a capella*, and closely related to flamenco. Most of the *cofradías* carry two *pasos*: the first, the Paso de Cristo, depicts a scene between the Last Supper and the Resurrection, and the second, called the Paso Palio, carries the Virgin, weeping at the death of her son. Both are ornately carved and gilded, but it is the second *paso* that draws all eyes as each *cofradía* vies to produce the most beautiful Virgin, resplendent in a richly embroidered cape and covered by a swaying canopy. There are two main contenders in this beauty contest: La Macarena (*see* p.126) and her rival from across the river in Triana, La Esperanza de Triana (*see* p.122). But, in Sevilla, everyone has a Virgin, and the crowds will wait for hours to see 'their' Virgin pass.

The most important *cofradías* – El Silencio, El Gran Poder, La Macarena, El Calverio, La Esperanza de Triana and Los Gitanos – are given top billing and process on Good Friday morning, the high point of Semana Santa. The heavy floats are carried by 20 to 30 *costaleros*, for whom it is a great honour to be chosen and who practise for weeks ahead of time. It's hard, hot and claustrophobic work hidden beneath the *paso*, and it's essential that their moves are synchronized and guided by the black-suited *capataz* (overseer). Around the floats are the Nazarenos in their macabre pointed hats and masks, carrying candles and banners. The Penitents, who follow the Paso de

at the turn of the 1400s, in a fit of pious excess, it was decided to build a new cathedral so grand that 'future ages shall call us mad for attempting it'. If they were mad, at least they were good organizers – they got it up in slightly over a century. The architects are unknown, though there has been speculation that the original master was either French or German.

The exterior, with its great rose window and double buttresses, is as fine as any of the Gothic cathedrals of northern Spain – if we could only see it. Especially on the western front, facing the Avenida de la Constitución, the buildings close in; walking around its vast bulk, past the fence of Roman columns joined by thick chains, is like passing under a steep and ragged cliff. Some of the best original sculptural work is on the two portals flanking the main door: the **Door of Baptism** (left) and the **Door of Birth** (right), which are covered with elaborate terracotta figures sculpted by the Frenchman Lorenzo Mercadante de Bretaña and his follower Pedro Millán during the late 15th century. The groundplan of this monster, roughly 125m by 185m (400ft by

Cristo and bear wooden crosses, are often performing authentic acts of penitence and process barefoot (many others just want to dress up and be in the show). They also wear the long flowing robes and masks of the Nazarenos, but their hoods are not supported by the conical *antifaz* and so hang down at the back. The official procession route, scented with thick clouds of incense, runs along C/Sierpes to Plaza El Salvador and Plaza de San Francisco, and then to the enormous cathedral itself. Boxes are set up for important figures, while the streets and balconies are crammed with up to a million spectators, most men in blue suits and the ladies in black *mantilla* veils. Easter Sunday sees the first bullfight of the year.

After all the gloom and solemnity of Semana Santa, Sevilla erupts a week or two later in a week-long party – the April Feria. Another medieval institution, it was re-introduced to the city by a Basque and a Catalan in the mid-19th century. Originally a cattle market, nothing remains of its original purpose other than the circus-style striped tents, or *casetas*, which have become increasingly ornate through the years (prizes are awarded for the most beautiful) and are divided into two sections: the front has stalls for food and drink and the back is used for dancing. The drink, of course, is sherry, and calculations suggest that as much is drunk in this one week in Sevilla as the rest of Spain drinks in a year. Having the right connections, or *enchufe*, is supremely important: to be denied entrance to the most élite tents is to lose considerable face (it helps if you've made some local friends). The Feria now takes place in the *barrio* of Los Remedios, but the council is besieged by so many applications for *casetas* that it may have to move again. The streets are decorated with thousands of lanterns; horses and carriages push through dense, jubilant crowds, many people wearing traditional costume (the women's flamenco costumes are especially dazzling); and the nearby funfair reverberates with screams of laughter. The festivities begin with a ceremonial lighting of the lanterns at midnight on Monday and culminate in a firework extravaganza the following Sunday, which also marks the official opening of the bullfighting season at La Maestranza.

600ft), probably covers the same area as did the mosque. On the northern side, the **Court of the Orange Trees** (Patio de los Naranjos), planted accordingly, preserves the outline of the mosque courtyard. The Muslim fountain survives, along with some of the walls and arches. In the left-hand corner, the Moorish 'Gate of the Lizard' has hanging from it a stuffed crocodile, said to have been a present from an Egyptian emir asking for the hand of a Spanish infanta. Along the eastern wall is the entrance of the **Biblioteca Colombina**, a library of ancient manuscripts and an archive of Columbus's life and letters, founded by his son, who obviously inherited his father's itchy feet. He travelled with his father to the Indies, took expeditions to Africa and Asia, and was part of Charles V's entourage in Flanders, Germany and Italy. He collected over 20,000 volumes on his travels, and bequeathed them to the city when he died in 1539.

The cathedral's cavernous interior overpowers the faithful with its size more than its grace or beauty. The main altarpiece is the world's biggest *retablo*, almost 370m

(120ft) high and entirely covered with carved figures and golden Gothic ornaments; it took 82 years to make, and takes about a minute to look at. Just behind the Large Chapel (Capilla Mayor) and the main altar, the **Royal Chapel** (Capilla Real) contains the tombs of San Fernando, conqueror of Sevilla, and of Alfonso the Wise; Pedro the Cruel and his mistress, María de Padilla, are relegated to the crypt underneath. Above the iron grille at the entrance to the Royal Chapel, the Moor Axataf hands over the keys of the city to a triumphant Fernando III. The art of the various chapels around the cathedral is lost in the gloom, but Murillo's masterpiece *La Visión de San Antonio* (1656) hangs in the Chapel of San Antonio (in the northern aisle), and a luminous, stark *retablo* depicting the life of St Paul by Zurbarán is fixed in the Chapel of San Pedro (to the left of the Royal Chapel). In the southern aisle, four stern pall-bearers on a high pedestal support the **tomb of Christopher Columbus**, although his bones were shifted, lost and rediscovered with such regularity that it is impossible to know with any certainty whose remains are borne so ceremoniously aloft. The pall-bearers represent the kingdoms of Castile, León, Navarra and Aragón. Columbus has been something of a refugee since his death. In the 16th century his remains were moved from Valladolid to the island of Santo Domingo, and after Dominican Independence from there to Havana cathedral. In 1899, after Cuba became independent, he was brought to Sevilla, and this idiosyncratic monument was put up to honour him. In the Dominican Republic, they'll tell you Columbus is still buried in Santo Domingo. Of course, most Spaniards are convinced that Columbus was born in Spain, not in Genoa, so it is appropriate that the life of this most elusive character should have mysteries at both ends.

Most of the cathedral's collections are housed in a few chambers near the entrance. In the **Chapter House**, which has an Immaculate Conception by Murillo, Sevilla's bishop can sit on his throne and pontificate under the unusual acoustics of an elliptical Baroque ceiling. The adjacent **Sacristy** contains paintings by Zurbarán, Murillo, Van Dyck and others, most in dire need of restoration. Spare a moment for the reliquaries. Juan de Arfe, maker of the world's biggest silver monstrances, is represented here with one that is almost a small palace, made with 410kg (900lbs) of silver and complete with marble columns. Spain's most famous, and possibly most bizarre, reliquary is the **Alfonsine Tables**, filled with over 200 tiny bits of tooth and bone. They were said to have belonged to Alfonso the Wise and were made to provide extra-powerful juju for him to carry into battle. (Interestingly, the term 'Alfonsine tables' also refers to the famous astronomical tables made for the same king by Jewish scholars of Toledo, until the 1600s used all over Europe to calculate eclipses and the movements of the planets.)

The Archive of the Indies (Archivo de Indias)

Closed for restoration; information **t** *95 421 12 34.*

In common with most of its contemporaries, parts of Sevilla's cathedral were public ground, and were used to transact all sorts of business. A 16th-century bishop put an end to this practice, but prevailed upon Philip II to construct next to the cathedral an

Exchange (Lonja), for the merchants. Philip sent his favourite architect, Juan de Herrera, then still busy with El Escorial, to design it. The severe, elegant façades are typical of Herrera's work, and the stone balls and pyramids on top are practically the architect's signature. By the 1780s, little commerce was still going on in Sevilla, and what was left of the American trade passed through Cádiz. Also, two foreigners, a Scot and a Frenchman, had had the gumption to publish histories of the Indies unflattering to the Spanish, so Charles III converted the lonely old building to hold the **Archive of the Indies**, the repository of all the reports, maps and documents that the Crown had collected during the age of exploration. Inside, a glorious staircase of rosy jasper marble leads handsomely to the upper floors, where the artefacts and treasures are stored in almost six miles of 18th-century Cuban mahogany and cedar-wood shelves.

The Alcázar

Open summer Tues–Sat 9.30–7, Sun and hols 9.30–5; winter Tues–Sat 9.30–5, Sun and hols 9.30–1.30; closed Mon; adm.

It's easy to be fooled into thinking this is simply a Moorish palace; some of its rooms and courtyards seem to come straight from the Alhambra (*see* pp.293–8). Most of them, however, were built by Moorish workmen for **King Pedro the Cruel** of Castile in the 1360s. The Alcázar and its king represent a fascinating cul-de-sac in Spanish history and culture, and allow the possibility that al-Andalus might have assimilated its conquerors rather than been destroyed by them.

Pedro was an interesting character. In Froissart's *Chronicle*, we have him described as 'full of marveylous opinyons...rude and rebell agaynst the commandements of holy churche'. Certainly he didn't mind having his Moorish artists, lent by the kings of Granada, adorn his palace with sayings from the Koran in Kufic calligraphy. Pedro preferred Sevilla, still half-Moorish and more than half-decadent, to Old Castile, and he filled his court here with Moorish poets, dancers and bodyguards – the only ones he trusted. But he was not the man for the job of cultural synthesis. The evidence, in so far as it is reliable, suggests he richly deserved his honorific 'the Cruel', although to many underdog *sevillanos* he was Pedro the Just. Long before Pedro, the Alcázar was the palace of the Moorish governors. Work on the Moorish features began in 712 after the capture of Sevilla. In the 9th century it was transformed into a palace for Abd ar-Rahman II. Important additions were made under the Almohads, since the Alcázar was their capital in al-Andalus. Almost all the decorative work you see now was done under Pedro, some by the Granadans and the rest by Muslim artists from Toledo; altogether it is the outstanding production of *mudéjar* art in Spain.

The Alcázar is entered through the little gate on the Plaza del Triunfo, on the southern side of the cathedral. The first courtyard, the **Court of León**, has beautiful arabesques, with lions amid castles for Castile and León; this was the public court of the palace, where visitors were received, corresponding to the Mexuar at the Alhambra. At the far end of the courtyard is the lovely façade of the interior palace, decorated with inscriptions in Gothic and Arabic script.

Much of the best *mudéjar* work can be seen in the adjacent halls and courts; their seemingly haphazard arrangement was in fact a principle of the art, to increase the surprise and delight in passing from one to the next. Off the Court of León is the **Hall of Justice**, with a stunning star-shaped coffered ceiling, where Pedro I passed the sentence of death on his brother, who had had the temerity to have an affair with Pedro's wife (*see* Convent of Santa Clara, p.126). Behind it, the secluded **Court of Plaster** is largely a survival of the Almoravid palace of the 1170s, itself built on the site of a Roman *praetorium*. The **Court of the Maidens**, entered through the gate of the palace façade, is the largest of the courtyards and is named after the young Christian women who were given as brides as peace offerings to the Moors. The Islamic motto 'None but Allah conquers' is entwined with the heraldic devices of the Kingdom of Castile and León, and the gallery was added during the reign of Charles V. The courtyard leads to the **Hall of the Ambassadors**, a small domed chamber that is the finest in the Alcázar despite the jarring addition of heavily carved balconies from the time of Philip II. In Moorish times this was the throne room. Another courtyard, the **Court of the Dolls**, once the hub of the palace's domestic life, takes its name from two tiny faces on medallions at the base of one of the horseshoe arches – a little joke on the part of the Muslim stone-carvers; to find them will bring luck (look on the right-hand arch of the northern gallery). The columns come from the ruins of Medinat al-Zahra.

Spanish kings couldn't leave the Alcázar alone. Fernando and Isabel spoiled a large corner of it for their **Casa de Contratación**, a planning centre for the colonization of the Indies. There's little to see in it: a big conference table, a model of the *Santa María* in wood, and a model of the royal family (Isabel's) in silver.

Charles V, who was married here in 1526 to Isabelle of Portugal, added a **palace** of his own, as he did in the Alhambra. This contains a spectacular set of **Flemish tapestries**

The Worst Man in the World

Life does imitate art, sometimes, and it seems that rather than serving as a model for Tirso de Molina, Miguel de Mañara (*see* p.120) saw the play, *El Burlador de Sevilla*, in 1641 when he was fourteen years old, and decided that he himself would become Don Juan. His story is as *sevillano* as anyone could ask, but this Mañara was in fact a Corsican, the son of a wealthy landowner living in Spain. The Corsicans are almost as proud of him as they are of Napoleon.

Like Napoleon, he wasn't the most amazing of physical specimens, with unprepossessing features arranged around a big Corsican nose, but his intensity and force of character were always enough to get him in the door, and usually well beyond it. The first notorious scandal he caused in Sevilla was taken right out of the play. He seduced a woman named Doña Teresita Sánchez who was legendary for her chastity and virtue, and then killed her father when he caught them together in her bedroom. With the police on his heels, he managed to escape and joined the Spanish army fighting in the Netherlands, where he performed with such conspicuous bravery that eventually the charges against him were dropped, and he returned to Sevilla.

There were bigger escapades to come. Mañara travelled to Corsica, where he was not known, and seduced his own cousin. Then he went back to Sevilla and had

showing finely detailed scenes of Charles' campaigns in Tunisia. Upstairs, you can take a guided tour of the royal apartments (an extra €3) if the royal family are not at home; the Alcázar is the oldest palace in use in Europe. Most of the furnishings are 19th-century, but there are some remarkable 15th- and 16th-century *artesonado* ceilings and you can also see Isabel La Católica's chapel and Pedro the Cruel's bedroom.

Within its walls, the Alcázar has extensive and lovely **gardens**, with reflecting pools, avenues of clipped hedges, and lemons and oranges everywhere. The park is deceptively large, but you can't get lost unless you find the little **labyrinth** near the pavilion built for Charles V in the lower gardens. Outside the walls, there is a formal promenade called the **Plaza Catalina de Ribera** with two monuments to Columbus, and the extensive **Jardines de Murillo**, bordering the northern wall of the Alcázar.

From the Cathedral to the River: El Arenal

Avenida de la Constitución, passing the façade of the cathedral, is Sevilla's main street. Between it and the Guadalquivir is the neighbourhood of **El Arenal**, once the city's bustling port district, thronged with sailors, shopkeepers, idlers and prostitutes. Those colourful days have long passed – even its old name, 'Baratillo' meaning 'shambles', was changed in the 18th century by writers in search of a more romantic past. El Arenal means, poetically, 'expanse of sand', referring to its isolation outside the old Arabic city perimeter, when only a slim stretch of wall along the river protected it from invaders. Now it is a quiet, tranquil district with small shops and cafés, without the distinction of the Santa Cruz quarter, but with an earthy charm all of its own. Heading down to the river, you will pass through one of the few surviving rampart

another go at Doña Teresita, who after her father's murder had become a nun. God, apparently, had had enough of Miguel de Mañara, and He sent him a vision of his own death and funeral, late at night on the corner of Sevilla's Calle del Ataúd and Calle de la Muerte (Street of the Coffin and Street of Death) and the old rake – he had reached the ripe old age of 21 – was frightened sufficiently to send a letter to Doña Teresita explaining his designs, and how he had planned to abandon her. The shock of learning that he had never really loved her was too much, and she died that night.

Mañara resolved to reform, and because this is Sevilla his redemption took a form as extreme as his former life of evil. At first he married, and behaved himself, but the visions of his own funeral kept recurring, and he eventually joined the fraternity of the Santa Caridad and took it over as prior. Here Mañara became a local legend. He spent his entire fortune on this hospital, and was known for personally caring for the sick during a plague, feeding the poor and comforting the afflicted; he even extended his pity to Sevilla's dogs, building the low trough in the convent wall to give them a drink. His confessions are still kept at the hospital's archive, and he is buried near the chapel entrance in a tomb, where he himself ordered the inscription: 'Here lie the ashes of the worst man the world has ever known.' There was a movement to make Mañara a saint, but so far he has only reached the title of Venerable.

gates leading to the old port area, the **Gate of Olive Oil** (Postigo del Aceite), a 16th-century remodelling of an old Moorish gate, with long vertical grooves for slotting in flood barriers when the river sporadically burst its banks. The city's coat of arms was added in the refurbishment, along with a little chapel.

Hospital de la Caridad

Open Mon–Sat 9–1.30 and 3.30–6.30, Sun 9–1; adm; ***t*** *95 422 32 32.*

Behind a colourful façade on C/Temprado is the **Charity Hospital**, built in 1647 in the old warehouse area which used to back on to the port. This piece of ground was used for hanging criminals until the 15th century, when the Cofradía de la Caridad sought permission to give the dead a Christian burial and provide shelter for the poor. The original hospital was established in the docklands Chapel of San Jorge, before its reconstruction in infinitely grander style during the 17th century. The new, improved hospital's benefactor was a certain Miguel de Mañara (*see* 'The Worst Man in the World', p.118), a reformed rake who has been claimed (erroneously, as the dates just won't add up) as the prototype for Tirso de Molina's Don Juan.

Though it still serves its intended purpose as a charity home for the aged, visitors come to see the art in the hospital chapel. The entrance is through a shadowy magenta and ochre courtyard with a double gallery, palms, fountains and panels of 17th-century Dutch Delft tiles brought from a convent in Cádiz. Much of the chapel's art has gone, unfortunately – in the lobby they'll show you photographs of the four Murillos stolen by Napoleon. The remaining eight in the series still hang here, a cosy group of saints and miracles, among them St Isabel of Hungary tending the poor, and a wild-eyed Moses drawing water from the rock. Murillo, a close friend of Mañara, and a prominent lay brother, was also responsible for the *azulejo* panels on the chapel façade depicting a rampant St Jorge, St James and three, overwrought virtues, Faith, Hope and Charity. Among what remains inside are three works of art, ghoulish even by Spanish standards, that reflect the funereal obsessions of Miguel de Mañara, who commissioned them. Juan de Valdés Leal (1622–90) was a competent enough painter, but warmed to the task only with such subjects as you see here: a bishop in full regalia decomposing in his coffin, and Death snuffing out your candle. Even better than these is the anonymous, polychrome bloody Jesus, surrounded by smiling Baroque *putti*, who carry, instead of harps, whips and scourges. Murillo's reported judgement on these pictures was that 'one has to hold one's nose to look at them'.

The Mint (Casa de la Moneda) and the Tower of Gold (Torre del Oro)

On C/Santada stands the renovated **Tower of Silver** (Torre de la Plata) and, along from it on C/Hubana, the **Mint**, rebuilt in the 16th century from a 13th-century Muslim watchtower, to cope with the flood of precious metals pouring in from the Indies. Here, the gold and silver marks of the Spanish empire were minted in dizzying quantities. Picture the scene when the annual silver fleet came in: for over a century the fleet's arrival was the event of the year, the turning point of an annual feast-or-famine cycle when debts would be repaid, and long-deferred indulgences enjoyed.

The Moorish **Tower of Gold** (***t*** *95 422 24 19; open Tues–Fri 10–2, weekends 11–2; closed Aug; adm*), which takes its name from the gold and *azulejo* tiles that covered its 12-sided exterior in the days of the Moors, stands on the banks of the Guadalquivir. The tower, built by the Almohads in 1220, was the southernmost point of the city's fortifications. In times of trouble a chain would be stretched from the tower and across the Guadalquivir; in 1248 the chain was broken by an attacking fleet led by Admiral Ramón de Bonifaz, the supply route with Triana was cut off and Sevilla fell. The interior now houses the small **Museo Marítimo** (*open Tues–Sat 10–2, Sun 10–1*), with plans, models, documents, weapons and maps of the golden age of the explorers.

The Cathedral of Bullfighting

On the river, just north of the tower, is another citadel of *sevillano* charm. **La Maestranza bullring**, with its blazing white and ochre arches, is not as big as Madrid's, but it is still a lovely building, and perhaps the most prestigious of all *plazas de toros*. It was begun in 1760 under the auspices of the aristocratic equestrian society of the Real Maestranza de Caballería (who still own it) in order to practise equestrian displays, including bullfights, and it was largely responsible for raising the profile of an otherwise dying and insalubrious neighbourhood. The Carlist Wars got in the way and the bullring was, amazingly, not finished until 1880, which is why it took on its characteristic oval shape – to squeeze itself in among the surrounding buildings. Today it is known as the 'cathedral of bullfighting' and is particularly celebrated for its extraordinary acoustics; it is said that every rustle of the matador's cape can be heard. From April until September, it carries a packed schedule; if you like to watch as your *rabo de toro* (oxtail) is prepared, you may be fortunate enough to see a *corrida* while in town (*see* 'Bullfighting', pp.52–3 and p.110). Inside is the **Museo Taurino** (***t*** *95 422 45 77; open daily 9.30–2 and 3–7, or 9.30–3 when a bullfight is being held; adm*), with a small shop, and displays of antique posters, portraits of celebrated bullfighters, the mounted heads of famous bulls, elaborate costumes and other memorabilia. Carmen stands haughtily outside, hand on hip, surveying the bullring which saw her tragic end in Bizet's opera. The large, modern, circular building on the Paseo del Cristóbal Colón which echoes the shape of La Maestranza is the **Theatre of Maestranza** (*information* ***t*** *95 422 33 44, www.maestranza.com*), a grand opera house built for Expo '92.

Triana

Across the Guadalquivir from the bullring is the neighbourhood of Triana, an ancient suburb that takes its name from the Emperor Trajan. Until the mid-19th century it was joined to the city centre by a pontoon, a flimsy string of boats that would get washed away by the frequent floods; finally, in 1852, the first fixed bridge was constructed, officially named the Bridge of Isabel II, but known to all as the **Bridge of Triana**. Even now, some people quickly glance at the carved lion's head at the Triana end of the bridge: an old superstition warns that, if the water rises to the lion's mouth, Sevilla will be flooded again. The bridge culminates in Plaza del

Altozano, with a statue of the famous bullfighter Juan Belmonte (1892–1962), whose motto was purportedly 'stop, pacify and control'. He looks as if he could manage it still.

The neighbourhood has a reputation for being the 'cradle of flamenco'. Queipo de Llano's troops wrecked a lot of it at the beginning of the Civil War, but there are still picturesque white streets overlooking the Guadalquivir.

On the riverbank on the right-hand side of the Bridge of Triana (with the bridge at your back) is the Paseo Nuestra Senora de la O, a charming avenue where a colourful and cheap produce market is now held. On the same spot, five centuries ago, the Castle of San Jorge, originally built by the Moors, became the infamous **Castle of the Inquisition**, a prison for those accused of Judaism, heresy and witchcraft. Sevilla's first auto-da-fé was held here in 1481 and the castle was destroyed only in 1820, when the Inquisition was finally abolished. The air used to be thick with fumes from the kilns which clustered around this part of town, and the streets around C/Castilla and C/San Jorge are still some of the best for finding Triana ceramics. The area's workmen make all Sevilla's *azulejo* tiles.

C/Betis, right on the river on the left-hand side of the Bridge of Triana, is one of the liveliest streets, with a string of popular bars and restaurants with wonderful views. The Feria de la Velá is held here in July, in honour of Triana's patron saint, Santa Ana, with dancing, buskers and street vendors. A gunpowder factory once stood here, until it exploded, catapulting dozens of people into the river.

The C/Pureza, behind it, leads to the Plaza de Santa Ana and one of the oldest Christian churches in the city. Towards the end of the 13th century, Alfonso X was miraculously cured of a strange disease of the eye and ordered the construction of a church in thanks. Built around 1276, the simple, Gothic church of **Santa Ana** holds a 16th-century *retablo* by Pedro de Campaña, and a fabulous *azulejo*-tiled tomb by Nicoloso Pisano. The most famous treasure is the enormous silver monstrance which forms part of Triana's Corpus Chico procession. The square around the church becomes especially animated during big festivals, particularly around Corpus Christi and Christmas, when it erects a huge nativity scene.

Back on C/Pureza, there stands the lovely **Chapel of the Virgen de la Esperanza** (*open Mon–Sat 9–1 and 5.30–9, Sun 9–1*), home to Triana's celebrated weeping figure of the Virgin of Hope, main rival to the equally famous figure in the *barrio* of La Macarena (*see* p.126) during the Semana Santa processions and celebrations. The chapel is also known as the Chapel of Sailors (Capilla de los Marineros), who would come here to pray for a safe return from their voyages, and from where mass used to be bellowed, so that all the sailors in the galleons moored along the river could hear.

Triana was traditionally a rich recruitment area for the ships setting out to discover new lands and fabulous treasures. C/Rodrigo de Triana is named after a local sailor who voyaged to the Indies with Columbus and first spied the New World. Another chapel popular with seafarers is the chapel of the **Convent of Remedios** in the Plaza de Cuba; sailors would blast their cannons in homage to the Virgen de Los Remedios (Virgin of Redemption) as they passed in their galleons, and pray for her protection on their Atlantic voyages. The convent later became the Hispano-Cuban Institute for the History of America, but Franco closed it down after a tiff with Fidel Castro.

The street leading off the Plaza de Cubana into the relatively new suburban quarter of Los Remedios is named after **Juan Sebastián Elcano**, who sailed with Magellan on his fateful voyage round the world. Two hundred and sixty-five sailors left Sevilla in 1519 and, after they had battled their way around the Cape of Good Hope, Magellan was killed in the Philippines; Elcano took command of the last remaining ship and limped home with just 18 sailors three years later. Also near the Plaza de Cubana is **C/Salado**, undistinguished by day but the best place for dancing *sevillanas* by night.

Northwest of the Cathedral: Art and the Auto-da-fé

Back across the river, over the Bridge of Triana, you'll approach the **San Eloy** district, full of raucous bars and hotels. On C/San Pablo is **La Magdalena** (1704), rebuilt by Leonardo de Figueroa on the ruins of the Dominican Convent of San Pablo, itself fused with an even older mosque. The eccentric Baroque façade is decorated with sundials, and the colourful dome is supported by long-suffering South American Indians. Among the art inside are two paintings of the life of St Dominic by Zurbarán, and gilded reliefs by Leonardo de Figueroa. Above the door is a hint of the church's nefarious past: the shield of the Inquisition. Heresy trials took place in this church and the condemned were led through the Door of the Jews, since closed up and hidden behind a chapel. Heretics were then burned in the Prado de San Sebastián or in the Plaza de San Francisco, expressly remodelled for the purpose. Many of the paintings and frescoes celebrate the triumph of the Catholic faith and the suppression of heresy, including a mural by Lucas Valdés, son of Valdés Leal, depicting an auto-da-fé. The face of the accused was scratched out by his outraged descendants, and restorers had to fill in the blank.

Fine Arts Museum (Museo de Bellas Artes)

Open Tues 3–8, Wed–Sat 9–8, Sun 9–2, closed Mon; adm, free to EU citizens.

This excellent collection is housed in the **Convent of Merced** (1612), on C/San Roque, expropriated for the state in 1835. It is set around three courtyards, the first of which is handsomely decorated with lustrous tiled panels taken from Sevilla's convents. There are some fine medieval works: some naïve-looking virgins, and an especially expressive triptych by the Master of Burgos from the 13th century. **Pedro Millán**, one of the most influential sculptors of the period, is well represented; the *Burial of Christ* is haunting and, in another sculpture, a mournful Christ stares in disbelief at the gash in his side. The Italian sculptor **Pietro Torrigiano** (the fellow who broke Michelangelo's nose, and who died here, in the Inquisition's prisons) has left an uncanny, barbaric wooden **St Jerome**. This saint, Jerónimo in Spanish, is a favourite in Sevilla, where he is pictured with a rock and a rugged cross instead of his usual lion. Torrigiano's *Virgen de Belén* (*c.* 1525) has a luminous clarity and stillness. There is a comprehensive collection of altarpieces and *retablos* from this period, with fiery scenes of hell and damnation, set off by the decapitated head of John the Baptist leering through a glass case. Through another of the lovely courtyards planted with orange trees, the main staircase, known as the Imperial Staircase, and richly decorated in the Mannerist style with swarms of angels, leads to a room full of the works of the most mannered of them all, **Murillo** (a *sevillano*, buried in Santa Cruz). Among the paintings is an Immaculate Conception and many other artful missal-pictures, accompanied by a number of pieces by the prolific painter Valdés Leal. Much more interesting are the works of **Zurbarán**, who could express spirituality without the simpering of Murillo or the hysteria of the others. His series of female saints is especially good, and the *Miracle of St Hugo* is perhaps his most acclaimed work. An altarpiece he sculpted for the Monasterio Cartujo de Santa María de las Cuevas (*see* p.130) has also found its way here. Occasionally even Zurbarán slips up; you may enjoy the *Eternal Father* with great fat toes and a triangle on his head, a *St Gregory* who looks like the scheming Church executive he really was, and the wonderful *Apotheosis of St Thomas Aquinas*, in which the great scholastic philosopher rises to his feet as if to say 'I've got it!' The room is dominated by an astounding *Cristo Crucificado* (*c*.1630–40). Don't miss El Greco's portrait of his son Jorge, or the wonderful stark portraits by Ribera. There are also works by Jan Brueghel, Caravaggio and Mattia Preti, and a less interesting section of 19th- and 20th-century works, mainly portraits of coy *sevillanas*, fluttering their fans or dandling pooches, and dashing dandies, swaggering in their finery.

North of the Cathedral: the Heart of the City

Sevilla's business and shopping area has been since Moorish times the patch of narrow streets north of La Giralda. **Calle Sierpes** ('Serpent Street') is its heart, a sinuous pedestrian lane lined with every sort of old shop, named after an ancient inn sign which depicted the jaws of a snake – or perhaps just because it is so winding. Just to the north, **El Salvador** is the city's second-biggest religious building after the cathedral, a fine Baroque church by Leonardo de Figueroa. It is picturesquely mouldering, its once-vibrant 'bull's blood' plasterwork now faded to a dusky rose. On the left is a door leading to the **Patio de los Naranjos**, with dilapidated Roman columns and arches that are all that remain of what was once the city's principal mosque (and before that a Visigothic cathedral and before that a Roman basilica) in a neat patchwork of pragmatic expropriation across two millennia and at least four sets of religious belief. The old minaret was turned into the belfry. The square in front of the church is one of Sevilla's liveliest, with *movida* kids sprawling on the church steps, and throngs of people sipping chilled sherry from the tiny *bodeguitas* opposite.

East of the Plaza del Salvador is little **Plaza Alfalfa**, now another vibrant nightspot, along with **Plaza de la Encarnación** a couple of streets to the north. The Plaza Alfalfa, once the site of the Roman forum and medieval markets selling meat and *alfalfa*, is at the heart of the city's oldest merchant district, with narrow half-timbered houses jostling for space on the tiny streets. Many of the narrow streets and squares in this district are named after the trades that were once carried out here, like the C/de la Pescadería, once the scene of a busy fishmarket, and tiny Plaza del Pan, where the bakers plied their trade.

Not far from the Plaza de la Encarnación, on bustling C/Cuna, is the **Palace of the Countess of Lebrija** (Palacio de la Condesa de Lebrija; *open Mon–Fri 10–1.30 and 5–8, Sat 10–2, closed Sun; adm, guided visits of apartments extra;* **t** *95 421 81 83, www.palaciodelebrija.com*). The Condesa de Lebrija was one of Spain's first female architects and an inveterate hoarder: she transformed her family home (a 16th-century palace) with thousands of archaeological odds and ends discovered at the excavations in Itálica (*see* p.134) and around Seville. Copies of fine Roman mosaics cover the entire first floor, while the original pieces hang, framed, on the walls. The vestibule glows with thousands of brightly coloured *azulejo* tiles, painted in Triana in the 18th century. A collection of tiny artefacts, also gleaned from Itálica, includes a handful of engraved signet rings made from cornelian, agate and glass, and shards of pottery (the prettiest are from Arabic pots which gleam like mother-of-pearl). The private apartments are open to visitors, and offer a glimpse into the world of an unconventional Sevillana aristocrat. Back out on C/Cuna are a number of Sevilla's fanciest flamenco shops, with all kinds of dresses and accessories.

On the **Plaza Nueva**, Sevilla's modern centre, you can see the grimy **City Hall** (Ayuntamiento), with a fine, elaborate Plateresque façade, built as the brand-new home for the town councillors in 1564, after Charles V complained about the shabbiness of their former home. The **Plaza de San Francisco**, which spreads out on the other side of the City Hall, was remodelled at the same time in order to serve as a suitably grand backdrop for the city's processions and its executions. From here, Avenida de la Constitución changes its name to C/Tetuán. Sevilla has found a hundred ways to use its *azulejos*, but the best has to be in the **billboard** on this street for 1932 Studebaker cars – so pretty that no one's had the heart to take it down.

La Macarena and Around

The northern end of Sevilla contains few monuments, though most of its solid, working-class neighbourhoods are clustered around Baroque parish churches. The **Alameda de Hércules** has been adorned since the 16th century with statues of Hercules, the mythical founder of the city, and Julius Caesar, credited with building the city's walls. This is the centre of one of the shabbier, yet most appealing, parts of the city, with a smattering of laid-back bars, music shops and cafés now paving the way for a new wave of gentrification. A fashionable promenade until the late 19th century, it nose-dived into disrepute when the bordellos and gambling dens took over at the end of the 19th century, and then had another brief flicker of glory as one of the foremost flamenco venues in Andalucía in the early 1900s. Statues of two of flamenco's finest performers, Aurora Pavón and Manolo Caracol, stand at either end of the avenue, which is currently half-hidden behind scaffolding while a major facelift is carried out. It can still be seedy and occasionally slightly threatening at night, but the neighbourhood bars are very popular with Sevilla's hip, arty crowd.

The earthy *barrio* of La Feria, next to El Arenal, is a delightfully old-fashioned, mercantile quarter, once the district of artisans and wool craftsmen, made up of a patchwork of crooked streets around the wide boulevard of C/de la Feria itself. Thursday mornings are particularly lively, animated by **El Jueves**, the celebrated antiques and bric-a-brac market, which has been going strong since the 13th century.

Santa Clara and **San Clemente** are two interesting 13th-century monasteries in this area, both established soon after Fernando III's victory over the Muslims in 1289; the former includes one of Sevilla's best *artesonado* ceilings and a Gothic tower built by Don Fadrique. There were two Don Fadriques, both of whom came to sticky ends, and both of whom are responsible for the tower according to separate legends. The first was Fernando III's son, who built his palace on this spot and carried on an affair with his widowed stepmother, to the disgust of his brother, who had him executed; the second was Pedro the Cruel's brother, who began an affair with Doña Blanca, Pedro's abandoned wife, for which he too lost his head. This isn't the only dramatic tale which clings to the convent: Pedro I, an infamous womanizer, pursued a terrified gentlewoman named Doña María, stripped her husband of his lands and property and executed him. Doña María took refuge in the convent and disfigured herself by throwing burning oil on her face. At least this story doesn't have an entirely sad ending: eventually her lands were returned to her and she founded the convent of Santa Iñes in 1374. Her tomb is opened annually on 2 December and her body is said never to have decomposed. The convent of **Santa Clemente** is the city's oldest, built on the remains of a Moorish palace; once a rich convent which enjoyed royal patronage, it was stripped of its lands during the Napoleonic occupation, when the nuns were ousted and the buildings were seconded for use as a warehouse and prison. A beautiful 16th-century *mudéjar* coffered ceiling and handsome frescoes by Valdés Leal and his son managed to survive the sacking.

Also near the Alameda de Hércules is the imposing **Basilica of Jesús de la Grand Poder**, a favourite spot for *sevillano* weddings. The basilica contains a celebrated and much revered 17th-century statue of the same name by Juan de Mesa. It is solemnly paraded through the streets on Good Friday morning.

North of C/San Luís, some of the city's **Moorish walls** survive, near the **Basilica of La Macarena** (*open daily 9–1 and 5–9; adm for museum*), which gives the quarter its name. The basilica, a garish 1940s neo-Baroque construction luridly frescoed with puffs of fluorescent angels, is the home of the most worshipped of Sevilla's idols, a delicate Virgin with glass tears on her cheeks who always steals the show in the Semana Santa parades. Like a film star she makes her admirers gasp and swarm around her, crying '*¡O la hermosa! ¡O la guapa!*' ('O beautiful Virgin! O lovely Virgin!'). Fleets of veiled old ladies jostle for the closest position to her feet, and twitter over the thousands of photographs laid out in the shop. The small adjacent **museum** (*entrance inside the chapel*) is devoted to her costumes, a breathtaking giant-sized Barbie wardrobe of superbly embroidered robes encrusted with gold and jewels, and solid gold crowns and ceremonial paraphernalia. Also here are the elaborately carved and gilded floats which take part in the Semana Santa parades; the first depicts the moment when Pontius Pilate passed the sentence of death on Christ, and the second carries the Virgin herself, weeping for the death of her son.

South from here, along C/San Luis, you'll pass another Baroque extravaganza, Leonardo de Figueroa's **San Luís**, built for the Jesuits (1699–1731), with twisted columns and tons of encrusted ornament. Lovely **San Marcos**, down the street, has an elaborate façade with a graceful combination of Gothic and Moorish elements, and one of Sevilla's last surviving *mudéjar* towers. The austere interior, with its soaring wooden roof supported by beautifully carved and decorated supporting beams, is adorned with elegant, white, Moorish horseshoe-shaped arches. Just east is the **Convento de Santa Paula**, with a finely detailed doorway with pink and blue inlaid tiles by Francisco Pisano and Pedro Millán (1504), and a pretty, much embellished openwork bell tower. You can take an excellent guided tour of the interior or just stop off at the little shop selling the jams and confectionery made by the nuns. Another post-1492 palace with *mudéjar* decoration, west on C/Bustos Tavera, is the huge **Palace of the Ladies** (Palacio de las Dueñas; *admission by appointment only; ask at the tourist office*).

Santa Cruz and Beyond

If Spain envies Sevilla, Sevilla envies **Santa Cruz**, a tiny, exceptionally lovely quarter of narrow streets and whitewashed houses. It appears to be the true homeland of everything *sevillano*, with flower-bedecked courtyards and iron-bound windows, though there is something unnervingly pristine about it. This is hardly surprising given that it was calculatedly primped up between 1912 and 1920 by the Ministry of Tourism in order to give visitors something to gawp at. Before 1492, this was the Jewish quarter of Sevilla; today it's the most aristocratic corner of town (and the most touristy). In the old days there was a wall around the *barrio*; today you may enter through the Murillo Gardens, the C/Mateos Gago behind the cathedral apse, or from the **Patio de las Banderas**, a pretty Plaza Mayor-style square next to the Alcázar. In the heart of this area lies the **Hospital de los Venerables** (***t*** *95 456 26 96; open daily 10–2 and 4–8; adm*), a former home for the elderly and now an art gallery set around a delightful courtyard. On the eastern edge of the *barrio*, **Santa María la Blanca** (on the street of the same name) was a pre-Reconquista church; some details remain, but the whole was rebuilt in the 1660s, with spectacular rococo ornamentation inside and paintings by Murillo. His former home, near little Plaza Alfara and the Murillo Gardens, has become a small **museum** devoted to his life and art.

On the eastern fringes of the old town, Santa Cruz fades gently into other peaceful, pretty areas – less ritzy, though their old streets contain more palaces. One of these, built by the Dukes of Medinaceli (1480–1571), is the **House of Pilate** (Casa de Pilatos; ***t*** *95 422 52 98; open daily 9–7; Tues 1–5; adm*) on Plaza Pilatos, one of Sevilla's loveliest hidden corners. The site once belonged to a judge who was condemned to death for heresy and had his lands confiscated by the Inquisition. They were snapped up by Don Pedro Enrique, the governor of Andalucía, who began construction of a palace in 1481, of which only the dauntingly named Chapel of Flagellation remains. His son, yet another Don Fadrique, was responsible for the present pleasing jumble of *mudéjar* and Renaissance work, with a lovely courtyard. It was constructed just after his return from a pilgrimage to Jerusalem, where, so the story goes, he was so struck by the Praetorium, Pontius Pilate's official residence, that he decided to model his palace at home on it. The entrance, a mock-Roman triumphal arch done in Carrara marble by sculptors from Genoa, is studded with Crusaders' crosses in commemoration of the pilgrimage. Each year in March, a Vía Crucis, following the Stations of the Cross, takes place between the House of Pilate and the Cruz del Campo, apparently the same distance as that between Pontius Pilate's house in Jerusalem and Mount Calvary. The entrance arch leads through a small courtyard into the **Patio Principal**, with 13th-century Granadan decoration, beautiful coloured tiles, and rows of Roman statues and portrait busts. These form a perfect introduction to the dukes' excellent collections of antique sculpture in the surrounding rooms, many with splendid coffered ceilings, including a Roman copy of a Greek *herm* (boundary marker, with the head of the god Hermes), imperial portraits, and a bust of Hadrian's boyfriend, Antinous. There is a series of delightful **gardens and courtyards** cooled with trickling fountains and bowers; the rose garden is especially lovely, particularly in spring, when the walls erupt in a blaze of purple bougainvillea. There is an optional tour of the **private apartments** upstairs (*tour in Spanish only*). You can see 18th-century furniture (particularly impressive in the dining hall), paper-thin porcelain from England and Limoges, fanciful Japanese vases and a rather humdrum collection of paintings ranging from portraits of stolid dukes and duchesses to a bullfight (set in Madrid) by Goya.

Behind the House of Pilate, **San Estebán**, rebuilt from a former mosque, has an altarpiece by Zurbarán. Farther up on noisy, traffic-filled Avenida de Luís Montoto are the forlorn remains of an Almoravid **aqueduct**.

Nudging up against the House of Pilate is the convent of **San Leandro**, founded in 1295, although this building dates from 1369, and has been considerably embellished and refurbished since. The original convent stood in the Field of Martyrs outside the city walls, but was brought in from the cold when the nuns complained of constant attacks from bandits and appealed to the king; Pedro I magnanimously donated them a piece of land confiscated from a 'disloyal' subject. Only the entrance courtyard can be viewed most of the year, but the richly endowed church, with two beautiful *retablos* by Juan Martínez Montañes, opens on the 22nd of each month, when hordes of supplicants descend to petition Santa Rita de Casia, the enormously popular patron saint of lost causes. On C/Águilas, **San Ildefonso** has a pretty polychrome 18th-century façade, and two perky towers.

South of the Cathedral

Sevilla has a building even larger than its cathedral – twice as large, in fact, and probably better known to the outside world. Since the 1950s it has housed parts of the city's **university** and it does have the presence of a college building, but it began its life in the 1750s as the state **Tobacco Factory** (Fábrica de Tabacos). In the 19th century, it employed as many as 12,000 women to roll cigars. (One of its workers, of course, was Bizet's Carmen.) These sturdy women, with 'carnations in their hair and daggers in their garters', hung their capes on the altars of the factory chapels each morning, rocked their babies in cradles while they rolled cigars, and took no nonsense from anybody. Next to the factory, the **Hotel Alfonso XIII**, built in 1929, is believed to be the only hotel ever commissioned by a reigning monarch – Alfonso literally used it as an annexe to the Alcázar when friends and relations came to stay. This landmark is well worth a visit, if you're not put off by an icy doorman. To the west of the hotel lies the Baroque **Palacio de San Telmo**, originally a naval academy, which became the court of an offshoot of the royal family in the mid-19th century. The dowager duchess María Luisa Fernanda de la Bourbon donated the elegant 19th-century ornamental gardens, the Delicias Gardens, to the city in 1893, and they formed the basis of the lovely city park which would bear her name.

María Luisa Park

For all its old-fashioned grace, Sevilla has been one of the most forward-looking and progressive cities of Spain in the 20th century. In the 1920s, while they were redirecting the Guadalquivir and building the new port and factories that are the foundation of the city's growth today, the *sevillanos* decided to put on an exhibition. In a tremendous burst of energy, they turned the entire southern end of the city into an expanse of gardens and grand boulevards. The centre of it is the **Parque de María Luisa**, a paradisiacal half-mile of palms and orange trees, covered with flowerbeds and dotted with hidden bowers and pavilions, one of the loveliest parks in Europe. Two of the largest pavilions, built by Aníbal González, on the **Plaza de América** have been turned into museums. The **Archaeological Museum** (Museo Arqueológico; ***t*** *95 423 24 01; open Tues 3–8, Wed–Sat 9–8, Sun and hols 9–2, closed Mon and Aug; adm, free to EU citizens*), with an impressively dour neo-Plateresque façade, has an excellent collection of pre-Roman jewellery and icons, and some tantalizing artefacts from mysterious Tartessos. The Romans are represented, as in every other Mediterranean archaeology museum, with copies of Greek sculpture and oversized statues of emperors, but also with a mosaic of the Triumph of Bacchus, another of Hercules, architectural fragments, some fine glass, and finds of all sorts from Itálica and other nearby towns. Across the plaza, the **Museum of Popular Art and Customs** (Museo de Artes y Costumbres Populares; ***t*** *95 423 25 76; open Tues 3–8, Wed–Sat 9–8, Sun and hols 9–2, closed Mon; adm, free to EU citizens*), in the Mudéjar Pavilion, with a gleeful motif of tiny unicorns and griffons dancing across blue tiles, is Andalucía's attic, with everything from ploughs and saucepans to flamenco dresses and exhibits from the city's two famous celebrations, Semana Santa and the April Feria.

The Plaza de España

In the 1920s at least, excess was still a way of life in Sevilla, and to call attention to the **Exposición Iberoamericana** they put up a building even bigger than the Tobacco Factory. With its grand Baroque towers (stolen gracefully from Santiago de Compostela), fancy bridges, staircases and immense colonnade, the Plaza de España is World's Fair architecture at its grandest and most outrageous. Much of the fanciful neo-Spanish architecture of 1930s Florida and California may well have been inspired by this building. The Fair, as it turned out, was a flop; attendance proved disappointing, and when it was over Sevilla was left nearly bankrupt. The dictator, Primo de Rivera, who was himself from Jerez, and who had put a lot of money and effort into this fair to show off his native region, died while it was still running, at the lowest depths of unpopularity. For all that, the *sevillanos* are glad they at least have this building and its park to show for the effort. They gravitate naturally to it at weekends, to row canoes in the Plaza's canals and nibble curious pastries. One of the things Sevilla is famous for is its painted *azulejo* tiles; they adorn nearly every building in town, but here on the colonnade a few million of them are devoted to maps and historical scenes from every province in Spain.

La Cartuja and Contemporary Art

The Isle of La Cartuja was part of the Expo '92 site, but it has become seedy and rundown since and nothing seems to work, including the rusting cable car which once hoisted visitors across the river. Some of the original Expo pavilions are now devoted to holding business fairs and conferences, and another section has become the **Isla Mágica** funfair (*open April–Oct Mon-Fri 11–7, Sat–Sun 11–10, until midnight daily in August; adm. Hours change regularly; for information check www.islamagica.es*).

Infinitely more interesting is the monastery of **Santa María de las Cuevas y la Cartuja** (*St Mary of the Caves; aka Centro Andaluz de Arte Contemporáneo; open Tues–Fri 10–9, Sat 11–9; Sun 10–3m, closed Mon; guided visits twice-daily, call for times,* ***t*** *95 503 70 70*), the partially restored Carthusian monastery where Columbus once stayed while he mulled over his ambitions and geographical theories. Pottery kilns proliferated here from the 12th century, and the Virgin is said to have appeared in one of the workshops. A Francisan hermitage was established in honour of the vision and, in 1399, Gonzalo de Mena, the archbishop of Sevilla, founded the Cartuja monastery. It grew to become a virtually self-sufficient walled city, giving refuge to spiritual figures such as Teresa de Jesús as well as all the Spanish monarchs who passed through Sevilla. At the peak of its affluence, the monastery was richly endowed with masterpieces by great artists from Zurbarán to Murillo. Since then, sadly, the building has suffered numerous indignities; the monks were driven out by Marshal Soult, who used it as a garrison during the Napoleonic occupation of 1810–12 and is responsible for the damage to the extraordinary *artesonado* ceiling in the refectory – his troops used the gable for target practice. As if this wasn't enough, the city sold it off to Liverpudlian Charles Pickman in the 1830s, who turned it into a ceramics factory. The brick kilns still soar above the monastery garden, which is full of orange trees.

Now the monastery is home to the **Andalucían Centre of Contemporary Art** (*opening times as above*), the only contemporary arts centre in Andalucía and one of the most singular and absorbing anywhere. The atmospheric ruins of the monastery itself serve as a palimpsest of the waves of invaders who have stripped it bare of most of its treasures, and yet, despite them, it retains a hushed and reverent stillness;

among the art now displayed on the ruined walls is a series of eight blazing paintings by José Manuel Bioto, in hazy, dreamy ochres and indigoes, in the main chapel, and a limpid collection of Japanese-inspired panels in St Anne's Chapel, where Columbus was once laid to rest. Attached to the monastery complex are the main exhibition galleries, in an unobtrusive, light-filled, modern building entered through a courtyard draped in a forest of vines. These are devoted to temporary exhibitions which focus on both emerging and established Andalucían artists and international artists who develop projects designed specifically for the space; this is one of the most engaging and vibrant places in Spain to see contemporary art and it shouldn't be missed.

Sevilla Province

Heading South

If you're travelling south on your way to Jerez or Cádiz, stops at a few towns on the way will make an interesting alternative to the big four-lane highway. **Alcalá de Guadaira**, off the N334, is jocularly known in Sevilla as Alcalá de los Panaderos ('of the bakers'), as it used to supply the city with its daily bread. Its **castle** is the best-preserved Almohad fortress in Andalucía. Just outside Utrera, the tiny village of **Palmar de Troya** received a visit in 1968 from the Virgin Mary (to little girls, as usual) which led to the founding of a new church, the Orden de la Santa Faz, a vast complex

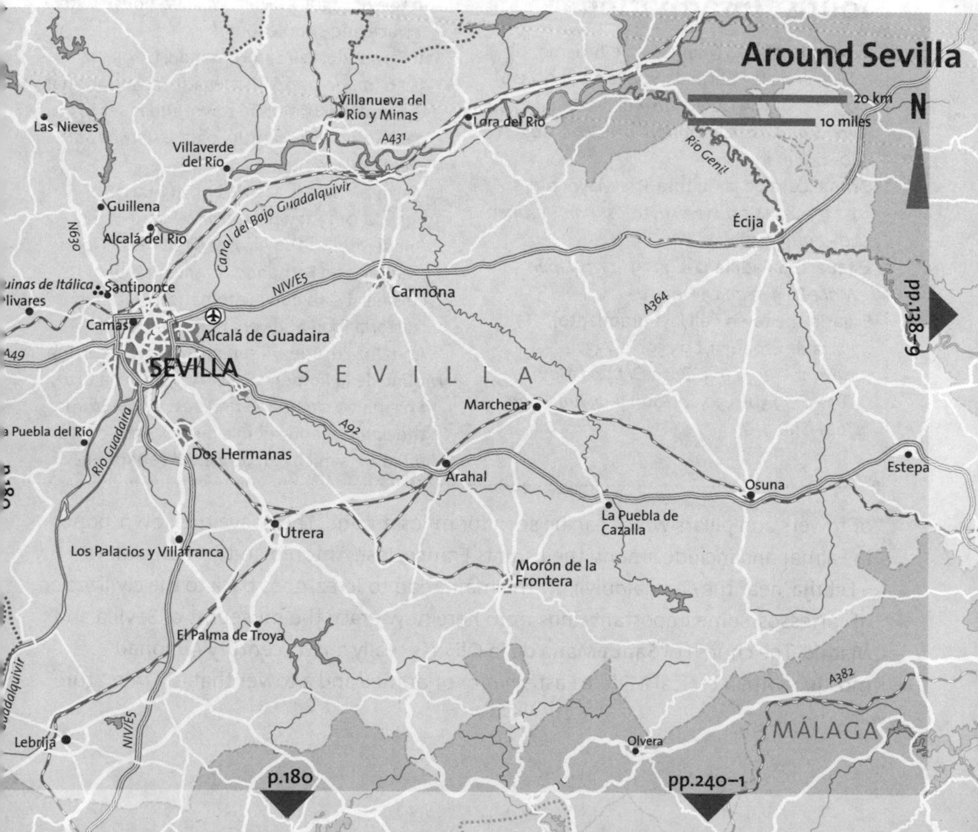

Getting There

There are two ways to go, both of approximately equal length. The **train**, and most of the **buses**, take the duller route through the flat lands along the Guadalquivir. The only landmark here is the Spanish-Moorish castle of Almodóvar del Río, perched overlooking the river. The southern route (the NIV) also follows the Guadalquivir valley, but the scenery is a little more varied, and the road passes through two fine towns, Carmona and Écija. There are regular buses from Sevilla to these towns, from where you can easily find connecting buses for Córdoba.

Getting Around

There is no train service for the towns around Sevilla, but plenty of **buses**. Itálica is on the Ctra Menda, with local buses leaving every half-hour from the Plaza de Armas, near the Puerto del Cachorro; the main highway east and south is the NIV.

Tourist Information

Carmona: Oficina Municipal de Turismo, Alcázar de la Puerta de Sevilla s/n, **t** 95 419 09 55, **f** 95 419 00 80, *carmona@andal.es, www.andal.es/carmona. Open Mon–Sat 10–6, Sun 10–3.*

Osuna: Casa de la Cultura, Pza Mayor s/n, **t/f** 95 582 14 00, *www.ayto-osuna.org. Open 10–2 and 5–7.*

Estepa: C/Saladillo 12, **t** 95 591 27 71. *Open Mon–Fri 9–2 and 3–10.*

Écija: in the town hall (ayuntamiento), Plaza de España 1, **t** 95 590 29 33, *turismo@ecija.org. Open Oct and May Tues–Fri 9.30–1.30, Sat–Sun 9–2; June–Sept Tues–Sun 9–2.*

Where to Stay and Eat

Carmona ✉ 39554

There are several *casas rurales* around Carmona: ask the tourist office for a full list.

★★★★★**Palacio Casa Carmona**, Pza de Lasso 1, **t** 95 419 10 00, **f** 95 419 01 89, *www.casadecarmona.com, reserve@casadecarmona.com* (*luxury*). Lovingly restored by Marta Medina and her artist son Felipe, this 16th-century palace is the last word in refined good taste.

★★★★**Parador Alcázar del Rey Don Pedro**, Argollón s/n, **t** 95 414 10 10, **f** 95 414 17 12, *carmona@parador.es* (*expensive*). Occupying a section of Cruel Pete's summer palace, the finest in Andalucía for style and comfort. It has superlative views, a garden, pool and luxurious furnishings; good value.

★★★★**Hotel Alcázar de la Reina**, Pza de Lasso 2, **t** 95 419 62 00, **f** 95 414 01 13 (*moderate*). Set in a beautiful old house, with one of the best restaurants in town, **La Ferrara** (*see below*).

★**Pensión Comercio**, C/Torre del Oro, **t/f** 95 414 00 18 (*inexpensive*). One of the few *pensiónes* in town; a typical whitewashed house with a terrace and simple rooms.

San Fernando, Pza San Fernando, **t/f** 95 414 35 56 (*moderate*). This elegant restaurant has the best reputation in town, and is set in a handsome 16th-century palace. *Closed Sun eve, Mon and Aug.*

La Ferrara, Pza de Lasso 2, **t** 95 419 62 00, **f** 95 414 01 13, *www.alcazar-reina.es (moderate)*. In the Alcázar de la Reina Hotel, rivalling San Fernando for the quality of its cuisine. It's an odd combination of Italian trattoria food and very fine traditional Andaluz cuisine, all served in a lovely setting.

Molino de la Romera, C/Sor Ángelá de la Cruz, **t** 95 414 20 00 (*moderate*). Just down from the *parador* and set in a historic 15th-century building, which can be visited separately.

of towers and pillars which can be seen for miles around. They have their own 'pope' in Palmar and include among their saints Franco, José Antonio and Ramon Llull.

Lebrija, near the Guadalquivir off the main road to Jerez, goes back to the civilization of Tartessos; some important finds from here now grace the museums of Sevilla and Madrid. The church of **Santa María de la Oliva** is really a 12th-century Almohad mosque, with a typical Middle Eastern roof of domes and a tower that is a miniature

Offers superb food and some of the best views in town. Specializes in local meats.

El Ancla, C/Bonifacio IV s/n, **t** 95 414 38 04 (*moderate*). A traditional seafood restaurant. *Closed Sun eve and Mon.*

La Cueva, Barbacana Baja 2, **t/f** 95 419 18 11 (*inexpensive*). Situated just below the city walls, these whitewashed caves have a heavy emphasis on pork and an extensive vegetable menu.

Marchena ✉ 39554

★★**Ponce**, Pza Alvarado 2, **t** 95 484 31 80 (*inexpensive*). The only central accommodation, this simple *pensión* has basic rooms with or without bathrooms.

★★**Hostal Los Ángeles**, on the Ctra Sevilla–Málaga, Km 67, **t** 95 484 70 88 (*Inexpensive*). Basic, road-side hotel but quite lively.

Los Muleros, Travesía de San Ignacio, **t** 95 484 61 20 (*inexpensive*). Try local specialities here.

Casa Carrillo, C/Las Torres 39 (*inexpensive*). A classic in Marchena, with excellent tapas and creative local dishes in the *comedor*.

Osuna and Estepa ✉ 41640

★★★★**Palacio Marqués de la Gomera**, C/San Pedro 20, **t** 95 481 22 23, **f** 95 481 02 00, *www.hotelpalaciodelmarques.com* (*expensive*). A beautiful conversion of one of the town's more impressive mansions dating from the 18th century. There is a good restaurant attached, with an emphasis on traditional Mediterranean cooking.

Caballo Blanco, C/Granada 1, **t** 95 481 01 84 (*inexpensive*). Centrally located, clean and comfortable, with a garage.

★★**El Balcón de Andalucía**, Avda. Andalucía 11, **t** 95 591 26 80 (*cheap*). The best of a handful of hotels in Estepa,with a pool and garden.

Doña Guadalupe, C/Pza Guadalupe, **t** 95 481 05 58. Has very good reputation and excellent home-made desserts. *Closed Tues.*

Écija ✉ 41400

The hotels are mostly motels on the outskirts, serving traffic on the Madrid–Cádiz highway.

★★**Hotel Platería**, C/Platería 4, **t/f** 95 590 27 54 (*inexpensive*). Just off the main square with a lovely marble courtyard and helpful service; probably the best in town.

★★**Ciudad del Sol**, Avda Miguel de Cervantes 48, **t** 95 483 03 00, **f** 95 483 58 79 (*inexpensive*). A friendly place with air-conditioned rooms and a decent restaurant, the Casa Pirula.

★★**Astigi**, Ctra Madrid-Cadiz, km 450, **t** 95 596 50 55 (*moderate*). A road-side alternative, if the others are full.

Pensión Santa Cruz, Romero Gordillo 8, **t** 95 483 02 22 (*inexpensive*). A minute's walk from the main plaza, in a back street behind the fabulously named Gasolina Bar (try the veal, they cook it at your table) you will find this delightful little place with simple rooms that open out to the tiled courtyard.

Las Ninfas, Palacio de Benamejí, C/Cánovas del Castillo 4, **t** 95 590 45 92 (*expensive*). The setting is stylish and subtle, the food light, with an emphasis on fish. You may also spot the four marble nymphs (hence the name) which once stood in the Pza de España.

Bodegón del Gallego, C/Arcipreste Aparicio 3, **t** 95 483 26 18 (*moderate*). One of the best places to eat in town, serving stylish *andaluz* dishes.

Pasareli, Pasaje Virgen del Rocío, **t** 95 483 20 24 (*inexpensive*). Looks like any modern cafeteria in the heart of town, but there's a surprisingly efficient little restaurant tucked away in the corner, where you can eat well from a large selection for under €10

El Bisturí, Pza de España 23, **t** 95 483 10 66. Situated back on the main *plaza* and specializing in food from across Spain.

version of La Giralda, built in the 19th century. The main altarpiece is a work of Alonso Cano – but Lebrija is better known for its wine and ceramics, and as a lively centre of flamenco, with an annual festival called the Caracol.

Take care before you start any rambles in the countryside; this area south of Sevilla contains some of the best-known ranches where fighting bulls are bred, and the bulls are always allowed to run free.

Itálica

Open Tues–Sat 9–5.30, Sun 10–4; adm, free to EU citizens; **t** *95 599 65 83.*

Eight kilometres north of Sevilla, in the direction of Mérida, the only significant Roman ruins in Andalucía are at Itálica. The first Roman colony in Spain, this city was founded in the 3rd century BC by Scipio Africanus as a home for his veterans after their victory in the Punic Wars; a Tartessian town may have originally occupied the site. Itálica thrived in the imperial age. The Guadalquivir had a reputation for constantly changing its course in the old days, and this may explain the presence of two important cities so close together. Three great emperors, Trajan, Hadrian and Theodosius, were born here, as were the poet Lucan and the moralist Seneca. The biggest ruins are an **amphitheatre**, with seating for 40,000, some remains of temples, and a street of villa foundations.

The village of **Santiponce**, near the ruins, has a fine Gothic-*mudéjar* monastery built for the Cistercians in 1301, using surviving columns and other materials from the ruins. **San Isidoro del Campo** has a gruesome St Jerome on the altarpiece, carved in the 1600s by Juan Martínez Montañés (1566–1649).

From Sevilla to Córdoba

Carmona

The first town along the NIV, Carmona, seems like a miniature Sevilla. It is probably much older. Remains of a Neolithic settlement have been found around town; the Phoenician colony that replaced it grew into a city and prospered throughout Roman and Moorish times. Pedro the Cruel favoured it and rebuilt most of its **Alcázar**. Sitting proudly with views over the valley, this fortress is now a national *parador*.

Carmona is well worth a day's exploration. Its walls, mostly Moorish fortifications built over Roman foundations, are still standing, including a grand gateway on the road from Sevilla, the **Puerta de Sevilla** (**t** *95 414 08 11; open Tues–Sat 10–6, Sun 10–3; adm, free to EU citizens*). You can climb to the top of the Torre del Oro next to the Puerta de Sevilla (entrance through the tourist information office) for fantastic views. Continue through the arch and up to the palm-decked Plaza de San Fernando, where the under-16s and over-60s gather; the Ayuntamiento here has a Roman mosaic of Medusa in its courtyard (**t** *95 414 00 11; open Mon–Fri 8–3*).

Nearby, the **Casa Palacio del Marqués de las Torres** (**t** *95 414 01 28; open Mon, Wed–Sun 11–2 and 6.30–9.30, Tues 10–2; adm, free Tues*) is now the town's excellent and engaging history museum. Set around a pair of pretty patios linked with winding staircases, the galleries are stacked full of thoughtful and well laid-out exhibits on the town's history over the last few thousand years. There's plenty for kids, with interactive exhibits clearly labelled in English and Spanish.

Head up Calle Martín López to the lofty 15th-century church of **Santa María** (*open April–Sept Mon–Fri 9–2 and 5.30–7.30, Sat 9–2; Oct–March Mon–Fri 9–2 and 5–7, Sat 9–2; closed mid-Aug–mid-Sept; adm*), built on the site of an old mosque.

The old quarters of town have an ensemble of fine palaces, and *mudéjar* and Renaissance churches. On one of these, **San Pedro** (1466) (just outside the city walls by the Puerta de Sevilla, *open Thurs–Mon 11–2; adm*), you'll see another imitation of La Giralda, La Giraldilla – though she has a cleaner exterior and is not as fussily ornate as her big sister.

Carmona's prime attraction is the **Roman necropolis**, a series of rock-cut tombs off the Avenida Jorge Bonsor, a good 10-minute walk from the centre. Some, like the 'Tomb of Servilia', are elaborate creations with subterranean chambers and vestibules, pillars, domed ceilings and carved reliefs (***t** 95 414 08 11; open 15 June–15 Sept Tues–Fri 8.30–2, Sat 10–2; 16 Sept–14 June Tues–Fri 9–5, Sat 10–2; adm*). Near the entrance to the site are remains of the Roman amphitheatre, forlorn and unexcavated. There's a small **zoo** and conservation centre to the west of the town centre (***t** 95 419 16 96; open daily 11–9; adm*), which promotes the reintroduction of endangered species to their natural habitat.

Twenty-eight kilometres south of Carmona on the C339, **Marchena** still retains many of its wall defences dating from Roman times, with later Moorish and Christian additions. Of its gates, the arch of **La Rosa** is best, and in the **Torre del Oro** there is an archaeological museum. The Gothic church of **San Juan Bautista** has a *retablo* by Alejo Fernández and a sculpture by Pedro Roldán. There's also a small museum with a collection of paintings by Zurbarán. Nearby **El Arahal** is a bleached white town well worth visiting for its Baroque monuments, notably the church of **La Victoria** of *mudéjar* origin.

Osuna and Estepa

From here, you can continue on the N333 back towards Écija and Córdoba, or take a detour eastwards on the N334 to **Osuna**. Founded by a busy, go-ahead governor named Julius Caesar, this was an important Roman military centre for the south of Spain, and survives as an attractive little city of white houses with characteristic *rejas* over every window. Osuna was an aristocratic town after the Reconquista, home of the objectionable Dukes of Osuna who lorded it over much of Andalucía. Their 'pantheon' of tombs may be seen in the fine Renaissance **Colegiata** church (*open Oct–April 10.30–1.30 and 3.30–6.30; May–Sept 10–1.30 and 4–7, closed Sun afternoons in July and Aug; adm*) on a hill on the west side of town. Inside is a memorable Crucifixion by José Ribera, and four other works of his in the high altar *retablo*. Behind the church is the old university building, founded in 1548 and now serving as a school. Several decorative façades of 16th-century mansions can be seen along the **Calle San Pedro**. Osuna has a little **archaeology museum** (Plaza de la Duquesa Invierno, *open Tues–Sun Oct–April 11.30–1.39 and 4.30–6.30; May and Sept 11.30–13.30 and 5–7; June–Aug 10–2; adm*) in the **Torre del Agua**, part of the old fortifications, and a museum of dubious art in La Encarnación convent, a Baroque work of the late 18th century; the cloister is done out in ceramic tiles (*open Oct–April 10.30–1.30 and 3.30–6.30; May–Sept 10–1.30 and 4–7, closed Sun afternoons in July and Aug; adm*).

Back on the N334 you'll come to **Estepa**, a smaller version of Osuna known for its Christmas biscuits (*polverones* and *mantecados*), and the mass suicide of its inhabitants, who preferred not to surrender to the Roman enemy in 208 BC. Above the town are the remains of a castle with a well-preserved Almohad keep. The two Baroque showpieces are the churches of **El Carmen**, in the main square, with a spectacular façade, and the 18th-century **Virgen de los Remedios**.

Écija

Écija makes much of one of its nicknames, the 'city of towers', and tries to play down the other – the 'frying pan of Andalucía', which isn't exactly fair. Any Andalucían town can overheat you thoroughly on a typical summer's day and, if Écija is a degree hotter and a little less breezy than most, only a born Andalucían could tell the difference. Ask one and you'll soon learn that the Andalucians are the only people yet discovered who talk about the weather more than the English.

Nowadays you'll be put off by the clinical outskirts of the town and by the ill-concealed gas-holders; all was once forgiven when you reached the **Plaza de España**, which was one of the loveliest in Andalucía, charmingly framed by tall palms with an exquisite fountain at its centre (now in safe-keeping). However, the local council have taken it upon themselves to construct an underground car park beneath the plaza – a project unlikely to be completed for a few years. In the meantime the square lies hidden behind a 6ft-high concrete wall. The Ayuntamiento stands at one end and, if you ask politely, you may be able to look at a Roman mosaic in the council chamber, lovingly described by Laurie Lee in *A Rose For Winter*. The façade of the 18th-century **Santa María** wouldn't look out of place in a Sergio Leone movie. Most of the **towers** are sumptuously ornate, rebuilt after the great earthquake of 1755 – the one that flattened Lisbon. Santa María has one, along with **San Juan Bautista**, gaily decorated in coloured tiles, and **San Gil**. This last is the highest of the towers, and within are paintings by Alejo Fernández and Villegas Marmolejo (*all monuments open 10–1; free*).

Écija also has a set of Renaissance and Baroque palaces second in Andalucía only to those in Úbeda; most of these showy façades can be seen on or near the **Calle Emilio Castellar**. Worth visiting is the **Palacio de Benamejí** (*open Tues–Fri 9.30–1.30 and 4.30–6.30, Sat–Sun 9–2; free, €1 for mirador*), dating from the 18th century, where you can find some interesting archaeological remains, part *mudéjar*, part Baroque, some Roman mosaics, and various reliefs, coins and glass. You can also climb up to the mirador for fabulous views. The town is also rediscovering its equestrian roots, and there is a horse-riding school nearby, **Tierra de Caballos** (***t*** *95 590 07 21, www.ecija.org*), which offers riding for non-beginners.

The **Peñaflor Palace** (1728) on Calle de Castellar – now a library – is one of the outstanding works of Andalucían Baroque, with its grandiose façade and lovely patio. In the evening the town buzzes. After the big-city crush of Sevilla, you might find that this is the perfect place to spend a couple of days – busy enough to be interesting, but not too frantic.

Córdoba and Jaén

10

The Río Guadalquivir was al-Andalus's great highway, lined with tall water wheels and prosperous farms, while its barges carried the luxuries of the East up to the caliphs and their court. For all the noise on the Costas, this valley remains the heart of real Andalucía. Right in the centre of it lies a marvel, Córdoba, a citadel of pure Andalucían *duende* that guards at its heart one of the most fascinating buildings on the planet. North of Córdoba is the Sierra Morena, famous for good hunting and cured hams, as well as Belalcázar with its remarkable castle. To the south it's mostly

Córdoba and Jaén

Highlights

1 La Mezquita: Córdoba's great mosque
2 Lonely castles of the Valle de los Pedroches
3 Frothy Baroque in Priego de Córdoba
4 Úbeda, city of Renaissance palaces and churches
5 Hiking in the Sierra de Cazorla

endless rows of olive trees, though there are beauty spots such as the natural park in the Sierras Subbeticas, and fine, busy towns like Lucena and Priego de Córdoba.

From there, it's a slow, leisurely journey up the valley of the slow, leisurely Río Guadalquivir, passing a few million more olive trees and, in places, endless miles of sunflowers, a grand sight in the early summer. Jaén with its famous cathedral is here, though the main attractions are two lovely, out-of-the-way towns with exceptional ensembles of Renaissance architecture: Baeza and Úbeda.

Andalucía has two natural wonders, in two of the nation's 10 national parks. The low one of course is the wetlands of the Donaña near Sevilla, and the high one rises to meet the sources of the Guadalquivir: the mountain ranges of the Sierra de Cazorla and Sierra de Segura, both gorgeous, unspoiled, and home to one of the richest and most diverse collections of wildlife in Europe.

Córdoba

There are a few spots around the Mediterranean where the presence of past glories becomes almost tangible, a mixture of mythic antiquity, lost power and dissipated energy that broods over a place like a ghost. In Istanbul you can find it, in Rome, or among the monuments of Egypt, and also here on the banks of the Guadalquivir at Córdoba's southern gate. Looking around, you can see reminders of three defunct empires: a Roman bridge, a triumphal arch built for Philip II and Córdoba's Great Mosque, more than a thousand years old. The first reminds us of the city's beginnings, the second of its decline; the last one scarcely seems credible, as it speaks of an age when Córdoba was one of the most brilliant metropolises of all Europe, city of half a million souls, a place faraway storytellers would use to enthral audiences in the rude halls of the Saxons and Franks. The little plaza by the bridge concentrates melancholy like a magnet; there isn't much left for the rest of the town. Córdoba's growth has allowed it a chance to renovate its sparkling old quarters and monuments and with the new prosperity has come a contentment the city hasn't known since the Reconquista.

Everyone who visits Córdoba comes for the Great Mosque, but you should spare some time to explore the city itself. Old Córdoba is one of the largest medieval quarters of any European city, and certainly the biggest in Spain. More than Sevilla, it retains its Moorish character, in a maze of whitewashed alleys opening into the loveliest patios in all Andalucía.

History

Roman **Corduba**, built on a prehistoric site, was almost from the start the leading city of interior Spain, capital of the province of Hispania Ulterior, and later of the reorganized province of Baetica. Córdoba had a reputation as the garden spot of Hispania; it gave Roman letters Lucan and both Senecas among others, testimony to its prominence as a city of learning. Córdoba became Christianized at an early date. Ironically, the True Faith got its comeuppance here in 572, when the Arian Visigoths under

Leovigild captured the city from Byzantine rule. When the Arabs conquered, they found it an important town still, and it became the capital of al-Andalus when Abd ar-Rahman established the Umayyad emirate in 756.

For 300 years, Córdoba enjoyed the position of unqualified leader of al-Andalus. It is impossible to take the chronicles at face value – 3,000 mosques and 80,000 shops, a library of 400,000 volumes, in a city stretching for 16km along the banks of the Guadalquivir. We could settle for half these totals, and still be impressed. Beyond doubt, Córdoba was a city without equal in the West as a centre of learning; it would be enough to mention two 12th-century contemporaries: **Averroës**, the Muslim scientist and Aristotelian philosopher who contributed so much to the rebirth of classical learning in Europe, and **Moses Maimónides**, the Jewish philosopher (and later personal physician to Saladin in Palestine) whose reconciliation of faith and reason were assumed into Christianity by St Thomas Aquinas. Medieval Córdoba was a great trading centre, and its luxury goods were coveted throughout western Europe; the old word *cordwainer* is a memory of Córdoba's skill in leatherwork. At its height, picture Córdoba as a city of bustling international markets, great palaces, schools, baths and mosques, with 28 suburbs and the first street lighting in Europe. Its population, largely Spanish, Moorish and Arab, included students and merchants from all over Europe, Africa and Asia, and an army and palace secretariat made up largely of slaves and black Africans. In it Muslims, Christians, and Jews lived in harmony, at least until the coming of the fanatical Almoravids and Almohads. We can sense a certain decadence; street riots in Córdoba were an immediate cause of the break-up of the caliphate in 1031, but here, as in Sevilla, the coming of the **Reconquista** was an unparalleled catastrophe.

When **Fernando III** 'the Saint' captured the city in 1236, much of the population chose flight over putting themselves at the mercy of the priests, although history records that he was unusually tolerant of the Jews. It did not last. Three centuries of Castilian rule sufficed to rob Córdoba of all its glories and turn it into a depressed backwater. Only in the last hundred years has it begun to recover; today Córdoba has also become an industrial city, though you wouldn't guess it from its sympathetically restored centre. It is the third city of Andalucía, and the first and only big town since Franco's death to have elected a communist mayor and council.

La Mezquita

Ticket booth on the Patio de los Naranjos. Open Mon–Sat 10–7, Sun 2–7 in summer; 10–5.30 in winter; adm; **t** *95 747 05 12. Museo Diocesano open Mon–Sat 9.30–3; free with adm to Mezquita.*

La Mezquita is the local name for Abd ar-Rahman's **Great Mosque**. Mezquita means 'mosque' and even though the building has officially been a cathedral for more than 750 years, no one could ever mistake its origins. **Abd ar-Rahman I**, founder of a new state, felt it necessary to construct a great religious monument for his capital. As part of his plan, he also wished to make it a centre of pilgrimage to increase the sense of divorce from eastern Islam; Mecca was at the time held by his Abbasid enemies.

Córdoba
SANTA MARIA DE TRASIERRA
GLORIETA PRETORIO
Convento de Merced/ Diputación de Córdoba
AVENIDA DE AMÉRICA
GTA. MARGARITAS
Bus Station
RENFE Train Station
AV. GRAN CAPITAN
Jardines de La Agricultura
AV. CERVANTES
AV. RONDA TEJARES
C. JOSÉ CRUZ CONDE
AVENIDA MEDINA AZAHARA
AVENIDA REPÚBLICA ARGENTINA
PASEO DE LA VICTORIA
C. CONCEPCIÓN
C. DE GONDOMAR
PZA LA TENDILL
San Nicolás
PÉRES DE CASTRO
C. DE SEVILLA
C. JESÚS MARIA
LOPE DE HOCES
C. BARROSA
CALLE DE ANTONIO MAURA
AV. GRAN
Plaza de Toros
PZA COSTA DEL SOL
Casa del Indiano
F. RUANO
C. BUEN PASTOR
B. BELMONTE
Almodóvar Gate
C. ALMANZOR
PLAZA BENAVENTE
VIA PARQUE
Synagogue
Museo Taurino
AV. DOCTOR FLEMING
PLAZA JUDÁ LEVI
La Mezqu
C. DE TORRIJOS
AV. CONDE DE VALLELLANO
AVENIDA DEL AEROPUERTO
AMADOR DE LOS RÍOS
Triun
Waterwheel
Alcázar de los Reyes Cristianos
AVENIDA DEL ALCÁZAR
N
AV. CORREGIOR
Moorish Walls (ruins)
500 metres
500 yards

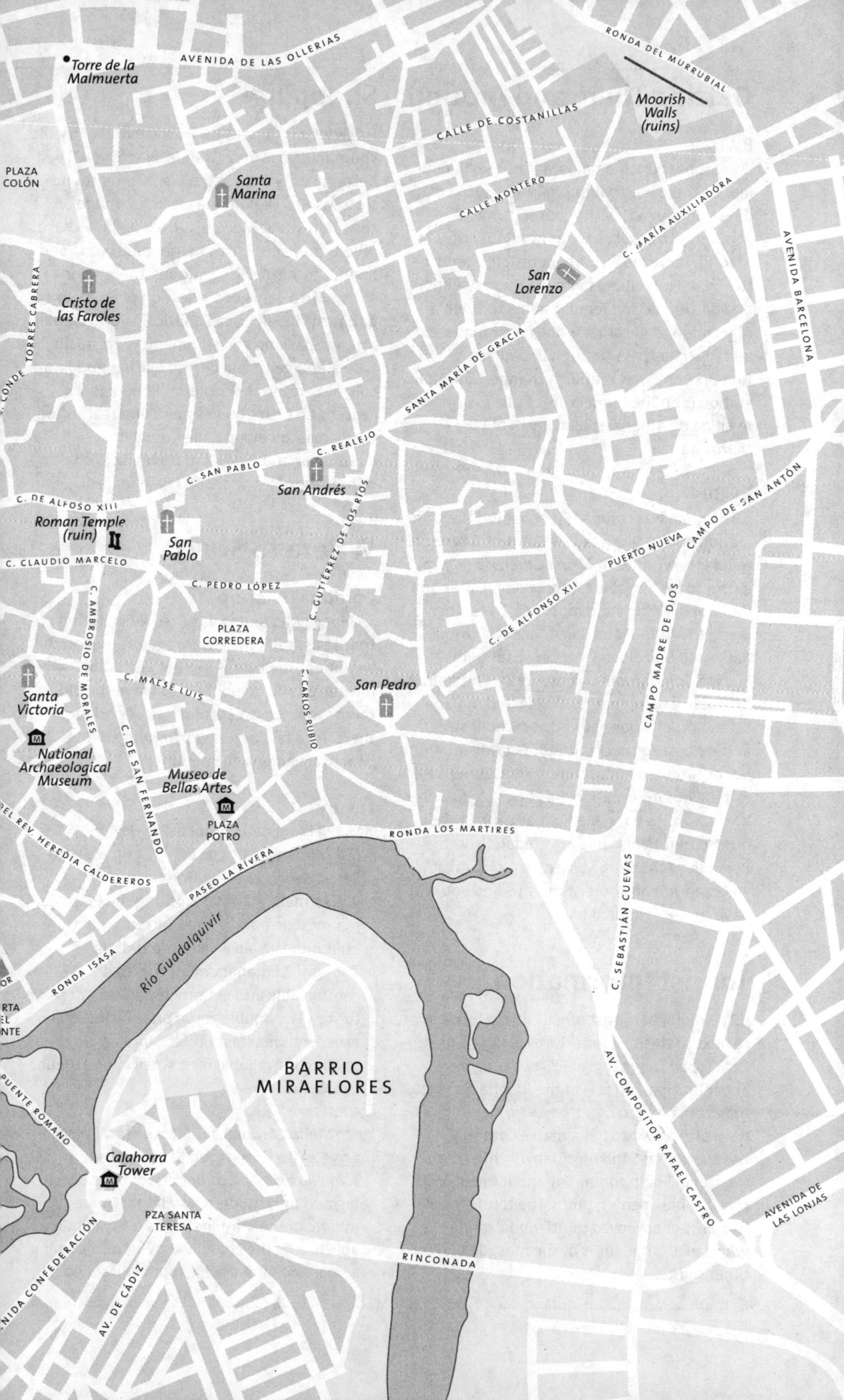

Torre de la Malmuerta
AVENIDA DE LAS OLLERIAS
RONDA DEL MURRUBIAL
Moorish Walls (ruins)
CALLE DE COSTANILLAS
PLAZA COLÓN
Santa Marina
CALLE MONTERO
C. MARÍA AUXILIADORA
AVENIDA BARCELONA
San Lorenzo
Cristo de las Faroles
CONDE TORRES CABRERA
SANTA MARÍA DE GRACIA
C. REALEJO
C. SAN PABLO
San Andrés
C. DE ALFOSO XIII
Roman Temple (ruin)
San Pablo
C. GUTIÉRREZ DE LOS RÍOS
CAMPO DE SAN ANTÓN
PUERTO NUEVA
C. CLAUDIO MARCELO
C. PEDRO LÓPEZ
C. DE ALFONSO XII
CAMPO MADRE DE DIOS
PLAZA CORREDERA
C. AMBROSIO DE MORALES
C. MAESE LUIS
C. CARLOS RUBIO
San Pedro
Santa Victoria
National Archaeological Museum
C. DE SAN FERNANDO
Museo de Bellas Artes
PLAZA POTRO
DEL REV. HEREDIA CALDEREROS
RONDA LOS MARTIRES
PASEO LA RIVERA
C. SEBASTIÁN CUEVAS
Río Guadalquivir
RONDA ISASA
BARRIO MIRAFLORES
PUENTE ROMANO
AV. COMPOSITOR RAFAEL CASTRO
Calahorra Tower
AVENIDA DE LAS LONJAS
PZA SANTA TERESA
RINCONADA
AV. DE CÁDIZ

Getting There and Around

By Train

Córdoba is on the major Madrid–Sevilla rail line, so there are about 12 trains a day in both directions by AVE, with a journey time of 43mins from Sevilla and 1hr 40mins from Madrid. There are also frequent *Talgo* services to Málaga (about 2hrs 15mins), Cádiz, Valencia and Barcelona, and regular trains to Huelva, Algeciras and Alicante. Trains for Granada and Algeciras pass through Bobadilla Junction, and may require a change. Córdoba's station is on the Glorieta Tres Culturas, off Avenida de América, 1.6km north of La Mezquita.

By Bus

The main bus station is just behind the train station on the Glorieta Tres Culturas. There are regular services with Alsina Graells (**t** 95 740 44 79) to Sevilla (at least three daily), Granada, Cádiz and Málaga and most nearby towns. Buses to Madrid (one daily), Valencia (three daily) and Barcelona (two daily): for general bus information call **t** 95 740 43 83. The train is probably a better bet for Sevilla and Málaga.

The Córdoba bus network is complicated and it's best to check with tourist information about times and departure points. Otherwise call the bus information line, **t** 95 740 40 40. If you want to go to Medinat al-Zahra, take bus No.01 for Villarubia or Veredón (from República Argentina at Medina Azahara); it will drop you off short of the site, and you will have to walk about 2km.

Tourist Information

The regional tourist office is on C/Torrijos 10 next to the Mezquita, **t** 95 747 12 35, **f** 95 749 17 78 (*open summer 9.30–8; winter 9.30–6*). The municipal office is in the Judería on Plaza Judá Leví, **t** 95 720 05 22, *www.turiscordoba.es*. It's worth a visit to get a map – Córdoba has the biggest and most labyrinthine old quarter in Spain containing monuments with changeable opening times. The tourist office has a list of approved multilingual guides who can arrange tours of the mosque and other sights.

Shopping

Córdoba is famous for its silverwork – try the shops in C/José Cruz Grande, where you'll get better quality than in the old quarter round the mosque. Handmade **crafts** are made on the premises at Meryan, Calleja de las Flores 2, where they specialize in embossed wood and leather furniture. For **antiques**, there's one shop with a very good selection of Spanish art and furniture in Plaza San Nicolás, and they'll arrange packing and shipment. High-quality ladies' and gents' suede and **leather goods** are sold at Sera, on the corner of Rondo de los Teares and Cruz Conde. The mainstream shopping areas are along Calle Conde de Gondomar and Calle Claudio Marcelo on either side of the Plaza de las Tendillas.

Where to Stay

Córdoba ✉ 14000

Near La Mezquita, of course. Even during big tourist assaults the advantages outweigh the liabilities. However, if this area is full, or if you have a car and do not care to brave the old town's narrow streets and lack of parking, there are a few hotels worth trying in the new town and on the periphery.

Luxury

★★★★**NH Amistad Córdoba**, Pza de Maimónides 3, **t** 95 742 03 35, **f** 95 742 03 65. Sensitively converted from an old *palacio*, with a main entrance fronting the Plaza de Maimónides, and a back entrance neatly built into the old wall of the Judería. Thoughtful management makes it a comfortable and extremely convenient place to stay. The double-room price includes an excellent breakfast buffet. Underground parking is available for a small supplement.

Expensive

★★★★**Meliá Córdoba**, Jardines de la Victoria, **t** 95 729 80 66, **f** 95 729 81 47, *www.solmelia.es, melia.cordoba@solmelia.es*. A big and ugly modern hotel right in the middle of the gardens. It has every conceivable luxury the chain is known for, including a pool and TV. A double room will set you back €126 – worth it for the car park alone, some would consider.

★★★★**El Conqistador**, C/Magistral González Francés 15, **t** 95 748 11 02, **f** 95 747 46 77, *conquist@teleline.es*. Rooms look out onto the floodlit walls of La Mezquita, literally just a few metres from your balcony. The breakfasts are ample, though the service is old-fashioned in the worst sense; but there is an underground car park.

★★★★**Las Adelfas**, Avda de la Arruzafa s/n, **t** 95 727 74 20, **f** 95 727 27 94, *adelfas@arrakis.es*. A modern hotel 5 minutes north of the train station, set in spacious gardens with a pool and beautiful views over Córdoba; definitely worth considering if you visit in summer.

★★★★**Parador de la Arruzafa**, Avda de la Arruzafa, **t** 95 727 59 00, **f** 95 728 04 09, *www.parador.es*, *cordoba@parador.es*. In common with much of the chain, service in this hotel on the outskirts of town seems to be improving. It isn't in an historic building, but offers a pool, tennis courts and air-conditioned rooms with a view.

★★★**Maimónides**, C/Torrijos 4, **t** 95 747 15 00, **f** 95 748 38 03. Totally refurbished a couple of years ago, this is right next to the mosque. A favourite with the package-tour market, though with underground parking.

★★**Lola**, C/Romero 3, **t** 95 720 03 05, **f** 95 742 20 63, *www.hotelconencantolola.com*. This hotel sits right in the heart of the old Jewish quarter in a lovingly restored old house with many of the original fittings and furniture, including old Bakelite phones. There are just eight rooms, each individually decorated. All rooms are doubles, but they vary in size, so ask to see them first if at all possible. Avoid the cheaper, smaller ones and go for the suite, which has a tiny terrace and a view of the tower of the Mezquita. Breakfast is served on the roof terrace or below. There is a parking arrangement with the **El Conquistador** (*see* above).

Hesperia Córdoba, Avda Fray Albino 1, **t** 95 742 10 42, **f** 95 729 99 97, *hhes-cordoba@adv.es*. Well placed just over the Roman bridge with pool, parking and fine views across the river to the city, but it's a pretty soulless upmarket establishment.

Moderate

Al-Mihrab, Avda del Brillante, km 5, **t/f** 95 727 21 98, *www.bd-andalucia.com*. Situated just 5km from the centre of town, this beautiful Modernista-style hotel is full of neo-*mudéjar* decoration. It's a listed building, and offers peace and a view of the Sierra Morena. It's very good value, too.

★★★**Posada de Vallina**, C/Corregidor Luis de Cerda 83, **t** 95 749 87 50, **f** 95 749 87 51, *www.hotelvallina.com*. One of the nicest hotels to have sprung up in the past few years, directly opposite La Mezquita. An old inn dating from Roman times, there are just 15 rooms, all sparkling clean and tastefully designed, some with mosque views, others facing the patio. Attached is a good restaurant (*see* below).

★★**Hotel Mezquita**, Pza Santa Catalina, 1, **t** 95 747 55 85, **f** 95 747 62 19. Right next to the El Conquistador, a converted 16th-century mansion sympathetically restored and with many of the original paintings and sculptures. Fantastic value for its location. The only drawback: no garage.

★★**Albucasis**, C/Buen Pastor 11, **t/f** 95 747 86 25. Situated in the Judería, near La Mezquita, this former silversmith's is an attractive, affordable and immaculate place with a charming flower-filled courtyard; it's one of the prettiest hotels in Córdoba. *Closed Jan–mid-Feb.*

★★**Marisa**, C/Cardenal Herrero 6, **t** 95 747 31 42, **f** 95 747 41 44. A simple but well-run establishment opposite the Patio de los Naranjos. The location is the only real amenity, but it will just do for the price.

★★**Hotel González**, C/Manrique 3, **t** 95 747 98 19, **f** 95 748 61 87. On the edge of the Judería. Some rooms contain family antiques and the arabesque patio houses a popular restaurant.

Inexpensive

★★**Hostal El Triunfo**, C/Corregidor Luís de Cerda 79, **t** 95 749 84 84, **f** 95 748 68 50. Right by the mosque, this is a perfectly decent no-frills option with a pleasant restaurant on its patio.

★**Hostal Magdalena**, C/Muñices, 35, **t** 95 748 37 53. Good for those who don't mind a 10-minute walk through the picturesque backstreets into town. It's in a quiet location where there's no trouble parking.

★**Hostal Seneca**, C/Conde y Luque 5 (just north of La Mezquita), **t** 95 747 32 34. A real find among the inexpensive *hostales*, with a beautiful patio full of flowers, nice rooms and sympathetic management. Not surprisingly, it's hard to get a room.

★**Hostal El Portillo,** C/Cabezas 2, **t** 95 747 20 91. Close to the mosque, this pretty little *hostal* has been refurbished and offers simple rooms around a small patio.

Cheap

Plenty of other inexpensive *fondas* can be found on and around Calle Rey Heredia – also known as the street with five names – so don't be thrown by all the different signs.

★**Hostal Rey Heredia**, C/Rey Heredia 26, **t/f** 95 747 41 82. A good-value *hostal* set around a shady patio: the nicest rooms have tiny balconies. The shared bathrooms are all spotlessly clean.

Fonda Agustina, C/Zapatería Vieja, **t** 95 747 08 72. Clean and central.

Maestre, C/Romero Barros 16, **t** 95 747 53 95, **f** 95 747 53 95. Two establishments on the same street, offering a range of rooms from doubles to small apartments; all have private bathrooms and those in the hotel have air conditioning. It is popular with backpackers, so make a reservation to avoid disappointment.

Hostal Martínez Rücker, C/Martínez Rücker 14, **t** 95 747 25 62. The cheapest place in town with tiny box-like rooms around a pretty Moorish-style courtyard filled with flowers.

★**La Fuente**, C/San Fernando, 51, **t** 95 748 78 27, **f** 95 748 78 27. A very pleasant budget option on the way to the Plaza del Potro, with rooms set round a large patio. The only drawback is that it's on a noisy road.

Eating Out

Córdoba is the heart of a wine-growing region; there are a few *bodegas* in town that appreciate visitors, including the Bodega Campos, C/Lineros 32, **t** 95 747 41 42, and the Bodega Guzmán, C/Judíos 7, which both have restaurants serving their own wines.

Expensive

El Churrasco, C/Romero 16, **t** 95 729 08 19. Located in an old town house in the heart of the Jewish quarter, this has always been one of Córdoba's most celebrated restaurants. Small, intimate, and just a little bit cliquey, it specializes in grilled meats – *churrasco* is the name of the grill the meat is cooked on, and by extension the piece of grilled meat itself. Unfortunately, success seems to have gone to its head and the service is rushed and unpleasant. A pity, because it is reputed to have the best cellar in Andalucía, and In winter braziers are put under tables making it possible to dine on the patio all year round, *Closed Aug*.

El Caballo Rojo, C/Cardenal Herrero 28, **t** 95 747 53 75. Another of Córdoba's best-known restaurants, its menu is supposed to be based on traditional *andaluz* cooking and old Arab recipes – *salmorejo* with cured ham, artichokes in Montilla wine, Mozarabic angler fish – but it has rather lost its way.

Almudaina, Jardines de los Santos Mártires 1, **t** 95 747 43 42. Set in an attractive old house dating from the 16th century. Its menu varies from day to day, depending on market availability, and special attention is paid to local produce. Look out for *ensalada de pimientos, alcachofas a la Cordobés*, and *lomo relleno a la Pedrocheña*, which are above average. *Closed Sun June–Sept, and Sun eve the rest of the year*.

Moderate

Posada de Vallina, C/Corregidor Luís de Cerda 83, **t** 95 749 87 50, **f** 95 749 87 51. Has fine service and offers free *finos* and nibbles as aperitifs. The setting is lovely, around the hotel patio, but the food lacks subtlety. It will fill you up though: great hunks of meat or a whole partridge with a smattering of chips.

El Burlaero, C/la Hoguera 5, **t** 95 747 27 19. Adjoining El Caballo Rojo, with the advantage of a courtyard. Specialities include run-of-the-mill *rabo de toro, paloma torcaz, perdiz, jabalí*.

Rincón de Carmen, C/Romero 4, **t** 95 729 10 55. Family-run, noisy and full of atmosphere. The local dishes are prepared as well as at any establishment in the city, and the prices are low. It also has a very pleasant (and slightly more peaceful) café attached.

El Somontano, Plaza del Escudo, **t** 95 748 65 54. A modern place way off the tourist trail in the new part of town, serving a fine selection of reasonably priced fare, including lamb, rabbit and venison.

Bodega Campos, C/Lineros 32, **t** 95 747 41 42. This handsome old *bodega* also offers excellent Cordobesa cuisine: try the artichokes cooked with local wine or the stuffed pork.

Casa Pepe de la Judería, C/Romero 1, **t** 957 20 07 44. With pretty tile decoration and a flower-filled patio, this is a beautiful, friendly little spot. Tasty, unusual tapas at the bar (wash them down with a glass of manzanilla from the barrel) or a fine restaurant serving regional cuisine.

El Barril, C/Concepción 16, **t** 95 748 67 94. A classic, crammed with old barrels and photos; try local wines and great tapas, or go straight for the *rabo de toro* or excellent seafood.

Inexpensive

El Tablón, Cardenal González 79, **t** 95 747 60 61. Just around the corner from La Mezquita, this characterful restaurant offers one of the best bargains in the city, with a choice of *menús del día* or *platos combinados* at less than €10, glass of wine included.

Los Patios, C/Cardenal Herrero 18, **t** 95 747 83 40. The best of several good options on Calle Cardenal Herrero, right by the Mezquita.

Taberna San Miguel, Plaza San Miguel 1. Better known as El Pisto, or the barrel, this is perhaps the best known *bodega* in town (and because of this it has, unfortunately, become a bit touristy, and the staff can be unpleasant). It's a big old barn of a place with decent tapas, lots of little rooms and *montilla*.

Bodega Guzmán, C/Judíos 7. Another good *bodega* worth seeking out; it's a shrine to bullfighting with a collection of memorabilia inside.

Bodegón Rafaé, on the corner of Calle Deanes and Buen Pastor. Take it or leave it, this place has true *bodega* food and atmosphere. Sausages drape from barrels, religious figurines hang next to fake bulls' heads, the radio and TV are on simultaneously; *rabo de toro* with a glass of wine at one of the vinyl-topped tables will cost next to nothing.

Bar Sociedad de Plateros, C/San Francisco 6, **t** 95 729 05 47. Another popular place with good tapas and cheap wine. It started out in the mid-19th century as a society to help struggling silversmiths and has since branched out into the *bodega* business; there are now nine dotted across the city.

Casa Matías, C/Nogal 16, **t** 95 727 76 53. Laid-back locals' bar with excellent tapas and a pretty *comedor* serving traditional *cocina Cordobesa* and lovely home-made desserts.

Entertainment

Córdoba is the birthplace of Paco Peña – one of Spain's most famous modern flamenco maestros. Paco Peña is part of a long tradition of Córdoba flamenco and the city is a good place to catch some great players and dancers in more authentic venues than, say, Sevilla. If you love flamenco, July is the best time to visit the city, during the guitar festival, when flourishes and trills drift out of every other room in Córdoba's White Neighbourhood and there are several concerts every night. At other times, wait until midnight and then head for one of the secluded little flamenco bars tucked away throughout the city. These include:

Peña Flamenca Fostorito, C/Ocaña 4 (near the Plaza de San Agustín).

Peña Flamenca Las Orejas Negras, Avda Carlos III 18 (in Barrio Fátima).

Tablao Cardenal, C/Torrijos 10, t 95 748 33 20 (strategically positioned next to the tourist office).

Though flamenco may be more authentic in Córdoba than in Sevilla, the bar nightlife is less lively. The most popular bars with locals are the street bars (*terrazas*) in Barrio Jardín, northwest of the Jardínes de la Vitoria, on the Avenida de la República end of Camino de los Sastrés. **El Loro Verde** and the **Albaicín** are two of the busiest. Barrio El Brillante, northwest of the Plaza Colón is full of upper-middle-class Spanish in the summer, particularly the nightclubs and bars found around Plaza El Tablero.

Islam was never entirely immune to the exaltation of holy relics, and there is a story that Abd ar-Rahman had an arm of Mohammed to legitimize his mosque as a pilgrimage site. The site, at the centre of the city, had originally held a Roman temple of Janus, and later a Visigothic church. Only about one-third of the mosque belongs to the original. Successive enlargements were made by Abd ar-Rahman II, al-Hakim, and al-Mansur. Expansion was easy; the plan of the mosque is a simple rectangle divided into aisles by rows of columns, and its size was increased to serve a growing population simply by adding more aisles. The result was one of the largest of all mosques, exceeded only by the one in Mecca. After 1236, it was converted to use as a cathedral without any major changes. In the 1520s, however, the city's clerics succeeded in convincing the Royal Council, over the opposition of the Córdoba city government, to allow the construction of a choir and high altar, enclosed structures typical of Spanish cathedrals. Charles V, who had also opposed the project, strongly reproached them for the desecration when he saw the finished work – though he himself had done even worse to the Alhambra and Sevilla's Alcázar.

Most people come away from a visit to La Mezquita somewhat confused. The endless rows of columns and red and white striped arches make a picture familiar to most of us, but actually to see them in this gloomy old hall does not increase one's understanding of the work. They make a pretty pattern, but what does it mean? It's worth going into some detail, for learning to see La Mezquita the way its builders did is the best key we have to understanding the refined world of al-Andalus.

Before entering, take a few minutes to circumnavigate this massive, somewhat forbidding pile of bricks. Spaced around its 685m (2050ft) of wall are the original entrances and windows, excellent examples of Moorish art. Those on the western side are the best, from the time of al-Mansur: interlaced Visigothic horseshoe arches, floral decorations in the Roman tradition, and Islamic calligraphy and patterns, a lesson in the varied sources of this art.

The only entrance to the mosque today is the **Puerta del Perdón**, a fine *mudéjar* gateway added in 1377, opening on to the **Patio de los Naranjos**, the original mosque courtyard, planted with orange trees, where the old Moorish fountain can still be seen. Built into the wall of the courtyard, over the gate, the original minaret – a legendary tower said to be the model for all the others in al-Andalus – has been replaced by an ill-proportioned 16th-century bell tower. From the courtyard, the mosque is entered through a little door, the **Puerta de las Palmas**, where they'll sell you a ticket and tell you to take off your hat. Inside, it's as chilly as Sevilla cathedral.

Now here is the first surprise. The building is gloomy only because the Spanish clerics wanted it that way. Originally there was no wall separating the mosque from the courtyard, and that side of the mosque was entirely open. In the **courtyard**, trees were planted to continue the rows of columns, translating inside to outside in a remarkable *tour-de-force* that has rarely been equalled in architecture. To add to the effect, the entrances along the other three walls would have been open to the surrounding busy markets and streets. It isn't just a trick of architecture, but a way of relating a holy building to the life of the city around it. In the Middle East, there are many medieval mosques built on the same plan as this one; the pattern originated with the first Arabian mosques, and later in the Umayyad Mosque of Damascus, one of the first great shrines of Islam. In Turkey they call them 'forest' mosques, and the townspeople use them like indoor parks, places to sit and reflect or talk over everyday affairs. In medieval Christian cathedrals, whose doors were always open, it was much the same. The sacred and the secular become blurred, or rather the latter is elevated to a higher plane. In Córdoba, this principle is perfected.

In the aesthetics of this mosque, too, there is more than meets the eye. Many European writers have seen it as devoid of spirituality, a plain prayer-hall with pretty arches. To the Christian mind it is difficult to comprehend. Christian churches are modelled after the Roman basilica, a government hall, a seat of authority with a long central aisle designed to humble the suppliant as he approaches the praetor's throne (altar). Mosques are designed with great care to free the mind from such behaviour patterns. In this one, the guiding principle is a rarefied abstraction – the same kind of abstraction that governs Islamic geometric decoration. The repetition of columns is like a meditation in stone, a mirror of Creation where unity and harmony radiate from innumerable centres. Another contrast with Christian churches can be found in an obscure matter – the distribution of weight. The Gothic masters of the Middle Ages learned to pile stone upwards from great piers and buttresses to amazing heights, to build an edifice that aspires upwards to heaven. Córdoba's architects amplified the height of their mosque only modestly by a daring invention – adding a second tier of arches on top of the first. They had to, constrained as they were by the short columns they were recycling from Roman buildings, but the result was to make an 'upside-down' building, where weight increases the higher it goes, a play of equilibrium that adds much to the mosque's effect. There are about 580 of these columns, mostly from Roman ruins and Visigothic churches the Muslims pulled down; originally, legend credits La Mezquita with a thousand. Some came from as far as Constantinople, a present from the emperors. The same variety can be seen in the capitals – Roman, Visigothic, Moorish and a few mysteries.

The *Mihrab* and Later Additions

The surviving jewel of the mosque is its *mihrab*, an octagonal chamber set into the wall and covered by a beautiful dome of interlocking arches, added in the 10th century under al-Hakim II. A Byzantine emperor, Nikephoras Phokas, sent artists to help with its mosaic decoration, and a few tons of enamel chips and coloured glass cubes for them to work with. That these two states should have had such warm relations isn't that surprising; in those days, any enemy of the pope and the western Christian states was a friend of Constantinople. Though the *mihrab* is no longer at the centre of La Mezquita, it was at the time of al-Hakim II; the aisle extending from it was the axis of the original mosque.

Looking back from the *mihrab*, you will see what once was the exterior wall, built in Abd ar-Rahman II's extension, from the year 848. Its gates, protected indoors, are as good as those on the west façade, and better preserved. Near the *mihrab* is the **Capilla de Villaviciosa**, a Christian addition of 1377 with fancy convoluted *mudéjar* arches that almost succeed in upstaging the Moorish work. Behind it is a small chapel, usually closed off. Fortunately, you can see most of the **Capilla Real** above the barriers; its exuberant stucco and *azulejo* decoration are among the greatest works of *mudéjar* art. Built in the 14th century as a funeral chapel for Fernando IV and Alfonso XI of Castile, it is contemporary with the Alhambra and shows some influence of the styles developing in Granada. Far more serious intrusions are the 16th-century **Coro** (choir) and **Capilla Mayor** (high altar). Not unlovely in themselves, they would not offend anywhere but here. Fortunately, La Mezquita is so large that from many parts of it you won't even notice them. Begun in 1523, the **Plateresque Coro** was substantially altered in the 18th century, with additional stucco decoration, as well as a set of Baroque choir stalls by Pedro Duque Cornejo. Between the Coro and Capilla Mayor is the **tomb of Leopold of Austria**, Bishop of Córdoba at the time the works were completed (and, interestingly, Charles V's uncle). For the rest of the Christian contribution, dozens of locked, mouldering chapels line the outer walls of the mosque. Never comfortable as a Christian building, today the cathedral seems to be hardly used at all, and regular Sunday masses are generally relegated to a small corner of the building.

Around La Mezquita

The masses of tatty souvenir stands and third-rate cafés that surround La Mezquita on its busiest days unwittingly recreate the atmosphere of the Moorish *souks* that once thrived here, but walk a block in any direction and you'll enter the essential Córdoba – brilliant whitewashed lanes with glimpses into dreamily beautiful patios, each one a floral extravaganza. One of the best is a famous little alley called **Calle de las Flores** ('Street of the Flowers') just a block northeast of La Mezquita, although sadly its charms are diminished by the hordes of tourists who flock to see it.

Below La Mezquita, along the Guadalquivir, the melancholic plaza called **Puerta del Puente** marks the site of Córdoba's southern gate with a decorative **arch** put up in 1571, celebrating the reign of Philip II. The very curious Churrigueresque monument next to it, with a statue of San Rafael (the Archangel Raphael), is called the **Triunfo** (1651). Wild Baroque confections such as this are common in Naples and southern Italy (under Spanish rule at the time); there they are called *guglie*. Behind the plaza, standing across from La Mezquita, is the **Archbishop's Palace**, built on the site of the original Alcázar, the palace of Abd ar-Rahman.

The **Roman bridge** over the Guadalquivir probably isn't Roman at all any more; it has been patched and repaired so often that practically nothing remains of the Roman work. Another statue of Raphael can be seen in the middle – probably replacing an old Roman image of Jupiter or Mercury. The stern-looking **Calahorra Tower**, built in 1369 over Moorish foundations, once guarded the southern approaches of the bridge and has been in its time a girls' school and a prison; now it contains a gimmicky **Museo Vivo de Al-Andalus** (*open daily Oct–April 10–6; May–Sept 10–2 and 4.30–6.30; adm*), with a high-tech multivision spectacle (*at 10.30, 11.30, 12.30, 5, 6, and 7 in summer; 11, 12, 1, 3, and 6 in winter*) where you are asked to strap on infrared headphones for a virtual reality tour through the city's history.

Just to the west, along the river, Córdoba's **Alcázar de los Reyes Cristianos** (*open Tues–Sat 10–2 and 5.30–7.30, Sun and hols 9.30–3; adm*) was rebuilt in the 14th century and used for 300 years by the officers of the Inquisition. There's little to see as it's now mainly used for official functions, but you can potter about the remnants of the Baños Reales (Royal Baths) with their star-shaped roof openings, and admire a series of Roman mosaics in the Salón de los Mosaicos. Sadly, the wonderful view of La Mezquita and the town from the belvedere atop the walls is currently clogged up with scaffolding from on-going restoration. The scented **gardens** (*same admission times as Alcázar*) are peaceful and lovely, an Andalucían amenity much like those in Sevilla's Alcázar. The gigantic stone figures of Columbus and the Catholic Kings are impressive. On the river's edge you'll see an ancient **water wheel**. At least some of the Moors' talent for putting water to good use was retained for a while after the Reconquista. This is the mill that disturbed Isabel's dreams when she stayed at the Alcázar; it was rebuilt only in the early 1900s. Just around the corner from the Alcázar on Avenida Doctor Fleming, the **Baños Califales** were opened to the public in August 2002 and are still being excavated (*tickets available only from the Alcázar, see above, opening times as for Alcázar*). This vast, elaborately decorated bath complex was probably built in the 10th century. The finest surviving decoration is in the marble-columned Sala Templada, where the caliph would soak under stellar skylights.

If you continue walking along the Guadalquivir, after about a kilometre you'll come to Parque Cruz Conde and the **Parque Zoológico**, a small zoo (*open daily 10.30–9, adm*) set in gardens with about 200 species including elephants, tigers, llamas and reptiles.

The Judería

How lovely is Thy dwelling-place O Lord of Hosts!
My soul grows weak and longs for Thy courtyards.

Hebrew inscription on synagogue wall

As in Sevilla, Córdoba's ancient Jewish quarter has recently become a fashionable area, a nest of tiny streets between La Mezquita and Avenida Dr Fleming. Part of the Moorish walls can be seen along this street, and the northern entrance of the Judería is the old **Almodóvar gate**. The streets are tricky, and it will take some effort to find Calle Maimónides and the 14th-century **synagogue** (***t*** *95 720 29 28, open daily except Mon 10–2 and 3.30–5.30; Sun 10–1.30*), after which you will find yourself repeatedly back at this spot, whether or not you want to be there.

The diminutive Córdoban synagogue is one of the two oldest and most interesting Jewish monuments in Spain (the other is the Tránsito in Toledo). Set back from the street in a tiny courtyard, it was built in the Granadine style of the early 14th century and, according to Amador de los Ríos, dates from 1315. After the expulsion, it was used as a hospital for hydrophobes, and later became the headquarters of the cobblers' guild. There is an interesting plasterwork frieze of Alhambra-style arabesques and Hebrew inscriptions. The recess for the Ark (which contained the holy scrolls) is clearly visible, and the ladies' gallery still intact. Despite few obvious signs of the synagogue's original function, its atmosphere is still charged; it is somehow easy to imagine this small sanctum as a focus of medieval Jewry's Golden Age, a centre of prayer and scholarship spreading religious and moral enlightenment. While modern Córdoba has no active Jewish community, several *marrano* families live in the city and can trace their ancestry to the pre-expulsion age. Some have opened shops in the *Judería* selling 'Judaica', which ranges from tacky tourist trinkets and tapes of Israeli folk songs, to beautiful Jewish artefacts worked from Córdoban silver. You'll find several in the **Zoco**, a little shopping alley opposite the synagogue.

On Calle Ruano Torres, the 15th-century **Casa del Indiano** is a palace with an eccentric façade. On Plaza Maimónides is the **Museo Municipal de Arte Cordobés y Taurino** (***t*** *95 720 10 56; open Tues–Sat 10–2 and 4.30–6.30; 5.30–7.30 in winter; Sun 9.30–2.30; adm*) with its beautiful courtyard – not surprisingly it's a museum dedicated to the bullfights. Manolete and El Cordobés are the city's two recent contributions to Spanish culture; here you can see a replica of Manolete's sarcophagus, the furniture from his home and the hide of Islero, the bull that did him in, along with more bullfight memorabilia than you ever thought existed. The turn-of-the-last-century Art Nouveau posters are beautiful, and among the old prints you can pay homage to the memory of the famous taurine malcontent Moñudo, who ignored the *toreros* and went up into the stands after the audience.

White Neighbourhoods

From the mosque you can walk eastwards through well over a mile of twisting white alleys, a place where the best map in the world wouldn't keep you from getting lost and staying lost. Though it all looks much the same, it's never monotonous. Every little square, fountain or church stands out boldly, and forces you to look at it in a way different from how you would look at a modern city – another lesson in the Moorish aesthetic. These streets have probably changed little since 1236, but their best buildings are a series of **Gothic churches** built soon after the Reconquista. Though small and plain, most are exquisite in a quiet way. Few have any of the usual Gothic sculptural work on their façades, to avoid offending a people accustomed to Islam's prohibition of images. The lack of decoration somehow adds to their charm. There are a score of these around Córdoba, and nothing like them elsewhere in the south of Spain. **San Lorenzo**, on Calle María Auxiliadora, is perhaps the best, with a rose window designed in a common Moorish motif of interlocking circles. Some 15th-century frescoes survive around the altar and on the apse. **San Pablo** (1241), on the street of the same name, is early Gothic (five years after the Christian conquest) but contains a fine *mudéjar* dome and ceiling. Others include **San Andrés**, on Calle Varela, two streets east of San Pablo, **Santa Marina** on Calle Morales, and the **Cristo de los Faroles** on the Plaza Capuchinos, with a strange and much-venerated statue of Christ of the Lanterns outside. Have a look inside any you find open; most have some Moorish decoration or sculptural work in their interiors, and many of their towers (like San Lorenzo's) were originally minarets. **San Pedro**, off Calle Alfonso XII, was the Christian cathedral under Moorish rule, though largely rebuilt in the 1500s.

The neighbourhoods have other surprises, if you have the persistence to find them. **Santa Victoria** is a huge austere Baroque church on Calle Juan Valera, modelled after the Roman Pantheon. Nearby, on Plaza Jerónimo Páez, a fine 16th-century palace houses the **National Archaeological Museum** (*t* *95 747 10 76, open Wed–Sat 9–8, Sun 9–3; adm, free to EU citizens*), the largest in Andalucía, with Roman mosaics, a two-faced idol of Janus that probably came from the temple under La Mezquita, and an unusual icon of the Persian *torero*-god Mithras; the museum also holds some Moorish-looking early Christian art, and early funeral steles with odd hieroglyphs. The large collection of Moorish art includes some of the best work from the age of the caliphate, including finds from Medinat al-Zahra. At the entrance is a small gallery with a plaque dedicated to 'Franco Caudillo de España' but it's always closed.

East of the Calle San Fernando, the wide street that bisects the old quarter, the houses are not as pristinely whitewashed as those around La Mezquita. Many parts are a bit run down, which does not detract from their charm. In the approximate centre of the city is the **Plaza de la Corredera**, which is an enclosed 'Plaza Mayor', like the famous ones in Madrid and Salamanca. This ambitious project, surrounded by uniform blank façades (an echo of the *estilo desornamentado*) was never completed. Now neglected and a bit eerie, the city is apparently being rehabilitated a little at a time. Continuing south, the **Museo de Bellas Artes**, (*t* *95 747 33 45, open Tues 3–8, Wed–Sat 9–8, Sun 9–3; adm, free to EU citizens*) is on the lovely Plaza del Potro (mentioned by Cervantes, along with the little *posada* that still survives on it); its collections include works of Valdés Leal, Ribera, Murillo and Zurbarán, two royal portraits by Goya, and works by Córdoban artists of the 15th and 16th centuries. Beware the 'museum' across its courtyard, dedicated exclusively to the works of a local named Julio Romero de Torres, the Spanish Bouguereau. Much prized by the Córdobans, this turn-of-the-last-century artist's *œuvre* consists almost entirely of naked ladies. Eastwards from here, the crooked alleys continue for almost a mile, as far as the surviving stretch of **Moorish walls** along Ronda del Marrubial.

Plaza de las Tendillas

The centre of Roman Corduba has, by chance, become the centre of the modern city. Córdoba is probably the slickest and most up-to-date city in Andalucía (Sevilla would beg to differ), and it shows in this busy district of crowded pavements, modern shops, cafés and wayward youth. The contrast with the old neighbourhoods is startling, but just a block off the plaza on Calle Gondomar the beautiful 15th-century **Church of San Nicolás** will remind you that you're still in Córdoba.

In the other direction, well-preserved remains of a collapsed **Roman temple**, one of the most complete Roman monuments in Spain, have been discovered on the Calle Nueva near the *ayuntamiento*. The city has been at work reassembling the walls and columns and already the front pediment is partially complete, though its setting, in the middle of what looks like an abandoned building site, makes it a far from captivating sight.

Next to the **Plaza de Colón**, a park a few blocks north of the Plaza de las Tendillas, the **Torre de Malmuerta** ('Bad Death') takes its name from a commander of this part of the old fortifications who murdered his wife in a fit of passion; it became the subject of a well-known play by Lope de Vega, *Los Comendadores de Córdoba*.

Across the plaza is a real surprise, the rococo **Convento de la Merced** (1745), an enormous building that has recently been restored to house the provincial government and often hosts cultural exhibitions on various subjects. Don't miss it. The façade has been redone in its original painted *esgrafiado*, almost decadently colourful in pink and green, and the courtyards and grand staircases inside are incredible – more a palace than a monastery.

Medinat al-Zahra

Open Tues–Sat 10–2 and 4–6.30, 6–8.30 in summer, Sun 10–2; ***t*** *95 732 91 30.*

Eight kilometres northwest of the centre of Córdoba, Caliph Abd ar-Rahman III began to build a palace in the year 936. The undertaking soon got out of hand and, with the almost infinite resources of the caliphate to play with, he and his successors turned Medinat al-Zahra ('City of the Flower', so named after one of Abd ar-Rahman's wives) into a city in itself, with a market, mosques, schools and gardens, a place where the last caliphs could live in isolation from the world, safe from the turbulent street politics of their capital. Hisham II was kept a virtual prisoner here by his able vizier, al-Mansur.

The scale of it is pure *Arabian Nights*. One chronicler records an ambassador, being taken from Córdoba to the palace, finding his path carpeted the entire 8km (5 mile) route and lined with maidens to hold parasols and refreshments for him.

Stories were told of the palace's African menageries, its interior pillars and domes of crystal, and curtains of falling water for walls; another fountain was filled with flowing mercury. Such carrying-on must have aroused a good deal of resentment; in the disturbances that put an end to the caliphate, Medinat al-Zahra was sacked and razed by Berber troops in 1013.

After having served as a quarry for 900 years it's surprising anything is left at all; even under Muslim rule, columns from the palace were being carted away as far as Marrakech. But in 1944 the royal apartments were discovered, with enough fragments to permit a restoration of a few arches with floral decorations. One hall has a roof on, and more work is under way, but as yet the rest is only foundations.

North of Córdoba

The N432 out of Córdoba leads north to the Sierra Morena, the string of hills that curtain the western part of Andalucía from Extremadura, Castilla and La Mancha. This area is the **Valle de los Pedroches**, fertile grazing land for pigs, sheep and goats and an important hunting area for deer and wild boar – though it's a sad fact that most Spaniards are still irresponsible sportsmen and the Andalucían hunter, a mild-mannered plumber or tobacconist during the week, will take a gun in his hand on Sunday and kill anything that moves. Thousands of these animals are stalked and shot in the numerous annual hunts, or *monterías*. The Valle de los Pedroches is also healthy hiking territory, but keep yourself visible at all times – you don't want to be mistaken for someone's supper.

Getting There and Around

Although **buses** do run from Córdoba up into the Sierra Morena and villages of Los Pedroches, they are infrequent and very time consuming. To explore the best parts, you really need a **car**.

Where to Stay

North of Córdoba there's nothing in the way of deluxe accommodation, but the area has a reasonably wide selection of one- and two-star hotels.

★★**San Francisco**, Ctra Villanueva de la Serena–Andújar, km 129, **t** 95 710 14 35 (*moderate*). A quiet place in a listed building with tennis courts; situated 2.5 km out of Pozoblanco.

★★★**Finca del Río**, outside Fuente Obejuna, **t** 92 463 66 01, **f** 92 463 67 70 (*moderate*). This old *cortijo* on the borders of Badajoz province in Extremadura has been converted into a lovely hotel with all the amenities, including a swimming pool; open in the summer only, but at a very reasonable rates.

★★**Sierra de Cardeña**, C/Modesto Aguilera 29, off the main square in Cardeña, **t** 95 417 43 09, **f** 95 717 43 09 (*inexpensive*). Offers decent rooms and a restaurant.

Hostal Cardeña, Cardeña, **t** 95 717 41 07, **f** 95 717 44 84 (*cheap*). A very pretty whitewashed old building right on the main square.

★**El Comendador**, C/Luis Rodriguez 25, Fuente Obejuna, **t** 95 758 52 22, *hotelcomendador@hotmail.com* (*cheap*). An adequate place to stay in Fuente Obejuna; the rooms are pretty basic and there is a damp feel about it, but the building itself, with a pretty patio, is lovely.

Hostal Javi, C/Córdoba 31, Bélmez, **t** 95 757 30 99, **f** 95 758 04 98 (*cheap*). An excellent value *hostal* in Bélmez which has sparkling plushly decorated rooms of hotel quality with TV, minibar and large bathrooms, set round a delightful vine-covered staircase; with parking and a pretty patio.

★★**Siena**, C/Negrillos 1, Bélmez, **t** 95 758 00 34 (*cheap*). A modest hotel with air-conditioned rooms, and a little café-bar.

La Bolera, C/Padre Torrero 17, Belalcázar, **t** 95 714 63 00 (*cheap*). A basic place in Belalcázar; food is available in the numerous bars around the main square.

Volao, C/Perralejo 2, Villanueva de Córdoba, **t** 95 712 01 57. Offers no frills for its very cheap rooms.

★★**El Sol**, C/Sol 24, Peñarroya-Pueblonuevo, **t** 95 756 20 50 (*inexpensive*). This is central, with refurbished, en suite rooms and though there's no reason to stay in Peñarroya-Pueblonuevo, you may like to use it as a base for your day trips.

★**Sevilla**, C/Miguel Vigara 15, Peñarroya-Pueblonuevo, **t** 95 756 01 00, **f** 95 756 23 07 (*inexpensive*). This is a comfortable place to stay, offering rooms with bath and even a small pool.

Eating Out

This area is famed throughout Andalucía for its supreme quality *jamón ibérico* (locally cured ham) and suckling pig; the excellent *salchichón* from Pozoblanco; and the strong, spicy cheese made from ewes' milk. Sadly it is often difficult for visitors to the region to sample them. There are no outstanding restaurants around, and even indifferent ones are pretty thin on the ground. Driving off into the countryside in search of gastronomic delight can be a risky business; and, though it's true that it occasionally pays rich dividends, to be sure of eating really well you should head for the tapas bars in the villages or, better still, grab some goodies from a supermarket and have a picnic out on the slopes.

Bar Lucas, Pza de la Independencia, in Cardeña (*inexpensive*). If you are in Cardeña, this bar is a good place to eat and drink, with a very reasonably priced menu.

Gran Bar, C/Córdoba, **t** 95 758 01 99. The best restaurant in Bélmez. *Closed Mon.*

There aren't many eating options in **Pedroche**, besides a couple of basic bars on the Plaza de las Siete Villas which do a well-priced *menú del día*: **Restaurante Ali**, **t** 95 713 73 27, or **Hornos Cano**, **t** 95 713 73 29.

A road winds 73km up to **Bélmez**, with its Moorish castle perilously perched on a rock, from which there are panoramic views over the surrounding arid countryside. **Peñarroya-Pueblonuevo** is a dull industrial town that has fallen into decline, but is useful here as a reference point. Sixteen kilometres west on the N432, the village of **Fuente Obejuna** is best remembered for the 1476 uprising of its villagers, who dragged their tyrannical lord from his palace and treated him to a spectacularly brutal and bloody end. His sacked palace was replaced by a church, which still has its original polychromed wooden altar and painted altarpiece. The event is the subject of the drama *Fuente Ovejuna* by Lope de Vega. The village also has an Art Nouveau mansion, **Casa Cardona**, which would be more at home in Barcelona than here. Now sadly in a bad state of disrepair, its flourishes and cornices and multi-coloured windows hint at a more prosperous time. Near the village are some excavations of Roman silver mines.

It's well worth making the trip 40 km north of Peñarroya to **Belalcázar** and one of the most extraordinary castles in Andalucía. **El Castillo de Sotomayor** stands just outside the village and bears down on it like some malevolent force. In any other part of Europe this would be a high point on the tourist trail, but here, in one of the least visited corners of the province, it stands decayed and forlorn. Situated on an outcrop of rock and built on the ruins of an old Moorish fortress, work began on the castle early in the 15th century on the orders of Gutierre de Sotomayor, who controlled the whole of this area. A palace was added in the 16th century, but its dominant feature is the 46m- (150ft-) high **Torre del Homenaje**, and its wonderfully ornate carvings. The castle remained in the family until the Peninsular War when it was badly damaged. Sadly, it is not open to the public, but can be tramped around to get an idea of its size; all around lie remnants of the earlier fortress. The present owner has declined various offers to sell to an Arab buyer or to turn it into a *parador*, a shame really as it would surely be one of the most spectacular in Spain. The village itself has a pretty main square dominated by 15th-century **Iglesia de Santiago el Mayor**, with its later Gothic facade. Just outside the village is the convent of **Santa Clara de Columna**, founded in 1476 and still in use, though it is open to visits. The ruins of an old monastery, San Francisco, are nearby.

The CP236 heads east from here across an unremarkable landscape to the tiny village of **Santa Eufemia**, some 26km away. The ruins of a medieval castle stand just outside the village, nestling in a cleft in the rocks which rise spectacularly above it. There's a 15th-century Gothic-*mudéjar* church, **La Encarnación**, and a well-preserved gate in the main square, as well as some good walking routes available from the *ayuntamiento*, in Plaza Mayor.

From here you could head down to the village of **Pozoblanco** (take the N502 then the A420), famous for the last *corrida* of the renowned bullfighter Francisco Rivera, better known as Paquirri. Gored, he died in the ambulance on the way to Córdoba; presumably bouncing around on those roads didn't help. Paquirri's widow, the singer Isabel Pantoja, soared to even greater heights of popularity on his death, with the Spanish public obsessed as ever by the drama of life and mortality.

Pedroche, 10km away, is a sleepy little village with a fine 16th-century Gothic church with a proud, lofty spire, and a Roman bridge. This place too has had its fair share of drama – in 1936 communist forces shot nearly a hundred of the menfolk; their deaths are commemorated by a plaque on the side of the church. Just outside the village lies the **Ermita de Piedras Santas**, a nondescript 16th-century building with some pretty atrocious art inside; it becomes the scene of a pilgrimage on 8 September. As many as 50,000 people from the villages around Pedroche come here to pay their respects to their *patronada*. Beyond the villages of **Villanueva de Córdoba** and **Cardeña** to the east is the **Parque Natural de Sierra Cardeña** – rolling hills forested in oak, more stag-hunting grounds and ideal rambling terrain.

South of Córdoba

This is the heart of Andalucía, a vast tract of bountiful hills covered in olive groves and vines. The area is more densely populated and a bit more prosperous than most of the region's rural districts. The towns are closer together, all white, and all punctuated by the warm sandstone of their palaces and towers. Some did well even in Andalucía's grim 18th century (Osuna under its haughty dukes, and Priego de Córdoba with its once-famous textiles); others haven't enjoyed good fortune since the passing of the Moors. Some towns inspired poets and novelists, others are famous for leather or barrels. Along the way, on what we hope will be a properly Spanish picaresque journey through a region few tourists enter, there will be flamingos, dolmens, rococo frippery, memorabilia of Julius Caesar, a cask of *amontillado*, a pretty fair canyon, and 139 gargoyles.

The Cordobés Subbética and La Campiña

Here in the heartland of Andalucía lies the **Parque Natural de las Sierras Subbéticas de Córdoba** – a succession of wooded hills that dip into the valleys of the rivers Zagrillo, Salado and Caicena. The landscape of oak trees, olive groves and much shrubland is home to eagles, falcons and vultures, rabbit and partridge, adders, field mice, bats and badgers; the rivers and small lakes dotted around brim with bass, perch and trout. Most tourists miss these untouched corners of Andalucía, where the people are God-fearing and industrious, and where the visitor is welcomed but watched carefully.

Twenty kilometres north of Estepa at **Puente Genil**, an old Moorish-style mill still turns in a pretty setting along the Río Genil. In the town is the 15th-century church of **La Concepción**, but the town's latter-day claim to fame is as a food-manufacturing centre. Semana Santa here is a big affair, and people come from all over the province to see the very colourful procession in Roman costume and Biblical dress.
An old railway line connecting Puente Genil with Linares has been turned into a walking route with each of its old stations refurbished into restaurants and cafés, one of which, La Cantina, can be found just outside the small village of **Doña Mencia**.

Tourist Information

Baena:Plaza de España 5, **t** 95 767 19 46.
Cabra: C/Santa Rosalía 2, **t** 95 752 01 10, *www.cabra.net. Open Mon–Fri 10–1.30 and 6–8, Sat and Sun 10–1.30.*
Lucena: in the Castillo Moral, Pza Nueva 1, **t** 95 751 32 82. *Open Mon–Fri 9–2, and 6–9, Sat, Sun and hols 11–2 and 7–9. www.turlucena.com*
Montilla: in the Casa del Inca, C/Capitán Alonso de Vargas 3, **t** 95 765 24 62, *www.emontilla.com. Open Mon–Fri 10–2, Sat and Sun 11–2.*
Priego de Córdoba: C/Río 33, **t** 95 770 06 25, *www.apriego.com. Open Tues–Sat 10–1.30 and 5–7.30, Sun 10–1.*
Puente Genil: Contraalmirante Delegado Parejo 1, **t** 95 760 28 51.
Rute: C/del Mercado s/n, **t** 95 753 91 08.
Zuheros: Ctra Zuheros-Baena, **t** 95 769 47 75, *www.zuheros.com, turismo@zuheros.com.*

Where to Stay and Eat

Lucena ✉ 14900

★★★★**Santo Domingo**, C/El Agua 12, **t** 95 751 11 00, **f** 95 751 62 95, *hsantodomingo@husa.es* (*expensive*). Part of the Husa chain and set in a former palace, this is the best hotel in the area. It has all the four-star amenities, except a pool, at very good prices.

★★**Los Bronces**, on the Córdoba-Málaga road, **t** 95 751 62 80, **f** 95 750 09 12 (*moderate*). Your next best bet, with pool, TVs and a very good restaurant.

★★**Baltanás**, Avda del Parque s/n, **t** 95 750 05 24, **f** 95 750 12 72, *baltanas@amike.com* (*inexpensive*). Try here only if the others in the range are full. Close to the centre.

Pensión Sara, C/Cabrillana 49, **t** 95 751 61 51 (*cheap*). The best budget option, with perfectly good rooms, all en suite and clean, and a good pizzeria restaurant below.

★★**Xenil**, C/García Lorca 3 (in Puente Genil), **t** 95 760 02 00, **f** 95 760 58 75 (*moderate*). The only hotel in Puente Genil.

Priego de Córdoba ✉ 14800

★★★**Villa Turistica de Priego**, 7km beyond Priego de Córdoba towards Zagrilla, **t/f** 95 770 35 03, *alonatur@arrakis.es* (*moderate*). Set in its own very pretty grounds with a pool, tennis and numerous other activities; the best place to stay in this area.

★★**Río Piscina**, Ctra Monturque–Alcalá la Real, km 44, **t** 95 770 01 86, **f** 95 754 09 77 (*inexpensive*). Another rural retreat 1.5kmoutside town with a small pool and tennis court, at reasonable rates.

Pensión Rafi, C/Isabel la Catolica 4, **t** 95 754 07 49, **f** 95 754 07 49, *hotelrafi@arrakis.es* (*cheap*). A good budget option in Priego de Córdoba itself, with satellite TV and phone; there's a good little restaurant attached.

Andalucía, C/Río 13, **t** 95 754 01 74 (*cheap*). A basic alternative in the centre.

Posada La Niña Margarita, in Los Villares (5km from Carcabuey on the road towards Rute), **t** 95 770 40 54, **f** 957 52 93 22 (*cheap*). A real rural retreat set in a small valley of streams and olive groves, where you can rent a cottage or stay in the Posada itself. There is a restaurant and bar attached.

El Aljibe, C/Abad Palomino 7, **t** 95 770 18 56 (*moderate*). Probably the best place to eat in Priego de Córdoba, built over an Arabic cistern (*aljibe*) with tapas and full meals at reasonable prices.

El Virrey, C/Solana 14, **t** 95 754 30 03 (*moderate*). Another good restaurant with a wide selection of regional meat and fish.

Aguilar ✉ 14920

Aguilar has a number of places, but none offering any luxury.

Hostal Queen, C/Pescaderías 6, **t** 95 766 02 22 (*inexpensive–cheap*). The best place to stay, with a café attached and TVs in the rooms.

La Casona, just off the main road and towards Puente Genil, **t** 95 766 04 39 (*moderate*). A very good restaurant which specializes in *churrascos*.

Montilla ✉ 14550

★★★**Don Gonzalo**, Ctra Madrid–Málaga, km 447, **t** 95 765 06 58, **f** 95 765 06 66 (*moderate*). Part of the Husa chain, on the main road outside Montilla, with gardens, swimming pool and tennis court.

★**Hotel los Felipes**, C/San Francisco Solano 27, **t** 95 765 04 96 (*inexpensive*). Looks pretty grim from the outside but in fact has a lovely old-fashioned dining room (*cheap*) and a piano bar.

★**Alfar**, Ctra Madrid–Málaga km 441, **t** 95 765 11 20 (*inexpensive*). Also on the main road outside Montilla, with a pool.

Hostal Bellido, C/Enfermería 57, **t** 95 765 19 15, *hbellido@teleline.es* (*inexpensive*). Has basic rooms set round a pretty patio.

Finca Buytrón, C/Gran Capitán 24, **t** 95 765 01 52, **f** 95 765 01 52, *fincabuytron@navegalia.com* (*inexpensive*). About 3km from Montilla, dating from the 16th century. It has eight double rooms (four en suite), a pool, library and an open fire.

Cortijo El Pinar, about 7km from town, **t** 95 747 22 60. A refurbished farmhouse with three separate houses; has a patio, barbecue area, kitchen and a pool.

Las Camachas, Ctra Madrid–Málaga, **t** 95 765 00 44, **f** 95 765 03 32 (*expensive*). A winner of various cuisine medals. Wash down tasty fish dishes with a glass of the local brew.

Baena ✉ 14850, Cabra ✉ 14940

★★★**La Casa Grande**, Avda Cervantes 35 (Baena), **t** 95 767 19 05, **f** 95 769 21 89, *www.lacasagrande.es* (*expensive–moderate*). This is the best place to stay in Baena, set in a restored old mansion, with the original chandelier in the lobby and a fine restaurant.

★★**Iponuba**, C/Nicolás Alcalá 7 (Baena), **t** 95 767 00 75, **f** 95 769 07 02, *iponuba@interbook.es* (*moderate*). Comfortable, central and with a café attached.

★★**Rincón**, Llano Rincón 13 (Baena), **t** 95 767 02 23 (*cheap*). The budget option in Baena, near the centre, with a tapas bar and restaurant.

★★**Zuhayra**, C/Mirador 10 (in Zuheros), **t** 95 769 46 93, **f** 95 769 47 02, *www.zuheros.com* (*inexpensive*). A comfortable hotel with a restaurant attached.

Casa Morejón, C/Obispo Cubero 1 (in Doña Mencía), **t** 95 767 61 69 (*cheap*). One of the cheapest *pensiónes* in all Andalucía, where a room with bath in low season will set you back a staggering €10.

El Granaíno, C/Barriada Estación, s/n, **t** 95 766 70 74 (*cheap*). The only place to stay in Luque; basic.

Casa del Monte, Plaza de la Constitución, **t** 95 767 66 75 (in the *almacén*). Probably your best bet to eat out in Baena.

Casa Luís, Pza Alcalde de la Moneda 4, Baena. A cosy, traditional spot for an *aperitivo* and some tapas.

Huerta de San Rafael, Ctra Badajoz–Granada (in Luque), **t** 95 766 74 97. Finding a good roadside *venta* such as this (serving regional specialities at giveaway prices) is a real boon in this area.

Cabra has a couple of places to stay in town, both pretty basic and *cheap*.

Guerrero, C/Pepita Jiménez 7, **t** 95 752 05 07.

San José, Avda Fuente del Río, **t** 95 752 03 68.

Mitra, Ctra Úbeda-Cabra, **t** 95 752 96 00, *www.hotelmitra.com* (*inexpensive*). Modern, roadside hotel just outside Cabra with a café-restaurant and all mod-cons.

Entertainment and Nightlife

Lucena has quite a lively nightlife with a number of bars, pubs and tea rooms, many of them on and around the main square. The *turismo* even supplies a *Ruta de la Tapa*, a bit like a pub crawl but with food, which includes most of the bars in town. Some worth checking out include:

El Encuentro, C/Ballesteros (just off the old square). Tea rooms and a bar set round a patio in a run-down old house; often has live bands at weekends.

Al Jai, C/Canilejas 4. In a faux-Alhambra design, with music and various teas.

Azúcar, C/General Lozano 8. A friendly, laid-back bar full of locals.

El Gambrinus, C/Montenegro 14. A lively bar which attracts a smart crowd and specializes in seafood tapas.

El Bulevar, C/Canilejas 18. One of the places to head for if you want music; there's a bar and a dance floor with loud music.

El Sinagoga, C/Juan Valera. Plays a mix of 70s and 80s music till late.

La Manzana de Adán, Avda de la Guardia Civil 7, **t** 95 750 19 35. A big disco and entertainment complex just out of Lucena, beyond the park. Popular with a younger crowd.

La Jaima, on the way up to the shrine. In summer this is a huge open-air disco in an olive grove with bedouin-style tents.

Further east of Puente Genil, **Lucena** is one of the centres of a great wine-growing region. The town is not known for its beauty, but for making the biggest wine barrels in Andalucía, and as the birthplace of the Baroque architect Hurtado Izquierdo. He produced the incredible La Cartuja chapel in Granada, though he is not responsible for Lucena's wonderful Baroque *sagrario* chapel in the church of **San Mateo**. Before the Reconquista, Lucena seems to have been an autonomous Jewish republic, and many families claim Jewish ancestry: a quick flick through the phone book reveals numerous Isaacs, Israels and Aarons. The town makes much of its Jewish and Moorish past; its tourist logo uses both the crescent moon of Islam and the Star of David, and there is the appropriately named **Festival de las Tres Culturas**, which the town hall are thinking about turning into an annual event. Two other festivals worth timing your visit for are the jazz festival held at the end of May and a piano festival throughout August, set in the surrounds of the castle. Lucena was also a major trading centre and its small industries still thrive today, notably furniture-making, and the manufacture of brass, copperware and barrels. All this has made the town one of the most prosperous in Andalucía, and crime and unemployment stand at virtually nil while property prices in the centre soar. On the Plaza de España is a battered castle; it was here in the **Tower of Moral** that Granada's last king, Boabdil el Chico was imprisoned by Fernando in 1483. Now it's home to the tourist office and a small archaeological museum (*open same hours as tourist office*).

Twenty kilometres south of here, the town of **Rute** produces the potent spirit *anís*, and has a museum which charts its history (*Paseo del Fresno 2,* **t** *95 753 81 43; open daily 9–2 and 5–8, but confirm hours with tourist office*). It also has a **donkey sanctuary** (*follow signs for ADEBO, Asociación para la Defensa del Borrico; visits 9–noon only*) above the town, endorsed by Queen Sofía, no less. The road from the sanctuary wends its way round one of the largest reservoirs in Spain, **Embalse de Iznájar**, which takes meltwater from the Sierra Nevada. It is named after the town tumbling down one of its shores. **Iznájar** itself is topped by a magnificent **Alcazaba** complex dating from the 8th century, with the **Iglesia de Santiago** added some 800 years later. Both can be visited; ask for the keys at the *ayuntamiento*, and leave your transport below – the road up is torturously steep and narrow.

Right at the centre of Andalucía, fittingly set in olive groves and vineyards, and with view of the Sierra Nevada to the southeast and the Guadalquivir valley to the north, is **Cabra**, 10km north of Lucena on the C340. As you enter the town turn left towards the buildings above it, which include a **castle** that once belonged to the dukes of Cabra; opposite is the 16th-century **Iglesia de la Asunción**, a former mosque and a good example of the local Baroque architecture. Inside are 44 red marble pillars and an impressive 18th-century *retablo*. On the way out of town on the A340 towards Priego de Córdoba you'll pass a series of swimming pools; they mark a natural spring, **La Fuente del Río**, source of the River Cabra. A few kilometres further is the turn-off for the hilltop shrine of the Virgin of the Sierra, from where you'll get extraordinary views across the mountains. The Virgin is celebrated in the town from 3–8 September, and there's an even wilder Gypsy Pilgrimage to the shrine in mid-June.

Priego de Córdoba

Priego de Córdoba lies at the foot of the highest mountain in the province, **La Tiñosa**, and has a famous ensemble of Baroque churches, monasteries and fountains; the best is the **Asunción** church (*open summer Tues–Sun 11–2 and 5.30–8; winter 10.30–1.30 and 4–7*) with a sumptuous stucco interior and, in its Sagrario chapel (designed by Francisco Javier Pedrejas), perhaps the finest example of Baroque frippery in all Andalucía: cherubs and angels look down beatifically from an outrageously frothy ceiling, a golden balcony lines the dome and light pours in from the high windows. The other churches can't quite live up to this, but if you are in a Baroque mood look out for the **Aurora**, Carrera de Álvarez, where every available bit of ceiling space is decked out in flourishes; and **Iglesia de las Mercedes**, Carrera de las Monjas, whose interior is another brilliant white Pedrejas creation. In the church of **San Pedro**, on the square of the same name, is an image of the Immaculada, a work attributed to Alonso Cano, and an ornate Baroque altar by the *sevillano* master Hurtado Izquierdo.

The Asunción sits just off the Plaza Abad Palomino, which is flanked along one side by a Moorish castle, remodelled in the 13th and 14th centuries; it is privately owned and cannot be visited. Behind the church lies the prettiest part of town, **Barrio de la Villa**, a maze of tiny winding streets bedecked with pot plants and little squares. The *barrio* gives on to the edge of town with views across the olive groves. Follow this road round and you will end up in the Puerta del Sol and Priego's pretty gardens.

The town's other pride is the Baroque **Fuente del Rey**, at the end of Calle Río: three connecting fountain pools lined with 139 gargoyles, and a centrepiece of Neptune and Aphrodite on a horse-drawn carriage – unfortunately it's now rather dirty and neglected. The town has wonderful fancy grillework around its windows and ornate front doors, as displayed along Calle Río. No.33, as well as housing the town's *turismo*, is also the birthplace of Niceto Alcalá Zamora, the president of the Spanish Republic from 1931–6. The building has been carefully preserved and recreated with much of the president's original furniture and documents lining the walls.

Zuheros to Montilla

From Cabra the A316 heads northeast towards Baena, through the heart of the Subbética. You can make a number of detours on the way, the most rewarding of which would be to **Zuheros**, about 2km along the CO241. The village clings to an escarpment, topped by the ruins of a Moorish castle, and is set against a backdrop of jagged cliffs. As with so many of these tiny villages, there is not a great deal to do but gawp at the views and perhaps stop for a quick drink. There is a pretty church, **La Virgen de los Remedios**, a brand new museum of local arts and customs in the Casa Grande, and another small museum displaying some of the finds from a cave 4km above the town: **La Cueva de los Murciélagos**, 'Cave of the Bats' (*guided tours in Spanish April–Sept Tues–Thurs, Sat and Sun hourly 11–1 and 4–6; adm; ring ahead for winter hours,* **t** *95 769 45 45*). It has a few faint cave paintings, the odd bit of bone, a number of weird stalagmite and stalactite formations, and a distinct lack of bats. If you've seen the caves at Nerja, Aracena or Gibraltar, this is a poor relation. Just before the caves is a *mirador*, with a spectacular view to the town.

Some 5km northwest of Zuheros is another pretty village, **Doña Mencía**, where novelist Juan Valera lived for several years. His former home has been turned into a small museum. The town is named after the wife of Alvar Pérez de Castro, a captain under Fernando III, who also rebuilt the castle. From here the road wends its scenic way out of the Subbética to **Baena**, a town of major importance in Moorish times, now squeezing out olive oil in remarkable quantities. The town has an official *denominación de origen* (DO) which grades its olive oils from the basic stuff we use for cooking to the top-notch oils, used for tapas or in gazpacho. A clean, tightly packed town with narrow, whitewashed streets, there is little to detain you but the ruins of a Moorish castle and a fine 18th-century arcaded building, once a warehouse and now a cultural centre and tapas bar (the Mesón Casa del Monte) on the Plaza de la Constitución. C/Juan Rabadan connects this with the Plaza de España, supposedly the town centre but little more than a road junction. Baena sees most of its visitors arrive for the Holy Week celebrations, when a deafening drum-rolling competition is held to see who can play the longest and the loudest; it lasts *two days*.

Twenty-two kilometres northwest from Cabra is **Aguilar de la Frontera**, another attractive wine town (producing *solera fina*, mostly) perched on a hill. It has an unusual octagonal plaza (a copy of the one in Antequera), and the Renaissance church of **Santa María del Soterraño**. It also has a number of *bodegas* which can be visited, including **Toro Albalá** (***t*** *95 766 00 46, www.talbala.com*), which is just off the main road to Málaga, on the turn-off to Puente Genil. On the outskirts of the town, on the way to Puente Genil, are a number of permanent and seasonal semi-saline lakes, the largest of which is the **Laguna de Zóñar**. During the winter months, the lakes are home to a large number of migrating birds, including white-headed ducks, marsh and Montagu harriers and flamingoes. About 3km along this road is a **visitor centre** (***t*** *95 733 52 52, open Fri 4–6, Sat and Sun 10–1 and 4–6*), which supplies walking routes and information.

From Aguilar it's a short hop up the road to the prince of the wine-producing towns, **Montilla**, sitting on a rise amidst endless acres of vines. Although *amontillado*, a pale dry sherry, takes its name from this town, the wine produced here is not a sherry, in that no extra alcohol is added to fortify it, unlike in Jerez. The town is refreshingly short of Baroque churches, but its *bodegas* can be visited to sample the good stuff. A small **museum** is dedicated to Garcilaso de la Vega, Hispano-Inca son of a *conquistador* and chronicler of the Inca civilization in the 16th century. The 1512 Gothic convent of **Santa Clara** is worth a visit for its *mudéjar* roof and Baroque altarpiece. The town is believed to be the site of the Battle of Munda, where former governor Caesar's men finally put paid to the Spanish followers of Pompey.

From Córdoba to Úbeda

In this section of the Guadalquivir valley the river rises into the heights of the Sierra Morena; endless rolling hills covered with neat rows of olive trees and small farms make a memorable Andalucían landscape. The three large towns along the way, Andújar, Bailén and Linares, are much alike, amiable industrial towns still painted a gleaming white.

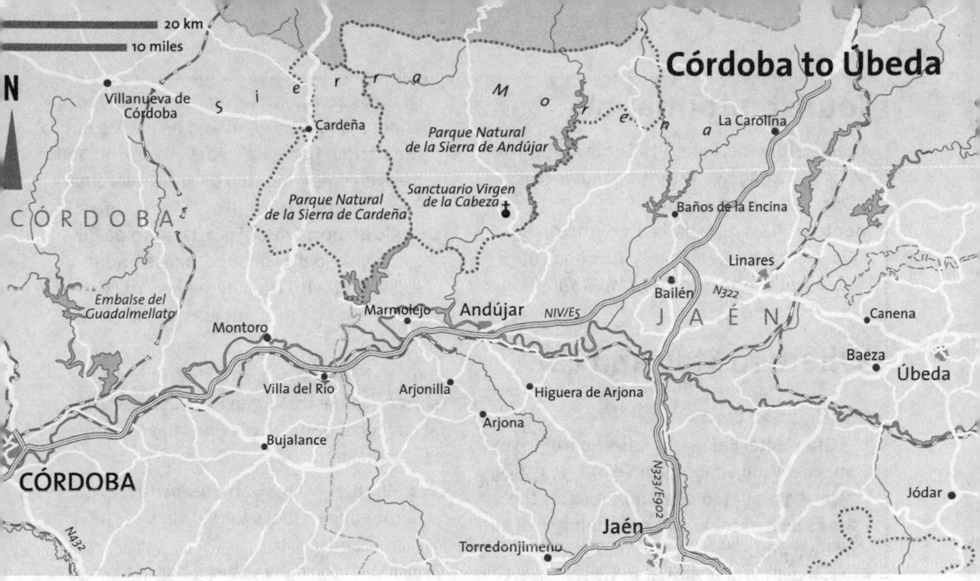

The Gateway to Andalucía

This area is Andalucía's front door. The roads and railways from Madrid branch off here for Sevilla and Granada. Many important battles were fought nearby, including Las Navas de Tolosa near La Carolina, in 1212, which opened the way for the conquest of al-Andalus; and Bailén, in 1808, where a Spanish-English force gave Napoleon's boys a sound thrashing and built up Spanish morale for what they call their War of Independence.

The NIV snakes along the Guadalquivir valley, and 42km east of Córdoba it brings you to the delightfully placed town of **Montoro**, sitting on a cliff overlooking a bend in the river. The facetious-looking tower that rises above the whitewashed houses belongs to the Gothic church of **San Bartolomé** in Plaza de España. Also in the square is the 16th-century **Ducal Palace**, now the *ayuntamiento*, with a Plateresque façade. The beautiful 15th-century bridge that connects Montoro to its suburb, Retamar, is known as the **Puente de Las Donadas**, a tribute to the women of the village who sacrificed their jewellery to help finance its construction. Seek out the kitsch **Casa de las Conchas**, C/Criado 17 (signposted from the Plaza de España), a house and courtyard done out in hundreds of thousands of sea shells gathered from the beaches of Spain by Francisco del Río over the past 40 or so years. He will show you round for a small fee and flog you a postcard.

Approaching **Andújar**, a further 35km down the NIV, you'll find the countryside dominated by huge, blue sunflower-oil refineries like fallen space stations. Sunflowers, like olives, are a big crop in the region and much in evidence in late summer. Nothing remains of Andújar's Moorish castle, but there are a couple of surprises in this town which might tempt you to linger a while. The church of **Santa María**, in the plaza of the same name, has in one chapel the *Immaculate Conception* by Pacheco, Velázquez's teacher, and in another the magnificent *Christ in the Garden of Olives*, by El Greco. You may wonder how on earth an El Greco got here? One reason

Tourist Information

Andújar: Torre del Reloj/Pza Santa María s/n, **t** 95 350 49 59, *www.turismoandujar.com. Open Tue–Sat 10–2 and 5–8.*

Montoro: Plaza de España 8, **t** 95 716 00 89. *Open Mon, Wed, Fri 8.30–3; Tues and Thurs 10–2 and 5–6.30; Sat 10–1; closed Sun.*

Where to Stay and Eat

Andújar ✉ 23740

★★★**Gran Hotel Balneario**, Calvario 101 (10km outside Andújar at Marmolejo), **t** 95 354 09 75, **f** 95 351 74 33 (*moderate*). Probably the area's best hotel, with a swimming pool and its own grounds.

★★★**Del Val**, C/Hnos del Val 1, **t** 95 350 09 50, **f** 95 350 66 06, *hdeval@ofijaen.com* (*moderate*). Just outside town, on the corner of the road up to the sanctuary, with a swimming pool and its own grounds.

★★**Don Pedro**, C/Gabriel Zamora 5, **t** 95 350 12 74, **f** 95 350 47 85 (*inexpensive*). The best place to stay in Andújar itself, situated in the centre of town, with pleasant rooms and a tavern-style restaurant that specializes in game dishes (*moderate*). It also has a disco attached.

★★**La Fuente**, C/Vendederas, **t** 95 350 46 29, **f** 95 350 19 00 (*inexpensive*). Clean and friendly *pensión* with a garage and a good restaurant (*moderate*) attached.

★**Logasasanti**, C/Doctor Fleming 5, **t** 95 350 05 00, **f** 95 350 50 05 (*moderate–inexpensive*). Another respectable, central option, though slightly more basic.

★★**Montoro**, Madrid–Cádiz road, km 358, **t** 95 316 07 92 (*inexpensive*). A basic option on the main road outside Montoro.

The restaurants at the Don Pedro and La Fuente hotels are particularly good. Otherwise try:

Restaurante Madrid–Sevilla, Plaza del Sol 4, **t** 95 350 05 94 (*expensive*). Patronized by the king and queen of Spain, and so called for its position on the old road. Run by the indefatigable Manuel Gómez Sotoca, it's a favourite with the hunting fraternity, as well as the royals. Fresh fish is brought in daily and game features heavily on the menu, which changes according to Snr Sotoca's mood. Choose what you want and he'll whip out to the kitchen to create it for you himself. Your meal is complemented by an extraordinary wine selection from all over the country.

Caballo Blanco, C/Monjas 3, **t** 95 350 02 88 (*cheap*). An old-fashioned, unassuming restaurant with friendly service. You won't get anything fancy, but everything is fresh and tasty.

If you have the desire to stay up by the shrine at Nuestra Virgen de la Cabeza there are a few options, all of which have restaurants attached.

★**La Mirada**, **t** 95 354 91 11 (*inexpensive*). As its name suggests, has a good view of the shrine, and a pool.

Pensión Virgen de la Cabeza, t 95 312 21 65 (*inexpensive*).

Los Pinos, **t** 95 354 90 23. A good restaurant on the road up to the sanctuary; also has rooms and rents out a rural retreat.

El Rancho, opposite Los Pinos, **t** 95 354 91 10. Serves a good selection of game and fish at reasonable prices.

Bailén ✉ 23710

★★★**Bailén**, Ctra NIV, km 296, **t** 95 367 01 00, **f** 95 367 25 30 (*moderate*). Just outside Bailén in an old *parador* and with pleasant gardens, air conditioning and a swimming pool. It also houses a restaurant and tapas bar.

★★★**Cuatro Caminos**, C/Sebastián Elcano 40, **t** 95 367 02 19, **f** 95 367 30 38 (*inexpensive*). Better placed near the centre and much cheaper, with a café attached, but no pool.

Baños de la Encina ✉ 23710

★★★**Hotel Baños** C/Cerro Llamada s/n, **t** 95 361 40 68, *www.hotelbanos.com* (*moderate*). The only hotel in town; very comfortable rooms with beautiful views over the surrounding sierra. Hiking and other activities can be arranged, and it houses the town's best restaurant.

La Encina, C/Consultorio 3, **t** 95 361 40 98 (*inexpensive*). Has views of the castle and does a well-priced *menú*.

Mesón del Duque, **t** 95 361 30 26 (*inexpensive*) At the top of town, opposite the Ermita

Jesús del Llano; its rather grand name belies its simple and reasonably priced country cooking.

Mirasierra, Bailén s/n, **t** 95 361 31 20 (*inexpensive*). This restaurant is worth trying for local dishes.

La Carolina ✉ 23200

★★★★**Perdiz**, Ctra NIV, km 268, **t** 95 366 03 00, **f** 95 368 13 62, *www.nh-hoteles.es* (*expensive*). A classic stopover for travellers between Andalucía and northern Spain with an appealing, coaching-inn ambience. It's got a pretty good restaurant too and, as its name ('partridge') implies, it serves seasonal game dishes (*moderate*).

★★**Orellana Perdiz/Orellana Perdiz II**, Ctra NIV, km 265, **t** 95 366 12 51, **f** 95 366 21 70, *www.orellanaperdiz.com* (*moderate*). Although more or less devoid of character, has good facilities including parking, a pool and tennis.

El Retorno, C/General Sanjurjo 5, **t** 95 366 16 13 (*cheap*). The best of the budget options in town with an attractive flower-fringed patio, clean, quiet rooms, and a friendly proprietor.

Los Jardineros, C/General Sanjurjo, **t** 95 366 08 12 (*inexpensive*). Next door, and slightly more basic.

Gran Parada, Avda Lindez Vilches 9, **t** 95 366 02 75 (*cheap*). If everything else is booked, try here as a last resort.

La Toja, Avda Juan Carlos 1, **t** 95 366 10 18 (*moderate–inexpensive*). Set back from the main street behind steel doors, this large, open-plan restaurant serves good local fare (game) at a reasonable price.

Linares ✉ 23700

★★★**Aníbal**, C/Cid Campeador 11, **t** 95 365 04 00, **f** 95 365 22 04 (*moderate*). The jumbo hotel in town.

★★★**Victoria**, C/Cervantes 7–9, **t/f** 95 369 25 00, *victoriahotel@terra.es* (*moderate*). Rather characterless, standard three-star place, but clean and friendly with large rooms.

★★**Cervantes**, C/Cervantes 23, **t** 95 369 05 00, **f** 95 369 00 96, *hotelcervantes@teleline.es* (*moderate*). Although slightly old-fashioned, it is probably better value than the Victoria, with spotlessly clean rooms set round a pretty patio.

Baviera, C/Virgen 25, **t** 95 360 71 15 (*inexpensive*). Decent budget hotel with plenty of mod-cons, including Internet access.

Mesón Campero, Ctra Pozo Ancho 5, **t** 95 369 56 22. Excellent grilled meats, and a big terrace have made this a hit with locals. *Closed Mon and Easter.*

Entertainment and Nightlife

Andújar ✉ 23740

Habana, C/Emperador Trajano. A café-bar that attracts a young crowd; the place to come for a late-night *copa*.

Escena, Pso del Castillo (in the old cinema). A more sophisticated spot.

OTK Cheroly, C/Emperador Adriano. The big disco in town, attracting a pretty young crowd.

Los Romeros, Alto Santo Domingo. Flamenco can be found here – ask at the bar nearby, Memphis, for times.

Baños de la Encina ✉ 23710

There are a small number of places to try for after-dinner drinks and more.

Lipika, Pso de Llana s/n. A pub/disco.

Pub La Colmena, C/Valdeloshuertos 12.

Discoteca El Pinar, C/Migaldías 15.

La Carolina ✉ 23200

Taberna del Arte, C/Real 5 (just down from Pza de Ayuntamiento), **t/f** 95 368 12 27. For late-night drinking, especially at the weekends; adorned with bullfighting posters and photos. The bar breaks into song every Friday and Saturday in celebration of the local pilgrimage to Nuestra Virgen de la Cabeza. Reasonably priced tapas and *raciones* are served.

Linares ✉ 23700

For a few late-night *copas*, C/Cervantes has two good options.

Long Rock, C/Cervantes 13.

Mas Tomate. A disco next door.

given is that the Río Guadalquivir, upon which the town stands, was once navigable as far as Andújar and as result the town grew rich through trade with the Americas. Many merchants and nobility settled here, one of whom, so legend has it, donated the painting to the church in lieu of a cash gift. This also accounts for the large number of palaces and mansions – though, due to shortage of funds, many are falling into dis-repair and are not open to the public.

The **Casa de Albarracín**, which dates from the 16th century and used to be the town hall, stands opposite the church of **Santa María**. The coat of arms has long since disappeared – pulled down by a departing nobleman or ordered off by an angry king. Nearby stands the **Torre del Reloj**, where the minaret of the Moorish mosque once stood. It was finished in 1534 and sports a fabulous imperial coat of arms symbolizing the town's loyalty to the then king, Charles V. The *torre* now houses the *turismo*, which has a mountain of information about the town and offers free walking tours if you ring ahead. It also offers maps and information on walking trails in the Sierra de Andújar, a natural park which forms part of the Sierra Morena.

From here it's a short walk to the Plaza de España, which is dominated by the current *ayuntamiento*, housed in what was the town's playhouse. Beside it is **San Miguel**, the oldest church in town, dating from Visigothic times. Inside is a beautiful choir with wrought-iron balustrades, the front carved in walnut. The tower outside the church leans slightly, a result of the Lisbon earthquake of 1755. The pink building on the other side of the square is the post office, with an arch leading through to the Plaza de la Constitución.

Andújar also has a small **archaeological museum** (*open Tues–Fri 7–9; Sat–Sun 11–1, **t** 95 350 06 03*) housed in another fine building, the Palacio de los Niños de Gomez, which stands just behind a part of the Moorish city wall. Inside are a number of local ceramics and artefacts dating from Roman times. The exterior of the palace is decorated with two incongruous, and rather camp, figures, which are supposed to represent South American Indians.

Around Andújar

Just before Andújar, off the NIV, lies the tiny spa village of **Marmolejo**, where the mineral water of the same name is bottled. There is little there to detain you, but a good hotel (*see* under 'Andújar' in 'Where to Stay', above) and the spa itself, which lies 2km into the mountains and is open from May to the end of October. From Marmolejo you could rejoin the NIV or take a detour through endless olive groves to two pretty villages: **Arjonilla**, a production centre of olive oil, which you can smell on the way into town, and **Arjona** a few kilometres on. This village was once topped by a Moorish castle, but all that remains today is the heavily restored church of Santa María, and the 17th-century chapel opposite. The walk up is worth it, however, for the wonderful views. Below is a pretty square, Plaza de la Constitución.

Another possible diversion, 30km north of Andújar on the J501, is the **Santuario de la Virgen de la Cabeza**. It's worth packing a picnic and enjoying the drive; when you get there you'll be rewarded with panoramic views, though there is very little left of the 13th-century sanctuary, which was blown to bits by Republicans after being seized by pro-Franco guards near the start of the Civil War. The present building and surrounds are a grotesque mish-mash of fascistic architecture, similar in style to El Valle de Los Caídos, Franco's tomb outside Madrid. In the crypt below there is a collection of photos and walking aids hanging from the walls, representing those who the Virgin has cured or those who have promised to make a pilgrimage if the Virgin helps them out of a sticky situation.

One of Andalucía's biggest fiestas is the annual *romería* to the sanctuary on the last Sunday in April, when half a million pilgrims trek up on foot, horseback, carts and donkeys. The celebrations begin the week before with various competitions held in the town centre. On the Thursday, thousands of Andújarans dress up in traditional Andalucían dress and layer the ground outside the Capilla del Virgen de la Cabeza, in C/Ollerías, with a blanket of flowers. The next day the streets, resonant with music, fill with people parading in costume on horseback. The pilgrimage proper begins early on the Saturday morning, leaving Andújar for the sanctuary along various routes, including the old Roman road. The halfway point is **Lugar Nuevo**, near an old Roman bridge, where pilgrims stop for a giant picnic, before arriving at the sanctuary that night where an hourly mass begins. Finally, on Sunday morning the Virgin is brought out of the sanctuary and paraded down the hill, where she has various objects – including young children – thrown at her to be blessed. Of course all this means big business, and the sanctuary is spawning a village at its feet, with restaurants, bars and hotels to cater for the pilgrims.

Back on the NIV, 27 km further east is the modern, unprepossessing town of **Bailén**. The tomb of the Spanish general Francisco Javier Castaños (1756–1852), who so cleverly whipped the French troops and sent Napoleon back to the drawing board, is in the Gothic parish church of the **Encarnación**, which also has a sculpture by Alonso Cano. But don't dally here – the real treat is to be found 11km to the north on the NIV at **Baños de la Encina**, where the 10th century oval Moorish castle is one of the best preserved in all Andalucía. Dominating the town, the castle has 14 sturdy, square towers and a double-horseshoe gateway, scarcely touched by time, and from the walls you get a sweeping vista of the olive groves and distant peaks beyond Úbeda. The castle has no set opening hours – enquire at the *ayuntamiento* on the Plaza de la Constitución (***t*** *95 361 30 04*) for the key.

An arduous hour's trek from Baños, through difficult, hilly terrain, lies the natural refuge of **Canforos de Peñarrubia**, with its remarkably preserved Bronze Age paintings of deer and scenes of animal-taming. Serious hikers should ask for a guide at the *ayuntamiento*.

Twenty kilometres north of here on the NIV is **La Carolina**, a model of 18th-century grid planning. The village owes its existence to forward-thinking Carlos III, who imported a few thousand German artisans in the late 1700s and set them to work excavating the lead and copper mines, tilling the fields and herding sheep. A side effect of this colonization was supposed to be the decline of banditry in the then wild and unpopulated hills. But within two generations almost all the Germans had died off or fled. The town and surrounding area are best known now as a big game-hunting reserve, particularly for partridge – that is to say, not *big game*, but a big reserve.

From Bailén the N322 heads eastward to the mining town of **Linares**, birthplace of the guitarist Andrés Segovia, who later moved on; others weren't so lucky – in 1947 the great bullfighter Manolete had an off day and met his end on the horns of a bull in the ring here.

If things had gone well for him, he might have gone to view the finds from the Roman settlement of nearby Castulo, housed in the town's **archaeology museum**, but unfortunately the last thing he saw was probably the ornate Baroque portal of the hospital **San Juan de Dios**. From Linares it's a 27km run to Úbeda; a little more than halfway you'll pass an elegant castle at **Canena**.

Baeza

Campo de Baeza, soñaré contigo cuando no te vea
(Fields of Baeza, I will dream of you when I can no longer see you)
Antonio Machado (1875–1939)

Sometimes history offers its recompense. The 13th-century Reconquista was especially brutal here; nearly the entire population fled, many of them moving to Granada, where they settled the Albaicín. The 16th century, however, when the wool trade was booming in this corner of Andalucía, was good to Baeza, leaving it a distinguished little town of neatly clipped trees and tan stone buildings, with a beautiful ensemble of monuments in styles from Romanesque to Renaissance. It seems a happy place, serene and quiet as the olive groves that surround it.

The prettiest corner of the town is **Plaza del Pópulo**. It is enclosed by decorative pointed arches and Renaissance buildings, and contains a fountain with four half-effaced lions; the fountain was patched together with the help of pieces taken from the Roman remains at Castulo, and the centrepiece, the fearless lady on the pedestal, is traditionally considered to be Imilce, the wife of Hannibal.

Heading north on the Cuesta de San Felipe, which can be reached by the steps leading off the Plaza del Pópulo, you pass the 15th-century **Palacio de Jabalquinto** (*open 10–1 and 4–6; closed Wed*), with an eccentric façade covered with coats of arms and pyramidal stone studs (a Spanish fancy of that age; you can see others like it in Guadalajara and Salamanca). The *palacio* was built in the 15th century by the Benavides family, and is now a seminary. Its patio is open to the public and boasts a beautiful two-tiered arcade around a central fountain, as well as a fine carved Baroque staircase. Adjoining the *palacio*, the 16th-century **Antigua Universidad** was a renowned centre of learning for three hundred years, until its charter was withdrawn during the reign of Fernando VII. It has since been used as a school; its indoor patio, like that of the Jabalquinto, is open to the public (*open 10–1 and 4–6, closed Wed*). The school has found latterday fame through Antonio Machado, the *sevillano* poet who taught there (1913–19). His most famous work of prose, *Sentencias, donaires, apuntes y recuerdos* (1936), draws on his experiences in Baeza.

Getting There and Around

By Train

Come to Baeza by train at your own risk. The nearest station, officially named Linares-Baeza, **t** 95 365 02 02, is far off in the open countryside, 14km away. A bus to Baeza usually meets the train, but if you turn up at night or on a Sunday you may be left stranded at the station.

By Bus

Baeza's bus station, **t** 95 74 04 68, is a little way from the centre on Avda Alcalde Puche Pardo. Baeza is a stop on the Úbeda–Córdoba bus route, with 12 a day running to Jaén (1½hrs); eight to Granada (2hrs); two to Cazorla and one to Málaga (4–5hrs).

Tourist Information

Pza del Pópulo (also known as the Plaza de los Leones), **t** 95 374 04 44. *Open Mon–Fri 9–2.30, Sat 10–1; closed Sun.*

Internet: Speed Informática, Pso de la Constitución (next to the employment office), **t** 95 374 70 05.

Where to Stay and Eat

Baeza ✉ 23440

*****Hotel Palacete Santa Ana**, C/Santa Ana Vieja 9, **t** 95 374 16 57, **f** 95 340 77 65, *www.palacetesantana.com, info@palacetesantana.com* (*moderate*). A lavishly restored noble palace where politicians and leading *toreros* seek privacy – the closest thing you'll get to stepping back into the 18th century. There are just 14 bedrooms, reached by a marble staircase, all of them different and stuffed full of original mirrors, paintings and sculptures, but with all mod cons. There are two dining rooms, two living rooms, an indoor and outdoor patio, a *terraza* on the roof and a cellar below where *dueña* Ana María Rodríguez organizes flamenco shows. The attention to detail here is extraordinary and the price for such splendour a giveaway.

*****Hotel Confortel Baeza**, C/Concepción 3, **t** 95 374 81 30, **f** 95 374 25 19, *comerbaeza@ctv.es* (*moderate*). The second-best choice in Baeza, situated behind the Iglesia del Hospital de la Purísima Concepción, near the Plaza de España. The hotel is set in a monasterial building and the rooms open on to a peaceful arched quadrangle.

*****Complejo Turistico Hacienda La Laguna**, Ctra Baeza–Jaen km 8, Puente del Obispo, **t** 95 377 10 05, **f** 95 312 71 72, *www.rgo.net/lalaguna* (*moderate*). A delightful rural hotel in an old *cortijo* with two pools and lots of activities and amenities for kids and adults.

*****Juanito**, Avda Arca del Agua s/n, **t** 95 374 00 40, **f** 95 374 23 24, *juanito.baeza@via.goya.es* (*inexpensive*). Has rooms with bath plus its own pool, but the hotel is rather run down; situated on the road leaving Baeza in the direction of Úbeda.

*****Hospedería Fuentenueva**, Pso Arca del Agua s/n, **t** 95 374 31 00, **f** 95 374 32 00, *www.fuentenueva.com* (*moderate*). On the same road, this is a more upmarket place set in its own grounds and with a pool attached.

****Comercio**, C/San Pablo 21, **t** 95 374 01 00 (*cheap*). A comfortable lodging where Machado stayed, and perhaps even penned a few poems.

Pensión El Patio, C/Conde Romanones 13, **t** 95 374 02 00 (*cheap*). This Renaissance mansion set around a courtyard is a good budget bet.

Andrés de Vandelvira, C/San Francisco 14, **t** 95 374 75 19 (*expensive*). A restaurant inside the San Francisco convent with tables filling the arched quadrangle; for more intimacy, dine upstairs. *Closed Sun afternoon.*

Juanito, Pso Arca del Agua s/n, **t** 95 374 00 40, **f** 95 374 23 24, *juanito.baeza@via.goya.es* (*expensive*). This hotel's restaurant is worth trying – it's in the Michelin guide.

La Gondola, Portales Carbonerías 13, **t** 95 374 29 84 (*moderate*). Set back from the main Paseo, with an emphasis on heavy meats and *churrascos*.

Sali, C/Cardenal Benavides 15, **t** 95 374 13 65 (*moderate*). Fish and shellfish feature with game dishes like partridge in brine; opposite the town hall. Good value *menú* at €11.

Casa Pedro, C/Cardenal Benavides 11, **t** 95 374 80 87 (*inexpensive*). Next door to Sali; has a *menú* for under €10.

A right turn at the next corner leads to the 16th-century Santa Iglesia **cathedral** (*open 10–1 and 5–7, 4–6 in winter; closed Wed*) on Plaza Santa María, a work of Andrés de Vandelvira. This replaced a 13th-century Gothic church (the chancel and portal survive), which in turn took the place of a mosque; a colonnade from this can be seen in the cloister. For the best show in town, drop a coin in the box marked *custodia* in one of the side chapels; this will reveal, with a noisy dose of mechanical *duende*, a rich and ornate 18th-century silver tabernacle. The fountain in front of the cathedral, the **Fuente de Santa María**, with a little triumphal arch at its centre (1564), is Baeza's landmark and symbol. Behind it is the Isabelline Gothic **Casas Consistoriales**, formerly the town hall, while opposite stands the 16th-century seminary of **San Felipe Neri** (also known as the Antonio Machado International University), its walls adorned with student graffiti in bull's blood. It's curiously reminiscent of the rowing eights' hieroglyphics which cover the quadrangle walls of the sportier Oxbridge colleges.

The Paseo de la Constitución, at the bottom of the hill, is Baeza's main, albeit quiet, thoroughfare, an elegant rectangle lined with crumbling shops and bars. Two buildings are worthy of note: **La Alhóndiga**, the 16th-century, porticoed corn exchange and, almost opposite, the **Casa Consistorial**, the 18th-century town hall. Just behind the Paseo, in Plaza Cardenal Benavides, the façade of the **Ayuntamiento** (1599) is a classic example of Andalucían plateresque, and one of the last. From here it's a short walk to the 16th-century **Convento de San Francisco**, which now houses an excellent restaurant (*see* above). At the end of the Paseo, the inelegant but always lively Plaza de España marks the northern boundary of historic Baeza and is home to yet more bars.

Úbeda

Even with Baeza for an introduction, the presence of this nearly perfect little city comes as a surprise. If the 16th century did well by Baeza, it was a golden age here, leaving Úbeda a 'town built for gentlemen' as the Spanish used to say, endowed with one of the finest collections of Renaissance architecture in all of Spain. Two men can take much of the credit: Andrés de Vandelvira, an Andalucían architect who created most of Úbeda's best buildings, and Francisco de los Cobos, imperial secretary to Charles V, who paid for them. Cobos is a forgotten hero of Spanish history. While Charles was off campaigning in Germany, Cobos had the job of running Castile. By the most delicate management, he kept the kingdom afloat while meeting Charles's ever more exorbitant demands for money and men. He could postpone the inevitable disaster, but not prevent it. Like most public officials in the Spanish 'Age of Rapacity', though, he also managed to salt away a few hundred thousand ducats for himself, and he spent most of them embellishing his hometown.

Like Baeza, Úbeda is a peaceful and happy place; it wears its Renaissance heritage gracefully, and is always glad to have visitors. Slowly, it's gearing up for them. Tourism is less of a novelty here than it was even a couple of years ago, and a tour bus of camera-wielding Japanese trying to negotiate the delicate Renaissance plazas is

Getting There and Around

Úbeda's **bus** station, C/San José, **t** 95 375 21 57, is at the western end of town, and various lines connect the city directly to Madrid, Valencia and Barcelona, at least once daily. There are more frequent buses to Baeza, (16 daily, 20mins), Córdoba (3 daily, 2½hrs), Jaén (8 daily, 1½hrs) Granada (2 daily, 2½hrs) and Sevilla (3 daily). Cazorla and other villages can easily be reached from Úbeda.

Tourist Information

Palacio Marqués de Contadero, C/Baja del Marqués 4 (off the Plaza del Ayuntamiento), **t** 95 375 08 97. *Open Mon–Sat 9–3*, otubeda@andalucia.org.

Where to Stay and Eat

Úbeda ✉ 23400

★★★★**Parador de Úbeda**, Pza de Vázquez de Molina s/n, **t** 95 375 03 45, **f** 95 375 12 59, *ubeda@parador.es* (*expensive*). In a 16th-century palace with a glassed-in courtyard, one of the loveliest and most popular of the chain. All the beamed ceilings and fireplaces have been preserved and the restaurant is the best in town (which isn't saying a lot), featuring local specialities for around €25 for a full dinner. Ask to see the ancient wine cellar.

★★**Palacio de la Rambla**, Pza del Marqués 1, **t** 95 375 01 96, **f** 95 375 02 67 (*expensive*). A romantic and slightly less expensive choice in the historic heart of the town, set in a magnificent ivy-clad Renaissance mansion where the Marquesa de la Rambla lets out beautiful double rooms (ask for 106) surrounding a courtyard.

★★★★**Álvar Fáñez**, C/Juan Pasquau 5 (just off the Plaza San Pedro), **t/f** 95 379 60 43, *alvarfanes@de.com* (*moderate*). Another handsomely converted ducal palace, with 11 tastefully decorated (albeit slightly austere) rooms, and a lovely *terraza* with views over the rooftops to the olive groves and the hills. The delightful old patio looks as it did 400 years ago. There is also a café serving excellent tapas and a good restaurant in the cellar. The hotels organizes cultural and environmental excursions.

★★★**María de Molina**, Plaza del Ayuntamiento, s/n, **t** 95 379 53 56, **f** 95 379 36 94, *www.hotel-maria-de-molina.com* (*moderate*). Probably has the edge over the others in terms of position, just behind the main square. The patio has been modernized, and is a little too prettified, but the 20 rooms have some original furniture and paintings, all with

not an uncommon sight. But it's still easy to understand the Spanish expression '*irse por los cerros de Úbeda*' ('take the Úbeda hill routes'). It basically equates to getting off the subject or wasting time and arose many years ago after Úbeda gradually lost traffic to more commercial routes. Legend has it that a Christian knight fell in love with a Moorish girl and was reproached for his absence by King Fernando III. When questioned about his whereabouts during the battle the knight idly replied, 'Lost in those hills, sire'.

Úbeda today leaves no doubt about its political colours. In the **Plaza de Andalucía**, joining the old and new districts, there is an old metal statue of a fascist Civil War general named Sero glaring down from his pedestal. The townspeople have put so many bullets into it, it looks like a Swiss cheese. They've left it here as a joke, and have merrily renamed another square, from Plaza del Generalíssimo to Plaza 1 de Mayo.

The Torre de Reloj, in the Plaza de Andalucía, is a 14th-century defensive tower now adorned with a clock. The plaque near the base, under a painting of the Virgin, records lovely bathrooms. Also with café and very good restaurant: try the roasted kid leg or the deer loin.

★**La Paz**, C/Andalucía 1, **t** 95 375 21 40 (*inexpensive*). A recently renovated hotel with large rooms, and good amenities.

★**Pensión Victoria,** C/Alaminos 5, **t** 95 375 29 52 (*cheap*). A simple *pensión* in an unremarkable building, but it's friendly, central and good value. All rooms are en suite.

★★**Sevilla**, Avda Ramón y Cajal 9, **t** 95 375 06 12 (*cheap*). You can get a clean and pleasant double with bath for very good rates here – air conditioning is extra.

Castillo, Avda Ramón y Cajal 20, **t** 95 375 04 30 (*inexpensive–cheap*). With a café attached, satellite TV and air conditioning.

★★**Hotel Consuelo**, Avda Ramón y Cajal 12, **t** 95 375 08 40, **f** 95 375 68 34 (*inexpensive*). Rooms here are a bit fancier.

Apart from the *parador*, there are few good restaurants in Úbeda.

El Marqués, Pza Marqués de la Rambla 2, **t** 95 375 72 55 (*expensive*). A smart, modern restaurant with a big reputation but little atmosphere. It's a favourite for business lunches.

Cuzco, Parque Vandelvira 8, **t** 95 375 34 13 (*inexpensive*). Serves local dishes and standard *andaluz* fish and meat menus. It's menu of the day includes two courses and wine.

El Seco, C/Corazón de Jesús 8 (near the Plaza Ayuntamiento), **t** 95 379 14 72 (*inexpensive*). A small dining room with reasonable food, and a little terrace overlooking the square.

Mesón Navarro, Plaza del Ayuntamiento, **t** 95 379 06 38. Pricier, but has more atmosphere than most.

El Gallo Rojo, C/Manuel Barraca 16, **t** 95 375 20 38 (*inexpensive*). During the daytime you'll find plenty of characters at the bar, and it's a lively place in the evening with excellent tapas and a restaurant.

Mesón Gabino, Fuenteseca s/n, **t** 95 375 42 07. Also good for tapas and light meals.

El Olivo, Avda Ramón y Cajal 6, **t** 95 375 20 92 (*inexpensive*). Plates are piled high at this simple local restaurant.

Hostal Sevilla, Avda Ramón y Cajal 20, **t** 95 375 06 12. The restaurant at this *hostal* is good value and worth a try.

The bar scene is fairly advanced in Úbeda.

Lupo, Plaza de San Pedro. This bar boasts a state-of-the-art interior.

Siglo XV, Calle de Muñoz García (Úbeda's liveliest street after dark). Set in a Gothic building which used to be a brothel.

Bar Palacio, Calle Trinidad (in the courtyard of the Palacio de los Bussianos). Stop off here for pre-dinner drinks.

There are plenty of buzzy *terrazas* along Av del Cristo Rey in summer.

a visit of Charles V. From here, Calle Real takes you into the heart of the old town. Nearly every corner has at least one lovely palace or church on it. Two of the best can be seen on this street: the early 17th-century **Palacio de Condé Guadiana** has an ornate tower and distinctive windows cut out of the corners of the building, a common conceit in Úbeda's palaces. Two blocks down, the **Palacio Vela de los Cobos** (*ask at the tourist office for opening hours*) is in the same style, with a loggia on the top storey. Northeast of here, on C/Cervantes, lies a small **museum** (*open Tues–Sun 11–1 and 5–7; adm*) with the tiny monastic cell where San Juan de la Cruz (St John of the Cross) died of cancer and ulceration of the flesh in 1591. Friar John, much persecuted in his lifetime because of his unorthodox teachings, is one of Spain's most illustrious poets and mystics.

The home of Francisco de los Cobos's nephew, another royal counsellor, was the great **Palacio de las Cadenas**, now serving as Úbeda's *ayuntamiento* and tourist office, on a quiet plaza at the end of Calle Real. The side facing the plaza is simple and dignified but the main façade, facing the **Plaza Vázquez de Molina** (*open daily 10–2 and 5–9*), is a stately Renaissance creation, the work of Vandelvira.

Plaza Vázquez de Molina

This is the only place in Andalucía where you can look around and not regret the passing of the Moors, for it is one of the few truly beautiful things in all this great region that was not built either by the Moors or under their influence. The Renaissance buildings around the Palacio de las Cadenas make a wonderful ensemble, and the austere landscaping, old cobbles and plain six-sided fountain create the same effect of contemplative serendipity as any chamber of the Alhambra. Buildings on the plaza include: the church of **Santa María de los Reales Alcázares**; a Renaissance façade on an older building with a fine Gothic cloister around the back; the *parador*; two sedate palaces from the 16th century, one of which, the **Palacio del Marqués de Mancera**, can be visited (*open daily 10am–11am*); and Vandelvira's **Sacra Capilla del Salvador** (*open 10–2 and 5–7.30; adm*), begun in 1540, the finest of Úbeda's churches, where Francisco de los Cobos is buried.

All the sculpture on the façades of Úbeda is first-class, especially the west front of the Salvador. This is a monument of the time when Spain was in the mainstream of Renaissance ideas, and humanist classicism was still respectable. Note the mythological subjects on the west front and inside the church, and be sure to look under the arch of the main door. Instead of Biblical scenes, it has carved panels of the ancient gods representing the five planets; Phoebus and Diana with the sun and moon; and Hercules, Aeolus, Vulcan and Neptune to represent the four elements. The interior, with its great dome, is worth a look despite a thorough sacking in 1936 (the sacristan lives on the first door on the left of Calle Francisco Cobos, on the north side of the church). Behind El Salvador, the **Hospital de los Honrados** has a delightful open patio – but only because the other half of the building was never completed. South of the plaza, the end of town is only a few blocks away, encompassed by a street called the **Redonda de Miradores**, a quiet spot favoured by small children and goats, with remnants of Úbeda's wall and exceptional views over the Sierra de Cazorla.

Úbeda's Pottery

Traditional dark green pottery, fired in kilns over wood and olive stones, is literally Úbeda's trademark. You'll see it all over town – try to pick up some authentic pieces before they become available in Habitat. Tito, on the Plaza Ayuntamiento, is a class establishment that produces and fires pieces on the premises. The designs are exquisite and are packed and shipped all over the world.

Highly recommended is a visit to the potters' quarter around the Calle Valencía, a 15-minute stroll from the Plaza del Ayuntamiento. Heading northeast to the Plaza 1 de Mayo, cross the square diagonally and leave again by the northeast corner, along the Calle Losal to the Puerta de Losal, a 13th-century *mudéjar* gate. Continue downhill along the Calle de Merced, passing the Plaza Olleros on your left, and you come to Calle Valencia. Nearly every house is a potter's workshop; all are open to the public and you will soon find your own favourite. Ours is at No.36, where Juan José Almarza runs his family business, handed down through several generations. Juan spent two years in Edinburgh and is possibly the only potter in the province of Jaén with a Scottish accent.

Beyond Plaza Vázquez de Molina

Northeast of El Salvador, along **Calle Horno Contado**, there are a few more fine palaces. At the top of the street, on Plaza 1 de Mayo, is the 13th-century **San Pablo** church (*open 7–9pm*), much renovated in the 16th century; inside is an elegant chapel of 1536, the Capilla del Camarero Vago. On the same square is the elegant town hall, dating from the 16th century. North from here along C/Cervantes is the Casa de Mudéjar, with a pretty courtyard containing the town's small **archaeological museum** (*open Tues 3–8, Wed–Sat 9–8, Sun 9–3*). **San Nicolás de Bari** (*open daily 8.30–9.30*), further north, was originally a synagogue, though nothing now bears witness to this. It was confiscated in 1492, which has left it with one Gothic door and the other by Vandelvira, who oversaw the reconstruction.

Take the road west from here, C/Condesa, and you will pass yet more fine palaces, Casa del Caballerizo Ortega, Palacio de los Bussianos, on C/Trinidad, and near it **Trinity Church** (*open daily 7.20pm–8.30pm*). On the western outskirts of town, near the bus station on Calle Nueva is Vandelvira's most remarkable building, the **Hospital de Santiago** (*open Mon–Fri 8–3 and 3.30–10, Sat and Sun 11–3 and 6–9.30*). This huge edifice has been called the 'Escorial of Andalucía'. It has the same plan as San Nicolás de Bari, a grid of quadrangles with a church inside. Oddly, both were begun at about the same time, though this one seems to have been started a year earlier, in 1568. Both are supreme examples of the *estilo desornamentado*. The façade here is not as plain as Herrera's; its quirky decoration and clean, angular lines are unique, more like a product of the 20th century than the 16th century.

Around Úbeda: the Sierra de Cazorla

If you go east out of Úbeda, you'll be entering a zone few visitors ever reach. Your first stop might be the village of **Torreperogil**, where the Misericordia growers' co-operative in the Calle España produces first-class red and white wines, such as their *tinto El Torreño*, at a modest price. The **Sierra de Cazorla**, a jumble of ragged peaks, pine forests and olive-covered lowlands, offers some memorable mountain scenery, especially around **Cazorla**, a lovely, undiscovered white village of narrow alleys hung at alarming angles down the hillsides, with a strangely alpine feel to it. Cazorla's landmarks are a ruined Renaissance church (again, by Vandelvira) half-open to the sky, and its castle. But there's an even better castle, possibly built by the Templars, just east of town. **La Iruela** is a romantic ruin even by Spanish standards, with a tower on a dizzying height behind. Beyond La Iruela is the pass into the Sierra, the wild territory of hiking, hunting and fishing.

All of this area is poorly served by public transport and you will need a car to explore far-flung villages such as **Hornos** and **Segura de la Sierra**, both topped with Moorish castles. The latter is a pretty little town, untouched by tourism, with a number of monuments on show, including some Moorish baths and a pretty Renaissance fountain. The road from here heads north to **Siles**, surrounded by embattlements and a lookout tower, before leaving the park via **Torres de Albánchez**, with more Moorish castle remains.

Tourist Information

Cazorla: Pso del Santo Cristo 17, **t** 95 371 01 02, *www.acazorla.com*; and a Natural Park Tourist Office at C/Martínez Falero 11, **t** 95 372 01 25.

Segura de la Sierra: C/Regidor Juan de la Isla 1, **t** 95 348 07 84.

Where to Stay and Eat

Cazorla ✉ 23470

Cazorla has a surprising number of hotels, both in town and up in the mountains.

*****Parador El Adelantado**, **t** 95 372 70 75, **f** 95 372 70 77, *cazorla@parador.es* (*expensive*). Tucked about 8 km inside the park, the *parador* is a mountain chalet with 33 rooms, a pool set right on the cliff edge and a cosy log fire. It is agreeably remote and has an appealing, if slightly institutional, feel to it. Its setting, however, is without equal; if budget allows, this is the obvious choice as a base for exploring the National Park. The restaurant is one of the best in the area, serving up lots of game dishes. There is a good-value set menu for around €20.

Molino La Fárraga, Camino de la Hoz s/n, **t/f** 95 372 12 49, *www.molinalafarraga.com*. A charming bed-and-breakfast in an old converted windmill with a pool and lovely gardens. North American owner.

Hotel Ciudad de Cazorla, Plaza de la Corredera 9 (right on the main square), **t** 95 372 17 00, **f** 95 372 04 20, *ciudad-de-cazorla@ciudaddecazorla.com* (*moderate*). The best hotel in town, with the sheer cliffs as a dramatic backdrop. The rooms are functional but undistinguished, but has the advanage of a swimming pool.

****Hotel Guadalquivir**, C/Nueva, 6, **t/f** 95 372 02 68, *info@hguadalquivir.com* (*inexpensive*). The next best option, with 12 comfortable rooms in a good spot near the centre.

****Parque**, C/Hilario Marcos 62, **t/f** 95 372 18 06 (*inexpensive*). One of a number of options along C/Hilario Marcos, with mod cons like phones and TV; all rooms en suite.

***Don Diego**, C/Hilario Marcos 163, **t** 95 372 05 31, **f** 95 372 05 45 (*inexpensive*). A comfortable little hotel.

Pension Limas, C/Hilario Marcos 175, **t** 95 372 09 09, **f** 95 372 19 09 (*inexpensive*). Similar, with a café attached.

***Mirasierra**, Santiago de la Espada, Ctra Cazorla–Pantana del Tranco, km 20, **t** 95 371 30 44 (*cheap*). In a beautiful setting 20km north of Cazorla, on the road to the dam and reservoir at El Tranco; with a restaurant.

La Iruela, a small village 1km from Cazorla along the Ctra de la Sierra, also has a couple of possibilities:

*****Peña de las Halcones**, Travesía Camino La Iruela s/n, **t** 95 372 02 11, **f** 95 372 13 35 (*moderate*). A relatively sophisticated place with wonderful views, a pool, garden and minibars in all of the rooms.

****La Finca Mercedes**, Ctra de la Sierra, **t** 95 372 10 87, *info@lafincamercedes.com* (*inexpensive*). Offers modest rooms, some with tremendous views. Its small dining room has the best kitchen in the area.

There are a few rural hotels near Segura where you can get away from it all:

***Hospedería de Montaña Río Madera**, Ctra de Río Madera, **t/f** 95 312 62 04 (*inexpensive*). In a lovely setting, this place offers all the mod cons, including a pool, at a reasonable price.

Hospedería Morceguillinas, along the road to Beas, **t** 95 312 61 52, **f** 95 349 62 84 (*inexpensive*). Offers similar facilities in another pretty setting.

El Mesoncillo, in La Platera (a few km from Hornos), **t** 64 681 02 52. A set of self-catering cottages with great views, log fires and lots of chunky wooden furniture – the perfect place to come if you want to get away from it all.

The mountain ranges of Cazorla and Segura make up one of the 10 national parks in Spain. The **Cazorla National Park** covers over half a million acres, and teems with wild boar, deer, mountain goat, buck and moufflon, while rainbow trout do their best to outwit anglers. The park abounds with mountain streams and is the source of the mighty Guadalquivir, nothing more than a trickle over a couple of stones at this point.

A hike in search of the source of Andalucía's greatest river is desperately romantic (a good map will direct you). Visitors interested in flora and fauna will find the area one of the richest in Europe, with a variety of small birdlife that's hard to match, as well as larger species such as eagles, ospreys and vultures.

Jaén

In the middle of the vast tracts of olive groves upon which its precarious economy depends is Jaén, the most provincial of all the Andalucían capitals. Jaén lacks the Renaissance charms of Úbeda or Baeza, but it is a decent, modern town, not quite as unattractive as many guidebooks claim; easily explored on foot in one day, along pleasant pedestrian walkways.

Jaén was the first capital of the kingdom of Granada and the old Arab quarter is a part of the town that is well worth a visit. Its weaving, narrow, paved lanes are at the foot of the hill crowned by the 13th-century Moorish castle of **Santa Catalina**, built by ibn-Nasr (***t** 95 321 91 16, open summer 10.30–1.30, winter 10–2, closed Wed*). Towering above the town, it's an ideal place to take in the views of the countryside and the

Olive Oil

Olive oil is an important part of Jaén cuisine and contributes to dishes such as *espinacas jiennenses* (spinach Jaén-style) and *ajilimojili* (potatoes, red peppers, oil and vinegar). There's even a dessert called *ochío* – oil cakes covered by a layer of salt and paprika. *Pipirrana* is considered a local speciality with peppers, tomatoes, onions, hard-boiled egg and tuna fish. It's especially popular in the summer. During the winter try *migas de pan* or breadcrumbs, usually served with pieces of pork, though also as a sweet dish eaten like popcorn. Wherever you eat, look out for Jaén black pudding, a concoction of pork, beef, garlic, paprika, nutmeg and sherry, *cabrito asado* (roast baby kid with garlic) and *chorizo*. The clay *cazuela* bowl gives its name to a savoury cake made from chickpeas, aubergine, marrow and sausage, topped with sesame seeds. As you might expect, olive oil is extremely inexpensive all over the province of Jaén; in the country you might stumble across a local co-operative which sells it even more cheaply than do the shops. Look out for really superior extra virgin oils, such as Oro Mágina, with its virtually nought per cent acidity.

But there's more in the olive than just the oil in these parts. Increasingly, Andalucía, the 'Saudi Arabia of olive oil', is finding ways to use the rest of the squeezed-out fruit. It's a good thing they have, since a single co-operative can pile up over 10,000 tons of it a year. In the old days farmers used to dry them out in cakes and use them for fuel, and now they're running a 12-megawatt power station near the village of Benameji, south of Córdoba. It's worked so well that plans have been made to build another one near Jaén, and the company that designed them is exporting the process to other countries around the Mediterranean. It's just another example of the new Spain at work – with over a thousand big windmills, and half of Europe's solar power, they're the EU leader in renewable energy.

Getting There and Around

Jaén has direct **rail** links only with Córdoba (three trains daily) and Madrid (about six). The RENFE station is on the Paseo de la Estación, the main street, at the northern edge of town, by the Plaza de la Concordia. **Buses** are the best bet – Jaen is a real transport hub. The bus station is on the Avenida de Madrid, near the tourist office. Buses run to Úbeda via Baeza (12 daily); Granada (14 daily); Málaga (4 daily); Córdoba (8 daily); Almeria (2 daily).

Tourist Information

C/Maestra 13, a small street near the cathedral, **t** 95 324 26 24/95 319 04 55. *Open Mon–Fri 10–7 (10–8 in summer); Sat, Sun and hols 10–1.*

Where to Stay

Jaén ✉ 23000

******Parador Castillo de Santa Catalina**, in the castle overlooking Jaén, **t** 95 323 00 00, **f** 95 323 09 30, *jaen@parador.es* (*expensive*). General Charles de Gaulle spent time here working on his memoirs. The management could do with an overhaul but the views are unsurpassable.

*****Infanta Cristina**, Avda de Madrid s/n, **t** 95 326 30 40, **f** 95 327 42 96, *directorhic@swin.net* (*expensive*). The best hotel in town with big, comfortable rooms, a pool and a good restaurant.

*****Europa**, Plaza de Belén 1, **t** 95 322 27 00, **f** 95 322 26 92, *pemana@ofijaen.com* (*moderate*). A functional and modern business hotel, run by the excellent Husa chain.

*****Condestable Iranzo**, Pso de la Estación 32, **t** 95 322 28 00, **f** 95 326 38 07 (*moderate*). A good mid-priced hotel, with a pleasant café attached.

*****Xauen**, Pza de Deán Mazas 3 (near Plaza Constitución), **t** 95 324 07 89, **f** 95 319 03 12 *hotelxauen@amsystem.es* (*moderate–inexpensive*). Another conveniently placed major hotel.

***Hostal Renfe**, Pso de la Estación s/n, **t** 95 327 46 14 (*inexpensive*). Right next to the station, but clean, bright and good value.

***La Española**, Bernardo López 9, **t** 95 325 02 54 98 (*cheap*). Pretty gloomy old mansion, but offers rooms with or without bath for a rock bottom price.

Eating Out

Café Zeluan, Plaza San Francisco. This Art Deco café is a good spot to linger over breakfast.

Casa Vicente, C/Francisco Martín Mora 1, **t** 95 323 22 22 (*expensive–moderate*). Come here for a wide-ranging menu of local specialities, mainly meat and fish, though it's somewhat gloomy (tourists out the back, locals at the front, seems to be the rule). During the summer, get a table outside in the courtyard. *Closed Sun.*

Mesón Neyra, Pasaje Neyra s/n, **t** 95 324 07 63 (*moderate*). Rustically decorated, this welcoming restaurant serves classic Jiennese cuisine. Try the *habas fritas de Jaén*, or the roast suckling pig.

For less formal dining, there are numerous excellent tapas bars in the streets around the cathedral, in particular: C/Maestra and Arco del Consuelo, and Plaza de la Constitución and along the narrow alley, Calle Nueva, which leads off it. What nightlife there is centres around the streets at the bottom end of Pso de la Estación, bordered by C/Andalucía and the train station. Try INN at No.54.

mountains beyond. The city's pride is its monumental **cathedral** on Plaza Santa María (*open summer daily 8.30–1 and 5–8; winter Mon–Fri 8.30–1 and 4–9, Sat and Sun 9–1 and 5–7; free*), begun in 1548 by Andrés de Vandelvira. His work inside has suffered many changes, and the façade isn't his at all; not begun until 1667, Eufrasio López de Rojas's design was the first genuine attempt at Baroque in Andalucía, decorated with extravagant statuary by Pedro Roldán. There's a small museum inside (*open Tues–Sat 10–1 and 4–7; adm*), with a dull collection of local art and some rather more striking religious statuary. Adjacent to the cathedral is the **Iglesia del Sagrario**, with a neoclassical interior designed by Ventura Rodríguez. On Calle Martínez Molina, west of the cathedral, the **Palacio de Villardompardo** (*t 95 323 62 92; open Tues–Fri 9–8, Sat and Sun 9.30–2.30; adm, free to EU citizens*) has been beautifully restored to hold the extensive and engaging **Museum of Arts and Popular Customs**, and the smaller and less interesting Museo de Arte Naïf. The real attraction is the **Baños Árabes**, well-preserved ruins of 11th-century Moorish baths, complete with cold rooms, hot rooms and a tepidarium, discovered underneath.

Jaén has a number of churches, convents, monasteries and fine palaces worth seeking out. Near the cathedral, on C/Pescadería, is the 17th-century Palacio de los Vilches, and in the Plaza de San Francisco is the beautiful **Palacio Provincial**, where the regional *ayuntamiento* is based. Dating from the 19th century, the building has a fine central patio. Of the monasteries, perhaps the finest is that of **Santo Domingo**, in the street of the same name, which began life as a 14th-century monastery, before becoming the town's university and then the headquarters of the Inquisition; it now houses Jaén's historical archive. The façade is by Vandelvira. A few streets down is another monastery, **Santa Clara**, the town's oldest; inside is an odd figure of Christ made out of bamboo, Latin American in origin. Opposite stands the church of **San Bartolomé**, which has a fine *mudéjar* ceiling and the wonderful *Cristo de la Expiración*, by Martínez Montañés. The town's oldest church is **La Magdalena**, at the top of town on C/Molino Condesa. It dates from the 16th century and is built over an old mosque: the former minaret is now its belltower. The exterior is Gothic; inside there are a number of paintings, including *La Magdalena*, by Mateo de Medina. The area in which it stands was once the old Roman part of town.

Jaén's modern quarters can be a bit dreary, and peculiar at the same time. The centre, **Plaza de las Batallas**, has an extremely silly winged statue atop a pedestal, commemorating past victories over the Moors. Nearby, on the broad Plaza de la Estación, there is a good, but rather old-fashioned, archaeological collection in the **Museo Provincial** (*t 95 325 06 00; open Tues 3–8, Wed–Sat 9–8, Sun 9–3; adm, free to EU citizens*).

If you're on the way to Granada, a possible detour is to **Alcalá La Real**, with an unusual town square and the picturesque **Castillo de la Mota** on top of a hill. The **Castillo de Solera**, in the tiny village of Solera just east of Huelma, is an even finer sight; the castle seems to grow out of its narrow crag. Like Cazorla, the views are breathtaking but it will be some trouble to get up to them on foot.

Huelva, Cádiz and Gibraltar

11

Huelva, Cádiz and Gibraltar

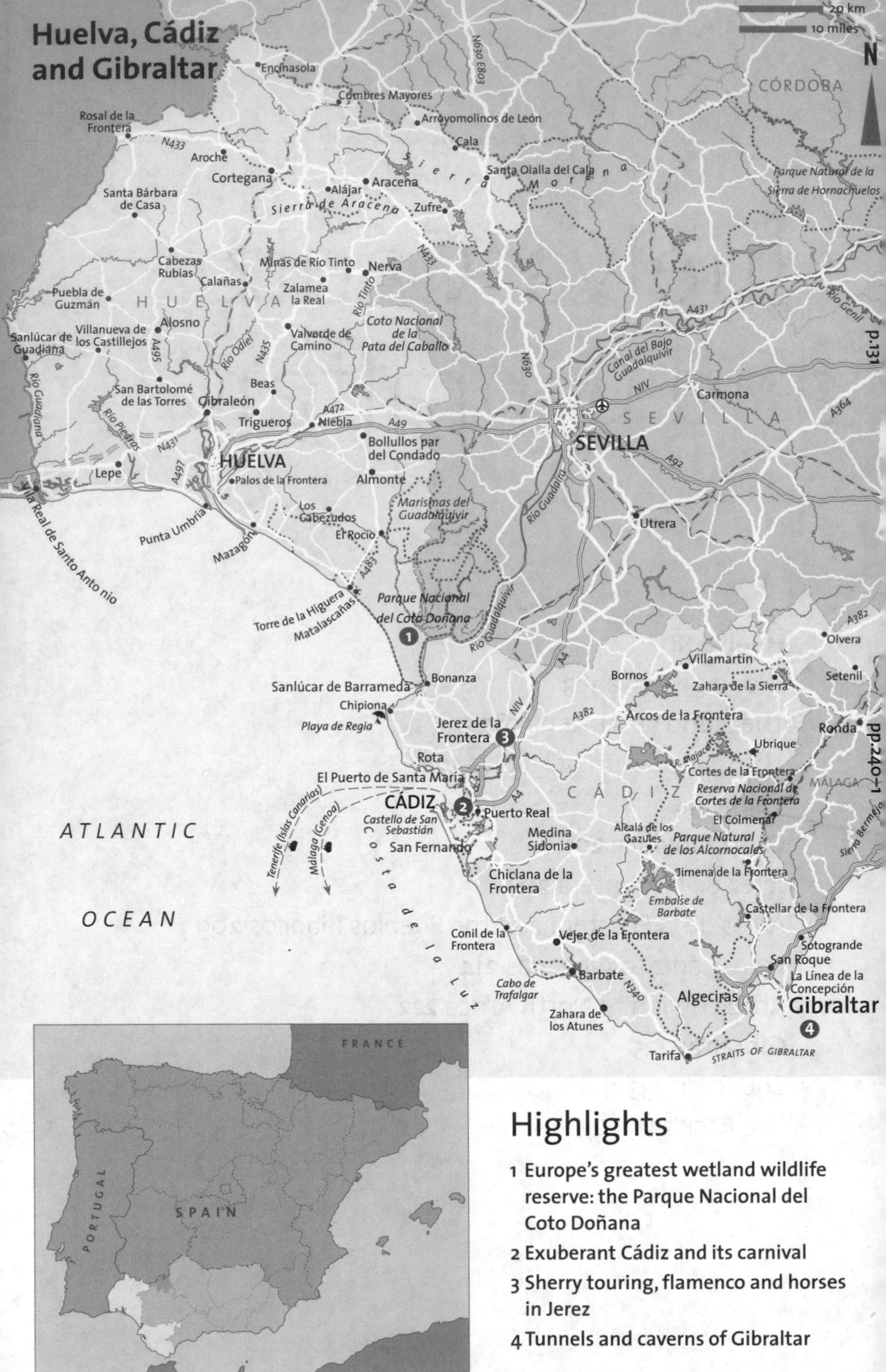

Highlights

1 Europe's greatest wetland wildlife reserve: the Parque Nacional del Coto Doñana

2 Exuberant Cádiz and its carnival

3 Sherry touring, flamenco and horses in Jerez

4 Tunnels and caverns of Gibraltar

Everyone has heard of the Costa del Sol, but there is a good deal more to Andalucía's coasts than just that narrow strip of salty Babylon – about 640km of it, from the empty spaces of Huelva to the empty spaces of Almería. The western half of this stretch is Andalucía's Atlantic coast, from Portugal to the Straits of Gibraltar; it's not all that scenic, but it has plenty of long golden beaches that haven't yet become too crowded. The image-makers of the Spanish Tourism Ministry have bestowed upon it the name Costa de la Luz.

The piquant, sea-washed town of Cádiz is its major attraction. After Cádiz comes a glass of sherry (or two) in Jerez de la Frontera. Here the mountains begin to close in, with their white villages. Back on the coast, there is a clutch of growing resorts including windsurf city, Tarifa; then Algeciras, a port town with the promise of a side-trip to Morocco, or to Ceuta, a tiny remnant of Spain's colonial empire in Africa. Finally we stop for meat and two veg in Gibraltar.

Huelva

A Huelva una vez y nunca vuelvas.
(One trip to Huelva and you don't go back.)

This Andalucían saying does seem a little unkind, but the provincial capital is full of factories and freshly laid cement; from the outskirts it looks like some dilapidated Slovak town. Hit the centre however and, small as it is, it boasts an incongruously large number of fur shops and amusement arcades. (History will probably prove that Las Vegas was actually founded by a Huelvan.) Huelvans are an isolated bunch, flanked and maybe intimidated by the presence of haughty Sevilla on one side and the expanse of Portugal on the other. They are nonetheless friendly and welcoming, and fervent in their desire to play a more important role in the future of Spain.

The town's tourist brochure, in a unique and disarmingly modest display of candour, states that Huelva 'has no particular historic interest'. The town was severely damaged by the earthquake of 1755, explaining the near-absence of anything older than that; exceptions include the 16th-century Baroque church of **San Pedro** and the newly renovated **Museo Provincial**, Alameda Sundheim 13 (*open Tues–Sat 9–8, Sun 9–3, closed Mon*). The town's theatre is an Art Deco aberration that resembles an

Chocos and *Choqueros*

Huelvan cuisine is based on fish and sausages – white, horseshoe-shaped, smoke-cured salami and blood sausgage. The Huelva hills are home to the Iberian pig, which has a justifiably high reputation for the quality of its pork; the local ham is a fine aromatic meat. Huelvans are also known as *choqueros*, because of their love for *chocos*, small cuttlefish; but just as popular is *mojama*, an expensive, salty fish delicacy of raw wind-dried tuna. Although Condado de Huelva is near to Jerez, it is still within Huelva province and provides decent white table wine and *finos* such as Condado Pálido and Condado Viejo.

Getting There and Around

By Train

The railway station is on the Avenida de Italia, 5mins from the centre of Huelva; there is a daily *Talgo* to Sevilla and Madrid (change at Linares for Granada and Almería), apart from the regular services to Sevilla, from where there are connections to Cádiz, Jerez, Córdoba and other points in Andalucía and Barcelona. There are also regular trains to Ayamonte, on the Portuguese border.

By Bus

The bus station is on Avda Doctor Rubio s/n, **t** 95 924 56 14. There are services to Sevilla, Granada, Cádiz and Algeciras, and other destinations within the province: Ayamonte, Isla Cristina, Punta Umbria, Mazagón and Matalascañas on the coast, less frequently to Nerva and the mountain villages to the north. The nearest **airport** is Sevilla.

Tourist Information

Avda de Alemania 12, **t/f** 95 925 74 03. *Open weekdays 9–7, Sat 10–2, closed Sun. www.huelvainformacion.es, www.todohuelva.com.* Huelva has a few Internet cafés: try **@IberMed**, C/Vázquez López, Galería Comercial, in front of Gran Teatro, **t** 95 925 14 10. *Open 10–12.*

Where to Stay

Huelva ✉ 21000

★★★★**NHLuz Huelva**, Alameda Sundheim 26, **t** 95 925 00 11, **f** 95 925 81 10 (*luxury*). Situated near the Columbus monument, with air-conditioned rooms, pool and tennis.

★★★**Tartessos**, Avda Martín Alonso Pinzón 13, **t** 95 928 27 11, **f** 95 925 06 17 (*moderate*). Another giant: comfortable and central with a renowned restaurant (*see* below).

★★★**Monte Conquero**, C/Pablo Rada 10, **t** 95 928 55 00, **f** 95 928 39 12 (*moderate*). The slightly pricier option in this category, just outside the old town centre to the north, with parking.

★★**Costa de la Luz**, C/José María Amo 8, **t/f** 95 925 64 22 (*inexpensive*). In a good spot bang in the centre of town, a few minutes walk from the theatre.

★★**Los Condes**, Alameda Sundheim 14, **t** 95 928 24 00, **f** 95 928 50 41 (*moderate*). A bit further out, but offers more comforts, such as a minibar and parking.

★★**Pensión La Vega**, Pza Independencia 15, **t** 95 924 15 63 (*cheap*). At the bottom of the scale with rooms for less than €30, but don't expect any home comforts.

Eating Out

Huelva packs some surprises in the culinary department; its markets keep the restaurants well supplied with gleaming fresh seafood, and Huelvans like to eat out.

El Estero, Avda Martín Alonso Pinzón 13, **t** 95 925 65 72 (*moderate*). Part of the Hotel Tartessos and generally regarded as one of the best restaurants in town; specialities include *dorado al horno*, local pork dishes, peppers stuffed with prawns, and delicious home-made puddings such as *Charlotte de chocolate blanco*.

Casa Calvino, C/Tendeleras 9, **t** 95 924 98 36 (*inexpensive*). Friendly, family-run restaurant serving delicious seafood and roasted meats in a tiny little dining room.

El Portichuelo, Avda Martín Alonso Pinzón, **t** 95 924 57 68 (*moderate*). A local classic, serving up excellent local grilled meat (*carnes a la brasa*). There's a very popular tapas bar, too.

Las Candelas, Ctra Punta Umbría (at the Aljaraque crossing 7km out of town), **t** 95 931 83 01 (*inexpensive*). Perfect seafood at affordable prices. *Closed Sun.*

Italian ice-cream parlour, but the real curiosity of Huelva is the **Barrio Reina Victoria**, a neighbourhood constructed by and for the employees of the English Río Tinto mining company in the 19th century. The company houses, now in a state of disrepair, sport gable ends and chimney pots in true English suburban style. (You may still see the Río Tinto Company mentioned in the business pages. In the 1900s they were running one of the biggest copper mines in the world here; when the deposits gave out, they opened a new one in Zambia.) Just out of townis the 36m (118ft) statue of Columbus, sculpted by Gertrude Whitney and presented to Spain by the USA in 1929.

The town also boasts an 18th-century cathedral, **La Merced**, off Paseo de la Independencia, and next door the recently opened **University of Huelva**, in an old hospital. Columbus-philes might also wish to trek up to the top of town to visit the **Santuario de Nuestra Señora de la Cinta**, off Avda de la Cinta, a 15th-century building commemmorated in traditional *azulejo* tiles by Daniel Zuloaga. Columbus prayed at this chapel, among others, before his epic voyage to the New World.

Around Huelva

Twenty-seven kilometres east of Huelva on the N431 you may visit the once-important town of **Niebla**, now forgotten behind its decayed Romano-Moorish walls. There's a Roman bridge and some interesting old churches and Moorish buildings. The **Santa María de la Granada** is a church and mosque which came about in the same way as Cordoba's Mezquita – by fusing the two religious buildings together (a key is available from the town hall).

Huelva province is making great attempts to cash in on its Columbus legacy and has published a guide to the area, *Columbus Territory* (free from most tourist offices in the province), detailing an itinerary which takes in the key spots associated with the great explorer, who set out on his first voyage to the New World from **Palos de la Frontera**, 5km southeast of Huelva. The town today is a rather uninspiring place, but it does have a number of key monuments associated with Columbus, including the church of **San Jorge**, where Columbus took mass before setting sail, and the fountain, **La Fontanilla**, which supplied water for the journey. Just beyond is a small park built to mark the quincentenary of Columbus's departure. Along C/Colón, at No.24, there is a small **museum** (*open Mon–Fri 10–2*) dedicated to Martín Alonso Pinzón, who was captain of the *Pinta* on Columbus's first voyage to America.

Tourist Information

Ayamonte: Avda Ramón y Cajal s/n, 21400 Ayamonte, **t** 95 947 09 88. *Open Mon–Fri, summer 10–2 and 5–9, winter 9.30–1.30 and 4.30–8.30.*

La Rábida: Paraje de la Rábida, **t** 95 953 11 37.

Moguer: C/Andalucía 5, **t** 95 937 18 98.

Punta Umbría: Avda Ciudad de Huelva, s/n, **t** 95 931 46 19.

Fiestas: Fiesta de Virgen de Montemayor in Moguer when the streets fill with horses.

Where to Stay and Eat

Ayamonte ✉ 21400

There's a line of fine little restaurants along the plaza, on the Paseo de la Ribera.

★★★★**Parador de Ayamonte**, El Castillito, **t** 95 932 07 00, **f** 95 932 07 00, *ayamonte@parador.es* (*expensive–moderate*). Not on the beach but it has a big pool and is on the edge of the Guadiana river, with views over the sea. Although it occupies the site of a long-gone Moorish castle, the *parador* was built more recently in 1966.

★★★**Don Diego**, C/Ramón y Cajal s/n, **t** 95 947 02 50, **f** 95 932 02 50 (*moderate*). The next best option in town, a '60s-style hotel.

★**Europa**, Avda de la Playa 45, **t** 95 947 12 39 (*cheap*). One of the cheaper options.

★**Marqués de Ayamonte**, C/Trajano 12, **t** 95 932 01 25 (*inexpensive–cheap*). A good basic option just off Pza de Ribera.

Casino España, Paseo de la Ribera (*moderate*). With its cool arches and terrace, this is a good place to try shellfish and *paella*.

Casa Barberi, Plaza de la Coronación 12–13, **t** 95 947 02 89 (*moderate*). You can peep through the palm trees at Portugal from this award-winning local restaurant.

Casa Luciano, C/Palma 2, **t** 95 947 10 71 (*moderate*). Excellent seafood, fish stews, and a good-value *menú* at less than €20.

Mesón la Casona, C/Lusitania 2, **t** 95 932 10 25 (*inexpensive*). A simple place which does a good *menú* for less than €10 with seafood featuring heavily; there is a patio inside. Tasty tapas are available at the bar, too.

Passage Café, Pza de la Laguna 11, **t/f** 95 947 10 81 (*inexpensive*). A good place to start the evening.

The limited nightlife is centred around C/Médico Rey García,down from Pza Ribera.

Sacapuntas, C/Médico Rey García. One of the numerous *bares de copas* in this area, a big and trendy place.

Pub Apoca, Ruelle de Portugal. At the end of Médico Rey García, looking across the Río Guadiana to the lights of Portugal.

Papaya, C/Médico Rey García. Nearby, and a bit smarter.

5 Mentario, C/Médico Rey García. A disco pub.

Ciber, Ruelle de Portugal. An Internet café-bar.

Palos de la Frontera, Moguer ✉ 21400

La Pinta, C/Rábida 75, **t** 95 935 05 11, **f** 95 953 01 64 (*moderate*). The best place to stay in town, with plenty of facilities and a very nice restaurant.

Pensión La Niña, C/Juan de la Cosa 37, Palos de la Frontera, **t** 95 953 03 60 (*inexpensive*). Cheaper, but slightly out of town.

Pensión Platero, C/Aceña 4, Moguer, **t** 95 937 21 59 (*cheap*). The best basic option in town, in a pretty *andaluz* house.

Hostal Pedro Alonso Niño, C/Pedro Alonso Niño 13, Moguer, **t** 95 937 23 92 (*cheap*). Another basic place with a little patio.

La Parrala, Pza de las Monjas 22, **t** 95 937 04 52 (*moderate*). The best place to eat, set on an attractive plaza.

Isla Canela ✉ 21400

★★★★**Riu Canela**, Pso de los Gavilanes s/n, **t** 95 947 71 24, *www.riu.com* (*luxury*). A luxurious faux-Moorish pile with 350 rooms, pools, gardens, tennis, shops,near the beach.

★★★★**Riu Atlántico**, Punta del Moral s/n, **t** 95 962 10 00, **f** 95 962 10 03, *www.riu.com* (*expensive*). Marginally cheaper but no less impressive than its cousin, with all the same amenities and a large lobby and pool.

Espuma del Mar, Pso de los Gavilanes s/n, **t** 95 947 72 85 (*moderate*). Serves simple, fresh seafood from this stretch of the coast.

Borelon, **t** 95 947 71 47 (*inexpensive*). A pizza-café actually on the beach in Isla Canela.

Isla Cristina ✉ 21410

★★Paraíso Playa, Avda de la Playa s/n, **t** 95 933 18 73, **f** 95 934 37 45, *hparaiso@retemail.es* (*moderate*). Provides all kinds of amenities, including a pool, for a reasonable price.

★★Los Geranios, Avda de la Playa s/n, **t** 95 933 18 00 (*moderate*). Another beachside option.

Casa Rufino, Ctra de la Playa, **t** 95 933 08 10, **f** 95 934 34 70 (*moderate*). The best food in Isla Cristina is to be found here. *Lunch only except during Semana Santa and in summer.*

Acosta, Pza del Caudillo 13, **t** 95 933 14 20 (*inexpensive*). A local favourite for fresh fish and Andalucian stews. *Closed Mon in winter.*

Paraíso Playa, Avda de la Playa, **t** 95 933 18 73 (*inexpensive*). The restaurant at this hotel serves a reasonable lunch for less than €12 between Holy Week and September on its pretty terrace.

La Rábida ✉ 21810

★★★Hostería de La Rábida, **t** 95 935 03 12 (*inexpensive*). A small and comfortable inn next to the monastery. Fewer rooms, and popular, so book ahead for high season.

★★Hotel Hacienda Santa María, on the road to Palos, **t** 95 953 00 01, **f** 95 935 04 99 (*inexpensive*). Has more amenities but a lot less character.

Punta Umbría ✉ 21100

The choice is wider at Punta Umbría. All these little resorts have cheaper hotels within reasonable distance of the beaches. In the busy season, phone ahead.

★★El Ayamontino, Avda Andalucía 35, **t** 95 531 14 50, **f** 95 531 03 16 (*moderate*). Has a good restaurant; but a fair walk from the beach.

★★Ayamontino Ría, Avda de la Ria 1, **t** 95 531 14 58 (*moderate*). Sister hotel to El Ayamontino, and better located.

★★Hostal La Playa, Avda Océano 95, **t** 95 531 01 12 (*inexpensive*). Open all year and one of the best bargains on the beach.

Youth Hostel, Avenida del Océano 13, **t** 95 931 16 50, **f** 95 931 42 29, *www.interjoven.com* (*cheap*). For those on a very tight budget.

El Paraíso, Ctra de Huelva–Punta Umbría, km 11, **t** 95 931 27 56 (*moderate*). Regarded as one of the best seafood restaurants in the region by locals. Two dining rooms, one beachy, the other quite elegant, serve fresh seafood.

La Esperanza, Pza Pérez Pastor 3, **t** 95 931 10 45 (*inexpensive*). Long popular, with satisfying well-cooked dishes at reasonable prices.

El Ayamontino, Avda Andalucía 35, **t** 95 931 14 50 (*inexpensive*). Serves tasty fish soup, bream and rather tough sirloin steaks.

Bar Antonio, Combes Punzones 10, **t** 95 931 41 32 (*inexpensive*). A small eaterie by the port.

Bar Clukibito. A boat moored by the port, off Pza Pérez Pastor, where most of the night-time action can be found.

Puntamar. One of a number of disco-bars along Avda Andalucía.

El Rompido ✉ 21459

Large-scale tourism has yet to take off here and accommodation is limited. Places to eat are lined along the main street in the lower part of the village, beside the beach.

★Hacienda San Miguel, El Rompido, km 2, **t/f** 95 950 42 62, *www.turandalucia.com* (*moderate*). A very pleasant and friendly hotel 2km from the village, with restaurant.

★La Galera, Ctra a Cartaya, **t** 95 939 91 76 (*cheap*). The budget option, also out of town.

La Ola (*inexpensive*). One of several reasonably priced fish restaurants by the beach.

Cambe II (*inexpensive*). A fish restaurant that doubles as an ice-cream parlour.

La Antilla ✉ 21449

La Antilla has a limited number of places to stay, all of which are booked up over summer.

★★Lepe Mar, C/Delfin 12, **t** 95 948 10 01, **f** 95 948 14 78 (*moderate*). The best hotel on the seafront, with parking, café and bars.

★★Pensión La Antilla, Pza de la Parida, **t** 95 948 00 56, **f** 95 948 00 88 (*inexpensive*). One of several places clustered around the bus stop.

★★Hostal Azul, La Parada 9, **t** 95 948 07 00 (*inexpensive*). Central, not far from the beach.

The road from La Antilla loops round to Lepe via the small fishing village of El Terron, on the banks of another small natural park. There is nowhere to stay, but there are a couple of good and *inexpensive* places to eat: **La Aucla**, on the harbour and **La Barca**, in the village.

A few kilometres on from Palos, along a road lined with ceramics depicting each of the 50 states of the USA, and set in a forest of pines, lies the **Monasterio de Santa María de la Rábida** (*visits hourly by guided tours only, Tues–Sun 10–1 and 4–7, or 4–6.15 in winter; donation requested*), where Columbus planned his epic journey. The rooms he used are maintained much as they were then, and can be viewed on a 45-minute tour, which also takes in an alabaster Virgin from the 14th century, the *mudéjar* cloisters and various frescoes painted by Daniel Vázquez Diaz. The **Muelle de las Carabelas** (*open April–Sept Tues–Fri 10–2 and 5–9, Sat–Sun 11–8; Oct–March Tues–Fri 10–2, Sat–Sun 11–8; adm*), between the monastery and the river, features three full-size models of the ships that made the voyage, together with replicas of 15th-century quayside bars.

North of Palos lies **Moguer**, a pretty whitewashed village where *La Niña* was built before the river silted up and, along with Palos, where most of the crew were recruited for the voyage, including Juan and Pedro Alonso Niño, the captain and pilot of *La Niña*. Moguer was also home to Nobel Prize-winning poet **Juan Ramón Jiménez**; his house, in the street of the same name, is now a **museum** (***t** 95 937 21 48; open 10.15–1.15 and 5.15–7.15, Sun 10–2; adm*), a Baroque building full of his notepads, books and documents. He is buried with his wife, Zenobia, in a cemetery on the eastern edge of town. You can also visit the 14th-century convent of **Santa Clara** (***t** 95 937 01 07; open 11–1 and 5–7, Sun and Mon 11–1; adm*), which is now a sacred art museum with a series of exquisite cloisters. The 18th-century **Iglesia de Santa María de Granada** has a belltower similar in design to the Giralda, while nearby, on Pza del Cabildo, is the beautiful **town hall**, described by Michael Jacobs in his book *Andalucía* as 'the finest neoclassical building in the whole of Huelva province'.

West of Huelva

Coming from Huelva by bus to **Ayamonte**, you'll be deposited next to the pretty square behind the harbour filled with small boats, which you can eye from the comfort of one of the *azulejo* benches. If you're on your way to Portugal, walk through the square and follow the signs for about 500m, where a flat-bottomed boat (*information **t** 95 947 06 17*) will be waiting to take you and 40 cars across the narrow stretch of the Guadiana river to the Portuguese town of **Vila Real de Santo António**. (If you are interested in a boat cruise up the Guadiana, call **t** 95 947 16 30). Most people now take the bridge across, which passes by the Portuguese border town of **Castro Marim**. The back streets of Ayamonte are not without character and there are plenty of little cafés where you can sit and muse, or bring your diary up to date. The town's major monument is the **Church of Las Augustias**, a Baroque-*mudéjar* pile, dedicated to the town's patron saint: her fiestas are celebrated at the start of September. Just across the water, the beaches of **Isla Canela** and **Punta del Moral** are more popular with Spaniards than with foreigners. Both lie just a few kilometres from the town centre through a small natural park, **Marismas de Isla Cristina** (*see* p.192). This fragile eco-system is under threat from burgeoning development on all sides, perhaps most acutely in Punta del Moral where a number of huge hotel complexes are under construction. Isla Canela is more restrained, a sleepy collection of bars, restaurants and apartments dominated by the vast faux-Moorish Riu Canela hotel (*see* 'Where to

Stay', pp.184–5). If you find yourself here around Easter time, Isla Cristina's Holy Week processions rival even those of Sevilla – it would be worth planning a visit for these alone. The working port is one of the most important in Spain: the catch ends up on Madrileños lunch tables via the early morning trains; get up early (5am) to see the boats come in.

Heading back east to Huelva, along the N431, you'll pass the sleepy town of **Lepe**, for some reason the butt of Andalucían jokes. Rather sportingly, every May the *leperos* hold a festival of humour – and even if they mind the abuse, they're laughing all the way to the bank, for the ever-abundant strawberry, orange and asparagus crops in this area have made the town very wealthy. (Those silver lakes you see along the road are actually tinted plastic sheets protecting the strawberries.)

This stretch of road between Huelva and Ayamonte has no real attraction for the tourist – orange groves interspersed with derelict buildings, scrapyards and mudflats. South of Lepe on the coast are two spots worth a visit – **La Antilla**, with its fine white sandy beach (EU Blue Flag), and **El Rompido**, a pleasant little place that is now being developed for tourism. The main development is taking place a few kilometres further on, at **El Portil**, a bland and ugly place. Further east, the peninsula of **Punta Umbría** is one of the main tourist resorts of the area; its long sandy beaches offer all types of water sports.

The Sierra de Aracena

If you have a car you can comfortably explore the little-visited mountain villages in the Sierra de Aracena, less than a two-hour drive from the capital. The N435, passing through beautiful forests of holm oaks and cork trees, leads you to the heart of this area, through mountainous countryside and evermore scenic views.

Aracena

Aracena makes a good base from which to explore the Sierra. Just 70km from the Portuguese border, Aracena became part of Spain in the 13th century and fell under the control of the Knights Templars. They built the **Iglesia de Nuestra Señora del Mayor Dolor**, which stands in the grounds of the Moorish castle above town. This fine medieval church has a *mudéjar* tower, once the minaret of the mosque which stood here before. Beneath it lies the region's major draw, the **Gruta de las Maravillas** (***t** 95 912 82 55; open 10–1.30 and 3–6; adm*), a series of cavernous natural chambers with underground lakes. Local legend has it that the caves, which rival Nerja's for their extraordinary beauty, were discovered by a shepherd late in the 19th century. They have since seen a flood of visitors.

The town has a number of other churches, including the **Ermita de Santa Catalina**, which was once a synagogue, and the unfinished Iglesia de la Asunción, which you pass on the way up to the ruins of a **Moorish castle**, once occupied by the Templars. The Ermita forms the focus for the town's main fiesta, the pilgrimage to the Sanctuary of the Virgin, which is held on 8 September and involves brotherhoods

from neighbouring villages dressing up in traditional costume and riding horseback to the top of the hill. Another hermitage nearby is also worth visiting, with its 13th-century Gothic carvings and wonderful views over the mining lands of **Río Tinto**, excavated as early as Phoenician and Roman times, and bought by a British company in the late 19th century. Twelve kilometres away, to the west on the bumpy H521, is the pretty village of **Alájar**, worth a stop for its natural caves, the **Sillita del Rey** and the **Salón de los Machos**, which form part of the **Peña de Arias Montano**, a spot long revered for its mystical qualities, and named after Benito Arias Montano, an adviser to Philip II who came here to meditate and study the Bible. The king is said to have joined him at one point, hence the name of one of the caves.

The **Minas de Río Tinto** is a small, shabby mining town set in an area scarred by open mines and lakes, once owned by the Río Tinto Mining Company and now gradually sliding into the history books. The town itself is worth a stop for just two things, the mining museum and the former British colony of **Bella Vista**. Now signposted as El Barrio Inglés at the lower end of town, Bella Vista is a collection of Edwardian-gabled houses like the ones in Huelva, only set round an English-style village lawn, straight out of the Surrey countryside. It was built for the Río Tinto bosses, presumably to alleviate homesickness. **Museo Minero** (*Plaza del Museo,* **t** *95 959 00 25; open daily 10–3; adm*), set in the old mining hospital at the top of town, is a painstaking account of the mining practices which have taken place in this area since Roman times. There are artefacts, Roman coins, a collection of semi-precious stones and some fascinating photos of miners through several generations. There are also various account ledgers and a hospital ledger detailing the grim accidents suffered by miners. The centrepiece is two British-built locomotives and a sumptuous carriage, the Maharajah's Carriage, built for (but never used by) Queen Victoria for a trip to India. The museum also organizes trips to the open-cast mines, including the **Corte Atalaya**,

Tourist Information

Aracena: Pza San Pedro s/n, **t** 95 912 82 06. *Open Mon–Sat 10–2.30 and 4–6.30*. For information on the Natural Park, there's a visitor's centre at Edificio Cabildo Viejo, Plaza Alta, s/n, **t** 95 912 8825.

Jabugo: C/Carratera 9, **t** 95 912 11 32.

Where to Stay and Eat

Aracena ✉ 21200

★**Finca Buen Vino**, Los Marines, Huelva, **t** 95 912 40 34, **f** 95 950 10 29, *www.buenvino.com* (*expensive*). A grand guesthouse up in the Sierra Morena (6km from Aracena), run by a locally well-known English family. Lunch is served beside the pool; dinner is taken with the family. *Book in advance*.

★★★**Finca Valbono**, Ctra de Carboneras 1, **t** 95 912 77 11, **f** 95 912 76 79 (*moderate*). This place is a much better bet than staying in the town's lacklustre hotels; very friendly, sparkling clean and in the heart of the hills, with a pool and restaurant. Also has self-catering apartments.

★★**Sierra de Aracena**, Gran Vía 21, **t** 95 912 63 00, **f** 95 912 62 18 (*inexpensive*). A modern place with reasonable rooms.

★★**Los Castaños**, Avda de Huelva 5, **t** 95 912 63 00, **f** 95 912 62 87 (*inexpensive*). Fairly gloomy rooms overlooking the main street.

Sierpes, C/Mesones s/n, **t** 95 911 01 47 (*inexpensive*). A classic, central restaurant serving local specialities.

Restaurante Casas, C/Pozo de la Nieve 37, **t** 95 912 80 44 (*moderate–inexpensive*). At the entrance to the caves in Aracena, styled after a traditional *venta*, serving Sierra pork every which way you can think of.

Almonaster la Real ✉ 21290

★**La Cruz**, Pza del Llano 8, **t** 95 914 31 35 (*cheap*). A basic but more than adequate hostal off a tiny square.

Hotel Casa García, Avda de San Martín 2, **t** 95 913 04 09 (*hotel inexpensive, restaurant moderate*). At the entrance to the village. An upmarket place with a delightful courtyard, serving various regional pork dishes and fish at a reasonable price. Rooms are pretty functional, though.

Jabugo and Galaroza ✉ 21290

★★**Galaroza Sierra**, Ctra Sevilla-Lisboa, km 69, Galaroza, **t** 95 912 32 37, **f** 95 912 32 36 (*inexpensive*). Offers good-vaue rooms with a view in a wonderful location in the heart of the Sierra de Aracena y Picos de Aroche Park.

La Aurora, C/Barco 9, **t** 95 912 11 46 (*cheap*). Jabugo's small friendly *pensión*, offering rooms with bath.

Other clean but fairly basic options in Galaroza include (both inexpensive):

Hostal Venecia, Ctra Sevilla-Lisboa 14, **t** 95 912 30 98. Roadside hotel with a decent inexpensive restaurant.

Hostal Toribio, Iglesia 1, **t** 95 912 30 73. More central, with a restaurant attached.

Mesón Cinco Jotas, Ctra de San Juan del Puerto s/n (in Jabugo), **t** 95 912 10 71 (*moderate*). Here they smoke their own hams and export them to every corner of Spain, and beyond. It is now part of a chain covering all of Spain.

Bodega Jamón, Ctra de San Juan del Puerto s/n (in Jabugo), **t** 95 912 15 96 (*inexpensive*). Alternatively, try this place next door to Mesón Cinco Jotas, serving much the same fare but at a cheaper price and with a lovely shaded patio attached.

the largest in Europe. You would probably be better off stopping at the *mirador*, signposted just before the village, where you can view the entire weird landscape yourself.

At El Chorro, a waterfall near the town of **Santa Ana La Real**, the road forks north to **Jabugo**, a centre of *jamón* production, and west to **Almonaster la Real**, a pretty village with Roman origins and later Arabic influence – 'al' derives from the Arabic *al-munia*, meaning fortress. Its chief feature is the 10th-century mosque, one of a handful of rural mosques in Andalucía. Its lines follow that of the Mezquita in Córdoba, perfect Moorish arches supported by slim columns. There is a fountain in the corner, and you

Alájar ✉ 21290

★★★**La Posada**, Médico Emilio González s/n, **t** 95 912 57 12 (*inexpensive*). The only place to stay in town, situated in a historic building, with more facilities than you'd expect for the price – minibar, phone, café.

There's not much in the way of nightlife, but some good local bars are on the main square.

Cortegana ✉ 21230

★★**La Posada de Cortegana**, Ctra El Repilado-La Corte km 2.5, **t** 95 950 33 01, **f** 95 950 33 02 (*moderate–inexpensive*). An old inn tucked away in the hills, with gardens, a pool, bike hire facilities and comfortable, well-equipped rooms.

Cervantes, Cervantes 27, **t** 95 913 15 92 (*cheap*). Very basic rooms, mostly without bath.

Restaurante La Placeta, Plaza del Divino Salvador 4, **t** 95 913 13 17 (*inexpensive*). Popular local restaurant right by the church.

Restaurante El Aceitón, Avda de Portugal s/n, **t** 95 913 13 56 (*inexpensive*). Cortegana's smartest restaurant, where you'll dine well on regional dishes including wild mushroom soup (*sopa de setas*) and cured hams.

Cumbres Mayores ✉ 21380

Mayma, Pso Andalucía, **t** 95 971 05 92 (*inexpensive*). Has clean, cool rooms with bath; situated in the main square.

Togahilo, Antonio Machado 47, **t** 95 971 00 06 (*cheap*). On the way out of town, with extremely basic rooms with bath.

Eating and drinking options are limited to the *pensiónes*, or you could try the **Pata Chica**, C/Machado 1, **t** 95 971 04 32 (cheap).

Fuenteheridos ✉ 21292

Villa Turística, Ctra Sevilla-Lisboa, km 97, **t** 95 912 52 02, **f** 95 912 51 99 (*moderate*). A slightly soulless, but upmarket with a bar, café and restaurant, and all the mod cons.

Pensión Carballo, La Fuente 16, **t** 95 912 51 08 (*cheap*). The budget option in town; just six clean and basic rooms. The friendly owners can arrange trips in the surrounding Sierra.

El Barrio, C/Esperanza Bermúdez s/n (on the road leading up from the main square), **t** 95 912 50 33 (*inexpensive*). Serves a good selection of well-priced tapas and main meals, including *carnes a la brasa*.

El Ricco, C/Esperanza Bermúdez s/n. The disco-bar next door, where you can go for a few after-dinner *copas*.

Rosal de la Frontera ✉ 21250

Pensión Frontera, Avda de Portugal 109, **t** 95 914 10 28 (*cheap*). This central place is the best the town has to offer; with bath.

El Mirador de la Frontera, Avda de Sevilla 60, **t** 95 914 14 08 (*cheap*). Even cheaper, but very basic.

Zufre ✉ 21210

La Posá, C/Cibarranco 5, **t** 95 919 81 10 (*cheap*). A simple pension in the town centre; the only place to stay.

Casa Pepe, C/Portales 10, **t** 95 919 81 28. Brick-lined restaurant serving tasty local dishes.

Aroche ✉ 21240

★★**Picos de Aroche**, Ctra de Aracena 12, **t** 95 914 04 75 (*inexpensive*). A basic pension on the main road into town. Restaurant attached.

Pensión Romero, Paseo Ordóñez Valdés 44, **t** 95 914 00 22. The cheapest option;basic, but central, with a bar-restaurant.

Santa Olalla del Cala ✉ 21260

Carmelo, C/Marina Española 23, **t** 95 919 01 69. (*inexpensive*). In the town centre with a café attached.

can climb up the minaret which looks across the bullring to a parkland of blue and green oak-covered hills. The town itself has a number of medieval buildings and contains some fine examples of *mudéjar* and Gothic architecture, as well as the 14th-century church of **San Martín** and the **Puerta del Perdón**, in Manueline style.

The road from here to **Cortegana** passes right through pig territory, so drive slowly and look out for herds sheltering from the sweltering heat under the oaks. Cortegana is topped by a restored medieval castle and contains a fine *mudéjar* church, **Iglesia del Divino Salvador**, a national monument dating from the 16th century. From here you might be best off heading back east to Jabugo. If you do decide to press on, the N433 will take you past fields full of mean-looking *toros bravos* (fighting bulls): stop to take snaps by all means, but don't venture into the fields for a closer look.

In **Aroche**, further west, the white houses bask in the sun under the remains of an Almoravid fortress with ten towers, containing a bullring. The town is just outside the Picos de Aroche National Park and about 25km from the border. There's a small municipal archaeological museum and the tiny **Museo del Rosario** – yes, a rosary bead museum with more than 1,300 rosaries donated by, among others, JF Kennedy, Franco, Mother Teresa and Nixon. The pilgrimage of San Mamés, a horseback procession, takes place on the third weekend in August (*information from the town hall in Pza Juan Carlos*).

The **Picos de Aroche National Park** might not have the drama or arresting beauty of the Serranía de Ronda or the Sierra de Grazalema, but it is equally as pretty in its own way, with tiny villages nestling among forests of oak and pine, home to herds of black pigs and *toros bravos*, with vultures, eagles and kestrels soaring overhead. The last bears were killed just a few years ago, but in the remoter parts of the park wolves are still said to prowl, and there are even a few recorded Iberian lynx still in existence.

The main road back towards Huelva passes through the charming little village of **Galaroza**, surrounded by willow and ash forest, and crossed by a pretty stream. Continuing east will take you to **Fuenteheridos**, another picturesque village with a number of water-inspired sights, including the Fuente de Doce Canos, a 12-spring fountain in the main square, with a Baroque wooden sculpture.

To the southeast of Aracena, the N433 passes **Higuera de la Sierra**, dominated by a pretty Baroque church. Its Epiphany festival is the oldest in Spain. Four kilometres on lies the turning for the spectacular cliff-top village of **Zufre**, with a number of important monuments including a church, built over a mosque, with a *retablo* by Alonso Cano. The crumbling town walls date from the 12th century. Forests of gall and holm oak separate Zufre from **Santa Olalla del Cala**, dominated by a 13th-century Moorish castle. The church below is built over a synagogue, the anchor inside a reminder of the time when Santa Olalla served as the base for the marine infantry during the Napoleonic wars. Two kilometres north is the turn-off for **Cala**, with a 14th-century church, and the Cerro del Bujo viewpoint at **Arroymolinos de León**

Aracena to Cumbres Mayores

An alternative and less plied route heads north from Aracena via Carboneras to the borders of Extremadura. This is prime pig-spotting territory and, in summer, the landscape is reminiscent of the African bush, with parched reservoirs and scrubby brown hills. The road ends up at **Canaveral de León**, allegedly famous for its gazpacho but not much else. You are best off continuing towards **Cumbres Mayores**, the largest of three villages with Cumbres (heights) in their name, all three famous for their sausages. In Cumbres Mayores there is a magnificent 13th-century **castle** built by Don Sancho IV 'El Bravo' during a war with Portugal. It has nine sides and eight turrets and was declared a national monument in 1895 by Alfonso XIII. To visit enquire at the *ayuntamiento* for the keys. Next door is the church of San Miguel, which marks the start of a marked hour-long walking tour. From here you could press on another 23km to **Encinasola**, which lies at the crossroads to Extremadura and Portugal and has a number of monuments, including a 10th-century Muslim fortress.

The Coast South of Huelva

El Rocío and its Pilgrimage

Twenty-three kilometres south of Huelva, along the coastal route, is **Mazagón**, a family resort surrounded by pine trees and lovely beaches. From here it's a straight shot to **Torre de la Higuera**, and the big hotel developments around the endless **Matalascañas Beach**, the most international of Huelva's resorts. This is the dead end of the coastal highway; the only place you can go is the tiny inland village of **El Rocío**, which would not even be on the map were it not for the annual *romería* at Pentecost, the biggest and perhaps the oldest in Spain. The place is empty the rest of the year, but at Pentecost its population swells to the hundreds of thousands. Three great processions (featuring the traditional covered wagons) begin in the Triana district of Sevilla, Sanlúcar de Barrameda and Huelva, and are managed by the religious confraternity, the *hermandades*.

No one knows exactly how long the *romería* of El Rocío has been going on; processions in honour of the Virgin Mary are often descendants of ancient pagan festivals. In its modern version, it is traced to the 1400s, when a shepherd from the nearby village of Villamanrique found an image of the Virgin in a hollow tree. Miracles followed, and a chapel was built to house the image. The Lady has acquired many names over the centuries: first Nuestra Señora de las Rocinas, then Virgen del Rocío, 'Virgin of the Dew'; today she is commonly called simply the White Dove, *La Paloma Blanca*.

Every year pilgrims bring their families for a few days of music and merry-making in the fields; it is traditional to arrive in a horse- or ox-drawn covered wagon, decorated with flowers and streamers – the wagons are to hold all the food and drink, for this pilgrimage is as serious a party as the April Fair in Sevilla. Campfires burn all night, and the atmosphere is pure electricity.

Las Marismas

Add the water of the broad Guadalquivir to this flat coastal plain, and the result is southern Europe's greatest marshland wildlife reserve. Las Marismas is another world, a bit of the Everglades in a country better known for hot dry mountains. Hundreds of species of migratory birds pass through in the spring and autumn – storks among them – but Las Marismas has a fantastically varied population of its own: rare golden eagles, snowy egrets, flamingos, griffin vultures, tortoises, red deer, foxes and European lynx. All these fauna have been responsible for keeping the area relatively undisturbed; for centuries it was an aristocratic hunting preserve, belonging originally to King Alfonso X, later to the Dukes of Medina Sidonia, and finally to William Garvey, one of the sherry barons of Jerez. Much of the territory around the park is still held in private hunting preserves.

Tourist Information

Mazagón: Edificio Mancomunidad Moguer–Palos, **t** 95 937 60 44 (in the same building as the police station).
Matalascañas: Urbanización Playa de Matalascañas, **t** 95 943 00 86.
El Rocío: Avda de la Canallega s/n, **t** 95 944 26 84. *Open Mon–Fri 10–2.*

Where to Stay and Eat

Mazagón ✉ 21130

Mazagón has a number of restaurants and cafés around Avenida Fuente Piña. There's not much to distinguish between them but at least they're lively.

********Parador Mazagón**, Ctra Huelva–Matalascañas s/n, **t** 95 953 63 00, **f** 95 953 62 28, *mazagon@parador.es* (*expensive*). In an attractive pine-tree setting, looking down onto Mazagón beach, this modern *parador* is the best option, with pleasant gardens, pool and air-conditioned rooms.

El Remo, Avda Conquistadores 123, **t** 95 953 61 38 (*inexpensive*). A good *chiringuito* restaurant, with a *terraza*, specializing in sardines and fresh local fish.

Matalascañas ✉ 21760

There are a number of resort hotels at Matalascañas, predictably packed during the high season.

****El Cortijo**, Sector E–P Arcelas 15/49, **t** 95 944 87 00, **f** 95 944 83 75, *sunnahoteles@sunnahoteles.com* (*expensive*). A pleasant alternative to the resort hotels, this one is 5 minutes from the beach, and has facilities for horse riding.

Tamarindos, Avda de las Adelfas 31, **t/f** 95 943 01 19 (*moderate–inexpensive*). Clean *pensión*, near the beach and the town centre; all rooms come with bath. Prices almost double between June and Sept.

El Duque, Rafael Pinto 1, **t** 95 943 00 58 (*inexpensive*). A reasonable choice at the other end of the scale.

Da Pino, Edificio Barlovento, Paseo Marítimo Caño Guerrero, **t** 95 944 04 37 (*moderate*). An Italian restaurant with pastas, excellent salads and steaks. *Closed Mon, Christmas*.

Freiduría Los Galanes Fausto, Plaza del Pueblo, **t** 95 944 81 22 (*inexpensive*). Has a lovely terrace where you can enjoy your seafood at leisure.

Las Dunas, opposite Las Dunas beach, **t** 95 944 81 47 (*cheap*). A café-bar with a patio and outside seating.

For nightlife, try all along the street into town, and in season all along Pso Marítimo; some possibilities are **Pub L'Enfant, Colos** and **Habana.**

El Rocío ✉ 21750

*****Puente del Rey**, Avda de Canaliega 1, **t** 95 944 25 75, **f** 95 944 20 20 (*moderate*). Offers all kinds of amenities such as riding tours in the Coto Doñana National Park, language courses and even guitar lessons. Prices quadruple during the pilgrimage.

****Toruño**, Pza Acebuchal 22, **t** 95 944 23 23, **f** 95 944 23 38, *toruño@antonia.com* (*moderate*). In a good spot near the town centre; again, prices quadruple when the pilgrimage is in flow.

Cristina, C/Real 32, **t** 95 944 24 13 (*cheap*). Run by a lady of the same name, this appears to be the only hotel which doesn't take undue advantage of pilgrims.

As in the Everglades, wildlife congregates around 'islands' among the wetlands; here they're called *corrales*, built of patches of dune anchored by surrounding shrubs and stands of low pines. Also like the Everglades, Las Marismas is threatened by development from growing resorts like Matalascañas. This has become Spain's top environmental concern, and the government has limited coastal development, setting aside a large slice of the area as the **Parque Nacional del Coto Doñana**.

Doñana was closed to visitors in 1998; a chemical factory spilt thousands of tons of toxic mud into the Río Guadalquivir, and hence the park, causing an ecological disaster, though the area has now been thoroughly cleaned up. The **Centro de**

Recepción de Acebuche (*t 95 944 87 11*), about half-way between El Rocío and Matalascañas, runs Land Rover tours around the park. It also upkeeps a number of hides from which to observe the wildlife, and there are some signposted walks from the visitor's centre. Keep in mind that the 'wetlands' are largely dry in the summer. Whenever you come, bring mosquito repellent and watch out for quicksand. At **La Rocina** is the next visitors' centre (*t 95 944 23 40, km 16*), reached by going north along the A483. It also details a signposted walk and offers access to the **Palacio de Acebrón**.

Cádiz

If Cádiz were a tiny village, the government would immediately declare it a national monument and put up a sign. It's a big, busy seaport, though, and the tourist business generally leaves it alone. It's a pity, for Cádiz is one of the most distinctive Spanish cities, worth spending a few days in even if there are few 'sights'. The city is a small peninsula, resembling a sturdy galleon patiently waiting to put to sea, packed tightly and pounded by the rough Atlantic breakers on all sides. It comes in colours – a hundred shades of off-white – bleached and faded by sun and spray into a soft patina, broken only by the golden dome of a rambling Baroque cathedral that would be a civic misfortune anywhere else, but seems inexplicably beautiful here.

History

Cádiz modestly claims to be the oldest city in western Europe. It's hard to argue; the Phoenician city of **Gadir** has a documented foundation date of 1100 BC and, while other cities have traces of older settlements, it would be difficult to find another city west of Greece with a continuous urban life of at least 3,000 years. Gadir served as the port for shipping Spanish copper and tin, and was undoubtedly the base for the now-forgotten Phoenician trade routes with west Africa and England – and possibly even for explorations to America. Cádiz, however, prefers to consider Hercules its founder, and he appears on the arms of the city between his famous pillars.

Under Roman rule **Gades**, as it was called, was a favoured city, especially under Julius Caesar, who held his first public office here. Scant remains of the Roman theatre were discovered in 1980. **Jazirat Qadis**, as it was known to the the Moors, never was an important centre. Alfonso X conquered it for Castile in 1262, and began its cathedral. The city remained out of the spotlight until the 16th century, when the American trade and Spain's growth as a naval power made it a major port once again. Two of Columbus's four trips to the new world started from here. Sir Francis Drake visited in 1587 and, as every school child knows, 'singed the King of Spain's beard'. Later British admirals followed the custom for the next two centuries, calling every now and then for a fish supper and an afternoon's sacking, notably in 1596, when under the Earl of Essex half the town was burned down; when the British were away, Barbary pirates took their place, and the city had to beat off their raids several times in the 1500s. The years after 1720, when Cádiz controlled the American market, shaped its present character. Street names like Calle Conde O'Reilly (an Irish-born royal governor who did a lot

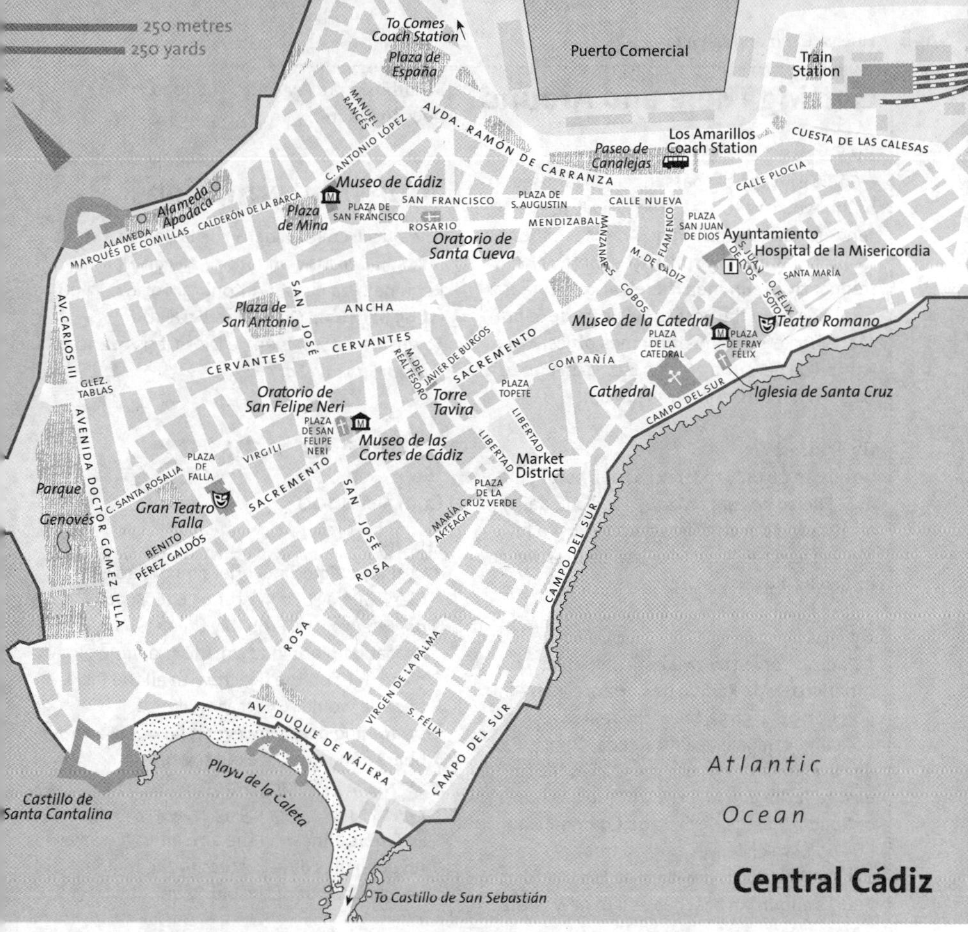

for Cádiz) and a statue of one José MacPherson y Hemas testify to the contacts the city enjoyed with the outside world, and it became the most liberal corner of Spain.

The Napoleonic Wars brought the pesky Brits back to plague the city again in 1797 and 1800. Its shining hour came in 1812, when the first Spanish constitution was declared here, and the city became the capital of free Spain. Understandably, Cádiz suffered after the restoration of the old absolutist government in 1823, when the constitution was abolished. Worse troubles were to come; the loss of most of Spain's colonies in America was a heavy blow, and the city declined further when its port became too outdated to handle modern ships. That was remedied in time to give the city of the constitution one further indignity – it was here that Franco ferried his Moroccan army into Spain in 1936, leading to the fall of most of Andalucía.

The approach to Cádiz is a dismal one, through marshes and saltpans cluttered with power lines and industrial junk. After this, you must pass through a long, narrow strip of land full of modern suburbs before arriving at the **Puerta de Tierra**, entrance to the old city on the peninsula. Almost everything about warfare in the 18th century had a certain decorum to it, and Cádiz's gates and formidable **land walls** (1757), all well preserved, are among the most aesthetically pleasing structures in town.

Getting There and Around

By Ferry

Cádiz isn't the big passenger port it used to be, but you can still take the weekly ferries to Tenerife – Las Palmas – and Arrecife in the Canary Islands. They run a little more frequently in summer. There's also a regular ferry ride from the port to El Puerto de Santa María. **Tickets**: Trasmediterránea office, Avda Ramón de Carranza 26, **t** 95 622 74 21/**t** 902 45 46 45, *www.trasmediterranea. com*.

By Train

You can go only to Jerez (20 daily, stopping at El Puerto de Santa María), Sevilla (8 daily) and Madrid directly. The station is just a few blocks from the Plaza San Juan de Dios, in Pza de Sevilla, **t** 95 625 43 01.

By Bus

Cádiz is served by two bus companies: **Los Amarillos**, Avda Ramón de Carranza 31 (by the port), **t** 95 628 58 52, takes the route west to Rota and Sanlúcar de Barrameda; **Comes**, Pza de Hispanidad 1, **t** 95 621 17 63, takes the route east to Tarifa and Algeciras. It also has buses to Ronda, Málaga, Seville and Córdoba. City bus no.1, which leaves from in front of Comes, will take you from the Plaza de España to Cádiz's suburban beaches and to new Cádiz.

Secorbus, from Pza Elio s/n, **t** 902 22 92 92, goes to Madrid.

Tourist Information

Andalucía: Calle Calderón de la Barca 1, **t** 95 621 13 13. *Open Mon and Sat 9–2, Tues–Fri 9–7.*

Regional: Pza de San Antonio 3, **t** 95 622 13 08, **f** 95 621 46 34. *Open Mon–Fri 8–3.*

Town: Pza de San Juan de Dios 1, **t** 95 624 10 01. *Open Sun and Sat 5–8.*

Where to Stay

Cádiz ✉ 11000

Luxury

★★★★**Playa Victoria**, Glorieta Ingeniero La Cierva 4, **t** 95 620 51 00, **f** 95 626 33 00, *hpv@teleline.es*. Probably the most upmarket place in town, this is a huge glitzy place right on the beach, with all the facilities you would expect, including a swimming pool. However it lacks the atmosphere of being in the old town.

★★★★**Meliá La Caleta**, Avda Amílcar Barca 47, **t** 95 627 94 11, **f** 95 625 93 22, *www.solmelia.es*. Offers almost all the amenities (bizarrely, no pool) plus direct access to the main beach, also out of the old town.

It's a great city for exploring. The old city is a maze of lanes bathed in soft lamplight after dusk, when the numerous cafés fill up with young, exuberant *gaditanos*. A walk through the myriad cobbled streets, past solid doors carved from the trees of South American forests, and balconies spilling over with flowers, will take you back to the time when mighty Cádiz bustled with industry as the gateway to the Americas. Keep an eye out for the little plaques – marking the birthplaces of, amongst others, Manuel de Falla, and Miranda, the first president of Venezuela – and reminders of what an important role this small city has often played. Note the houses, too, in a style unique to Cádiz, with roof-terraces and Moorish-looking turrets. You can walk around Cádiz in about an hour, past parks like the **Alameda Apodaca**, and forts of the 18th century.

Plaza San Juan de Dios and Around

From the Puerta de Tierra, the Cuesta de las Calesas leads down to the port and rail station, then around the corner to **Plaza San Juan de Dios**, the lively, palm-shaded centre of Cádiz, flanked at the end by the enormous ayuntamiento, with most of the restaurants and hotels on the surrounding streets. Two blocks away is the **cathedral**,

Expensive

★★★★**Parador Hotel Atlántico**, Avda Duque de Nájera 9, **t** 95 622 69 05, **f** 95 621 45 82, *cadiz@parador.es*. Another good *parador* set in a modern building with wonderful views over the Atlantic and a large outdoor pool. The suites at the front of the building are especially nice, and don't cost much more.

Moderate

★★★**Francia y París**, Pza San Francisco 2, **t** 95 622 23 48, **f** 95 622 24 31. A quiet, well-run hotel around the corner from Plaza de Mina.

★★**Pensión Bahia**, C/Plocia 5, off Plaza San Juan de Dios, **t** 95 625 90 61, *hostelbahia@terra.es* (*moderate*). Has a/c in the rooms with TV.

★**Imares**, San Francisco 9, **t** 95 621 22 57, **f** 95 621 22 58 (*inexpensive*). Small hotel with comfortable rooms.

Centro Sol, C/Manzanares 7, **t** 95 628 31 03, *centrosol@wanadoo.es*. A bit ramshackle, but in the heart of the city, with café.

On the other side of the Puerta de Tierra, in the new part of Cádiz, there's just as much choice. The Paseo Marítimo is lively, so don't feel you're missing out if you stay here. The following hotels are of a similar standard, both with garages and cafés attached:

★★**Regio**, C/Ana de Viya 11, **t** 95 627 93 31.

★★**Regio 2**, Avda Andalucía 79, **t** 95 628 30 08, **f** 95 625 30 09. Both *moderate*.

Cheap

There will be no problem finding cheaper rooms – lots of sailors pass through here. Some of the cheapest places are near the Plaza San Juan de Dios in the old town. Otherwise look for the *camas* signs and take your pick.

★**Pensión Fantoni**, Flamenco 5, **t** 95 628 27 04. Full of tiles and cool marble with a breezy roof terrace. Rooms available with or without bath.

Pensión España, Marqués de Cádiz 9, **t** 95 628 55 00. Offers reasonable doubles, with bath available; right in the centre of the old town.

Pensión Colón, Marqués de Cádiz 6, **t** 95 628 53 51. Well situated in the old town opposite a good delicatessen; rooms without bath.

Marqués, Marqués de Cádiz 1, **t** 95 628 58 54. In an old mansion; only one room has an en suite bathroom. Recently repainted and a good cheap option.

Eating Out

Dedicated foodies should look out for a useful little booklet called *Cadiz's Gastronomic Guide* (€1.50), available from the tourist office, with descriptions of local specialities, recipes, lists of tapas bars and restaurants, and a guide to the various food festivals in the Cádiz region. Also, it's worth noting that many of

on a small plaza. Thorough restoration of this ungainly bulk has not destroyed its ingratiating charm. It was begun in 1722, at the height of Cádiz's prosperity. Funds soon started running short, sadly enough; if original architect Vicente Acero had had his way, he might have made this as fanciful a work as his cathedral in Guadix. Neglected for centuries, the crumbling stonework was corroding in Cádiz's salty air, before the damage was undone by a lengthy and expensive restoration project, now virtually completed. Of the paintings within, Zurbarán's *Santa Úrsula* stands out. The composer Manuel de Falla, author of *Noches en los jardines de Espāna (Nights in the Gardens of Spain)* has his tomb in the cathedral crypt (*open weekdays 10–1*). The **Museo de la Catedral** (*t 95 625 98 12; open Tues–Fri 10–1.30 and 4.30–7, Sat–Sun 10–1; adm*) has a lot of ecclesiastical gold and silverware, paintings by Murillo, Zurbarán and Alejo Fernández, and painted panels and an ivory crucifix by Alonso Cano.

Just behind the cathedral is the simple **Iglesia de Santa Cruz**, the 'old cathedral', on Plaza de Fray Félix (*open daily 9.30–1 and 6.30–9, closed Fri afternoon*). Begun in the 13th century on the remnants of a mosque, it was virtually destroyed when the Duke of Essex and his armies sacked the city in 1596. Most of what you see was rebuilt or the finest restaurants have tapas bars, including **El Faro**, **El Balandro** and **El Sardinero**.

Expensive

El Faro, C/San Félix 15, **t** 95 621 10 68. Generally regarded as the best restaurant in town. It is now part of a chain including **Ventonillo El Chato** (*see* below) and **El Faro de El Puerto** (*see* El Puerto de Santa María section). Come here to explore the amazingly wide range of seafood fished from this part of the Atlantic – things that we don't even have names for in English such as *mojarras* and *urtas*. There are also more recognizable varieties as well as a selection of meat dishes.

Ventorillo del Chato, Vía Augusta Julia, Cortadura, **t** 95 625 00 25, *ventorillodelchato @raini-computer.net*. This rustic place on the road to San Fernando claims to have been around for more than 200 years and is still going strong.

El Balandro, Alameda Apodaca 22, **t** 95 622 09 92. Situated by the Alameda Apodaca walls, with an upstairs dining room that looks over to Puerto de Santa María.Serves a mix of seafood and Spanish specialities.

Moderate

El Candil, Javier de Burgos 19, **t** 95 622 19 71. If you feel like you really can't look at another fish, try this place.

El Sardinero, Pza San Juan de Dios 4, **t** 95 628 25 05. One of the oldest restaurants in the city, with a variety of Basque and *andaluz* dishes. Outside tables available.

Achuri, C/Plocia 15, **t** 95 625 36 13. Just off Pza de San Juan de Dios. Another old restaurant, popular with the locals, and specializing in Basque and Andalucían dishes.

Arte Serrano, Pso Marítimo 2, **t** 95 622 72 58. In newer Cádiz, along the Paseo Marítimo, there's a wide choice of restaurants, nearly all with terraces or outside seating. This one specializes in meats from the Sierra.

El Brocal, Avda José León de Carranza 4, **t** 95 625 77 59. Serves meat with a North African and Greek bias; behind the sea front, opposite the football stadium. *Closed Sun.*

Casa Grimaldi, C/Libertad 9 (in the market district), **t** 95 622 83 16. Offers delicious fresh fish and seafood from the Bay at very reasonable prices. Great tapas, too.

La Montanera, C/Sacramento 39, **t** 95 622 06 00, and C/Reina Victoria, **t** 95 628 48 51. Two of the Fogon de Mariana chain (there are others in San Fernando and Jerez), which offer large chunks of meat like *jamón* and *chorizo* at reasonable prices.

Inexpensive

Mesón Miguel Ángel, Pza de Mina 1, **t** 95 621 35 00. A slightly more upmarket place than

added in the 17th century, including the theatrical Baroque *retablo* behind the main altar. A couple of blocks east of the cathedral, on the Campo del Sur, is the **Teatro Romano** (*open Tues–Sun 11–1.30*), a restored Roman theatre built by a *gaditano*, Lucio Cornelio Balbo, and dating from the 1st century BC. Excavations have revealed the stands and a large section of an interior gallery. The idea was to extend the city into the area that today comprises the *barrios* of Santa María and El Pópulo. The theatre backs onto the latter, an atmospheric maze of streets and old *palacios* that have changed little since medieval times, now crammed full of tiny bars and dilapidated blocks of flats.

Continuing westwards, the **Plaza Topete** was named after a *tophet*, the Phoenician temple dedicated to that nasty habit of theirs – sacrificing first-born babies; remains of one were found here (lately, some historians have begun to doubt that the Phoenicians and Carthaginians were really so brutish; they suspect that the children buried here died natural deaths, and that the stories about child-sacrifice were only propaganda spread by the Greeks). Now, this area is Cádiz's almost excessively colourful **market district**, spread around a wonderful, dilapidated old market building.

the others, which serves good value *plato combinados*, as well as a cheap *menú*.

Café la Galeona, C/San Francisco, opposite C/Ramón y Cajal. A delicatessen and café with a very cheap *menú*.

Tapas and *Freidurías*

Freiduría Cervecería Las Flores, Plaza San Juan de Dios 4, **t** 95 628 25 05. Fried fish was invented in Cádiz, and nothing beats digging into a paper cone (*cartucho* or *papelón*) filled with freshly caught and battered fish. Here, you can swig beer on the terrace, while sampling the fried shrimps or cuttlefish.

Bahía. Avda Ramón de Carranza 29, **t** 95 628 11 66. A classic, close to the port; try the famous spare ribs (*costillas de cerdo*).

Piccola, C/San José 4, **t** 95 622 50 99. A tiny bar serving up excellent tapas including spicy *pulpo a la gallega*. You can even finish up with an ice-cream.

La Parra del Veedor, C/Plata 2, **t** 956 22 40 21. Next door to a *freiduría*, you can pick up your *papelón de pescaíto frito* and munch it over an ice-cold beer.

Nightlife

The town abounds with bars; the best area to find a bit of *marcha* outside summertime is around the university buildings, particularly Pza San Francisco and Pza España and the streets off and between them, including C/San Francisco and C/Rosario.

Over the summer months the nightlife shifts to the beach area in the new part of town, The area along the Pso Marítimo flanking Playa de la Victoria is particularly lively.

There is also a substantial gay scene in Cádiz; for information call COLEGA (Colectivo de Lesbianas y Gais de Andalucía), *www.colegaweb.net*, **t** 95 622 62 62.

O'Connells, Pza San Francisco. An Irish theme bar which serves a bizarre combination of Guinness and tapas.

Peña de Cazadores, C/San Francisco 5. Old, atmospheric and, as the name suggests, dedicated to hunting, with numerous heads of dead animals hanging from the walls to underline the point.

Taberna La Manzanilla, C/Feduchy 18, off C/Rosario. A wonderful old place serving all the varieties of sherry you could wish for, with a limited range of tapas. The glass cabinets display ancient bottles, and a room at the back contains even older, dustier ones: ask if you can have a peek.

Bunker-Bank, C/Manuel Rances s/n. One of the trendiest Cádiz disco-bars.

Bodega Nicanor, C/Rosario 8. Lively little *bodega*. *Open Thurs–Sun only*.

A few blocks west, the little church of **San Felipe Neri** on Calle Sacramento (*open Mon–Sat 10–1; adm*) is an unprepossessing shrine to the beginnings of Spanish liberty. On 29 March 1812 an assembly of refugees from Napoleon's occupation of the rest of Spain gathered here, set up the Cortes and wrote a constitution declaring Spain an independent republic, guaranteeing full political and religious freedom. Though their constitution, and their revolution, proved stillborn, it was a notable beginning for Spain's struggle towards democracy. Big marble plaques, sent as tributes, cover the church's façade. Inside is a beautiful *Immaculate Conception* by Murillo.

Around the corner, Cádiz's very good municipal museum, **Museo de las Cortes de Cádiz**, C/Santa Inés (***t** 95 622 17 88; open 15 June–15 Sept Tues–Fri 9–1 and 5–7, Sat–Sun 9–1; 16 Sept–14 June Tues–Fri 9–1 and 4–7, Sat–Sun 9–1; closed Mon and hols*), has a huge Romantic-era mural depicting the 1812 event. In front of it, in the main hall, is the museum's star exhibit, a 15m (50ft) **scale model of Cádiz**, made entirely of mahogany and ivory by an unknown obsessive in 1779. Nearly every building is detailed – Cádiz hasn't changed much since. Among a collection of portraits of Spanish heroes is the

Goat Cuisine

One of Cádiz's most well-known dishes is *berza* – a cabbage-based stew. Goat's cheese is called Cádiz cheese here, produced in the mountains where it is semi-cured and develops a yellow colour. Cheese from Grazalema is made only in the spring and must be consumed within two months. For dessert try an almond pastry (*torta de almendra*) from the local convents.

Duke of Wellington, who in Spain carried the title of Duke of Ciudad Rodrigo. The best picture, also from that era, shows Hercules about to give Napoleon a good bashing.

It's a short walk from here to the **Torre Tavira**, on C/Marqués del Real Tesoro 10 (***t*** *95 621 29 10; open 16 Sept–14 June 10–8; 15 June–15 Sept 10–6; adm*), the highest tower in the city, which is grafted onto an 18th-century mansion, and has a *cámera oscura* giving wonderful views over the city. Walking back down Sacramento will take you to the Plaza de Falla and the huge neo-*mudéjar* **Gran Teatro Falla** (***t*** *902 10 12 12, for details of performances*), named after the composer, who was born in a house in the Plaza de Mina.

Plaza de Mina and Around

On this lovely square, in the northwestern corner of the peninsula, you'll find the **Museum of Fine Arts and Archaeology** (*open Wed–Sat 9–8, Tues 2.30–8, Sun 9.30–2.30; adm*), also referred to as the **Museo de Cádiz**. The archaeology section contains a Phoenician sarcophagus, Phoenician jewellery, Roman pottery and Greek ceramics; among the statues there's a dumb-looking Emperor Trajan with a big Roman nose. But best in the museum are the paintings: some Murillos and some very good paintings, including *Four Evangelists* and *John the Baptist* by Zurbarán. On the top floor are unaffectedly charming puppets and stage sets from a Cádiz genre of marionette show called *Tía Norica*, still performed in these parts.

Around the corner, on Calle Rosario, the 18th-century **Oratorio de la Santa Cueva** (*open Tues–Fri 10–2 and 5–8, Sat and Sun 10–1; adm*) has emerged from an immaculate restoration to provide a gleaming, frilly backdrop for three Goya frescoes (the only ones in Andalucía): the *Miracle of the Loaves and Fishes*, *The Parable of the Wedding Guest* and the *Last Supper*, completed after he was stricken with the illness that left him completely deaf.

Beaches

The old town beach, **Playa de la Caleta**, may not be large nor particularly clean, but it is lovely at dusk when the brightly painted fishing boats are pulled up onto the shore. Set against a backdrop of great architecture, including the florid turn-of-the-century domes of the old *balneario* (spa), it's a sheltered crescent of sand, sandwiched between the **Castillo de Santa Catalina** and the **Castillo de San Sebastián**, the latter at the end of a long pier. You can visit the former (*open daily 10.30–8*). **Playa de Santa María del Mar** starts just outside the old town and becomes **Playa de la Victoria**, a long stretch of sand packed in season and flanked by bars, restaurants and kiosks.

Cádiz Province

Like those to the east, the beaches around Cádiz are popular mostly with Spaniards and are more crowded, at least in summer. Just the same, the beaches are lovely and huge, and the towns behind them relatively unspoiled; there may be few better places in Spain to baste yourself, with plenty of opportunities for exploring *bodegas*.

Sanlúcar and Rota

Sanlúcar de Barrameda makes *manzanilla*, most ethereal of sherries. It is known as the port that launched Magellan on his way around the world, and Columbus on his second voyage to the Indies and third to America, and for its annual horse races on the beach; Sanlúcar is also the birthplace of the artist-writer Francisco Pacheco, Velázquez's teacher. The town has a certain crumbling colonial charm and an exceptionally pretty main square, **Plaza de Cabildo**. Off nearby Plaza Roque, where a plaque commemorates Pacheco, is the town's market, one of the biggest in Andalucía and a delight to stroll around to soak up the myriad smells and sounds. From here

Tourist Information

Sanlúcar de Barrameda: Calzada del Ejército s/n, **t** 95 636 61 10, **f** 95 636 61 32. *Open Mon–Fri 10–2 and 5–7, Sat, Sun and hols 10–1.30 and 4–6.30.*

Rota: C/Luna 2 (in the palace), **t** 95 684 61 74, **f** 95 692 81 16. *Open daily 9–2 and 5–7.*

El Puerto de Santa María: C/Luna 22, **t** 95 654 24 75, **f** 95 654 22 46, *www.elpuertosm.es. Open daily 10–2 and 6–8.*

Chipiona: Pz. Andalucía s/n, **t** 95 637 28 28, **f** 95 637 50 02. *Open Mon–Fri 10–2 and 5–7, Sat–Sun 11–1.*

Puerto Real: C/de la Plaza 44, **t** 95 647 28 95, **f** 95 647 31 08. *Open Mon–Fri 10–1.30.*

Where to Stay

It's no problem finding a place to stay in the coastal resorts, especially in the high season; little old ladies meet the buses to drag you off to their *hostales*. The resorts around Cádiz are seasonal and many close during the winter.

Sanlúcar ✉ 11540

*****Los Helechos**, Pza de Madre de Dios 9, **t** 95 636 76 55, **f** 95 636 96 50 (*moderate–inexpensive*). In the old part of town and built around two courtyards, this is the most delightful hotel in Sanlúcar.

*****Tartaneros**, Tartaneros 8, **t** 95 636 20 44, **f** 95 638 53 78 (*moderate*). Another good option set in a neoclassical *palacio*.

****Hotel Posada de Palacio**, C/Caballero 11, **t** 95 636 48 40 (*moderate*). A quirky, family-run hotel in another converted *palacio*, with antique-filled rooms around a pretty patio.

Hostal La Blanca Paloma, Plaza San Roque 9, **t** 95 636 36 44 (*cheap*). Or, in contrast to the Tartaneros, you could try this unglamorous *hostal*, the only place in town suitable for those on a tight budget.

Chipiona ✉ 11550

*****Cruz del Mar**, Avda Sanlúcar de Barrameda 1, **t** 95 637 11 00, **f** 95 637 13 64, *www.hotelcruzdelmar.com* (*moderate*). Has a pool, garden and satellite TV. Right on the beach.

******Nuestra Señora del Rocío**, Avda de la Cruz Roja; **t** 95 637 70 71, **f** 95 637 30 35, *mfturis@futurnet.es* (*luxury–expensive*). A newish hotel and supposedly the best in town, but it's a funny old place, crammed onto the seafront, with a tiny pool just off the main road and small rooms with views of the car park. Over-priced for what's on offer.

*****Brasilia**, Avda del Faro 12, **t/f** 95 637 10 54 (*moderate*). In its own grounds with a decent-sized pool and pleasant restaurant.

*****Playa de Regla**, Pso Costa de la Luz, **t** 95 637 27 69, **f** 95 637 09 36, *www.hotelplaya.com* (*inexpensive*). Next door, rooms

C/Bretones leads up to the church of **Nuestra Señora de la O** (*open Mon–Sat 10–1, Sun 10–12, closed Thurs*) with its fine *mudéjar* portal and 16th-century coffered ceiling. Beside the church you will find the **Palace of the Dukes of Medina Sidonia** *(guided tours Sun and Mon, call to book a place **t** 95 636 01 61)*, who owned the town. The building dates from the 16th century and has an extensive private archive including copious notes on the Armada. Nearby is the 19th-century **Montpensier Palace** (*open 8–2.30*), with its extensive library and paintings by Murillo, El Greco, Rubens and Goya. To the west, along C/Caballero lies the **Palace of Orleans and Bourbon** (Palacio de Orléans y Borbóns), (*open daily except Thurs, guided visits at 10:30, 11:30, 12:30, and 13:30*), which was built by the Duke of Montpensier in the 19th century and is now the town hall. Go back east past the church and you will come across the ruins of the 15th-century Moorish castle, which is closed for interminable restoration works. Below here lies C/Ancha, the scene of much merriment on 15 August (*see* below).

The town has a number of sherry houses which you can visit, although you usually need to book tours in advance. The biggest is **Antonio Barbadillo**, C/Sevilla 1 (***t*** *95 638*

here cost a bit less for many of the same facilities, except a pool.

*****Al Sur**, Avda Sevilla 101, **t** 95 637 03 00. www.hotelalsur (*moderate*). With a pool and garden. Very reasonable at the price.

***Paquita**, Francisco Lara 26, **t** 95 617 02 06 (*inexpensive*). A modest *hostal* typical of what you'll find in these modest resorts. All rooms have bathrooms, TVs and a/c.

San Miguel, Avenida de la Regla 79, **t** 95 637 29 76 (*inexpensive*). A prettier budget option, and also near the beach.

Pinar de Chipiona, **t** 95 637 23 21. A campsite 3km outside of Chipiona, towards Rota.

Rota ✉ 11520

*****Playa de la Luz**, on the beach at Arroyo Hondo, **t** 95 681 05 00, **f** 95 81 06 06, *www.hotelplayadelaluz.com* (*expensive*). A sports-orientated modern resort hotel with a lovely pool and gardens.

******Duque de Nájera**, C/Gravika 2, **t** 95 684 60 20, **f** 95 681 24 71, *www.hotelduquedenajera.com* (*expensive*). In the centre, with pool, minibar, satellite TV, sauna and gym.

*****Caribe**, Avda de la Marina 60, **t** 95 681 07 00, **f** 95 681 01 36 (*expensive–moderate*). A slightly cheaper option in the town centre, also with pool, TV and terrace.

Pensión la Española, C/Garcia Sánchez 9, **t** 95 681 00 98 (*inexpensive*). Basic,but in a mansion with a campsite in the grounds.

Camping Puntador, **t** 95 681 33 03. A campsite just out of the town.

El Puerto de Santa María ✉ 11500

******Hotel Monasterio San Miguel**, C/Larga 27, **t** 95 654 04 40, **f** 95 654 26 04, *monasterio@jale.com* (*luxury–expensive*). This 16th-century former monastery is the loveliest place to stay around here. It's marvellously soothing with tranquil cloisters, religious artefacts and a swimming pool discreetly placed where the vegetable garden used to be. The beautiful restaurant, **Las Bóvedas**, is excellent (*see* below).

******Meliá Caballo Blanco**, Avda de Madrid 1, **t** 95 656 25 41, **f** 95 656 27 12 (*expensive*). Set in a picturesque spot, this hotel is less pricey and also worth a try; facilities include a pool, café with terrace and parking.

******Puerto Sherry**, Avda Libertad s/n, **t** 95 687 20 00, **f** 95 685 33 00 (*expensive*). In the marina area with two pools, one heated.

*****Santa María**, Avda de la Bajamar s/n, **t** 95 687 32 11, **f** 95 687 36 52, *www.hotelsantamaria.es* (*moderate*). A 17th-century palace with swimming pool.

*****Los Cántaros**, Curva 6, **t** 95 654 02 40, **f** 95 654 11 21, *www.hotelloscantaros.com* (*moderate*). Pitchers (*cántaros*) were once made here, but now it's an elegant, modern hotel in the town centre near the action; with parking and restaurant.

55 00, tours Mon–Sat 12–1; adm), which makes the bulk of the *manzanilla*; try also **La Guita**, C/Misericordia (**t** *95 631 95 64, free*), another delicious make, and **Hidalgo La Gitana,** C/Banda de la Playa 42, one of the oldest *bodgegas* (**t** *95 638 53 04, tours Mon–Fri at 12.30; adm*).

Although its beaches are not major-league, Sanlúcar has always been a popular summer destination with Spanish holidaymakers for its excellent cheap seafood. The Bajo de Guía is a particularly charming fishing district, and from here you can take the motor boat over to **Coto Doñana** for a four-hour trip up the river, including two stops and two guided walks. (*Two boats daily; tickets from Fábrica de Hielo, Bajo de Guía,* **t** *95 636 38 13, open Mon–Sat 9–7.*)

If you have an afternoon to spare, amuse yourself by visiting the public fish auction in **Bonanza**, 4km away. **Chipiona** is a family resort, full of small *pensiónes* and *hostales*, with a good beach at **Playa de Regla** near the lighthouse, and a couple of *bodegas*; try **César Florido**, Padre Lerchundi 35–37 (**t** *95 637 12 85, only large groups in summer*), or **Mellodo Martín**, Ctra Chipiona-Nola 3 (**t** *96 637 01 97*).

*****Puertobahía**, Avda de La Paz 38, Urbanización Valdelagrana, **t** 95 656 27 21, **f** 95 656 12 21, *www.hotelpuertobahia.com* (*expensive–moderate*). A big, modern resort hotel set on the beach.

Pensión Manolo, C/Jesús de los Milagros 18, **t** 95 685 75 25 (*inexpensive*). At the lower end of the scale, near the port.

Hostal Loreto, C/Ganado 17, **t** 95 654 24 10 (*inexpensive*). A good budget option, set in a converted 18th-century mansion with plenty of knick knacks and bullfighting posters. Some rooms are huge.

Eating Out

Many of the restaurants in this area – informal cafés where you can pick out the fish you like– are open only during the summer.

Rota ✉ 11520

Casa Bigote, Bajo de Guía, **t** 95 636 26 96 (*expensive–moderate*). Famous throughout Andalucía for its delicious appetizers, classic dishes of the region, and the best seafood in all its varieties; the crayfish are a must, and you can try the local *manzanilla* with the day's catch. You may find you'll need more than one visit, as the tapas selection in the bar opposite is extensive and excellent. Get there early for a table. *Closed Sun.*

Mirador de Doñana, Bajo de Guía, **t** 95 636 42 05 (*moderate*). Casa Bigote's main rival down on the beach, this is another popular bar and restaurant with a panoramic view across to the bird reserve. Try *cigalas* (crayfish), *angulas* (baby eels) and *nido de rapé a la Sanluqueña*, a nest of straw potato chips, deep-fried with monkfish.

Bar El Fresquito, C/Mina, 38, **t** 95 681 64 14. In Rota the cuisine is heavily influenced by the presence of the naval base pizza and Chinese restaurants alongside the usual seafood. There are, however, a number of good tapas bars, including this one.

Casa Balbino, Pza Cabildo 11. The best tapas bar in Sanlúcar, with bulls' heads and faded posters; varied tapas, inevitably fish-dominated, all washed down by chilled *manzanilla*. It's full most of the time but it is worth hanging around for a table as this is infinitely superior to others in the square.

Bar La Concha, Plaza Bartolomé Pérez 8, **t** 95 681 27 04. Another old-fashioned tapas bar, full of locals sipping *manzanilla*.

Chipiona ✉ 11550

Chipiona is full of reasonably priced seafood restaurants where you can try the town's sweet *moscatel* wine or the dry *manzanilla* from nearby Sanlúcar.

El Gato, C/Pez Espada 9–11, **t** 95 637 07 87 (*moderate*). One of the best restaurants in

Next, on the edge of the bay of Cádiz, comes **Rota**, a bigger, flashier resort with the best and longest beach on the coast; the town is pretty, though it's a bit overbuilt. It's also full of Americans from the largest naval base in the region, just outside town. This was the key base Franco gave up in the 1953 deal with President Eisenhower; in the 1980s, when Spain was debating its future role in NATO, the Americans made it unpleasantly clear that this base was not a subject for negotiation, although in the 1986 NATO referendum this region turned out the highest 'yes' vote in Spain. In recent years, however the numbers at the base have fallen by about a third.

Of the fiestas, the most famous involves horse racing along the beach at the end of August. It's a beautiful sight that has its origins in the middle of the 19th century when the Spanish aristocracy stayed here. The town sends a few brotherhoods to El Rocío in May; at the end of that month is the **Feria de la Manzanilla**, which sees horseriding, bullfights, Andalucían dress and vast quantities of sherry; 15 August sees C/Ancha covered with a pretty carpet of faux-flowers (in fact sawdust); a wonderful Flamenco festival takes place in July, **Noches de Bajo de Guía**; and in mid-October there's a **Feria de Tapas**, where you can sample the town's wonderful food.

Chipiona, serving up *sopa de mariscos* (shellfish soup) and other delicious fish dishes.

La Pañoleta, C/Isaac Peral 4-6, **t** 95 637 37 71 (*moderate*). Specializes in shellfish and *guisos marineros* such as *chocos en salsa*.

Bar El Carmen, Paseo Marítimo, Cruz del Mar 24, **t** 95 637 19 52 (*inexpensive*). A low-key tapas bar and restaurant with tables overlooking the beach.

Bar El Toro, on the Pso Marítimo (*inexpensive*). A good, honest place which does fabulous *langostinos* and has a wide selection of sherries, all at a reasonable price.

Discoteca Bugui 2, C/El Castillo. There are a couple of discos in town including this one, but most of the action in season takes place along the seafront or on C/Isaac Peral.

El Puerto de Santa María ✉ 11500

The town's speciality is *urta*, like a sea bream, and there is a fiesta in mid-August to celebrate this tasty fish. Apart from the excellent *bodegas* and simple beach cafés, El Puerto has some deservedly popular restaurants.

Hacienda El Pinar, Viejo de Nota, **t** 95 685 42 04, **f** 95 685 23 39, *www.haciendaelpinar.com* (*expensive*). The palace belonging to the Osborne family (of sherry fame); if you ring ahead, you can dine in memorable surroundings (minimum 8 people).

La Goleta del Puerto, Ctra de Fuentebravía km 0.75, **t** 95 685 42 32 (*expensive*). The most successful restaurant with simple but well-prepared seafood dishes, especially the fish cooked in salt, the *tosta de salmón* and the porgy in brandy. *Closed Mon except in July and Aug*.

El Faro de El Puerto, Ctra de Rota km 0.5, **t** 95 687 09 52, **f** 95 654 04 66 (*expensive*). The other El Faro (the original is in Cádiz), also with an excellent reputation for its regional cuisine, serving some of the finest seafood in the province.

Las Bóvedas, C/Larga 27, **t** 95 654 04 40 (*expensive*). In the former monastery of San Miguel, this is one of the most charming and romantic restaurants in town, with exquisite seafood and *andaluz* specialities.

Guadalete, Avda de la Bajamar 14, **t** 95 687 02 98 (*inexpensive*). Attracts crowds for its shrimps, sole and clams – a thoroughly professional joint down on the riverside quay that's been getting it right for decades. *Closed Mon and 15–29 Nov.*

Romerijo's, at Ribera del Marisco 1, **t** 95 654 12 54 (*inexpensive*). The liveliest place to dine, where you can eat the freshest of fish and seafood at the tables outside or enjoy a take-away wrapped in a paper cone. Everyone throws discarded shells into the red buckets on each table and munches their way through one of the five kinds of prawn on offer. A kilogram of shellfish is enough for four people.

El Puerto de Santa María and Puerto Sherry

Across the bay from Cádiz lies **El Puerto de Santa María**, the traditional port of the sherry houses in Jerez, which has quite a few *bodegas* of its own – **Osborne**, C/Los Moros s/n (***t*** *95 686 91 00; adm for tours*), and **Terry**, C/Tonelero s/n (***t*** *95 685 77 00; adm for tours*), among other famous names. It's one of the prettiest towns on the whole of the Costa de la Luz, a maze of narrow streets crammed with low white washed houses and Baroque mansions meandering down to the port. The town has some interesting churches, some mansions of the Anglo-Spanish sherry aristocracy, and the fine, restored 13th-century *mudéjar* **Castillo de San Marcos** *(open Tues–Sat 10–1.30; adm, free on Tues)*. To get a taste of what the town was like in the glory days of the 18th century, visit the **Casa de los Leones**, C/La Placilla 2 (*open 10–2 and 6–8*), where there's a permanent exhibition on the Baroque era. The century-old **bullring** (*open 11–1.30 and 6–7.30, except when there's a bullfight*) ranks with those of Sevilla and Ronda in prestige. El Puerto itself isn't a big resort, but it's a typical town of Cádiz province, with bright bustling streets, excellent restaurants and some good beaches.

Puerto Sherry is a modern marina, built in the late 1980s, and a pleasant place to spend an afternoon or evening. It has yet to reach its potential (or occupancy) so it's a little lacking in character.

Jerez de la Frontera

The name is synonymous with wine – by the English corruption of Jerez into sherry – but besides the *finos, amontillados, olorosos* and other varieties of that noble sauce, Jerez also ships out much of Spain's equally good brandy. Most of the well-known companies, whose advertising is plastered all over Spain, have their headquarters here, and they're quite accustomed to taking visitors – especially English ones – through the *bodegas*. Don't be shy. Most are open to visitors between 9am and 1pm on Mondays to Fridays, though not in August, or when they're busy with the *vendimia* (harvest) in September. Admission prices are around €3 upwards and usually include tasting sessions. Many are located out of town as land prices in the centre rise. However, booking is strongly advised – numbers are restricted on guided tours and many people who fail to reserve places are turned away.

One of the most interesting *bodegas* to visit is that belonging to **González Byass**, C/Manuel María González 12 (***t*** *95 635 70 00, www.gonzalesbyass.es*). The tour includes a visit to the old sawdust-strewn *bodega* that has held the sherry *soleras* for two centuries; the casks have been signed by many famous visitors over the years, from Orson Welles to the Hollywood swimming star Esther Williams. The tour ends at the *degustacíon*, where the motto is, 'If you don't have a *copa* at eleven o'clock, you should have eleven at one'. The tour also includes a video of the production process, with cellarmen demonstrating their skill at pouring sherry from distances of a metre or more into the small *copitas* (in order to aerate the wine). **John Harvey**, C/Arcos 54 (***t*** *95 634 60 04*), is another *bodega* well worth a visit – watch out for the alligator at

Getting There and Around

Cádiz is the base for visiting Jerez and the coasts. The Amarillo company provides regular **buses** from Cádiz to all the coastal towns, and at least five daily to Jerez. Infrequent buses connect Jerez with Rota, Sanlúcar and El Puerto. Almost all the Sevilla–Cádiz buses stop in Jerez and El Puerto, as do the trains. There are frequent connections for Arcos de la Frontera and Ronda and one bus a day to Córdoba and Granada. Jerez stations for buses and **trains** are together on the eastern edge of town, **t** 95 633 79 75.

There's a regular **ferry** service from El Puerto to Cádiz – more fun than the bus. Parking can be hard to find if you're in a **car** but it is sometimes best to be based in Jerez for the surrounding area to avoid the queues on the roads into Cádiz.

Tourist Information

Town: C/Larga 39, **t** 95 633 11 50/95 633 17 31, *www.webjerez.com. Open Mon–Fri 9–2 and 4–7.*

Where to Stay

Jerez ✉ 11400

In Jerez, there are many unremarkable hotels. The two top hotels are close to the centre of town, convenient for the fair and the Spanish Riding School.

Expensive

★★★★**Jerez**, Avda Alcalde Álvaro Domecq 35, **t** 95 633 06 00, **f** 95 630 50 01, *www.jerezhotel.es*. Has a pool and tennis courts and is set in lovely tropical gardens, but is no bargain.

★★★★**Royal Sherry Park**, Avda Alcalde Álvaro Domecq 11, **t** 95 631 76 14, **f** 95 631 13 00, *www.sherryparkhotel.com*. A modern place set in a park a little closer to town, with a pool and a restaurant, El Abaco.

Moderate

★★★**Doña Blanca**, C/Bodega 11, **t** 95 634 87 61, **f** 95 634 85 86. The most pleasant three-star place, refurbished, in the heart of town; clean and modern with its own parking – extremely useful in this town.

★★★**Serit**, C/Higueras 7, **t** 95 634 07 00, **f** 95 634 07 16, *hostalserit@redicom.es*. In the centre of town; comfortable rooms and parking.

★**Trujillo**, C/Medina 36, **t** 95 634 24 38. A decent little hotel in an old townhouse, at the lower end of this price bracket.

Inexpensive–Cheap

★★**Virt**, C/Higueras 20, **t** 95 632 28 11. A middle-range bargain *pensión* with a/c.

★**Las Palomas**, C/Higueras 17, **t** 95 634 37 73. Very good value, although just out of the centre, with a tiled patio full of plants.

★**San Andrés I and II**, C/Morenos 12 and 14, **t** 95 634 09 83. Basic rooms around a pretty flower-filled patio for reasonable prices.

Youth Hostel, Avda Carrero Blanco 30, **t** 95 614 32 63, *www.interjoven.com*. A modern building with a pool – but it's 2km south of the centre.

Eating Out

Even in a region of Spain known for the late hours it keeps, Jerez seems to go a step further. It's not at all unusual here to sit down to lunch at 3.30pm. Don't even think about dinner until after 10pm.

Expensive

El Bosque, Avda Álvaro Domecq 26, **t** 95 618 08 80/95 630 70 30. Beautifully situated in woods near the Parque de González Montoria, yet only a short distance from

the end of the tour. Others include **Sandeman**, C/Pizarro 10 (***t** 95 631 29 95, www.sandeman.com*), and **Williams and Hombert**, Ctra Nac. IV km 641.7 (***t** 95 635 34 06*). The *Semana Santa* festival in Jerez is more intimate than Sevilla's, but in its way just as splendid. The nightly processions escorting the saint and Madonna images create a city-wide pageant. Late in the night, returning home through the backstreets, town; formal, elegant, well-known but slightly dull. The seafood is good; try *langostinos de Sanlúcar, tortillas* of baby shrimps, monkfish in shellfish sauce or strawberry *gazpacho*. *Closed Sun*.

Moderate

Tendido 6, Circo 10, **t** 95 634 48 35. Closer to town, by the bullring, this place has a covered patio with adjoining dining room, decorated on a *feria* theme, with bullfight memorabilia on the walls. Here the emphasis is on robust helpings of traditional food. *Closed Sun*.

Gaitán, Gaitán 3, **t** 95 634 58 59. One of the favourite dining places in town, a couple of streets behind the tourist office, Gaitán is a tiny place with a big reputation. Try the bull's tail *a la jerezana*. *Closed Sun eve*.

La Mesa Redonda, C/Manuel de la Quintana 3, **t** 95 634 00 69. Near the Avenida Jerez hotel, this beautifully decorated restaurant has antique furniture and paintings, giving the impression of an old aristocratic Jerez home. It has a first-class kitchen serving excellent game and seasonal specialities, and takes its food seriously. For our money it's the best restaurant in Jerez. Reservations essential. *Closed Sun and Aug*.

Bodegón La Aldana, C/Manuel Ríos Ruiz s/n, **t** 95 630 73 85. A local favourite, this traditional tapas bar and restaurant serves up delicious *platos caseros* and a tasty selection of tapas.

Inexpensive

Bar Juanito, Pescadería Vieja 8 and 10, **t** 95 633 48 38. The best among a clutch of tiny tapas bars on Pescadería Vieja, a passage off the Plaza del Arenal. Try the *alcachofas* en salsa or the *costillas en adobo* (marinaded grilled pork chops). It is a crush at lunchtime; arrive early (*opens at 8pm*) if you want a table.

La Taberna Marinera, Plaza Rafael Rivero 2, **t** 95 633 44 27. One of a number of good tapas bars in Plaza Rivero, just behind the Alameda Cristina. It's small inside but during summer everyone spills out onto the square.

La Parra Vieja, C/San Miguel 9, **t** 95 633 53 90. A traditional old restaurant and tapas bar where you can try fish or meat *a la parilla* – grilled over charcoal.

There are many street *bodegas* where you can try the whole spectrum of the area's produce. Two central places to try are:

Alcazaba, Medina 19, **t** 956 33 29 60.

La Tasca, Edificio Jerez 74, **t** 95631 03 40.

Nightlife

Jerez has a great nightlife, but it's spread out all over the city. A good place to start for early evening *copas* is Plaza Canterbury, opposite the Williams and Humbert Bodega, near the bullring on C/Paul. Around this are a number of bars, clubs and discos, including **Graffton St**, C/Zaragoza 27, which has live music on Thursdays; and a bit further north, in Avda de Mejico, you'll find **Moet Moet**, where the clientele is a bit older, and **Sala Mol**, a disco. Nearer the centre there are a couple of other discos: **Copola**, in Pza Aladro, near the Palacio Domecq, and **Oh**, in C/Porvera; expect the usual diet of dodgy Spanish techno.

Jerez is justly famous for flamenco and, unlike in Sevilla where many *tublaos* will be overpriced and catering for busloads of tourists, here you will find the real thing; but you've got to look for it (and don't expect it to happen just because it's advertised). Here are a selection of venues, mostly situated in the Gypsy quarter:

El Laga de Tío Parilla, Pza del Mercado, **t** 95 633 83 34. *Free on Thur, Fri and Sat*.

La Taberna Flamenca, Augostillo de Santiago 3.

El Rincón del Duende, C/Muro 19.

Los Cerinicalos, C/Sánchez Vizcaino 20.

Los Jerales, Pza Cocheras 20.

Bar Nochiero, Velázquez 20.

they are serenaded by impromptu solo voices; for the finest singers, the whole procession halts in appreciation.

Business is not as good as it was, for sherry sales are falling worldwide, but Jerez is growing. It's an extremely attractive town, at least in the centre, and it has a few lovely buildings for you to squint at after you've done the rounds of the *bodegas*. Two in particular are worth a look: the **Ayuntamiento** in Plaza de la Asunción, a fine example of Renaissance architecture dating from the 16th century, and **Palacio Domecq**, at the start of the Alameda, an 18th-century palace built by the sherry clan. Jerez's landmark is **La Colegiata** (also called San Salvador), the town's cathedral, a curious pseudo-Gothic church with a separate bell tower and Baroque staircase; though begun in the 13th century, its façade, largely the work of Vicente Acero, was not completed until 1750. Works inside include a Madonna by Zurbarán and sculptures by Juan de Mesa. Nearby, on the central Plaza de los Reyes Católicos, **San Miguel** (begun in 1482) (*open Mon–Sat 8–9, Sun 9–1*) changes the scene to Isabelline Gothic – a fine example of that style, with a florid *retablo* inside. There is a Moorish **Alcázar** at the end of Calle Pérez Galdós (*open May–15 Sept daily 10–8, except Sundays from June 15–Sept 15 when it's only open 9–3; 16 Sept–April 10–6; adm*), with a tower and some remains of the baths, a *cámera oscura* with wonderful views over the city, an art gallery and a well-preserved mosque. **La Atalaya**, at Palacio de Cervantes 3 (***t*** *95 618 21 00*), is an interesting clock museum with more than 300 timepieces from around the world (unfortunately closed at the time of writing). The excellent **archaeology museum**, opposite San Mateo on Plaza del Mercado (*open Tues–Fri 10–2 and 4–7, Sat–Sun and hols 10–2.30; adm*), contains a number of Greek and Roman artefacts in a very pretty restored 18th-century mansion. One of the higlights is a menacing Greek warrior's helmet, discovered in the river, and dating back to the 7th century BC. The top floor is devoted to Arabic ceramics and other finds from the Alcázar.

Outside town, on the road to Medina Sidonia, is the **Cartuja de la Defensión**, a 15th-century monastery with the best Baroque façade (added in 1667) in Andalucía – a sort of giant *retablo* with sculptures by Alonso Cano and others. This is still a working monastery, and you'll need special permission to go inside. There is little reason to; what was the main attraction, a great altarpiece by Zurbarán, is scattered to the four winds – you can see panels in the museums of Sevilla and Cádiz. The church is currently closed for restoration work, but do, however, visit the gardens and patio (*open Mon–Fri 9.30–11.15 and 12.45–6.30; book visits in advance,* ***t*** *95 615 64 65*). Nearby is the **Yeguada de la Cartuja** (***t*** *95 616 28 09, www.yeguadacartuja.com*), a centre for the breeding of the beautiful Jerezano horses, which you can see being put through their paces at 11am on Saturdays throughout the year.

Jerez also boasts a clutch of quirky little **museums**, devoted to things as diverse as wine labels (*Museo de Etiquetas de Vino, in the Garvey bodega at Ctra N.IV,* ***t*** *95 631 96 50*), bullfighting (*Museo Taurino, C/Pozo del Olivar,* ***t*** *95 632 30 00; open Mon–Sat 10–2*), and costumes (*Museo de Traje Corto, C/Bizcocheros 3,* ***t*** *95 634 61 74, book visits in advance*). There is also a **zoo and botanical garden** (***t*** *95 618 23 97; open summer daily 10–8; winter Tues–Sun 10–6, adm*), just out town on the curiously named C/Taxdirt.

Horses and Flamenco

While in Jerez, look out for exhibitions scheduled at the **Real Escuela Andaluz del Arte Ecuestre**, Avda Duque de Abrantes (***t*** *95 631 11 11,* ***f*** *95 630 99 54, www. real escuela.org*). Jerez's snooty wine aristocracy takes horsemanship very seriously; they have some of the finest horses you're likely to see anywhere, and they know how to use them. You can see them tarted up like Tío Pepe bottles at the annual **Horse Fair** during the first half of May. The origin of this fair can be traced back to the 13th century, and its events include jumping, classical riding, harness riding and Andalucían country riding. Being an Andalucían fair, it is provides a good excuse for attending the *corrida*, drinking plenty of sherry and, of course, joining in the flamenco extravaganza. There are also a number of events during the *fiestas de otoño* in September and October, including sherry tasting and horse racing in the main square. Every Thursday (and on Tuesday from March to October) there is a spectacular 'horse ballet' at 12 noon. The show runs for about 1½ hours with a short interval (there's a bar which serves sherry), and afterwards you are free to wander through the stables to meet the stars of the show. Additionally, there are tours between 11am and 1pm weekdays except Thursdays. Check with the tourist information for details of any special shows and wear something warm during the winter months.

One of Jerez's attractions is its contrasts – as well as being home to the wealthiest Spaniards, it also has a large Gypsy population who live in the warren of streets stretching up from the cathedral to the Barrio Santiago. Here you can find the **Flamenco Centre**, Palacio Penmartín, Pza de San Juan 1 (***t*** *95 632 27 11, http://caf.cica.es; open Mon–Fri 9–2, closed for two weeks during Aug*), housed in one of the most beautiful buildings of the old part of the city; the centre hosts different shows and activities throughout the year – concerts, exhibitions, seminars and video shows – in an effort to promote and prolong the art. You might also be able to locate a flamenco show which hasn't been put on solely for tourists (*see* 'Nightlife' p.207). There's also a spectactular **flamenco festival** held at the end of February or early March, and Friday nights are flamenco nights throughout the city in August. The area's main sight is the 15th-century church of **Santiago**, a wonderfully preserved Gothic pile (*visits at time of Mass, or call ahead,* ***t*** *95 618 08 39*).

Arcos de la Frontera and the *Pueblos Blancos*

Starting from Jerez, **Arcos de la Frontera** is the first of the *pueblos blancos* (white towns) you come to and one of the most spectacular, hanging on a steep rock with wonderful views over the valley of the Guadalete from the *mirador* near the Plaza del Ayuntamiento. The narrow streets twist and turn like an oriental maze, an inheritance from its Moorish past. Follow the long street up to the castle and you'll be rewarded with panoramic views in all directions. The older sections of town under the castle contain some ancient palaces and the Isabelline-Gothic **Santa María de la Asunción**, next to which is a rectangular esplanade hanging over the cliff above the Guadalete. Way below stretches the river and its fertile valley.

Arcos's history is full of feud and conflict. Its name is derived from the Roman *Arx-Arcis*, meaning 'fortress on high'. The town was an important centre for the Moors, a seemingly impregnable eyrie that was the capital of its own kingdom in the age of the *taifas*, ruled by the Berber king, Bem Jazrum, who built the now privately owned *castillo* in the eleventh century. Alfonso the Wise was smart enough to capture the town in 1264, dismantling the beautiful Moorish mosque in typical Spanish style and replacing it with the church of **Santa María de la Asunción** (*open Mon–Fri 10–1 and 3.30–6.30, Sat 10–1.30; adm*), which squats on the northern side of the Plaza del Cabildo, the old town's car park. The church's southern plateresque façade is impressive, as are the 14th-century *mudéjar* wall paintings inside and the gilt altarpieces by Andrés Benítez. The crucifixes on the walls cover bits of saint, entombed in the superstructure in an attempt to make the church holier than its arch-rival – the 18th-century church of **San Pedro** (*open Mon–Fri 10–1 and 4–7, Sat 10–2; adm*), perched on the clifftop to the east. A feud between them in the 18th century became so intense that the churches turned to the Vatican for adjudication. Santa María still proudly displays the papal decree which declares it the winner – it hangs on the wall next to the glass case containing the grey and withered, yet undecomposed, body of an obscure St Felix. St Peter's parishioners were so disgusted that they refused to pronounce the name of their rival, and addressed their prayers to 'St Peter, Mother of God' or 'The Divine Shepherdess', rather than to 'Mary, Mother of God'.

San Pedro may have lost the holiness competition but it nonetheless contains the town's most important religious art: two paintings of San Ignacio and La Dolorosa by Velázquez's teacher, Pacheco. They hang on either side of the 16th-century *retablo*, the oldest in the province.

The town's most venerated relic, a 17th-century Jesús Nazareno (Christ Carrying the Cross) by Jacomi Verdi lies hidden within yet another holy shrine, the 16th-century **Convent of San Augustín** at the eastern end of the town (*open Wed–Mon 10.30–12.30 and 4–6.30*). It is also possible to see the beautiful and ornate *retablo* in the church of the **Convent of Mercedarias Descalzas** on Calle Maldonado, which only opens once a week, for Sunday Mass at 9am. At other times the convent and the nuns remain ensconced behind heavy iron bars, and communication with the outside world is carried out through a rotating grill, through which the sisters pass handmade sweets.

Arcos has one of the region's most elaborate and colourful Easter parades. Fighting bulls are let loose in the streets and those who choose not to be chased by them can watch the procession of priests in purple twist their way through the incense-filled streets carrying heavy gilt images of Christ covered in flowers and lit by tall candles. There's also a flamenco festival around the beginning of August.

East into the Sierra de Grazalema

Further east, **Grazalema** is another lovely village, full of flowers and surrounded by pine woods. It is considered by many to be the archetypal Sierra town, and its peaceful beauty is in perfect accord with its surroundings. Grazalema has been famous for hand-woven blankets since Moorish times, and they are still made here on big old wooden looms. The town's heyday was from the end of the 18th century to the middle of the 19th, when a resurgence in the demand for blankets swelled the population to more than 9,000, compared to today's 2,400. The **Iglesia de la Encarnación**, beside the hotel on the Plaza Pequeña, is the oldest church in the town, with *mudéjar* designs dating from the 17th century, though it suffered badly during both the War of Independence and the Civil War. Flanking the far end of the main

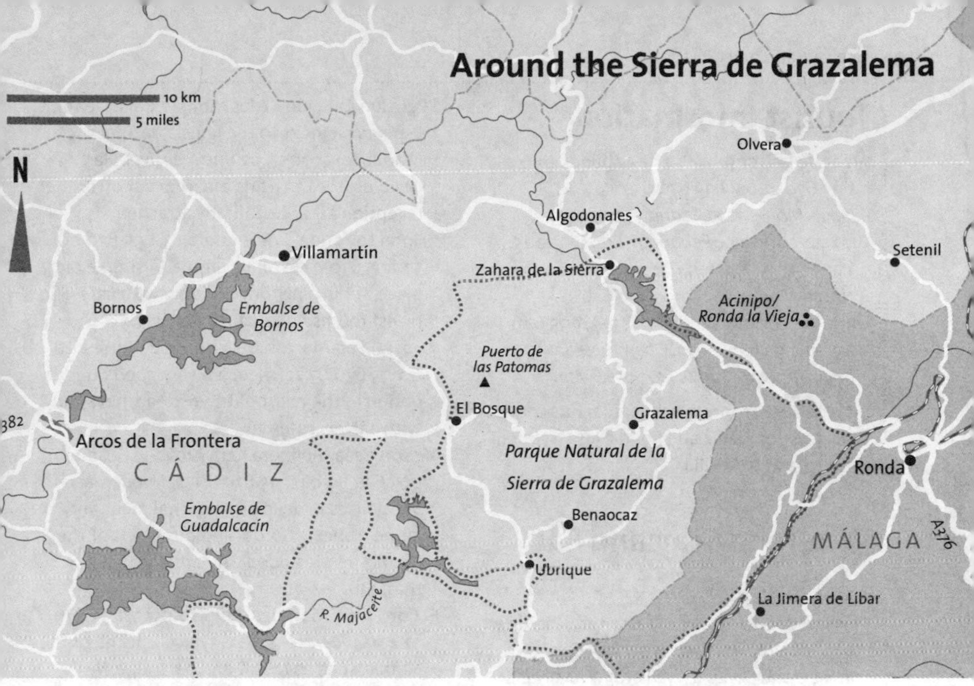

square, Plaza de España, is the 18th-century **Nuestra Señora de la Aurora**, unusual for its octagonal plan. The roads leading off the plaza are especially pretty, lined with little shops and bars, and leading to Plaza de los Asomaderos, a viewing area which doubles as a market on Tuesdays. C/Juan de la Rosa continues up to the top of town, and the 18th-century chapel of **San José**, originally a Carmelite convent. Beside the chapel is a campsite office which can provide you with details of walks and horse-trekking.

The **Sierra de Grazalema** is one of the most stunning and ecologically important parks in Spain. Consisting mainly of limestone formed in the Jurassic and Triassic ages, the park is a micro-climate with the highest average rainfall in Spain; many pre-Ice Age species of plants and trees have survived, including the Spanish fir, or *pinsapo*. This rare tree grows only above 1,000m (3,200ft), and elsewhere it can only be found in the nearby reserve of Las Nieves and the Urals. Animal life includes golden eagles, common vultures, mountain goats and, in the high peaks, ibex. There are wonderful walks and activities such as pot-holing, caving, hang-gliding and horse riding. It is bounded by some of the prettiest *pueblos blancos* in Andalucía. For horse riding, contact **Al-hazan** (***t*** *95 623 42 35*), off the CA5311 Grazalema-Ribera del Gaidovar road.

Nearby **Zahara** ('flower' in Arabic) is a quiet town perfumed by orange groves, at the foot of a hill crowned by a medieval castle, which the Christians captured from the Moors towards the end of the 15th century. Despite the fact that the centre has been classified as a national monument, upon closer inspection there is not much more to the town save the views. Zahara is another good base for walks into the deep mountain gorges of the national park, including the stunning **Garganta Verde**, which leads to a little monastery.

Tourist Information

Arcos de la Frontera: Pza de Cabildo s/n, **t** 95 670 22 64, **f** 95 670 09 00. *Open Mon–Sat 10–2 and 3.30–7.30.*

Grazalema: Pza de España 11, **t** 95 613 22 25, **f** 95 613 20 28. *Open Tue–Sun 10–2 and 5–7, closed Mon.*

Ubrique: C/Morena de Mora 19-A, **t** 95 646 49 00, **f** 95 646 26 59. *Open Tues–Sat 10–2 and 4.30–7.30, Sun 10–2, closed Mon.*

Arcos de la Frontera has regular bus connections to Jerez, Cádiz and Ronda; less frequent connections to Sevilla.

Where to Stay and Eat

Arcos ✉ 11630

★★★**Parador de Arcos de la Frontera**, Pza de Cabildo s/n, **t** 95 670 05 00, **f** 95 670 11 16, *arcos@parador.es* (*expensive*). A lovely place, and it's quite popular so book ahead. Request a room with a view, and even if you don't stay, sit over a coffee in the café – a picture window looks out over the entire plain.

★★**Cortijo Faín**, Ctra de Algar, Km 3, **t/f** 95 623 13 96 (*expensive*). Offers 10 rooms and suites set in a 17th-century country house.

★★★**Peña de Arcos**, C/Muñoz Vázquez 42, **t** 95 670 45 32, **f** 95 670 45 02 (*expensive–moderate*). A tastefully designed building with all the amenities, but down in the new town.

★**Marqués de Torresoto**, Marqués de Torresoto 4, **t** 95 670 07 17, **f** 95 670 42 05 (*moderate*). Another excellent choice in an aristocratic, 17th-century mansion, wonderfully situated in the historic quarter of Arcos near the Ayuntamiento.

★★**El Convento**, C/Maldonado 2, **t** 95 670 23 33, **f** 95 670 41 28, *elconvento@viantil.com* (*moderate*). The place to stay in the old town if the *parador* is full (which it frequently is), sharing the views but at half the price and with an excellent restaurant attached (*see* below).

★★★**Los Olivos**, San Miguel 2, **t** 95 670 08 11, **f** 95 670 20 18 (*moderate*). A comfortable and more reasonably priced three-star place.

★**Pensión Callejón de las Monjas**, Calle Deán Espinosa 4 (next to the Iglesia de Santa María), **t** 95 670 23 02 (*inexpensive*). Has doubles from €33, and a barber's shop in the reception area. Restaurant attached.

★**Hotel La Fonda**, C/Corredara 83, **t** 95 670 00 57, **f** 95 670 07 21 (*inexpensive*). A simple old place, set in a historic building with café. The nicest rooms have little balconies.

★**Hostal San Marcos**, C/Marqués de Torresoto 6, **t** 95 670 07 21 (*cheap*). A very good budget option in the heart of town; clean, new and with a lively café-bar.

Mesón de la Molinera, Ctra Arcos–El Bosque, **t** 95 670 80 02, **f** 95 670 80 07 (*moderate*). Specializes in delicious regional meat and game dishes; affords fabulous views of the town. There's a good value *menú* at less than €10.

El Convento, Marqués de Torresoto 7, **t** 95 670 32 22 (*moderate*). Offers typical cuisine of the Sierras, such as rabbit and partridge, in a 16th-century nobleman's house with a beautiful traditional *andaluz* patio.

Parador de Turismo, Pza del Cabildo, **t** 95 670 05 00 (*moderate*). Probably the second best place to eat in town (after Mesón de la Molinera); the *menú de degustación* is good value. No reservations taken.

El Telescopio, Ctra Arcos–El Bosque 3, **t** 95 670 24 61 (*moderate*). Another reasonable option, with wonderful views from the terrace and good local dishes.

Peña Flamenca, Pza de la Caridad, **t** 95 670 12 51. Arcos is not renowned for its late-night activities, but there are a couple of flamenco bars, including this place, and a Flamenco Festival in July and August.

There are several bars along C/Sevilla for a late-night copa: try **La Cabaña**. The discos are mainly around Avda Duque de Arcos; Caramba and Quo Vadis have terraces.

El Bosque ✉ 11670

★★**Las Truchas**, Avda de la Diputación s/n, **t** 95 671 60 61, **f** 95 671 60 86 (*moderate*). Situated just outside El Bosque, which is a delightful little village set amongst verdant forests (providing shady relief from the sun-blasted landscapes of the rest of this area) and the Río Majaceite, which is stuffed full of trout. There is a pool and excellent restaurant specializing in – you guessed it – fresh trout *a la serranía*. There are lots of walking routes possible from this spot.

Grazalema ✉ 11610

****Hotel Puerta de la Villa**, Plaza Pequeña 8, **t** 95 613 24 06, **f** 95 613 20 87, *www.grazhotel.com* (*expensive*). This is the best place to stay and eat. Light, spacious rooms with outstanding views and all the mod cons. The hotel is just off the main square and is an excellent base for exploring the surrounding countryside. Has a tiny pool, gym, sauna and the best restaurant in town, **La Garrocha** (*see* below).

Hotel Villa Turística de Grazalema, C/Olivar s/n, **t** 95 613 21 36 (*moderate*). One of the comfortable, government-run self-catering places, which you will pass on the approach into town. Includes apartments with Jacuzzi.

****La Casa de las Piedras**, C/las Piedras 32, **t** 95 613 20 14 (*inexpensive*). The cheaper, functional option, just above the main square.

La Garrocha, Plaza Pequeña 8, **t** 95 613 24 06, **f** 95 613 20 87, *www.grazhotel.com* (*expensive*). Probably the best restaurant in town, featuring *andaluz* dishes of fresh fish, meat and vegetables, prepared in an innovative way; attached to **Hotel Puerta de la Villa** (*see* above).

Elsewhere, most of the food and drink options can be found in the streets leading off Plaza de España, particularly C/Agua and around the delightful palm-shaded Plaza Andalucía.

El Torreón, C/Agua 44, **t** 95 613 23 13 (*moderate*). Probably your best option in this area, a beautiful, traditional restaurant with local trout, steak and chicken featuring on the reasonably priced menu.

Cádiz el Chico, Pza de España 8, **t** 95 613 20 27. Back on the main square, offering an *inexpensive menú* of local dishes and an excellent wine list.

Grazalema has a surprising number of **bars** for such a small place, most of them to be found on C/Agua.

Villaluenga del Rosario ✉ 11611

Hostal Villaluenga, **t** 95 646 19 12 (*inexpensive*). You might like to base yourself at this *hostal* to explore nearby prehistoric sites. The village itself is a tiny place seemingly cut out of the limestone.

Zahara, Algodonales, Olvera and Setenil ✉ 11192

****Arco de la Villa**, Pso Nazarí s/n (Zahara), **t** 95 612 32 30, **f** 95 612 32 44 (*moderate*). A fantastic location built into the cliff edge above the town and below the ruined castle, although it is let down by a rather pedestrian design, an uninspiring restaurant and basic rooms (all with bath). Part of the local Tugasa chain.

****Hostal Marqués de Zahara**, San Juan 3, **t/f** 95 612 30 61 (*inexpensive*). A cheaper option with rooms set round an inner courtyard off the main square.

****Hostal Alameda**, C/Constitución 12, in Algodonales, **t** 95 613 72 29 (*inexpensive*). A basic place but with lovely views over the square and the hills behind the town.

****Sierra y Cal**, Avda Nuestra Señora de los Remedios 4, in Olvera, **t** 95 613 03 03, **f** 95 613 05 83 (*inexpensive*). Comfortable with all mod cons and a good restaurant.

Hostal Maqueda, C/Calvario 35, in Olvera, **t** 95 613 07 33 (*cheap*). Offers rooms without bath for less than €30.

El Almendral, Ctra Setenil–Pto del Monte; **t** 95 613 40 29, **f** 95 613 44 44 (*inexpensive*). The only place to stay in Setenil, though for a pensión it has a surprising number of amenities including a pool, tennis courts, disco and café.

Zahara has limited eating possibilities; all the hotels have restaurants, or there is a small tapas bar, **El Mirador**, on the main square.

Fiestas

Grazalema: Last Sunday of May: Romería de San Isidro Labrador, a celebration of the sun and the earth. Third week of July: Fiestas del Carmen, culminating in the Lunes del Toro, a traditional local festival. Third week of August: Las Fiestas Mayores/Feria de Grazalema. Sept 8: El Virgen de los Ángeles, the town's patron saint.

Zahara: June: Romería de Arroymolinos; Fiestas de Agosto.

Algodonales has nothing more to it than a long square topped by the pretty church of **Santa Ana**, a few cafés and a couple of places to stay, but it's got a stunning setting in the shadow of a stony outcrop. You would do better stopping at **Olvera**, once a famous bandits' hideout, and now a beautiful place poised high on a hilltop with a memorable silhouette – its 12th-century **castle** and 17th-century church, **La Encarnación**, sticking up bravely over the gleaming spiral of whitewashed houses.

To the south is **Benaocaz**, which has a small museum of local archaeological finds. Nearby **Ubrique** hangs over the Río Majaceite; though a growing industrial town, best known for its leatherwork, it still manages to retain some of its medieval charm.

Halfway between Olvera and Ronda is **Setenil**, a peculiar village with some of its streets lining the walls of a gorge. The houses are tucked under the overhanging rock, and their front doors overlook a stream. The village's proper name is Setenil de las Bodegas – it was once a wine-producing centre, until all its vines were killed off by the phylloxera in the 1890s, initiating a period of poverty and decay from which the place has only lately been recovering.

From Cádiz to Algeciras

The green, hilly countryside of this region looks a lot like the parts of Morocco just across the straits. The hills force the main road away from the sea, leaving a few villages with fine beaches. These make good places to take time out from your over-active holiday; the problem is they're hard to reach unless you have a car.

Beyond the marshland around Cádiz, you'll see the turn-off for **Sancti Petri**, a small village with a ruined castle on an island off the beach and a little fishing harbour where the trawlers are now outnumbered by yachts. The village is being swallowed up by the neighbouring soulless tourist resort of Novo Sancti Petri, where the admittedly glorious long sandy beaches are lined with endless banal new developments. Next along the coast is **Conil**, with a tiny harbour and what remains of the town's fishing fleet. It's a very popular resort for Spanish families, thanks to its vast, shallow bay. It is always crammed in August, when you'll have virtually no chance of finding anywhere to stay, but you can count on some pretty lively nightlife, especially along the Paseo Marítimo.

Twenty-three kilometres inland along the A390 is **Medina Sidonia**. This is one of the prettiest whitewashed towns, far less visited than Vejer (*see* below). It is set on top of a hill in the middle of rolling fields; on a clear day you can see the mountains of the Serranía de Ronda. Its origins stretch to Roman and Phoenician times but its modern history dates from 1440, when it was handed over to Don Juan de Guzmán, who became the first Duke of Medina Sidonia. The town saw royal patronage for many years, although today it has a slightly dusty and neglected feel. There are a few monuments that stand out, including the 16th-century church of **Santa María la Coronada** in Plaza Iglesia Mayor, where the tourist office is located. It has a huge carved *retablo* inside stretching from floor to ceiling. Climb the hill and you will reach the ruins of the Moorish castle. The town also has three well-preserved Moorish gates, Puertas de

Belén and del Sol, and the the 10th-century **Arco de la Pastora**, perhaps the best preserved. The 17th-century **Ayuntamiento**, in fine Renaissance style, is in the Plaza de España, in the lower part of town.

The main attraction back on the coastal road is **Vejer de la Frontera**, whitest of the 'white villages' of Andalucía, strangely moulded around its hilltop site like a Greek island town. The village was probably a Carthaginian citadel before becoming the Roman town of Besipo. Now it couldn't be more Moorish in its feel; a Moorish castle dominates the village and the 13th-century Gothic church, built over the site of a mosque, lies deep within the town's sparkling clean, narrow whitewashed streets. In the upper part of town you can see the original Moorish gates. Even the locals seem close to their Muslim past. Until fairly recently women in Vejer wore the *cobija*, a piece of dark cloth like a Muslim *heshab* that covers the face, leaving only the eyes exposed. There's a seldom-visited beach 9km away at **El Palmar** and, nearby, a Roman aqueduct in the beautiful village of **Santa Lucía**. From Vejer the C343 goes down to the modern town of **Barbate**, whose income comes not from tourists but tuna. Twice a year large shoals of them pass here, to be slaughtered in a bloody ambush similar to the *mattanza* off the coast of Sicily. It's a small, scrubby working town, full of canning factories and cheap apartment blocks, but the fish restaurants and tapas bars along the Paseo Marítimo are all excellent.

Just inland from Barbate, not far from Vejer de la Frontera, is **MMAC** – look for signs for Montenmedio, on the main road N-340, km 42.5 (***t** 95 645 12 16, open Tues–Sun 10–1.30 and 5.30–8.30*). It is a striking and original contemporary art centre with a twist: the landscape itself has become a 'gallery' for a collection of permanent site-specific sculptures and installations.

A small road leads west out of Barbate to the summer resort of **Los Caños de Meca**, traditionally busy in the height of summer with tourists from Sevilla and Cádiz. The trendy, hippy crowd have moved on to Tarifa now, and in recent years, Germans have adopted the place as their haven. Half an hour's walk west of here takes you to **Cape Trafalgar**, where Nelson breathed his last in 1805. Spaniards remember this well; it was mostly their ships that were getting smashed, under incompetent French leadership. Every Spaniard did his duty, though, and with their unflappable sense of personal honour the Spanish have always looked on Trafalgar as a sort of victory.

Zahara de los Atunes

Ten kilometres south of here is another developing resort, **Zahara de los Atunes** ('of the tunas'). This is one of the most unspoilt coastlines in southern Spain, with miles of fine sandy beach that will be all yours in spring and autumn. The town was the birthplace of Francisco Rivera, or Paquirri, the famous bullfighter. Today it is fairly tranquil, with a few small hotels and restaurants. There's little to see or do other than laze around on the beach and watch the sun sinking into the sea whilst sipping a beer. However, a huge new *urbanización*, Nueva Zahara, is being built on the Atlanterra road, and numerous large hotels are beginning to spring up, with the whole area rechristened the 'Costa de Zahara'.

Tarifa

Tarifa, at the tip of Spain and of Europe, looks either exotic and evocative, or me rely dusty and dreary, depending on the hour of the day and the mood you're in. You might even think you've arrived in Africa, it's so bleached by sun and salt. The town is one of the top destinations in Europe for windsurfing; the *levante* and *poniente* winds are relentless in their attack on this coast and the associated young crowd has fomented a lively bar scene. Tarifa has also become a very popular spot for whale-watching tours: several companies run them, including the excellent Whale Watch España (***t** 636 47 65 44/95 662 70 13*). Other tours are run by the Foundation for Information and Research on Marine Mammals (FIRMM; ***t** 95 662 70 08/619 45 94 41*).

The town has a 10th-century Moorish **castle**, much rebuilt, and the site of the legend of **Guzmán el Bueno**. In 1292, this Spanish knight was defending Tarifa against a force of Moors. Among them was the renegade Infante Don Juan, brother of King Sancho IV, who had Guzmán's young son as a prisoner, and threatened to kill him if

Getting There and Around

By Train

Trains go to Ronda and Granada from Algeciras, and from there to all points in eastern Andalucía; there is a daily *Talgo* to Madrid and points north. The station is across from the bus station.

By Bus

Buses to Algeciras from the Comes station in Cádiz are frequent enough, but services to coastal resorts like Conil, Barbate and Zahara are less so (two per day). Algeciras's bus station is in the Hotel Octavio complex, C/San Bernardo; there are buses to La Línea (for Gibraltar) about every half-hour, and connections to the Costa del Sol.

By Boat

FRS, **t** 95 668 18 30, *www.frs.es*, runs ferries between Tarifa–Algeciras, and Tarifa–Tangiers. It also offers guided one- or two-day trips to Tangiers.

Tourist Information

Algeciras: Juan de la Cierva s/n, by the port, **t** 95 657 26 36, **f** 95 657 04 75. *Open Mon–Fri 9–2, Sat 10–1.*

Barbate: C/Ramón y Cajal 45, **t** 95 643 10 06. *Open Mon–Fri 8–3.*

Chiclana: Alameda del Río s/n, **t/f** 95 653 59 69. *Open Mon–Sat 10–1.30 and 6.30–8.30; closed Sat pm in winter.*

Conil: Carretera El Punto s/n, **t** 95 644 05 01, **f** 95 644 05 00. *Open Mon–Sat 9.30–1.30.*

Medina Sidonia: Pza Iglesia Mayor s/n, **t/f** 95 641 24 04. *Open daily 10–1.30 and 4.30–7.*

San Fernando: C/Real 24, **t** 95 689 74 30, **f** 95 688 99 64. *Open Mon–Fri 9.30–1.30.*

San Roque: C/San Felipe 7, **t** 95 678 09 27. *Open Mon–Fri 9–3.*

Tarifa: northern end of Paseo Alameda, outside the western wall of the old town, **t/f** 95 668 09 93, *www.tarifa.net*. *Open Mon–Fri 10.30–2 and 6–8 summer; 10.30–2 and 5–7 in winter.*

Vejer: C/Marqués de Tamarón 10, **t** 95 645 01 91, **f** 95 645 11 49. *Open Mon–Fri 9–2 and 5–9, Sat–Sun 11–2 and 6–9.*

Where to Stay and Eat

Conil ✉ 11140

A pretty resort popular with Spanish and refreshingly undeveloped (as yet). The town boasts some of the best beaches along the coast and one of the finest hotels.

****__Fuerte Conil__, Playa Fontanilla s/n, **t** 95 644 33 44, **f** 95 644 23 00, *www.fuertehoteles.com* (*moderate*). Faux-Moorish, in soft colours, stylish and subtly luxurious, and set in its own grounds with the rooms ranged round a huge outdoor pool. There is also an indoor pool, tennis courts, a gym, and a diving school.The restaurant and bar are excellent, with everything at a reasonable price. It is the winner of Spain's first environmental award for hotels.

***__Flamenco__, Fuente del Gallo s/n, **t** 95 644 07 11, **f** 95 644 05 42, *www.partner-hoteles.com* (*expensive*). Slightly out of town, but with all the facilities including indoor and outdoor pool, direct beach access, tennis, golf and comfortable rooms.

Hostal Diufain, Cañada del Rosal s/n, **t** 95 644 25 51, **f** 95 644 30 30 (*inexpensive*). Surprisingly luxurious for a *hostal*, this is built in a hacienda style on the top of a hill overlooking the town; small rooms but a big pool and pleasant café.

Venta Melchor, Cádiz-Málaga highway, km 18, **t** 95 644 50 07 (*expensive*). The best seafood place, though it's out of town. Family-run and dating from 1950, they still serve the freshest seafood from the area as well as delicious homemade *postres*.

La Villa, Plaza de España 6, **t** 95 644 10 53 (*inexpensive*). A small restaurant and bar in town with a good range of seafood tapas.

Guzmán did not surrender. Guzmán's response was to toss him a dagger. His son was killed, but Tarifa did not fall. Fascist propaganda recycled this legend for the 1936 siege of the Alcázar in Toledo, with the Republicans in the villain's role.

El Rincón de Villa (*inexpensive*). A basic place, with very reasonably priced tasty tapas.

Plaza Sta Catalina and the streets off it, particularly C/Ancha, are where the later night action takes place. Try **Café Habana**, where you can also get Internet access, or **La Botellita**, in the square, and **La Cochera**, **El Paso** and **La Calle**, all in C/Ancha. The town's disco **Em**, is also down here, in C/Goya.

Medina Sidonia ✉ 11170

*Venta el Molino**, Avda Al-Andalus s/n, **t** 95 641 03 00 (*inexpensive*). Slightly out of the centre; basic but friendly.

Pensión Napoleón, C/San Juan 21, **t** 95 641 01 83 (*cheap*). In a good location near the centre; the budget option.

La Duquesa, Ctra Medina–Benalup, km 3, **t** 95 641 08 36, **f** 95 641 20 00 (*moderate*). Set in a converted farmhouse in the middle of bull-breeding territory, this restaurant offers superb local cooking with the emphasis on game, including pheasant, partridge and deer, served with fresh vegetables from its own fields.

Cádiz, Pza Espana, **t** 95 641 02 50 (*inexpensive*). Has a lovely shaded patio and serves some good local dishes including partridge, rabbit and stew.

Vejer de la Frontera ✉ 11150

***** Convento de San Francisco**, La Plazuela s/n, **t** 95 645 10 01, **f** 95 645 10 04 (*moderate*). A delightful place; a restored former convent with tastefully designed rooms, lots of original furniture and an excellent restaurant, **El Refectorio** (*moderate*).

Trafalgar, Plaza de España 31, **t** 95 644 76 38 (*moderate*). A traditional restaurant set in a small townhouse, serving up imaginative *andaluz* cuisine. They make their own ice-creams and sorbets, too.

Zahara and Los Caños de Meca ✉ 11393

****Antonio II**, Urb. Atlanterra 1, **t** 95 643 93 46, **f** 95 643 91 35, *www.antoniohoteles.com* (*expensive–moderate*). Recently built to cater for a new influx of tourists. Set back from the beach, with lovely views along the coast, light airy rooms and a large pool area; excellent value just out of season.

****Melía Atlanterra**, Bahía de la Plata, **t** 95 643 90 00, **f** 95 643 90 51, *www.solmelia.es* (*expensive–moderate*). The big resort complex at the Bahía de la Plata; it offers a variety of sports and recreational activities. *Closed Nov–April*.

Gran Sol, on the beach at the end of C/Sánchez Rodríguez, **t** 95 643 93 58 (*expensive–moderate*). In Zahara itself, this is a better option, with comfortable air-conditioned rooms with TV, a fairly good restaurant and a pool.

***Hotel Pozo del Duque**, Ctra Atlanterra 32, **t/f** 95 643 90 97 (*moderate*). Offers spacious rooms with a terrace and sea view, large dining rooms, a pool and is on the beach.

***Porfirio**, Ctra Atlanterra 33, 200m from the beach, **t** 95 644 95 15, **f** 95 643 90 80, *porfirio@arrakis.es* (*moderate*). A delightful hotel built in Andalucían style with patios and 24 rooms arranged around a large pool and set in its own grounds. Bedrooms are with terraces and all mod cons, and there's a good, reasonably priced restaurant.

***Doña Lola**, Pza Thomson 1, **t** 95 643 90 09, **f** 95 643 90 08 (*moderate*). The prettiest hotel in town, with rooms set around a patio and overlooking a large pool.

Hotel Nicolás, C/María Luisa,15, **t** 95 643 92 74, **f** 95 643 94 31, *www.hotel-nicolas.tuweb.net*, *hotel-nicolas@terra.es* (*inexpensive*). Friendly, old-fashioned little hotel in the centre of the village, with a classic café-bar downstairs.

Antonio I, just in front of Antonio II (*see above*, *inexpensive*). The cheaper option, set on the beach, with a superb restaurant.

Camping Bahía de la Plata, **t** 95 643 90 40. A campsite at the south end of the village.

Antonio, Ctra Atlanterra, km 1, **t** 95 643 93 46 (*expensive*). Tourists flock to this restaurant on the beach for its high-quality fish and seafood.

Outside Tarifa, along the beaches west of the town, there are **ruins** of a once-sizeable Roman town, **Baelo Claudio** (*open Tues–Sat June–Sept 10–8; March–May and Oct 10–7; Nov–Feb 10–6; Sun and hols 10–2;* **t** *95 668 85 30; adm, free to EU citizens*). Baelo Claudio was founded in the 2nd century BC, and became important for the production

Casa Juanito, C/Sagasta 7, **t** 95 643 92 11 (*moderate*). One of the most popular restaurants in town – getting a table can be difficult. Excellent seafood, particularly the locally caught tuna.

Asador Sergio, El Pradillo 44, **t** 95 643 94 55 (*moderate*). Just out of the town centre, on the Atlanterra road, specializing in meat done Segovia-style, roasted pig, lamb and some seafood.

Los Tangos, C/Gobenardor Sánchez González, **t** 95 643 91 30 (*moderate–inexpensive*). On the beach in the castle walls, with a very nice *terraza*; also functions as a disco.

Bar Marisquería Porfirio, Plaza Tamarón, **t** 95 643 90 80. Serves excellent seafood in season.

Patio la Plazuela, Plaza Tamarón, **t** 95 643 90 09. Vegetarians won't be disappointed with the sumptuous pizza baked on the spot in Italian ovens.

Trafalgar, in Los Caños de Meca, **t** 95 644 76 38 (*inexpensive*). Inevitably, there had to be a Trafalgar here, set back from the seafront with a pleasant terrace; the menu concentrates on international fare. *Closed in winter.*

Pericayo, C/Ilustre Fregona (parallel with Main Street), **t** 95 643 93 15. Serves *sangría* and tasty tapas.

Tarifa ✉ 11380

Rooms are surprisingly and unnecessarily expensive in the 'recently discovered' resort of Tarifa; the same is true of Conil.

****Hurricane**, Ctra N340, km 76, **t** 95 668 49 19, **f** 95 668 03 29, *www.hotelhurricane.com* (*expensive*). Further along the coast, this English-owned place is popular with windsurfers and film stars; it's incredibly trendy but you pay for the privilege. *Closed Jan.*

Arte-Vida, Ctra Nacional 340, km 79.3, **t** 95 668 53 46, *www.hotelartevida.com* (expensive). Another trendy place for the 'boho-chic' crowd, this has stylish rooms set around a pool just back from a popular wind-surfing beach, and a sleek blue and white restaurant and cocktail bar with pale wicker furniture.

*****Balcón de España**, Ctra Cádiz–Málaga, km 77, **t** 95 668 43 26, **f** 95 668 04 72 (*moderate*). Situated in a pretty spot by the Playa de los Lances, between Tarifa and Punta Palomas to the west of town, this Dutch-owned place is one of the better options. It has two pools, a gym, tennis courts and horse-riding facilities. *Closed Nov–Mar.*

Hostal La Calzada, C/Justino Pertiñez 7, **t** 95 668 03 66 (inexpensive). Tucked away in the old town, with pretty rooms decorated with pine furniture and colourful prints.

Hostal Alameda, C/Santísima Trinidad 7, **t** 95 668 11 81 (*inexpensive–cheap*). One of the cheaper options in town; some of whose pleasant rooms have sea views.

Mesón de Sancho, Ctra N340, km 94, **t** 95 668 49 00, **f** 95 668 47 21 (*expensive*). One of the best restaurants in the area, attached to an equally good hotel. Especially pleasing in winter with its roaring fire, it specializes in home-cooked dishes – favourites are garlic soup, *urta* in cream sauce and *rabo de toro*.

Bar Restaurante Morilla, C/Sancho IV 2, **t** 95 668 17 57 (*inexpensive*). Classic *andaluz* restaurant and tapas bar with a terrace, serving good local seafood and other dishes.

Mandrágora, C/Independencía 3, **t** 95 668 12 91 (moderate). Charming brick-lined little resturant, with Moroccan-style dishes (some vegetarian) and friendly staff. Rather pricey for what's on offer, unfortunately.

Those seeking nightlife should wander around the old town, where the crowds congregate in the numerous bars from about 11pm; try **Café-bar Almedina**, C/Almedina 3, which does good tapas and cocktails in a red-painted, cushion-strewn cavern, before heading down to the beach-front disco, **El Balneario**.

Algeciras ✉ 11200

******Reina Cristina**, Pso de la Conferencia, **t** 95 660 26 22, **f** 95 660 33 23 (*luxury–expensive*). The hotel of the town's bygone elegance, scene of the Algeciras Conference of 1906 (which carved up Morocco) and a

of *garum*, a fish sauce that was one of the prized condiments of the Roman kitchen; preserved in jars, it was shipped from Andalucía all over the Empire. The town rose to prominence during the 1st century AD, when it was made a self-governing municipality under Emperor Claudius. Its decline began in the second half of the 2nd century hotbed of spies during the Second World War. W. B. Yeats spent a winter here.

★★★★**Octavio**, C/San Bernardo 1, **t** 95 665 27 00, **f** 95 665 28 02 (*expensive*). Borders the bus station and is within a few metres of the train station. Mod cons, but no pool.

★★★**Al Mar**, Avda de la Marina 2, **t** 95 665 46 61, **f** 95 665 45 01, *al-mar@eh.etursa.es* (*moderate*). Right on the seafront, above the busy arcades filled with cafés and ticket offices, and looking out over the port area.

★★**Hotel Marina Victoria**, next to Al Mar at Avda de la Marina 7, **t** 95 665 01 11, **f** 95 663 28 65 (*inexpensive*). A less salubrious option, but with good views over to the Rock.

★★★**Alborán**, Álamo Colonia San Miguel-Algeciras, **t** 95 663 28 70, **f** 95 663 23 20 (*expensive–moderate*). A wonderful building in classical Andalucían style, very atmospheric and keenly priced, with an indoor patio and porticoed terrace.

Versailles, Montero Ríos 12, **t** 95 665 42 11 (*inexpensive*). One of a cluster of convenient little *hostales* in the back streets behind the Avenida de la Marina.

There are lots of restaurants in Algeciras. The streets off Plaza Alta, particularly C/Alfonso XI, have a number of good ones.

Los Remos, at Villa Victoria (on the road out of San Roque to La Línea), **t** 95 669 84 12, (*expensive–moderate*). The most famous restaurant in the area, long-established and Michelin-rosetted. Set in a beautiful old house surrounded by lovely gardens, but in a horrible setting – in the shadow of the oil refineries; red carnivores beware – it serves mostly fish.

El Copo, Trasmayo 2 (near Los Barrios), **t** 95 667 77 10 (*moderate*). A good place to splash out. The restaurant is draped with fishermen's nets and takes pride in its enormous tanks of lobsters, sea urchins, spider crabs and mussels, so you can be sure that any fish or seafood dishes are supremely fresh. It serves a wide range of dishes, from fried sea nettles to *rabo de toro* and *solomillo*. If you get a chance take a look upstairs at the bullfighters' room and the room with a painted panorama of views from Palmones several hundred years ago. *Reservations essential. Closed Sun.*

Almazara, C/Alfonso IX 9, **t** 95 665 74 77 (*moderate*). One of the best restaurants in town, serving tapas at the bar and great steaks and fish in the tiny restaurant.

Asador Iruña, C/Alfonso IX 1, **t** 95 665 21 49 (*moderate*). Specializes in Basque dishes and serving tasty *pintxos*, Basque tapas of crusty bread with toppings, at the bar.

Pazo de Edelmiro, Plaza Miguel Martín 1, **t** 95 666 63 55 (*inexpensive*). Reliable workers' favourite, serving Galician dishes at very reasonable prices.

Casa Montes, C/San Juan 16, **t** 95 665 42 07 (*inexpensive*). A popular place with working people, where *urta* surfaces again, along with roast kid and poultry.

Alcalá de los Gazules ✉ 11180

★★**San Jorge**, Pso de la Playa s/n, **t** 95 641 32 55, **f** 95 642 01 75 (*inexpensive*). A friendly place with all the facilities and a good restaurant.

Hostal Pizarro, Pso de la Playa 9, **t** 95 642 01 03, **f** 95 642 01 75 (*cheap*). The cheaper version of the San Jorge and with a few less creature comforts, run by the same people.

Jimena de la Frontera ✉ 11330

Hostal El Anon, C/Consuelo 36, **t** 95 664 01 13, **f** 95 664 11 10, *elanon@mx3.redestb.es* (*moderate*). A delightful place with a series of pretty courtyards around which are ranged the rather basic rooms. There is a good restaurant and bar and even a pool on the roof with lovely views.

Los Arcos, Avda Reina de los Angeles 8, **t/f** 95 664 12 12 (*moderate*). A more basic option, without pool.

There are a couple of places to eat just round the corner from the main square, including **La Bodeguita**, a simple tapas bar, and **Vecina**, opposite, as well as **Bar Cuenca**, on the way into town.

due to an earthquake, and it was abandoned by the 7th century. What remains is all that makes up a Roman town; a court, temples, basilica, roads – and the fish factory. The beach, with its sand dune cascading down the western end, is rarely crowded.

Algeciras

Ask at the tourist office what there is to see and you'll be told, 'Nothing. Nobody ever stays here'. Once you've seen the town you'll understand why: it's a dump. Nevertheless, Algeciras has an interesting history, and an attractive setting opposite the Rock of Gibraltar if you can see through the pollution. It played a significant role in the colonization of the eastern Mediterranean, becoming an important port in the Roman era. From AD 713 on, it was occupied by the Moors, and its name derives from the Arabic *Al-Jazira al-Khadra* (Green Island). Today, apart from its importance as a port with regular connections to Ceuta, Tangier and the Canary Islands, Algeciras is a sizeable industrial centre. Its only recent claim to fame is its illustrious son Paco de Lucía, Spain's greatest guitarist. There's a small monument to him at the quayside.

The bustling, seedy port area has little attraction for the visitor, although the small bazaars in the side streets, selling Moroccan leather goods, may whet your appetite for a trip across the straits – you can see Morocco's jagged surreal peaks all along the coastal highway. It is also the centre of one of the busiest drug-smuggling routes in the world, and every stevedore and cab driver will be whispering little propositions in your ear if you look the type.

Inland, lying in a pleasantly wooded area, is **Los Barrios**, settled by refugees when Gibraltar was lost to the British; archaeological finds indicate that it was inhabited from earliest times. The parish church of **San Isidro** dates from the 18th century. There are two fairly decent beaches nearby – Guadarranque and Palmones.

On the N340 heading north, the road passes **San Roque**, with exceptional views over the bay of Algeciras and Gibraltar. Here are the ruins of *Carteya*, the first Roman settlement in the south of the peninsula. The 18th-century parish church of **Santa María Coronada** was built above the ancient hermitage of San Roque, and is worth a visit. This pretty little town is a relief after the more sordid quarters of Algeciras, and a bonus are the nearby clean beaches of Puente Mayorga, Los Portichuelos and Carteya.

Parque Natural de Los Alcornocales

This National Park spreads out above Algeciras and Tarifa, reaching as far as El Bosque. It is sparsely populated but does include the lovely white towns of Jimena de la Frontera and Alcalá de los Gazules. The name of the park refers to the cork oak, or *alcornoque*, which is spread right across the area, forming its largest forest in Europe. The park is an important spot for migratory birds coming over the Straits from Africa in spring and returning in autumn. March to May is the best time to spot species such as sea eagles and short-toed eagles as well as one of the largest groups of spotted vultures in Europe. Animals such as deer, boar and mongoose are also indigenous, as are trees including rhododendron, ash and hazel. It's a delight to explore on foot or by mountain bike, staying in one of the mountain villages, or on a leisurely day's drive from Algeciras or Tarifa. There is a park information office just outside Algeciras by the El Pelayo beach on the N-340 (***t*** *95 667 91 61*), which has guides to walking routes of varying difficulties within the park.

If you head north from Algeciras via Los Barrios, following the route Laurie Lee took in his book *A Rose for Winter*, the road winds through former bandit country before arriving at the village of **Alcalá de los Gazules**, which Lee described as 'a terraced town of bright white houses hung with red flowers and roofed with gold'. (Sadly, a motorway is currently being built, which will tear through the countryside between Algeciras and Cádiz.) Despite the bulldozers just out of sight, the village hasn't changed much in 70 years and there is not a great deal to see other than the church of **San Jorge** in the Plaza Alta, which affords wonderful views over the surrounding countryside. The church is usually closed but if you ask at the *turismo* in the Casa Consistorial, or at Bar Luna opposite, someone should be able to rustle up the key. Inside there are a couple of curiosities: an odd-shaped choir stall adjusted from four seats to three for Inquisition purposes and an effigy of San Cristóbal, heavily scratched by superstitious townsfolk. There's also one of a pair of paintings of San Estebán; the other resides in the Vatican.

Southwest along the CA3331 you come to **Jimena de la Frontera**, topped by an impressive Moorish castle, once owned by the Dukes of Medina Sidonia. Just outside the castle wall lie the ruins of the **Church of the Misericordia**, and a few kilometres away are some prehistoric caves with ancient wall paintings.

There is another 13th-century Moorish castle at **Castellar de la Frontera**, entirely circled by the castle walls, from where, on a clear day, you can see right across to Africa. During the 1970s, due to its primitive state, the old town was abandoned by its entire population, all of whom moved to Nuevo Castellar along the main road. It has been gradually repopulated though, mainly by Germans, who sit uneasily with the original populace down the road.

An Excursion to North Africa

The main reason for making the crossing to **Morocco** will be to take a look at the limited attractions of Tangier. Unfortunately, the real treasures are all far to the south, in Fez, Marrakech and the kasbahs of the Draa and Ziz valleys. But even an admittedly international city like Tangier will give you the chance to explore a fascinating society – and perhaps see a little reflection of the lost culture of al-Andalus. On the other hand, you could shop at Ceuta, one of Spain's last two *presidios* on the North African coast (the other is Melilla, further east along the coast: *see* p.264).

Ceuta

Every time the Spanish make self-righteous noises about getting Gibraltar back, someone reminds them about their two colonial leftovers on the North African coast, Melilla and Ceuta. Lately Colonel Qaddafi has also been heard from on the issue. Ceuta has a mainly Spanish population; that is why it was excluded from the 1955 withdrawal from the Spanish-Moroccan protectorate. They are the stumbling block, and some way will have to be found to accommodate them before the inevitable transfer of sovereignty. Ceuta is a pleasant enough town, but there's little reason to go there, perhaps only the impressive 16th-century **walls** and moat. The **Museo de Ceuta** (*open Mon–Fri 10–1 and 7–9 in summer, 5–9 in winter, Sat 10–2;*

adm) has rather dull exhibits on local history, and the **Museo de La Legión** (*open Mon–Sat 11–1 and 3–6*) is devoted to Spain's Foreign Legion (a band of cut-throats who became notorious during the Civil War under a one-armed, one-eyed commander named José Millán Astray; their slogan: 'Long live Death'). The **Parque Marítimo del Mediterraneo** is a massive watery theme park, with plenty of pools, a vast lake, botanic gardens, shops and restaurants. Like Andorra, Ceuta is a big, duty-free supermarket. You can easily cross into Morocco from here, though it's better to take the ferry to Tangier.

Tetuán and Tangier

Aside from its polluted river and contraband appeal Tetuán is a decent town, full of gleaming white, Spanish architecture; it has a famous market in its *medina*, a historical museum, and it's a good place to purchase Moroccan crafts. On the way into **Tangier**, note how the old Plaza de Toros has been turned into flats. Once in the square outside the port entrance, you may take your chances with the inexpensive hotels in the surrounding streets, or take a cab to fancier spots in the Europeanized districts. Tangier may not be as romantic as you expect; or you may find it more so. It is certainly exotic in parts. The wares in the markets of the *medina* are interesting, but the quarter itself is down-at-heel. Non-Muslims may not enter mosques in Morocco, but in the old governor's palace are two **museums** of archaeology and Moroccan art.

Hotels, restaurants, and everything else will be almost half as expensive as in Spain. The food has an international reputation; national dishes like couscous and *harira* can be superb but seldom are. Don't judge Morocco by Tangier and Tetuán, and don't even judge these places by first impressions. A little side-trip to Morocco may not be an epiphany, but think how much you'll regret it if you pass up the chance.

Getting There

By Ferry

Algeciras's *raison d'être* is its port, and there's no trouble getting a ferry either to Ceuta (with at least 10 crossings a day in summer) or to Tangier (6 crossings in summer). Ceuta is 1½hrs away by ferry, 30 mins by hydrofoil and Tangier is 2½hrs away, or 1hr on a the jetfoil. A jetfoil runs five times daily except Friday and Sunday. Among others, FRS Maroc, **t** 95 668 13 30, run a guided one- or two-day tour.

There are plenty of official Trasmediterránea agents at the port, as well as unofficial ticket booths along the N340, as far away as Estepona. They all look extremely dodgy, though they sell legitimate tickets. To avoid hefty commissions, buy directly from the Trasmediterranea office at the port (Recinto del Puerto s/n, **t** 902 46 45 45). You'll need your passport.There's also a summer hydrofoil service from Tarifa to Tangier and to Gibraltar.

Getting Around

If you're travelling from Ceuta, you'll have to take a **cab** or **city bus** (the one marked '*frontera*') to the border; after some border confusion, wait for the infrequent bus or negotiate a taxi trip to **Tetuán**, 30km away. There's no train from Tetuán to Tangier, but **buses** run regularly from the central bus station. They'll take you right to Tangier's port.

Tourist Information

Ceuta: Muelle Cañonero Dato s/n, **t** 95 650 14 10, *www.ciceuta.es*.
Tangier: 29 Boulevard Pasteur, **t** (039) 948 661, **f** (039) 948 050.
Tetuán: 30 Avenue Mohammed V, **t** (9) 96 44 07.

Where to Stay and Eat

Ceuta ✉ 51001

Finding a place to sleep here can be a problem as there are only a few hotels.

****__Parador La Muralla__, Pza de Nuestra Señora de África 15, **t** 95 651 49 40 (*expensive*). Offers the most comfort and luxury, with a pool and gardens.

****__Meliá Confort Ceuta__, Alcalde Sánchez Prados 3, **t** 95 651 12 00, **f** 95 651 15 01 (*expensive–moderate*). Big, bland chain with all the comforts including a pool.

*** **Ulises**, Camoens 5, **t** 95 651 45 40, **f** 95 651 45 46 (*moderate*). A reasonable choice, with a pool and restaurant.

Restaurante Mar Chica, Pza Rafael Gilbert 5, **t** 95 651 72 40 (*inexpensive*). A good place to meet the locals (and a strange bunch they are), with tasty sea food, paellas, tapas, and a good value *menú del día* at €15.

Al Andalus, Ctra Sanamaro-Pinogordo, s/n, **t** 95 651 39 21 (*moderate*). A romantic spot with sea veiws and Moroccan specialities.

El Rincón de Nacho, C/Padilla 4, **t** 95 651 57 84 (*inexpensive*). Tasty local sea food and home-made desserts.

El Portalón, C/Agustina de Aragón 2, **t** 95 651 75 00 (*inexpensive*). Tapas and seafood in a rustic little tavern in the old heart of Ceuta.

Some Moroccan Practicalities

Money

Wait until you get into Morocco to change money. Spanish travel agents will often change money at a dishonestly low rate, and the rates at the border crossings aren't much better. The currency is the *dirham*, lately about 16 to the pound, 10 to the dollar.

Dealers and Dealing

This corner of Morocco, being the fullest of tourists, is also full of English-speaking hustlers, particularly around the bus stations. Entertain no offers, especially of drugs or guided tours, and do your best to ignore them. The Moroccans don't like them either. Beyond that, you'll need your wits to bargain with merchants, taxi drivers and even hotel-keepers. There's no reason why you can't do this firmly and gracefully, but the whole process is tiring. Also, crime is a problem after dark in Tetuán and Tangier.

Gibraltar

At first sight it looks like a sphinx, crouching at the water's edge, her hindquarters resting in Europe, her head gazing over the sea and her forepaws stretching in front of her to form the most southerly part of our continent.

Alexandre Dumas, 1846

In under two hours, you can experience the ultimate culture shock: sailing from the smoky souks of Tangier to Algeciras, Spain, with time for *churros* and chocolate before the bus takes you off to a mysterious enclave of red phone booths, warm beer and policemen in silly hats.

The Spanish bus will really take you only as far as **La Línea** (*see* pp.242–3) (meaning 'the Line', after Gibraltar's old land walls), a town that has built up dramatically since the reopening of the Gibraltar border in 1985, though drug-crime and pickpockets are rife. Prices in Gibraltar are outrageous by Spanish standards, and if you are on a tight budget you might be best staying in La Línea – just keep an eye on your possessions.

It's only a short walk through the neutral zone into Gibraltar, where you'll be confronted immediately with one of the Rock's curiosities: as you enter British territory you find yourself looking down the noses of 737s and Tridents. Where else does a busy street cross an airport runway? The airport, built on landfill at right angles to the narrow peninsula (this area was included in the land ceded to Britain under the Treaty of Utrecht), symbolizes British determination to hold on during the years Franco was putting the squeeze on Gibraltar, and also points up the enclave's biggest problem – lack of space.

As well as large numbers of cigarette smugglers who cross the border with regularity (there is now an official restriction of two cartons), British residents living on Spanish soil cross in droves to stock up with life's comforts – items either unobtainable in Spain, or just too expensive – baked beans and Christmas crackers, cheddar cheese and headache pills, pickled onions and liver salts. Smugglers are even known to drive into Gibraltar with an empty tank, fill up with petrol (which is much cheaper than in Spain) only to recross the border, siphon off the petrol for resale, and return to Gibraltar. This often adds to the border queues, which can vary from a couple of vehicles to a four-hour tailback, depending on how thorough customs decide to be.

Other more discreet visitors come over to bank their 'black' (undeclared) money made in Spain, and take advantage of the no-questions-asked, tax-free, offshore investments. Needless to say, this gets the goat of the Spanish taxman. The other gripe is the political status of the Rock itself. Spain is like the little boy who kicks his ball into next door's garden, Britain the grouchy old bachelor who says, 'I'm keeping it.' The question of the Rock's sovereignty comes up annually; Spain asks for concessions; Whitehall merely smiles and says, 'Sorry, old chap'.

You'll soon find that Gibraltar has a unique mixture of people – mostly Genoese (who have been around for centuries), along with Maltese, Indians, Spaniards, Jews and Moroccans, all as British as Trafalgar Square; when a referendum on joining Spain was held in the 1960s, they voted it down by 99.6 per cent. The dissenters were

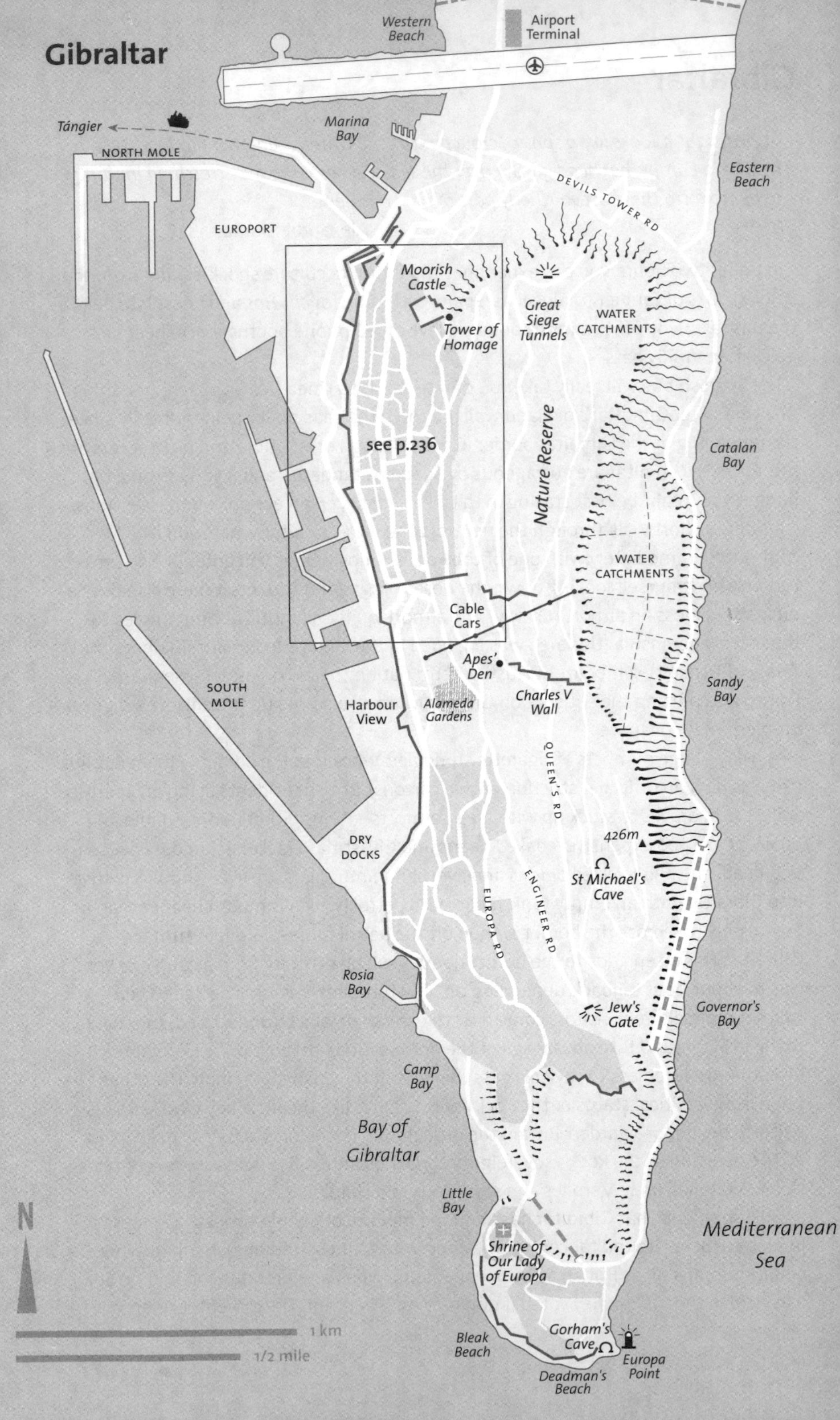
Gibraltar
Western Beach
Airport Terminal
Tángier
Marina Bay
NORTH MOLE
EUROPORT
DEVILS TOWER RD
Eastern Beach
Moorish Castle
Great Siege Tunnels
WATER CATCHMENTS
Tower of Homage
see p.236
Nature Reserve
Catalan Bay
WATER CATCHMENTS
Cable Cars
Apes' Den
Sandy Bay
SOUTH MOLE
Harbour View
Alameda Gardens
Charles V Wall
QUEEN'S RD
DRY DOCKS
426m
St Michael's Cave
ENGINEER RD
EUROPA RD
Rosia Bay
Jew's Gate
Governor's Bay
Camp Bay
Bay of Gibraltar
Little Bay
Mediterranean Sea
Shrine of Our Lady of Europa
N
1 km
1/2 mile
Bleak Beach
Gorham's Cave
Europa Point
Deadman's Beach

tagged *Las Palomas* (the pigeons), and some of these subsequently flew to Spanish climes; they are not missed in Gibraltar.

With English as their official language, most Gibraltarians are, however, bilingual. For many Gibraltarians, Spanish is used in everyday situations and particularly in moments of high emotion; English is generally reserved for more formal situations.

History

Some 50,000 years ago, when Spain was a cooler, more forested place, Neanderthal man was minding his own business in the caves around Gibraltar, long before Palaeo-Spaniards found the rest of Andalucía to be of any interest. The Rock's location, where the continents of Europe and Africa rub noses and the Atlantic Ocean and Mediterranean Sea meet, is one of the world's most important crossroads; as a consequence it has been fought over for centuries. **Calpe**, as the Greeks knew it, was, of course, one of the Pillars of Hercules, beyond which the jealous Phoenicians would permit no other nation's ships to trade. The other, less dramatic, pillar is **Mount Abyla** in Morocco, visible across the straits on clear days.

The Phoenicians may have been the first people to pass through the Straits into the Atlantic, where they traded down the African coast and probably travelled as far north as Britain. They used the Rock solely as a naval base and never entertained the thought of settling there, preferring the more hospitable land near the Bay. Similarly, under Roman rule from 190 BC onwards, there was no permanent settlement.

Six hundred years later the Vandal tribes surged through the Iberian peninsula on their way to North Africa, followed by the Visigoths, who remained as the most powerful local force until the late 7th century AD.

711–1462: Muslim Ascendancy

By the beginning of the 8th century the Moors were poised to invade the Iberian Peninsula, under the new and forceful banner of Islam. Having swept westward through North Africa from Arabia, converting the subjugated population by coercion, the Moors landed a small expeditionary force at what is now Tarifa in 710. The following year, Tariq ibn Ziyad led a determined Berber army of 7,000 men to the Rock that came to bear his name – *Jebel Tariq* (Tariq's Mountain). For the following six centuries Gibraltar remained under Moorish rule. As the Moors moved further north, Gibraltar remained a vital camp, but it was not until 1160 that any sort of permanent settlement was established, under the orders of the Almohad Caliph Abdul Mamen.

Throughout the Moorish occupation of Andalucía, Gibraltar faced a number of sieges at the hands of Moorish caliphs fighting amongst themselves over its control and Christian Spaniards trying to win it back. Guzmán el Bueno seized it for Castile in 1309, and in the centuries that followed it was one of the major battlegrounds of the Mediterranean. It was not until 1462 that the Rock was finally wrested from the Moorish grasp by Enrico IV, King of Castile. (The day of liberation was 29 August, the feast day of St Bernard, the patron saint of Gibraltar.)

Getting There and Around

By Air

There are at least three daily flights from London (Heathrow and Gatwick, run by British Airways in partnership with GB Airways); twice-weekly flights from Manchester and regular flights from Casablanca and Tangier. British Airways has check-in facilities at Victoria, meaning you don't see your luggage again till you arrive. Monarch Airlines also runs regular flights to Gibraltar. **Information**: British Airways, **t** 79 300, **f** 51 562. Monarch Airlines, **t** 47 477, **f** 70 154.

By Sea

There are usually at least three ferries a week from Gibraltar to Tangier and from Tangier to Gibraltar. The fares are expensive, like everything else in Gibraltar. FRS run a high-speed crossing (80mins) but the ferry journey is usually 2–2½hrs. You'd be slightly better off doing it from Algeciras. Bland Line also also run a ferry service; phone for details. **Information**: FRS, **t** 95 668 18 30, *www.frs.es*, (office in Tarifa); TourAfrica, **t** 77 666, **f** 76 754, *tourafri@gibnet.gi*. Bland Line, **t** 77 050, **f** 44 011, *jpg@gibnet.gi*.

By Bus

There is a direct **bus** service between Gibraltar and the Costa del Sol. Gibraltar's tiny buses also serve the frontier, which is only 800m from the town centre.

By Taxi

There is a taxi tour of the Rock, taking in all the sites and lasting about 1½ hours. The charge is about £20, plus additional costs per passenger to include compulsory admission to the Nature Reserve. It's part of a scheme by the taxi drivers' cartel and should be resisted: you can always take the cable car and walk! Gibraltar's taxis also serve the frontier, although iit's only a ½-mile walk from the town centre.

If you are coming by **car** leave it in La Línea, as there are frequently long delays while customs check the day-trippers' stash of goodies in *both directions*.

Information: John L. López, **t** 72 726, *www.gibraltar-rock-tours.com*; Gibraltar Taxi Association, 12 Waterport, **t** 70 052, **f** 76 986, *gibtaxiass@gibnynex.gi*; Gibraltar mini-cab, **t** 79 999.

Tourist Information

Gibraltar Information Bureau, Duke of Kent House, Cathedral Square, **t** 74 950, **f** 74 943, *tourism@gibraltar.gi, www.gibraltar.gi*.

Local Information Bureaux: Market Place, **t** 74 982; Gibraltar Museum, 18–20 Bomb House Lane, **t** 74 805 (*all open weekdays 10–6 and Sat 10–2*). There are booths within the airport terminal and at Waterport coach park, **t** 47 671.

Internet

Café Cyberworld, Unit 14–16, Ocean Heights Gallery, Queensway, **t** 51 416, *cybercafe@gibnet.gi*, £4.50 per hour.

General Internet Business Centre, **t** 44 227, **f** 79 992, *gibc@gibnet.gi*.

Currency

The enclave has its own currency, the Gibraltar pound (which is tied in value to the

1462–1704: The Key of Spain

In 1469 a royal decree proclaimed the son of the Duke of Messina as the rightful owner. Queen Isabel granted the Rock a coat of arms, still used today, with the inscription 'Seal of the Noble City of Gibraltar, the Key of Spain'.

During this time of Spanish occupation the town was divided into three districts: *Villavieja* (the old town), *Barcina* ('wicker basket' – one was used to display the remains of the captured Count of Niebla) and *Turba*, which can be translated as 'mob'; but these names have now disappeared. This was a fairly tranquil period by Gibraltarian standards, until one fine day in 1540 when, as the townsfolk were going

British pound sterling), as well as its own stamps – don't be stuck with any currency when you leave, as it's hard to get rid of anywhere else, especially in Britain! These days, most shops and restaurants in Gibraltar are perfectly happy to take euros, stirling or Gibraltarian money.

Telephones

If you are calling the Rock from elsewhere, the international calling code from Spain to Gibraltar is **t** (9567), and **t** (350).

Shopping

Expats residing in Spain flock across the border to pick up familiar brand-name groceries and household items at British prices; the real bargains are to be had in the top range of luxury goods. Remember that Gibraltar is VAT-free, and savings can be considerable. Here is a selection – but shop around for the best bargains.

Antiques: Lladro, 265 Nao/280, Lalique, Jasons.

Cashmere: Carruana, 181 Main Street (jerseys, suits and fabrics).

Cuban cigars and perfume: S M Seruya, 165 and 187 Main Street, and Stagnetto's, 56 Main Street.

Electronics: 140 Wingsway.

Gifts: 170 Tagore (jewellery, *objets*, silver); The Body Shop, 164 Main Street.

Jewellery: Sakata, 92 Main Street; The Red House, 66 Main Street; The Jewel Box, 148 Main Street, 8 Queensway Quay (cultured pearls, Cartier, Rolex, diamonds, gold).

Menswear: García, 192 Main St (Daks, Burberry, etc.).

Porcelain: Omni, 182 Main Street.

Where to Stay

Gibraltar's hotels have all undergone an extensive refurbishment programme, which has served to modernize and improve most of them; however, it has also put the prices up.

Luxury

Eliott Hotel, Governor's Parade, **t** 70 500, **f** 70 243, *eliott@gibnet.gi, www.gibraltar.gi/eliotthotel*. Offers sterile anonymity for the businessman, along with air conditioning, sauna, Jacuzzi, very pleasant rooftop pool and bar.

Expensive

Rock Hotel, 3 Europa Road, **t** 73 000, **f** 73 513, *rockhotel@gibnynex.gi, www.rockhotel gibraltar.com (20% discount for online bookings)*. A resort hotel of long standing, up on the heights – about halfway up, under the cable car and near Gibraltar's casino. Considering its position and its history, this should be one of the world's great 'colonial' hotels, but sadly it isn't. Visiting dignitaries and the occasional celebrity stay here (past guests include Lennon and Yoko Ono, Winston Churchill, Sean Connery, Errol Flynn), leaving their autographs on the bar menu There's a pool, landscaped gardens and rooms with sea view and balconies, and a very pleasant café with sea views to North Africa and Spain.

★★★★**Caleta Hotel**, Sir Herbert Miles Road, on Catalan Bay, **t** 76 501, **f** 42 143, *www.*

about their daily business, a fleet of 16 galleys, manned by 2,000 men, took them by surprise. These were the hordes of the infamous **Barbarossa**, who operated out of North African bases, raiding ships for goods and slaves; the pirates had decided to break with tradition and sack Gibraltar, having heard of the great booty to be gained.

The horror of that day stands out in Gibraltar's chequered history – a day of slaughter, rape and looting. Some were lucky enough to escape the carnage in the safety of the castle, but most were either killed or taken into slavery. The pirates headed straight for the Shrine of Our Lady of Europa at Europa Point and the Franciscan convent in the town (both well stocked with gold, jewels and precious *caletahotel.com*. If you need a beach, this resort hotel is very modern and recently upgraded. There are rooms with balconies, a pool, good restaurants, and a bar.

Moderate

Bristol, 8–10 Cathedral Square, **t** 76 800, **f** 77 613, *bristhtl@gibnet.gi, www.gib.gi/bristolhotel*. In the heart of town, with a swimming pool, and TV in all rooms.

Continental, 1 Engineer Lane, **t** 76 900, **f** 41 702. Just off Main Street and not quite as comfortable, with a tacky fast-food restaurant on the ground floor.

Inexpensive

Queen's Hotel, just outside the old city walls on Boyd Street, PO Box 99, **t** 74 000, **f** 40 030, *queenshotel@bignynex.gi*. Crumbling and pretty characterless but has less expensive accommodation than other places, and there are good views of the Rock and bay.

Cannon Hotel, 9 Cannon Lane (just off Main Street), **t** 51 711, **f** 51 789, *www.cannonhotel.gi*. You could also try this centrally located hotel with patio, bar and restaurant.

Cheap

Stay in La Línea, if you're on a budget, and you can bear the place. Prices in Gibraltar are two to four times what they would be for comparable hotels in Spain.

The Gibraltar Youth Hostel, Line Wall Road (near the harbour), **t** 51 106. The one opportunity for a cheap room in Gibraltar; they will put you up for around £7 per person per day. Understandably, it is usually full (often with school trips).

Eating Out

Food in Gibraltar is no longer restricted to authentic pub grub and fish n' chips (although both are still available). For the best restaurants on the Rock, get out of the environs of Main Street and head for the recently developed Queensway Quay or the more established Marina Quay, where you will find a good selection of fish, Italian and even tapas restaurants. There are around 360 pubs in Gibraltar, many serving food in one form or another.

See also **Food and Drink** chapter, pp.70–1.

Expensive

Rock Hotel, 3 Europa Road, **t** 73 000, **f** 73 513, *www.rockhotelgibraltar.com*. Arguably the most pleasant place for lunch; its colonial-style décor and discreet waiters set the scene for Gibraltar's answer to Raffles in Singapore. The steaks are flown in fresh from the UK daily.

International Casino Club, 7 Europa Road, **t** 76 666, **f** 40 843. The restaurant in the casino club is popular among the locals, and you won't find a better place for five-star service. Concerned with maintaining high standards, the management used to have a strict ruling on dress – even local celebrities have been turned away for inappropriate attire. Sadly, such standards have slipped and this dress code is no longer enforced, but the food is still as good and there is also often live entertainment. There's a wide range of international dishes on offer, and the terrace has great views overlooking the Bay and Algeciras – a perfect place to watch the sun go down on the Atlantic, if not on the Empire.

coins) and stripped them bare, before making off across the Bay for further pillaging and merrymaking. Overconfidence proved to be their undoing, for the Christian fleet anchored in Tarifa had time to sail along the coast and cut off their escape route. A bloody battle ensued, and what was left of Barbarossa's mob fled back to the sanctuary of its North African ports with just 75 captives in tow. But Gibraltar was left in ruins. From this time on, the Rock was heavily fortified and became an important naval base for Spain's explorations to the Americas, but life was far from peaceful, as a pirate of a different ilk, Sir Francis Drake, would drop in occasionally.

Country Cottage, 13–15 Giros Passage, **t** 70 084. In a lane off Main Street, complete with antique furnishings and Olde Worlde atmosphere. The menu includes sole mornay, shrimp, and meat dishes from *brochettes* to Angus steaks.

Moderate

El Patio, 54 Irish Town, **t** 70 822. A reasonably pleasant spot, if overpriced; it offers Basque cuisine and Mediterranean fish specialities. Particularly popular with the business community, this place fills up at lunchtime. *Closed Sat lunch and Sun.*

La Bayuca, 21 Turnbulls Lane, **t** 75 119. A long-time favourite, not least because of its owners Tita and Johnnie; the walls are lined with photos of its more famous customers, and the décor is pleasantly rustic. The menu is lacklustre: steaks, chicken, fish, and some Mediterranean dishes. *Closed Sun lunch and Tues.*

Strings, 44 Cornwall's Parade, **t** 78 800. A small, intimate place, serving international dishes: smoked salmon, gravadlax, shrimp in wine sauce. *Closed Mon.*

Sax, International Commercial Centre. A piano bar and restaurant that attracts a young crowd; expect queues at weekends. The fare is mixed – English, Mexican, Italian – and the lunchtime menu is particularly recommended; light snacks are also available, and there's live music two evenings a week. *Closed Sun lunch.*

Maharaja, 5 Tuckey's Lane, **t** 75 233. One of a few Indian restaurants; this one has the simplest furnishings of the lot, and offers some of the best food. The service is efficient and friendly, and all the old Indian favourites can be found on the menu.

Bianca's, 6–7 Admiral's Walk, **t** 73 379, **f** 79 061. Come here to sit out and watch the yachts or plane-spot while eating reasonably priced fish, meat and pizza.

Da Paolo, The Tower, Admiral's Walk, **t** 76 799. Our favourite place to eat in Gibraltar, with well-prepared fish specialities, such as fillet of John Dory in dill sauce, a particularly good Spanish wine list, a fine view and enough characters passing through to add interest.

The Little Mermaid, 4–5 Admiral's Walk, **t** 77 660. Danish business interests in the area contributed to the opening of this refreshing addition to the ethnic culinary scene. The interior is sleek and modern, and all the usual Scandinavian specialities appear, including marinated herring, salmon and prawns; help your open sandwiches down with an Aalborg Akvazit and Tuborg chaser, instead of wine.

Waterfront Bar/Restaurant, Queensway Quay, **t** 45 666. Set in a good spot, right on the marina, with good food at reasonable prices; try the excellent *moules marinières*. The mussels are caught from within the bay in season and twice the size of anything you can get back home.

The Maasai Grill, Queensway Quay, **t** 73 546. Serves good Indian food. *Closed Sun.*

Casa Pepe, Unit 18, Queensway Quay, **t** 46 967. Probably Gibraltar's best tapas bar, specializing in paella, *jamón iberico* and fresh fish dishes in taberna-style surroundings. *Closed Wed.*

Raffles, Queensway Quay, **t** 40 362. An extensive choice of tasty English and Spanish dishes at reasonable prices, with paellas and summer barbecues as specialities of the house.

The beginning of the 18th century brought the **War of the Spanish Succession**, with Britain on the side of the Habsburgs against the French. Admiral Sir George Rooke, commanding the Anglo-Dutch fleet, tried to take Toulon and Barcelona and, having failed on both counts, took Gibraltar instead. At the time (1704), Gibraltar was held by forces loyal to the French claimant to the Spanish throne. Rooke offered the inhabitants two choices – to pack their bags and leave, or swear allegiance to the Habsburg claimant. Most opted for the former, probably hoping that the tide of war would change.

Seawave, 60 Catalan Bay Village, **t** 78 739. Serves generous helpings of fresh local fish at reasonable prices with a terrace looking out towards Spain.

La Mamala, Catalan Bay Village, **t** 72 373. A smarter place at the top of the road; also offers a selection of local fish.

Inexpensive

Cheers Brasserie, G1 Cornwall Centre, **t** 79 699. Fills up with tourists at lunchtime and is a popular meeting place, where you can enjoy the large terrace and soak up the sun. The tired snacks include club sandwiches, a variety of salads, and chilli, as well as full English breakfasts.

The Clipper, 78B Irish Town, **t** 79 791. A gastro-pub which is popular with Gibraltarians and visitors alike for its roast beef and lasagne.

The Royal Calpe, 176 Main Street, **t** 75 890. Another pub where the grub, served piping hot, is authentically English and popular with all.

Bull and Bush, 30 Parliament Lane, **t** 72 951. For a parting memory of Gibraltar, drop into this patriotic pub, complete with portrait of the queen. Drinks are chalked up on a slate as in days of yore. Pictures of England and English pubs cover the walls; and there are no tapas in sight

Entertainment and Activities

Many companies offer **guided tours** of Gibraltar and its sights; Bland Travel, Cloister Building, Irish Town, **t** 77 012, also runs a 'Trafalgar Tour' from Rosia Bay to Tarifa in Algeciras during the summer months. There are large populations of whales (although sightings are not that common) and dolphins within the Bay and the Straits of Gibraltar, which makes it an excellent place to see these mammals. A number of companies offer tailored tours for dolphin viewing (the best are listed below). For sports enthusiasts the waters are ideal for activities ranging from windsurfing to scuba-diving. In Marina Bay you can charter yachts or cabin cruisers.

Dolphin Safari, **t** 71 914, **f** 47 326, mobile **t** 607 290 400, *www.dolphinsafari.gi.is*. The original tours, on a glass-bottomed boat.

Nautilus IV, based in Marina Bay, **t** 73 400, *www.dolphin.gi*. Offers tours in a semi-submersible boat, where you can ride above or watch the dolphins through an under-water viewing cabin.

Dive Charters, Marina Bay, **t** 45 649, *www.divegib.gi*, PADI centre. Try here for diving. There are some excellent dive spots off Gibraltar and, not surprisingly, plenty of wrecks, including aircraft.

Rentabike, **t** 70 420. The best bet for moped or scooter hire.

Nightlife

Corks, 79 Irish Town, **t** 75 566. Try this place for a change from the numerous pubs; also serves food.

Casino, 7 Europa Road, **t** 76 666. Gibraltar's late-nightlife happens here – dress well and take lots of cash.

There are a handful of clubs in Gibraltar. Try the **Cool Blues Café**, 310 Main St, **t** 43 111; **The Midnight Club**, 1 Reclamation Rd, **t** 41 458; **Sax II**, Unit F6 International Commercial Centre Building, **t** 52 555; or the **Factory of Sound**, Winston Churchill Ave.

1704 to the Present: British Colonial Rule

With Gibraltar in British hands, the grateful Habsburgs handed it over 'in perpetuity' as a reward, under the 1713 **Treaty of Utrecht**. It was a crucial acquisition; Britain's imperial expansion across the Mediterranean would have been inconceivable without it. Peace did not last long, however, and the Spanish laid siege to the Rock with the aid of French forces in 1727. Destruction was again suffered by the townsfolk, and the area around what is today Casemates Square was completely flattened.

From this point we can trace the mixed heritage of the present population, for after the disappearance of the original Spanish inhabitants it became necessary to import a workforce from around the Mediterranean, especially Genoa. This force helped strengthen the city's defences; Ragged Staff Wharf was constructed, new barracks were built and a number of Spanish churches were turned into accommodation for the troops. New batteries were put up – Montague, Orange and King's Bastion, Devil's Tongue on the Old Mole, Grand Battery north of Grand Casemates with the adjacent Couvreport and King's Lines above, Willis's, Catalan and Green's Lodge Batteries on the Upper Rock, and the Advance Batteries at Europa Point.

The Great Siege, 1779–83

The preparations proved justified. In 1779 a combined Spanish and French force began the worst siege ever experienced by the population. Yet both fortifications and people endured under the command of Lord Heathfield, and the phrase 'safe as the Rock of Gibraltar' came into common use as a result. Gibraltar's rock tunnels and galleries also date from this time. Their construction allowed the gun batteries to take up defensive positions at more commanding heights. The tunnelling continued after the Great Siege, opening up what is known as St George's Hall, a large chamber under 'the Notch'. Now there are approximately 50km of tunnels; Gibraltar is still very well defended.

The Napoleonic Wars, 1799–1815

After a decade of uneasy peace the Gibraltarians were once again in the thick of things – this time at the outbreak of the Napoleonic Wars between Britain and France. For once, Spain was an ally, and it can even be assumed that the people of the Rock actively welcomed the hostilities. Business perked up remarkably – repairing ships, supplying the Royal Navy with food and ammunition, and auctioning off the contents of ships captured by the British fleet. On 21 October 1805, Nelson and his 27 'Wild Geese' triumphed at **Trafalgar**, an event still celebrated in Gibraltar. The admiral was killed during the engagement and his body was borne back to Rosia Bay in a cask of brandy (whence the naval term 'Nelson's Blood'). Ten years later, the end of the war heralded the start of a long period of peace and prosperity for Gibraltar, by which time the population was firmly established in occupations that relied not only on the military presence, but also on external trade.

1814 saw the appointment of Sir George Don as lieutenant governor, a man of considerable calibre. By this time the population had swelled to 10,000, and was badly in need of an efficient civil administration. The new governor embarked on an ambitious programme of improvements: hospitals were built, public gardens laid out, opportunities created for business and trade. Life became peaceful and prosperous.

The World Wars, 1914–45

During the two World Wars, Gibraltar provided a safe harbour where the Allies could repair ships and replenish stocks. In the Second World War many of the civilians were evacuated to safer spots, notably the UK, Madeira, Jamaica and Morocco. (Those who ended up in Morocco were forced to move on again when the Vichy government made it clear they were not welcome.) The airstrip was built at this time, which meant the disappearance of the cricket and football pitches. The miles of tunnels under the Rock were developed further, and used for food storage, hospitals and military headquarters. The invasion of Africa, **Operation Torch**, was spearheaded through Gibraltar, where Eisenhower and his advisers completed much of the planning.

The Question of Sovereignty

By the time the war ended, the Gibraltarians had developed an even deeper sense of identity, partly through being separated from their homeland. In 1950 the Duke of Edinburgh inaugurated the first elected Legislative Council, and in 1964 Gibraltar was granted domestic autonomy, with the UK retaining responsibility for foreign affairs and defence. The 1968 referendum on sovereignty led to the introduction of a new constitution the following year, which entrenched the British promise never to surrender the sovereignty of Gibraltar against the wishes of her people. As a direct consequence, General Franco closed the border, and it did not open again until 1985. This had a profound effect on the population and served only to strengthen its resolve, and deepen the rift with Spain.

Far from being dismayed at the closure of the frontier, many older Gibraltarians were actually disappointed when it was reopened, feeling that they had lost their safe little haven, their isolated 'English village'. They now face the future with some trepidation, always suspicious of their next-door neighbour; they insist on the retention of the wire fence between the two states. The British government is eager to reach an agreement with Spain, an important EU partner, and, in June 2002, it announced that shared sovereignty of the island seemed to be the only way forward. This caused uproar in Gibraltar, and a referendum was called by Gibraltar's chief minister, Peter Caruana: 99 per cent of Gibraltarians voted against the plan. Once again, the British and Spanish governments are forced back to the drawing board.

The Future

Space is at a premium in Gibraltar. Most of the prime parts were owned by the Ministry of Defence (MOD), which has now agreed to confine its operational needs to smaller areas, and has handed the rest over to the Gibraltar government. Since 1990 the scale of the British military presence has been drastically diminished and the three services amalgamated under one command. To give an indication of the severity of the cuts, in 1983 MOD spending was equal to 78 per cent of Gibraltar's GDP; it had dropped to less than 5 per cent by the millennium. This retrenchment has released a certain amount of land and housing for civilian use and prompted successive governments to look elsewhere for income. The existing space was never likely to accommodate the level of growth planned by the socialist GSLP government that took office in the late 1980s. They began an ambitious and extensive programme of land reclamation which continues today and was responsible for Europort, the large complex of commercial offices south of North Mole, which is now the heavily promoted financial heart of Gibraltar. The Rock's banking deposits increased from £1 billion in 1990 to £3 billion in 1996 and they continue to rise under the present government, the GSD, which touts the Rock as a base for the establishment of financial services.

Gibraltar is also involved in a number of refurbishment and renovation projects designed to smarten up the whole place, the first of which was the pedestrianization of Main Street and the refurbishment of Casemates Square. All the hotels have been spruced up, thanks to a £5 million loan from the last administration, though this has led to a number of upgradings and a corresponding increases in rates. There is a spanking new coach park and cruise terminal to deal with the 300 liners which dock here. And the next project is to spruce up the border to present visitors with a good first impression. The reclamation programme has also seen an extension of the industrial zone to the old dockyard region, where new warehousing, light industrial units and ship-repair facilities unite under the name of Harbour View. The programme has also seen the development of Queensway Quay into a smart residential and dining area, with some of the best places to eat on the Rock.

The third phase of Gibraltar's expansion caters for tourism and recreation on the Mediterranean side, at Catalan Bay. In 1999, there were four million visitors to Gibraltar. The latest plan is to join the three beaches on the Eastern side – Sandy Bay, Catalan Bay and Eastern Beach – and make a long sea-front promenade, most of which has already been built, along the entire length. These programmes for housing, industrial and commercial enterprise, and tourism are part of an overall government strategy to create a strong economy underpinned by foreign investment. Geographically, economically and politically, there is no earthly reason why Gibraltar should not flourish as a kind of Monaco of the Southern Mediterranean.

The Town

> *... a cosy smell of provincial groceries. I'd forgotten how much the atmosphere of home depended on white bread, soap and soup squares.*
>
> Laurie Lee, *As I Walked Out One Midsummer Morning*

Despite a degree of bad press, Gibraltar is still much more than just a perfect replica of an English seaside town. The town itself is long and narrow, strung out along **Main Street**, which has most of the shops and pubs. The harbour is never more than a couple of blocks away, and the old gates, bastions and walls are fun to explore.

The short tunnel at **Landport Gate** will probably be your entry point if on foot; dating from the 18th century, it was for a long time the only entrance by land. It leads to **Casemates Square**, one-time parade ground and site of public executions, and now a bustling trading centre. **Grand Casemates** itself, part of the town's defences and barracks, used to provide seedy accommodation for Gibraltar's 2,000-strong Moroccan labour force, but it has been revamped and they now stay elsewhere. **King's Bastion** is now used as an electricity generating station, but probably started out as an ancient Arab gate, added to by the Spanish in 1575 and further extended in the 18th century by the British under General Boyd. It played an important defensive role at the time of the Great Siege, and it was from this spot that General Elliott commanded during the fierce fighting in 1782. **Ragged Staff Wharf** takes its name not

Gibraltar Town

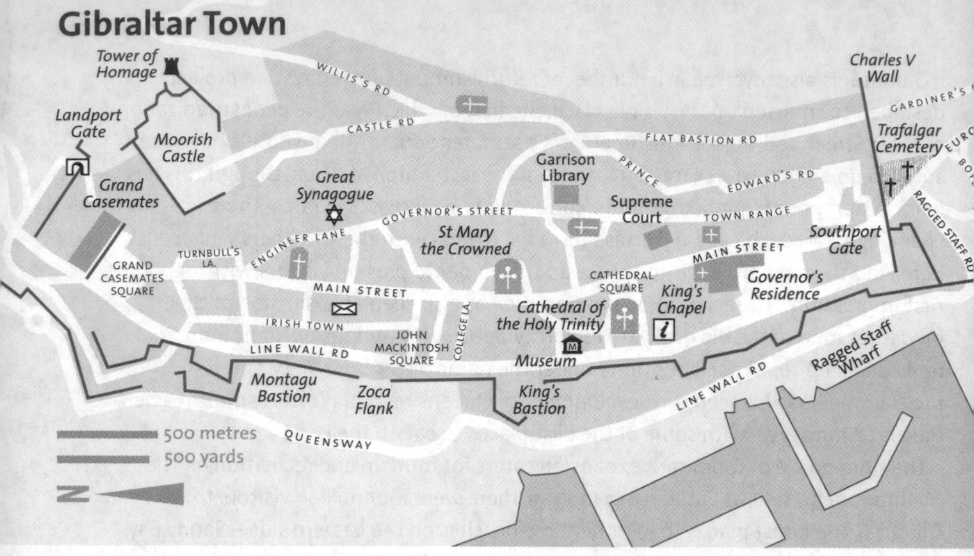

from the sartorial deficiency of its troops, but either from the flagstaff that marked safe passage into the harbour or from an emblem on the arms of the House of Burgundy, to which Charles V belonged.

Near the centre of town, off Line Wall Road, you should spare a few minutes for the small but excellent **Gibraltar Museum**, 18–20 Bomb House Lane (*open Mon–Fri 10–6, Sat 10–2, closed Sun; adm*), which offers a painstakingly detailed room-sized model of the Rock as it was in the mid-1800s, and a thorough schooling in its complicated history. The museum is built over the remains of **Moorish baths**, with Roman and Visigothic capitals on its columns. It also contains a replica of the female skull found in Forbes Quarry in 1848, a find that predates the Neanderthal skull found in Germany by eight years. (Perhaps Neanderthal Man should be known as Gibraltar Woman.) Other exhibits include archaeological finds from Gibraltar's caves; an Egyptian mummy found floating in the Bay by local fishermen, dating from 750 BC and probably from Thebes; a natural history collection; and a gallery devoted to Gibraltar artists – among them Gustavo Bacarisas, Mania and Olimpia Reyes.

In Library Street, in the grand building that was once the Governor's Residence, is the **Garrison Library**, built during the Great Siege in the hope of preventing boredom in sieges to come. Here there are extensive archives on Gibraltar's history. Nearby are the offices of *The Chronicle*, which reported Nelson's victory off Trafalgar. The **Supreme Court** looks diagonally across the street to the 16th-century former Franciscan convent, now the **Governor's Residence**, where the changing of the guard takes place (*check with tourist office for times*). If it's bucketing down, an occurrence frequent in winter months, you can watch these serious proceedings from the warmth and comfort of the Angry Friar, the pub on the corner.

Southport Gate, at the top of Main Street, was built in 1552, during the reign of Charles V and has additions from the 19th century; the wall stretching east from the gate is Charles V's Wall, which ends just short of the water catchments at Philip II's Arch. Beyond the gate you can wander through the small, shady Trafalgar Cemetery, which in fact has the remains of only two sailors from the Battle of Trafalgar, and where sad little inscriptions tell of children killed by disease, and of young men who met their bloody end at sea. The Alameda Gardens, a few yards away, are more cheerful; you can stop in to see the exotic flora before taking the cable car up the Rock to the Apes' Den (*see* below).

The cathedral of **St Mary the Crowned** (between Main Street and Cannon Lane) stands on the site of the chief mosque of Gibraltar, of which some remains can still be seen. The Anglican cathedral of the **Holy Trinity** (off Main Street, near the museum) was consecrated in 1838, and in Engineer Lane the **Great Synagogue**, rebuilt in 1768, is attended by Gibraltar's 700-strong Jewish community. **King's Chapel**, part of the Franciscan convent, was one of the few buildings left standing at the end of the Great Siege, and was an earlier sanctuary for those sheltering from the attack by Barbarossa and his pirates, although the place itself was looted. Legend has it that the chapel is haunted by the grey nun, Alitea de Lucerna, whose family forced her into convent life because they disapproved of her lover. He, however, managed to sneak into the convent, dressed as a Franciscan friar, and the two continued their relationship until, inevitably, they were discovered. The lover drowned as they tried to escape, and poor Alitea remained to stalk the cloisters, bemoaning her lost love.

The Rock

The famous silhouette, surprisingly, does not hang over the seaward edge, but faces backwards towards La Linea. From 500 yards up, the views from the upper part of the Rock are magnificent: the Costa del Sol curves away to the east, the mountains of Morocco sit in a purple haze across the narrow Straits to the south; and way below, where the Mediterranean opens out into the wide and wild Atlantic, tiny toy-like craft plough through the waters in full sail. The Rock's entire eastern face is covered by the **water catchment system** that supplies Gibraltar's water – an engineering marvel to equal the tunnels. The upper part of the Rock has been turned into a **nature reserve** (*open Mon–Sat 9.30 to 7; adm*), which can be reached by cable car (***t** 77 826, leaves every 15 mins 9.30–6, last cable car down at 5.45; adm; closed Sundays*) or through the entrance at Jews' Gate, on the hairpin bend where Engineer and Queen's Roads meet.

Apart from views of a panoramic variety, admission to the reserve will get you a look at Gibraltar's best-known citizens. The **Apes' Den** is halfway up the Rock where you can see Barbary apes, a species of tailless macaque. These gregarious monkeys are much more common on the African side of the straits and in Europe are unique to Gibraltar. There is an old saying that, as long as they're here, the British will never leave. Understandably, they're well cared for, and have been since the days of their great benefactor, Winston Churchill. The Gibraltarians are fond of them, even though (as a local guidebook solemnly notes) they 'fail to share the same respect for private property' as the rest of us. Now that most of their feeding grounds have been built over, they are on the dole, and it's fun to watch them when the official Keeper of the Apes comes round at feeding time. Legend has it that the apes, two packs of them numbering 60 in all, travel to and from their native Morocco by an underground tunnel in the rock. In fact, they were brought over from Africa in ships.

Nearby are remains of a **Moorish wall** and, a short walk to the south, **St Michael's Cave**, a huge cavern of delicate stalactites, now sometimes used as an auditorium. Lower St Michael's Cave was accidentally discovered when the caves were being converted into a military hospital during the Second World War. It contains a huge **underground lake** that is seldom visited (*tours by appointment only; call* ***t*** *55 606,* ***t*** *73 527 or* ***t*** *55 120*). In the 19th century wealthy merchants would rent the cave out for extravagant parties; it was also a favourite venue for illegal duels, away from the censorious eye of the authorities. It's now used for concerts and fashion shows, but do bring a waterproof hat if you attend one of these – the roof leaks (*son et lumière shows can be pre-arranged*).

At the northern end of the Rock, facing Spain, are the Upper Galleries, now called the **Great Siege Tunnels**, an extensive section of the original British tunnels, which were hacked and blown out of the rock during the Great Siege – the work of Sergeant Major Ince, who was rewarded for his labours with a plot of farming land and a race-horse. (Horseracing and hunting were extremely popular; the airport was once the site of a racecourse.) Open to visitors, the Galleries have wax dummies of 18th-century British soldiers hard at work digging and blowing up Spaniards. From here it's a short walk down to the **Moorish castle** probably founded in the 8th century by Tariq ibn-Ziyad, but its best-known feature, the **Tower of Homage**, dates from the 14th century when Abd Hassan recaptured Gibraltar from the Spanish. At present Gibraltar's **prison** is housed in the keep, but hopes are that this will be moved to a new military building. Unfortunately, some rather short-sighted town planning allowed a housing estate to be built within the castle's boundaries, again high-lighting Gibraltar's acute need of space. Just down from here is Gibraltar's last red phone box, on the steps up from Castle Road.

Away from the nature reserve, to the south of the promontory, is the **Shrine of Our Lady of Europa**, adopted as a Catholic chapel in 1462, after which a flame was kept continuously alight – a predecessor to the present lighthouse at Europa Point. Close to the shrine fragments of a Moorish pavement can still be seen. Also nearby is the **Ibrahim-al-Ibrahim Mosque**, a gift from King Fahd of Saudi Arabia used by the thou-sands of Moroccans working on the Rock; it's Europe's most southerly mosque. **Gorham's Cave**, by the shore near Europa Point, was almost certainly inhabited by Neanderthal man. Extensive digs have uncovered important archaeological finds, largely of the animal-remains variety.

If you want to sit on a beach, Gibraltar has a few, but they're all on the eastern side, opposite the town, and accessible by bus. **Catalan Bay** and **Sandy Bay** are both a little built-up and crowded, the former slated for even greater development in the near future. **Eastern Beach** (dubbed 'Margate' in the 19th century) is better, though unfor-tunately it's next to the airport

The Bay of Gibraltar is a favourite playground of schools of dolphins, who on a good day will put on a show for the camera-toting bipeds on the shore (*see* 'Entertaiment and Activities', p.232).

Málaga: The Costa del Sol

12

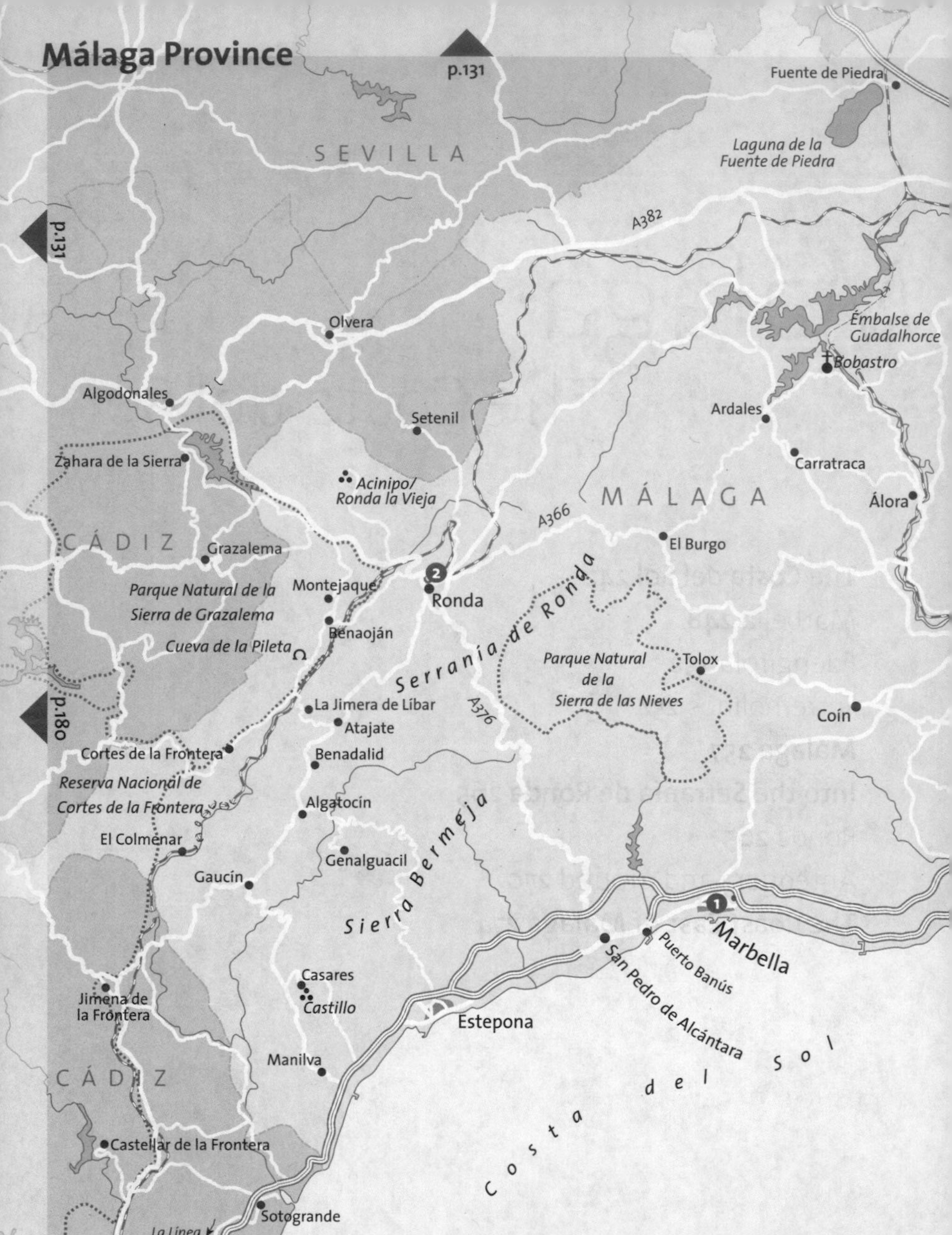

At first glance, it doesn't seem the speculators and developers could have picked a more unlikely place to conjure up the Mediterranean's biggest holiday playground. The stretch of coast between Gibraltar and Málaga is devoid of beautiful scenery, and its long beaches come in a uniformly dismal shade of grey. Spain's low prices are one explanation, and the greatest number of guaranteed sunny days in Europe another. The reason it happened here, though, is breathtakingly simple – cheap land. Forty

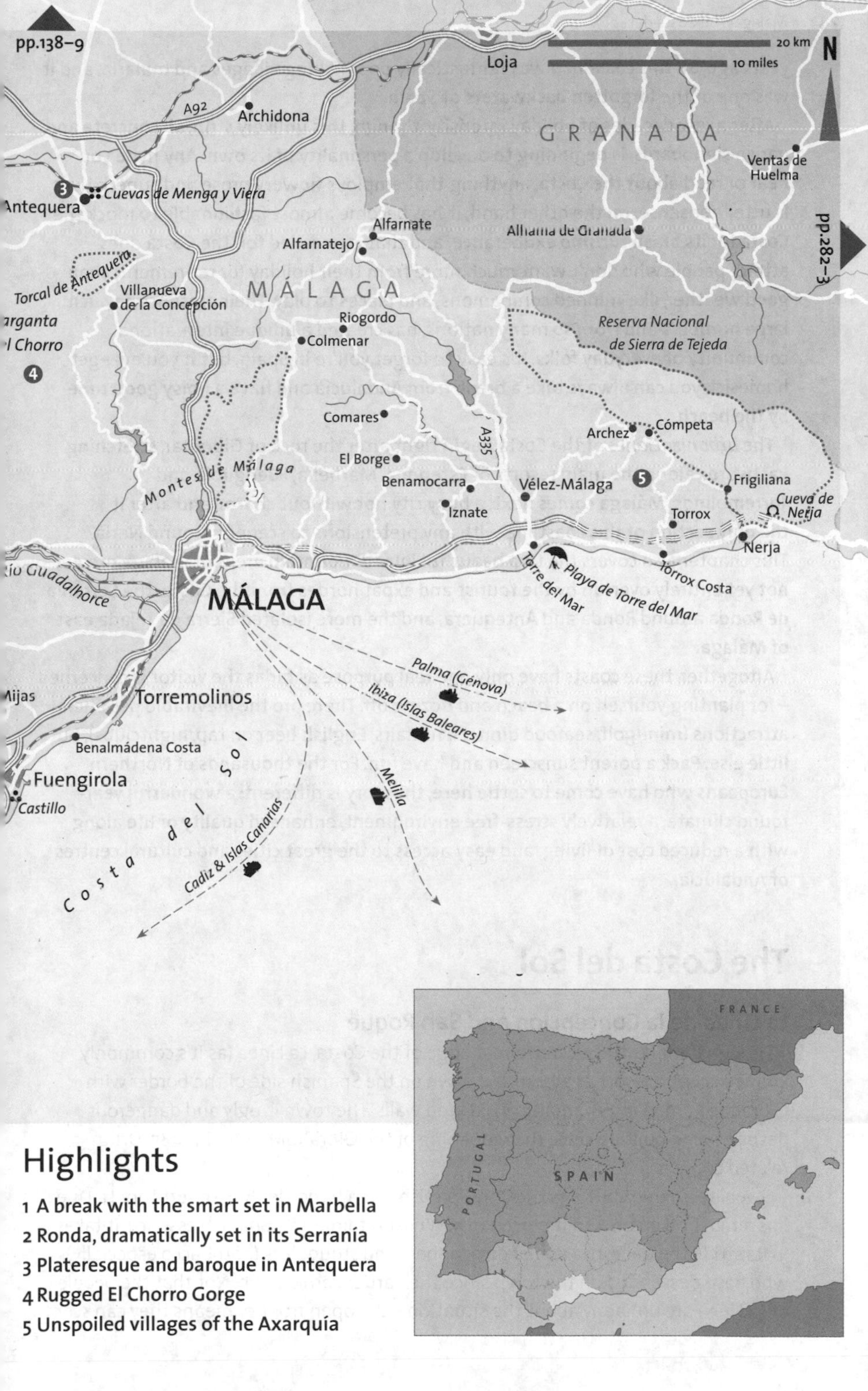

Highlights

1 A break with the smart set in Marbella
2 Ronda, dramatically set in its Serranía
3 Plateresque and baroque in Antequera
4 Rugged El Chorro Gorge
5 Unspoiled villages of the Axarquía

years ago, all this coast had was fantastically poor fishing villages and malaria, and it was one of the forgotten backwaters of Spain.

After a few decades of holiday intensity, though, this unlikely strip, all concrete and garish signboards, is beginning to develop a personality of its own. Any hype you hear or read about the Costa, anything that employs flowery prose and superlatives, is utter nonsense; on the other hand, it has become almost fashionable to mock the Costa for its brash *turismo* exuberance, and that is uncalled for. The Costa does attract people who don't want much more from their holiday (or retirement) than good weather, like-minded companions, and places to play. Their presence, in such large numbers and from so many nations, has created a unique international community of everyday folks. It's easy to forget you're in Spain, but if you ever get homesick you can always take a break from Andalucía and have a noisy good time by the beach.

The *urbanizaciones* of the Costa begin right after the rock of Gibraltar, stretching eastwards along the main resorts of Estepona, Marbella, Fuengirola and Torremolinos. Málaga comes next, a busy city not without charm, and after it the only section of this coastline with any pretensions to scenery, around Nerja. This chapter also covers the two beautiful inland mountain areas of Málaga province, not yet entirely overrun by the tourist and expat hordes from the Costa: the Serranía de Ronda around Ronda and Antequera, and the more isolated Sierra de Tejada east of Málaga.

Altogether, these coasts have only one real purpose as far as the visitor is concerned – for planting yourself on a beach and dozing off. There are the inevitable peripheral attractions (mini-golf, seafood dinners, funfairs, English beer on tap, nightclubs), but little else. Pack a potent sunscreen and have fun. For the thousands of Northern Europeans who have come to settle here, the story is different: a wonderful year-round climate, a relatively stress-free environment, enhanced quality of life along with a reduced cost of living, and easy access to the great cities and cultural centres of Andalucía.

The Costa del Sol

La Línea de la Concepción and San Roque

Though it marks the westernmost edge of the Costa, La Línea (as it's commonly known) is not a resort at all, but the town on the Spanish side of the border with Gibraltar, named after Gibraltar's old land walls. The town is ugly and dangerous despite being built up since the reopening of the Gibraltar border in 1985. Drug-related crime is rife.

Given its unique status as the only Spanish town to border British territory, La Línea has almost taken on a split personality. Whilst retaining its Spanish essence, it takes in its stride the daily invasion of day-trippers and smugglers (of tobacco especially), who have descended on the town since the barrier came down. Not that the people of La Línea are unhappy about the situation – the open frontier means they can scoot

Getting There and Around

By Bus

Two bus companies serve La Línea: Transportes Comes runs the service to Algeciras (every 30mins) and points west; and the Portillo company serves the Costa del Sol, Málaga and Madrid. The bus station, **t** 95 617 23 96, is on the Plaza de España, just off La Línea's central square. From here it's a 6min walk to the border with Gibraltar.

By Train

The nearest railway station, 12km away at San Roque-La Línea, has services to Ronda, with connections to other destinations in Andalucía.

Tourist Information

Avda 20 de Abril, just off the Plaza de la Constitución (next to the bus station), **t** 95 676 99 50, **f** 95 676 72 64. *Open Tues–Fri 9–7, Sat 10–2, Mon 9–3.*

Where to Stay and Eat

La Línea ✉ 11300

The only reason to stay in La Línea is that it is cheaper than staying in Gibraltar (although more expensive than surrounding villages because of its proximity to the Rock). The hotels here are mostly as dull as the town. Eating out is cheaper than in Gibraltar, particularly if you want to spoil yourself on fish.

★★★**AC Hotel La Línea**, Los Caireles 2, **t** 95 617 55 66, **f** 95 617 15 63 (*expensive*). Has a first-class view of the Rock and the Bay of Algeciras. The bullfighter El Cordobés used to stay here, but now it's part of a massive chain.

★★★**Mediterráneo Costa**, Paseo Marítimo s/n, **t** 95 617 56 66, **f** 95 610 54 44 (moderate). A modern hotel overlooking the bay.

★**La Campana**, C/Carboneros 3 (just off the main plaza), **t** 95 617 30 59 (*inexpensive*). This *pensión* is the best bargain in town; there's a good little restaurant downstairs with a cheap *menú del día*.

★★**Hotel Florida**, C/Sol 1, **t** 95 617 13 00 (*inexpensive*). Well placed, though recommended only if you are on a budget.

La Marina, Paseo Marítimo, **t** 95 617 15 31 (*moderate*). The speciality here is a favourite of the southern coast of Spain: grilled sardines on a spit.

El Mirador, Playa Sta Bárbara, **t** 95 617 08 91 (*inexpensive*). As its name might suggest, this restaurant is in an excellent position to view the Rock; specializes in paella.

Mesón La Jerezana, C/San Pablo, 6, **t** 95 676 34 91. On the central pedestrian thoroughfare, this serves simple, inexpensive *raciones*.

La Perrada, Pza de la Iglesia (*inexpensive*). Offers tasty tapas at reasonable prices.

over in their coffee breaks to buy up tax-free goods and off-the-peg clothing, hoping that Spanish customs aren't too rigorous in their searches on the way back.

But the *linenses* are still guarded about their colonial neighbours, and not for reasons of politics. They have in the past had to suffer the jolly old British tradition of street brawls involving servicemen, although admittedly this practice is now in decline due to the lack of remaining soldiers and vigilant military police. La Línea's reputation is not exactly unblemished either – stray too far from the centre of town or the waterfront after dark, and there are some exceedingly seedy people skulking in dark doorways, hungry for your money, whether by selling you drugs or stealing your wallet.

There is little to detain you in La Línea. Only the 19th-century church of **La Inmaculada**, with its Baroque-style altar; and the **Cruz Herrera Museum**, tucked away in a modern delapidated building just off the main square, Plaza de la Constitución, on Calle Carboneros.

San Roque, just 8km away, is infinitely more attractive, perched on a hilltop and with a typically *andaluz* maze of steep, narrow streets lined with whitewashed houses sprouting flowers from the balconies. It was founded by Gibraltarians, who rejected a British offer to remain on the Rock when it was captured in 1704 and established their own colony while they waited for Spanish rule to be restored. They didn't get the island back, and suffered a second British invasion instead: this time from affluent 20th-century second-homers who bought up much of the property and built a ring of luxurious villa developments. San Roque doesn't have much in the way of sights, but you can gaze out at Gibraltar from the *mirador* (half-hidden behind the smoke billowing from the San Roque oil refinery on the outskirts of La Línea), and take a look at the local curiosity in the town hall: the Pendón de Gibraltar, a pennant traditionally believed to have been embroidered by Juana la Loca, the supposedly mad daughter of Queen Isabel.

Sotogrande to Marbella

Thirty years ago Gibraltarians who had money bought villas in Algeciras or San Roque. Nowadays they prefer **Sotogrande**, a relatively old-established British enclave 10 minutes along the Costa from Gibraltar, where middle- and upper-middle-class Brits who don't go to Tuscany for their holidays have established a comfortable, manicured and totally un-Spanish colony. Apart from some big houses and a couple of polo fields, this glorified *urbanización* isn't nearly as interesting as the rather forbidding barriers at the entrance would suggest. The more recent **Puerto Sotogrande**, 10km east along the coast, is an up-and-coming marina complex with restaurants, shops and apartments. It could be worth a stop for lunch to break the drive along the Costa.

The first town of any note you will come to is unprepossessing **Manilva**, where there are ruins of a **Roman spa**. The old spring still pours out strange, sulphurous water, and the locals still drop in to bathe. **Sabinillas**, Manilva's coastal extension, is making valiant attempts to transform itself into a resort, with hotels, a golf course and a marina popping up. There is an 18th-century fort, and of course a number of built-up beaches. Historically, Manilva was linked with **Casares**, up in the Sierra Bermeja, a typical white Andalucían village perched on a steep hill under the ruins of its castle. The village, which was granted independence in 1796, has several monuments, a restored house belonging to Blas Infante's uncle, and a collection of Roman ruins.

Estepona, the first of the big resort towns east of Gibraltar, is also the quietest. Unfortunately the big developers have moved in, concrete blocks are sprouting up all over the place and the town is losing its former appeal. The biggest attraction appears to be a nudist beach and club, **Costa Natura** (incidentally, the oldest in Spain of any size), although a touch of its past fishing-village simplicity has returned, now that the bypass diverts the horrendous traffic which used to slice through the centre of town.

The **Paseo Marítimo** has been completely refurbished since the great cut in traffic and makes for a very pleasant evening stroll, where you can stop in at any of the cafés

Getting There and Around

By Bus

The Portillo bus company has the franchise for this stretch of coast; and with the growth of tourism its service has become almost like a city bus-line, stopping every few hundred yards in the developed areas between Algeciras and Málaga. Be sure to check how long your bus will take to arrive if you're planning an intercity journey, and change to an express service if necessary.

There's never too long a wait in either direction. San Pedro is where the buses branch off for Ronda, an easy destination from any town on the coast. You can also go directly to Sevilla or Madrid from the bus station in Marbella, Avda del Trapiche, **t** 95 276 44 00.

By Train

The N340 connects all the towns and villages along the coast , though at Fuengirola you can pick up a suburban train, which runs a regular service to Málaga. It stops at Torremolinos and most other points in between (including the airport).

By Car

There is also the motorway, rather confusingly called the N340 or E15, but with a *peaje* or toll system. It bypasses all the towns, and is fast and usually empty.

Tourist Information

Casares: Town Hall, C/Fuente 24, **t** 95 289 40 56.

Estepona: Avda San Lorenzo 1, **t** 95 280 20 02, **f** 95 279 21 81. *Open Mon–Fri 9–6, Sat 9–1.30; closed Sun.*

San Pedro de Alcántara: Avda Marqués del Duero 69, **t** 95 278 52 52.

To discover what's on, check the local publications – *Lookout*, a magazine for the British on the Costa, *The Entertainer* or *The Reporter*; a weekly English edition of Málaga's newspaper *Sur*, which appears every Friday; and various local entertainment guides.

Where to Stay and Eat

Manilva ✉ 29691

★★★★**Duquesa Golf and Country**, **t** 95 289 12 11 (*expensive*). This is *the* place to stay – located in the marina area, and with all the facilities you would expect.

Hostal Buenavista, Iglesia 29, in Sabinillas, **t** 95 289 12 11 (*Inexpensive*). A non-descript *pensión* in town.

Hostal Sibajas, Pza San Luis de Sabinillas, **t** 95 289 02 59 (*inexpensive*). Another basic option in town.

Manilva has a surprising number of decent restaurants, most near Castillo de la Duquesa.

Mesón del Castillo, C/Miramar 12, **t** 95 289 07 66 (*moderate*). Offers *rabo del toro*, as well as fish and shellfish specialities.

Hachomar, San José 4, **t** 95 289 03 47 (*moderate*). Specializes in seafood.

Estepona ✉ 29680

The main road to Estepona from Marbella has some of the finest hotels along the Costa del Sol, most of which have their own beach and extensive facilities, but be warned: this sort of splendour does not come cheap. The town has a dearth of quality hotels, although there are a number of two-star places.

★★★★★**Las Dunas Beach Hotel and Spa**, Ctra 340, km 163, **t** 95 279 43 45, **f** 95 279 48 25, *www.las-dunas.com* (*luxury*). One of the 'Leading Hotels of the World', and with prices to match (over €600 for a double in high season), complete with health spa plus

and bars that line its length. The old town remains a pleasant, quiet place, with narrow streets and some very pretty squares including **Las Flores**, bursting with palms and flowers and fringed by some good bars and restaurants, and **Plaza del Reloj**, named after the 15th-century clock tower, all that remains of a church built by Henry IV of Castile. It has a modern bullring, a covered market on C/Castillo and a marina, the **Puerto Deportivo**, where you can grab a beer and a bite to eat while you all the treatments, restaurants, bars, live music, vast pool.

*******Kempinski Hotel**, Ctra 340, km 159, **t** 95 280 95 00, **f** 95 280 95 50, *www.kempinski-spain.com* (*luxury*). About half the price, but almost as luxurious, offering a private beach, health and beauty centre and a number of quality restaurants.

*******Gran Hotel Playabella**, Ctra 340, km 163, **t** 95 288 08 68, **f** 95 288 02 68, *www.hotelesplaya.com* (*luxury*). A modern resort hotel set in tropical gardens, with sleek, stylish rooms with sea views. Sailing, tennis, 3 outdoor pools and tennis courts, plus 40 golf-courses almost on the doorstep.

******Hotel Atalaya Park**, Ctra 340, km 169, **t** 05 288 90 00, **f** 95 288 90 19, *www.atalaya-park.es* (*luxury*). The biggest along this stretch, with 900 rooms, and despite one less star than the Kempinski,this is in fact a bit pricier. However, if you are a sports fan then this is the one to go for: nine tennis courts, a football pitch, athletics track, basketball, volleyball and one of the best golf courses on the Costa.

******El Paraíso**, Ctra 340, km 168, **t** 95 288 30 00, **f** 95 288 90 02, *www.hotelparaiso costadelsol.com* (*luxury*). Set back from the sea but with a golf course, swimming pool, gardens, health centre, restaurants, tennis courts and more.

****Dobar**, Avda de España 178, **t** 95 280 06 00 (*inexpensive*). Functional and the best value in terms of location, situated right on the seafront.

****Aquamarina**, Avda San Lorenzo 32, **t** 95 280 61 55, **f** 95 280 45 98 (*moderate–inexpensive*). Just down from the *turismo*, with clean, spacious doubles, many with balconies, all with bath and air conditioning and a stone's throw from the beach.

***Buenavista**, Paseo Marítimo 180, **t** 95 280 01 37 (*inexpensive*). The best bet for a modicum of concrete splendour near the beach.

There are plenty of inexpensive *hostales* both in the town and on the beach.

***El Pilar**, Pza de las Flores 10, **t** 95 280 00 18 (*inexpensive*). Overlooking Estepona's prettiest square.

***La Malagueña**, C/Castillo 1, **t** 95 280 00 11 (*inexpensive*). Next to El Pilar and offering much the same for the same price.

There are lots of restaurants in and around Estepona, some of them very good indeed. Fish, of course, is the town's speciality, particularly *fritura malagueña, and espetos de sardinas*.

Típico Andaluz, **t** 95 280 18 02, and **Bodega Sabor Andaluz**, **t** 95 279 10 30. A pair of restaurants at the far end of C/Caridad, offering wonderful *embutidos* such as *jamón iberico* and *queso manchego*.

La Casa de Mi Abuela, C/Caridad 54, **t** 95 279 19 67 (*moderate*). Offers a selection of grills, including Argentinian-style *churrasco*.

Taberna Marinera, **t** 95 279 63 26 (*moderate*). One of many restaurants at the marina specializing in fish.

La Sal, Edificio Montemayor Cancelada, **t** 95 388 83 69. Diminutive, pretty restaurant serving up some of the finest local dishes in town. Try the excellent paellas and *fideuás*.

Mesón Genaro, C/Lozano (*inexpensive*). Offers very reasonably priced tapas, such as *chorizo, morcillo* and *pulpo*.

La Taberna Real, C/Real 24, **t** 60 759 28 46 (*inexpensive*). Good tapas and home-cooking (including couscous on Wednesdays).

San Pedro de Alcántara ✉ 29670

*****El Pueblo Andaluz**, Avda Luís Carrillo Benítez, **t** 95 278 05 97, **f** 95 278 91 04, *commercial@globales.com* (*expensive–moderate*). A pretty place near

study the classy yachts. And, for a glimpse of how it all once was along this coast, get down to the port, at the far west side of town, to watch the fishing boats come in from about 6am. On the way out of town towards Cádiz are a number of towers – lookout points dating back to Roman times and refurbished by the Moors as a defence against pirates.

the beach built around an old Andalucían home with a pool, playground, restaurant and garden.

★★★**Cortijo Blanco**, **t** 95 278 09 00, **f** 95 278 09 16, *commercial@globales.com* (*expensive–moderate*). Near El Pueblo Andaluz, of a similar quality and run by the same management, but with a few extra facilities such as parking and a nursery. It also allows pets.

★**Marta**, C/Lagasca 24, **t** 95 278 33 36 (*cheap*). One of several *hostales* in town.

There is a wide variety of bars and restaurants in San Pedro itself, on the 'Ronda Road' as you leave towards the Sierras, and in Nueva Andalucía, a vast area of beautiful countryside between San Pedro and Marbella which boasts a great deal of high-quality residential development.

Alfredo, Avda Andalucía, Local 8, **t** 95 278 61 65 (*moderate*). A choice selection of fresh grilled fish and meats; the lively atmosphere buzzes.

Méson El Coto, **t** 95 278 66 88 (*moderate*). A handsome Andalucían house with magnificent views over sea and mountains and a top-class kitchen specializing in delicious grills and seasonal game. It is situated 6km above town on the road to Ronda so you'll need a car or taxi.

El Gamonal, Ctra Ronda–Camino La Quinta, **t** 95 278 99 21 (*moderate*). A very pretty Spanish restaurant, specializing in roasts. Cosy inside, with a flowering terrace, it is tucked inside Nueva Andalucía near La Quinta. *Closed Wed.*

Ogilvy & Mailer, **t** 95 281 53 98 (*moderate*). On a charming site by Los Naranjos Country Club, stylish without claiming to be particularly Spanish; serves some of the finest and most innovative Mediterranean food on the coast, accompanied by Carol Mailer's carefully selected wines. A memorable evening here is surprisingly reasonable for this kind of quality. *Closed Sun.*

Entertainment and Nightlife

For a place supposedly in the shadow of its wild sister up the road in Marbella, **Estepona** has a lot to offer, especially at the weekends. Since C/Real was pedestrianized the town centre has exploded with clubs and bars.

La Jerezana, C/Extremadura. A shrine to legendary flamenco star el Camarón de la Isla, who died of a heroin overdose. There are pictures of him all over the walls; if you hang around long enough you may be treated to some impromptu hand clapping and guitar.

97, C/Caridad 97. One of a number of good bars along this street, many with an emphasis on food.

Cue, C/Real. Minimalist and chic.

There are a few discos in town, including the trendy **Melodie Cool** (C/Real, just behind the seafront) and **Niágara** (Avda Juan Carlos I), but for later night action head to the marina where there are a number of other discos, including **Chico Diez** and **Mambo**. In summer, there's the massive outdoor disco **El Campo**.

Sports and Activities

Escuela de Arte Ecuestre, Rio Padrón Alto, Ctra 340, km 159, **t** 95 288 47 02. A horse-riding school built in traditional *andaluz* style.

Estepona Golf, **t** 95 211 30 08.

Happy Divers Club, Hotel Atalaya, Ctra N340, km 168, **t** 95 288 90 00, **f** 95 280 81 66, *www.happy-divers-marbella.com*. Scuba-diving centre offering a number of courses and excursions; also has a branch at the marina.

San Pedro de Alcántara along the coast is a little fancier, though still pleasingly unsophisticated to look at. Most of the town is a fair distance from the beaches (though walkable). From here the only good road through the mountains will take you to Ronda and its surrounding villages – the best excursion you can make from the Costa.

Marbella

Marbella finds herself more or less in the middle of the stretch of coast said to be the fastest-growing area in Europe, so it is not without its growing pains. Until recently, zoning laws were permissive to the point of being totally ineffective and developers, eager to make a quick profit, threw up one unattractive building after another. But for every ugly development there is a stunningly beautiful one, carefully preserving Andalucían tradition and delightfully landscaped with trees, lawns and flowering shrubs. So, despite her limited charm for the 'serious' traveller, Marbella continues to thrive, and the fun-loving teenager she was is now turning into a respectable matron. Wild parties, eccentric ways and a live-for-today attitude have given way to serious business, fuelled by the property boom on the Costa del Sol in the 1980s.

Marbella is the smartest, most expensive and complex resort in Spain. When you arrive, you might find yourself asking why – its appeal is not obvious. When you get to know it, this in itself becomes one of Marbella's greatest attractions. The place has been much maligned and, it's true, over-developed, but the old quarter of town, with the pretty orange-blossom scented **Plaza de los Naranjos** as its centrepiece, is still a delight, as whitewashed and charming as Andalucía at its most typical, and without being too cutesy or tripperish – at least out of season. The self-contained *urbanizaciones* around Marbella and the continuing expansion of Puerto Banús and its surrounding area have actually done the old town a favour, reducing the number of chi-chi shops and 'returning' Marbella to the Spanish whose home it is. If you are ever in doubt as to whether Spaniards actually live here, come in May when Marbella's *feria* is in full swing – it's an event you're unlikely to forget.

Nonetheless, for the earnest tourist there is not a great deal of point in spending time in the town. You'll pay high prices without getting in on the action, which takes place in a score of private clubs, private villas and private yachts. There are a couple of attractions worth a visit: in the heart of the old town, the **Museo del Grabado** on C/Hospital Bazán (*open Tues–Sat 10–2 and 5.30–8.30; adm*) is housed in an immaculately restored 16th-century hospital and has an extensive collection of etchings by Dalí, Miró and Picasso among others. Dedicated fans of the Bonsai tree can make a pilgrimage to the **Museo del Bonsái** in the Parque del Arroyo de la Represa (*open 10.30–1.30 and 5–8.30 in July and August; 10.30–1.30 and 4–7 during the rest of the year; adm*). Two kilometres south of Marbella is the new **mosque**, financed by King Abdulaziz al-Saud, who also built himself a palace (in the style of the White House) next to it and occasionally turns up with a fleet of limousines and an army of staff.

Few foreigners actually live in old Marbella itself; self-styled artists and flashy bachelors take studios in **Puerto Banús**, English and Scandinavian golfers head for 'Golf Valley' in **Nueva Andalucía**, and well-heeled, well-dressed French, Italians and Germans heave-ho at the **Marbella Club** and **Puente Romano**, both situated a few miles west of town. **Puerto Banús** is the brilliantly designed, ancient-looking (but modern) development 6km to the west, with a marina full of gin palaces; don't pass up the chance of spending an afternoon or evening in one of the many waterside

Getting There and Around

By Bus

Marbella is well connected by bus, with frequent Portillo services trundling into town (if you are coming from Estepona or San Pedro de Alcántara), or into the new bus station north of the town on C/Trapiche.

By Car

The N340 connects all the towns and villages along the coast, passing just north of the centre of Marbella. There is also the motorway, rather confusingly called either the N340 or E15. It is usually fast and empty, but has a *peaje* or toll system.

Tourist Information

Marbella: Glorieta de la Fontanilla, **t** 95 277 14 42. *Open Mon–Fri 9.30–9.30 or 9.30–8.30 in winter, and Sat 10–4 or 10–2 in winter.* There's also an office on Pza Los Naranjos, **t** 95 282 35 50.

Puerto Banús: Avda Principal, **t** 95 281 74 74.

Where to Stay

Marbella ✉ 29600

There are fewer hotels than you might imagine in the Marbella area, where villa life is very much the form. Don't count on finding a room at any price during the season; package tours have taken over here just as they have in the resorts to the east, and most places are booked pretty solidly.

Luxury

★★★★**Los Monteros**, Ctra Cádiz, km 187 (6km east of Marbella), **t** 95 277 17 00, **f** 95 282 58 46, *www.monteros.com*. One of the oldest hotels in these parts, and for many the best-loved. Its beach club is the height of restrained luxury and room prices include green fees at the hotel's own Río Real golf course.

★★★★★**Meliá Don Pepe**, Avda José Meliá, **t** 95 277 03 00, **f** 95 277 99 54, *www.solmelia.com*. Another luxury, family-orientated hotel, facing out over the sea. It has a large sports complex, including an 18-hole golf course, 11 tennis courts, 5 squash clubs, a riding school, heated pool, gym and sauna.

★★★★★**Puente Romano**, Ctra Cádiz, km 1/8, **t** 95 282 09 00, **f** 95 277 57 66, *www.puenteromano.com*. One of the most beautiful, if not the most expensive, hotels. Its name comes from the genuine Roman bridge incorporated into its lovely surroundings.

★★★★**Marbella Club Hotel**, Boulevard Príncipe Alfonso de Hohenlohe, **t** 95 282 22 11, **f** 95 282 98 84, *www.marbellaclub.com*. Alfonso de Hohenlohe's jet-set retreat, which put Marbella on the map in the late 1950s, is still going strong and is Marbella's most sophisticated hotel. A week with full board would have cost you less than £4 per person in 1959; not so now.

Expensive

★★★★**El Fuerte**, Avda El Fuerte s/n, **t** 95 286 15 00, **f** 95 282 44 11, *www.fuertehoteles.com*. Ideally placed next to the Marbella shopping centre, at the end of the promenade overlooking the sea.

★★★**Las Chapas**, Ctra Cádiz, km 192, **t** 95 283 13 75, **f** 95 283 13 77. A nearly self-sufficient holiday complex with opportunities for tennis, golf and water sports; situated right on the beach on the coastal highway, 8km to the east of Marbella.

Moderate

★★★**Don Miguel Club Med**, **t** 95 277 28 00. If screaming infants and round-the-clock disco beats are your thing, you could do worse than try here. In the hills above Marbella (you won't need the address), Club Med does everything for you, from meeting you at the airport and minding your children to escorting you to the bullfight. It's likely to be a little regimented for some, but the food is sensational, at least in quantity. It helps if you speak French.

Inexpensive

Surprisingly, there is a wide selection of *hostales* in the €30–50 range, most of them in the old town, around Calle Peral and Calle San Francisco.

★★**Hostal Enriqueta**, Los Caballeros 18, **t** 95 282 75 52. Particularly well placed, near the Plaza Los Naranjos, with rooms set around a patio.

★★**Hotel Paco**, C/Peral 16, **t** 95 277 12 00. An adequate two-star option (*open April–mid-Oct*).

Cheap

Hostal de Pilar, C/Mesconcillo 4, **t** 95 282 99 36. British-run and popular mostly with young budget travellers. Lively bar, too.

Albergue Juvenil Marbella, C/Trapiche 2, **t** 95 277 14 91, **f** 95 286 32 27. A youth hostel with rooms for 2–6 and a pool.

Eating Out

There's a wealth of places to suit all tastes and pockets in and around Marbella.

Expensive

Hostería del Mar, Avda Cánovas del Castillo 1A, **t** 95 277 02 18. In summer you can dine on the patio looking onto the swimming pool, while the restaurant is cosy inside in winter. Specialities include chicken and prawns Catalan-style, stuffed quail, roast duck in a sauce of *cassis* and candied figs. *Open evenings only, closed Sun.*

El Portalón, Ctra de Cádiz 178, **t** 95 282 78 80. Opposite the Marbella Club. This has become one of the most exclusive and talked-about restaurants on the Costa del Sol. The freshest local produce is used in the creative, contemporary cuisine with a Basque flavour. And if you've had enough of seafood, it's got the perfect antidote with excellent roast meats.

Villa Tiberio, Ctra Cádiz km 178.5, **t** 95 277 17 99. A well-appointed restaurant with affordable prices, soft music and luxurious surroundings. Your Italian host will kiss you (if you're female) on both cheeks, whether or not he has ever clapped eyes on you before. Good *antipasto* dishes include the *bresaola con aguacate* (thinly sliced cured beef with avocado), and delicious pasta. Main courses are good, too, though less adventurous.

La Meridiana, Camino de la Cruz s/n (just behind the mosque), **t** 95 277 61 90. Marbella's most expensive and glamorous restaurant, offering international cuisine and designer dishes such as salad of monkfish marinated in dill, or braised veal sweetbreads with grapefruit. *Open eves only in summer.*

Francis Butler's Rustic Farmhouse, Finca Besaya, Río Verde Alto, **t** 95 286 13 82. Butler is usually a charming host and the Baroque farmhouse interior is a magnificently tasteful testament to his background as a former West End theatre designer. There's a terrace overlooking the avocado trees and several rooms littered with antiques and warmed by open fires during the winter. He serves an international cuisine which includes duck breast in mango sauce and an exquisite chocolate sorbet, and if the mood takes him he will do a couple of party pieces for you; high camp is the order of the day. Reservations essential (if only to ask for directions). *Open eves Wed–Sat.*

Toni Dalli, The Oasis Club, Ctra Cádiz, km 176, **t** 95 277 00 35. Another special outing in Marbella, this restaurant is housed in a Moorish mansion with a central courtyard and a magnificent view of the beach. The owner, Dalli, a retired Italian opera singer, often entertains his customers personally with an aria; otherwise there's the regular lively showbiz band to tap your toes to. Italian food is obviously the order of the day.

La Hacienda, Ctra Cádiz, km 193, Urbanización Las Chapas, **t** 95 283 11 16. This Relais et Châteaux establishment east of Marbella is frequently described as the best restaurant on the Costa del Sol. It prides itself on its super-fresh ingredients, but the service can be surly and the atmosphere strained. Try the hake in wine sauce, river crab and mushroom salad, fresh pasta, home-made ice cream. Dining out on the terrace, among the statues and stone arches, will set you back around €60. *Closed Mon and Tues, Sept–June and 14 Nov–21 Dec.*

Santiago, Pso Maritímo 5, **t** 95 277 00 78. Try this long-established place for the best *paella* in Marbella, suckling pig, or white beans with clams – in fact some of the best

Spanish cooking on the coast. One room is dedicated to the late Camilo José Cela, Nobel prize-winning novelist, who visited often.

La Torre, Muelle de Honor, Club de Mar, Puerto Banús, **t** 95 281 15 61. At the end of the marina with wonderful views out to sea, and excellent seafood, but at a price.

Silk's, Muelle de Levante, Puerto Banús, **t** 95 281 41 88. A French restaurant concentrating on lobster, caviar and champagne, currently in vogue with the more-money-than-sense set.

Moderate

La Pesquera, Plaza de la Victoria s/n, **t** 95 277 80 54. One of the oldest *marisquerías* in Marbella, serving some of the best-value seafood meals in the area.

La Relojera, Puerto Pesquero, **t** 95 277 14 47. Sit on the roof terrace overlooking the fishing port and watch the trawlers head out to sea while dining on tasty barbecued fish.

Dalli Pasta Factory, Avda Fontanilla s/n, in the centre of Marbella, **t** 95 277 67 76. Toni Dalli seems to be building an empire around Marbella, and no one begrudges him and his three charming sons their well-deserved success. This restaurant serves fresh pasta, delicious *antipasto* and a spicy *tagliolini rabiaha* (pasta with prawns and chillis). You can eat well with wine for a very reasonable price here. In Puerto Banús the Dalli brothers' Pasta and Pizza factories stand next door on Calle Rivera.

Restaurante Mena, Plaza de Los Naranjos 10, **t** 95 277 15 97. Has a good reputation, serving superb *paella*, fish and seafood plus roast leg of yearling lamb and Châteaubriand.

Brasserie Vinoteca, Ctra Cádiz 176.5, **t** 95 277 12 11. Delicious grilled meat and seafood, a lengthy wine list and more than 40 kinds of cigars on offer.

Inexpensive

The tapas bars of Marbella are excellent, both in the old town and in the streets behind the Alameda, such as Calle Carlos Mackintosh. Plenty of inexpensive places, mostly specializing in seafood, can be found in the area around Calle Aduar. Many of the inexpensive beach restaurants that run the length of the coast, known as *chiringuitos*, are open year-round. You won't go far wrong anywhere with a plate of grilled sardines, but some places are inevitably better than others.

Balcón de la Virgen, C/Remedios 2, **t** 95 277 60 92. Charming little restaurant set in a 17th-century house in the old town. Good *cazuelas* (stews) and desserts.

Freiduría Miraflores, Avda del Mercado 22, **t** 95 282 68 02. You'll be lucky to get a seat at this Marbellan favourite: excellent *pescado frito* at a great price.

Casa La Vieja, Calle Aduar 18, **t** 95 282 13 12. Serves up a good plate of mixed fish.

Victor's Beach, Urbanización El Ancón. West of Marbella, attracting a young and trendy crowd in summer.

Entertainment and Nightlife

Most action will be found in Puerto Banús, with its late bars, discos and piano bars. The best bars in the old town are concentrated on and around the Pza de los Naranjos, and slightly off to the west at Pza de los Olivos.

Sinatra's, Puerto Banús, at the main entrance to the port. The classic hang-out of the see-and-be-seen set.

Salduba Bar. Next door to Sinatra's and slightly less crowded.

Night Café. A café by day and club by night.

La Notte, Camino de la Cruz, **t** 95 277 61 90. The customers here are younger and trendier than in the past; situated above the mosque, opposite Puente Romano hotel.

In Marbella itself action can be found in the streets leading up from the Pso Marítimo and around the Puerto Deportivo. The Calle Peral has lots of hip bars; try **Alaska**, **Moloko** or the disco **Cúpula**. A good place to start the evening on this street is the relaxed Arab-style tea room **La Tetería**.

Atrium, C/Gregorio Marañon 11. A place to investigate for early drinks; super-hip and pricey, with outdoor seating and foliage.

Havana, around the corner on C/Ortega y Gasset. Attracts an older crowd.

Olivia Valere, Ctra de Istán, km 0.8. Very slick and incredibly expensive.

cafés here, ogling all the yachts and some of the people. It also has one of the biggest El Corte Inglés stores in Spain, almost every designer clothes shop you can imagine, a huge cinema and numerous Internet cafés.

Fuengirola

You should come on a package tour if you find Fuengirola and Torremolinos to your taste. That's what these places are for, and you would get a better deal. If you're just passing and want to rest in anonymity by the beach, there are some possibilities.

Thirty years ago, Fuengirola was a typical whitewashed Spanish fishing village. It's still white, but hardly typical, and even less Spanish. With the miles of speculative *urbanizaciones* that surround it, it would be easy to be unkind to Fuengirola except that everyone there seems to be having such a good time. The town, and its adjacent community of **Los Boliches**, may be the only place in Spain where you'll see a sign in a shop-window reading '*Se habla español*'; the laid-back international community

Tourist Information

Fuengirola: Avda Jesús Santos Rein 6, in an old railway station, **t** 95 246 76 25. *Open daily 9.30–1.30 and 4–8, Sat mornings only*.

Mijas: Plaza de la Virgen, **t** 95 248 59 00.

Where to Stay

Fuengirola ✉ **29640**

Luxury

*******Byblos Andaluz**, Urbanización Mijas Golf, **t** 95 247 30 50, **f** 95 247 67 83, *www.byblos-andaluz.com*. This haven of peace and tranquillity with a spa and thalassotherapy centre is only 5km from the centre of Fuengirola, with every imaginable luxury and a glamorous clientele.

Expensive

******Las Palmeras**, Paseo Marítimo s/n, **t** 95 247 27 00, **f** 95 247 29 08. A massive, modern beachfront hotel with all the trimmings from a pool to tennis courts. Prices drop by more than half out of season.

Moderate

It's difficult to tell one new holiday hotel from the next, but for the best deals a few places do stand out.

*****Florida**, Pso Marítimo, **t** 95 247 61 00, **f** 95 258 15 29, *florida@spa.es*. Has a pool and gardens, and though not luxurious is still a comfortable enough place.

****Cendrillón**, Ctra Cádiz km 213, **t** 95 247 53 16, **f** 95 247 87 97. Much the same as the Florida, only with tennis courts.

****Más Playa**, Urbanización Torreblanca del Sol, **t** 95 247 53 00, **f** 95 247 87 97. Next door to Cendrillón, both places on the beach, popular with families.

Inexpensive

***Yamasol**, Avda Ramón y Cajal, **t** 95 258 44 00. Clean and functional; typical of the many inexpensive *hostales* around the centre of Fuengirola and in the suburb of Los Boliches to the north.

Eating Out

Dining in Fuengirola is an experience; you can choose from Indonesian to Belgian without going broke. There are plenty of choices along Calle del Hambre, which means 'hungry street', and Calle Moncayo, known as 'fish alley'.

Expensive

Portofino, Edificio Perla 1, Pso Marítimo, **t** 95 247 06 43. A popular restaurant where Italian specialities head the list. *Closed Mon*.

appreciates a good joke. The shops of the old village have been transformed into pubs, English bookshops, travel agencies and Swiss, Chinese, Belgian, Italian, Moroccan and even Spanish restaurants, but there's something genuine in the atmosphere of this casual European village – now grown into a fair-sized city. Today the Spaniards live mostly in town, picnicking and sunbathing on their flat roofs or balconies; the foreigners drive in from the *urbanizaciones* for pub-hopping or to shop in the vast hypermarkets. The centre is becoming ever more determinedly multi-national and multilingual, while upwardly mobile Spaniards are buying their way into the *urbanizaciones*. In another 20 years Fuengirola might be quite an interesting place. The best place to observe this curious community is at the Tuesday **market**.

Unlike other resorts on the Costa, there are some things to see – the Moorish **Castillo de Sohail** above town, a bullring, even the brand new façade of a **Roman temple**. In Roman times there were important marble quarries in the mountains near here, and off the coast divers recently discovered a wreck with these stones, bound for somewhere else; they've been salvaged and assembled on a spot near the beach.

Valparaíso, Ctra de Mijas, km 4, **t** 95 248 59 96. Just outside Fuengirola, on the mountain road to Mijas; one of the most attractive and popular restaurants in the area, with bars, terrace, swimming pool and an extensive international menu. Starters are labelled 'temptations' and women are given menus without the prices, but it's a favourite haunt – with foreign communities in particular. *Closed Sun except July–Oct.*

Café Royal, Avda del Sol, Benalmádena Costa, **t** 95 244 60 00, **f** 95 244 57 02. In attractive surroundings at Hotel Torrequebrada, with a fine view over the curve of the coastline, serving international cuisine. Once you've paid large sums for your meal, you can join the high rollers and blow more at the casino.

Moderate

Raj, C/Asturias 3, **t** 95 258 45 96. An attractive Indian restaurant – a welcome addition to Fuengirola's already cosmopolitan culinary scene. Decorated with charming *objets d'art* brought back from India, the cuisine is from the north of the subcontinent.

La Casa Vieja, Avda los Boliches, **t** 95 258 38 30. Excellent, imaginative *andaluz* dishes in a traditional turn-of-the-century house.

Casa Navarra, Ctra de Mijas (near Valparaíso), km 4, **t** 95 258 04 39. Serves Navarrese cuisine, including huge steaks and delicious fish that you can choose yourself. Try the *merluza* in prawn and parsley sauce. *Closed Tues.*

Dany, Paseo Marítimo s/n, Edificio de Jean Luís, **t** 95 247 34 85. A classic spot for tasty *fritura de pescaítos*, or fish baked slowly in rock salt.

Inexpensive

La Cepa, Plaza Constitución, in Fuengirola. The place to come if you fancy a bit of pub grub while you observe movements on the plaza.

La Plaza, Pza de la Constitución 9, **t** 95 246 33 59. An alternative with a commanding view of the entire square; cyber café upstairs.

Hermanos Blanco, Pso Marítimo. Typical of the many *chiringuitos* in the Los Boliches area.

Entertainment and Nightlife

Fuengirola might not rock like Torremolinos and Marbella, but it does have its fair share of drinking establishments and *discotecas*. In the centre, these are concentrated in and around the streets of Pza Constitución, and include the inevitable slew of 'authentic' Irish pubs and English bars. Off the Pso Marítimo, C/Martínez Catena is the place to be, with bars, discos and numerous restaurants vying for punters. Try **El Botijo**, C/Capitán, a stylish cocktail bar, or **The Cotton Club**, Avda Condes San Isidro, a late-night café-bar serving snacks.

Mijas

Visitors from Fuengirola totally overwhelm the village of Mijas, 3km up in the hills above town, but at dusk it returns to the hands of the foreign residents, who count for 90 per cent of the village's population. To escape the coastal sprawl, visitors drive up here by the coachload to find *real* Spain, and a typical Andalucían village, which it obviously is not, nor has it been for 30 years. Yet it's still a pretty place with a promenade offering a view out to sea, a votive shrine to the Virgin, lots of pine woods, dozens of photogenic souvenir shops and 'officially licensed *burro* taxis' to take you around. The munchkin-sized whitewashed **bullring** sees its fair share of action throughout the year, but the town's museum of miniature curiosities is hard to take, even as a joke.

Torremolinos

All sources agree about Torremolinos, the 'fishing village' immortalized in James Michener's *The Drifters*. The oldest and biggest resort town on the Costa, it has become a ghastly, hyperactive, unsightly holiday inferno. In other words, it has character. Torremolinos isn't at all interested in our opinion, though, or in yours either; it's doing quite well with its endless screaming blocks of bars, shopping centres and concrete hotels.

For those who want to spend their holiday in the fast lane, in a raucous, international, entirely synthetic environment, this is the place. In the summer, the tourists, hustlers, Gypsies, drug-pushers, sailors and an assortment of others mingle in the streets and the movement is fast and furious between the bars. The predominant language is English, but a dozen others can be heard in the space of a few steps. To escape this horde step down to one of the beach cafés, popular day and night; if your luck is in, you'll be treated to some of the local street performers sharing their talents: an *anís*-soaked troubadour mangling an aria, cigarette dangling from his lower lip, or a transvestite flamenco dancer, whirling between the passing cars, his grim-looking mother handing round the hat. This is all received with good humour by the Spaniards, even if some of the tourists look a bit nonplussed.

Part of Torremolinos' character arises from its status as capital of what the newspapers used to call the 'Costa del Crime'. Literally thousands of clever bank-heisters, conmen and embezzlers, mostly from Britain, once added to the local colour, courtesy of Spain's traditional unwillingness to conclude extradition treaties with other nations. Now that an agreement with Britain has been reached, the crooks have had to move along as their visas ran out. There are still plenty of other types left – smooth operators of uncertain nationality, religious cult agents, hedonists of all shapes and sizes, and other European detritus. They're only the surface, though; the most noticeable segment of an enormous permanent and transient population is made up of gawking sun-seekers from every corner of Europe. On the outskirts of Torremolinos welcome signs proclaim 'City of Tourists'. In summer, Torremolinos becomes the third largest city in Andalucía, when the 36,000 residents are joined by some quarter of a

Tourist Information

La Carihuela: Borbollón Bajo, **t** 95 237 29 56.
Bajondillo/Playamar: Plaza de las Comunidades Autónomas, **t** 95 237 19 09.
Benalmádena: Avda Antonio Machado 14, **t** 95 244 24 94.
Torremolinos: Pza de la Independencia, **t** 95 237 42 31.

Where to Stay

Torremolinos ✉ 29620

In Torremolinos and its neighbouring stretch of tourist sprawl, at Benalmádena Costa, the possibilities are endless, though these, too, will probably be packed with package tours.

Expensive

There are a number of swanky four-star hotels in Torremolinos, all offering much the same – swimming pool, air-conditioned rooms and dull hotel food.

★★★★**Pez Espada**, Avda Salvador Allende 11, **t** 95 238 03 00, **f** 95 237 28 01, *www.medplaya.com*. The hotel which started it all off – built in 1959, it was the first luxury hotel to appear in the city, and it put Torre on the map. Fading now, but still of a high standard and in a good spot just out of the town centre and near the beach.

★★★★**Royal Al-Andalus**, C/Al Andalus 3, **t** 95 238 12 00, 95 238 19 06, *www.royalpremier hoteles.com*. Just off the main road towards Benalmádena and set in its own grounds, complete with huge pool and sea-facing rooms with balcony.

★★★★**Alay**, Avda Alay s/n, **t** 95 244 14 40, **f** 95 244 63 80. In a good location just above the Puerto Marina, but you pay for the privilege.

★★★★**Aloha Puerto**, Salvador Allende 53, **t** 95 238 70 66, **f** 95 238 57 01 *www.solmelia.es*. Another pricey option, nearer Benalmádena. Prices drop from €150 in July and August, to less than €90 in winter.

Moderate

★★★★**Hotel Cervantes**, C/Rió Cañoles 1, **t** 95 238 40 33, *www.hotelcervantestorremolinos.com*. Just a few yards from the heart of the action, this hotel is surprisingly reasonable (except in August) and offers all the creature comforts you would expect, with two pools (one indoor, one out), big rooms with balconies, a disco, restaurant, café and a very good restaurant of the same name.

★★★**Sol Príncipe**, Pso Colorado 26, **t** 95 238 41 0, **f** 952 388 075. A comfortable hotel in a quiet corner of the Playamar area (2km from the centre), with three pools and a good restaurant.

★★★**Hotel Picasso**, C/María Barrabino, **t** 95 238 76 00. For its location in the centre of town, and overlooking the main square, this is very reasonably priced; rooms with balcony.

★★★**Griego Mar**, Avda Sorolla 7, **t** 95 238 54 55, **f** 95 238 46 38, *griego@marconfort.com*. A faceless tower block at the top of town offering all mod cons.

★★★**Hotel Adriano**, Avda de los Manantiales 1, **t** 95 205 08 38, **f** 95 238 63 07. In a good spot – albeit slightly noisy – but this is Torre and you're not here to get away from it all. All rooms come with bath, air conditioning, phone and TV.

★★★**Eurosol**, Residencial Eurosol, Bl. 93–95 (out towards Benalmádena), **t** 95 238 21 19. More apartment blocks set in their own grounds and a short walk from the beach.

★★★**Sol Patos**, **t** 95 244 19 90, **f** 95 244 29 29, *sol.patos@solmelia.es*. One of several three- and four-star hotels along the N340 (Ctra Cádiz), all offering much the same quality.

Inexpensive

Budget places are few and far between in this area, and most are placed some way out of town. Some of the good bargains can be found out towards La Carihuela, along Avenida Carlota Alessandri.

★★**Miami**, C/Aladino 14, in La Carihuela, **t** 95 238 52 55. Perhaps Torremolinos's last secret. The house was built as a holiday villa by Picasso's cousin Manolo Blasco, and is quite charming despite its shabbiness.

★★**Victoria**, C/ Hoyo, Urb. Los Naranjos 10, (opposite the bus station), **t** 95 238 19 34. Whether staying a few days or just passing through, this *hostal* is pleasant, conveniently placed and reasonably priced.

Hotel Guadalupe, Bajondillo, C/Peligro 15, **t/f** 95 238 19 37. Near the beach and away from the mayhem.

Hotel Micaela, C/Bajondillo 4, **t** 95 238 33 10, **f** 95 237 68 42. Clean and has rooms with bath; just down from C/San Miguel.

Eating Out

Expensive

Frutos, Ctra Cádiz, km 235, **t** 95 238 45 30. A popular restaurant on the main *carretera* (next to Los Álamos petrol station), with high-quality food at reasonable prices generous portions: leg of lamb, suckling pig, Málaga fry, *tocino de cielo* – not a hint of *nouvelle cuisine*.

La Cónsula/Escuela de Hostelería de Málaga, Finca La Cónsula, Churriana, **t** 95 262 25 62. Located in a beautiful colonial-style house where Hemingway used to stay, this is an interesting dining experience. The hotel school's students prepare delectable lunches featuring innovative *andaluz* recipes. Booking essential.

Moderate

Mar de Alborán, Hotel Alay, Avda de Alay 5, Benalmádena Costa, **t** 95 244 64 27, **f** 95 244 63 80. Highly recommended for excellent Basque and Andalucían cuisine, this is a restaurant where the food, prepared by chef Álvaro Arriaga, gets better and better. *Closed Sun and Mon*.

Casa Guaquín, C/Carmen 37, **t** 95 238 45 30. The best seafood restaurants are in La Carihuela, along the beach from Torremolinos, and this one is very good indeed; try such specialities of the Costa as 'fish baked in salt' – it's a bit of an acquired taste.

Casa Juan, C/de San Ginés 20, **t** 95 237 35 12. Run by Guaquín's cousin, with similar fare at affordable prices.

La Jábega, Paseo Marítimo, La Carihuela, **t** 95 238 63 75. Another good place on the beach, with fish, of course, and a wide variety of starters and shellfish.

El Mero, Puerto Deportivo de Benalmádena, **t** 95 244 07 52. An excellent seafood and shellfish restaurant in a wonderful setting overlooking the marina.

Venta los Piños del Coto, Cañada de Ceuta s/n, Churriana, **t** 95 243 58 00. To escape the bedlam of Torre, head up into the hills to this rambling, ranch-type restaurant run by a Hispano-German couple; it's a 10min drive. The spacious, attractive interior has stained-wood ceilings and a log fire for cold winter evenings. The menu is devoted to meat in large quantities, especially roast lamb. *Closed Mon and Tues*.

Inexpensive

Mesón Gallego Antoxo, C/Hoxo 5, **t** 95 238 45 33. A short walk from the Torremolinos bus station, this is a typical Spanish restaurant with a beautiful interior and charming little courtyard. There's a wide choice of fish, many dishes cooked to Galician recipes. Your wine will be served in the traditional Galician ceramic jug, and the drinking vessels resemble large finger bowls.

El Vietnam del Sur, Pso del Colorado, Urbanización Playamar, Bloque 9, **t** 95 238 67 37. If you've never had the Vietnamese variations on Chinese cuisine, so popular in France, try this place – the food is delicious and affordable. *Closed Jan and Feb*.

Bodega Quitapenas, on the central steps down to the beach. Sit outside this *bodega* back in town for a cheap aperitif – everybody passes this way.

La Chacha, Avda Palma de Mallorca, 3, **t** 95 238 49 10. A real old-style *comedor* where you can choose from *gambas* and *pulpo* as you sit at the bar.

Entertainment and Nightlife

Torremolinos was once a byword for hedonistic fun, but the party is beginning to move on. There are a few discos in town, but the best action is to be found 3km down the road at Puerto Marina in Benalmádena. Torre is currently awash with English theme bars on C/San Miguel and Pza de la Independencia – take your pick, if that's your thing.

In town there are loads of enormous clubs along the Avda Palma de Mallorca: try **The Palladium**, in the style of a Roman bath, complete with pool and bars; **Voltage**, for hard-core homegrown techno; or **Fun Beach**, the biggest club in Spain, with seven dance-floors and six bars.

Activities on the Costa

There are bullrings in Marbella, Fuengirola, Estepona, Mijas (a square one!) and Benalmádena Costa, though *corridas* are infrequent and the really serious action occurs in the big ring in Málaga. For music on the Costa del Sol, there are concerts at the Casa de Cultura and Salón Varietés in Fuengirola and the Mijas Arts Centre, and at the Nueva Andalucía bullring near Marbella, among others; many also offer art exhibitions and guitar and dance courses. For sports, there are around sixty golf courses on the Costa, though green fees are a little dear; tennis at many of the hotels, most open to the public; even snooker clubs (in Fuengirola). Of course all the water sports are popular; you can always make arrangements for equipment or instruction through your hotel. There are casinos at Benalmádena Costa (the Torrequebrada, on the coastal highway), and at Puerto Banús (the Casino de Marbella, at Torre del Duque), where the stakes are quite a bit higher.

For kids there's a Disneyland-style amusement park at Benalmádena Costa called Tivoli World with a Wild West area, Chinese pagodas, Cinerama, flamenco and can-can shows as well as the Sea Life Park, where you can take a journey to the bottom of the sea. Also, a modern zoo in Fuengirola, Super Bonanza cruise boats for leisurely excursions between Torremolinos and Puerto Banús, and horse riding from the El Castillo Salvador stables outside Fuengirola. There is also horse riding at Finca La Perita (*t 95 247 10 34*), and at Rancho Antonio (*t 639 50 55 91*). The Aquapark in Fuengirola has slides and rides to keep the little ones amused for an afternoon.

million tourists. There are around 70 hotels to deal with them, offering 34,000 beds on a daily basis; 40 per cent of the total bed space in the Costa del Sol.

In recent years the city has made attempts to cloak itself in green; in among the concrete blocks there are now a surprising number of leafy spaces. The tree-lined Paseo Marítimo – an uninterrupted 6km stretch leading to the Puerto Marina at Benalmádena – makes a pleasant stroll. The marina is Torre's answer to Marbella's Puerto Banús, another spot for sophisticated dining and yacht-gazing. **Benalmádena** itself was where Fernando and Isabel chose to defend this stretch of the coast, and it claims an ancient history going back as far as the Phoenicians. There's the **Castillo del Bil Bil** – of Moorish origins and now used to stage concerts – a bullring, and the **Museo Arqueólogico** (*currently closed for restoration, **t** 95 244 85 93, museo@benalmadena.com*), which has various artefacts from Latin America.

Málaga

Much-maligned Málaga, capital not only of the Costa del Sol, but also of crime and sleaze in southern Spain, is making a determined effort to improve its reputation and attract more tourists. In the past, a visit to the swish department store El Corte Inglés, may have been the only reason a tourist considered spending any time here at all.

To miss Málaga, however, means to miss the most Spanish of cities, certainly on the Costa del Sol. Whatever you may think of the place, it is alive and real: ungainly cranes

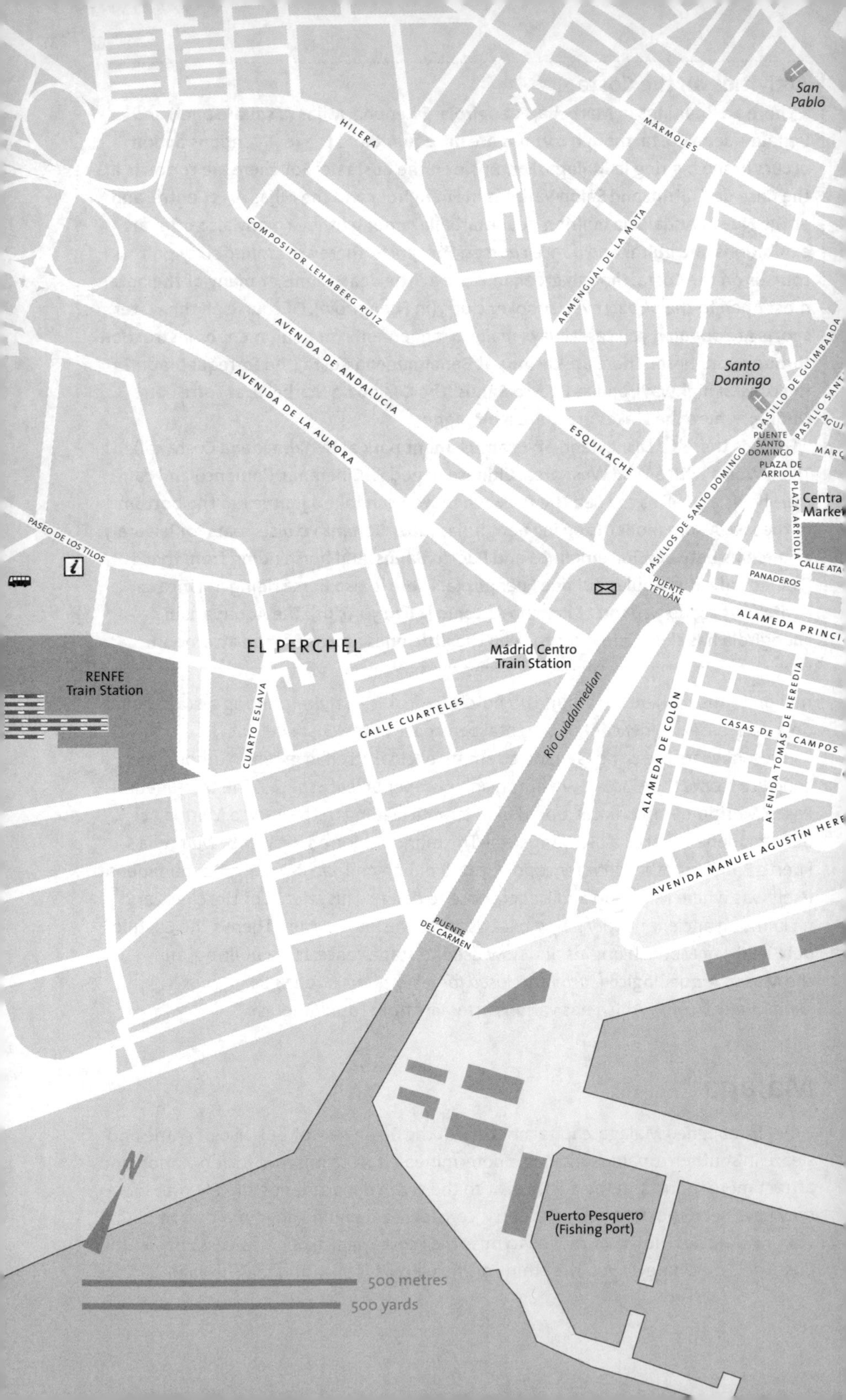
San Pablo
Mármoles
Hilera
Compositor Lehmberg Ruiz
Armengual de la Mota
Avenida de Andalucia
Avenida de la Aurora
Esquilache
Santo Domingo
Pasillo de Guimbarda
Puente Santo Domingo
Plaza de Arriola
Plaza Arriola
Pasillos de Santo Domingo
Central Market
Paseo de los Tilos
Calle Ata
Panaderos
Puente Tetuán
Alameda Princi
El Perchel
Mádrid Centro Train Station
RENFE Train Station
Cuarto Eslava
Calle Cuarteles
Río Guadalmedian
Alameda de Colón
Avenida Tomás de Heredia
Casas de Campos
Avenida Manuel Agustín Here
Puente del Carmen
N
Puerto Pesquero (Fishing Port)
500 metres
500 yards

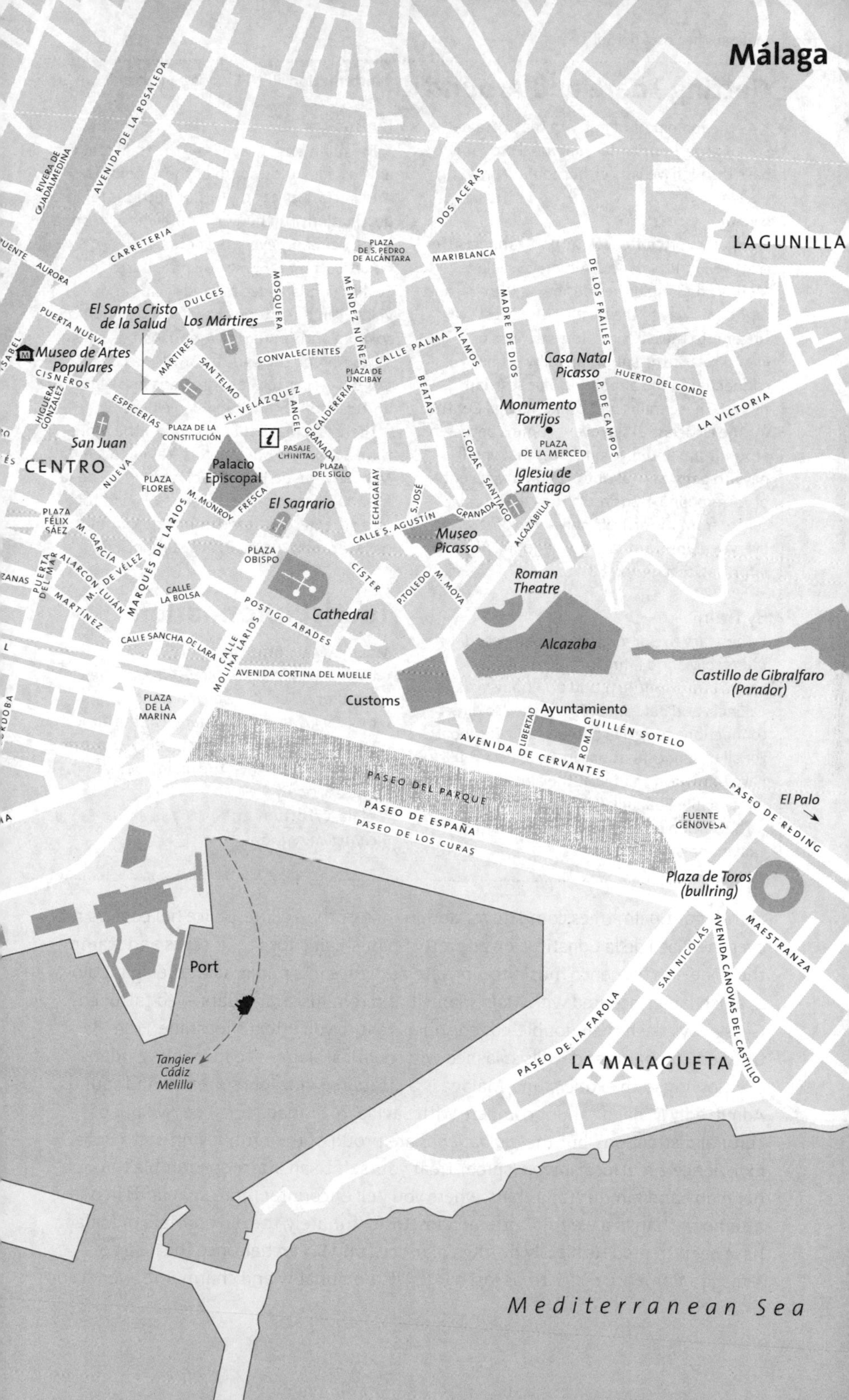
Málaga
LAGUNILLA
CENTRO
LA MALAGUETA
El Santo Cristo de la Salud
Los Mártires
Museo de Artes Populares
San Juan
Palacio Episcopal
El Sagrario
Cathedral
Museo Picasso
Casa Natal Picasso
Monumento Torrijos
Iglesia de Santiago
Roman Theatre
Alcazaba
Castillo de Gibralfaro (Parador)
Customs
Ayuntamiento
Plaza de Toros (bullring)
El Palo
Port
Tangier
Cádiz
Melilla
Mediterranean Sea
PLAZA DE S. PEDRO DE ALCÁNTARA
PLAZA DE UNCIBAY
PLAZA DE LA CONSTITUCIÓN
PASAJE CHINITAS
PLAZA DEL SIGLO
PLAZA FLORES
PLAZA FÉLIX SÁEZ
PLAZA OBISPO
CALLE LA BOLSA
PLAZA DE LA MERCED
PLAZA DE LA MARINA
FUENTE GENOVESA
AVENIDA DE LA ROSALEDA
RIVERA DE GUADALMEDINA
CARRETERIA
AURORA
DULCES
PUERTA NUEVA
CISNEROS
HIGUERA GONZÁLEZ
ESPECERÍAS
MÁRTIRES
SAN TELMO
MOSQUERA
CONVALECIENTES
MÉNDEZ NÚÑEZ
DOS ACERAS
MARIBLANCA
CALLE PALMA
ALAMOS
MADRE DE DIOS
DE LOS FRAILES
HUERTO DEL CONDE
P. DE CAMPOS
LA VICTORIA
H. VELÁZQUEZ
ÁNGEL
CALDERERÍA
GRANADA
BEATAS
T. COZAR
SANTIAGO
ECHAGARAY
S. JOSÉ
CALLE S. AGUSTÍN
ALCAZABILLA
NUEVA
M. MONROY
FRESCA
MARQUÉS DE LARIOS
M. GARCÍA
ALARCÓN
M. DE VÉLEZ
PUERTA DEL MAR
M. LUJÁN
MARTÍNEZ
CÍSTER
P. TOLEDO
M. MOYA
POSTIGO ABADES
CALLE SANCHA DE LARA
CALLE MOLINA LARIOS
AVENIDA CORTINA DEL MUELLE
LIBERTAD
ROMA
GUILLÉN SOTELO
AVENIDA DE CERVANTES
PASEO DEL PARQUE
PASEO DE ESPAÑA
PASEO DE LOS CURAS
PASEO DE REDING
MAESTRANZA
SAN NICOLÁS
AVENIDA CÁNOVAS DEL CASTILLO
PASEO DE LA FAROLA

Getting There and Around

As the main port of entry to the Costa del Sol and southern Andalucía, you'll probably pass through Málaga either coming or going.

By Air

Málaga's often frenetic airport connects the city to Madrid, Valencia, Almería, Sevilla, Melilla and Tangier, besides being the charter-flight gateway to the Costa. The easiest way to get into the city, or to Torremolinos or Fuengirola, is the suburban railway line, connected to the airport via a pedestrian flyover. These trains (get off at Málaga Centro for the city centre) run every 30mins between around 7am and 11.30 pm: after that you'll have to get a taxi (about €12 to Málaga centre or Torremolinos). Bus no.19 runs to the city centre from the arrivals hall approximately every 30mins from 7am and 11.30pm. **Airport information, t** 95 204 88 04.

By Train

There are five or more daily high-speed trains to Madrid (4hrs 10mins), plus four normal trains (7½hrs), and two trains a day to Valencia and Barcelona. There are also direct connections to Sevilla (2½ hrs) and Córdoba. For all other destinations in Andalucía you'll have to make a change at the almost inescapable Bobadilla Junction.

The station is off Calle Cuarteles on the Explanada de la Estación. **Information:** RENFE **t** 902 240 202.

By Bus

The main bus station is by the train station at Pso de los Tilos, south of the Avenida de Andalucía, **t** 95 235 00 61. Connections for local destinations run hourly; for provincial destinations, generally every 1–2 hours.

Portillo, **t** 95 236 01 91, operate buses to Sevilla, Ronda, Algeciras and towns and villages in the interior. Bacoma, **t** 95 231 88 28, to Álora and Ronda; Los Amarillos, **t** 95 231 59 78, to Antequera, Carratraca; Alsina Graells, **t** 95 231 04 00, to Granada, Nerja and Almería, and also for Alicante and Barcelona.

There's a smaller bus station – little more than a string of bus shelters – along Avenida Manuel Agustín Heredia (close to Plaza de la Marina). Buses for Torremolinos, Fuengirola and other resorts leave from here, but most pass through the main bus station.

Tourist Information

Málaga: Main office at Avda Cervantes 1, **t** 95 260 44 10. *Open Mon–Sat 8–8.* There's another office at Pasaje Chinitas 4, **t** 95 221 34 45; a small branch at the airport, **t** 95 204 84 84, ext. 58617 (*open 9–2 except Sun*), and a booth at the main bus station, **t** 95 235 00 61.

Melilla: C/Fortuny 21, **t** 95 267 54 44, *dsi@camelilla.es.*

and elegant palm trees compete for dominance of the skyline; police helicopters roar over the Plaza de la Constitución as pretty Spanish girls toss their skirts and stamp their heels to flamenco music, to a private audience in a public square; elegant old Spanish ladies, scented with *Maja* soap, sit and reminisce, and dark-eyed tattooed Gypsy boys flash their double-edged smiles to lure you into a shoeshine. From its tattered billboards and walls splashed with political slogans to its public gardens overflowing with exotic fauna, Málaga is a jamboree of colours, aromas and sounds. Admittedly Málaga cannot compete with Sevilla or Granada for sheer wealth of cultural distractions, but the *malagueños* are proud of their fun-loving metropolis. To experience a real local *juerga* (spree), treat yourself to an afternoon ramble through her many and famous tapas bars, where you will encounter more Spaniards in one afternoon than in a week in Torremolinos. Unfortunately, the old quarters of Málaga have been treated ruthlessly by town planners, and **El Perchel**, once the heart of Málaga's flamenco district, has lost a lot of its personality and charm. The Avenida de

Where to Stay

Málaga ✉ 29000

Luxury

★★★★**Parador de Gibralfaro**, Castillo de Gibralfaro, s/n, 29016, **t** 95 222 19 02, **f** 95 222 19 04, *gibralfaro@parador.es*. Up in the old Moorish castle above the city, with a swimming pool; offers the best view of Málaga, and is one of the nicest places to stay, following an expensive facelift. Lunching on its terrace is unforgettable.

★★★★**Larios**, Marqués de Larios 2, **t** 95 222 22 00, **f** 95 222 24 07, *www.hotel-larios.com*. Well appointed and extremely comfortable (cheaper rates at weekends).

★★★★**AC Málaga Palacio**, Avda Cortina del Muelle 1, **t** 95 221 51 85, **f** 95 222 51 00, *mpalacio@ac-hoteles.com*. Now part of the ultra-modern AC chain, with an excellent location at the top of the Alameda, and sweeping views over the port. Try to get a room on an upper floor.

Expensive

★★★★**Parador de Málaga Golf**, Apartado de Correos 324, **t** 95 238 12 55, **f** 95 238 89 63, *malaga@parador.es*. A modern resort hotel, just beyond the airport, with a heavy emphasis on golf. Also has a swimming pool. Good value.

★★★**Hotel Don Curro**, C/Sancha de Lara 7, **t** 95 222 72 00, **f** 95 221 59 46. Excellently situated just behind the Alameda and a few hundred yards from the cathedral. Bar, restaurant and bingo hall attached.

★★★★**NH Málaga**, Avda Río Guadalmedina s/n, **t** 95 207 13 23, **f** 95 239 38 62, *nhmalaga@nh-hoteles.es*. Slightly out of the centre overlooking Málaga's empty river bed. Part of an excellent chain, with all modern amenities.

★★★**Parador**, Avda Cándido Lobera (in Melilla), **t** 95 268 49 40, **f** 95 268 34 86, *melilla@parador.es*. Offers panoramic views over the walled town of Melilla, one of Spain's *presidios* on the African coast.

Moderate

★★**Ánfora**, C/Vallesca 16 (in Melilla), **t** 95 268 33 40. A reliable, unremarkable hotel. There are also quite a few modest *hostales* scattered around Melilla.

★★**Hotel Carlos V**, C/Císter 10, **t** 95 221 41 20. Convenient location, and well-equipped rooms for a modest price. The garage is an extra plus.

Inexpensive

★★**Alameda**, C/Casa de Campos 3, **t** 95 222 20 99. Reasonable if unexceptional rooms with or without bathrooms in the city centre.

★★**Castilla**, C/Córdoba 7, **t** 95 221 86 35. Along with the Guerrero, which is in the same building, this is a well-run establishment.

Casa Huéspedes Bolivia, Casa de Campos 24, **t** 95 221 88 26. Spotlessly clean and central.

Andalucía cuts through this old district and then becomes the Alameda Principal and the Paseo del Parque. The essence of Málaga is within this limited area, from the elegant Avenida de Andalucía to the seedy, teeming neo-Moorish market on the Calle Atarazanas.

You may find it difficult to decide whether you love or loathe this city – will you notice the two snarling drivers impatient for the green light, or the two old gentlemen sipping sherry in the doorway of a cool, dark *bodega*, hung with *serrano* hams and lined with wine casks?

The Heart of Málaga

As the Avenida de Andalucía, the main road from the west, crosses the dry rocky bed of the Guadalmedina river, it becomes the **Alameda Principal**, a majestic 19th-century boulevard. North of the Alameda is the **Plaza de la Constitución**, in the heart of the commercial centre, and the Pasaje Chinitas, an all-and-sundry shopping arcade. One

Any place on or around the Alameda will be decent, but avoid the cheap dives around the train station.

Eating Out

Expensive

Adolfo, Paseo Marítimo Ruiz Picasso 12, **t** 95 260 19 14. A smart restaurant in a perfect location on the Malagueta beach; excellent grilled meats as well as seafood.

El Compá, C/La Bolsa 7, **t** 95 222 97 06. An excellent restaurant, specializing in fresh local fish and with a large wine selection; situated just behind the Alameda.

Monte Sancha, C/Monte Sancha 16, **t** 95 260 31 76. Fashionable, elegant restaurant serving original and creative cuisine.

Café de Paris, C/Vélez-Málaga 8, **t** 95 222 50 43. Perhaps the best place in Málaga to try truly innovative Mediterranean cuisine, accompanied by an excellent wine list.

Moderate

Mesón El Chinitas, C/Moreno Monroy 4–6, **t** 95 221 09 72. A local legend, with bull-fighting posters and flamenco memorabilia. There's a pricey, smart restaurant, and very good tapas at the bar. A lovely terrace, too.

Mesón Astorga, C/Gerona 11, **t** 95 234 25 63. A really atmospheric *malagueño* restaurant that's on the up and up – a good place to enjoy a long, late lunch.

Antonio Martín, Playa de la Malagueta, **t** 95 222 21 13. *Malagueños* flock to the Paseo Marítimo and the El Palo district east of town, on Sunday especially, to fill up the many beachfront restaurants. This place is a favourite, with fish and rice dishes as the basis of the menu; try scrambled eggs with baby eel and salmon, or gilthead cooked in salt. *Closed in winter.*

El Cabra, C/Copo 21, Pso El Pedregal **t** 95 229 50 70. Another good choice by the beach, with a more expensive range of seafood.

Casa Pedro, C/Quitapenas 57, El Palo, **t** 95 229 00 13. You may well be deafened by the din as you tuck into skewered sardines or Sierra-style monkfish. *Closed Mon eve.*

Inexpensive

La Tetería, C/San Agustín 9. Málaga is also, slowly, discovering its Moorish roots, and a number of Moroccan-style tea rooms have opened. This one serves various couscous dishes, cakes and mint tea.

Café Cosmopolita, C/Marqués de Larios. Start your day with breakfast at this café, where tables spill onto the pavement and surround the wooden horseshoe bar inside. Service is outrageously slow but at least this allows you to relax over a paper from the kiosk next door, or watch the shoeshine boys at work on customers' footwear.

El Corte Inglés, Avda de Andalucía, **t** 95 230 00 00. The department store has three restaurants and bars on the top floor, as well

of the clothes shops bears a commemorative plaque – it's the original site of the Café Chinitas, where bullfighters and flamenco singers would gather in the old days; the spirit of it was captured by García Lorca. The Alameda continues into the Paseo del Parque, a tree-lined promenade that runs along the port area, and leads to the city's **bullring**, built in 1874 with a capacity of 14,000, and very much in use today. Nearby is the **English cemetery**. William Mark, the 19th-century consul, so loved Málaga that he described it as a 'second paradise', and encouraged his fellow countrymen to join him here. In 1830 he founded this cemetery, allowing a decent burial to Protestants. Hans Christian Andersen declared he could 'well understand how a splenetic Englishman might take his own life in order to be buried in this place'. Its sea views, however, have long since been blocked by buildings, and sadly, it is about to be closed.

High above the oldest part of Málaga is the Moorish **Alcazaba** (*entrance on Plaza de la Duana, off C/Alcazabilla; open Tues–Sat 9.30–7; adm*). Under the Moors, Málaga was the most important port of al-Andalus, and from contemporary references it seems as El Club de Gourmets, where you could put together some luxurious ingredients for a very special picnic.

Antigua Casa de Guardia, Alameda 18, **t** 95 221 46 80. For sherry, shrimps and a marvellous atmosphere, come here and choose a drink from one of the 20 or so barrels lining the bar, with names like Pajarete 1908 and Guinda; a glass of sherry and a dozen mussels will set you back less than €5.

Legado Celestial, C/Peregrino 2, **t** 95 235 15 21. A good little vegetarian place, with a buffet menu of tofu dishes, salads and freshly squeezed juices.

Café con Libros, C/Granada 63, **t** 95 220 47 17. Laid-back, cosy café with books and magazines, sofas and good range of teas and cakes - try the chocolate banana cake.

Bar Lo Güeno, Marín García 9. Head here for tapas – it's literally a hole in the wall serving imaginative *raciones* and a decent selection of wines.

Orellana, C/Moreno Monroy 5. One of the city's oldest and most classic tapas bars (they still offer a free *tapa* – or 'lid' – with your first glass of sherry).

Mesón la Aldea, C/Esparteros 5, **t** 95 222 76 89. A great tapas restaurant, with a speciality of the house you won't find anywhere else in Málaga: *carne al curry*. Try also the *flamenquín de carne*, a cheese and ham dish.

Rincon de el Tillo, C/Esparteros, **t** 95 222 31 35. A more upmarket *taberna* opposite Mesón la Aldea.

La Arkesama, C/Cervantes 10, **t** 95 221 79 26. Full of hams, cheese and a traditional atmosphere at a reasonable price.

Nightlife

Málaga has a buzzing summer club scene. On Friday or Saturday nights, it's hard to move through the streets between Plaza de la Constitución and Plaza de Siglo. Hundreds of trendy Spaniards spill out of a bewildering variety of street bars and clubs. Some of the best bars are to be found in and around Pza de Uncibay, C/Granada and in Pza de la Merced. A few bars and disco bars can also be found down by the bullring. In the summer, the action moves out to the city beaches, particularly Pedragalejo and El Palo.

Bar Pim Pi, C/Granada. A good place to start your nocturnal wanderings – a small doorway leads into a courtyard with rooms off every angle – cellars, patios, balconies – where the beautiful *malagueños* come out to play.

Gibralfaro Bar, Pasaje de Chinitas. Anything can happen in this appealingly scruffy bar; you might be treated to some impromptu flamenco, and it's always buzzing.

El Cantor de Jazz, C/Lazcano 7, **t** 95 222 28 54. Smoky, sophisticated jazz joint, with live acts on Thursdays.

Liceo, C/Beatas 21, **t** 95 260 14 60. One of the trendiest of the many bars lining C/Beatas.

also to have been one of its most beautiful cities. King Fernando thoroughly ruined it in the conquest of 1487, and after the expulsion of the Moors in 1568 little remained of its ancient distinction. Little, too, remains of the Alcazaba, except a few Moorish gates, but the site has been restored to a lovely series of terraced **gardens**, full of fountains and bird song. At the top there used to be a small **archaeological museum**, now empty although there are plans to create a new home here for the relics from the Phoenician necropolis found on the site and lists of Moorish architectural decoration salvaged from the ruins. The top of the Alcazaba also affords fine views over Málaga, framed by horseshoe arches, and there is a half-ruined **Roman theatre** next to the main entrance on the lower slopes of the hill, which is still being excavated (*open for guided visits Mon–Thurs 9–6, Fri 9–2*). Behind the Alcazaba you can make the long dusty walk to the the **Gibralfaro** (*open 9.30–9; adm*), the ruined Moorish castle that dominates the city, or pick up a shuttle bus from outside the Alcazaba ticket office (*at least ten daily in summer*).

Just below the Alcazaba, overlooking the Paseo del Parque, note the chunky Art Nouveau **Ayuntamiento**, one of the more unusual buildings in Málaga. On the opposite side of the Alcazaba is the **Museo de Bellas Artes**, C/San Agustín 8, in a restored 16th-century palace. It is currently being turned into the city's Picasso museum, due to open in October 2003. Picasso was a native of Málaga, though once he left it at the age of 14, he never returned. The artist's birthplace, **Casa Natal Picasso**, which now incorporates the **Municipal Picasso Foundation**, is just around the corner on Plaza de la Merced (*t 95 206 02 15; open summer Mon–Sat 10–9, Sun 10–2; winter Mon–Sat 10–8, Sun 10–2*), and has a small exhibition space on the ground floorwith a handful of works by Picasso and his peers (minor works by González, Miró, and Dalí), plus a gift shop with posters and all kinds of knick knacks stamped with a Picasso design. The upper floors have black and white photographs of Picasso at work, and a collection of his illustrations for *Le Chant des Morts*, a book of poetry by Pierre Reverdy.

Málaga's **cathedral** (*open Mon–Sat 9–6.45, closed Sun; adm*) is a few blocks away on Calle Molina Larios. It's an ugly, unfinished 16th-century work, immense and mouldering. Known as *La Manquita* (the one-armed lady), the only interesting feature is the faded, gaudy façade of the **sacristy**, left over from the earlier Isabelline Gothic church that once stood here.

Next to the dry river bed, the **Museo de Artes Populares**, Pasillo de Santa Isabel 10 (*open 10–1.30 and 4–7; closed Sat afternoon and Sun; adm*), occupies a restored 17th-century inn with a collection of household bric-a-brac. The **Jardin Botánico Historico La Concepcíon** (*t 95 225 21 48; open 10–5.30; adm*), an old farm 7km north of Málaga on the new road to Granada, has been transformed into Spain's second most important botanical gardens. They were founded in the mid-19th century by Jorge Loring and Amalia Heredia, who encouraged ships' captains to bring them plants from around the world. The gardens passed on to the Echevarría family, who eventually could no longer afford their upkeep, and by the time Málaga city council bought the gardens in 1990 they had grown into a virtual jungle. After much pruning, they were re-opened in 1994 and display a variety of plants from around the world, including a 700-year-old Canary Islands Dragon Tree (which could live up to 2,000 years).

For some reason the tourist industry has neglected the areas east of the city. There are a few resorts strung out along the coastal highway, notably **Torre del Mar**, but they are all grim-looking places: little bits of Málaga that escaped to the beach. Nearby are some scanty remains of a Greco-Phoenician settlement called **Mainake**.

Melilla

Nobody ever goes to Melilla, the more obscure of Spain's two remaining *presidios* on the North African coast. It's a long boat ride from Málaga, or a slightly shorter one from Almería, and onward destinations are severely limited. Morocco's big towns are far away, though you may consider Melilla as a quieter, less exasperating way to slip into Morocco than Tangier or Tetuán (*see* p.223), with their hustlers and aggravations. The town itself is prettier than Ceuta, hiding behind stern-looking fortifications over the water's edge, a mile-long beach spreading awkwardly from the walls.

Into the Serranía de Ronda

The Serranía de Ronda is a region of difficult topography, and it made life difficult for most would-be conquerors. A band of southern Celts gave the Romans fits in these mountains; various Christian chieftains held out for centuries against the Moors, and to return the favour the Moors kept Castile at bay here until 1485, just seven years before the conquest of Granada.

Ronda

Ronda, the only city in the Serranía, is a beautiful place, blessed with a perfect postcard shot of its lofty bridge over the steep gorge that divides the old and new towns. Because of its proximity to the Costa del Sol, it has lately become the only really tourist-ridden corner of the interior. The town's monuments are few; what Fernando the Catholic didn't wreck in 1485, the French finished off in 1809. Ronda saw plenty of trouble in the Civil War, with hundreds of bodies tossed into the gorge (the exact numbers, and who was doing the tossing, depend on who is telling the story).

Don't be discouraged from a visit; the views from the top of the city alone are worth the trip. One of the best places from which to enjoy them is the **Alameda del Tajo**, a park on the edge of the **Mercadillo**, as the new town is called. At its northern end is the 16th-century Carmelite **Convento de la Merced** on the plaza of the same name, where the nuns will sell you sweeties. Next to it, Ronda has one of Spain's oldest and most picturesque bullrings. The 1785 **Plaza de Toros**, the 'cathedral of bullfighting', stages only about three *corridas* a year – including *La Goyesca* at the beginning of September, in traditional 18th-century costume – but it still has great prestige: the art of bullfighting was developed here. There's also a small bullfighting **museum**, Virgen de la Paz 15 (*open daily 10–8; adm*), which has a selection of pictures, costumes and photos, including those of Orson Welles, who wished his ashes to be scattered in the bullring, and Ernest Hemingway, who mentions the bullring in *Death in the Afternoon*.

Ronda's other landmark, the **Puente Nuevo**, was built at the second try in 1740 – the first one immediately collapsed. The bridge's two thick piers descend almost 92m (300ft) to the bottom of the narrow gorge. The main square, **Plaza de Socorro**, is where most of the town comes out before dinner. It is flanked by a church, **Nuestra Señora del Socorro**, and a number of bars and restaurants both on and off the side streets. Crossing the bridge into the **Ciudad** (old town), a steep path heads downwards to a clutch of 18th-century palaces: the **Palacio de Salvatierra**, a Renaissance mansion still used as a private house (*once open to visitors but currently closed although there are plans to start the tours again; contact the tourist office*), and the **Casa del Rey Moro** (*gardens open daily 10–8; adm*), built over Moorish foundations. Around the corner is the new **Museo Lara** (*open daily 10-8; adm*), a fascinating collection of archeological bits and bobs, pistols, paintings, clocks and old cameras housed in the sumptuous 18th-century Casa Palacio de los Condes de la Conquista.

Getting There and Around

By Bus

Without a car in this region, you'll be depending on buses, run by Amarillos, **t** 95 218 70 61, or Portillo, **t** 95 287 22 62. From Ronda you can go directly to Jerez, Cádiz, Málaga, Sevilla and most of the towns along the Costa del Sol. Ronda has connections to villages in the hinterlands – usually only once a day, so if you're day-tripping, make sure there's a return. Ronda's bus station is in the new town, on the Plaza de Concepción, Glorieta Redondo 2, **t/f** 95 287 26 57.

By Train

Ronda has trains, too; there are at least three a day for Algeciras but no direct trains to Málaga (the bus is the best bet), with connections at Bobadilla Junction for Madrid and the other cities of Andalucía. Some trains stop at Gaucín and Setenil. The station is on the edge of town at Avda Alférez Provisional s/n, **t** 902 24 02 02.

By Car

When you are travelling by **car**, be warned that some streets of the Serranía towns and villages are very narrow, and difficult for a large vehicle to negotiate.

Tourist Information

Ronda: Plaza de España 1, **t** 95 287 12 72. *Open Mon–Fri 10-2 and 4–7, Sat 10–3*. Paseo de Blas Infante (by the bullring), **t** 95 218 71 19. *Open Mon–Fri 9.30–7.30, Sat–Sun 10–2 and 3–6.30.*

Where to Stay and Eat

Ronda ✉ 29400

Ronda has a wide choice in all ranges. There are dozens of small *hostales* and *camas* over bars – most of them quite agreeable – on all the side streets of Calle Jerez in the Mercadillo.

****Parador de Ronda**, Pza de España, **t** 95 287 75 00, **f** 95 287 81 88, *ronda@parador.es* (*expensive*). This newish *parador* preserves the façade of the old town hall, but is painfully modern inside. It is the flagship of the *parador* chain; comfort and service are excellent, and the views from the duplex suites are matchless. The restaurant has an excellent-value menu.

****Reina Victoria**, Avda Fleming, **t** 95 287 12 40, **f** 95 287 10 75 (*expensive*). A fine and handsome old hotel, which can no longer afford to rest on its laurels. Built by the British around the turn of the century as a retreat for the military in Gibraltar, and now run by the Husa chain, the hotel has lovely views over the cliffs; the German poet Rainer Maria Rilke stayed here for a season in 1912, and wrote some of his best-known works; his room 208 is preserved as a museum.

****Hotel Maestranza**, C/Virgen de la Paz 24, **t** 95 218 70 72, **f** 95 219 01 70, *info@hotelmaestranza.com (expensive)*. This former residence of Pedro Romero, the legendary bullfighter, is one of the best

From the garden of the Casa del Rey Moro there is a stairway – 365 steps cut out of the rock, called the **Mina** – that takes you down to the bottom of the gorge. Here there is a **Moorish bridge** and well-preserved remains of a **Moorish bath** (*t 95 287 77 85; open Tues– 9.30–1.30 and 4–6, Wed–Sat 9.30–3.20; adm*). Inside you can make out the individual pools and changing rooms and see the graceful arches, reminiscent of a mini-Mezquita. Further down from the Casa del Rey Moro you reach the Puente Viejo and the Puente de San Miguel, beyond which the city walls start; you can walk along the walls, with views out over the *vega*. Across the Puente Viejo, to the north, is the Gothic-*mudéjar* **Convento de San Francisco**, founded by Fernando and Isabel in 1485. It has an arch with florid decoration and sports the coat of arms of the Franciscan monks. From here, a pleasant walk back up to town runs via the **Jardines Ciudad de Cuenca**, a series of tiered viewing platforms on the side of the gorge.

options in town. It is in an excellent position just yards from the bullring and the heart of town, and with all the four-star comforts you would expect, including the use of a country club with pool and tennis courts. It also has a good restaurant, **Sol y Sombra**.

Enfrente Arte, C/Real 42, **t** 95 287 47 33, **f** 95 287 72 17, *elfrente@teleline.es* (*expensive*). A stylish small hotel, situated in an old inn at the foot of the cliffs. You'll pay a relatively big sum for a not very big room, although this does include drinks and most food, and it has a very nice pool.

******Hotel San Gabriel**, C/Marqués de Moctezuma 19, **t** 95 219 03 92, **f** 95 219 01 17, *www.hotelsangabriel.com* (*moderate*). Probably the loveliest hotel in town in terms of décor, service, atmosphere and value; a private house from 1736 before conversion to a hotel in 1998. Wood panelling and old prints line the walls, plus billiards, café and a lovely, shaded patio. Bedrooms are individually designed

Hotel Don Miguel, Plaza de España 4, **t** 95 287 77 22, **f** 95 287 83 77, *www.dmiguel.com* (*moderate*). Very good value for such a great spot on the cliff edge and opposite the *parador*. With excellent restaurant.

Alavera de los Baños, C/San Miguel s/n, **t/f** 95 287 91 43, *www.andalucia.com/alavera* (*moderate*). A beautiful little whitewashed-hotel with beamed ceilings and gardens. Slightly inconvenient in that it's at the bottom of town, right next to the Moorish baths, but it is in a pretty setting and has a pool, restaurant and rooms with *terrazas* to watch the sunrise over the hills.

*****Polo**, C/Mariano Soubirón 8, **t** 95 287 24 47, **f** 95 287 24 49 (*moderate*). A busy little place in the centre of town, with pretty blue and white rooms at a modest price – which makes it popular with tour groups.

****Royal**, C/Virgen de la Paz 42, **t** 95 287 11 41 (*inexpensive*). In a good spot near the bullring in the old town.

Hostal El Tajo, C/Cruz Verde 5, **t** 95 287 40 40 (*inexpensive*). A simple, modest *hostal* with recently refurbished rooms with TV and a/c.

Hostal Ronda Sol, C/Almenda 11, **t** 952 87 44 97, (*cheap*). A friendly little place for those on a tight budget; rooms without bath.

There are also a number of places around Ronda – in Cortes de la Frontera, Benarraba, Genalguacil, Montejaque and Jimera de Líbar.

*****Palacete de Mañara**, Pza de la Constitución 2, Montejaque, **t** 95 216 72 52, **f** 95 216 74 08, *hotelpalacete@ole.com* (*moderate*). A really delightful little place, built in a former palace with eight large, individually designed rooms and a pretty patio with a small pool and an excellent restaurant.

****Hotel Banú Rabbah**, C/Sierra Bermeja s/n, Benarraba, **t/f** 95 215 02 88, *www.hbenarraba.es* (*moderate*). Has a huge swimming pool which you can spot from the main road, attached to a very reasonably priced and comfortable hotel on the edge of the pine forest, with a nice restaurant attached.

In the old town, **Palacio de Mondragón**, Pza Mondragón (*open Mon–Fri 10–7, Sat–Sun 10–3; adm*), is one of Ronda's most beautiful palaces, where Fernando and Isabel bedded down on their visits; now it's the town's museum with local finds and some well-preserved patios and woodwork. Just east of here is the town's main church, **Santa María La Mayor** (*open daily 10–7; adm*), still retaining the mihrab and minaret of the mosque it replaced, and with an interior apparently inspired by Granada's cathedral and the ruins of the **Alcázar**, blown up by the French. Also in the old town is the **Casa Juan Bosco**, C/Tenorio 20 (*open 9–6; adm*), a 19th-century mansion that is now a college, with beautiful gardens and fountains, while the **Museo del Bandolero**, C/Armiñan 59 (*open daily summer 10–8, winter 10.15–6.30; adm*), up from the Arab walls, offers a look at the region's past of banditry.

For wonderful views of the town, head out of Ronda on the C/Torrejores towards Algeciras and take a right towards the **Iglesia de la Virgen de la Cabeza** (*open Mon–Fri*

Centro de Iniciativas Turisticas, C/Montes de Oca 18, Málaga, **t** 95 227 62 29, *www.ruralandalus.es*. Genalguacil has no hotels, but it does have a wealth of *casas rurales*. Contact this central reservation office for details (online booking available). There are also a number of *casas rurales* in Jimera de Líbar.

Quite a few really inferior tourist restaurants have been opening in conspicuous places to take advantage of day-trippers from the Costa: watch out.

Tragabuches, C/Jose Aparicio 1, **t** 902 40 42 00, **f** 95 287 86 41 (*expensive*). This is a *cuatro tenedores* place, Spain's top award for a restaurant, so you know you are in for a treat. Chef Sergio López is a rising star and a winner of one of the country's most prestigious culinary awards, the *Bidasoa*. The food is traditional *andaluz* cuisine combined with some unexpected flavours: duck's liver with curry and chocolate, for example, or white garlic soup with herrings, eggs and figs. The warm chocolate soufflé and ice-cream pud is out of this world. Accompanied by a superb wine list. *Closed Mon.*

Escudero, Chalet del Tajo, Pso de Blas Infante 1, **t** 902 43 45 45, **f** 95 287 45 32 (*expensive*). Under the same management, but a totally different style of restaurant, serving more traditional food such as roasts and grills and with probably the best view in town, just behind the bullring.

Duquesa de Parcent, C/Tenorio 12, **t** 95 219 07 63, **f** 95 287 27 16 (*expensive*). The place you can see from the bridge, with three tiered terraces perched above the gorge. This 19th-century house has been sumptuously renovated inside, and features grilled pork and lamb and fish in saltcrust as the house specials. It's ideal for an early-evening drink as you watch the sun set over the mountains.

Casa Santa Pola, C/Sta Domingo 3, **t** 95 287 92 08, **f** 95 287 93 28 (*expensive–moderate*). Set in a 9th-century Moorish mosque, with a terrace overlooking the river, and great décor inside; the food is traditional *andaluz* and Rondan – roast meats and fresh fish. Flamenco show on Fridays and Saturdays (ring ahead for details).

Don Miguel, Villanueva 4, **t** 95 287 10 90 (*moderate*). At the hotel of the same name. Some of the best meals Ronda can offer, overlooking the gorge next to the famous bridge; they also have a bar built into the bridge itself.

Doña Pepa, Plaza del Socorro 10 (overlooking the square), **t** 95 287 47 77, **f** 95 287 53 80, *restopepa@ronda.net* (*moderate*). A good bet around the Mercadillo, with quail sautéed in garlic, and partridge.

La Farola, Plaza de Carmen Abela s/n. A friendly, family-run bar serving a great range of tapas, and some home-cooked dishes.

Relax Café Bar, C/ Los Remedios 27, t 952 877 207. Mellow, friendly vegetarian café, with wooden tables and ochre walls. Good sandwiches, juices and cakes.

El Refugio, C/Duende 4, Genalguacil, **t** 95 215 21 30 (*moderate*). At this restaurant in

10–2 and 5–7.30, Sat–Sun 10–3; adm), which is about 2km away. The building dates from the 9th century and is built into the rock. Come towards sunset when the dying rays illuminate the rock. There are some excellent walking trails around Ronda – including one to the chapel of Virgen de la Cabeza – which are described in leaflets available from the tourist office, or online at *www.turismoronda.org*.

Around Ronda

Besides the opportunities for walks in and around the valleys under Ronda, an interesting excursion can be made to an area of curiosities 15–20km west of town. The hills around the hamlet of **Montejaque** are full of caves. Two of them, the **Cueva del Gato** and **Cueva del Hundidero**, both full of stalactites and odd formations, are connected. A little stream, the Gaduares, disappears into one and comes out in the

Genalguacil you can try the local mushrooms (in season) and other regional dishes.

Benaoján ✉ 29370

★★★**Molino del Santo**, Bulevar de la Estación, **t** 95 216 71 51, **f** 95 216 73 27, *www.andalucia.com/molino* (*moderate*). A converted water mill beside a mountain stream, close to the Pileta caves and with a spring-fed swimming pool. The kitchen serves up local ingredients. It's friendly and intimate and offers details on excursions – hiking, cycling and mini-bus nature tours in the Grazalema National Park.

Casitas de la Sierra, **t** 95 216 73 92, **f** 95 216 72 99 (*inexpensive*). Offers fully furnished village houses with all mod cons; a cheaper and more rustic option.

Benalauría ✉ 29491

Mesón La Molienda, C/Moraleda 59, **t** 95 215 25 48 (*moderate*). A restaurant with rooms, set in an old olive mill; it specializes in mountain dishes with a Moorish influence. The views across the Serranía from this eagle's nest are magnificent.

Gaucín ✉ 29400

Cortijo El Puerto del Negro, Ctra El Colmenar, **t/f** 95 215 12 39. Below the village, on an exclusive residential estate set within a 50-hectare farm, with a country-house atmosphere. There are independent cottages in the grounds which can be rented. With billiard room, swimming pool, tennis court, formal Andalucían garden and stunning views of Gibraltar.

El Pilar, Ctra Ronda-Algeciras, opposite petrol station, **t** 95 215 13 47 (*inexpensive*). A real workman's *comedor*, but with a nobleman's view from the terrace on a sunny day. Offers an excellent-value lunch with wine.

La Fructuosa, C/Luís de Armiñan 67, **t** 95 215 10 72. Widely regarded as one of the best restaurants in the area, a great place for a romantic dinner or a lazy lunch. It also offers beautifully decorated rooms painted in deep Mediterranean colours. Fabulous views from the roof terrace.

El Burgo ✉ 29420

La Casa Grande, C/Mesones 1, **t** 95 216 02 32, **f** 95 216 01 81, *www.hotel-lacasagrande.com* (*moderate*). The best place to stay; spotlessly clean and done out in an old style with beams and brickwork and a wonderful shaded patio.

Nightlife

Ronda doesn't really rock, but there are one or two late night bars dotted around.

Tacones, C/Mariano Soubirón 4 (at the top end of the Alameda). Quite trendy, with good music and Internet access; there is a slightly more upbeat bar opposite.

Café las Bridas, C/Los Remedios 16/18. One of several bars on this busy street. This one has a flamenco flavour – but also does Guinness on tap.

other. Five kilometres south, past the village of **Benaoján**, the **Cueva de la Pileta** has some 25,000-year-old art – simple drawings in black of animals and magic symbols (***t** 95 216 73 43; open 10–1 and 4–7; guided tours on the hour; adm*).

Twelve kilometres west of Ronda, off the road to Grazalema, are the Roman ruins of **Acinipo** known locally as Ronda la Vieja, with a theatre and stage building like Mérida's. If you have a car or even a bicycle, take the 40km 'scenic route' along the spectacular C341, which leaves Ronda to the southwest. It's a breathless roller-coaster ride through the heart of the **Serranía de Ronda**. From Benaoján the road wends down towards **Cortes de la Frontera**, a village founded by the Phoenicians, with a wonderful main square surrounded by old mansions adorned with the previous owners' coats of arms. It's worth making a brief detour to **Jimera de Líbar**, which has an ancient castle of Moorish and Roman origins. From Jimera you can strike out on a number of walking routes (*information from the ayuntamiento,* **t** *95 218 00 04*). From Cortes the MA512 twists and turns via the tiny village of El Colmenar. You'll pass by the villages of Atajate, Benadalid and Algatocín before reaching the ancient village of **Gaucín**. This agreeable but undistinguished place has become a magnet for a certain kind of American and English expat who came here in the 1970s and '80s looking for the 'real' Spain. From their balconies, they have remarkable views of Gibraltar and the African coast over the peaks of the Serranía.

On the way back to Ronda stop in at the tiny village of **Genalguacil**, east along the MA536 after Algatocín. The village has been turned into an open-air art museum, with sculptures of wood, ceramics, iron and pottery brightening up the streets and squares until a permanent home can be found for them.

The scenery of the Serranía is justly famous; mountains and ravines sprinkled with tiny white villages nestling under crags, hair-raising mountain passes and a wilderness where vultures, golden eagles and ibex can be spotted. Much of it has been turned into nature reserves: to the east lies the **Reserva Nacional de Serranía de Ronda**, to the southeast the **Reserva Nacional de Cortes de la Frontera**, and to the northeast, the **Parque Natural Sierra de Grazalema** (*see* pp.209–14). There are a vast number of walking routes and plenty of outdoor activities such as rock climbing, potholing and horse riding to detain you, as well as natural sights: caves, gorges, lakes and rivers. There are also some wonderful restaurants and hotels tucked away in the hills and villages. Local tourist offices will supply you with walking maps of the area.

Ronda to Málaga

A far more relaxing and scenic route to Málaga than the hectic N340 takes you inland along the twisting and turning A366: all stone outcrops and dark hills. The road passes by a little-known nature reserve, **Sierra de las Nieves**, which has a 5,000-hectare wood of Spanish pine trees that can be traced back to prehistoric times, as well as a number of birds including goshawks, sparrowhawks and falcons. The first place of any note is **El Burgo**, a typical white town nestling in a valley. From here you can strike out on a number of walks or stop for a bite to eat. The road passes the northern limit of the path before dropping down towards the dusty town of **Coín** and then east to Málaga or west to Marbella.

Antequera and Around

Known in Roman times as *Antiquaria*, it was the first of the Granadan border fortresses to fall to the Reconquista, in 1410, although subsequently it was retaken by the Moors and lost again. The centre of a leather-tanning industry, set below an outcrop overlooking the *vega*, Antequera is one of the architectural showpieces of the entire region, with an impressive ensemble of 16th- to 18th-century buildings. The Nájera Palace houses the **Municipal Museum** (*open Tues–Fri 10–13:30 and 4–6, Sat 10–1.30, Sun and hols 11–1.30; adm*), with many religious works including a St Francis by Alonso Cano and a Roman bronze of a young boy, known as 'Ephebus of Antequera'.

Getting There and Around

By Train

Antequera is on the rail line from Algeciras to Granada, and there are easy connections to all points from nearby Bobadilla Junction. The station is on Avenida de la Estación, **t** 902 24 02 02.

By Bus

Lots of buses go to Málaga and Sevilla, fewer to Granada and Córdoba, as well as to Olvera, Osuna and the other villages of the region. The bus station, **t** 95 284 19 57, is at Campillo Alto s/n, at the top of town, near the *parador*.

Tourist Information

Antequera: Pza San Sebastián 7, **t** 95 270 25 05. *Open 10–2 and 5–8.*

Archidona: Plaza Ochavada 2, **t** 95 271 64 79. *Open Mon–Fri 10–1.30, Sat 11–2.*

Where to Stay and Eat

Antequera ✉ 29200

****Hotel Golf Antequera**, Urbanización Santa Catalina s/n, **t** 95 270 45 31, **f** 95 284 52 32, *www.hotelantequera.com*. A brand new modern complex with gym, sauna, pool, and restaurant. As of early 2003, the golf course wasn't quite finished.

***Parador de Antequera**, Pso García del Olmo s/n, **t** 95 284 02 61, **f** 95 284 13 12, *antequera@parador.es* (*expensive–moderate*). A plain, modern building but with the most comforts in Antequera, including a pool; reasonably priced.

***Hotel Las Villas de Antikaria**, Ctra de Córdoba 3, **t** 95 284 48 99, **f** 95 284 56 21, *www.hotellasvillas.com* (*moderate*). A modern place lacking much character but with an excellent restaurant and bike hire, but no pool.

***Hotel Mesón Papabellotas**, C/Encarnación 5, **t** 95 270 50 45, **f** 95 270 48 42 (*moderate*). Excellently situated in the heart of the old town, the hotel is a converted whitewashed townhouse.

Hotel Castilla, C/Infante de Fernando 40, **t** 95 284 32 48, **f** 95 284 30 90 (*moderate*). Set in a completely new building, but in the heart of the old town, with air conditioning, bath and satellite TV.

*Manzanito**, Pza San Sebastián, **t** 95 284 10 23 (*inexpensive*). One of the best budget choices in the town centre. The management also runs a good restaurant beneath.

*Hotel Nuevo Infante**, C/Infante de Fernando 5, **t** 95 270 02 93, **f** 95 270 00 86 (*inexpensive*). Small apartments in the centre, equipped with kitchens.

Pension Madrona, C/Calzada 25, **t** 95 284 00 14 (*cheap*). Clean and basic; does good *churros* and breakfasts.

Caselio de San Benito, Ctra M-C, km 108, **t** 95 211 11 03 (*expensive*). One of the finest restaurants in the area, appearing in two of Spain's top gourmet guides.

El Angelote, C/Encarnación (corner of Coso Viejo), **t** 95 270 34 65 (*moderate*). An excellent restaurant set in the heart of the old town near the Palacio de la Nájera, serving delicious *Antequerana* dishes.

La Espuela, Pso María Cristina s/n, Pza de Toros, **t** 95 270 34 24 (*moderate*). The only restaurant in Spain actually located inside a bullring – *rabo de toro* is usually the dish

Up the Cuesta Zapateros is the 16th-century **Arco de los Gigantes**, meant as a sort of triumphal arch for the seldom-victorious Philip II; next to it, the ruins of a Moorish fortress offer views over the town to one of the main landmarks of the area: **La Peña de los Enamorados** (Lovers' Rock), halfway between the town and Archidona. It looks like the head of a sleeping giant and is known colloquially as 'Franco's nose', but it got its name from the legend of a Moorish girl who fell in love with a Christian boy; realizing they could never be together in life, they threw themselves from the rock. Nearby is the plateresque church of **Santa María La Mayor** (*open Tue–Fri 10.30–2 and 4.30–6.30, Sat 10.30–2, Sun 11.30–2*), attached to which is an art restoration centre.

of the day. There's another branch on C/San Augustín 1, **t** 95 270 30 31.

Nightlife is centred up and down the C/Alameda, which has a number of *tapas* bars and pubs.

Mollina ✉ 29532

*****Hotel Molino de Saydo**, Ctra de Málaga km 146, **t** 95 274 04 75, **f** 95 274 04 66, *saydo@arrakis.es* (*moderate*). A wonderful hotel set in its own grounds overlooking the *vega*. The traditional rooms are set around a patio, and there's a bar, restaurant and Olympic-sized swimming pool.

Archidona ✉ 29200

*******La Bobadilla**, Finca La Bobadilla, **t** 95 832 18 61, **f** 95 832 18 10, *www.la-bobadilla.com* (*luxury*). Turn off the road at the sign for Villanueva de Tapia, halfway to Loja. This plush hotel is an honest attempt at reconstructing the typical Andalucían *pueblo*, complete with Moorish touches, and set in 250 hectares of Mediterranean oak forest. The sports facilities are outstanding and include tennis, archery, gym, pools, horse-riding and clay-pigeon shooting, and there are no fewer than three award-winning restaurants.

****Hotel Escua**, **t** 95 271 43 76 (*moderate*). On the outskirts of town, this agreeable hotel offers attractive, welcoming rooms and the owners can organize all kinds of activities. The restaurant is equally good.

***Las Palomas**, Ctra Jerez–Granada, km 177, **t** 95 271 43 26 (*cheap*). The best bet if you are on a budget.

El Central, C/Nueva 49, **t/f** 95 271 48 11. This is the best restaurant in town, just up from the square. It serves seafood, tapas and regional wines. Try the speciality *púrra*, a kind of thick gazpacho.

Villanueva de la Concepción ✉ 29230

Casa de Elrond, Barrio Seco, **t/f** 95 275 40 91, *elrond@mercuryin.es*. An English-run *andaluz*-style guest house, set in gardens, by El Torcal National Park; family and double rooms all en suite, with pool.

Álora and Carratraca ✉ 29200

***El Príncipe**, C/Antonio Riobo 9, **t** 95 245 80 20 (*inexpensive*). This is *the* place to stay in Carratraca – in season it's always advisable to book well in advance as it's popular with spa visitors.

Guadal Arte, C/Baños 3, **t** 95 245 83 40 (*inexpensive*). Delicious Malagueña recipes with a hint of Morocco in some dishes. Save room for the home-made desserts, and enjoy the fabulous views from the terrace.

***Durán**, C/La Parra 9, Álora, **t** 95 249 66 42 (*inexpensive–cheap*). A reasonable, basic option in the centre of Álora.

El Chorro ✉ 29552

La Garganta, **t** 95 249 51 19, **f** 95 249 52 98. The best option if you want to stay near the gorge; offers excellent apartments with kitchen and lounge areas, great views, a rooftop pool and a good restaurant attached.

Ardales ✉ 29550

*****La Posada del Conde**, Pantano del Chorro 16 & 18, **t** 95 211 24 11, **f** 95 211 28 05, *(moderate)*. A lovely hotel wonderfully situated on the reservoir; large doubles – bright, clean and tastefully designed – with balconies and a good restaurant.

Next to the church are some recently discovered **Roman baths** (*termas romanas*), still glittering in places with faded mosaics. To the east of the square lies **La Iglesia del Carmen** (*open Mon 11–2, Tues–Fri and Sun 10–2, Sat 10–2 and 4–7; adm*), which has one of Andalucia's finest Baroque altars. At the **Museo Convento de Las Descalzas** (***t** 95 284 19 59*) on the Plaza de las Descalzas, you can visit the museum of religious art, or pick up some sweet treats from the cloistered nuns. To the west of the Alcazaba, on the Plaza de Portichuelo, is one of the prettiest churches in Antequera, **Capilla de la Virgen de Socorro**, or 'Portichuelo' for short, with a combination of architectural styles from Baroque to *mudéjar*.

Heading northwest out of Antequera into the gentler hills flanking the southern slopes of the Guadalquivir valley, you'll be on your way to Sevilla via the villages of Estepa and Osuna (*see* pp.135–6). If you're going that way, turn off the N334 at Fuente de Piedra and you'll come to the **Laguna de Fuente de Piedra**, one of Europe's largest breeding grounds for flamingos from March to September.

If you wish to stay in the area, you could do much worse than **Mollina**, a tiny village at the top of Málaga province. It has a history dating back to Neolithic times, while its name comes from Norman times when it was known as Mollis, or 'drizzle', as in olive oil. There are some 40 caves at **La Sierra de la Camorra**, about 6km north of the village, and a 17th-century church, **Nuestra Señora de la Oliva**. Roman monuments include the 2nd-century **Mausoleum de la Capuchina**, and the 3rd-century **Castellum de Santillon**, in the park 3km from town.

East of Antequera

The Romans may have given Antequera its name, 'old town', and there was probably a settlement here some centuries before the arrival of the Phoenicians. Another possibility is that the name is related to *anta*, the local word for dolmen. Just out of town are the Neolithic monuments known as the **Cuevas de Menga**, the 'first real architecture in Spain'. They are hardly as impressive as the *talayots* and *taulas* of the island of Menorca, but there's nothing like them elsewhere on mainland Spain. Le Corbusier came here in the 1950s, as he said, 'to pay homage to my predecessors'. There are three, dating from anything between 4500 BC and 2500 BC. The two largest, the **Menga** and **Viera** dolmens (*open Tues–Sat 9–3, Sun 10–2*), are covered chambers about 21m (70ft) long, roughly elliptical and lined with huge, flat stones; other monoliths support the roof-like pillars. Nearby at **El Romeral**, under a mound and in the grounds of a sugar factory, the third of these temples has two chambers with domed ceilings. Originally the mound would have been about 100 yards in diameter, as big as Newgrange in Ireland. All three have figures and symbols etched around the walls.

Fifteen kilometres east of Antequera on the N342 is **Archidona**. The town overlooks acres of olive trees, but its main feature is the unique, octagonal Plaza Mayor, the **Ochavada**. Built between 1780 and 1786 by Francisco Astorga and Antonio González, it is one of the loveliest plazas in Andalucía, and was built using stones from **El Torcal**. In nearby **Loja** is the 16th-century church of **San Gabriel**, which has a cupola attributed to Diego de Siloé. The town's other main sites, which can be seen on the approach from Antequera, are the hilltop ruins of its Moorish castle and, just below, the **Santuario de la Virgen de Gracia** (*open daily Nov–Jan 9–2 and 3–7, May–Aug 7–2 and 5–10, Feb–Apr and Sep–Oct 8–2 and 4–8*), a simple brick building built over a mosque. Inside is a font, a gift from Queen Isabel. The views across the *vega* to the **Peña de los Enamorados** and the olive-tree clad slopes are impressive.

South of Antequera

The sierras between Antequera and Málaga contain some of the remote villages of the region and offer some spectacular scenery – almond trees, cacti, olive groves and mountains that drop steeply away to the silver ribbon of a stream down below. A natural park has been laid out around the rock formations at **El Torcal**, a tall but hike-able mountain with unusual red limestone crags (*info centre open daily 10–5; for guides call* **t** *95 260 22 79*). The nearest town is **Villanueva de la Concepción**. Here you should take the MA424 and travel south for about 17km. You will be rewarded with **Almogía**, presenting a dramatic spectacle overlooking a high ridge. From 15–18 August this place comes to life with dancing in the streets in celebration of San Roque and San Sebastián. The best views are from the ruined tower.

A more roundabout route south from Antequera will take you to the town of **Álora**. Originally a Roman settlement and one of the last towns to be held by the Moors, it is mainly of interest now as the point where you should turn northwest towards one of Andalucía's natural wonders. **El Chorro Gorge**, in the deep rugged canyon of the Río Guadalhorce, has sheer walls of limestone tossed about at crazy angles. It used to be possible to circumnavigate it on a concrete catwalk called **El Camino del Rey**, built in 1920 for Alfonso XIII, and poorly maintained ever since. It's currently closed for repairs, after several terrible accidents. El Chorro has a train station on the Antequera–Málaga line. If you're not up to stopping, you can get a good view of the gorge from the train as it weaves in and out of the tunnels.

If you have time to explore this region, seek out the church of **Bobastro**, a 9th-century basilica cut out of bare rock; it supposedly contains the tomb of ibn-Hafsun, the Christian emir who founded a short-lived independent state in the mountains around 880. Some remains of the city and fortress he built can be seen on the heights nearby. The lakes, which are also visible, were created as part of a big hydro-electric scheme, but their shores, surrounded by gentle hills, make an ideal place to have a lazy picnic.

From Bobastro follow the road to **Carratraca**, a spa town from Greek and Roman times, though its heyday was in the 19th and early 20th centuries. Visitors included Byron, Dumas, Rilke and Napoleon III's Spanish wife, the Empress Eugénie, who gadded about everywhere else in Europe and lived to the age of 94. Though its heyday has now passed, the town is famous for its Passion play. As part of their Semana Santa celebrations, 140 of the villagers perform *El Paso* in the bullring. From here the road twists and turns its way back to Álora.

The Coast East of Málaga

Vélez-Málaga and the Axarquía

Torre del Mar, the first resort east of Málaga, is a carbon copy of any of the Costa del Sol towns, with grey-sand beaches and the usual concrete monstrosities lining the seafront, but if anything, lacking the party atmosphere of the others. The town has attempted a bit of prettification with a long, tree-lined promenade, and there are some lovely views to the Sierra de Tejeda. From Torre del Mar you can make a short detour inland to **Vélez-Málaga**, lying in a fertile valley at the foot of the Axarquía mountain area. The new town holds no particular charm, but the old part tells of its

Getting There and Around

The Portillo and Alsina Graells **buses** from Málaga or Motril serve Nerja, Almuñécar and Salobreña, and connections can be made from these towns to the interior villages. Note that long-distance buses along the coast do not usually stop at these towns. Almuñécar's buses set off from Avda Juan Carlos I, **t** 95 863 01 40.

Tourist Information

Almuñécar: Avda de Europa (in the small Moorish palace), **t** 95 863 11 25, **f** 95 863 15 07. *Open Mon–Sat 10–2 and 5–8.*

Frigiliana: Pza del Ingenio s/n, **t** 95 253 31 26.

Herradura: Avenida Prieto Moreno (by the market) **t/f** 95 864 04 25.

Nerja: Puerto de Mar 2, **t** 95 252 15 31. *Open weekdays 10–2 and 5–7, Sat 10–1.*

Salobreña: Pza de Goya s/n, **t** 95 861 03 14, *salobre@redestb.es. Open Mon–Fri 9.30–1.30 and 4.30–7, Sat 9.30–1.30; closed Sun.*

Torre del Mar: Avda de Andalucía 92, **t** 95 254 11 04.

The tourist information offices have a map with general information about the Axarquía and a number of routes to follow.

Where to Stay and Eat

Torre del Mar ✉ 29740

★★★★**Hotel Husa Mainake**, C/Copo s/n, **t** 95 254 72 46, **f** 95 254 15 43, *mainake@husa.es* (*expensive*). The best hotel in the area, 100yds from the beach. It has all the amenities, including a pool on the roof.

★★**Miraya**, C/Patrón Veneno 6, **t** 95 254 59 59, **f** 95 254 55 15 (*moderate*). Virtually on the beach; friendly, with clean, bright rooms, all en suite, and a café.

★**Hostal Generalife**, C/Patrón Veneno 22, **t** 95 254 33 09. The *inexpensive* beachside option.

Vélez-Málaga ✉ 29700

★★**Hotel Dila**, Avenida Vivar Téllez 3, **t** 95 250 39 00 (*inexpensive*). Offers clean, basic rooms with baths.

Benamocarra ✉ 29719

★★★**Cerro La Jaula**, **t/f** 95 253 56 85 (*moderate*). A wonderful place to stay or eat, just outside the town, on its own hill. It has incredible views, a pool and 10 spacious rooms. The restaurant serves excellent local dishes at reasonable prices; try the gazpacho and *conejo*. (Down the hill towards town is a flamenco bar, on C/Grupo Cerro.)

Moorish past; the castle, **La Fortaleza** (of which a restored tower remains, set in pretty gardens), was one of the last Moorish outposts to fall to Christian forces during the campaigns of Isabel and Fernando. Below the castle, the church of **Nuestra Señora de la Encarnación** has had a chequered career – first as a Visigothic church, then a mosque, then a church again when the town was recaptured by Christian forces in 1487. In town there are a number of sites, none particularly outstanding: the **Hospital de San Juan de Dios**, C/Confrade, founded by Fernando and Isabel, used as a theatre in the 17th century, and now an old people's home; the 15th-century **Convento de San Francisco**, on Pza de San Francisco, and a Baroque church with a *mudéjar* courtyard.

Just to the west of Vélez is **Benamocarra**. Although not as dramatically placed as towns further inland, it is mercifully free of tourist buses and retains much of its character. The main church, **Iglesia Santa Ana**, dates from 1505 and was restored in 1949; its tower and main nave, which is octagonal, are in *mudéjar* style. Close by is **Iznate**, which has several monuments, including the castle of Omar Ben Hafsun, the rebel Andalucían leader, and a *mudéjar* church. Iznate is most famous for its riotous grape festival, **Fiesta de la Uva Moscatel**, held on 5 August, where you can join the locals in a food and drink blowout from eight till late, with music and prizes.

Comares ✉ 29195

El Molino de los Abuelos, Plaza 2, **t** 95 250 93 09, **f** 95 221 42 20, *info@molino-abuelos.com* (*moderate*). Possibly the best-situated hotel in the region: an old olive-pressing mill which has been beautifully converted into a small hotel. There are five rooms and three apartments, all individual, but the ones to go for are the front-facing double or the suite, which look right out across the valley. For a few more euros, book the apartment with a Jacuzzi set in an alcove with windows all round. The restaurant below serves a fine selection of reasonably priced local dishes.

Sedella ✉ 29215

Casa Pinta, located just outside Sedella, **t** 95 250 89 55, (*inexpensive*). The best place to stay in the area is this dramatically located, English-run hotel; it's friendly and very reasonable with an excellent restaurant and a pool that looks out across the sierras.

Competa ✉ 29754

*****Hotel Balcon de Competa**, C/San Antonio 75, **t** 95 255 35 35, **f** 95 255 35 10, *www.hotel-competa.com* (*inexpensive*). Has fantastic views, a restaurant, café and pool. Also offers activities such as horse-riding, safaris, hiking and golf. For longer stays ask about the self-catering apartment.

Archez ✉ 29753

Posada-Mesón Mudéjar, C/Álamo 6, **t** 95 255 31 06, **f** 95 255 30 19, *archez@sopde.es* (*inexpensive*). A delightful restored 17th-century building converted into a hotel; all five rooms have bath, phone and a/c plus a restaurant with local dishes.

Canillas de Aceituno ✉ 29716

Hostal Canillas, t 95 251 81 02 (*cheap*). This village, apparently untouched by tourism, has this one little place to stay above a shop on a quiet street. Also has apartments to let.

Torrox-Costa ✉ 29793

****Hotel Nuval**, Cortijo Amaya, **t** 95 253 02 45, **f** 95 253 13 14 (*moderate*). Close to the beach and set in a lovely garden with a pool. The *cortijo* is a restored farmhouse, with big rooms and a good restaurant; rooms can also be hired on a reduced weekly rate.

Nerja ✉ 29780

******Parador de Nerja**, Playa de Burriana, C/Almuñécar 8, **t** 95 252 00 50, **f** 95 252 19 97, *nerja@parador.es* (*expensive*). A luxurious place; modern and newly renovated.

A less-explored region than the Serranía de Ronda, but no less beautiful, is the **Axarquía**, a collection of tiny whitewashed villages surrounding Vélez-Málaga on the slopes of the **Sierra de Tejeda**, a national park. To really explore, you will need your own car as public transport links are scarce. Some towns, such as Frigiliana (*see* p.279) and Torrox, both of which are a short drive from the coast, have suffered the same fate that befell Mijas, above Torremolinos, and are consequently overrun with tourists throughout the day. Press on into the hills, however, and you will find little gems like Competa and Almáchar – famous for sweet wines and flower displays respectively (*see* below) – and **Comares**, perched atop one of the highest peaks and with one of the best-positioned hotels in the entire valley (*see* 'Where to Stay', above). Situated on the C340 (north of Vélez), Comares is known as the 'Balcón de Axarquía', with views from the platform in the main square across the valley and towards the coast. The town was of strategic importance during Moorish times and was one of the bases of Omar ben Hafsun; there are the ruins of a Moorish castle at its highest point.

West of Vélez, **Almáchar** is an exquisite little village of tumbling houses and winding streets, best explored on foot. Leave your car at the top of town near what was the old bus shelter and head down C/Eugenia Ríos. In spring and summer, the

★★★★**Balcón de Europa 1**, Pso Balcón de Europa, **t** 95 252 08 00, **f** 95 252 44 90, *balconeuropa@spa.es* (*expensive*). Though not as luxurious as the *Parador*, the beautiful location on the 'balcony of Europe' in the town centre and the reasonable rates make the difference. Both hotels have lifts down to the beaches under Nerja's cliffs.

★★★**Plaza Cavana**, Plaza Cavana, **t** 95 252 40 00, **f** 95 252 40 08, *hotelplazacavana@inforegocio.com* (*moderate*). Just a few minutes walk from the Balcón de Europa, with air conditioning and two pools.

★**Portofino**, Puerta del Mar 2, **t** 95 252 01 50 (*moderate*). A slightly over-priced option for what's offered, set right on the beach.

★★**Hostal Marissal**, Balcón de Europa 3, **t** 95 252 01 99 (*inexpensive*). Excellent location and value; sea views, a/c and TV; with café.

Hostal Miguel, C/Almirante Ferrandíz 31, **t** 95 252 65 35 (*inexpensive–cheap*). Central and friendly, with rooms with or without bath.

Udo Heimer, Pueblo Andaluz 27, **t** 95 252 00 32 (*expensive*).For a special dinner: a tranquil, elegant restaurant serving contemporary Spanish cuisine on the terrace.

Casa Luque, Plaza de Cavana 2, **t** 95 252 10 04 (*moderate*). One of the finest restaurants in Nerja, with superb views and a buzzy tapas bar, too.

La Marina, Plaza de la Marina, **t** 95 252 12 19 (*inexpensive*). A family favourite, serving a wide range of fish and seafood tapas.

El Candil, **t** 95 252 07 97 (*moderate–inexpensive*). Has a good selection of Spanish dishes in a lovely setting, in a square just off the Balcón.

Frigiliana ✉ 29788

★★★**Los Caracoles**, Ctra. km 4.6, **t** 95 203 06 80, *loscaracoles@ari.es* (*moderate*). Slightly out of town on the road to Torrox; set amongst olive groves with beautiful views, this is a lovely spot, with Gaudí-inspired designs.

★**Las Chinas**, Pza Capitán Cortés 14, **t/f** 95 253 30 73 (*inexpensive*). At present, the only hotel in the town itself; clean and hospitably run by Miguel and Puri, who can tell you all about the village.

La Posada Morisca, **t** 95 253 41 51 (*moderate*). A delightful rural hotel in the hills about 2km from Frigiliana, with just a dozen rooms, a garden, pool and excellent restaurant.

Frigiliana is full of restaurants; some of the best include:

La Bodeguilla, C/El Garral 2, **t** 95 253 34 28 (*inexpensive*). Serves typical mountain food.

Santo Cristo, Ctra Frigiliana–Torrox, **t** 952 53 40 65 (*inexpensive*). A cosy restaurant serving barbecued fish and lamb on a terrace

town is a riot of colours, with flowers spilling from every balcony, patio and window box (look for the plaques dotted about town commemorating individual streets for their displays). The **Iglesia San Mateo**, Plaza de España, is worth a peek, as are the small gardens at the bottom of the C/Forfe where, legend has it, a Moor hid some treasure that has never been found. Nearby **El Borge** is smaller and not as immediately pretty but it does have a lovely church, **Nuestra Señora de Rosario**, which has a *mudéjar* ceiling, two octagonal towers and a small crypt containing some dusty old bones, which Carlos III had a hand in sealing in 1787.

From Comares you could press on to **Colmenar**, a dusty town on the borders of Málaga province and a centre for honey production; otherwise you could head back down the hill and east via Riogordo to **Alfarnate**, which claims the oldest inn in Andalucía, the 13th-century **Venta de Alfarnate**, which doubles as a museum about the various *bandoleros* who frequented the place.

Another Axarquía route, perhaps less dramatic and a great deal shorter, begins on the coast east of Vélez and winds through **Salares** and **Sedella**, two of the prettiest villages in the area. Both have churches built on Moorish foundations, Santa Ana and San Andrés respectively, the former still bearing an old Moorish minaret. Continue on

El Tangay, Avda Andalucía, **t** 95 253 30 49. A favourite among locals.

Almuñécar ✉ 18690

There are plenty of hotels to be found in Almuñécar in the old town, with cheaper ones around the Plaza de la Rosa.

******Hotel Helios**, Paseo San Cristóbal, **t** 95 863 44 59, **f** 95 863 44 69 (*expensive–moderate*). The town's smartest hotel, with a pool.

****Casablanca**, Plaza San Cristóbal 4, **f** 95 863 55 75 (*moderate–inexpensive*). A family-run pseudo-Moorish affair with rooms looking out to sea or to the castle and the sierras.

***Hotel San Cristóbal**, Plaza San Cristóbal, **t/f** 95 863 36 12 (*inexpensive*). A cheaper option, with sea-facing rooms and balconies.

Los Geranios, Pza Rosa 4a, **t** 95 263 07 24 (*moderate*). Owned by a Hispano-Belgian couple; the menu is international, with a Spanish bias. *Closed Sun and Nov*.

Bodega Francisco, C/Real 15, **t** 95 263 01 68 (*inexpensive*). A wonderful watering hole serving tapas and the usual *andaluz* staples.

***Hotel La Tartana**, C/San Nicolás de la Herradura, *www.hotellatartana.com*, **t/f** 95 864 05 35. The only hotel in the pretty little bay of La Herradura, where development has, for once, been kept under control. Basic, spotless rooms and charming service.

Salobreña ✉ 18680

*****Salobreña**, outside the town on the coastal highway, **t** 95 861 02 61, **f** 95 861 01 01 (*moderate*). Close to the beach with pool and garden. The restaurant is also worth trying; it does barbecues in summer and the views are worth the price alone.

***Mari Tere**, Ctra de la Playa 7, **t** 95 882 84 89, **f** 95 861 01 26. A *hostal* near the beach with doubles and bath, and a restaurant.

Camping El Peñón, **t** 95 861 02 07. A campsite near the beach. *Closed Nov–March*.

Mesón de la Villa, Plaza F. Ramírez de Madrid, **t** 95 861 24 14 (*moderate–inexpensive*). The best restaurant in town, serving up local fish dishes and *rabo de toro*. *Closed Wed*.

There are also a number of good *chiringuitos* along the beach during the season.

Activities

La Herradura, effectively a suburb of Almuñécar but far less developed, mainly consists of beach-front restaurants, a wind-surfing school and a diving centre – **Centro de Buceo**, Pso de Andrés Segovia 13, **t** 95 864 06 57, **f** 95 864 06 49, *www.buceolaherradura.com*. In summer the water is clear with a visibility of up to 25m (80ft); it's teeming with fish and sea cucumbers.

to **Competa**, a truly lovely old village known principally for its sweet wines; the grapes are sun-dried to sweeten and fortify them. Its big wine fiesta is held on 15 August in the main square. As has happened with many Andalucían villages near the coast, northern invaders have discovered its charm, Brits and Danes particularly. Beyond Competa begin the wilds of the **Reserva Nacional de Sierra de Tejeda**; you'll have to leave your car to explore it, though, and strong comfortable shoes are recommended. To get back to the coast, take the MA137 through beautiful vine-clad slopes to **Torrox**, another Nordic enclave with a history dating back to 2000 BC, and continue down to **Torrox-Costa**, an expanding resort 8km from Nerja.

Alhama de Granada

For a further detour into the mountains, you can tackle the 50km drive along the C335 (becoming the C340 at Ventas) from Vélez over the Sierra to **Alhama de Granada**. The road snakes its way up through olive trees, trickling streams and rocky gulches; but pay close attention – there are some helter-skelter turns. Alhama balances precariously on a rocky lip and looks down to the deep grass-banked gorge, through which the Alhama runs. Up here you're away from it all. 'Oh, for my Alhama', was the lament of Boabdil el Chico, who had to abandon this beauty spot to the Christians in 1482. The town's 17th- to 18th-century church of **El Carmen** has a terrace from which you can enjoy the panorama.

No prizes for guessing the town's other attractions – the remains of a Moorish castle, in the main square, and a 15th-century parish church, a gift to the town from Fernando and Isabel. The Catholic Kings' Granada architects, Enrique de Egas and Diego de Siloé, both worked on it. Alhama has been famous since Roman times for its spa waters; ask at the modern spa, the Hotel Balneario, to see the **Roman and Moorish baths** beneath.

Nerja

Approaching this town, the scenery becomes impressive as the mountains loom closer to the sea. Sitting at the base of the Sierra de Tejeda, Nerja itself is pleasant and quiet for a Costa resort. In Moorish times the town was a major producer of silk and sugar, an industry that fell into rapid decline after their departure. An earthquake in 1884 partially destroyed Nerja, and from then to the early 1960s it had to eke a living out of fishing and farming.

Its attractions are the **Balcón de Europa**, a promenade with a fountain overlooking the sea, and a series of secluded beaches under the cliffs – the best are a good walk away on either side of the town. A few kilometres east, the **Cueva de Nerja** (*open daily 10–12 and 4–6.30; adm*) is one of Spain's fabled grottoes, full of Gaudíesque formations and needle-thin stalactites – one, they claim, is the longest in the world. The caves were discovered in 1959, just in time for the tourist boom, and they have been fitted out with lights and music. The caves were popular with Cro-Magnon man, and there are some Palaeolithic artworks. Occasionally, this perfect setting is used for ballets and concerts.

A scenic 7km drive north of Nerja on the MA105 finds pretty **Frigiliana**, a pristine whitewashed village of neat houses, cobbled streets and a large expat population. There are splendid views down to the eastern coast, especially from the ruins of the Moorish fort. This was the site of one of the last battles between Christians and

Málaga Virgen and Moorish Tarts

Two grapes, muscatel and Pedro Ximénez, define Málaga province wines and sherries. All are sweet and enjoyed with gusto in bars, and the best known are the Málaga Virgen. Fish and seafood dominate cuisine in Málaga but there are plenty of gazpachos, particularly *ajo blanco con uvas* – a creamy white soup made from almonds and garlic with grapes. Prawns and mussels are plump and, served simply with lemon, are divine. Virtually every tapas bar serves anchovies called *boquerones*; in Málaga *fritura mixta* is one of Spain's culinary art forms.

Nearly every village in the province has its own dessert, usually influenced by the Moors. Try the almond tarts in Ardales, the honey-coated pancakes in Archidona and the mixture of syrup of white roses, oil and eggs called *tocino de cielo* in Vélez. There again, you can always substitute pudding for a sweet Málaga dessert wine – delicious sipped with dry biscuits.

Moriscos in 1569; the story of the battle is retold on ceramic plates around the village's old quarter. Nowadays, Frigiliana is like an English colony rather than an inland Andalucían village.

Almuñécar and Salobreña

The coastal road east of Nerja, bobbing in and out of the hills and cliffs, is the best part of the Costa, where avocado pears and sugar cane keep the farming community busy; however the next resort, **Almuñécar**, is a nest of dreary high-rises around a beleaguered village. Even so, this former fishing village has a lot to offer, not least the fact that Laurie Lee immortalized it in *As I Walked Out One Midsummer Morning*, describing his experiences just prior to the outbreak of the Civil War, and in *A Rose For Winter*, when he returned some 20 years later. Although the hotel where he stayed, 'a white, square crumbling hotel where I had previously worked as a porter and a minstrel', is long gone and replaced by an apartment block, there is a plaque in the square in front which mentions his books. Lee was careful to disguise Almuñécar, calling it 'Castillo' due to its strong resistance against Franco's forces, so there is no mention of individual bars or restaurants. He does, however, speak of the castle in ruins, a fairly accurate description today. Lee *aficionados* may also like to visit the pretty **Ayuntamiento**, on Plaza de la Constitución (where the peasants raised flags before the town was overcome by fascists), and **Iglesia de la Encarnación**, Plaza Nueva, which the locals set alight during the uprising.

For an idea of the ancient history of the town, visit the **Cueva de los Siete Palacios**, where the town's **archaeological museum** (*open 10.30–1.30 and 6–8*) is based. Almuñecar was founded by the Phoenicians as *Sexi*, which can be confusing for the first-time visitor: the *ayuntamiento* has taken to putting up signs declaring certain areas 'Sexi'. The museum has artefacts from this period through to the Romans and the Moors, as well as an Egyptian vase fired between 1700 and 1600 BC for Pharoah Apophis I, and inscribed with the oldest written text found in Iberia.

The **castillo** is dominated by a huge tower, and used to contain the town's cemetery, which has recently been located out of town. Below it lies the **Parque Ornitológico** (*open summer 11–2 and 6–9; winter 10–2 and 4–8; adm*), which holds 1,500 birds from all over the world, and a cactus garden. Despite being the *granadinos*' favourite resort, Almuñécar's numerous beaches are pretty dire, consisting of black sand and pebbles, while the nudist stretch is disconcertingly called *El Muerto*, 'the dead'. Outside town are the remains of a Roman aqueduct. The prettiest place for a swim is the perfectly curved bay of **La Herradura** (which means 'horseshoe') on the western outskirts of town, a low-key resort with a couple of restaurants and *chiringuitos* on the beach.

Salobreña, where the road from Granada meets the coast, is much nicer than Almuñecar, though it may not stay that way. The village's dramatic setting, slung down a steep, lone peak overlooking the sea, is the most stunning on the coast, and helps to insulate it a little from the tourist industry. The beaches are about 2km away.

From here the next town is **Motril**, set back from the sea, with little to attract visitors; it's the centre of the coastal sugar-cane production, thanks to the gin family, Larios. The land between the town and the beaches is now one long *urbanizacion*.

Granada and Almería

13

Granada and Almería

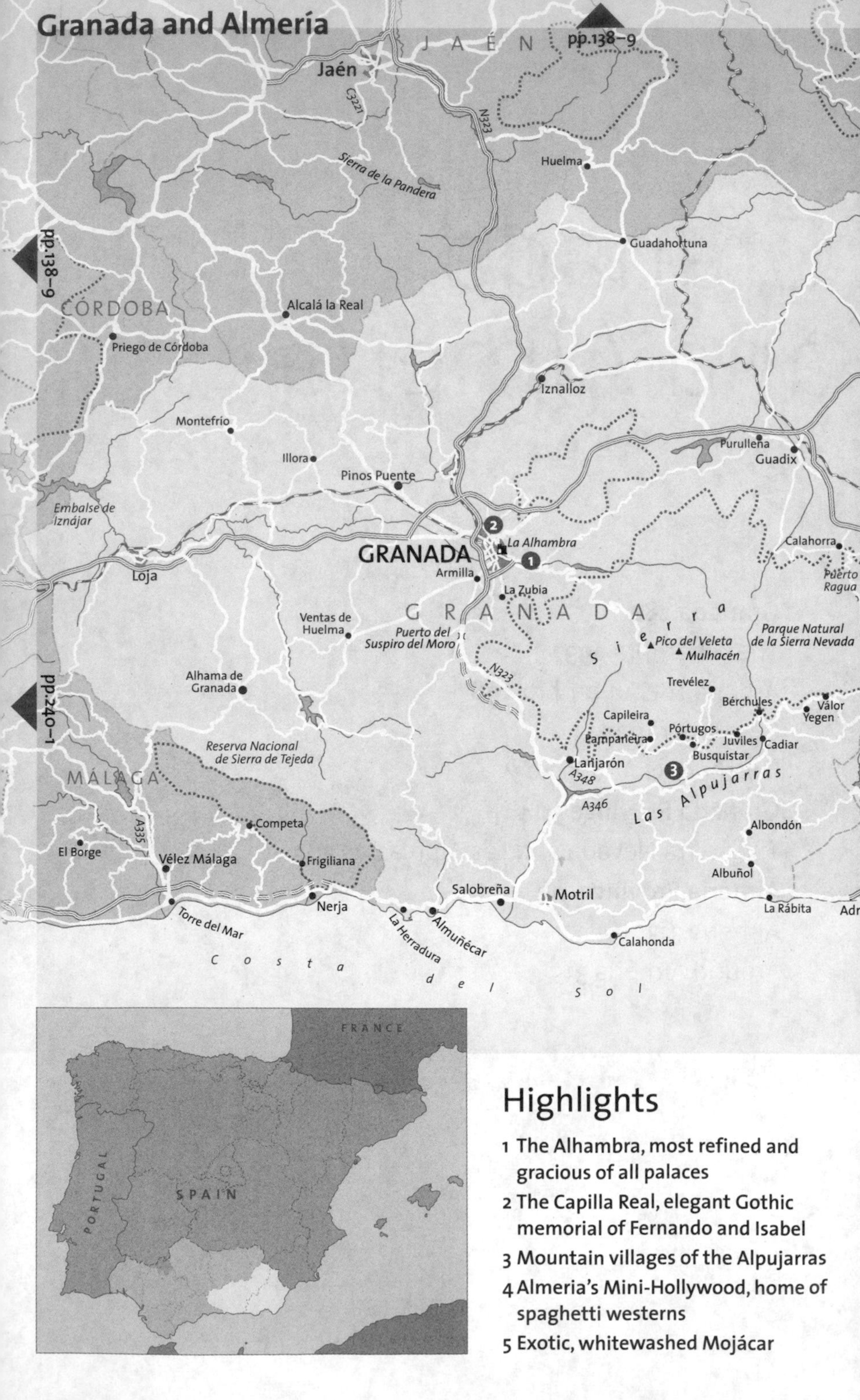

Highlights

1 The Alhambra, most refined and gracious of all palaces
2 The Capilla Real, elegant Gothic memorial of Fernando and Isabel
3 Mountain villages of the Alpujarras
4 Almeria's Mini-Hollywood, home of spaghetti westerns
5 Exotic, whitewashed Mojácar

Everyone who comes to Andalucía stops in to see the Alhambra in Granada, but there is infinitely more to this magical (though somewhat complex and introverted) city. Not content with having the biggest collection of wonders from Moorish al-Andalus, Granada also possesses the greatest monuments of the Christian Reconquista. The city where Fernando and Isabel chose to be buried is still a capital of romance, a city where 'Nights in the Gardens of Spain' is not merely a fantasy, but something encouraged by the tourist office.

Granada's setting is a land of excess, where Spain's tallest mountain, Mulhacén in the Sierra Nevada, stands only 40km from the sea – it has become something of a

tourist ritual to ski and swim on the same day. Mulhacén and its sister peaks provide the backdrop for the Alhambra, while their southern face overlooks the hidden villages of the Alpujarras, the last redoubt of the Moors in Spain.

Beyond the Sierra Nevada the landscapes merge into the arid expanses typical of southeastern Spain. Out in the dry and lonely eastern reaches of Granada's province, the main attraction is the bizarre cave-city of Guadix. The province of Almería is another world – perfect for the filming of Sergio Leone's spaghetti westerns and complete with its own 'Mini-Hollywood' at Tabernas. The highlights are Almería itself, and the exotic, whitewashed (and increasingly trendy) coastal resort of Mojácar.

Granada

Dale limosna mujer, que no hay en la vida nada
Como la pena de ser ciego y en Granada.
(Give him alms, woman, for there is nothing in life
so cruel as being blind in Granada.)

Francisco de Icaza

Upon arrival,pick up a copy of Washington Irving's *Tales of the Alhambra*. Every bookshop in town can sell you one in just about any language. It was Irving who put Granada on the map, and established the Alhambra as the necessary romantic pilgrimage of Spain. Granada, in fact, might seem a disappointment without Irving. The modern city underneath the Alhambra is a stolid, unmagical place, with little to show for the 500 years since the Catholic Kings put an end to its ancient glory.

As the Moors were expelled, the Spanish Crown replaced them with Castilians and Galicians from up north, and even today *granadinos* are thought of as a bit foreign by other Andalucians. Their Granada has never been a happy place. Particularly in the last hundred years it has been full of political troubles. Around the turn of the century even the Holy Week processions had to be called off for a few years because of disruptions from the leftists, and at the start of the Civil War the reactionaries who always controlled Granada made one of the first big massacres of Republicans. One of their victims was Federico García Lorca (*see* also p.304), the *granadino* who, in the decades since his death, has come to be recognized as one of the greatest Spanish dramatists and poets since the 'Golden Age'. If Irving's fairy tales aren't to your taste, consider Lorca, for whom Granada and its sweet melancholy are recurring themes. He wrote that he remembered Granada 'as one should remember a sweetheart who has died'.

History: the Nasrid Kingdom of Qarnatah

First Iberian *Elibyrge*, then Roman *Illiberis*, the town did not make a name for itself until the era of the *taifas* in the early 11th century, when it emerged as the centre of a very minor state. In the 1230s, while the Castilians were seizing Córdoba and preparing to polish off the rest of the Almoravid states of al-Andalus, an Arab chieftain named Mohammed ibn-Yusuf ibn-Nasr established himself around Jaén. When that town fell to the Castilians in 1235, he moved his capital to the town the Moors called *Qarnatah*. Ibn Nasr (or Mohammed I, as he is generally known) and his descendants in the Nasrid dynasty at first enjoyed great success extending their domains. By 1300 this last Moorish state of Spain extended from Gibraltar to Almería, but this accomplishment came entirely at the expense of other Moors. Mohammed and his successors were in fact vassals of the kings of Castile, and aided them in campaigns more often than they fought them.

Qarnatah at this time is said to have had a population of some 200,000 – almost as many as it has now – and both its arts and industries were strengthened by refugees from the fallen towns of al-Andalus. Thousands came from Córdoba, especially, and the Albaicín quarter was largely settled by the former inhabitants of Baeza. Although a significant Jewish population remained, there were very few Christians. In the comparatively peaceful 14th century, Granada's conservative, introspective civilization reached its height, with the last flowering of Arabic-Andaluz lyric poetry and the architecture and decorative arts of the Alhambra.

This state of affairs lasted until the coming of the Catholic Kings. Isabel's religious fanaticism made the completion of the Reconquista the supreme goal of her reign; she sent Fernando out in 1484 to do the job, which he accomplished in eight years by a breathtakingly brilliant combination of force and diplomacy. Qarnatah at the time was suffering the usual curse of al-Andalus states – disunity founded on the egotism of princes. In this fatal feud, the main actors were Abu al-Hasan Ali (Mulay Hassan in Irving's tales), king of Qarnatah, his brother El Zagal ('the valiant') and the king's rebellious son, Abu abd-Allah, better known to posterity as Boabdil el Chico. His seizure of the throne in 1482 started a period of civil war at the worst possible time. Fernando was clever enough to take advantage of the divisions; he captured Boabdil twice, and turned him into a tool of Castilian designs. Playing one side against the other, Fernando snatched away one Nasrid province after another with few losses.

When the unfortunate Boabdil, after renouncing his kingship in favour of the Castilians, finally changed his mind and decided to fight for the remnants of Qarnatah, Fernando had the excuse he needed to mount his final attack. Qarnatah was besieged and, after two years, Boabdil agreed to surrender under terms that guaranteed his people the use of their religion and customs. When the keys of the city were handed over on 2 January 1492, the Reconquista was complete.

Under a gentlemanly military governor, the Conde de Tendilla, the agreement was kept until the arrival in 1499 of Cardinal Ximénez de Cisneros, the most influential cleric in Spain and a man who made it his personal business to destroy the last vestiges of Islam and Moorish culture. The new Spanish policy – cultural genocide (*see* **History**, pp.37–9) – was as successful in the former lands of Granada as it was among those other troublesome heathens of the same period, the Indians of Central and South America. The famous revolt in Las Alpujarras (1568) was followed by a rising in the city itself, in the Albaicín. Between 1609 and 1614, the last of the Muslims were expelled, including most of those who had converted to Christianity, and their

Granada
Carretera de Murcia
Plaza Haza Grande
Moorish walls (ruins)
Sacromonte
Plaza Cruz de Piedra
San Luis
Cuesta del Chapiz
City University
Callejón de Lebrija
Plaza Castillas
San Salvador
Panaderos
Plaza Carniceros
Albaicín
Cuesta Algibe de Trillo
La Cartuja
Larga San Cristóbal
Plaza San Nicolás
Nuevo San Nicolás
Cuesta María de la Miel
Moorish walls (ruins)
Cuesta Alhacaba
Monasterio de Santa Isabel la Real
Cardenal Parrado
Real de Cartuja
Avenida de Murcia
Tiña
Hornillo de Cartuja
Hospital Real
Avenida Hospicio
Puerta de Elvira
Plaza San Miguel Bajo
San José
Plaza San José
Zenete
Pulianas
Plaza del Triunfo
Quirós
Plaza San Isidro
Avenida de Ancha de Capuchinos
Jardines del Triunfo
Calle de Elvira
Gran Via de Colon
Madrid
Doctor Guirao Gea
San Juan de Dios
Mano de Hierro
Plaza San Agustín
San Jerónimo
Santa Barbara
Basílica de San Juan de Dios
University
Avenida de la Constitucion
Gran Capitan
Misericordia
Plaza Lobos
Bus Stand
Av. Andaluces
San Jerónimo
Train Station
Avenida Fuente Nueva
Carril del Picón
Plaza Gran Capitán
Obispo
Melchor Almagro
Martínez Rosa
Plaza Albert Einstein
Calle Pedro Antonio de Alarcón
Camino Ronda

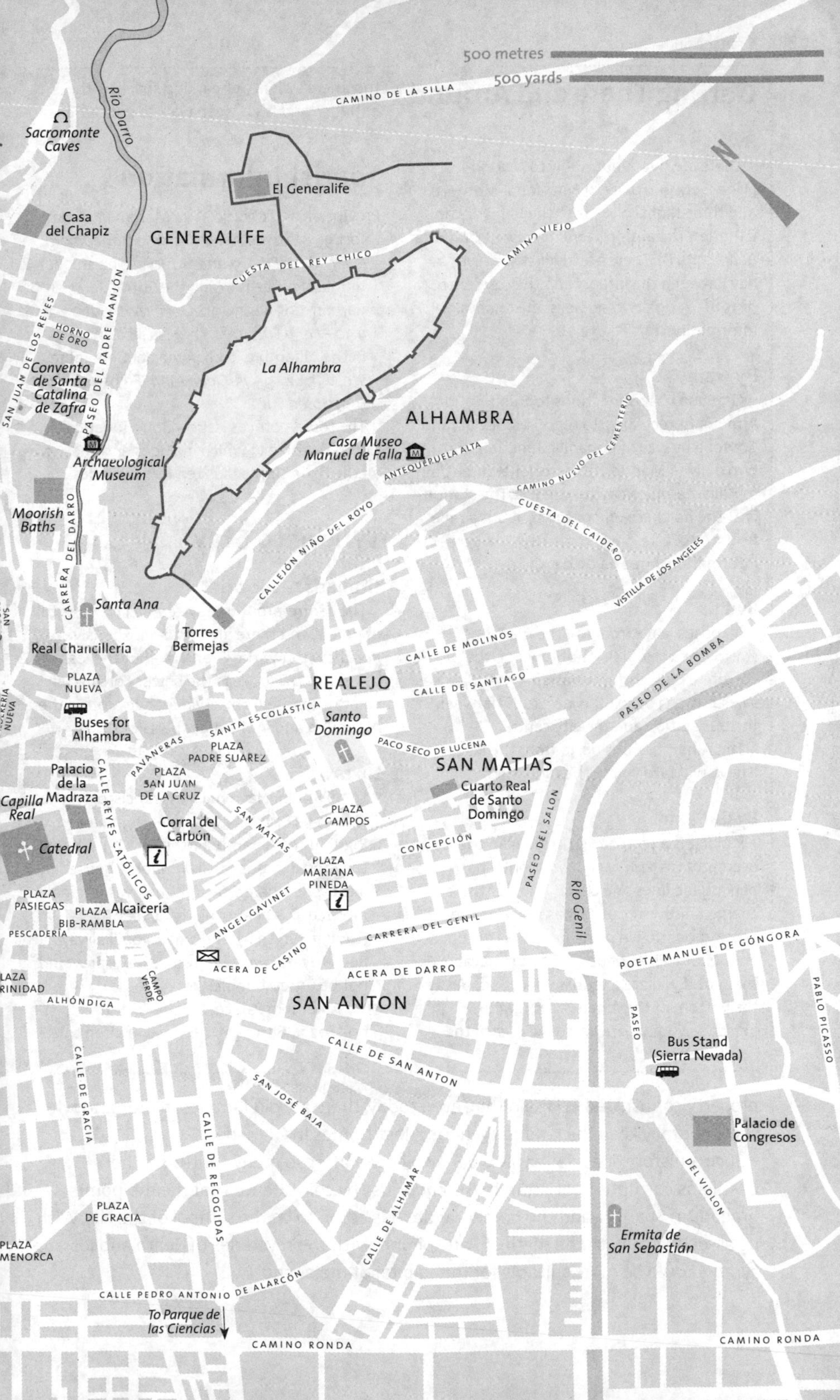

500 metres
500 yards
CAMINO DE LA SILLA
N
Río Darro
Sacromonte Caves
El Generalife
Casa del Chapiz
GENERALIFE
CUESTA DEL REY CHICO
CAMINO VIEJO
HORNO DE ORO
SAN JUAN DE LOS REYES
PASEO DEL PADRE MANJÓN
Convento de Santa Catalina de Zafra
La Alhambra
ALHAMBRA
Casa Museo Manuel de Falla
ANTEQUERUELA ALTA
CAMINO NUEVO DEL CEMENTERIO
Archaeological Museum
Moorish Baths
CARRERA DEL DARRO
CALLEJÓN NIÑO DEL ROYO
CUESTA DEL CAIDERO
VISTILLA DE LOS ANGELES
Santa Ana
Torres Bermejas
Real Chancillería
CALLE DE MOLINOS
PLAZA NUEVA
REALEJO
CALLE DE SANTIAGO
Buses for Alhambra
SANTA ESCOLÁSTICA
Santo Domingo
PASEO DE LA BOMBA
PAVANERAS
PLAZA PADRE SUAREZ
PACO SECO DE LUCENA
SAN MATIAS
Palacio de la Madraza
PLAZA SAN JUAN DE LA CRUZ
CALLE REYES CATÓLICOS
Cuarto Real de Santo Domingo
Capilla Real
SAN MATÍAS
PLAZA CAMPOS
Corral del Carbón
PASEO DEL SALON
Catedral
CONCEPCIÓN
PLAZA MARIANA PINEDA
Río Genil
PLAZA PASIEGAS
PLAZA BIB-RAMBLA
Alcaicería
ANGEL GAVINET
PESCADERÍA
CARRERA DEL GENIL
POETA MANUEL DE GÓNGORA
ACERA DE CASINO
ACERA DE DARRO
ALHÓNDIGA
CAMPO VERDE
SAN ANTON
PABLO PICASSO
PASEO
CALLE DE SAN ANTON
Bus Stand (Sierra Nevada)
CALLE DE GRACIA
SAN JOSÉ BAJA
CALLE DE RECOGIDAS
Palacio de Congresos
DEL VIOLON
CALLE DE ALHAMAR
PLAZA DE GRACIA
PLAZA MENORCA
Ermita de San Sebastián
CALLE PEDRO ANTONIO DE ALARCÓN
To Parque de las Ciencias
CAMINO RONDA
CAMINO RONDA

Getting There and Around

By Air

There are two flights daily to Madrid (*Mon–Sat*), two daily to Barcelona (*Mon–Fri*) and three flights a week to the Balearics and Canaries. The airport is 16km west of Granada, near Santa Fé. There are at least six buses a day between the airport and the city centre (**t** 95 813 13 09); two services on Sundays. **Information:** **t** 95 824 52 00.

By Train

Granada has connections to Guadix and Almería (three daily), to Algeciras, Sevilla, and Córdoba by way of Bobadilla Junction, and two daily to Madrid and Barcelona; three daily to Alicante, one a day to Valencia. The station is at the northern end of town, about a mile from the centre, on Avenida de Andalucía. **Information:** **t** 902 24 02 02.

By Bus

All buses leave from the the main bus station, on the outskirts of town on the Carretera de Jaén. **Information:** **t** 95 818 54 80; sales **t** 902 33 04 00. Bus no.3 runs between the bus station and the city centre.

The 'Alhambra' bus no.30 from the Plaza Nueva will take you to the Alhambra.

By Car

Parking is a problem, so if you plan to stay overnight make sure that your hotel has parking facilities and check whether there is a charge or not – it can cost as much as the accommodation in some places. Traffic police are vigilant. Fines of up to €120 are payable on the spot if you are a tourist. Ignore people at the bottom of the Alhambra trying to persuade you to park before you reach the top; there's plenty of parking space by the entrance and it's a steep walk to get there.

Tourist Information

Provincial tourist office, Pza Mariana Piñeda 10, **t** 95 822 21 02, *www.turismogranada.org*. *Open Mon–Fri 9–7 and Sat 10–2*. The smaller municial office is inside the Corral del Carbón, **t** 95 822 59 90. *Open Mon–Sat 9.30–7 and Sun 10–2*. There is also an office in the Alhambra itself: Avda del Generalife s/n, **t** 95 822 95 75. *Open Mon–Fri 9–4 and Sat 9–1; closed Sun*.

The tourist offices issue a Bono Turístico/ City Pass (€15.03) which includes entrance to all the main sights plus ten free bus rides.

Where to Stay

Granada ✉ 18000

The centre, around the Acera del Darro, is full of hotels, and there are lots of inexpensive *hostales* around the Gran Vía – but the less you see of these areas the better. Fortunately, you can choose from a wide range around the Alhambra and in the older parts of town.

Luxury

★★★★★**Parador Nacional San Francisco**, **t** 95 822 14 40, **f** 95 822 22 64, *granada@parador.es*. Right in the Alhambra itself, this is perhaps the most famous of all *paradores*, housed in a convent where Queen Isabel was originally interred. It is beautiful, very expensive (though worth it), and small; you'll always need to book well in advance – a year would not be unreasonable.

★★★★**Alhambra Palace**, C/Peña Partida 2–4, **t** 95 822 14 68, **f** 95 822 64 04. An alternative

property confiscated. It is said that, even today, there are old families in Morocco who sentimentally keep the keys to their long-lost homes in Granada.

Such a history does not easily wear away, even after so many centuries. The Castilians corrupted Qarnatah to *Granada*; just by coincidence that means 'pomegranate' in Spanish, and the pomegranate has come to be the symbol of the city. With its associations with the myth of Persephone, with the mysteries of death and loss, no symbol could be more suitable for this capital of melancholy.

choice very near the Alhambra; outrageously florid. Most rooms have terrific views.

★★★★**Meliá Granada**, C/Ángel Gavinet 7, **t** 95 822 74 00, **f** 95 822 74 03, *www.meliagranada.solmelia.com*. Within striking distance of the old and new parts of the city.

Expensive

★★★**Washington Irving**, Pso del Generalife 2, **t** 95 822 75 50, **f** 95 822 75 59, *hwirving@arrakis.es*. This old place on the slopes below the Alhambra is a little faded but still classy.

★**Hotel América**, Real de la Alhambra 53, **t** 95 822 74 71, **f** 95 822 74 70. Right beside the *parador* but up to a third of the price, with simple, pretty rooms and a delightful garden and patio. Book well in advance.

★★★**Palacio de Santa Inés**, Cuesta de Santa Inés 9, **t** 95 822 23 62, **f** 95 822 24 65, *www.palaciosantaines.com*. A 16th-century palace in the Albaicín with murals in the patio attributed to Alejandro Mayner, Rafael's disciple. Just nine rooms, some with priceless views of the Alhambra.

★★★★**Hotel Triunfo–Granada**, Pza del Triunfo 19, **t** 95 820 74 44, **f** 95 827 90 17, *h-triunfo-granada@granada.net*. Stands by the Moorish Puerta de Elvira at the foot of the Albaicín. Quiet, with a restaurant.

★★★★**Hotel Plaza Nueva**, Plaza Nueva 2, **t** 95 850 18 97, **f** 95 850 18 13, *www.hotelplazanueva.com*. An immaculate hotel right on the square, with rooms offering views of the Alhambra.

★★★★**Carmen**, Acera del Darro 62, **t** 95 825 83 00, **f** 95 825 64 62, *www.hotelcarmen.com*. If you are after luxury, but are not overly concerned about position, then this modern hotel offers sumptuous bedrooms and bathrooms, a rooftop suite and a pool.

Casa del Aljarife, Placeta de la Cruz Verde 2, **t/f** 95 822 24 25, *www.granadainfo.com/most*. This 17th-century Moorish house with tastefully refurbished rooms is one of a handful of hotels in the Albaicín, and one of the most delightful places to stay, with a view of the Alhambra. There are only three rooms so be sure to book in advance. The owners can arrange parking.

Casa Morisca, Cuesta de la Victoria 9, **t** 95 822 11 00, *www.hotelcasamorisca.com*. A beautiful converted 15th-century house just below the Alhambra, with a patio garden and cooly stylish rooms.

Moderate

★★★**Hotel Navas**, C/Navas 24, **t** 95 822 59 59, **f** 95 822 75 23. In an excellent spot; quiet rooms with a/c and a good-value restaurant.

★★★**Los Ángeles**, Cuesta Escoriaza 17, **t** 95 822 14 24, **f** 95 822 21 26. On the slopes below the Alhambra, with pool and a/c.

★★**Hotel Maciá Plaza**, Plaza Nueva 4, **t** 95 822 75 36, **f** 95 822 75 33, *maciaplaza@maciahoteles.com*. A good bet if you want a few more mod cons than the *hostales* and *pensiónes* in this area.

Pensión La Ninfa, C/Cocheras de San Cecilio 9, **t** 95 822 26 61. A very quirky hotel covered in ceramic plates, jars and other bits and bobs, overlooking the lively Campo del Principe. Simple restaurant across the square.

Cuevas El Abanico, Verea de Enmedio 89, **t** 95 822 61 99, *www.el-abanico.com*. Your very own cave in Sacromonte – caves sleep from 1–5 and have their own kitchen areas.

Inexpensive

The residential area around the Campo del Principe hides some possibilities.

Hostal Suecia, C/Molinos (Huerta Los Ángeles), **t/f** 95 822 50 44. A delightful budget option: clean, quiet, in its own grounds, with parking and views of the palace.

A Sentimental Orientation

In spite of everything, more of the lost world of al-Andalus can be seen in Granada than even in Córdoba. Granada stands where the foothills of the Sierra Nevada meet the fertile Vega de Granada, the greenest and best stretch of farmland in Andalucía. Two of those hills extend into the city itself. One bears the **Alhambra**, the fortified palace of the Nasrid kings, and the other the **Albaicín**, the most evocative of the 'Moorish' neighbourhoods of Andalucían cities. Parts of old Qarnatah extended down

Failing this, try around Plaza del Carmen:

★★Lisboa, Pza del Carmen 27, **t** 95 822 14 13, **f** 95 822 14 87. Adequate, if uninspiring.

★Hotel Niza, C/Navas 16, **t** 95 822 54 30, **f** 95 822 54 27. Good value but in a noisy location sandwiched between a number of bars.

Cheap

For cheap *hostales*, the first place to look is the Cuesta de Gomérez, the street leading up to the Alhambra from Plaza Nueva.

Viena, **t** 95 822 18 59. One of three good Austrian-run budget options around Cuesta de Gomérez; all are clean, friendly and functional.

Landázuri, Cuesta de Gomérez 24, **t** 95 822 14 06. A bit further up with a restaurant and a small roof terrace. Parking (€10).

★★Britz, Cuesta de Gomérez 1, **t** 95 822 36 52. Basic; no bath.

★★Navarro Ramos, Cuesta de Gomérez 1, **t** 95 825 05 55. Quiet and friendly. A good address for those on a tight budget.

Off Calle San Juan de Dios, in the university area, there are dozens of small *hostales* used to accommodating students:

★San Joaquín, C/Mano de Hierro 17, **t** 95 828 28 79. Has a pretty patio.

Hostal Angélica, C/Cristo de la Yedra 36, **t** 95 827 14 30. A couple of streets away from the Hospital Real.

Eating Out

Granada isn't known for its cuisine. There are too many touristy places around the Plaza Nueva, with very little to distinguish between them. Below are some better finds.

Expensive

Ruta del Veleta, Ctra de la Sierra, km 50, **t** 95 848 61 34. Some of the finest cooking in Granada can be found here; 5km from the city towards the Sierra Nevada.

Moderate

Sevilla, C/Oficios 12, **t** 95 822 12 23. The best-known and best-loved restaurant in Granada, where Lorca often met fellow poets. Although recent reports of the food have not been good, it retains its original character. *Closed Sun eve.*

Cunini, Pza de Pescadería 14, **t** 95 825 07 77. The *granadinos* trust dining out at this place, where the menu depends on availability. *Closed Mon.*

Mesón Antonio, Ecce Homo 6, **t** 95 822 95 99. There is no better in Granada for agreeable dining in an intimate family-run restaurant. *Closed Sun, July and Aug.*

Mirador de Morayma, Pianista García Carrillo 2, Albaicín, **t** 95 822 82 90. In a charming 16th-century house with views over the Alhambra from the top-floor dining room; *Closed Sun eve.*

Chikito, Pza de Campillo 9, **t** 95 822 33 64. Popular with *granadinos*, serving classic Granada dishes in an intimate atmosphere. Another of Lorca's erstwhile haunts.

Pilar de Toro, C/Hospital de Santa Ana 12, Plaza Nueva, **t** 95 822 38 47. In a converted 17th-century house with a trendy bar set round a romantic patio and more intimate dining upstairs.

Tendido 1, Avda. Doctor Oloriz 25, **t** 95 827 23 02. Huge, atmospheric restaurant right under the bullring itself.

Inexpensive

El Ladrillo, C/Panaderos del Albaicín s/n, **t** 95 829 26 51. In the heart of the Albaicín, this friendly restaurant has a pretty patio and serves up delicious soups, grilled meat and fish.

into the plain, but they have been largely submerged into the new city. How much you enjoy Granada will depend largely on how successful you are in ignoring the new districts, in particular three barbarically ugly streets that form the main automobile route through Granada: the **Gran Vía de Colón** chopped through the centre of town in the 19th century, the **Calle Reyes Católicos**, and the **Acera del Darro**. The last two are paved over the course of the Río Darro, the stream that ran picturesquely through the city until the 1880s. Before these streets were built, the centre of Granada was the

Jardines Zoraya, C/Panaderos del Albaicín, **t** 95 829 35 03. Another charming choice with garden. Pizzas as well as traditional fare.

Tapas Bars

Granada rivals Sevilla for its tapas and has a fine tradition of serving up mini-meals for the price of a drink. Areas worth exploring are the roads off the top end of Gran Vía and the Plaza Nueva, particularly Calles Almireceros, Joaquin Costa, Elvira and Cetti Meriem; around the cathedral, Plaza Bib-Rambla and C/Pescadería are particularly good. Leading up into the Albacín are a number of Moroccan-style tea bars, or *teterías*, where you can sip mint tea in Alhambra-style décor. Try in particular Calles Calderias Vieja and Nueva and Carcel Alta.

Castañeda, C/Almireceros 1–3. A great *andaluz* bar with tiles and huge barrels, serving up very generous and reasonably priced tapas

Las Tinajas, C/Martínez Campos 17. A classy, old-fashioned tapas bar and restaurant.

Bar Casa Julio, C/Hermosa s/n. This tiny locals' bar is tucked down a narrow passage. You don't choose tapas – they come free with your drink, but they're always good.

Bodega La Mancha, C/Joaquin Costa s/n. Another classic *andaluz* barwith *vermut* from the barrel, a good selection of wines and a wide variety of tapas and *raciones*.

Bar Gracia, C/Gracia 21. Delicious and creative tapas and *raciones* to the accompaniment of flamenco music. Occasional flamenco concerts downstairs.

La Fragua, C/Panaderos 14. At the top of the Alabaicín, this is a simple but popular local haunt with a young, hippyish crowd.

La Cava, Plaza del Realejo 5. A tiny wood-panelled wine-shop and deli with a good selection of wines and a few tapas.

El Bañuelo Tetería, C/Bañuelos. One of the most charming *teterías* in Granada, with quiet, cushioned nooks and silver teapots, Arabic cakes and views of the Alhambra.

Entertainment and Nightlife

Granada is one of the best places in Andalucía to catch flamenco. Though there are touristy shows in the caves of Sacromonte (the tourist office has a list), there are also some more spontaneous venues (but take care up here at night). Most of them are along Camino del Sacromonte. If you can, get recommendations from locals to find out who's performing while you are in town. Festival Discos, C/San Sebastián 10 (just off Pza Bib-Rambla), is a music shop with a friendly owner who is usually happy to make recommendations. Granada's nightlife is centred in the streets around the Plaza Nueva, and in the new part of town along C/Pedro Antonio de Alarcón (plenty of bars full of local teenagers and students).

El Camborio, Camino del Sacromonte, 47, Sacromonte. One of several discos popular with the locals in Sacromonte; always packed on Friday and Saturday nights.

Eshavira, Postigo de la Cuna 2, **t** 95 829 41 25, *www.eshavira.com*. A local institution, an old Moorish-style house with regular live flamenco, jazz and world music on Thursdays and Sundays. It's down a passage between C/Elvira and the Plaza Nueva.

Cervecería La Riviera, C/Cetti Meriem 7. This young bar is a good place to start the night.

Bar Makeba, Placeta Sillería 7. A tiny, packed bar in the heart of the city, with great African and Latin music, good cocktails and dancing later on (if you can find room).

Bar Candela, C/Sta Escolástica 11. Small, bohemian bar, with a great atmosphere.

Plaza Nueva, a square that is also partly built over the Darro. The handsome building that defines its character is the **Audiencia** (1584), built by Philip II for the royal officials and judges. **Santa Ana** church, across the plaza, was built in 1537 by Diego de Siloé, one of the architects of Granada's cathedral. From this plaza the ascent to the Alhambra begins, winding up a narrow street called the **Cuesta de Gomérez**, past guitar-makers' shops and Gypsies with vast displays of tourist trinkets, and ending abruptly at the **Puerta de las Granadas**, a monumental gateway erected by Charles V.

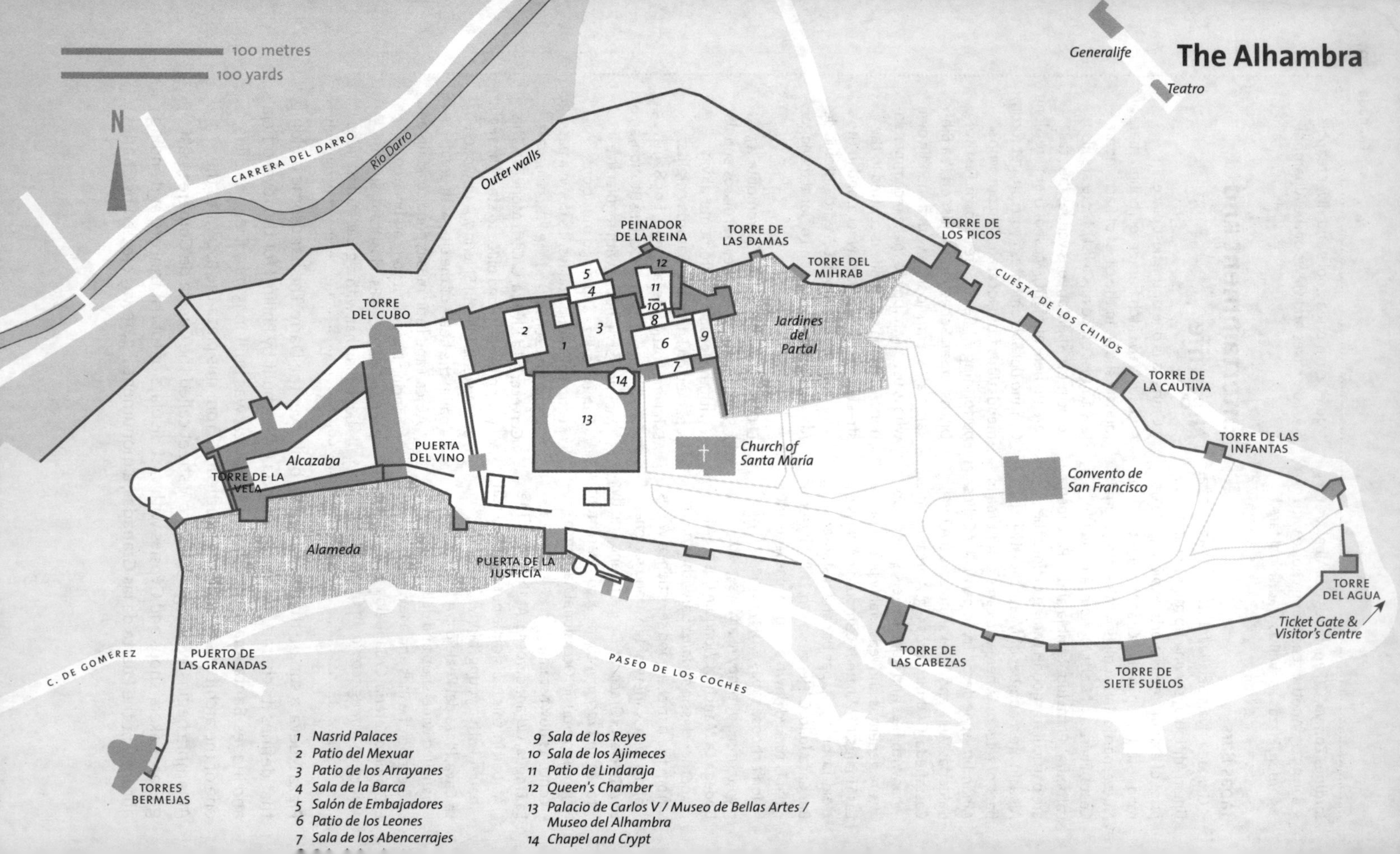
The Alhambra
100 metres
100 yards
N
CARRERA DEL DARRO
Río Darro
Outer walls
Generalife
Teatro
PEINADOR DE LA REINA
TORRE DE LAS DAMAS
TORRE DEL MIHRAB
TORRE DE LOS PICOS
CUESTA DE LOS CHINOS
TORRE DE LA CAUTIVA
TORRE DE LAS INFANTAS
TORRE DEL AGUA
Ticket Gate & Visitor's Centre
TORRE DEL CUBO
Jardines del Partal
PUERTA DEL VINO
Alcazaba
TORRE DE LA VELA
Church of Santa María
Convento de San Francisco
Alameda
PUERTA DE LA JUSTICIA
TORRE DE LAS CABEZAS
TORRE DE SIETE SUELOS
PUERTO DE LAS GRANADAS
C. DE GOMEREZ
PASEO DE LOS COCHES
TORRES BERMEJAS
1 Nasrid Palaces
2 Patio del Mexuar
3 Patio de los Arrayanes
4 Sala de la Barca
5 Salón de Embajadores
6 Patio de los Leones
7 Sala de los Abencerrajes
9 Sala de los Reyes
10 Sala de los Ajimeces
11 Patio de Lindaraja
12 Queen's Chamber
13 Palacio de Carlos V / Museo de Bellas Artes / Museo del Alhambra
14 Chapel and Crypt

The Alhambra

Open Nov–Feb daily 8.30–6, plus night visits on Fri and Sat 8pm–9.30pm, ticket office open daily 8–5 plus 7.30pm–8.30pm on Fri and Sat; March–Oct daily 8.30–9, plus night visits Tues–Sat 10pm–11.30pm, ticket office open daily 8–7 plus Tues–Sat 9.30pm–10.30pm; adm (discount with Granada City Pass, see Tourist Information above). Night visits only include entrance to the Nasrid Palaces. It is strongly advisable to book your tickets in advance: at www.alhambratickets.com, at any branch of the BBVA bank or by phone on **t** *902 224 460 (+34 91 346 59 36 from outside Spain).*

The grounds of the Alhambra begin here with a bit of the unexpected. Instead of the walls and towers, not yet even in view, there is a lovely grove of great elms, the **Alameda**, planted at the time the Duke of Wellington passed through during the Peninsular War. Take the path to the left – it's a stiff climb – and in a few minutes you'll arrive at the **Puerta de la Justicía**, the former entrance of the Alhambra. The orange tint of the fortress walls explains the name *al-hamra* (the red), and the unusual style of the carving on the gate is the first clue that here is something very different. The two devices, a hand and a key, carved on the inner and outer arches, are famous. According to one of Irving's tales, the hand will one day reach down and grasp the key; then the Alhambra will fall into ruins, the earth will open, and the hidden treasures of the Moors will be revealed. Follow the road uphill to the new car park and visitor's centre, where you'll find the ticket office and entrance. There are three routes around the Alhambra complex, all marked on the map that comes with the ticket. You will be given a time slot for entrance to the Nasrid Palaces, which could well start an hour or two after your entrance to the complex and should give you time to explore the Alcazaba and perhaps the Generalife before visiting the Palaces.

The Alcazaba

Not much remains of the oldest part of the Alhambra, out on the tip of the promontory. This citadel probably dates back to the first of the Nasrid kings. Its walls and towers are still intact, but only the foundations of the buildings that once stood within it have survived. The **Torre de la Vela** at the tip of the promontory has the best views over Granada and the *vega*. Its big bell was rung in the old days to signal the daily opening and closing of the water gates of the *vega*'s irrigation system; the Moors also used the tower as a signal post for sending messages. The Albaicín (*see* pp.298–300), visible on the opposite hill, is a revelation; its rows of white, flat-roofed houses on the hillside, punctuated by palm trees and cypresses, provide one of Europe's most exotic urban landscapes.

In front of the Alcazaba is a broad square known as the **Puerta del Vino**, so called from a long-ago Spanish custom of doling out free wine from this spot to the inhabitants of the Alhambra.

Palacios Nazaries (Nasrid Palaces)

You must enter the palace within the time slot printed on your ticket. Once in, you can stay as long as you like.

Words will not do, nor will exhaustive descriptions help, to communicate the experience of this greatest treasure of al-Andalus. This is what people come to Granada to see, and it is the surest, most accessible window into the refinement and subtlety of the culture of Moorish Spain – a building that can achieve in its handful of rooms what a work like Madrid's Royal Palace cannot even approach with its 2,800.

It probably never occurs to most visitors, but one of the most unusual features of this palace is its modesty. What you see is what the Nasrid kings saw; your imagination need add only a few carpets and tapestries, some well-crafted furniture of wood inlaid with ivory, wooden screens, and big round braziers of brass for heat or incense, to make the picture complete. Most of the actual building is wood and plaster, cheap and perishable, like a World's Fair pavilion; no good Muslim monarch would offend Allah's sense of propriety by pretending that these worldly splendours were anything more than the pleasures of a moment (much of the plaster, wood, and all of the tiles, are the products of careful restorations over the last 100 years). The Alhambra, in fact, is the only substantially intact medieval Muslim palace – anywhere.

Like so many old royal palaces (those of the Hittites, the Byzantines or the Ottoman Turks, for example), this one is divided into three sections: one for everyday business of the palace and government; the next, more secluded, for the state rooms and official entertainments of the kings; and the third, where few outsiders ever reached, for the private apartments of the king and his household.

The Mexuar

Of the first, the small Mexuar, where the kings would hold their public audiences, survives near the present-day entrance to the palace complex. The adjacent **Patio del Mexuar**, though much restored, is one of the finest rooms of the Alhambra. Nowhere is the meditative serenity of the palace more apparent (unless you arrive when all the tour groups do) and the small fountain in the centre provides an introduction to an important element of the architecture – water. Present everywhere, in pools, fountains and channels, water is as much a part of the design as the wood, tile and stone.

Patio de los Arrayanes (or Patio de Comares)

If you have trouble finding your way around, remember the elaborately decorated portals never really lead anywhere; the door you want will always be tucked unobtrusively to the side; here, as in Sevilla's Alcázar, the principle is to heighten the sense of surprise. The entrance to the grand Patio de los Arrayanes (Court of the Myrtles), with its long goldfish pond and lovely arcades, was the centre of the second, state section of the palace; directly off it, you pass through the **Sala de la Barca** (Hall of the Boat), so called after its hull-shaped wooden ceiling, and into the **Salón de Embajadores** (Hall of Ambassadors), where the kings presided over all important state business. The views and the decoration are some of the Alhambra's best, with a cedarwood ceiling and plaster panels (many were originally painted) carved with floral arabesques or Arabic calligraphy. These inscriptions, some Koranic scripture (often the phrase 'Allah alone conquers', the motto of the Nasrids), some eulogies of the kings, and some poetry, recur throughout the palace. The more conspicuous are in a flowing script developed by the Granadan artists; look closely and you will see others, in the angular Kufic script, forming frames for the floral designs.

In some of the chambers off the Patio de los Arrayanes, you can peek out over the domed roofs of the baths below; opposite the Salón de Embajadores is a small entrance (often closed) into the dark, empty **crypt** of the Palace of Charles V, with curious echo effects.

Patio de los Leones

Another half-hidden doorway leads you into the third and most spectacular section, the king's residence, built around the Patio de los Leones (Court of the Lions). Here the plaster and stucco work is at its most ornate, the columns and arches at their most delicate, with little pretence of any structural purpose; balanced on their slender shafts, the façades of the court seem to hang in the air. As in much of Moorish architecture, the overripe arabesques of this patio conceal a subtle symbolism. The 'enclosed garden' that can stand for the attainment of truth, or paradise, or for the cosmos, is a recurring theme in Islamic mystical poetry. Here you may take the 12 endearingly preposterous lions who support the fountain in the centre (under renovation) as the months, or signs of the zodiac, and the four channels that flow out from the fountains as the four corners of the cosmos, the cardinal points, or, on a different level, the four rivers of paradise.

The rooms around the patio have exquisite decorations: to the right, from the entrance, the **Sala de los Abencerrajes**, named after the legend of the noble family that Boabdil supposedly had massacred at a banquet here during the civil wars just before the fall of Granada; to the left, the **Sala de las dos Hermanas** (Hall of the Two Sisters). Both of these have extravagant domed *muqarnas* ceilings. The latter chamber is also ornamented with a wooden window grille, another speciality of the Granadan artists; this is the only one surviving in the Alhambra. Adjacent to the Sala de las dos Hermanas is the **Sala de los Ajimeces**, so called for its doubled windows. The **Sala de los Reyes** (Hall of the Kings), opposite the court's entrance, is unique because of the paintings on its ceiling (currently under restoration), works that would not be out of place in any Christian palace of medieval Europe. The central panel may represent six of Granada's 14th-century kings; those on the side are scenes of a chivalric court. The artist is believed to have been a visiting Spanish Christian painter, possibly from Sevilla. From the Sala de las dos Hermanas, a passage leads to the **Patio de Lindaraja** (or Mirador de Daraxa), with its fountain and flowers, Washington Irving's favourite spot in the Alhambra. Originally the inner garden of the palace, it was remodelled for the royal visits of Charles V and Philip V. Irving actually lived in the **Queen's Chamber**, decorated with frescoes of Charles V's expedition to Tunis – in 1829, apartments in the Alhambra could be had for the asking! Just off this chamber, at ground-floor level, is the beautifull **hammam**, the palace baths.

Follow the arrows out of the palace and into the outer gardens, the **Jardines del Partal**, a broad expanse of rose terraces and flowing water. The northern walls of the Alhambra border the gardens, including a number of well-preserved towers: from the west, the **Torre de las Damas**, entered by a small porch, the **Torre del Mihrab**, near which is a small mosque, now a chapel; the **Torre de los Picos**; the **Torre de la Cautiva** (Tower of the Imprisoned Lady), one of the most elaborately decorated; and the **Torre de las Infantas**, one of the last projects in the Alhambra (*c.* 1400).

Palacio de Carlos V

Anywhere else, this elegant Renaissance building would be an attraction in itself. Here it seems only pompous and oversized, and our appreciation of it is lessened by the mind-numbing thought of this emperor, with a good half of Europe to build palaces in, having to plop it down here – ruining much of the Alhambra in the process. Once Charles had smashed up the place he lost interest, and most of the palace, still unfinished today, was not built until 1616. The original architect, Pedro Machuca, had studied in Italy, and he took the opportunity to introduce into Spain the chilly, Olympian High Renaissance style of Rome. At the entrances are intricately detailed sculptural **reliefs** showing scenes from Charles's campaigns and military 'triumphs' in the antique manner: armoured torsos on sticks amidst heaps of weapons. This is a very particular sort of Renaissance fancy, arrogant and weird, and wherever it appears around the Mediterranean it will usually be associated with the grisly reign of the man who dreamt of being Emperor of the World. Inside, Machuca added a pristinely classical circular courtyard, based perhaps on a design by Raphael. For all its Doric gravity, the patio was used almost from its completion for bullfights and mock tournaments. In 1922, Lorca and the painter Ignacio Zuloaga organized a famous festival of flamenco here, with performances in the courtyard that contributed greatly to the revival of flamenco as a serious art.

The Museums

Museo de Bellas Artes, open Tues 2.30–6, Wed–Sat 9–6, Sun 9–2.30; adm, free to EU citizens. Museo de Alhambra, open Tues–Sat 9–2.30; adm included in Alhambra ticket. Free guided visits around museum Tues–Sat 11am–1pm.

On the top floor of the palace is the **Museo de Bellas Artes**, a largely forgettable collection of religious paintings from Granada churches. Downstairs, the **Museo de la Alhambra** contains perhaps Spain's best collection of Moorish art, including some paintings, similar to those in the Moorish palace's Sala de los Reyes. Also present are original *azulejo* tiles and plaster arabesques from the palace, and some exceedingly fine wooden panels and screens. There is a collection of ceramic ware with fanciful figurative decoration and some lovely astronomical instruments. One room contains four big copper balls stacked on a pole, a strangely compelling ornament that once stood atop a Granada minaret. These were a typical feature of Andalucían minarets and similar examples can be seen in Morocco today; Granada's great mosque had a big one designed to be visible to travellers a day's journey from the city.

Nights in the Gardens of Spain

The first proper garden in al-Andalus, according to legend, was planted by the first caliph himself, Abd ar-Rahman. This refugee from Damascus brought with him fond memories of the famous Rusãfah gardens in that city, and he also brought seeds of the palm tree to plant. As caliph, he built an aqueduct to Córdoba, partly for the city and partly to furnish his new Rusãfah; his botanists sent away for more palms, and also introduced the peach and the pomegranate into Europe.

Following the caliph's example, the Arabs of the towns laid out recreational gardens everywhere, particularly along the river fronts. The widely travelled geographer al-Shaquindi wrote in the 11th century that the Guadalquivir around Córdoba was more beautiful than the Tigris or the Nile, lined with orchards, vines, pleasure gardens, groves of citrus trees and avenues of yews. Every city did its best to make a display, and each had its district of villas and gardens. Sevilla's was in Triana and on the river islands. Valencia too, which had another copy of the Rusãfah, came to be famous for its gardens; poets called the city 'a maiden in the midst of flowers'.

All this gardening was only part of a truly remarkable passion for everything green. Andalucía's climate and soil made it a paradise for the thirsty Arabs and Berbers, and bringing southern Spain into the wider Islamic world made possible the introduction of new techniques, flowering plants and crops: rice, sugar, cotton, saffron, oranges (*naranja* in Spanish, from the Persian *nãrang*), even bananas. In the 12,000 villages of the Guadalquivir valley, Moorish farmers were wizards; they learned how to graft almond branches on to apricot trees, and they refined irrigation and fertilizing to fine arts (one manuscript that survives from the time is a 'catalogue of dung'; pigs and ducks were considered very bad, while the horse was best for almost all fields). Sophisticated techniques of irrigation were practised throughout al-Andalus, and everywhere the rivers turned the wooden water wheels, or *norias* (another Persian word, *nã'urãh*); one in Toledo was almost 62m (200ft) tall. No expense was spared in bringing water where it was needed; near Moravilla remains can be seen of a mile-long subterranean aqueduct, 9m (30ft) in width. The farmers had other tricks, mostly lost to us; it was claimed they could store grain to last for a century, by spreading it between layers of pomegranate leaves and lime or oak ash.

Flowers were everywhere. On the slopes of Jabal al-Warad, the 'Mountain of the Rose' near Córdoba, vast fields of these were grown for rose water; other blooms widely planted for perfumes and other products included violet, jasmine, gillyflower, narcissus, gentian and tulip. And with all the flowers and gardens came poetry, one of the main preoccupations of life in al-Andalus for prince and peasant alike. When Caliph Abd ar-Rahman saw his palm tree growing, he wrote a lyric in its honour:

In the centre of the Rusãfah I saw a palm tree growing,
born in the west, far from the palm's country.
I cried: 'Thou art like me, for wandering and peregrination,
and the long separation from family and friends.
May the clouds of morning water thee in thy exile.
May the life-giving rains that the poor implore never forsake thee.'

Behind Charles's palace a street leads into the remnants of the town that once filled much of the space within the Alhambra's walls, now reduced to a small collection of restaurants and souvenir stands. In Moorish times the Alhambra held a large permanent population, and even under the Spaniards it long retained the status of a separate municipality. At one end of the street, the church of **Santa María** (1581), designed by Juan de Herrera, architect of El Escorial, occupies the site of the Alhambra's mosque; at the other, the first Christian building on the Alhambra, the **Convento de San Francisco** (1495) has been converted into a *parador*.

Around the Alhambra

The Generalife

Currently closed for major restoration, otherwise, same as for the Alhambra; adm incl. in Alhambra ticket.

The Generalife (*Djinat al-Arif*: high garden) was the summer palace of the Nasrid kings, built on the height the Moors called the Mountain of the Sun. Many of the trillions of visitors the Alhambra receives each year have never heard of it, and pass up a chance to see the finest garden in Spain. To get there, it's about a 5-minute walk from the Alhambra along a lovely avenue of tall cypresses.

The buildings here hold few surprises if you've just come from the Alhambra. They are older than most of the Nasrid Palaces, which were begun around 1260. The gardens are built on terraces on several levels along the hillside, and the views over the Alhambra and Albaicín are transcendent. The centrepiece is a long pool with many water sprays that passes through beds of roses, although this is currently being restored to its original Moorish design. A lower level, with a promenade on the hill's edge, is broken up into secluded bowers by cypress bushes cut into angular walls and gateways. Beautiful as it is, there is no evidence that the original Moorish gardens looked anything like this; everything here has been done in the last 200 years.

If you're walking down from the Alhambra, you might consider a different route, across the Alameda and down through the picturesque streets below the Torres Bermejas, an outwork of the Alhambra's fortifications built on foundations that date back to the Romans. The winding lanes and stairways around Calle del Aire and Calle Niño del Rollo, one of the most beautiful quarters of Granada, will eventually lead you back down near the Plaza Nueva.

Albaicín

Even more than the old quarters of Córdoba, this hillside neighbourhood of whitewashed houses and tall cypresses has successfully preserved some of the atmosphere of al-Andalus. Its difficult site and the fact that it was long the district of Granada's poor explain the lack of change, but today it is becoming fashionable again.

From the Plaza Nueva, a narrow street called the **Carrera del Darro** leads up the valley of the Darro between the Alhambra and Albaicín hills; here the little stream has not been covered over, and you can get an idea of how the centre of Granada looked in centuries past. On the Alhambra side, old stone bridges lead up to a few half-forgotten streets hidden among the forested slopes; here you'll see some 17th-century Spanish houses with curious painted *esgrafiado* façades. Nearby, traces of a horse-shoe arch can be seen where a Moorish wall once crossed the river; in the corner of Calle Bañuelo there are well-preserved **Moorish baths** (*open Tues–Sat 10–2*).

Even more curious is the façade of the **Casa Castril** on the Darro, a flamboyant 16th-century mansion with a portal carved with a phoenix, winged scallop shells and other eccentric-looking devices that have been interpreted as elements in a complex mystical symbolism. Over the big corner window is an inscription reading 'Waiting for her from the heavens'. The house's owner, Bernardo de Zafra, was once a secretary to Fernando and Isabel, and he seems to have got into trouble with the Inquisition.

Casa Castril has been restored as Granada's **archaeological museum** (*t 95 822 56 40; open Tues 2.30–8, Wed–Sat 9–8, Sun 9–2.30; adm, free to EU citizens*) with a small collection of artefacts from the huge number of caves in Granada province, many inhabited since Palaeolithic times, and a few Iberian settlements. There is a Moorish room, with some lovely works of art, and finally, an even greater oddity than Casa Castril itself. One room of the museum holds a collection of beautiful alabaster burial urns, made in Egypt, but found in a Phoenician-style necropolis near Almuñécar. Nothing else like them has ever been discovered in Spain, and the Egyptian hiero-glyphic inscriptions on them are provocative in the extreme (translations given in Spanish), telling how the deceased travelled here in search of some mysterious primordial deity.

Farther up the Darro, there's a small park with a view up to the Alhambra; after that you'll have to do some climbing, but the higher you go the prettier the Albaicín is, and the better the views. Among the white houses and white walls are some of the oldest Christian churches in Granada. As in Córdoba, they are tidy and extremely plain, built to avoid alienating a recently converted population unused to religious imagery. **San Juan de los Reyes** (1520) on Calle Zafra and **San José** (1525) are the oldest; both retain the plain minarets of the mosques they replaced. Quite a few Moorish houses survive in the Albaicín, and some can be seen on **Calle Horno de Oro**, just off the Darro; on **Calle Daralhorra**, at the top of the Albaicín, are the remains of a Nasrid palace that was largely destroyed to make way for Isabel's **Convento de Santa Isabel la Real** (1501).

Here, running parallel to Cuesta de la Alhacaba, is a long-surviving stretch of Moorish wall. There are probably a few miles of walls left, visible around the hillsides over Granada; the location of the city made a very complex set of fortifications neces-sary. In this one, about halfway up, you may pass through **Puerta de las Pesas**, with its horseshoe arches. The heart of the Albaicín is here, around the pretty, animated **Plaza Larga**; only a few blocks away the **Mirador de San Nicolás**, in front of the church of that name, offers the most romantic view imaginable of the Alhambra with the snow-capped peaks of the Sierra Nevada behind it. Note the brick, barrel-vaulted fountain on the *mirador*, a typical Moorish survival; fountains like this can be seen

Tortilla al Sacromonte

Regional dishes include cod rissole soup, chick peas and onions, plus, of course, the famous *tortilla al Sacromonte* made from a delightful concoction of brains, lamb's testicles, vegetables and eggs. The name originates from the Sacromonte Gypsies. Broad beans Granadine, cooked with fresh artichokes, tomatoes, onions, garlic, breadcrumbs and a smattering of saffron and cumin, may seem less adventurous compared to *Sacromonte* but it's just as typical of Granada's dishes.

If you're in Las Alpujarras, try the fresh goats' cheese, and in Trevélez you'll be hard pushed to avoid its famous ham. But if you're west of Granada near Santafé, make a detour to sample its sumptuous *pionono*s – *babas* with cream.

throughout the Albaicín and most are still in use. Granada today has a small but growing Muslim community, including a substantial number of western converts, and a brand new mosque is rising up just off the *mirador*.

On your way back from the Albaicín you might consider taking a different route, down a maze of back streets to the **Puerta de Elvira**, one of the most picturesque corners of the neighbourhood.

Sacromonte

For something completely different, you might strike out beyond the Albaicín hill to the **Gypsy caves of Sacromonte**. Granada has had a substantial Gypsy population for several centuries now. Some have become settled and respectable, others live in trailers on vacant land around town. The most visible are those who prey on the tourists around the Alhambra and the Capilla Real, handing out carnations with a smile and then attempting to extort huge sums out of anyone dumb enough to take one (of course, they'll tell your fortune, too). The biggest part of the Gypsy community, however, still lives around Sacromonte in streets of some quite well-appointed cave homes, where they wait to lure you in for a little display of flamenco. For a hundred years or so, the consensus of opinion has been that the music and dancing are usually indifferent, and the Gypsies' eventually successful attempts to shake out your last *centimo* can make it an unpleasantly unforgettable affair. Hotels sell tours for around €25.

Nevertheless, if you care to match wits with the experts, proceed up the Cuesta del Chapiz from the Río Darro, turn right at the **Casa del Chapiz**, a big 16th-century palace that now houses a school of Arab studies, and keep going until some Gypsy child drags you home with him. The bad reputation has been keeping tourists away lately so it's now much safer and friendlier as the Gypsies are worried about the loss of income. Serious flamenco fans will probably not fare better elsewhere in Granada except during the festivals, though there are some touristy flamenco nightspots – the **Reina Mora** by Mirador San Cristóbal is the best of them. On the third Sunday of each month, though, you can hear a **flamenco Mass** performed in the San Pedro Church on the Carrera del Darro.

Central Granada

The old city wall swung in a broad arc from Puerta de Elvira to Puerta Real, now a small plaza full of traffic where Calle Reyes Católicos meets the Acera del Darro. Just a few blocks north of here, in a web of narrow pedestrian streets that make up modern Granada's shopping district, is the pretty **Plaza de Bib-Rambla**, full of flower stands and toy shops, with an unusual fountain supported by leering giants at its centre. This was an important square in Moorish times, used for public gatherings and tournaments of arms. The narrow streets leading off to the east are known as the **Alcaicería**. This area was the Moorish silk exchange, but the buildings you see now, full of tourist souvenir shops, are not original; the Alcaicería burned down in the 1840s and was rebuilt in more or less the same fashion with Moorish arches and columns.

The Cathedral

*Pza de Pasiegas, entrance on Gran Vía de Colón, **t** 95 822 29 59.*
Open Mon–Sat 10.45–1.30 and 4–8, Sun 6–8.

The best way to see Granada's **cathedral** is to approach it from Calle Marqués, just north of the Plaza Bib-Rambla. The unique façade, with its three tall, recessed arches, is a striking sight, designed by the painter Alonso Cano (1667). On the central arch, the big plaque bearing the words 'Ave María' commemorates the exploit of the Spanish captain who sneaked into the city one night in 1490 and nailed up this message up on the door of the great mosque this cathedral has replaced.

The other conspicuous feature is the name 'José Antonio Primo de Rivera' carved on the façade. Son of the 1920s dictator, Miguel Primo de Rivera, José Antonio was a mystic fascist who founded the Falangist Party. His thugs provoked many of the disorders that started the Civil War, and at the beginning of the conflict he was captured by the loyalists and executed. Afterwards his followers treated him as a sort of holy martyr, and chiselled his name on every cathedral in Spain. That you can still see it here says a lot about Granada today.

The rest of the cathedral isn't up to the standard of its façade, and there is little reason to go in and explore its cavernous interior or dreary museum. Work was begun in 1521, after the Spaniards broke their promise not to harm the Great Mosque. As in many Spanish cathedrals, the failure of this one stems from artistic indecision. Two very talented architects were in charge: Enrique de Egas, who wanted it Gothic, like his adjacent Capilla Real, and (five years later) Diego de Siloé, who decided Renaissance would look much nicer. A score of other architects got their fingers in the pie before its completion in 1703. Some features of the interior: the grandiose **Capilla Mayor**, with statues of the apostles, and of Fernando and Isabel, by Alonso de Mena, and enormous heads of Adam and Eve by Alonso Cano, whose sculptures and paintings can be seen all over the cathedral; the **Retablo de Jesús Nazareno** in the right aisle, with paintings by Cano and Ribera, and a St Francis by El Greco; the Gothic **portal** leading into the Capilla Real (now closed) by de Egas. At the foot of the bell tower is a **museum**; its only memorable work is a subject typical of the degenerate art of the 1700s – a painted wooden head of John the Baptist.

Capilla Real

C/de los Oficios, open daily 10.30–1 and 3.30–6.30, Sun 11–1; adm.

Leaving the cathedral and turning left, you pass the outsized **sacristy**, begun in 1705 and incorporated in the cathedral façade. Turn down Calle de los Oficios, a narrow lane paved in charming patterns of coloured pebbles – a Granada speciality; on the left, you can pay your respects to *Los Reyes Católicos*, in the Capilla Real. The royal couple had already built a mausoleum in Toledo, but after the capture of Granada they decided to plant themselves here. Even in the shadow of the bulky cathedral, Enrique de Egas's **chapel** (1507) reveals itself as the outstanding work of the Isabelline Gothic style, with its delicate roofline of traceries and pinnacles. Charles V thought it not monumental enough for his grandparents, and only the distraction of his wars kept him from wrecking it in favour of some elephantine replacement.

Inside, the Catholic Kings are buried in a pair of Carrara marble sarcophagi, decorated with their recumbent figures, elegantly carved though not necessarily flattering to either of them. The little staircase behind them leads down to the **crypt**, where you can peek in at their plain lead coffins and those of their unfortunate daughter, Juana the Mad, and her husband, Philip the Handsome, whose effigies lie next to the older couple above. Juana was Charles V's mother, and the rightful heir to the Spanish throne. There is considerable doubt as to whether she was mad at all; when Charles arrived from Flanders in 1517, he forced her to sign papers of abdication, and then locked her up in a windowless cell for the last 40 years of her life, never permitting any visitors. The interior of the chapel is sumptuously decorated – it should be, considering the huge proportion of the crown revenues that were expended on it. The iron *reja* by Master Bartolomé de Jaén and the *retablo* are especially fine; the latter is largely the work of a French artist, Philippe de Bourgogne. In the chapel's sacristy you can see some of Isabel's personal art collection – works by Van der Weyden, Memling, Pedro Berruguete, Botticelli (attributed), Perugino and others, mostly in need of some restoration – as well as her crown and sceptre, her illuminated missal, some captured Moorish banners, and Fernando's sword.

Across the narrow street from the Capilla Real, an endearingly garish, painted Baroque façade hides **La Madraza**, a domed hall of the Moorish *madrasa* (Islamic seminary) and one of the best Moorish works surviving in Granada. It's now the university shop, and you can visit the small patio to admire its delicate arches and the creamy, sculpted *muqarna* ceiling. The Christians converted it into a town hall, whence its other name, the Casa del Cabildo.

Across Calle Reyes Católicos

Even though this part of the city centre is as old as the Albaicín, most of it was rebuilt after 1492, and its age doesn't show. The only Moorish building remaining is also the only example left in Spain of a *khan* or *caravanserai*, the type of merchants' hotel common throughout the Muslim world. The 14th-century **Corral del Carbón**, just off Reyes Católicos, takes its name from the time, a century ago, when it was used as a coal warehouse. Under the Spaniards it also served time as a theatre; its interior courtyard with balconies lends itself admirably to the purpose, being about the same size and shape as a Spanish theatre of the classic age, like the one in Almagro (La Mancha). Today it houses a government handicrafts outlet, and much of the building is under restoration *(open Mon–Sat 9–7, Sun 9–2)*. The neighbourhood of quiet streets and squares behind it is the best part of Spanish Granada and worth a walk if you have the time. Here you'll see the *mudéjar* **Casa de los Tiros**, a restored mansion built in 1505 on Calle Pavaneras, with strange figures carved on its façade; it houses a small **museum** of traditional arts and customs (*open Mon–Fri 2.30–8*). **Santo Domingo** (1512), the finest of Granada's early churches, is just a few blocks to the south. Fernando and Isabel endowed it, and their monograms figure prominently on the lovely façade. Just north of here is the Campo del Príncipe, another delightful square frequented by students and crammed full of restaurants and cafés.

From here various winding streets provide an alternative ascent to the Alhambra. This neighbourhood is bounded on the west by the Acera del Darro, the noisy heart of modern Granada, with most of the big hotels. It's a little discouraging but, as compensation, just a block away the city has adorned itself with a beautiful string of wide boulevards very like the Ramblas of Barcelona, a wonderful spot for a stroll. The **Carrera del Genil** usually has some sort of open-air market on it, and further down, the **Paseo del Salón** and **Paseo de la Bomba** are quieter and more park-like, joining the pretty banks of the Río Genil.

Out in a modern park in the southern suburbs of the city is Granada's newest and most high-tech attraction: the Parque de las Ciencias (*open Tues–Sat 10–7, Sun and hols 10–3; adm*), which has an excellent and very child-friendly museum with plenty of interactive activities and exhibits, a planetarium, and IMAX theatre.

Northern Granada

From the little street on the north side of the cathedral, the Calle de la Cárcel, Calle San Jerónimo skirts the edge of Granada's markets and leads you towards the old **university** district. Even though much of the university has relocated to a new campus half a mile to the north, this is still one of the livelier spots of town, and the colleges themselves occupy some fine, well-restored Baroque structures. The long yellow College of Law is one of the best, occupying a building put up in 1769 for the Jesuits; a small botanical garden is adjacent. Calle San Jerónimo ends at the Calle del Gran Capitán, where the landmark is the basilica of **San Juan de Dios**, with a Baroque façade and a big green and white tiled dome. **San Jerónimo**, a block west, is another of the oldest and largest Granada churches (1520); it contains the tomb of Gonzalo de Córdoba, the 'Gran Capitán' who won so many victories in Italy for the Catholic Kings.

Here you're not far from the Puerta de Elvira, in an area where old Granada fades into anonymous suburbs to the north. The big park at the end of the Gran Vía is the

Jardines del Triunfo, with coloured, illuminated fountains the city hardly ever turns on. Behind them is the Renaissance **Hospital Real** (1504–22), designed by Enrique de Egas. A few blocks southwest, climbing up towards the Albaicín, your senses will be assaulted by the gaudiest Baroque chapel in Spain, in the **Cartuja**, or Carthusian monastery, on Calle Real de Cartuja (***t** 95 816 19 32; open Mon–Sat 10–1 and 4–8, Sun 10–12; adm*). Gonzalo de Córdoba endowed this Charterhouse, though little of the original works remain. The 18th-century chapel and its sacristy, done in the richest marble, gold and silver, and painted plaster, fairly oozes with a froth of twisted spiral columns, rosettes and curlicues. It has often been described as a Christian attempt to upstage the Alhambra, but the inspiration more likely comes from the Aztecs, via the extravagant Mexican Baroque.

Lorca

Outside Spain Federico García Lorca is popularly regarded as Spain's greatest modern dramatist and poet. The Spanish literati would acknowledge others from the generation of 1925 and from the previous generation of 1898 to have at least equal stature – the Galician dramatist and poet Ramón del Valle-Inclán springs to mind. But Lorca's murder certainly enhanced his reputation outside Spain. Under Franco, any mention of him was forbidden (understandably so, since it was Franco's men who shot him). Today the *granadinos* are coming to terms with Lorca, and seem determined to make up for the past. Lorca fans pay their respects at two country houses, now museums, where the poet spent many of his early years: the **Huerta de San Vicente** (***t** 95 825 84 66, www.huertadesanvicente.com; open for guided visits Tues–Sun July–Aug 10–3; April–June and Sept 10–1 and 5–8; Oct–Mar 10–1 and 4–7; adm*), on the outskirts of town at Virgen Blanca, and the **Museo-Casa Natal Lorca** at Fuente Vaqueros, the village where he was born, 17km to the west near the Córdoba road (***t** 95 851 64 53, www.museogarcialorca.org; open Tues–Sun, guided tours every hour Oct–March 10–1 and 4–6; April–June 10–1 and 5–7; June–Aug 10–2 and 5–7; adm*).

Granada Province

From everywhere in Granada, the mountains peer over the tops of buildings. Until the 20th century they were associated with the so-called icemen who made the gruelling journey to the peaks and back again with chunks of ice to sell in town. Today, Spain's loftiest peaks are more accessible.

The Sierra Nevada and Las Alpujarras

Dress warmly. As the name implies, the Sierra Nevada is snowcapped nearly all year, and even in late July and August, when the road is clear (*see* 'Getting Around', p.304) and you can travel right over the mountains to the valley of Las Alpujarras, it's as chilly and windy as you would expect it to be, some 3,300m (10,825ft) above sea level. These mountains, a geological curiosity of sorts, are just an oversized chunk of the Penibetic

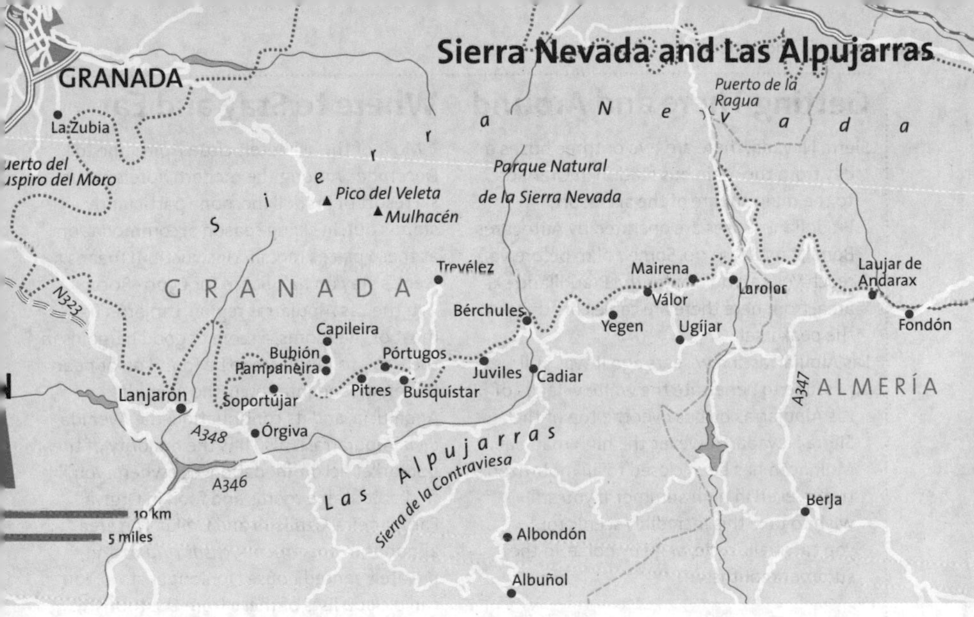

System, the chain that stretches from Arcos de la Frontera almost to Murcia. Their highest peak, **Mulhacén** (3,481m/11,420ft), is less than 40km from the coast. From Granada you can see nearly all of the Sierra: a jagged snowy wall without any really distinctive peaks. The highest expanses are barren and frosty, but on a clear day they offer a view to Morocco. Mulhacén and especially its sister peak **Veleta** (3,392m/ 11,125ft) can be climbed without too much exertion. Up until quite recently the area was fairly inaccessible and the facilities – certainly compared to Alpine standards – pretty basic. But the place has come on in leaps and bounds in the last decade – so much so that it was deemed good enough to host the 1995 World Skiing Championships (unfortunately postponed until 1996 owing to lack of snow). The Sierra Nevada cannot compete in terms of scale and variety with Alpine resorts but there are more than enough pistes to detain you for a long weekend.

If you're adventurous, you can continue onwards from Veleta down into **Las Alpujarras**, a string of white villages along the valley of the Río Guadalfeo, between the Sierra Nevada and the little Contraviesa chain along the sea coast. On the way to Las Alpujarras, just outside Granada, you'll pass the spot called **Suspiro de Moro**, where poor Boabdil sighed as he took his last look back over Granada (now, sadly, just a signpost on the motorway). His mother was less than sympathetic – 'You weep like a woman for what you were incapable of defending like a man', she told him. It gave Salman Rushdie the title for his novel *The Moor's Last Sigh* (1995). The last 33km of this route, where the road joins the Guadalfeo valley down to Motril, is one of the most scenic in Spain.

In Moorish times this was a densely populated region, full of vines and orchards. Much of its population was made up of refugees from the Reconquista, coming mainly from Sevilla. Under the conditions for Granada's surrender in 1492, the region was granted as a fief to Boabdil el Chico but, with forced Christianization and the resulting revolts, the population was exiled and replaced by settlers from the north.

Getting There and Around

Sierra Nevada: there are two or three buses a day from the main bus station in Granada, to the main square of the ski resort, Pradollano. Buses are operated by Autocares Bonal, **t** 95 827 31 00. Some 20km before you reach Veleta, you'll enter the Pradollano ski area; from here there are cable cars up to the peak itself.

Las Alpujarras: a few years ago it was still possible to penetrate the white villages of Las Alpujarras by bus over the top of the Sierra Nevada. However, the high road past Mulhacén has been closed to all motorized traffic, even in high summer. If you still wish to take this incredibly scenic route you can walk, cycle, or go by horse, in the summer months.

Tourist Information

Lanjarón: opposite the spa, on the right as you come in from Granada: **t** 95 877 02 82. Opening times vary.

Pampaneira: Parque Natural de la Sierra Nevada, Plaza de la Libertad s/n, **t** 95 876 31 27, **f** 95 876 33 01, *www.nevadensis.com. Open in summer Tues–Sat 10–2 and 4–7, winter 10–2 and 3–6, Mon and Sun all year 10–3.*

Órgiva: C/Lora Tamayo 17, **t** 95 878 44 84, *alta-alpujarra@asociacion-tierra.org*.

For skiing information contact the tourist office in Granada, or visit the excellent website *www.sierranevada.ski*. There's a central reservation number for accommodation and ski packages, **t** 902 70 80 90.

Where to Stay and Eat

Most of the ski hotels close from June to December. Among the modern hotels in the ski resort of Pradollano, none particularly stands out; in skiing season accommodation at these places (not inc. instruction) means a week's stay on half board for €500–800.

In the Las Alpujarras region, Lanjarón has most of the rooms; a score of good bargains in the €30–40 range are to be found on or near the main road into town, the Avenida Andalucía, and its continuation, the Avenida de la Alpujarra. It also has the majority of the upmarket accommodation. Elsewhere, you'll find acceptable rooms and food in Órgiva, Pampaneira, Capileira and Ugíjar. The area abounds in apartments, *casas rurales* and privately rented houses for longer stays. You can pick up lists of these from the tourism offices in the area, including Rustic Blue (**t** 95 876 33 81, *www.rusticblue.com*) and Global Spirit, Ctra. de la Sierra s/n, **t** 97 132 51 11, **f** 97 132 55 13, *www.global-spirit.com*, both in Bubión.

Lanjarón ✉ 18420

*****Nuevo Palas**, Avda de Alpujarra 24, **t** 95 877 00 86, **f** 95 877 12 83, *www.hotelnuevopalas.com* (*moderate*). The best in town; recently refurbished, comfortable rooms with views, pool, gym, games room and restaurant.

****Castillo Alcadima**, C/Francisco Tarrega 3, **t** 95 877 08 09, **f** 95 877 11 82, *www.alcadima.es* (*inexpensive*). Just down from the main road and occupying one of the best spots in town, with rooms set round a pool/dining area with views to the castle and across the valley. They also rent apartments for longer stays.

Though often described as one of the most inaccessible corners of Spain, this region has attracted growing numbers of visitors since Gerald Brenan wrote *South from Granada* and, more recently, Chris Stewart wrote *Driving Over Lemons* and its sequel, an account of setting up home in one of the remoter corners of this region. The roads wind past stepped fields, cascades of water, high pastures and sudden drops, and when the almond trees are in blossom it is at its most appealing. Unlike the other Andalucían villages with their red-tiled roofs, the *pueblos* of Las Alpujarras are flat-roofed. Though you won't be the only visitors to Las Alpujarras, the region is hardly spoiled; and with the villages relatively close to each other, and plenty of wild country on either side, it's a great spot for hiking or just finding some peace and quiet.

★**España**, Avda Andalucía 44, **t/f** 95 877 01 87 (*inexpensive*). Excellent value for what it has, which includes a pool and its own grounds.

Alcadima, C/Francisco Tarrega 3, **t** 95 877 08 09, **f** 95 877 11 82. This hotel restaurant offers good value and fine views.

El Rincón de Jamon, along the main road just beyond the España. For an altogether earthier experience, come here to enjoy a *copa* of *vino* and a few slices of *jamón* from Trevélez in spit-and-sawdust surroundings.

Órgiva ✉ 18400

★★★**Taray**, Ctra Talbate-Albuñol, km 18, **t** 95 878 45 25, **f** 95 878 45 31, *tarayalp@teleline.es* (*moderate*). On the road out of Órgiva, this is one of the best places to stay in the whole of this area: comfortable rooms in a *cortijo*-style hotel, set round a large pool, and with a bar and good restaurant.

★★**Hotel Alpujarras**, Ctra de Trevélez, **t** 95 878 55 49, *hotelalpujarra@terra.es* (*inexpensive*). The next best option, on the junction as you go into town, with restaurant.

El Molino de Benizalte, C/González Robles 12, **t** 95 878 57 45, *elmolino@turinet.net*. Friendly little B&B in a converted olive mill, with a patio garden, tiny pool and pretty terrace.

Ugíjar ✉ 18480

Hostal Vidaña, Ctra de Almería, **t** 95 876 70 10 (*inexpensive*). Serves up huge portions of delicious mountain fare, such as partridge, goat and rabbit; also provides basic accommodation.

Pedro, Fábrica de Sedas s/n, **t** 95 876 71 49 (*cheap*). Another good-value place to stay.

Aben-Humeya, Los Bolos, Válor, **t** 95 885 18 10. Excellent *alpujarraneña* cuisine in this tiny village north of Ugíjar; the wine list features a lot of locally grown organic wines.

Pampaneira ✉ 18411

Hostal Ruta de Mulhacén, Avda Alpujarra 6, **t** 95 876 30 10, **f** 95 876 34 46 (*cheap*). On the main road as you go through the town, this is simple but comfortable.

Hostal Pampaneira, José Antonio 1, **t** 95 876 30 02. Slightly cheaper and a bit more basic.

For food there are numerous options in the pretty main square, Plaza de la Libertad, none of them outstanding.

Bubión ✉ 18412

Villa Turística de Bubión, Barrio Alto s/n, **t** 95 876 31 11, **f** 95 876 31 36, *www.ctv.es/alpujarr* (*moderate*). Offers self-catering apartments with the advantages of a hotel. Prices depend on apartment size; most apartments have beautiful views.

Terrazas de la Alpujarra, Plaza del Sol s/n, **t** 95 876 30 34, **f** 95 876 32 52, *terrazas@teleline.es* (*cheap*). A perfectly acceptable budget option, with en suite rooms in the *hostal*, or excellent value apartments (*inexpensive*) with log fires and *terrazas* with breathtaking views across the valley.

As a place firmly on the tourist trail, Bubión has a number of good bars and restaurants.

La Artesa, C/Carretera 2, **t** 95 876 30 82 (*inexpensive*). Perhaps the best restaurant, serving hearty fare at a reasonable price.

Teide, C/Carretera, **t** 95 876 30 37. Another good restaurant.

CiberMonfi, Café Morisco, C/Alcalde Pérez Remón 2 (off the Plaza del Sol), **t** 95 876 30 53. Drink mint tea and surf the Net.

Lanjarón, the principle tourist centre in the region, has been attracting visitors to its spas since Roman times and now markets its bottled water all across Spain. It's not particularly attractive, just a strip of road lined with functional-looking spas. There are eight springs in all, each offering a different blend of natural minerals, while shops along the main street offer complementary remedies for whatever ails you. The ruined Moorish castle on the hill saw the Moors' last stand against the imperial troops on 8 March 1500. Well and truly Catholic today, Lanjarón's Semana Santa celebrations are the most famous in the province.

Órgiva was made the regional capital by Isabel II in 1839 and it remains the biggest town of Las Alpujarras today. There are few remains of its Moorish past; the castle of

Capileira ✉ 18143

★★★**Finca Los Llanos**, Ctra de Sierra Nevada, **t** 95 876 30 71, **f** 95 876 32 06 (*moderate*). A luxury option with a pool; its restaurant is known for its aubergines in honey.

Mesón Poqueira, Doctor Castilla, 6, **t** 95 876 30 48 (*cheap*). Rooms with a view, and a good restaurant.

Apartamentos Antonio y Susi, C/ Doctor Castilla, **t** 95 876 31 95. Apartment rental at modest prices.

Panjuila, on the road just outside the village. Nightlife is fairly limited in Capileira, but if you're here on a Thursday then track down this café-restaurant for some flamenco.

Pitres ✉ 18414

★★Hotel San Roque, C/ Cruz,1, **t** 95 885 75 28 (*inexpensive*). Simple whitewashed hotel, with airy rooms, beamed ceilings, and a good little restaurant (with vegetarian specialities).

Posada La Taha, Bancal de Perico s/n, **t/f** 95 834 30 41 (*cheap*). Rents out apartments in a typical Alpujarran house with garden.

Pórtugos ✉ 18415

★★**Nuevo Malagueño**, Ctra Órgiva–Trevélez, **t** 95 876 60 98 (*moderate*). Offers comfortable rooms and views over the Alpujarras.

Trevélez ✉ 18005

★★★**Alcazaba de Busquístar**, Ctra Órgiva-Láujar, km 37, **t** 95 885 86 87, **f** 95 885 86 93 (*moderate*). This is one of the best places to stay in the Alpujarras, despite the indifferent service. Rather confusingly, it is nowhere near Busquístar (but 4km beyond Trevélez). It is a new hotel arranged along traditional Alpujarran lines. It has apartments and studios, all with log fires, kitchen, phone and satellite TV. There is a heated indoor pool, squash court, excellent restaurant, three cafés and games room.

★**La Fragua**, C/San Antonio 4 (in the Barrio del Medio), **t** 95 885 85 73 (*inexpensive*). The best in town, with warm rooms and a good restaurant which concentrates on Alpujarras specialities (*moderate*).

Hostal Mulhacén, Ctra Ugíjar, **t/f** 95 885 85 87 (*cheap*). Well situated for hill walks and the annual all-night pilgrimage up Spain's highest mountain at midnight on August 4th. The *hostal* is also beside the river, where locals swim during the summer.

Casa Julio, Haza de la Iglesia s/n, **t** 95 885 87 08. Cosy bar-restaurant, with a beamed dining room in winter and a small terrace in summer; serves regional specialities.

Cadiar ✉ 18440

★★**Alquería de Morayma**, C/Alquería de Morayma, **t** 95 834 32 21 (*moderate*). A recreated *cortijo* with individual and charmingly decorated apartments for 2–6 people, a pool and good restaurant. The best place to stay in town.

Yegen ✉ 18460

El Rincón de Yegen, Camino de las Eras, **t** 95 885 12 70 (*moderate*). Despite its indifferent service, probably the best place to stay, just east of the village with a pool and a good restaurant. It also lets *casas rurales*.

Casas Blancas, C/Casas Blancas 24, in the nearby village of Mecina Bombarón, **t** 95 885 11 51 (*inexpensive*). A rural hotel which also lets studio rooms.

the Counts of Sástago may look the part but it dates from the 17th century. The Renaissance church has a carving by Martínez Montañés and there is an old olive mill just outside the town (*see* 'Where to Stay'). Órgiva springs to life on Thursdays, when everyone congregates for the weekly market. The town has become a magnet for New Age travellers and you can't fail to notice them or their beaten-up transit vans passing through the streets. Just outside town they have set up a wigwam village.

From here you'll have a choice of keeping to the main road for **Ugíjar** or heading north through the highest and loveliest part of the region, with typical white villages climbing the hillsides under terraced fields. **Soportújar**, the first, has one of Las Alpujarras' surviving primeval oak groves behind it. Next comes **Pampaneira**, a pretty

La Fuente, in the main square, **t** 95 885 10 67 (*cheap*). The budget option, just round the corner from Gerald Brenan's house, with a simple café-bar. Also rents apartments.

Laujar de Andarax ✉ 04470

★★**Villa Turística de Laujar**, Cortijo de la Villa (just outside the village), **t** 95 051 30 27, **f** 95 051 35 54, *villa_laujar@servimar.net* (*moderate*). Rents 31 apartments with open fires, satellite TV and terrace. Also has a pool, tennis, good restaurant and kids' play area.

★★**Almirez**, Ctra Laujar-Órgiva, km 1.6, **t** 95 051 35 14, **f** 95 051 35 61 (*inexpensive*). Relaxed, modern, family-run hotel in a beautiful setting with a pool and good restaurant.

Alhama de Almería ✉ 04400

★★**San Nicolás**, C/Baños s/n, **t** 95 064 13 61 (*moderate*). On the site of the original Moorish baths, offering comfortable rooms on its own grounds at reasonable prices.

Pradollano (Sol y Nieve) ✉ 18196

Most of what you'll need for skiing can be found here: ski hire shops rent out the entire kit (including clothes) for about €60. There is also what is reputed to be the biggest covered car park in Spain, with space for almost 3,000 cars. Ski passes cost between €10–20 a day, depending on the season. Seasoned Alpine skiers will not be hugely challenged by the slopes, but for the beginner the area is a dream, with plenty of wide gentle pistes. There is plenty to keep you occupied for two or three days, and the views from the top of Veleta, across to Morocco on clear days, are unsurpassable. All the hotels listed below are open year-round unless otherwise noted.

★★★**Kenia Nevada**, C/Virgen de las Nieves 6, **t** 95 848 09 11, **f** 95 848 08 07 (*expensive–moderate*). Alpine-style, with a Jacuzzi, pool, gym and sauna.

★★★**Hotel Parador**, on the main highway, **t** 95 848 06 61, **f** 95 848 02 12 (*expensive–moderate*). This hotel is one of the smaller and newer *paradores;* open all year.

★★★★**Meliá Sierra Nevada**, C/Pradollano s/n, **t** 95 848 04 00, *melia.sierra.nevada@solmelia.es* (*luxury–moderate*). The huge block back from the square; offers similar luxuries as above, at a slightly higher price.

★★★★**Maribel**, **t** 95 848 10 19, **f** 95 848 20 10, *hmaribel@eurocibes.es* (*luxury–moderate*). Prettier and more intimate with just 26 rooms but no pool.

★★★**Ziryab**, Plaza de Andalucía, **t** 95 848 05 12, **f** 95 848 14 15 (*expensive–moderate*). A dramatically situated hotel on the main square, with big, comfortable rooms and chunky wood furniture. Right by the car park.

★★**El Ciervo**, **t** 95 848 04 09, **f** 95 848 04 61, *www.eh.etursa.es* (*moderate*). Large *pensión*.

Albergue Universitario, Peñones de San Francisco, **t** 95 848 01 22 (*cheap*). Cheaper accommodation like this can be had in this village at the end of the bus route.

Most restaurants are open only in the skiing season, and most are a little pretentious – but that's ski resorts for you.

Ruta de Veleta, **t** 95 848 12 01 (*moderate*). This restaurant in Edificio Bulgaria is worth a try.

Rincón de Pepe Reyes, in Pradollano, **t** 95 848 03 94 (*inexpensive*). Good *Andaluz* dishes.

Borreguiles, halfway up Veleta, **t** 95 848 00 79. Take the cable car up to this frenetic café and sit out on the terrace to take in the view.

little town of cobbled streets and flowers. In the Plaza de la Libertad there's a museum dedicated to the customs and costumes of Las Alpujarras and a locally run office for the **Parque Natural de la Sierra Nevada**. All sorts of activities are on offer here, such as horse rides, skiing, hang-gliding, nature walks and caving expeditions. They also sell good maps of the park. If you'd prefer something more contemplative, the **Tibetan Monastery of Clear Light**, the birthplace of a reincarnated Spanish Tibetan lama, Osel, sits above the town on the sides of the **Poqueira Gorge**, complete with a visitor centre (*open daily 3–6*) offering courses in Mahayana Buddhism and retreats. To get there, take the road marked Camino Forestal, on the right just before the turn-off for Pampaneira; it's about 7km along a dirt track.

Bubión is a Berber-style village in a spectacular setting with a textile mill and tourist shops. All these villages are within sight of each other on a short detour along the edge of the beautiful (and walkable) ravine called **Barranco de Poqueira**. The last village on the mountain-pass route over Mulhacén and Veleta is **Capileira**, which sees more tourists than most. Its treasure, in the church of **Nuestra Señora de la Cabeza**, is a statue of the Virgin donated to the village by Fernando and Isabel. North from here a tremendously scenic road takes you up across the Sierra Nevada and eventually to Granada. In winter this pass is snowbound, and even in summer you need to take extra care – it's steep and dangerous with precipitous drops down the ravines. However, the beautiful scenery makes the risks worthwhile. The road is permanently closed to all motorized traffic, but you can do it on foot (about 5½ hours), by bike or on horseback. Alternatively, continue on the GR421 to **Pitres**, centre of a Hispano-Japanese joint venture that produces handcrafted ballet shoes, of all things. There is a ruined hilltop mosque, and the remains of a few other Moorish buildings.

The road carries on through the villages of **Pórtugos**, a pilgrimage centre for Our Lady of Sorrows, and **Busquístar**, before arriving in **Trevélez**, on the slopes of Mulhacén. Trevélez likes to claim it's the highest village in Europe. It's also famous in Andalucía for its snow-cured hams – Henry Ford and Rossini were fans – and a ham feast is held in their honour every August. Today Trevélez is full of tour buses, and a string of ugly developments has removed any charm it once had. This is the main starting point for climbers heading for the summit of Mulhacén and the other peaks in the Sierra Nevada, but, despite the tacky tourist shops, there's little to detain other visitors. From there the road slopes back downwards to **Juviles** and **Bérchules**, one of the villages where the tradition of carpet-weaving has been maintained since Moorish times. From here you can go down to **Cádiar**, the 'navel' of Las Alpujarras, as Gerald Brenan described it, a nondescript place with an attractive main square. Otherwize you can move along to Ugíjar, or cut down to the coast via **Albondón** and **Albuñol** (both famous for their rosé wines), finishing at **La Rabita**, in Almería.

The C332 from Bérchules takes you to **Yegen**, some 10km further, which became famous as the long-time home of Gerald Brenan. His house is still in the village – ask for 'La Casa del Inglés'. After that come more intensively farmed areas on the lower slopes, with oranges, vineyards and almonds; you can either hit Ugíjar or detour to the seldom-visited villages of **Laroles** and **Mairena** on the slopes of **La Ragua**, one of the last high peaks of the Sierra Nevada. In 1569 Fernando de Córdoba y Válor rallied the last remaining Moors in the area to revolt against the Christians; **Válor** is the site of the Moors' last stand. The events are recreated in the annual 'Moors and Christians' festival in September.

The A337 will take you north over the mountains and towards Guadix (*see* below). Further east, through countryside that rapidly changes from healthy green to dry brown, the road enters Almería province and the town of **Láujar de Andarax**. It was here that the deposed Boabdil planned on setting up his court to rule the Alpujarras after being expelled from Granada in 1492. But his plans were short-lived and in less than a year the Christian kings had reneged on their promise and expelled him: his last view of Spain was from Adra before he set sail for Africa.

A few kilometres on, the village of **Fondón** is of particular interest; an Australian architect, Donald Grey, and his Spanish partner, José Antonio Garvayo, have set up a school to teach the traditional crafts of ironwork, carpentry, tile- and brick-making, so most of the buildings have been restored, and Fondón is now a model village. The church tower was once a mosque's minaret. The road from here passes through some nondescript villages before arriving in **Alhama de Almería**, a spa town since Moorish times. You can take the waters here or drop down to the coast and Almería.

Around the Sierra Nevada

It's a better road entering Granada from the west than that leaving it to the east. Between the city and Murcia are some of the emptiest, bleakest landscapes in Spain. The first village you pass through is **Purullena**, long famous for its pretty ceramic ware; the entire stretch of highway through it is lined with stands and displays.

The poverty of this region has long forced many of its inhabitants to live in caves, and nowhere more so than in **Guadix**. Several thousand of this city's population, most of them Gypsies, have homes – complete with whitewashed façades, chimneys and television aerials – built into the hillsides. The cave dwellings have their advantages: they're warmer in the winter and cooler in summer than most Andalucían homes, relatively spacious and well ventilated – and all you need is a pick and shovel to create a new room. If you care to venture around the caves, largely concentrated in the Barrio de Santiago, beware of being lured into someone's home and charged an exorbitant fee. For a better understanding of troglodyte culture head to the **Cave Museum**, Plaza del Beato Poveda s/n (***t*** *95 866 08 08; open Mon–Sat 10–2 and 5–7, Sun 10–2; adm*).

Tourist Information

Guadix: situated on the edge of town on the Granada road, **t** 95 866 26 65, *www. guadixmarquesado.org. Open Mon–Fri 8–3.*

Where to Stay and Eat

Guadix ✉ 18500

★★★**Comercio**, C/Mira de Amezcua 3, **t** 95 866 05 00, **f** 95 866 50 72, *www.moebius.es/ hotelcomercio* (*inexpensive*). The best place to stay, in a refurbished mansion which has seen better days, with all mod cons.

★★**Mulhacén**, Avda Buenos Aires 41, **t** 95 866 07 50, **f** 95 866 06 61 (*inexpensive*). An acceptable alternative, near the train station, with a café.

★★★**Carmen**, Avda Mariana Pineda 61, **t** 95 866 15 00, **f** 95 866 01 79 (*inexpensive*). Has a TV and phone in each room and, rather incongrously, a tennis court.

Cuevas de Pedro Antonio Alarcón, Avda de Buenos Aires (just out of the centre), **t** 95 866 49 86, **f** 95 866 17 21 (*moderate*). For something completely different, you might like to try a night in a cave: the hotel comprises a series of luxuriously appointed caves complete with pool and a decent restaurant.

Baza ✉ 18800

★★**Robemar**, Ctra de Murcia 175, **t** 95 886 07 04, **f** 95 870 07 98 (*inexpensive*). The best place to stay, out of the centre, but it does boast a pool.

Pension Anabel, C/María de Luna 3, **t** 95 886 09 98 (*inexpensive*). All rooms are en suite with TV and phone; café attached.

Galera ✉ 18840

Casas Cuevas, C/Cervantes 11, **t** 95 873 90 68, *www.casas-cueva.es* (*moderate*). Another charming, comfortable cave hotel.

The centre of Guadix is dominated by a Moorish **Alcazaba**, largely rebuilt in the 16th century; near the arcaded central **Plaza Mayor** stands the huge **cathedral**, begun by Diego de Siloé, builder of Granada's cathedral, and given its magnificent façade in the 1700s by Andalucía's great rococo eccentric, Vicente Acero. The ornate church, and the imposing castle, appearing together out of the eroded hills make a striking sight.

Forty-six kilometres northeast on the A92N lies **Baza**, which was important in Moorish times as a centre of silk production, in Roman times when it was known as Basti and was capital of the area, and important also in prehistoric times as a centre for ancient Iberian tribes. Today it is an unassuming market town, worth an afternoon's wander. It too has a cave quarter, though not as extensive as Guadix, and a ruined Alcazaba. More rewarding though are the **Moorish baths** – some of the oldest in Spain, dating from at least the 10th century – which are still privately owned but can be visited (check with the *turismo*). But Baza is most famous for its **Dama de Baza**, an Iberian sculpture of a goddess dating from the 3rd or 4th century BC, unearthed nearby but now residing in Madrid; a copy can be seen in the local **archaeological museum** in Plaza Mayor (***t** 95 870 06 91*). There are a couple of other buildings worth seeking out, including the 16th-century **cathedral of Santa María** and the **Palacio de los Enriquez**, just off the main square, which dates from the 15th or 16th century and has many interesting Moorish-influenced designs. The town is bounded by a natural park which has many ancient settlements including cave dwellings found on nearby Mount Jabalcón, accessible from the village of **Zújar**.

From Baza the main highway heads into Almería towards Vélez-Rubio and Vélez-Blanco (*see* p.320). Alternatively you could make a detour to **Huéscar**, some 37km from Baza along the A92N then north along the A330 at Cúllar Baza. Huéscar has a stormy past. It constantly fell in and out of Moorish and Christian hands through the Middle Ages, suffering terribly in the Moorish uprising of the 16th century. As a result most of its buildings have been replaced with ugly modern blocks. However, seek out its church, **Santa María de la Encarnación**; both Diego de Siloé and Vandelvira had a hand in its construction. Near the village of **Galera**, about 7km to the south, are some hill-top caves which form part of the ancient Iberian settlement of Tútugi (5th to 6th century BC). **Orce**, to the east, is built round an old Alcazaba, which has been largely reconstructed.

There's not much else to distract you. If you're headed for Almería and the coast (N324), you'll pass near **La Calahorra**, with a spectacular Renaissance castle, and **Gérgal**.

Almería Province

At **Adra** you enter the province of Almería, the sunniest, driest and hottest corner of Europe. What they call winter here lasts from the end of November to March; scores of films (famously *Lawrence of Arabia*) have been shot here, taking advantage of the light and scenery. Until the 1970s the **Costa de Almería**, difficult of access and bereft of utilities, was untouched by tourism. Now, charter flights drop in from northern Europe, but compared to the region further west, it's pleasantly underwhelming.

Almería

Almería has been a genial, dusty little port since its founding by the Phoenicians, though for a short time in the 11th century, after the fall of the caliphate, it dominated this end of al-Andalus, rivalling Córdoba and Sevilla. The upper city, with its narrow streets, tiny pastel houses and whitewashed cave dwellings hugging the looming walls of the **Alcazaba** (*open daily 9–8.30; adm, free to EU citizens*), has retained a fine Moorish feel to this day. Built by Caliph Abd ar-Rahman II in the 10th century, the

Getting There and Around

By Air

Almería's airport is 8km from the city on the road to Níjar, **t** 95 033 31 11, **f** 95 021 38 59. There are charters from London, and regular connections with Madrid, Barcelona and Melilla. A bus runs from the airport tothe town every 30mins: the no 14, which leaves for the airport from Avda Federico García Lorca (next to Pizza Hut), **t** 95 022 14 22.

By Boat

Trasmediterránea, **t** 902 45 46 45, *www.trasmediterranea.com*, runs car ferries from Almería to Melilla on the North African coast and Nador in Morocco. There is one sailing daily to each destination all year round, plus an extra service to Melilla in summer. Book early to be sure of a place. Ferri-Maroc, **t** 95 027 48 00, run services at least twice-daily to Nador.

By Train

Almería's RENFE station is a block from the bus station, on Ctra Ronda, easy walking distance from the centre, **t** 902 24 02 02. There are daily regional and high-speed trains to Madrid, Barcelona and Valencia and overnight services to Córdoba and Sevilla.

By Bus

The bus station, on the Plaza Barcelona, **t** 95 021 11 35, has a daily service to the major cities of the Levante up to Barcelona; also to Madrid, Granada, Sevilla, Cádiz, Málaga and Algeciras. There are two buses daily to Adra; hourly connections to Aguadulce and Roquetas; five buses daily to Berja; at least three to Cabo de Gata, four to Mojácar, two each to Níjar and Tabernas and connections to Jaén and Guadix.

Tourist Information

Parque de Nicolás Salmerón at Martínez Campos, **t** 95 027 43 55, *almeria@andalucia.org*. *Open Mon–Fri 9–7, Sat and Sun 10–2.* There is also a municipal tourist office on Avda Federico García Lorca. Internet: Battlezone, C/de la Terriza 20; Cybercafé Abakan, C/Marcos 19.

Where to Stay and Eat

Almería ✉ 04000

Expensive

******Gran Hotel Almería**, Avenida Reina Regente 8, **t** 95 023 80 11, **f** 95 027 06 91. When on location in Almería, Hollywood denizens have traditionally checked in here. Rooms are plush, with a/c, and among the diversions are a pool and bingo hall.

Torreluz Hotel Complex, Pza de las Flores 1, **t/f** 95 023 43 99, *www.amtorreluz.com* (*expensive–inexpensive*). Another comfortable choice in town offering two-, three- and four star accommodation, all in the same pretty square. All three hotels offer parking, a/c, phone and TV; the four-star also has a pool. The hotels have an excellent restaurant, the Asador Torreluz, **t** 95 023 45 45.

El Bello Rincón, Ctra Nacional 340, km 436, **t** 95 023 84 27. Probably the best restaurant, with a beautiful views over the sea and wonderfully fresh seafood. *Closed Mon, July and Aug.*

Moderate

*****Costasol**, Pso de Almería 58, **t** 95 023 40 11. The city's other quality choice, located right where all the action is and with all three-star amenities.

Alcazaba was the most powerful Moorish fortress in Spain; today its great curtain walls and towers defend mostly market- and flower-gardens – nothing remains of the once-splendid palace. The main complex is divided into three distinct sections. The first and largest is reached through the Puerta de la Justicia, which opens out on to a large space consisting mainly of flower beds. It is hard to imagine that this once contained the military barracks as the first line of defence. The views from here, across the entire town to the sparkling sea, are extraordinary. The second level is where the Moorish baths and palaces, the private residences and leaders' homes once

Baños Sierra de Alhamilla, t 95 031 74 13, **f** 95 016 02 57. 7km from Almería at Pechina, look out for this beautifully restored 18th-century palace next to the thermal springs.

Bodegon La Gruta, t 95 023 93 35. Beside the Bello Rincón in a natural grotto, a decent restaurant serving mainly meat dishes and grills. *Closed Sun and Nov.*

Balzac, C/Gerona,29, **t** 95 026 61 60. A popular restaurant with a terrace, serving classic Mediterranean dishes with a French twist.

Merendero la Playa, Playa del Alquián, **t** 95 052 01 71. On the beach at Perdigal, this family favourite offers great tapas and more substantial seafood dishes, including a very fine *fritada de pescado fresco.*

Inexpensive

****HR Perla**, Plaza del Carmen 7, **t** 95 023 88 77. One of the city's original hotels, a solid place, with parking and a café.

***Sevilla**, C/Granada 25, **t** 95 023 00 09. The best in the range, in an excellent position just off the Puerta Purchena. It's been refurbished recently so each room has en suite bathrooms, TV and phone.

Almería also has plenty of *hostales* mainly concentrated around the Puerta de Purchena, Plaza San Sebastian and the streets off them.

***Maribel**, Avda. FG Lorca 153, **t** 95 023 51 73, **f** 95 023 51 66. Within easy walking distance of the bus and train stations, offering simple but adequate rooms.

Nixar, C/Antonio Vico 24, **t/f** 95 023 72 55. On a one-way street near the Alcazaba; basic but functional with a café attached.

The Bristol, Plaza San Sebastián 8, **t** 95 023 15 95. In a good position, just off the top of the Pso de Almería; all rooms en suite.

Tapas Bars

The city has a large number of tapas bars and restaurants, many of which are on a map available from the tourist office. Here is a selection to the west of Pso de Almería:

Casa Puga, C/Jovellanos 7. A family-run place, ancient, noisy and with a vast wine list.

Cerveceria La Estrella, Plaza del Carmen 2. By contrast, this *cervecería* is stylish, modern and attracts a thirty-something crowd.

Cafeteria Granada, C/Granada 26. Offers a wide range of tapas, *raciones*, *platos*, *dulces*, as well as Internet access; younger crowd.

Bodeguilla Ramón, C/Padre Alonso Torres 4. Atmospheric place with bullfight pictures, *azulejos* and a wide range of reasonably priced tapas; try their grilled *chorizo*.

Cerveceria La Charka, C/Trajano 8. Bright and noisy, as an honest tapas bar should be. Try the *gambas a la plancha* and *patatas bravas*.

There is also a number of tapas bars to the east of the Paseo:

La Tahona, C/Reyes Católicos 30. Has a big bar downstairs and a restaurant upstairs. Its faux-French bistro style is quite appealing, and there is a huge range of nibbles on offer.

El Quinto Toro, C/Juan Leal 6. Offers good tapas in an atmospheric setting.

Entertainment and Nightlife

There are plenty possibilities in the maze of streets to the west of the Paseo de Almería, between Puerta de Purchena and Plaza San Pedro and the streets off it. Plunge into these and you will stumble across numerous bars and discos. However, stick to the lit streets and note that the further west you go, the seedier it becomes.

stood, now an ugly open space resembling an archaeological dig – a few taped-off ruins and scratched-out signs the only indication of the glory that once stood here. The third level was added by the Catholic Kings and bears a coat of arms on the **Torre de Homenaje**. Look to the west of here and you will see **Barrio de La Chanca**, the poorest part of the city, where you can make out front doors leading into former cave dwellings. The main structure is joined to the northern hills by the **wall of Jayrán**, which rises up towards a high cross. This can be visited on the same ticket. Between the two is the **Centre for the Rescue of Animals of the Sahara**, where gazelles and other African animals are cared for: before going up, get permission from the centre's headquarters off the Avda de Federico García Lorca (*C/General Segura 1,* **t** *95 028 10 45*) – they'll give you a note permitting you to wander among the cages and enclosures of a wide variety of endangered animals, in an environment that must feel like home.

Almería's **cathedral** (**t** *60 957 58 02; open Mon–Fri 10–4.30, Sat 10–1; adm*), begun in 1524 on the site of a mosque destroyed by an earthquake, was built to defend marauding Berber pirates; its four mighty towers once held cannons. On the eastern wall you can make out the *indalo*, symbol of Almería, which was originally found in a cave some 4,000 years BC. On the front is another inscription, 'José Antonio Primo de Rivera' – rather bizarre considering Almería was a Republican stronghold and one of the last cities to fall to Franco. Inside there are a two paintings worth seeing, an Annunciation by Cano and an Immaculate Conception by Murillo, as well as a red and black marble altar; otherwise it's a huge and barren vault. Prettier, and boasting a fine carving of St James (Santiago) Matamoros ('Matamoros' means 'the Moor-slayer') and a minaret-like tower, is **Santiago El Viejo**, just off the Puerta de Purchena near the top of the Paseo de Almería. It's a bit unusual to find a pilgrimage church, complete with St James's cockle-shells, so far off the main routes.

Almería's small archaeological museum has been closed for some time and is in no danger of re-opening, but it contains remains from the remarkable Neolithic culture of Los Millares which flourished here about 3500–3000 BC. Neolithic fans will have to go to **Los Millares** itself (*open Tues–Sat 9.30–3.30; always ring ahead* **t** *608 95 70 65*), in stark, barren mountains about 25km north on the N324 at Santa Fé de Mondújar. Five thousand years ago this was rich farmland, and the people who lived here had the leisure to create one of the most advanced prehistoric civilizations in Spain. The burial mounds here are almost true temples, with interior passages and surrounding concentric stone circles, broken by concave semicircular entrances. Five millennia of erosion have made these difficult to discern, and you'll have an even harder time distinguishing the remains of the walled town that once stood nearby.

Around Almería

West of the provincial capital, near the border with Granada, is **Adra**, which was an ancient Phoenician town, and the last spot in Spain surrendered by the Moors at the moment Boabdil sailed from here to Africa. Though it's still basically a fishing and agricultural village, it has spawned **Almerimar**, a large new development of mostly

Tourist Information

Carboneras: Ayuntamiento, Plaza del Castillo 1, **t** 95 045 42 38. *Open summer only.*

Mojácar: Pza Nueva s/n, **t/f** 95 047 51 62, *www.mojacarvida.es. Open Mon–Fri 10–2 and 5–7, Sat 10–1; closed Sun.*

Sorbas: C/Terraplén 9, **t** 95 036 44 81.

Tabernas: Plaza Pueblo 1, **t** 95 036 53 39.

San José: C/Correos s/n, **t** 95 061 10 55.

Many of the smaller villages have *puntos de información*, small kiosks on the beach, open in season.

Where to Stay and Eat

Adra ✉ 04770

******Meliá Adra**, C/Fábricas 84, **t** 95 060 40 00, **f** 95 060 41 31 (*expensive–moderate*). Occupies a fine position away from the town, with views out to sea, plus two pools, one indoor and one outdoor.

Almerimar ✉ 04700

******Golf Almerimar**, **t** 95 049 70 50, **f** 95 049 70 19 (*expensive–moderate*). Now part of the Meliá chain of hotels, this is a very plush 38-room refuge, with tennis courts, swimming pool and recreational facilities in an attractive setting.

Roquetas de Mar ✉ 04740

This village has a vast number of top-end hotels to choose from, all offering more or less the same things – swimming pools (indoor and out), tennis, quality restaurants, but little character.

******Playacapricho**, Urb Playa Serena H-10, **t** 95 033 31 00, **f** 95 033 38 06 (*luxury*). One of two luxury options for the over-indulgent. It is worth noting that prices fall dramatically from October, when it is still searing hot in this part of the world.

******Mediterraneo Park Hotel**, Pez Espada s/n, **t** 95 033 32 50, **f** 95 033 33 21, *www. mediterraneo-park.com* (*expensive*). The best value, offering all the facilities at roughly half the price of the other four-star options.

For cheaper options try:

*****Sabinal**, Avda Gaviotas, **t** 95 033 36 00, **f** 95 033 35 33 (*moderate*). With pool.

Hostal El Faro, Avda Sabinal 190, **t** 95 032 10 15 (*inexpensive*). The budget option.

Aguadulce ✉ 04720

******Playadulce**, Avda El Parmeral, **t** 95 034 12 74, **f** 95 034 30 09 (*luxury*). Two pools set in its own grounds, a café, restaurant and tennis are some of the facilities on offer at this hotel.

******Meliá Almerimar**, **t** 95 049 70 07, **f** 95 049 71 46 (*expensive–moderate*). Even plusher, with more facilities including a covered pool; fractionally more expensive.

******Portomagno**, Pso Marítimo s/n, **t** 95 034 22 16, **f** 95 034 29 65 (*expensive–moderate*). Better placed and much cheaper.

Hostal Juan de Austria II, Avda de Carlos III 150, **t** 95 034 01 63, **f** 95 034 11 84, *laustria@ larural.es* (*inexpensive*). A comfortable budget choice with parking and satellite TV for all guests.

Níjar ✉ 04700

****Venta del Pobre**, C/Venta del Pobre, **t/f** 95 038 51 92 (*moderate*). Has en suite rooms with air conditioning, but just off the motorway.

Asensio, C/El Parque 2, **t** 95 036 03 65 (*cheap*). One of several basic *pensiónes* in town.

San José ✉ 04118

In San José you have a choice between either four-star luxury hotels or simple *hostales*; rather bizzarely there is nothing in between. For further options head up the coastline to Los Escullos, La Isleta, La Negra and Agua Amarga, where there are moderate options.

******Don Ignacio**, Pso Marítimo s/n, **t** 95 061 10 80, **f** 95 061 10 84, *donignacio@ servimar.net, www.servimar.net* (*luxury–expensive*). A huge modern luxury hotel and the only place right on the beach.

villas and flats, with a new marina and one of Spain's best golf courses. From here you can dip into the eastern Alpujarras to the pretty 'city' of **Berja**, with its palatial country homes; this area supplies most of northern Europe's Christmas grapes. The

Comfortable rooms with sea views and a small pool. Very good value out of season (mid-Sept–May, when it drops to inexpensive), overpriced in season. Restaurant and bar attached.

★★★**El Sotillo**, Ctra San Jose-Níjar, **t** 95 061 11 00, **f** 95 061 11 05, *sotillo@a2000.es* (*expensive–moderate*). The best place In town, a *finca*-style hotel set in its own grounds, with large reception areas, pool table, swimming pool, big bedrooms and a good restaurant There is also a stable offering horse riding.

★★**Hotel Atalaya**, C/Correos s/n, **t** 95 038 00 85, **f** 95 038 05 52 (*moderate*). This well-designed place is perhaps the next best option; all rooms have little *terrazas* looking out onto a very pretty courtyard. Good sized bedrooms with bath.

Agades, **t** 95 038 03 90 (*inexpensive*). Slightly out of town on the main road, but has the advantage of a pool, its own grounds, a café and airy rooms, some with *terrazas* and views.

Hostal Bahía, C/Correos s/n, **t/f** 95 038 03 06 (*inexpensive*). Simple but clean, friendly and bang in the centre of town, 100 yards from the beach and with a few rooms with balconies.

In San José there are two eating-out areas: the road into town or the harbour; the latter, with sea views is preferable.

La Cueva, on the harbour, **t** 95 038 01 54 (*moderate*). Slightly over-priced but with deliciously fresh fish, good house wines and decent meats; with a beautiful sea view over the *terraza*. Probably has the edge over the other options, which are much of a muchness.

Heladeria Vittoria, on the beachfront. Come here for ice cream and a superb champagne and sangría cocktail.

Mojácar ✉ 04638

★★★★**Parador Reyes Católicos**, just over the road from the beach, **t** 95 047 82 50, **f** 95 047 81 83, *mojacar@parador.es* (*expensive*). Probably the best option, a modern *parador* with a swimming pool in season, tennis courts, air conditioning and rooms where you can watch the sun rise from the comfort of your own balcony.

★★★**Indalo**, Pso del Mediterráneo 1, **t** 95 047 80 01, **f** 95 047 81 76 (*expensive–moderate*). Probably the next best option, with all mod cons including pool, tennis and sea views.

★★★**El Moresco**, Avda. D'Encamp, **t** 95 047 80 25, **f** 95 047 82 62 (*expensive–moderate*). Has the advantage of being open throughout the year, with indoor, outdoor and children's pools, as well as wonderful views. Prices plummet to inexpensive in low season.

★★**Virgen del Mar**, on the beach, **t** 95 047 22 22, **f** 95 047 22 11 (*moderate*). A good mid-priced option on the beach, but no pool. Good restaurant attached (*see* below).

Mamabel's, C/Embajadores 3, **t** 95 047 24 48 (*inexpensive*). A beach house owned by Belgian poet Jean-Marie Raths. Ask for Room No.1 if it's available – you're sure to like the view. Dinner is prepared here as well; seafood and couscous are served on Fridays.

Casablanca, Avda del Mediterraneo 383, **t** 95 047 24 74. All kinds of delicious goodies at this well-known local restaurant, including carpaccio of courgette, and great desserts.

Virgen del Mar, on the beach, **t** 95 047 22 22. Food on the beach is generally a sorry affair, with a rash of pizzerias and Chinese restaurants. However, this hotel restaurant with a lovely terrace and good fresh fish is an exception.

Turre ✉ 04638

Finca Listonero, Cortijo Grande, **t** 95 047 90 94 (*moderate*). A restored farmhouse on an estate in the peaceful Turre mountains, just a few kilometres away from Mojácar itself.

Garrucha ✉ 04630

El Almejero, Explanada del Puerto, **t** 95 046 04 05. A few kilometres north of Mojácar, this restaurant serves super-fresh and delicious seafood, with a view of the fishing port where the catch is landed.

bland, overbuilt resorts at **Roquetas de Mar** (more golfing) and **Aguadulce** (oldest and biggest course on the Almería coast) are easily reached from Almería by bus. Inland from these resorts is an encroaching sea of plastic – not coastal development, but agricultural plastic, allowing a good percentage of Europe's winter vegetables to grow on the otherwize barren land. The boom town of **El Ejido** – centre of 'plastic culture' (*plasticultura*) – has grown exponentially in the last 10 years from a relatively small village to the second biggest town after the region's capital, boasting a population of more than 50,000. A small few of these inhabitants are the new *plasticultura* millionaires, those who realized the potential of this once worthless land, exploiting the cheap labour of immigrants and itinerant workers. Shocking working conditions in the torpid air beneath hectares of plastic tents is causing uneasiness among the locals, with strikes and riots in recent years. Meanwhile the region's meagre water supply continues to be drained dry. The only relief from the encroaching plastic is a couple of **salt lakes** near Roquetas, a good spot for bird-watching.

Almería Inland

East of Almería the road goes through the **Alhamilla** – one of the driest, most rugged and lunar of the Spanish sierras – and on into **Tabernas**, Europe's only desert. The N340A passes through the dusty town of **Benahadux**, where you could take the N324 into the Almerían Alpujarras, and on through Rioja into an ever more arid and desolate landscape. About 24 km from Almería the road forks – east towards Sorbas (*see* below) and west towards the small village of **Gérgal**, above which a joint German-Hispano **observatory** was constructed in the late 1970s: they claim you can see the stars more clearly here than anywhere in Europe. It's actually a series of observatories, built on the highest peak of the Sierra, at an altitude of over 2,780m (9,000ft). The Spanish handled the infrastructure, the Germans built the telescopes. You can visit the site any time by following the signs just beyond Gérgal to Calar Alto, along a hair-raising 26km road.

More interesting sights lie to the east: just beyond the fork, off the main N340 (on some maps marked as the A370), lies **Mini Hollywood** (***t** 95 036 52 36; open summer 10–9; winter 10–7; adm exp*), the town built by Sergio Leone for such classics as Clint Eastwood's first vehicle, *A Fistful of Dollars*, and subsequent spaghetti westerns including *For A Few Dollars More* and *The Good, The Bad and The Ugly*. When Leone completed the trilogy the extras from those films decided to buy the place and run it as a tourist attraction rather then let it vanish into the desert, maintaining it and re-enacting various scenes from the films, with shootouts and mock hangings twice a day. Today it is run and owned by a hotel group (hence the astronomical admission prices – probably the highest for any attraction in Andalucía – but worth it for fans!). The area around the town itself is the setting for, most famously, *Lawrence of Arabia* and *Cleopatra*, and more recently *Indiana Jones and the Last Crusade* and *Conan the Barbarian*, among countless others. The reason Sergio Leone, David Lean and Steven Spielberg, chose this particular spot is its extraordinarily clear light and stark landscape: here the sun shines for 3,000 hours a year and just a few millimetres of rain fall. Sadly, this paucity of rain and relentless sunshine does little good for the animals living in the **zoo** attached to the town. There are some wonderful creatures here – black panthers, Siberian tigers, jaguars, lions and hippos, all living in cramped, searing conditions in cells surrounded by electric fences.

The main road east winds through the northern flanks of the sierra, passing first through **Tabernas**, a dusty, uninviting place, and then through a lush *huerta* of country estates before rising into a perfectly desolate region, where even in springtime green is a foreign colour.

Sorbas, with its hanging houses, is most impressive seen from the highway, but if you do care to stop there are a couple of buildings worth looking out for: two privately owned mansions on the main square, Plaza de la Constitución, belonging to the Dukes of Alba and Valoig, who own much of the land round here. A walk to the edge of town affords some great views across this bizarre landscape and precarious housing. The surrounding area forms part of the **Parque Natural de Karst En Yesos**, which has a series of caves that can be visited on a guided tour organized by the *turismo* (*see* p.316).

Between Tabernas and Sorbas a turn-off south along the AL102 will take you to the white village of **Níjar**. The road winds along for about 20km through some wonderful terrain, blasted and weirdly beautiful. As you begin to descend you will catch glimpses of the valley, now a sea of plastic. Níjar was recently a charming oasis in an arid setting where potters actively carried on a craft introduced by the Phoenicians, but the craftsmen and their cheap tapestries now attract coach-loads of tourists, who swamp the town most days. Federico García Lorca's play *Blood Wedding* was based on incidents that occurred here around the turn of the century. From Níjar it is a short drive to the coast.

The Almería Coast

The coastal road struggles out to the **Cabo de Gata**, a natural park with pretty beaches, a solitary lighthouse and crystal-clear waters, popular with divers. The area has two main resorts, the little town of Cabo de Gata itself and **San José**, beyond the lighthouse. Cabo de Gata and its extension, **La Almadraba de Monteleva**, have some fine beaches but little else to detain you. To get to San José you could walk, but it will take at least half an hour; to drive you have to double back on yourself – the road past the lighthouse is closed to traffic. San José is set round a small, dirty beach, used by its inhabitants as a dog toilet and general rubbish tip. Fortunately, better beaches lie either side; one of the loveliest is **Los Genoveses**, a delightful walk through scrub and cacti over the top of town.

The town itself is charming, though how long it will stay that way is unclear: signs of development are everywhere and the landscape is scarred with building sites and cranes. There are two diving schools, a number of good restaurants, a pretty harbour and some good, reasonably priced places to stay, especially out of season when prices plummet. From here you can walk or drive to numerous secluded beaches and delightful little villages including Los Escullos, La Isleta de Moro and Las Negras. One particularly pleasant drive is northeast along the small coastal road which rises through spectacular landscape after La Isleta, before dropping into the pretty **valley of Rodalquilar**. From here it's a few kilometres drive to Las Negras.

To reach one of the loveliest places in the park, take the unpaved but driveable road to **Agua Amarga**, a delightful town with a white-sand beach and transluscent waters protected by eroded cliffs. The park ends just north of here, before **Carboneras**, an ugly town made worse by a huge cement factory. Despite this it is being developed for tourism and marks the southern point of a stretch of development which is going the way of the Costa del Sol.

Mojácar

Isolated amidst the rugged mountains, on a hill 2km from the beach, trendy Mojácar has often been compared to a pile of sugar cubes. No town in Spain wears such a Moorish face, its little, flat-roofed, white houses stacked almost on top of one another. Before the equally white hotels were added to the scene a couple of decades ago, the women covered their faces with their veils when passing a stranger; a plaque by the fountain tells how the townspeople valiantly defended themselves against the army of the Catholic Kings.

Most unusually, the old women in the village used to paint a symbol known as the *indalo* (a stick figure with outstretched arms, holding up an arc) on their doors as a charm against the evil eye and thunderbolts. No one knows when this practice originated, though in the nearby caves of **Vélez-Blanco** Neolithic drawings of *indalos* dating from 3000 BC have led anthropologists to the conclusion that this is one of the few cases of a prehistoric symbol being handed down in one place for thousands of years. It is now the official symbol of Almería. Before the onslaught of tourism this was a grindingly poor place, with a population reduced to just 300, post-Civil War. Today it has been heavily prettified with pristine whitewashed houses and trinket stalls on every corner – better this, though, than the excesses of the beachfront. The coast road north to **Garrucha** is now an almost continuous stream of *urbanizaciones*; to the south it's bars, discos and English-run pubs.

There's nothing but empty space as far as the Andalucía-Murcia border (and well beyond it, for that matter). The nondescript village of **Palomares** occupied all the world's headlines for a while in 1966, when an American B-52 crashed nearby and littered the countryside and sea with live hydrogen bombs.

Language

Castellano, as Spanish is properly called, was the first modern language to have a grammar written for it. When a copy was presented to Queen Isabel in 1492, she understandably asked what it was for. 'Your majesty', replied a perceptive bishop, 'language is the perfect instrument of empire'. In the centuries to come, this concise, flexible and expressive language would prove just that: an instrument that would contribute more to Spanish unity than any laws or institutions, while spreading itself effortlessly over much of the New World.

Among other European languages, Spanish is closest to Portuguese and Italian – and of course, Catalan and Gallego. Spanish, however, may have the simplest grammar of any Romance language, and if you know a little of any one of these, you will find much of the vocabulary looks familiar. It's quite easy to pick up a working knowledge of Spanish; but Spaniards speak colloquially and fast, and in Andalucía they leave out half the consonants and add some strange sounds all of their own. Expressing yourself may prove a little easier than understanding the replies. Spaniards will appreciate your efforts, and when they correct you, they aren't being snooty; they simply feel it's their duty to help you learn.

There are dozens of language books and tapes on the market; one particularly good one is *Teach Yourself Spanish*, by Juan Kattán-Ibarra (Hodder & Stoughton). Note that the Spaniards increasingly use the familiar *tú* instead of *usted* when addressing even complete strangers.

For food and drink vocabulary, *see* 'Menu Reader', pp.68–71.

Pronunciation

Pronunciation is phonetic but somewhat difficult for English speakers.

Vowels

a short *a* as in 'pat'
e short *e* as in 'set'
i as *e* in 'be'
o between long *o* of 'note' and short *o* of 'hot'
u silent after *q* and gue- and gui-; otherwise long *u* as in 'flute'
ü *w* sound, as in 'dwell'
y at end of word or meaning *and*, as **i**

Diphthongs

ai, ay as *i* in 'side'
au as *ou* in 'sound'
ei, ey as *ey* in 'they'
oi, oy as *oy* of 'boy'

Consonants

c before the vowels *i* and *e*, it's a *castellano* tradition to pronounce it as *th*; many Spaniards and all Latin Americans pronounce it in this case as an *s*
ch like *ch* in 'church'
d often becomes *th*, or is almost silent, at end of word
g before *i* or *e*, pronounced as **j** (see below)
h silent
j the *ch* in loch – a guttural, throat-clearing *h*
ll *y* or *ly* as in million
ñ *ny* as in canyon (the ~ is called a tilde)
q *k*
r usually rolled, which takes practice
v often pronounced as *b*
z *th*, but *s* in parts of Andalucía

Stress

If the word ends in a vowel, an *n* or an *s*, then the stress falls on the penultimate syllable, otherwise stress falls on the last syllable; exceptions are marked with an accent.

If all this seems difficult, remember that English pronunciation is even more difficult for Spaniards; if your Spanish friends giggle at your pronunciation, get them to try to say *squirrel*.

Practise on some Spanish place names:

Madrid ma-DREED
León lay-OHN
Sevilla se-BEE-ah
Cáceres CAH-ther-es
Cuenca KWAYN-ka
Jaén ha-AIN
Sigüenza sig-WAYN-thah
Trujillo troo-HEE-oh
Jerez her-ETH
Badajoz ba-da-HOTH
Málaga MAHL-ah-gah
Alcázar ahl-CATH-ar
Valladolid ba-yah-dol-EED
Arévalo ahr-EB-bah-lo

Useful Words and Phrases

yes *sí*
no *no*
I don't know *No sé*
I don't understand Spanish *No entiendo español*
Do you speak English? *¿Habla usted inglés?*
Does someone here speak English? *¿Hay alguien que hable inglés?*
Speak slowly *Hable despacio*
Can you help me? *¿Puede usted ayudarme?*
Help! *¡Socorro!*
please *por favor*
thank you (very much) *(muchas) gracias*
you're welcome *de nada*
It doesn't matter *No importa/Es igual*
all right *está bien*
ok *vale*
excuse me *perdóneme*
Be careful! *¡Tenga cuidado!*
maybe *quizá(s)*
nothing *nada*
It is urgent! *¡Es urgente!*
How do you do? *¿Cómo está usted?*
or more familiarly *¿Cómo estás? ¿Qué tal?*
Well, and you? *¿Bien, y usted?*
or more familiarly *¿Bien, y tú?*
What is your name? *¿Cómo se llama?*
or more familiarly *¿Cómo te llamas?*
My name is ... *Me llamo...*
My number is ... *Mi nombre es...*
Hello *¡Hola!*
Goodbye *Adi s*
Good morning *Buenos días*
Good afternoon *Buenas tardes*
Good evening *Buenas noches*
What is that? *¿Qué es eso?*
What ...? *¿Qué ...?*
Who ...? *¿Quién ...?*
Where ...? *¿Dónde ...?*
When ...? *¿Cuándo ...?*
Why ...? *¿Por qué ...?*
How ...? *¿Cómo ...?*
How much? *¿Cuánto/Cuánta?*
How many? *¿Cuántos/Cuántas?*
I am lost Me he perdido
I am hungry *Tengo hambre*
I am thirsty *Tengo sed*
I am sorry *Lo siento*
I am tired (man/woman) *Estoy cansado/a*
I am sleepy *Tengo sueño*
I am ill *No me siento bien*
Leave me alone *Déjeme en paz*
good *bueno/buena*
bad *malo/mala*
slow *despacio*
fast *rápido/rápida*
big *grande*
small *pequeño/pequeña*
hot *caliente*
cold *frío/fría*

Numbers

one *uno/una*
two *dos*
three *tres*
four *cuatro*
five *cinco*
six *seis*
seven *siete*
eight *ocho*
nine *nueve*
ten *diez*
eleven *once*
twelve *doce*
thirteen *trece*
fourteen *catorce*
fifteen *quince*
sixteen *dieciséis*
seventeen *diecisiete*
eighteen *dieciocho*
nineteen *diecinueve*
twenty *veinte*
twenty-one *veintiuno*
thirty *treinta*
thirty-one *treinta y uno*

forty *cuarenta*
forty-one *cuarenta y uno*
fifty *cincuenta*
sixty *sesenta*
seventy *setenta*
eighty *ochenta*
ninety *noventa*
one hundred *cien*
one hundred and one *ciento-uno*
five hundred *quinientos*
one thousand *mil*
first *primero*
second *segundo*
third *tercero*
fourth *cuarto*
fifth *quinto*
tenth *décimo*

Time

What time is it? *¿Qué hora es?*
It is two o'clock *Son las dos*
... half past two *... las dos y media*
... a quarter past two *... las dos y cuarto*
... a quarter to three *... las tres menos cuarto*
noon *mediodía*
midnight *medianoche*
month *mes*
week *semana*
day *día*
morning *mañana*
afternoon *tarde*
evening *noche*
today *hoy*
yesterday *ayer*
soon *pronto*
tomorrow *mañana*
now *ahora*
later *después*
it is early *es temprano*
it is late *es tarde*

Days

Monday *lunes*
Tuesday *martes*
Wednesday *miércoles*
Thursday *jueves*
Friday *viernes*
Saturday *sábado*
Sunday *domingo*

Months

January *enero*
February *febrero*
March *marzo*
April *abril*
May *mayo*
June *junio*
July *julio*
August *agosto*
September *septiembre*
October *octubre*
November *noviembre*
December *diciembre*

Colours

red *rojo*
blue *azul*
green *verde*
yellow *amarillo*
orange *de color naranja*
pink *rosa*
purple *púrpura, morado*
brown *marrón*
black *negro*
grey *gris*
white *blanco*

Shopping and Sightseeing

I would like... *Quisiera.../Me gustaría*
Where is/are...? *¿Dónde está/están...?*
How much is it? *¿Cuánto vale eso?*
open *abierto*
closed *cerrado*
cheap *barato*
expensive *caro*
bank *banco*
beach *playa*
booking/box office *taquilla*
church *iglesia*
hospital *hospital*
money *dinero*
museum *museo*
theatre *teatro*
newspaper (foreign) *periódico (extranjero)*
police station *comisaría*
policeman *policía*
post office *correos*
postage stamp *sello*
sea *mar*

shop *tienda*
antique shop *anticuario*
bakery *panadería*
butcher's *carnicería*
confectioner's *confitería*
department store *grandes almacenes*
pharmacy *farmacía*
hairdresser's *peluquería*
hardware shop *ferretería*
jeweller's *joyería*
kiosk *kiosko*
market *mercado*
stationer's *papelería*
winery *bodega*
Do you have any change? *¿Tiene cambio?*
telephone *teléfono*
tobacconist's *estanco*
supermarket *supermercado*
toilet/toilets *servicios/aseos*
men *señores/hombres/caballeros*
women *señoras/damas*

Accommodation

Where is the hotel? *¿Dónde está el hotel?*
Do you have a room? *¿Tiene usted una habitación?*
Can I look at the room? *¿Podría ver la habitación?*
How much is the room per day/week? *¿Cuánto cuesta la habitación por día/semana?*
... with two beds *con dos camas*
... with double bed *con una cama grande*
... with a shower/bath *con ducha/baño*
... for one person/two people *para una persona/ dos personas*
... for one night/ one week *una noche/ una semana*

Driving

rent *alquiler*
car *coche*
motorbike/moped *moto/ciclomotor*
bicycle *bicicleta*
petrol *gasolina*
garage *garaje*
This doesn't work *Este no funciona*
road *carretera*
motorway *autopista*
Is the road good? *¿Es buena la carretera?*
breakdown *avería*
(international) driving licence *carnet de conducir (internacional)*
driver *conductor, chófer*
speed *velocidad*
exit *salida*
entrance *entrada*
danger *peligro*
dangerous *peligroso*
no parking *estacionamento prohibido*
narrow *estrecha/o*
give way/yield *ceda el paso*
road works *obras*

Note: Most road signs will be in international pictographs

Transport

aeroplane *avión*
airport *aeropuerto*
bus/coach *autobús/autocar*
bus/railway station *estación de autobuses/de ferrocarril*
bus stop *parada*
car/automobile *coche*
customs *aduana*
platform *andén*
port *puerto*
seat *asiento*
ship *buque/barco/ embarcadero*
ticket *billete*
train *tren*

Directions

I want to go to... *Deseo ir a.../Quiero ir a...*
How can I get to...? *¿Cómo puedo llegar a...?*
Where is...? *¿Dónde está...?*
When is the next...? *¿Cuándo sale el próximo...?*
What time does it leave (arrive)? *¿Parte (llega) a qué hora?*
From where does it leave? *¿De dónde sale?*
Do you stop at ... ? *¿Para en... ?*
How long does the trip take? *¿Cuánto tiempo dura el viaje?*
I want a (return) ticket to... *Quiero un billete (de ida y vuelta) a...*
How much is the fare? *¿Cuánto cuesta el billete?*
Have a good trip! *¡Buen viaje!*

here *aquí*
there *allí*
close *cerca*
far *lejos*
left *izquierda*
right *derecha*
straight on *todo recto*
forwards *adelante*
backwards *hacia atrás*
up *arriba*
down *abajo*
north (n./adj.) *norte/septentrional*
south (n./adj.) *sur/meridional*
east (n./adj.) *este/oriental*
west (n./adj.) *oeste/occidental*
corner *esquina*
square *plaza*
street *calle*

Restaurant Vocabulary

See also 'Menu Reader' in **Food and Drink** chapter, pp.65–72.

menu *carta/menú*
bill/check *cuenta*
change *cambio*
set meal *menú del día*
waiter/waitress *camarero/a*
Do you have a table? *¿Tiene una mesa?*
... for one/two? *... ¿para uno/dos?*
Can I see the menu, please? *Déme el menú, por favor*
Do you have a wine list? *¿Hay una lista de vinos?*
Can I have the bill (check), please? *La cuenta, por favor*
Can I pay by credit card? *¿Puedo pagar con tarjeta de crédito?*

The Beach

sand *arena*
sea *mar*
wave *ola*
seaweed *alga*
dune *duna*
high/low tide *marea alta/baja*
cove *cala*
bay *bahía*
lifeguard *vigilante*
lifeboat *lancha de socorro*
swimsuit *traje de baño*
sunbathe *tomar el sol*
sun cream *crema bronceadora*
tan *bronceado*
sunburn *quemadura*
sunglasses *gafas del sol*
parasol *sombrilla*
towel *toalla*

Clothing

clothing *ropa*
belt *cinturón*
blouse *blusa*
coat *abrigo*
raincoat *impermeable*
dress *vestido*
suit *traje*
jacket *chaqueta*
trousers *pantalón*
jeans *vaqueros*
T-shirt *camiseta*
skirt *falda*
shoes *zapatos*
socks *calcetines*
boots *botas*
underwear *ropa interior*
shorts *pantalón corto*
tennis shoes *zapatillas*
sweater *suéter*
tie *corbata*
handkerchief *pañuelo*
hat *sombrero*
scarf *bufanda*
vest *chaleco*
swimsuit *traje de baño*
gloves *guantes*
wallet *cartera*
purse *bolsa*

Animals

horse *caballo*
donkey *burro*
sheep *oveja*
deer *ciervo*
goat *cabro*
pig *cerdo*
cow *vaca*
bull *toro*
dog *perro*

cat *gato*
monkey *mono*
mouse *ratón*
rat *rata*
squirrel *ardilla*
snake *serpiente/culebra*
turtle/tortoise *tortuga*
lizard *lagarto*
frog *rana*
crocodile *cocodrilo*

Birds

bird *pájaro/ave*
eagle *águila*
vulture *buitre*
hawk *halcón*
owl *búho/lechuza*
pigeon *paloma*
sparrow *gorrión*
crow *cuervo*
starling *estornino*
parrot *loro*
swan *cisne*
seagull *gaviota*
cormorant *cormorán*
woodpecker *pájaro carpintero*
dove *paloma*
humming bird *colibrí*
chicken *gallina/pollo*
duck *pato*
pheasant *faisán*
goose *ganso*
turkey *pavo*

Glossary

corregidor: chief magistrate.
corrida de toros: bullfight.
cortijo: Andalucían country house.
cúpula: cupola; dome or rounded vault forming a roof or ceiling.
custodia: tabernacle, where sacramental vessels are kept.
diputación: seat of provincial government.
embalse: reservoir.
ermita: hermitage.
esgrafiado: style of painting, or etching designs in stucco, on a façade.
estilo desornamentado: austere, heavy Renaissance style inaugurated by Philip II's architect, Juan de Herrera; sometimes described as Herreran.
fandango: traditional dance and song, greatly influenced by the Gypsies of Andalucía.
feria: major festival or market, often an occasion for bullfights.
finca: farm, country house or estate.
fonda: modest hotel, from the Arabic *funduq*, or inn.
fuero: exemption or privilege of a town or region under medieval Spanish law.
grandee: select member of Spain's highest nobility.
hammam: Moorish bath.
Herreran: see *estilo desornamentado*.
hidalgo: literally 'son of somebody' – the lowest level of the nobility, just good enough for a coat of arms.
homage tower: the tallest tower of fortification, sometimes detached from the wall.
humilladero: Calvary, or stations of the Cross along a road outside town.
Isabelline Gothic: late 15th-century style, roughly corresponding to English perpendicular.
judería: Jewish quarter.
junta: council, or specifically, the regional government.
khan: inn for merchants.
Kufic: angular style of Arabic calligraphy originating in the city of Kufa in Mesopotamia, often used as architectural ornamentation.
lonja: merchants' exchange.
madrasa: Muslim theological school, usually located near a mosque.
majolica: type of porous pottery glazed with bright metallic oxides.
mantilla: silk or lace scarf or shawl, worn by women to cover their head and shoulders.
maqsura: elevated platform usually with grills.
matador: the principal bullfighter, who finally kills the bull.
medina: walled centre of a Moorish city.
mercado: market.
mezquita: mosque.
mihrab: prayer niche facing Mecca, often elaborately decorated in a mosque.
mirador: scenic viewpoint or belvedere.
monterías: hunting scenes (in art).
Moriscos: Muslims who submitted to Christianization to remain in al-Andalus after the Reconquista.
moufflon: wild, short-fleeced mountain sheep.
Mozarábs: Christians under Muslim rule in Moorish Spain.
mudéjar: Moorish-influenced architecture, characterized by decorative use of bricks and ceramics; Spain's 'national style' in 12th to 16th centuries.
muqarnas: hanging masonry effect created through multiple use of support elements.
ogival: pointed (arches).
parador: state-owned hotel, often a converted historic building.
paseo: promenade, or an evening walk along a promenade.
patio: central courtyard of a house or public building.
picador: bullfighter on horseback, who goads and wounds the bull with a *pica* or short lance in the early stages of a bullfight in order to weaken the animal.

Plateresque: heavily ornamented 16th-century Gothic style.
plaza: town square.
Plaza Mayor: main square at the centre of many Spanish cities, often almost totally enclosed and arcaded.
plaza de toros: bullring.
posada: inn or lodging house.
pronunciamiento: military coup.
pueblo: village.
puente: bridge.
puerta: gate or portal.
Reconquista: the Christian Reconquest of Moorish Spain beginning in 718 and completed in 1492 by the Catholic Kings.
reja: iron grille, either decorative inside a church or covering the exterior window of a building.
retablo: carved or painted altarpiece.
Los Reyes Católicos: The Catholic Kings, Isabel and Fernando.
romería: pilgrimage, usually on a saint's feast day.
sagrario: the chapel where the Holy Sacrament is kept.
sala capitular: chapterhouse.
sillería: choir stall.
souk: open-air marketplace found in Muslim countries.
stele: stone slab marking a grave or displaying an inscription.
taifa: small Moorish kingdom; especially one of the so-called Party Kingdoms which sprang up in Spain following the 1031 fall of the caliph of Córdoba.
taracea: inlaid wood in geometric patterns.
torero: bullfighter, especially one on foot.
torre: tower.
vega: cultivated plain or fertile river valley.

Further Reading

General and Travel

Baird, David, *Inside Andalusia* (Lookout Publications). Background reading. Glossy, full of history and anecdote.

Borrow, George, *The Bible in Spain*. One of the best-known travel books about Spain, opinionated and amusing; first published in 1842.

Brenan, Gerald, *The Face of Spain* (Penguin, 1987). An account of his journey through central and southern Spain in the spring of 1949; *South from Granada* (Penguin, 1998) Customs of rural Spain before the Civil War.

Chetwode, Penelope, *Two Middle-Aged Ladies in Andalusia*. A delightful bosom-heaving *burro*-back look at the region.

Elms, Robert, *Spain: A Portrait After the General* (Heinemann, 1992). Incisive, witty, honest look at the new Spain from one of Britain's foremost young travel writers.

Ford, Richard, *Gatherings from Spain* (Everyman). A boiled-down version of the all-time classic travel book *A Handbook for Travellers in Spain*, written in 1845. Hard to find but worth the trouble.

Gibson, Ian, *Lorca's Granada* (Faber and Faber, 1992). The city seen through its association with the poet.

Hooper, John, *The New Spaniards* (Penguin, 1995). A comprehensive account of contemporary Spanish life and politics. Well done.

Jacobs, Michael, *A Guide to Andalusia* (Viking, 1990). Informative and well-researched volume on history, culture and sights.

Josephs, Allen, *White Wall of Spain* (University Press of Florida, USA, 1990). An interesting collection of essays on Andalucían folklore, with a particular focus on religious festivals, flamenco and bullfights.

Lee, Laurie, *As I Walked Out One Midsummer Morning* and *A Rose for Winter*. Very well-written adventures of a young man in Spain in 1936, and his return 20 years later.

Stewart, Chris, *Driving Over Lemons* (Sort of Books, UK, 1999), *A Parrot in the Pepper Tree* (2002). A witty account of an Englishman and his wife setting up home in a farmhouse in Las Alpujarras, Granada. The sequel is just as good.

History

Brenan, Gerald, *The Spanish Labyrinth* (Cambridge, 1990). Origins of the Civil War.

Castro, Américo, *The Structure of Spanish History* (E. L. King, 1954). A remarkable interpretation of Spain's history, published in exile during the Franco years.

Cohen, J. M. (editor), *The Four Voyages of Christopher Columbus* (Penguin Classics). Accounts of all four of Columbus's voyages to the Indies, including passages from the explorer's own log entries.

Elliott, J. H., *Imperial Spain 1469–1714* (Pelican, 1983). Elegant proof that much of the best writing these days is in the field of history.

Gibson, Ian, *The Assassination of Federico García Lorca* (Penguin, 1983).

Mitchell, David, *The Spanish Civil War* (Harper Collins, 1983). Anecdotal; wonderful photographs.

O'Callaghan, J. F., *History of Medieval Spain* (Cornell University, 1983).

Thomas, Hugh, *The Spanish Civil War* (Penguin, 1990). The best general work.

Watt, W. H., and **Cachia, P.**, *A History of Islamic Spain* (Edinburgh University Press, 1977).

Art and Literature

Brenan, Gerald, *The Literature of the Spanish People* (Cambridge, 1951).

Burckhardt, Titus, *Moorish Culture in Spain* (Allen and Unwin, 1972). Indispensable for understanding the world of al-Andalus.

Cervantes, Miguel de, *Don Quixote* (Penguin, 2003). The early 17th-century Spanish classic.

García Lorca, Federico, *Three Tragedies* (Penguin, 1988); *Five Plays: Comedies and*

Tragi-comedies (Penguin, 2000); *Selected Poems* (Penguin, 2001); *Poem of the Deep Song* (City Lights, USA, 1987). Works by the great Andalucían playwright and poet, who was murdered by fascists in Granada.

Goodwin, Godfrey, *Islamic Spain* (Chronicle, 1991). From the informative 'Architectural Guides for Travellers' series. Covers all the significant Islamic buildings in Spain.

Hemingway, Ernest, *For Whom the Bell Tolls* (Vintage, 2000). Set in Andalucía during the Civil War. A young American volunteer experiences the dangers of war behind the lines, and discovers María.

Irving, Washington, *Tales of the Alhambra* and *The Conquest of Granada* (London, 1986).

Jimenéz, Juan Ramón, *Platero and I* and *Pepita Jimenéz*. Noble Prize-winning poet from Andalucía. The former of his works evokes the people and landscape of Andalucía through conversions with Platero, the poet's donkey.

Pérez Reverte, Arturo, *The Seville Communion* (Harvill Press, 1996). An entertaining, offbeat thriller about a Vatican priest sent to Sevilla to investigate mysterious going-on at a run-down church.

Rice, David Talbot, *Islamic Art* (Thames & Hudson, UK, 1975). A renowned introduction to the whole subject of Islamic art and architecture.

Index

Main page references are in **bold**. Page references to maps are in *italic*.

Andalucía touring atlas

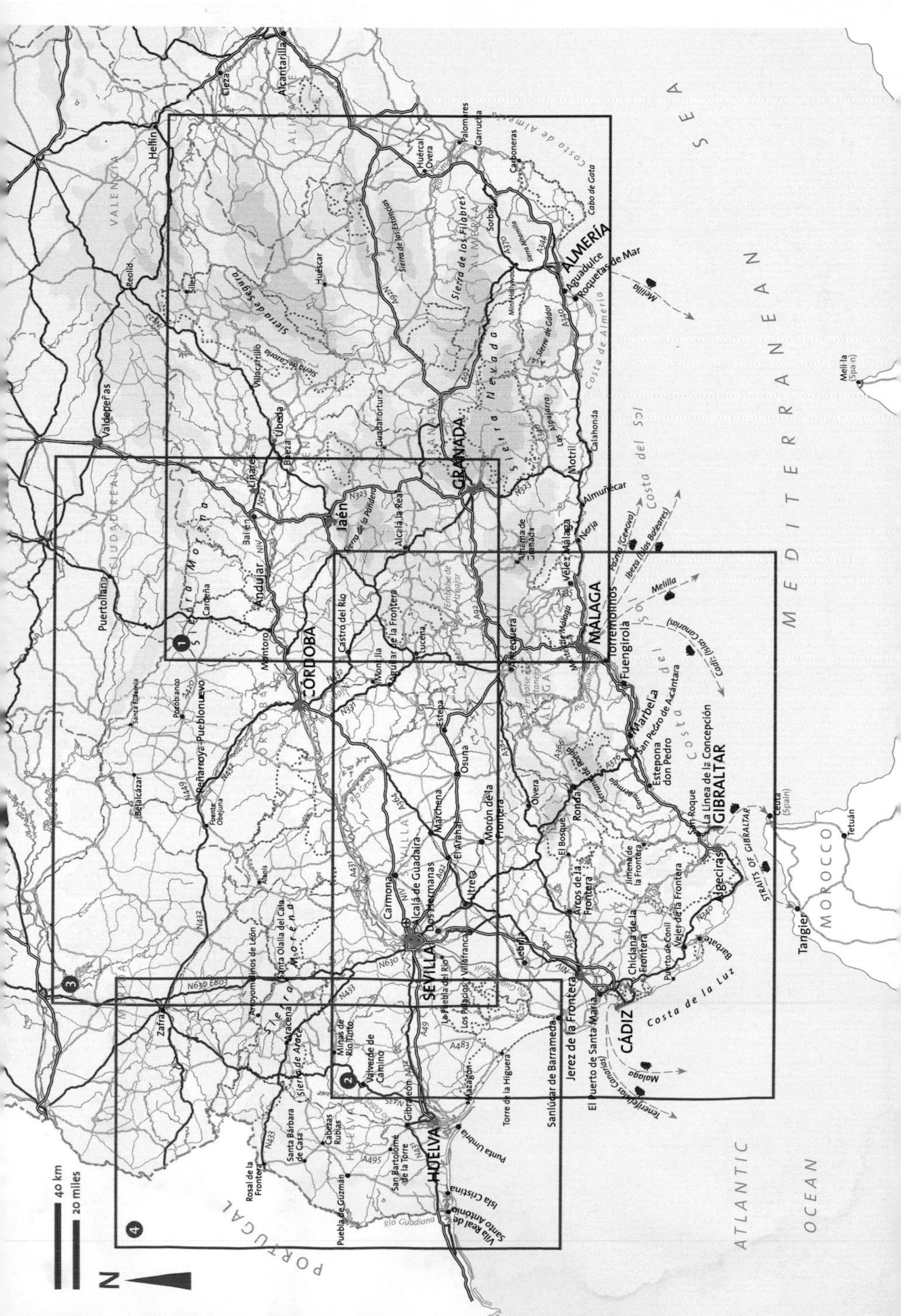

3
CIUDAD REAL
Desfiladero de Despeñaperros
Sierra Morena
Parque Natural de la Sierra de Andújar
La Carolina
Cardeña
Parque Natural de la Sierra de Cardeña
Sanctuario Virgen de la Cabeza
Baños de la Encina
NIV-E5
N322
Linares
Bailén
Andújar
NIV
Canena
Montoro
Marmolejo
Torreperogil
Baeza
Úbeda
Villa del Río
Arjonilla
Higuera de Arjona
Arjona
JAÉN
Bujalance
N323-E902
Jódar
A316
CÓRDOBA
Torredonjimeno
Jaén
Martos
C3221
Castro del Río
Solera
Sierra de la Pandera
Huelma
N323
Baena
Alcaudete
Doña Mencía
Guadahortuna
Cueva de los Murciélagos
Cabra
Alcalá la Real
Priego de Córdoba
Lucena
Parque Natural de la Sierra Subbética
N323-E902
Iznalloz
Rute
Montefrío
Purullena
Guadix
Illora
Pinos Puente
Embalse de Iznajar
GRANADA
2
Loja
A92
La Alhambra
Armilla
GRANADA
La Zubia
A92
Archidona
Sierra
Parque Natural de la Sierra Nevada
Ventas de Huelma
Puerto del Suspiro del Moro
Pico Veleta
A359
Mulhacen
N323
Trevélez
Alfarnate
Alhama de Granada
Alfarnatejo
Bérchules
Capileira
Bubión
Juviles
MÁLAGA
Pampaneira
Pórtugos
Soportújar
Pitres
Busquistar
Riogordo
Lanjarón
Colmenar
Orgiva
A348
Reserva Nacional de Sierra de Tejeda
N331
A346
Las Alpujarras
Comares
Sierra de la Contraviesa
Archez
Competa
A335
Montes de Málaga
El Borge
Frigiliana
Benamocarra
Vélez Málaga
Albuñol
Iznate
Torrox
Cueva de Nerja
Motril
Nerja
La Rábita
Torre del Mar
Torrox Costa
La Herradura
Almuñécar
Salobreña
Calahonda
MÁLAGA
Playa de Torre del Mar
Cádiz (Is. Canarias)
Palma (Genova)
Ibeza (Islas Baleares)
Melilla
Costa del Sol
Torremolinos
2

1
ALBACETE
Elche de la Sierra
Torres de Albanchez
Siles
Yeste
Segura de la Sierra
Beas de Segura
Hornos
Calasparra
Moratalla
Sierra de Segura
Villacarrillo
Caravaca de la Cruz
Cehegín
Coto Nacional de Cazorla
Sierra de Cazorla
C330
MURCIA
Cazorla
La Iruela
C3211
Quesada
Sierra de Espuña
Huéscar
Galera
Orce
Pozo Alcón
Vélez Blanco
Lorca
Cuevas de los Letreros
Vélez Rubio
C3211
N340-E15
Cúlla Baza
Embalse del Negratín
A92N
Sierra de las Estancias
Baza
Albox
Huércal Overa
Río Almanzora
Macael
Sierra de los Filabres
Palomares
A92
Calahorra
ALMERÍA
Garrucha
Puerto de la Ragua
Turre
Mojácar
Gérgal
Sorbas
A370
Tabernas
Laroles
Mairena
Laujar de Andarax
Mini Hollywood
Carboneras
Sierra Alhamilla
Níjar
Fondón
Sierra de Gádor
A347
A344
Costa de Almería
Berja
ALMERÍA
Parque Natural de Cabo de Gata-Níjar
Sierra del Cabo de Gata
Retamar
A340
Aguadulce
N
Cabo de Gata
Adra
Roquetas de Mar
Almerimar
Cabo de Gata
Costa de Almería
Melilla
20 km
10 miles

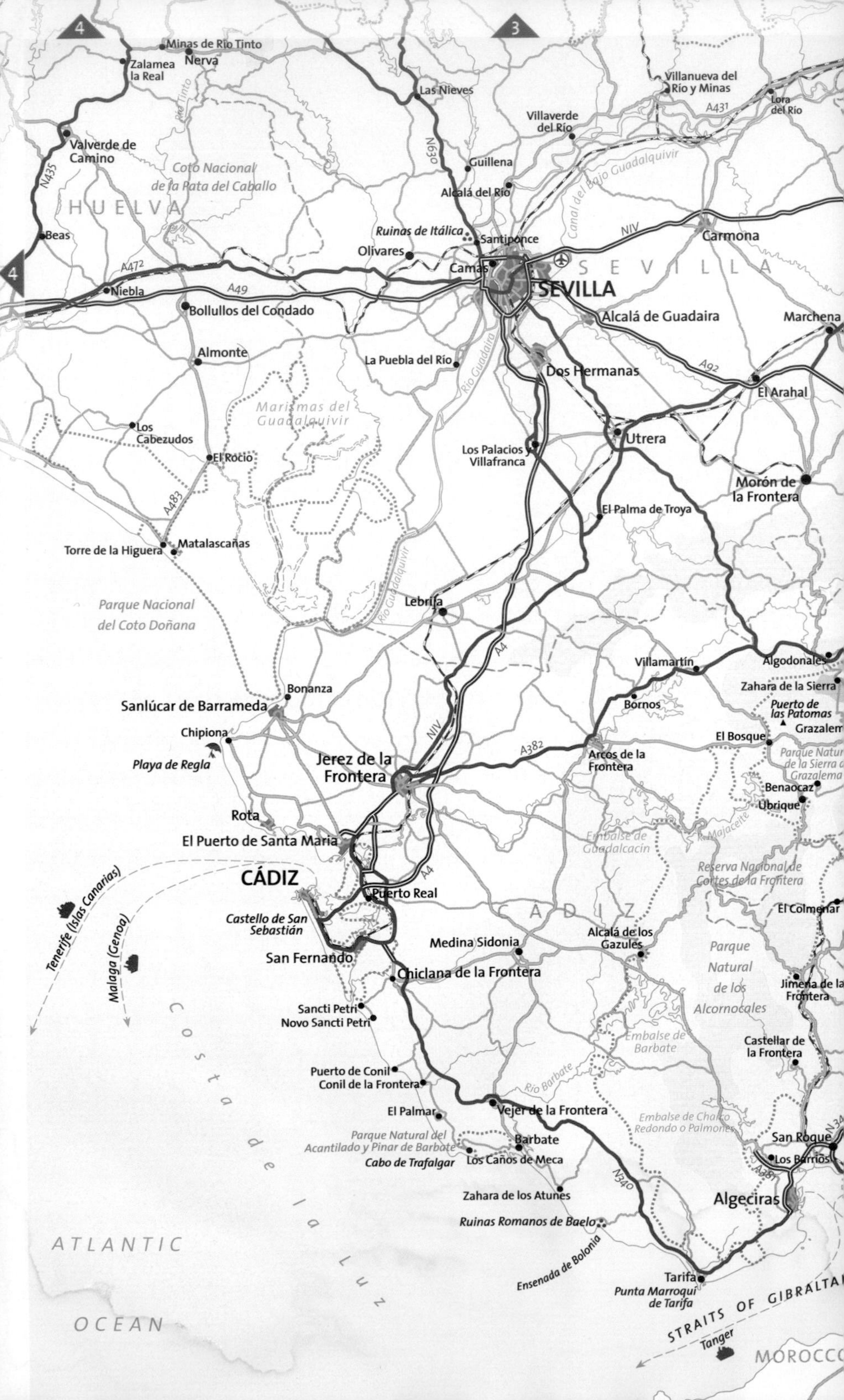

4
3
Minas de Rio Tinto
Nerva
Zalamea la Real
Las Nieves
Villanueva del Río y Minas
Lora del Río
A431
Villaverde del Río
Valverde de Camino
N435
N630
Coto Nacional de la Pata del Caballo
Guillena
Alcalá del Río
Canal del Bajo Guadalquivir
HUELVA
Beas
Ruinas de Itálica
Santiponce
NIV
Carmona
Olivares
Camas
SEVILLA
A472
Niebla
A49
Bollullos del Condado
Alcalá de Guadaira
Marchena
Almonte
La Puebla del Río
Río Guadaira
Dos Hermanas
A92
El Arahal
Marismas del Guadalquivir
Los Cabezudos
Utrera
Los Palacios y Villafranca
El Rocío
Morón de la Frontera
A483
El Palma de Troya
Torre de la Higuera
Matalascañas
Parque Nacional del Coto Doñana
Lebrija
Río Guadalquivir
A4
Villamartín
Algodonales
Bonanza
Zahara de la Sierra
Bornos
Sanlúcar de Barrameda
Puerto de las Palomas
Chipiona
Grazalema
El Bosque
Playa de Regla
A382
Arcos de la Frontera
Jerez de la Frontera
Parque Natural de la Sierra de Grazalema
Benaocaz
Ubrique
Rota
Río Majaceite
El Puerto de Santa Maria
Embalse de Guadalcacín
CÁDIZ
Reserva Nacional de Cortes de la Frontera
Tenerife (Islas Canarias)
Puerto Real
El Colmenar
Castello de San Sebastián
Malaga (Genoa)
Medina Sidonia
Alcalá de los Gazules
Parque Natural de los Alcornocales
San Fernando
Chiclana de la Frontera
Jimena de la Frontera
Sancti Petri
Novo Sancti Petri
Costa de la Luz
Embalse de Barbate
Castellar de la Frontera
Puerto de Conil
Conil de la Frontera
Río Barbate
El Palmar
Vejer de la Frontera
Embalse de Charco Redondo o Palmones
Parque Natural del Acantilado y Pinar de Barbate
Barbate
San Roque
Cabo de Trafalgar
Los Caños de Meca
Los Barrios
A381
N340
Zahara de los Atunes
Algeciras
Ruinas Romanos de Baelo
ATLANTIC
Ensenada de Bolonia
Tarifa
Punta Marroquí de Tarifa
STRAITS OF GIBRALTA
OCEAN
Tanger
MOROCCO

3
2
1
Palma del Río
La Carlota
Fernán Núñez
Castro del Río
CÓRDOBA
JAÉN
Río Genil
La Rambla
Montilla
Baena
Alcaudete
Écija
Doña Mencía
Aguilar de la Frontera
Cueva de los Murciélagos
Cabra
Priego de Córdoba
Parque Natural de la Sierra Subbética
Lucena
Puente-Genil
Rute
Montefrío
Casariche
Estepa
Osuna
La Puebla de Cazalla
Embalse de Iznájar
Loja
Fuente de Piedra
Laguna de la Fuente de Piedra
Archidona
GRANADA
Antequera
Cuevas de Menga y Viera
Alfarnate
Alfarnatejo
Alhama de Granada
Olvera
Embalse de Gaitanejo
Torcal de Antequera
Villanueva de la Concepción
Bobastro
Riogordo
Colmenar
Reserva Nacional de Sierra de Tejeda
Setenil
Ardales
Ronda la Vieja
Carratraca
Garganta del Chorro
Comares
Alora
Archez
Competa
Montes de Málaga
El Borge
El Burgo
Benamocarra
Vélez Málaga
Ronda
Iznate
Torrox
Montejaque
MÁLAGA
Benaoján
Serranía de Ronda
Parque Natural de la Sierra de las Nieves
Tolox
Río Guadalhorce
Cueva de a Pileta
Torre del Mar
Playa de Torre del Mar
Torrox Costa
La Jimera de Libar
Atajate
Coín
Palma (Genova)
Cortes de la Frontera
Benadalid
Ibeza (Islas Baleares)
Algatocín
Torremolinos
Melilla
Mijas
Genalguacil
Benalmádena Costa
Gaucín
Fuengirola
Castillo
Sierra Bermeja
Marbella
Puerto Banús
San Pedro de Alcántara
Casares
Castillo
Estepona don Pedro
Playa de Estepona
Cadiz (Islas Canarias)
Manilva
Sotogrande
Costa del Sol
La Línea de la Concepción
GIBRALTAR
Punta Grande de Europa
MEDITERRANEAN SEA
N
20 km
10 miles
Ceuta (Spain)
NIV-E5
N331
N432
A364
A92
A382
A359
A366
A376
A335
A49-E15
N340
E15

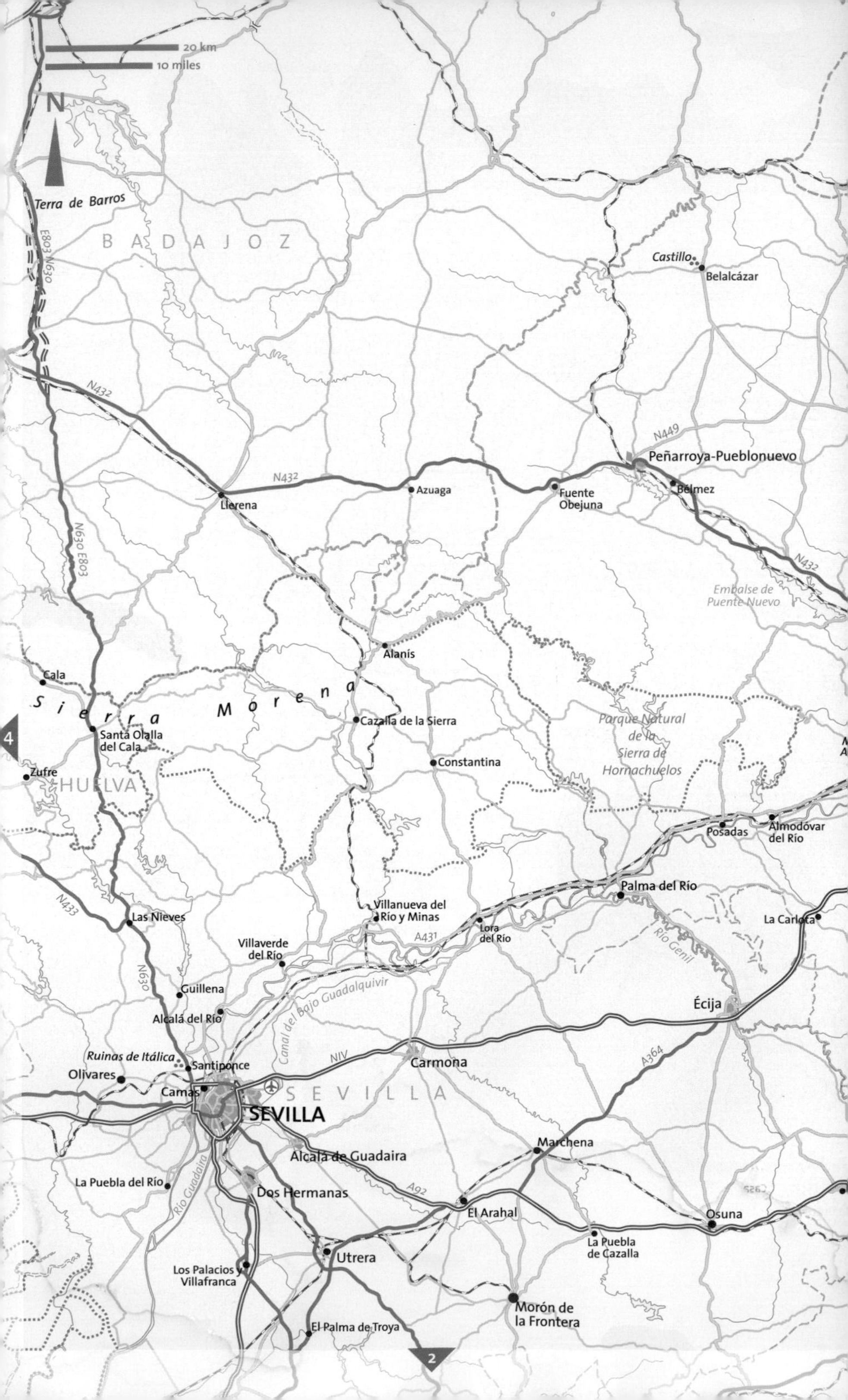

20 km
10 miles
N
Terra de Barros
BADAJOZ
E803 N630
Castillo
Belalcázar
N432
N449
Peñarroya-Pueblonuevo
Bélmez
N432
Azuaga
Fuente Obejuna
Llerena
N630 E803
N432
Embalse de Puente Nuevo
Alanís
Cala
Sierra Morena
Cazalla de la Sierra
Santa Olalla del Cala
4
Parque Natural de la Sierra de Hornachuelos
Constantina
Zufre
HUELVA
Posadas
Almodóvar del Río
Palma del Río
N433
Las Nieves
Villanueva del Río y Minas
La Carlota
A431
Lora del Río
Río Genil
Villaverde del Río
N630
Guillena
Canal del Bajo Guadalquivir
Écija
Alcalá del Río
A364
Ruinas de Itálica
NIV
Santiponce
Carmona
Olivares
Camas
SEVILLA
SEVILLA
Marchena
Alcalá de Guadaira
La Puebla del Río
Río Guadaira
Dos Hermanas
A92
El Arahal
Osuna
La Puebla de Cazalla
Utrera
Los Palacios y Villafranca
Morón de la Frontera
El Palma de Troya
2

3
Almagro
CIUDAD REAL
CM412
Gargantiel
Almadén
N420
Almodóvar del Campo
Puertollano
Convento Castillo de Calatrava la Nueva
Santa Eufemia
Pedroche
Pozoblanco
Desfiladero de Despeñaperros
A420
Sierra Morena
Villanueva de Córdoba
Parque Natural de la Sierra de Andújar
Cardeña
Parque Natural de la Sierra de Cardeña
La Carolina
NIV-E5
Baños de la Encina
Sanctuario Virgen de la Cabeza
Bailén
N322
Linares
1
Embalse del Guadalmellato
CÓRDOBA
Montoro
Marmolejo
Andújar
NIV
Canena
Villa del Río
Arjonilla
Higuera de Arjona
JAÉN
Medina Azahara
Arjona
Bujalance
N323-E902
CÓRDOBA
NIV-E5
N432
Río Guadajoz
A316
Torredonjimeno
Parque Natural de la Sierra Mágina
N331
Jaén
Castro del Río
Martos
C3221
Fernán Núñez
Sierra de la Pandera
N323
Baena
La Rambla
Montilla
Alcaudete
Doña Mencía
Aguilar de la Frontera
Cueva de los Murciélagos
Cabra
Alcalá la Real
Priego de Córdoba
Lucena
Puente-Genil
Parque Natural de la Sierra Subbética
N323-E902
Iznalloz
Rute
Montefrío
Casariche
Estepa
A92
Parque Natural de la Sierra de Huétor
Illora
Pinos Puente
Embalse de Iznajar
Loja
A92
GRANADA
La Alhambra
Fuente de Piedra
Armilla
MÁLAGA
Laguna de la Fuente de Piedra
A92
Archidona
GRANADA
La Zubia
2
1

4
20 km
10 miles
N
BADAJOZ
PORTUGAL
HUELVA
SEVILLA
ATLANTIC OCEAN
Barcarrota
Zafra
N432
EX112
Jerez de los Caballeros
EX101
Fregenal de la Sierra
Encinasola
Cumbres Mayores
N630 E803
Arroyomolinos de León
Parque Natural de la Sierra de Aracena
Sierra
Rosal de la Frontera
N433
Aroche
Cala
Jabugo
Galaroza
Carboneras
Corteganа
Fuenteheridos
Nuestra Señora de los Angeles
Aracena
Castillo
Almonaster la Real
Alájar
Gruta de las Maravillas
Santa Ana la Real
Santa Olalla del Cala
Santa Bárbara de Casa
Sierra de Aracena
Zufre
Higuera de la Sierra
3
Cabezas Rubias
Minas de Río Tinto
Nerva
Calañas
Zalamea la Real
Puebla de Guzmán
Río Tinto
Alosno
Valverde de Camino
Villanueva de los Castillejos
A495
Río Odiel
N435
Coto Nacional de la Pata del Caballo
Sanlúcar de Guadiana
San Bartolomé de la Torre
Río Guadiana
Beas
Olivares
Río Piedras
Gibraleón
Trigueros
A472
A49
Niebla
N431
Bollullos del Condado
Castro Marim
Lepe
Cartaya
Moguer
Ayamonte
HUELVA
Almonte
A497
Vila Real de Santo António
Isla Cristina
La Antilla
El Rompido
Palos de la Frontera
Monasterio de la Rábida
Playa Canela
Punta Umbría
Los Cabezudos
Marismas del Guadalquivir
Mazagón
El Rocío
Playa de Mazagón
A483
Torre de la Higuera
Matalascañas
Parque Nacional del Coto Doñana
Río Guadalquivir
Sanlúcar de Barrameda
Bonanza
2